Children in Therapy
Using the Family as a Resource

Children in Therapy
Using the Family as a Resource

C. Everett Bailey, Ph.D.
Editor

W.W. Norton & Company
New York • London

Copyright © 2000 by C. Everett Bailey

For information about permission to reproduce selections from this book, write to
Permissions, W. W. Norton & Company, Inc., 500 Fifth Avenue, New York, NY 10110

Composition by Paradigm Graphics
Manufacturing by Haddon Crafstmen

Library of Congress Cataloging-in-Publication Data

Children in therapy: using the family as a resource / C. Everett Bailey, editor.
p.   cm.
"A Norton professional book."
Includes bibliographical references and index.
ISBN 0-393-70289-8
1. Family psychotherapy. 2. Child psychotherapy. I. Bailey, C. Everett.

RC488.5 .C468 2000
616.89'156--dc21   00-038022

W. W. Norton & Company, Inc., 500 Fifth Avenue, New York, N.Y. 10110
www.wwnorton.com
W. W. Norton & Company Ltd., 10 Coptic Street, London WC1A 1PU

1 2 3 4 5 6 7 8 9 0

To my wife, Robin, for her love and friendship

To my children
Madeleine, Carter, Caroline, and Olivia

Contents

Acknowledgments

As John Donne stated most eloquently, "No man is an island." Certainly, no one could accomplish such an undertaking as editing a book without the help of many people. First of all I would like to thank Susan Munro at W. W. Norton for her interest and support in this project, and for her valuable edits and feedback. Also, a big thanks to Regina Dahlgren Ardini for her patience and constant, but gentle, reminders that helped guide the project through to completion.

Other people have been an inspiration for me in my work with children and their families. I am grateful to the pioneers in this area, including Lee Combrinck-Graham and Eliana Gil, who have paved the way and stressed the importance of working with families and children together in their own work. I would also like to thank my colleagues Kate Sori and Laura Johnson for their passion and enthusiasm in working with children and whose clinical work exemplifies what I am trying to accomplish in this book.

I particularly want to thank the outstanding authors who contributed chapters to this book. They certainly are an "all-star" cast. I could not have written a book that contained the knowledge, expertise, and experience that they possess and willingly share. I respect and value their professional and clinical work and their commitment to helping children and their families. I am honored that they would be willing to have their name and work associated with this project. It has been wonderful to work with them.

Finally, I want to thank my wife, Robin, whose support and encouragement has been invaluable throughout this project. Ironically, while I was spending late hours writing and editing this book on children and families (and getting messages from my seven-year-old son asking me when I was coming home), Robin took on the full responsibilities of taking care of our children. Thank you, Robin.

Contributors

Harlene Anderson, Ph.D., is a founding member of Houston Galveston Institute and Taos Institute, Houston, Texas.

C. Everett Bailey, Ph.D., is Assistant Professor in the Marriage and Family Therapy Program, North Dakota State University, Fargo, North Dakota.

Mary Jo Barrett, M.S.W., is Director of Training and Consultation, Center for Contextual Change, Skokie, Illinois.

Dean M. Busby, Ph.D., is Professor and Chair of the Human Development and Family Studies Department at Texas Tech University, Lubbock, Texas.

Joseph Cortese, L.C.S.W., is Co-Clincial Director, Center for Contextual Change, Skokie, Illinois.

Linda Stone Fish, Ph.D., is Associate Professor and Program Director, Marriage and Family Therapy Program, Syracuse University, Syracuse, New York.

Jill Freedman, M.S.W., is Co-Director of Evanston Family Therapy Center, Evanston, Illinois.

Eliana Gil, Ph.D., is Director of Abused Children's Treatment Services, Inova Kellar Center, Fairfax, Virginia.

Chandra M. Grabill, Ph.D., is a psychologist at Sexton Woods Psychoeducational Center, Chamblee, Georgia.

Mariellen Griffith, Ed.D., is a marriage and family therapist in private practice, Bloomington, Illinois.

Michelle Jensen, M.A., is Director of Residential Services, Northern Tier Children's Home Residential Services, Inc., Harrison Valley, Pennsylvania.

Laura M. Johnson, Ph.D., L.M.F.T., is Assistant Professor, Marriage and Family Therapy Program, Appalachian State University, Boone, North Carolina.

Susan M. Johnson, Ed.D., is Professor of Psychology and Psychiatry, University of Ottawa, and Director of the Couple and Family Therapy Clinic and Ottawa Couple & Family Institute, Ottawa, Ontario, Canada.

Nadine J. Kaslow, Ph.D., is Professor and Chief Psychologist, Emory Univer-sity School of Medicine Department of Psychiatry and Behavioral Sciences, Atlanta, Georgia.

James P. Keim, M.S.W., L.C.S.W., is an internationally known presenter in private practice in Ft. Collins, Colorado.

Kimberly T. Kendziora, Ph.D., is a research analyst at the American Institutes for Research, Washington, D.C.

Bonnie Klimes-Dougan, Ph.D., is Assistant Professor of Psychology, The Catholic University of America, Washington, D.C.

Alison C. Lee, Ph.D., is a registered psychologist and Vice President, Ottawa Couple and Family Institute, Ottawa, Ontario, Canada.

Kristen Marzolf, L.C.S.W., is Co-Clinical Director, Center for Contextual Change, Skokie, Illinois.

Lindi Ann Meadows, M.A., is a graduate student at Georgia State University, Atlanta, Georgia.

Richard L. Meth, M.S.W., Ph.D., is Clinical Director, Child and Family Services of Pioneer Valley, Springfield, Massachusetts.

Michelle B. Mintzer, M.D., is Psychiatrist, MHM Correctional Services Inc., Atlanta, Georgia.

Robert E. Nida, Ph.D., is Associate Professor, Department of Child Develop-ment and Family Relations, East Carolina University, Greenville, North Carolina.

Sarah Pierce, Ph.D., is Associate Professor, School of Human Ecology, Louisiana State University, Baton Rouge, Louisiana.

Michol Polson, Ph.D., is a marriage and family therapist at Family Resource Center, Idaho Falls, Idaho.

Tracey Reichert, M.A., is a family therapist and doctoral student at Syracuse University, Syracuse, New York.

Richard C. Schwartz, Ph.D., L.M.F.T., is Senior Staff Therapist, The Family Institute, Northwestern University, Evanston, Illinois.

Matthew D. Selekman, M.S.W., L.C.S.W., maintains a private practice and consultation service in Evanston, Illinois.

Virginia A. Simons, M.S.W., is Clinical Instructor, Case Western Reserve University, Family Medicine Department, Fairview Center for Family Medicine, Cleveland, Ohio.

Geoffrey L. Smith, M.A., is a marriage and family therapist at the Sex Abuse Treatment Program, Tulare Youth Service Bureau, Tulare, California.

Barbara Sobol, M.A., A.T.R., L.P.C., is Clinical Service Coordinator, Health and Human Services Community Partnership for Children, Youth and Families, Montgomery County, Maryland.

Catherine E. Ford Sori, Ph.D.(c), is Child and Family Associate, Cancer Support Center, Homewood, Illinois.

Sally St. George, Ph.D., is Associate Professor, Counseling and Human Development, Lindsey Wilson College, Columbia, Kentucky.

Joyce Thiessen-Barrett, M.Ed., is special education coordinator, Wichita Public Schools, Wichita, Kansas.

Jennifer Wainman-Sauda, M.A., is a family therapist at UNIVERA, Baldwinsville, New York.

Dan Wulff, Ph.D., is Assistant Professor, Kent School of Social Work, University of Louisville, Louisville, Kentucky.

Introduction
Helping Children Heal: The Role of Families in Children's Therapy

One day last summer, my children were playing outside together. My 6-year-old son, Carter, was taking small rocks from the side of the house and hitting them across the yard with a tennis racket, something he had been told not to do. Accidentally, one of the rocks hit 5-year-old Caroline in the forehead. Shocked, hurt, and with blood dripping down her face, Caroline shrieked in pain and started to cry. Olivia, my 4-year-old daughter, stood by and witnessed the traumatic event. As Caroline began to cry, Olivia empathically began to cry also. With tears rolling down her cheeks, Olivia rushed over and hugged Caroline in an attempt to comfort her. Hearing the screaming and crying, my wife, Robin, ran outside to find out what had happened (I was at work at the time). Noticing the blood, tears, and the "smoking gun" (Carter standing there holding the tennis racket), my wife pieced together what had transpired. She quickly embraced both Caroline and Olivia who were visibly shaken by the event. While understandably upset by the incident, her distress over Caroline's injury was compounded by the fact that Carter inflicted the wound. At the same time, though, Robin was impressed with Olivia's compassion for Caroline. This brief family incident elicited several different emotions and issues for each person involved. Carter felt guilty, shocked, and scared for the pain he caused his sister and his impending punishment. Caroline, physically and emotionally traumatized, felt rejected by her brother and wondered why he did this to her. Olivia, equally confused by the event, absorbed Caroline's distress. In addition, Robin and I experienced an array of emotions. Troubled by Carter's behavior, Robin wondered about her own adequacy as a parent. She felt helpless to relieve Caroline's pain and simultaneously felt guilty because she was not there to protect her. On the other hand, she felt some momentary satisfaction over Olivia's heartfelt response, which indicated that she was not a total failure as a parent. When I heard about the event I was angry at Carter and somewhat irritated with Robin for not monitoring our children's activities closer. I also felt a lack of control over what happened at home when I was at work. All of these emotions would be a normal response to such an unfortunate incident.

Although most presenting problems in therapy are much more serious and chronic in nature, such an incident illustrates several reasons why families should be involved in children's therapy. First, as this family episode depicts, children most often experience traumatic events within the context of their family. While growing up in families, children experience a myriad of hurts, disappointments, frustrations, and trials as they interact with family members. These wounds cut the deepest because they come from people they trust and depend on the most. Children expect family members to protect them from pain, not inflict it. These experiences, in what Napier and Whitaker (1978) referred to as the "family crucible," are often what lead to children's problematic behavior. Therefore, in trying to understand children's problems it is critical to assess the problem within the family context. In many cases, family interactions may be directly related to children's behavior (e.g., Caroline was upset because Carter hurt her). Research on family process supports this view. For example, research on marital conflict shows that it can lead to child maladjustment and children's behavioral problems (Cummings & Davies, 1994). Further research provides evidence that ineffectual parenting due to parental depression, anger, substance use, or other mental illness can lead to children's internalizing and externalizing problems (Bornstein, 1995). Sibling relationships can also be a factor in children's disruptive behavior (Brody & Stoneman, 1996). Thus, as family systems theory posits, in order to treat childhood disorders, clinicians must also assess and treat dysfunctional interactions within the family system. This is not to say that all children's problems are caused by family dysfunction. The issue is more complicated than that. However, if treatment focuses exclusively on the child, the child's symptoms maybe reduced but they are likely to return if the dysfunctional interactions within the family system are not addressed.

This incident with my children also portrays that such traumatic events do not just happen to individuals, they also happen to families. When distressing events occur to children within the family, they have a significant impact on other family members as well. Regardless of whether family members are directly involved in the interaction/event, witness it, or hear about it later, they also experience a range of emotions and reactions. Their reactions play an important part in how children respond to distressing circumstances.

In addition, family members are also affected when the child encounters a distressing event outside the family. The research literature has identified several factors, in addition to family functioning, that contribute to children's emotional and behavioral problems. These factors include the child's peer and friend relationships, school-related experiences, and larger cultural influences (e.g., minority and socioeconomic status) (Bornstein, 1995). Moreover, a child's behavior may be related to individual factors like the child's temperament (e.g., difficult temperament), transitioning to a new developmental stage (e.g., entering adolescence), or adjusting to a normative life event in a family (e.g., moving or having a baby). Whether family relationships, individual child factors, or influences external to the family are the genesis of the problem, other family members are directly affected by the child's struggles. Regardless of the source of the problem, the family's response to the child's behavior is a major factor on how the child deals with the problem. If family members do not respond in a way to enable the child to emotionally resolve the problem, family interactions can actually make the problem worse. If this happens, family members perpetuate a vicious cycle of attacking, blaming, and defending behaviors. This negative cycle fragments the family, isolating family members and weakening family bonds. Stuck in this pattern, the family becomes inflexible and incapable of drawing on their own resources and abilities to help the child adapt to or overcome his or her difficulties. This inflexibility puts quite a strain on other individuals in the family and their relationships. It can affect parents' individual functioning and erode parental self-confidence and self-efficacy as they struggle with the child's problem behavior. As parenting issues become a source of conflict in the marriage, additional stress is put on the marital relationship. Furthermore, children's problem behavior can fuel the rivalry and jealousies between siblings. When families eventually seek therapy they come feeling discouraged, confused, guilty, angry, and often desperate. As therapists it is important to remember that the family does not cause all children's problems even though family interactions may be related to the child's behavior. Nevertheless, therapy can transform negative family interactions into more supportive ones, enabling the family to be a positive resource to the child.

Another point that the story about my children illustrates is that families are a source of strength and support for children. Although our greatest pains often come from those closest to us, family members are also our greatest source of love, comfort, acceptance, and nurturing (e.g., Olivia and Robin's comforting Caroline). Most importantly, families are also a source of healing. A story I found (Sheehan, 1996) aptly illustrates this point. After their premature birth, Brielle and Kyrie Jackson, twin baby girls, were put in separate incubators to reduce the risk of infection. Kyrie, the larger one at two pounds and three ounces responded quite well and began to sleep and gain weight. Brielle, on the other hand, struggled to regulate her breathing and her heart rate. At one point Brielle's condition became critical. The nurse, having tried everything to stabilize Brielle's condition, remembered a new procedure she had heard about. She informed the parents that she was going to put Brielle in the same incubator with her sister Kyrie. When the nurse did this Brielle snuggled over to Kyrie and almost immediately became soothed. After a few minutes Brielle's blood-oxygen readings improved and her condition stabilized for the first time since she was born. As the two sisters lay there side by side, Kyrie picked up her tiny arm and wrapped it around her sister's shoulders. When therapists involve families in children's therapy, they help the child access the greatest healing source that child has: the child's family.

Involving the family in therapy also allows the therapist to be an advocate for the child within the family. Children hold the least power in the family system and their voices are the least heard. Therapists can elevate children's voices and help family members hear them and effectively respond to them. Working with the family as a unit, therapists can also identify ways that family members blame themselves or the identified child patient. Therapists can help family members decrease blaming attitudes and behavior, which tend to exacerbate the child's problem rather than solve it.

At the same time, therapists can help family members identify individual and family strengths. Highlighting strengths makes family members aware of the skills and resources they already have that can help them resolve the child's problem. In the process the family recognizes its resiliency and gains confidence in their ability to resolve any problems in the future. Ultimately it is children who will benefit in the long-term as family members increase their capacity to utilize their own assets. As therapists involve families in children's treatment to cultivate their strengths and garner their support, they can become an important resource in helping children heal.

Involving Families in Children's Therapy

Including both children and adults in the same session presents quite a challenge for any clinician. The difficulty is finding a mode of therapy that engages both of them. If traditional talk therapy is used, then children get bored and become more of a distraction in the session. If therapists use a medium that children are comfortable with, like play therapy, then parents feel uncomfortable and uncertain of their role in therapy. However, most clinicians who work with children do not include families in therapy. The main reason for this is that theoretically their interventions with children do not call for it. Child therapy is traditionally based on psychoanalysis or humanistic psychology, and has focused largely on the internal life of the child. Through the child's symbolic experiences, often expressed through play, therapists can understand the child's inner state. Through the therapeutic relationship and play therapy, therapists help children express and resolve their inner turmoil. Because therapy focuses on the child's inner experiences, parents or siblings are not generally involved in therapy (filial therapy is an exception; see Landreth, 1991). Another common approach to treating children's problems, developed by behavioral therapists is parent management training (PMT). PMT teaches parents behavior management techniques that they can use to alter their child's problem behavior. Typically, though, therapists focus interventions on the parents and do not involve children in treatment (Briesmeister & Schaefer, 1998).

Trained in family systems theory, marriage and family therapists would seem to be the most likely to involve families in children's therapy. Ironically, though, the marriage and family therapy (MFT) field as been strongly criticized for not involving children and families together in therapy (Combrinck-Graham, 1986, 1998; Diller, 1991; Nickerson, 1986). The MFT field has approached the issue of children and family therapy in two different ways. First, the MFT field has encouraged the practice of seeing families as a whole in therapy, which means including children even when the presenting problem was adult-oriented. Many of the early pioneers in family therapy stressed the value of including children in therapy sessions (Ackerman, 1970, Keith & Whitaker, 1981). Ackerman (1970) stated, "Without engaging the children in a meaningful interchange across the generations, there can be no family therapy" (p. 403). However, marriage and family therapists have been criticized for rarely including children in therapy and not being true to their family systems orientation when the presenting problem is adult-related (Bloch, 1976). In response to this criticism many authors have described the benefits of including children in adult sessions (Dare & Lindsey, 1979; Dowling & Jones, 1978; Guttman, 1975; Villeneuve & LaRoche, 1993). Others have examined and researched the reasons why marriage and family therapists exclude children from therapy (Diller, 1991; Johnson & Thomas, 1999; Korner & Brown, 1990).

The second way the MFT literature has addressed the issue of children and family therapy is by stressing the need to include other family members in treatment when the problem presented is child-related. (It is this issue that is the focus of this book.) Although marriage and family therapists are more likely to include children in therapy if the family presents with a child-oriented problem (Johnson & Thomas, 1999), they often dismiss children from therapy and focus treatment on the parent's family-of-origin or the marital relationship even when the presenting problem is child-related (Olson, 1970; Bloch, 1976; Combrinck-Graham, 1986). Olson (1970) explains that many of the early pioneers in family therapy believed that a problem child was a symptom of a dysfunctional family and, more specifically, the symptom of a troubled marriage. As a result, family therapists have centered treatment on the marital relationship, believing that the child's problem behavior would remit once the marriage was strengthened. Others have argued that the reason family therapists exclude children and concentrate on adult family members is because they are uncomfortable working with children (Diller, 1991; Johnson & Thomas, 1999). One of the major reasons for this discomfort is the lack of training in doing therapy with children (Combrinck-Graham, 1986; Doherty & Simmons, 1996; Hines, 1996; Korner & Brown, 1990). Even when family therapists do include children in a therapy session they often do not know how to engage them (Cederborg, 1997).

The practice of family therapy by MFTs, which entails involving children and other family members in treatment, is still criticized today. In a recent edition of the American Family Therapy Academy (AFTA) newsletter devoted to children in families, Combrinck-Graham (1998) censures therapists for not including family members when treating children. In her article "Where Have All the Family Therapists Gone?" she states that the family is often part of the problem and needs to be included in treatment so they can learn how to become part of the solution. "The most successful outcomes appear to be achieved when attachments are acknowledged, loyalties are realistically supported, and someone who loves the child 'best of all' is able to advocate for the child and provide protection and comfort" (p. 25). Although limited, there is some research on the practice patterns of MFTs and their use of family therapy. One national survey on MFTs reports that they only see families in 12% of their sessions, but see individuals 49% and couples 23% of the time (Doherty & Simmons, 1996). In another article using the same sample, Simmons and Doherty (1998) reported that there was no statistical difference between the frequency of family therapy done by MFTs and the amount done by psychologists, social workers, or counselors. These reports raise several questions about the practice of family therapy. If family therapists are generally excluding children from therapy and not seeing families as units, are they basically practicing marital or individual therapy with a family systems lens? This and similar questions need to be examined further by the MFT field.

Since most clinicians are not trained in both family therapy and child therapy, some have integrated the two modes of treatment. Some examples of approaches that include working with both children and families include filial therapy (Guerney & Guerney, 1987; Johnson, 1995), family play therapy (Gil, 1994), and parent-child interaction therapy (PCIT) (Eyberg & Boggs, 1998). Although each of the approaches include both children and adults in treatment they are also limited because either they do not address family dynamics (e.g., filial therapy and PCIT) or they do not incorporate the individual child's contribution to the problem (e.g., family play therapy). However, these approaches could be components of a more comprehensive treatment plan. Levant and Haffey (1981) suggested a more comprehensive approach that would include individual play therapy, marital therapy, and family therapy sessions as part of treatment. This concurrent approach allows therapists to assess the influence that the individual child characteristics, the parent-child dyad, the marital dyad, and family relationships have on the presenting problem. Unfortunately, over the last twenty years there has been very little literature on utilizing such a comprehensive treatment model with children. In general, there is a paucity of literature on how clinicians can involve family members to augment their work with children. An exception to this has been the work of Combrinck-Graham (1986, 1989) and Zilbach (1986, 1989), who have highlighted and discussed the importance of treating children within the context of the family. Another exception is Wachtel (1994), who integrates family systems theory, psychodynamic play therapy, and a cognitive-behavioral perspective to involve the child, parents, and family in children's treatment.

The Purpose of This Book

Although many clinicians see the therapeutic value of involving families in children's therapy, most are not trained to work with families and children together. As a result, therapists have not been able to draw on family members as a resource to help children. Yet "the family is a child's primary resource system" (Combrinck-Graham, 1989, p. ix). If we exclude families from our work with children, we exclude the greatest resource to help children. We also miss an opportunity to strengthen families and help them learn how to utilize their inherent abilities to heal themselves. Therapists can probably best serve children by helping families improve their capacity to effectively respond to children's distress.

The primary purpose of this book is to present ways that therapists can involve families and use them as a resource in their work with children. Since children do not respond well to traditional talk therapy, therapists are often at a loss for how to work with both adults and children in treatment. This is not to say that every session should be a family session. Rather, the goal of this book is to discuss ways therapists can effectively integrate family members into the overall treatment of children, which might also include individual sessions with the child. This will enable therapists to use the family as a resource and draw on the inherent strengths of children and families in order to help children heal.

Another purpose of the book is to help therapists highlight children's voices in therapy so that children's perspectives are acknowledged and respected within the family. Increased attention has been given to the voices of women and minorities in therapy, but very little attention has been given to increasing "the voices of children." In many ways our society still adheres to the saying "children are to be seen and not heard." This book is meant to explore ways that therapists can help families hear children's voices and understand their experiences within the family.

Overview of the Book

The book is broken down into three parts: Theoretical Perspectives, Content Areas, and Additional Perspectives. The theory section includes chapters on how to approach therapy with children from five different theoretical perspectives: solution-oriented brief therapy, narrative therapy, collaborative language systems therapy, internal family systems therapy, and emotionally-focused family therapy. Many of these new theories have not been applied to working with children and their families. What is similar about all these theories is that they do not focus on clients' or families' pathology. Instead, they build on clients' competencies and focus interventions on identifying the inherent strengths of individuals and families. In each of the theory chapters the authors provide some background and basic theoretical assumptions of the model and describe some of the techniques associated with the theory and how they could be applied to children. The chapters also include an extended case study illustrating how the theory and techniques were applied in a case that involved a child and his or her family. As part of the case study the authors explain what family members were involved and why they thought it was important to involve those family members. After describing the case, the authors explain theoretically what was most significant in helping the child and the family and why they thought certain interventions were effective.

The second part of the book deals with common disorders or problems that children might present with. The chapter authors describe how they assess children and what family dynamics are associated with the disorder. The main part of each chapter focuses on developing a treatment plan for a child with the disorder. The authors advise readers on who to invite to the first few sessions, how to involve family members in treatment, and how to work with other larger systems (e.g., schools, physicians, other mental health professionals). They suggest realistic treatment goals and progress for working with the child and his or her family. The authors also share some specific interventions that therapists can use and provide brief case examples to show their effectiveness in working with families who have a child with the respective disorder. Each chapter also references the current research related to the different childhood problems.

The last section covers five different topics related to working with children and their families. The chapter on family play therapy describes and illustrates different activities and techniques that therapists can use to involve the whole family in a play therapy session. The next chapter discusses the importance of involving fathers in children's therapy. When a parent is involved in a child's therapy it is often the mother; the father is excluded or resistant to participate. Current research is providing more and more evidence of the important role that fathers play in children's development. This chapter discusses the barriers and ways to overcome father's resistance to therapy. The author outlines and illustrates interventions clinicians can use to involve fathers in treatment and how children benefit from their involvement. The third chapter in this section pinpoints how clinicians can identify children's resilient factors and illustrates how they can be incorporated into treatment to facilitate the healing process for children and their families. The next chapter describes different developmental issues that clinicians should be aware of when working with children and how a developmental perspective can inform their assessment and treatment of children. Finally, the last chapter discusses the process of involving parents in their children's therapy. The authors describe and illustrate treatments that involve both parents and children in therapy. They also introduce and illustrate a multimodal approach for treating children that stresses parental involvement.

Conclusion

Today most scholars recognize the powerful influence of the family on children's behavior and development. Unfortunately though, therapists have primarily viewed the family's influence as the *source* of children's problems and largely overlooked the family as a resource to help children overcome their problems. Although, many therapists would probably agree that "it takes a family to heal a child," they still may be limited by individualistic theories and the lack of professional training in working with either children or families. As a result, many therapists probably wonder: How do I involve families in children's treatment? How do I work with both children and adults in the same session? Which family dynamics are associated with the different childhood disorders? How can I mobilize a family's emotional and relational resources to help children?

This text is meant to be a "hands-on" book to answer these questions and guide therapists in their efforts to involve families in children's therapy. Perhaps by involving families we can not only heal children, but we can also strengthen entire families and generations to come.

References

Ackerman, N. (1970). Child participation in family therapy. *Family Process, 30,* 403–410.

Bloch, D. (1976). Including the children in family therapy. In P. J. Guerin, Jr. (Ed.), *Family Therapy: Theory and practice.* New York: Gardner.

Bornstein, M. H. (Ed.). (1995). *Handbook of parenting.* Mahwah, NJ: Lawrence Erlbaum.

Briesmeister, J. M., & Schaefer, C. E. (Eds.). (1998). *Handbook of parent training: Parents as co-therapists for children's behavior problems* (2nd ed.). New York: Wiley.

Brody, G. H., & Stoneman, Z. (1996). A risk-amelioration model of sibling relationships: Conceptual underpinnings and preliminary findings. In G. H. Brody (Ed.), *Sibling relationships: Their causes and consequences* (pp. 231–247). Norwood, NJ: Ablex.

Cederborg, A. C. (1997). Young children's participation in family therapy talk. *American Journal of Family Therapy, 25,* 28–38.

Combrinck-Graham, L. (Ed.). (1986). *Treating young children in family therapy.* Rockville, MD: Aspen.

Combrinck-Graham, L. (Ed.). (1989). *Children in family contexts: Perspectives on treatment.* New York: Guilford.

Combrinck-Graham, L. (1998). Where have all the family therapists gone? *American Family Therapy Academy Newsletter, 72,* 25–27.

Cummings, E. M., & Davies, P. (1994). *Children and marital conflict: The impact of family dispute and resolution.* New York: Guilford.

Dare, C., & Lindsey, C. (1979). Children in family therapy. *Journal of Family Therapy, 1,* 253–269.

Diller, L. (1991, July/August). Not seen and not heard. *Family Therapy Networker, 15*(4), 18–27, 66.

Doherty, W. J., & Simmons, D. S. (1996). Clinical practice patterns of marriage and family therapists: A national survey of therapists and their clients. *Journal of Marital and Family Therapy, 22,* 9–25.

Dowling, E., & Jones, H. (1978). Small children seen and heard in family therapy. *Journal of Child Psychotherapy, 4,* 87–96.

Eyberg, S. M., & Boggs, S. R. (1998). Parent-child interaction therapy: A psychosocial intervention for the treatment of young conduct-disordered children. In J. M. Briesmester & C. E. Schaefer (Eds.), *Handbook of parent training: Parents as co-therapists for children's behavior problems* (2nd ed.). New York: Wiley.

Gil, E. (1994). *Play in family therapy.* New York: Guilford.

Guerney, L., & Guerney, B., Jr. (1987). Integrating child and family therapy. *Psychotherapy, 24,* 609–614.

Guttman, H. A. (1975). The child's participation in conjoint family therapy. *Journal of the American Academy of Child Psychiatry, 14,* 480–499.

Hines, M. (1996). Follow-up survey of graduates from accredited degree-granting marriage and family therapy training programs. *Journal of Marital and Family Therapy, 22,* 181–194.

Johnson, L. (1995). Filial therapy: A bridge between individual child therapy and family therapy. *Journal of Psychotherapy, 6,* 55–70.

Johnson, L., & Thomas, V. (1999). Influences on the inclusion of children in family therapy. *Journal of Marital and Family Therapy, 25,* 117–123.

Keith, D. V., & Whitaker, C. A. (1981). Play therapy: A paradigm for work with families. *Journal of Marital and Family Therapy, 7,* 243–254.

Korner, S., & Brown, G. (1990). Exclusion of children from family psychotherapy: Family therapists' beliefs and practices. *Journal of Family Psychology, 3,* 420–430.

Landreth, G. L. (1991). *Play therapy: The art of the relationship.* Bristol, PA: Accelerated Development.

Levant, R., & Haffey, N. (1981). Towards an integration of child and family therapy. *International Journal of Family Therapy, 3,* 130–141.

Napier, A. Y., & Whitaker, C. A. (1978). *The family crucible.* New York: Harper & Row.

Nickerson, E. (1986). Integrating the child into family therapy: The remaking of a for-adults-only orientation. *International Journal of Family Psychiatry, 7,* 59–69.

Olson, D. H. (1970). Marital and family therapy: Integrative review and critique. *Journal of Marriage and the Family, 32,* 501–538.

Sheehan, N. (May, 1996). A sister's helping hand. *Reader's Digest,* 155–156.

Simmons, D. S., & Doherty, W. J. (1998). Does academic training background make a difference among practicing marriage and family therapists? *Journal of Marital and Family Therapy, 24,* 321–336.

Villeneuve, C., & LaRoche, C. (1993). The child's participation in family therapy: A review and a model. *Contemporary Family Therapy, 15,* 105–119.

Wachtel, E. F. (1994). *Treating troubled children and their families.* New York: Guilford.

Zilbach, J. J. (1986). *Young children in family therapy.* New York: Brunner/Mazel.

Zilbach, J. J. (Ed.). (1989). *Children in family therapy: Treatment and training.* New York: Haworth.

Children in Therapy
Using the Family as a Resource

I
THEORETICAL PERSPECTIVES

1

Solution-Oriented Brief Family Therapy with Children

Matthew D. Selekman

Historically, therapeutic work with children has been a long-term endeavor in which the therapist serves as the main healing agent and the privileged expert. The use of empathy and interpretations of the child's play and art activity are the psychotherapist's main tools for helping fill psychic deficits (Kohut, 1971) and resolving conflicts. However, in today's managed health care environment, therapists have limited time to stabilize the child's symptoms and resolve family difficulties. Managed care companies are more likely to contract with therapists that provide goal-focused, action-oriented therapy approaches for children, than those that espouse a growth-oriented, long-term treatment philosophy for this population (Selekman, 1997).

In this chapter, I present an integrative solution-oriented brief family therapy approach that combines the best elements of modified traditional play and art therapy techniques with other compatible competency-based family therapy approaches (Selekman, 1997). After presenting a brief overview of this approach, I discuss ways to interview for change and present six major therapeutic tasks I frequently use with children and their families. A case example of a family plagued by alcoholism, depression, fetal alcohol syndrome, and long-standing parental marital difficulties will complete the chapter.

Theoretical Overview

The solution-oriented brief family therapy model (Selekman, 1993, 1997) expands on the basic solution-focused therapy model (Berg & de Shazer, 1993;

Berg & Miller, 1992; de Shazer, 1985, 1988, 1991, 1994), making it more flexible and adaptable to short-term clinical work with children and their families.
The solution-oriented brief family therapy approach encourages therapeutic
improvisation and active collaboration with involved professionals from larger
systems, such as school and medical personnel.

Key Assumptions

Five solution-oriented assumptions guide the therapist's thinking and activity
during sessions. Solution-oriented brief family therapy is not just a way of
doing therapy—it is also a philosophy about therapy.

Change is Inevitable

Change is a constant process. Often families are taking important steps toward
resolving or better coping with their difficulties well before they make their
first telephone call to our offices (Weiner-Davis, de Shazer, & Gingerich,
1987). Therefore, during the initial family session therapists should explore
what has already improved about the situation that brought them in for therapy.
The following questions can be asked:

- Since you first had the idea to call our clinic, or after you made the call,
  what have you noticed that's better about your situation?
- On a scale from 1 to 10, with 10 indicating that your situation is suffi-
  ciently resolved, what would you rate your situation today?
- How did you get your son to do that?
- What will you have to continue to do to get that to happen more often?

These questions empower clients by highlighting their creativity, strengths, and
resourcefulness.

Cooperation is Inevitable

All clients want to cooperate with their therapists, but we—like Miss Marple
and Sherlock Holmes—must look for and listen to clues that can guide us on
how to best cooperate with each family member. In any given interview, therapists need to closely observe themselves in relationship to their clients, carefully matching their questions and therapeutic tasks with the unique
cooperative response patterns of each family member. For example, with a
highly pessimistic parent, the therapist should ask questions like:

- I'm curious. What steps have you taken to prevent things from getting much worse?
- Some parents in your situation would have already thrown in the towel by now. What keeps you going?

An effective way to foster a cooperative therapeutic relationship with a child is to design and select tasks that fit with his or her unique learning style or intelligence area. Therapists can elicit information regarding a child's learning style and intelligence areas by asking questions such as:

- If someone stopped you on the street and asked you what you are most talented at doing, what would you tell this person?
- What are two of your biggest strengths?
- What are your favorite subjects in school?
- If you were to share something special about yourself with me, what would it be?
- How would you present it to me so I could learn best?

Gardner (1991) has identified seven human intelligences: language expression, logical-mathematical analysis, spatial-visual representation, musical thinking, kinesthetic-movement, interpersonal, and intrapersonal-introspective. A child who possesses strong spatial-visual processing abilities will respond best to tasks that draw on visual prowess and imagination powers, such as the imaginary time machine task (Selekman, 1997).

All Children Have the Strengths and Resources to Change

For the past two decades, I have worked with children of divorced, alcoholic, drug-abusing, or mentally ill parents. Despite the chaos, inconsistency, and disruption in their lives, these children have found effective ways to cope and courageously persevere. Just as one might ask parents about their past parenting successes, therapists can explore with children their unique coping and problem-solving strategies. To elicit these strategies, therapists can ask:

- When you are really sad, what do you do to make yourself happy?
- What do your parents do to help you be less angry?
- Which friend do you turn to first when you are upset?

Once the child's strengths, talents, and intelligence areas have been identified, the therapist can harness and utilize them in the problem area. For example, I used a video camera and drama in a session with an oppositional

11-year-old girl who was a talented singer and dancer to alter the parents' negative views and interactions with her. The girl spontaneously created a family
comedy show in the office and had her parents play different roles. The parents
were impressed by their daughter's creativity and appeared to enjoy themselves
in the session. Children can serve as the catalyst for bringing back humor, playfulness, and spontaneity in the family. And like shamans, they can often heal and
change their parents in more creative and effective ways then any therapist can.

Clients Succeed When their Goals Drive Therapy

Research indicates the need for client self-determination in the therapeutic
process. When clients think they have even modest personal control over their
destinies, they will persist at mastering tasks, do better at managing them, and
become more committed to the change process (Campbell, 1996; Miller,
1985). If we do not know where we are going with our clients we risk ending
up stuck or frustrated. Therefore, it is critical that we invite our clients to take
the lead in determining what they would like to change with their problem situations. Our main responsibility in the goal-setting process is to negotiate solvable, well-formed behavioral goals with our clients. It is of the utmost
importance to educate clients about pursuing small, realistic goals, especially
for families on managed health care plans. I like to ask clients the following
goal-setting questions:

- We have six sessions authorized. What would you like to work on chang-
  ing first?
- What will be a small sign of progress over the next week?
- How will you know you are really succeeding?
- What will you tell me you did?
- Let's say that this session today proved to be most helpful to you. What
  will have changed with your situation?

We will be better able to empower clients to succeed if we can elicit detailed
descriptions about what goal attainment will look like to them.

There are Many Ways to Look at a Problem

When clients seek professional help, often they are stuck viewing their problem situations in one way. Parents often seek "why" explanations or view the
problem as belonging only to the identified client. Our job as therapists is to
offer clients a multiplicity of views, which helps to loosen fixed beliefs that
have kept the families stuck. Positive relabeling can be helpful. For example, a
therapist can relabel an angry parent's behavior as exhibiting "concern and

commitment" or a child with ADD (attention-deficit disorder) as being "energetic." I like to share a different interpretation of the letters with the parents of children labeled as ADD: active, dynamic, determined. Sometimes parents get a laugh out of this positive relabeling of ADD and begin to look at their child in a different way. Like parents, therapists are also vulnerable to mental traps and becoming wedded to one way of looking at things. Therefore, it is crucial for therapists to be curious about second, third, or fourth explanations when trying to make sense of their clients' problem stories.

Applications

First-Session Tasks

With any given case, therapy begins with the therapist's gaining a clear definition from the family members about what they view as the problem. While gathering information in the family interview, the therapist listens carefully for key family beliefs, themes, language, attempted solutions, and how developmental, cultural, and gender issues contribute to the maintenance of the presenting problem. Once the family's problem story is clearly elaborated, the therapist elicits from family members detailed information about pretreatment changes (Selekman, 1997; Weiner-Davis et al., 1987) and past parental successes at resolving previous difficulties with their children. The next phase of the family interview involves negotiating a solvable treatment goal with the parents and the identified child. Solution-oriented questions like the miracle and scaling questions (de Shazer, 1988, 1991, 1994) are used to elicit the family's ideal treatment outcome picture and to negotiate a small, well-formed behavioral goal. With young children, I use imaginary wand questions (Selekman, 1997) to help them articulate their ideal outcome wishes. After delivering the compliments and tasks, I like to wrap up the session by asking the family: "What was this session like for you?" Their responses provide valuable feedback about how well they cooperated together and what was particularly helpful or not helpful to them.

Interviewing For Change

The solution-oriented therapist asks questions in a purposeful manner, carefully matching his or her questions with the unique cooperative response patterns of each family member. Interviewing in a purposeful manner is a circular process in which family members' verbal and nonverbal feedback guides the therapist toward future question category selections. The therapist needs to constantly be ready and willing to shift gears and move in any direction family members wish. With young children, the therapist must use concrete language and invite children to draw upon their great sense of imagination. Five major categories of questions I frequently use with children and their families follow.

Goal-Setting Questions

The *miracle question* (de Shazer, 1988) is a powerful interventive tool for eliciting family members' ideal treatment outcome pictures. The family is asked: "Suppose you were to go home tonight, and while you are sound asleep a miracle happens, and all of your problems are completely solved. What would be in each of your ideal miracle pictures?" To further clarify the picture, the therapist asks: "What would be different about your situation?" "What else would be better about it?" "When that happens, what effect would it have on your relationship?" "I'm curious—are any pieces of the miracle already happening now?" When asking the miracle question, the therapist has to be patient and wait for family members to respond. Once family members respond, the therapist can help them to expand on this positive view of the future.

With young children, I use *imaginary wand* or *crystal ball* questions (Selekman, 1993, 1997) to elicit their ideal wishes for themselves and their families. Since young children thrive on imagination, play, and pretending, they tend to respond better to these types of questions. Often, the young child's wishes have a profound impact on the parents' behavior, particularly if, for example, their arguing is scaring the child and affecting his or her ability to sleep at night. A 7-year-old depressed boy waved his imaginary wand and wished that his parents would "stop yelling" at him. When asked about how this change would make a difference for him, he said, "I would be happier." The son's disclosure helped the parents to become more aware of how their behavior affects their son's functioning. No parent likes to hear that his or her behavior is negatively affecting his or her child.

Scaling Questions

Scaling questions (de Shazer, 1988, 1991) can be used to help family members identify small, realistic behavioral goals. These questions also serve as a quantitative measure of progress toward the goal throughout the course of therapy. Some examples of scaling questions are:

• On a scale from 1 to 10, with 10 being that your son is doing his homework most of the time and 1 not at all, what would you have rated the situation a month ago? What about today?

- Let's say in one week he steps up to a 6. What will you tell me he did?
- On a scale from 1 to 10, with 10 being totally confident that you will resolve this difficulty with your daughter and 1 having no confidence at all, where are you today?

In some cases, I have the child scale a particular parental behavior he or she would like to see changed, such as nagging. Thus, both the parents and the child are simultaneously working on improving targeted goal areas. When working with very young children, I make the scale visual and draw on a flipchart or whiteboard a face at both ends of the scale. A 10 can be represented by a happy face and a 1 can be represented by a sad face.

Coping Questions

Coping questions (Berg & Miller, 1992) can be used with more pessimistic family members:

- What steps are you taking to prevent your situation from getting much worse?
- What other steps are you taking that seem to be helping?
- How has that made a difference?
- How did you get that to happen?

Coping questions tend to elicit family members' expertise in creative problem-solving. I ask coping questions when family members do not respond well to the miracle question. Often, pessimistic parents can better negotiate a realistic treatment goal following the use of coping questions.

Pessimistic Questions

Pessimistic questions (Berg & Miller, 1992; Selekman, 1993, 1997) can be very effective interventive tools for creating hope and possibilities with highly pessimistic parents who describe their presenting problems as chronic, oppressive, and out of control. Some examples of pessimistic questions are:

- The three of you have already had five counseling experiences. Why are you willing to give counseling another try?
- What has prevented you from throwing in the towel with your situation?
- What keeps you going?
- Is there anything you have tried to do that seems to have helped a little bit?

When the therapist cooperates with the parents' pessimistic position, the parents are more likely to feel supported and recognize some current strategies that are working for them. It is also helpful to explore any past successful parenting strategies they have used to resolve other behavioral difficulties. The therapist can then suggest that it may be worthwhile to experiment with applying a particular past successful strategy to the current presenting problem.

Reversal Questions

Reversal questions (Selekman, 1997) draw on the child's competencies and assist with the problem-solving process. Children by nature are very imaginative and creative and can offer ideas for tackling the various problems their families are struggling with. Reversal questions can effectively alter any outmoded beliefs the parents may have about the identified client. Some examples of reversal questions include:

- Billy, do you have any advice for your parents about how they can help you to do a better job of putting your toys away?
- Mary, do you have any advice for your mother about how we can get her to yell at you less?
- What do you think I should work on changing with your parents first that will help all of you get along better?

Therapeutic Tasks

In this section, I present six therapeutic tasks that I frequently use with children both in and out of family sessions. The first two tasks are geared for stuck parents who are oppressed by a tunnel-view of their children's behavior and need to learn new ways of problem-solving. The other four tasks capitalize on the child's expertise in helping to challenge family beliefs and unproductive interactions. Since it is beyond the scope of this chapter to provide an in-depth overview of all solution-oriented family play and art therapy tasks used in this model, interested readers may refer to Selekman (1997) for more detailed discussion of these tasks.

Observation Tasks

Observation tasks are most useful with parents who engage in a therapist-complainant relationship pattern of interaction (Berg & Miller, 1992; de Shazer, 1988; Selekman, 1993, 1997). Initially, these parents do not include themselves as part of the solution-construction process. Complainants can also be teachers and other school personnel or helping agents from larger systems. Typically, they want the therapist to correct or "fix" the child's disturbing behavior without their involvement in the problem-solving process. After I gather a wealth of information about the problem situation from the complainant, I give him or her the following experiment to further assist me in understanding the child's problematic behavior: "In order for me to have a more complete picture of (identified client's) behavior, I would like you to pretend to be Miss Marple/Sherlock Holmes over the next week. Pull out your imaginary magnifying glass on a daily basis and notice any encouraging steps that you see (identified client) take. Write down your observations and bring them to our next session together." Simply getting the complainant to refocus his or her attention on the child's competency areas and responsible behavior can lead to major changes in the parent's beliefs about and interactions with the child. Children can also make great super-sleuth detectives. For example, a 10-year-old client who was having behavioral problems in class was given the following observation task to perform for one day: "Notice two nice things that your teacher does that you like, write them down, and at the end of the school day tell your mom what those nice things were when she picks you up." This observation task proved to be successful in helping the client view her teacher in a more favorable way. The client's mother was also pleased with her daughter's willingness to take steps to try and improve her behavior in school.

Do Something Different

The do-something-different task (de Shazer, 1985, 1988; Selekman, 1993, 1997) is effective with parents who are predictable and entrenched in superresponsible-superirresponsible behavior or power-struggle interactive tangos with their children. When prescribing the do-something-different task, I share this with parents: "Your child has gotten your number. It is predictable; she can tell what is coming next by the look on your face or how you stand. Over the next week, I would like you to throw a monkey wrench into this problem situation and try a little experiment. Whenever your daughter tries to push your buttons, I want you to do something different from your usual course of action—maybe something wacky or off the wall, as long as it is different from what you usually do." Therapists should avoid, if possible, giving parents ideas about what they could do. It is best that parents tap their own right-brain, creative capacities with this task. Most parents who experience success with this task find it emotionally uplifting, fun, and empowering for them.

The Secret Surprise

The secret surprise task (de Shazer, 1985; Selekman, 1997) is useful with cases in which some improvement in the child's behavior has been reported and you wish to increase or amplify exception patterns of behavior. In this playful task, the child meets alone with the therapist and selects two surprising things she could do in one week to shock her parents in a positive way. The child is not to tell her parents what the surprises are. At the end of the week, playing detective, the parents try to guess what the surprises were. Most children tend to feel more secure and happy when they see their parents happy; this is why children usually have little difficulty following through with this highly effective task.

Imaginary Feelings X-Ray Machine

With very young children or children with somatic problems, grave difficulties expressing themselves, or who come from high-stress family environments, I like to utilize the imaginary feelings x-ray machine (Selekman, 1997) to help the family and myself gain access to the child's inner world. Using a long sheet of meat-wrapping paper or tagboard, I have the identified child client select a family member to draw an outline of the child's body while he or she is lying on the paper. Then I say to the child: "Imagine I have a special x-ray machine that can show us pictures of what your feelings look like. When I turn it on, what will we see?" Children often draw pictures that serve as metaphors for the family drama, such as erupting volcanoes to represent anger, a sad face, or scenes capturing negative family interactions that trouble them. The child's responses can prove to be a newsworthy experience for other family members and lead to improvements in family communications and symptom alleviation.

Invisible Family Invention

The invisible family invention (Selekman, 1997) is a playful task that draws on the child's creative capacities. Most children love to play with gadgets. With this task, the child is given an opportunity to invent a gadget, machine, or useful device that would benefit families just like his or her own. For example, an 11-year-old boy invented a "homework-doing machine," which was easy to program and could correctly complete homework assignments in any subject. Some children and their families take this task a step further and attempt to build the invisible invention at home. I often recommend that families try to secure U.S. patents for their creative inventions.

The Family Mural

The family mural task is an effective in-session family art activity that engages all family members in a fun and playful way. I have the family members draw on a long sheet of paper what they will be doing when they are defeating the problem. This task helps to alter family members' beliefs, to move the child out of the scapegoat role, and to generate group solutions for overcoming the problem. Family members can be asked to write titles by their pictures that capture the essence of their drawings and their family without the problem.

Case Illustration: "Alcohol Is Bad!" Empowering a Family on the Road to Success

One day I received a call from Joshua, a Jewish father who wanted to know if I was running a children of alcoholics group for latency-aged children at our social service agency. At the time, such a group did not exist, but I offered to see Joshua and his children as a family until I had enough participants to start a group. Joshua was quite concerned about his daughters, Jennifer, 11, and Abbie, 9, who were not their usual energetic and socially active selves anymore. Joshua felt they were both very depressed. Their mother, Mary, was an alcoholic, and they frequently cried about this.

Joshua's presentation of his family's difficulties suggested that alcohol was wreaking havoc in this family, and Joshua was taking preventative measures to save his children emotionally. I asked him if he had any other children. He reported having three sons: Steven, 10, Sidney, 8, and Harvey, 6. Harvey was a high-functioning child with fetal alcohol syndrome. When I asked Joshua who he wanted to bring in for our first family session, he felt it would be best to begin with Jennifer and Abbie. He was pretty convinced that Mary would not be joining them due to her frequent intoxication and her past negative treatment experiences. Mary had relapsed after a 28-day inpatient alcoholism treatment program and continued to drink to the present day. She had also failed to respond to two outpatient treatment experiences. Mary was Mexican-American and a former devout Catholic. When questioned about their cultural and racial differences, Joshua pointed out that this was not an issue for either one of them. In fact, they took their children to both church and synagogue for religious holidays. Apparently, the family used to go to church on a regular basis, but stopped attending services because of Mary's difficulties getting up in the mornings and staying sober in the evenings.

The First Family Interview

Present at the first family interview were Joshua, Jennifer, and Abbie. When I greeted them in the lobby, I noticed that the girls had been drawing in some notebooks they carried with them. During the session, both girls looked and verbalized being depressed about the home situation. They described times when they witnessed their mother too drunk to get out of bed, arguing with their father, and passed out in her vomit. Harvey, their brother with fetal alcohol syndrome, was described as a "big" behavioral problem for their mother to manage at home. Jennifer had the challenging task of supervising her younger siblings, cooking for the family, and keeping the household in order. Somehow Jennifer maintained both a straight-A average in school and an adult role at home!

I asked the family the imaginary wand question and the girls indicated that their mother would be functioning better and the family would be happier. Jennifer pointed out that her father would be "less nervous" and the boys would give her less trouble while she was supervising them. Joshua's first wish was that Mary would achieve abstinence from alcohol. Joshua added that he hoped that therapy would help his children to later avoid becoming alcoholics themselves or to hook up with alcoholic or drug-abusing men. In an attempt to elicit pretreatment change material from family members, I asked them if any of their wishes were occurring a little bit now. Not one family member reported any pretreatment changes. Efforts to negotiate a small, behavioral goal proved to be futile. The father viewed the main family problem as being Mary's alcoholism. I avoided asking scaling questions because I did not think they would be helpful.

In the last half-hour of the family session, I decided to try two therapeutic tasks. The use of the imaginary feelings x-ray machine proved highly successful with Abbie. Abbie took a risk and drew pictures right by her heart and her stomach. The picture depicted her desire to run away from home when her mother was highly intoxicated. She also drew a picture of her mother "throwing up to death" in the bathroom. We discussed her fears, sad feelings, and strong desire to see the family situation changed. Jennifer disclosed that there had been some times in the past when she felt like running away from home, too. Joshua found his daughters' disclosures to be quite newsworthy and he provided them with some fatherly support.

Following our discussion of the girls' x-rays, I asked Jennifer if she were to invent something that would benefit other families just like her own, what would her invention be and how would it work. Jennifer took a few minutes to get her creative juices flowing and then came up with the brilliant idea of a machine called "The Family Helper." Whenever family members were stressed or feeling bad, they could go into The Family Helper machine and come out feeling better. I invited Jennifer to discuss how her machine would benefit each family member. Her father would go in and come out "less nervous" after running a lot of errands. Abbie would go in and come out wanting to "go out" and "play more" with her friends. Her mother would go in and come out "not wanting to drink" because "her brain changed." With the help of the invisible family inventions task, Jennifer was clearly able to articulate the family's treatment outcome goals. At this point in the session, I asked scaling questions about each of these ideal outcome areas.

After complimenting the family on their tremendous courage, resiliency, and fine work with the in-session tasks, I asked them if they had a desire to build The Family Helper machine. Since Joshua was an auto mechanic and handy with his hands, he offered to help the girls out with this project. I encouraged Joshua to bring Mary in for our next scheduled appointment. The girls left our first session smiling and in much better spirits.

The Second Family Session

Apparently, right after our last session together Joshua and the girls went home and built The Family Helper machine out of large cardboard boxes. Whenever the girls felt sad or mad, they would go into the machine for a few minutes, and then come out and pretend to be in a happy mood. Through the help of the invisible family inventions task, the family had generated their own unique solution for combating emotional discomfort and stress. The family members' use of The Family Helper machine was a form of pattern intervention (O'Hanlon, 1987). They were disrupting their own negative thought patterns.

The second family session was held three weeks after the first due to scheduling conflicts and Mary's initial resistance to attend our meetings. Mary eventually agreed to accompany Joshua, Jennifer, and Abbie. Much to my surprise, Mary was alcohol-free and quite up front about her alcoholism and voiced a strong desire to see her children get the help they needed to learn how to better cope with her condition. Mary had achieved three weeks of abstinence from alcohol following a visit to her family physician who had prescribed Antabuse. According to Mary, her doctor was quite successful at getting her to commit to taking the Antabuse, along with Librium to combat withdrawal symptoms, and to schedule weekly visits with him to monitor for alcohol withdrawal complications. I asked Mary what she did not like about her past treatment experiences so that I would avoid making the same mistakes. Mary said she "hated to be confronted about being in denial" and adamantly refused to attend

Alcoholics' Anonymous meetings. She openly admitted that she had gone to two AA meetings in the past and found them to be "unhelpful." She did not "buy into" the 12-step philosophy.

With the daughters' permission, I showed Mary their feelings x-ray machine drawings. Mary was quite shocked by Abbie's drawings, particularly by her fear that Mary would die from alcoholism. With tearful eyes, Mary commented that it hurt her inside to see that the children were so troubled by her drinking. I addressed the issue of Jennifer's pseudo-adult caretaker role in the family and how it appeared that she was burning out. Mary voiced a strong desire to get back on track and take over more as a parent in the family. Mary was very pleased that her children enjoyed therapy and were getting something out of it; the children had raved to her about how much they had enjoyed the two tasks we did together and that it was helpful to talk about their problems.

Prior to concluding the session, I complimented Mary on her courage to get help for herself and her high level of commitment to her children. I complimented the girls on taking big positive risks with their mother by sharing their concerns with her and making good use of The Family Helper machine.

Since I was going on vacation for three weeks, I gave the family an observation task of keeping track on a daily basis the various things they were doing that was helping them cope better and succeed at resolving their difficulties. Mary was instructed to notice what she did daily to avoid the urge to drink. When clients are making great progress in treatment, you want to keep things simple and have them do more of what is working for them.

The Third Family Session

I began the third session by exploring with the family what further progress they had made while on vacation from therapy. Mary proudly proclaimed that she was "taking the Antabuse faithfully," which was helping her stay alcohol-free. Mary was also keeping busy so she would not have any free time to think about drinking. She also reported being less reactive to Harvey's impulsive behavior. Joshua pointed out that Jennifer and Abbie had "stopped crying and looked happier," and that Mary had taken over more of the household and parenting responsibilities. Joshua also reported that he was "less stressed out" and getting along much better with Mary. The family had also started going to church again, which in the past had brought them closer together as a family. The observation task and my using presuppositional language had encouraged the family members to become more aware of their strengths and resources.

I spent the majority of the session time amplifying and consolidating the family gains. I particularly underscored the children's success with The Family Helper machine and Mary's taking on more parenting responsibilities. To help consolidate family gains, I asked the following questions:

- What would you do to go backwards?
- How would you prevent a major backslide?
- If you were to gaze into my imaginary crystal ball three months down the road, what further changes do you see yourselves making?

I also asked the family when they wanted to get together again and they unanimously agreed that we would have our next session four weeks later since they were progressing so well. I like to give families vacations from therapy as a vote of confidence. I recommended that if family members wanted to do any work while on vacation, they could step into The Family Helper machine to "chill out" if things should get tense. I let the family know that change is three steps forward and two steps back, and that slips are part of the change process. By predicting and normalizing slips, clients will not feel like they have returned to square one if past problematic behavior returns.

The Fourth Family Session

When I met the family for the fourth session, I almost did not recognize them. Mary had just come from a job interview and was professionally dressed, the girls had big smiles on their faces, Joshua seemed to be in great spirits, and much to my surprise the three boys had joined them for our session. Up to this point, Mary and Joshua had left their sons at home under the supervision of their maternal grandmother. After highlighting all of the important family changes, I had the family create a mural depicting the various ways they will not allow alcohol to destroy their lives. The family got to work immediately and created a masterpiece. One of the most interesting scenes was Abbie's drawing. She drew herself both driving a car into and stabbing a monster that represented alcohol. While discussing her picture, she pointed out how the alcohol monster made her "mad." Jennifer drew a picture of her family having a great time on vacation; her parents were cuddled up together under a tree. The boys drew a giant bottle-shaped monster representing alcohol. They drew themselves inside helicopters dropping a special water-like solution that would turn alcohol into water onto the monster, thus rendering it powerless. Mary drew a gravestone for her father. Since achieving abstinence, Mary had been thinking a lot about her deceased father and the fact that she had not adequately mourned his death due to her alcohol abuse problem. Mary also disclosed that she had initiated this mourning process on her own with support from her mother. Throughout the discussion of the drawings, both the children and the parents spontaneously asked questions about each others' drawings. For the first time, family members were freely sharing their thoughts and feelings about the effects of alcoholism on all of them, including Mary.

After discussing everyone's drawings, I invited each family member to come up with a title for the new family they had become. Some of the titles were: "A Happy Story," "A New Beginning," "Staying Strong," and "Alcohol is Bad!" I complimented the family on their great teamwork, courage, and resilience. We mutually agreed that it was time for an extended vacation from therapy. The next appointment was scheduled for two months later. I reminded the family that slips go with the territory of change and should they occur, it is a sign that they are making progress. As I mentioned earlier, I did not want the family to be devastated by a slip or view this situation as disastrous. The family left quite confident that they would not go backward over the break period.

Case Summary

Two months later, the family returned eager to report their many changes. The greatest accomplishment was Mary's over four months of sobriety without one relapse! She also had landed a part-time job and regained her children's respect and trust as an authority figure in the family. The children were doing well in school. Joshua reported that he and Mary were a much more solid parenting team when disciplining the children. After amplifying and consolidating the wealth of changes, I asked the family what their consultation fee would be if I called upon them in the future to serve as expert consultants in helping me with other families oppressed by alcohol problems. The family kindly shared with me that there would be "no charge" for their services. We mutually agreed to stop therapy due to their progress.

Follow-up calls were made at three, six, and nine months. Each time, the parents indicated that they were going strong, no alcohol relapses had occurred, and the children were functioning quite well.

Case Discussion

In reflecting upon how this family had done so well so quickly, it was clear to me that I was working with a family that had a multitude of strengths. They possessed the six major characteristics that research indicates make up a strong family: time spent together, commitment, appreciation, communications, dealing with crisis in a positive way, and spiritual wellness (De Frain & Stinnett, 1992). Throughout the course of therapy, these characteristics empowered Joshua and his family to persevere and cope with high levels of stress. As is often the case growing up in an alcoholic family system, the unspoken rules are: "Don't feel," "Don't talk," and "Don't trust" (Black, 1981). Joshua's family was an exception to the rule. On a daily basis he made himself available to each of his children, listening to their concerns and playing with them.

The three family play and art therapy tasks employed with this family proved to be quite effective at eliciting the children's thoughts and feelings and contributed to the stabilization of their depressive symptoms. The children made excellent use of The Family Helper machine to challenge their negative thoughts and alter their unpleasant emotional states. In the second family session, showing the daughter's x-ray drawings to Mary opened up the lines of communication between them. Mary's teary eyes and sad tone of voice showed that she was very troubled by the effects of her drinking problem on the girls. Mary's powerful emotional experience with her daughters in the second session forced her to confront her commitment to the change process.

To further empower the family, I spent the majority of the latter sessions amplifying and consolidating their behavioral changes. At the same time, I addressed the likelihood of their experiencing slips despite the progress they were making; prediction is a useful therapeutic tool for keeping family members on their toes. Research indicates that clients who have made changes often worry about slipping back into old problematic patterns of behavior and have concerns about maintaining their therapeutic gains (Prochaska, Norcross, & DiClemente, 1994). However, I did not experience this with Joshua's family. In our last meeting together, each family member came in beaming with self-confidence and highly optimistic about future success.

Limitations of the Model

The solution-oriented brief family therapy approach can be quite effective with a wide range of children's problems. Like all therapy models, however, it is not a panacea for every child problem situation.

Families who describe their presenting problems as oppressive, chronic and having a life of their own do not respond well to solution-oriented questions. With these families, it may be more effective to externalize their problems

(White & Epston, 1990; White, 1995, 1988). For example, a child who has temper tantrum problems can be asked: "How long has the temper been pushing you around?" or "What does the temper coach you to say to your mother?" By externalizing the problem, family members will begin to view the problem situation differently, which will change their interactions as well.

Families who have experienced severe traumas and multiple treatment failures also do not initially respond well to solution-oriented therapy. The therapist must respectfully give them plenty of room to share their long stories of feeling demoralized and victimized by their problems and the treatment systems they have been involved with. If the therapist moves too quickly with these families and becomes a narrative editor (Anderson, 1996), they will feel slighted and misunderstood, and interpret the therapist's behavior as not taking their situation seriously. Therefore, the therapist needs to operate from a position of *not knowing* (Anderson & Goolishian, 1988) and ask open-ended questions to elicit further information about the ever-evolving client story, which can loosen up fixed beliefs and generate new narratives. Once change has occurred in both of these clinical case situations, the therapist can use solution-oriented questions to amplify family gains.

Matthew D. Selekman, M.S.W., L.C.S.W., maintains a private practice and consultation service in Evanston, Illinois.

References

Anderson, H. (1996). A reflection on client-professional collaboration. *Family Systems and Health, 14*(2), 193–203.

Anderson, H. & Goolishian, H. (1988). Human systems as linguistic systems: Preliminary and evolving ideas about the implications for clinical theory. *Family Process, 27*(4), 371–395.

Berg, I. K., & de Shazer, S. (1993). Making numbers talk: Language in therapy. In S. Friedman (Ed.), *The new language of change: Constructive collaboration in psychotherapy* (pp. 5–24). New York: Guilford.

Berg, I. K., & Miller, S. D. (1992). *Working with the problem drinker: A solution-focused approach.* New York: Norton.

Black, C. (1981). *It will never happen to me.* Denver, CO: M.A.C.

Campbell, T. (1996). Systemic therapies and basic research. *Journal of Systemic Therapies, 15*(3), 15–40.

DeFrain, J., & Stinnett, N. (1992). Building on the inherent strengths of families: A positive approach for family psychologists and counselors. *Topics in Family Psychology and Counseling, 1*(1), 15–26.

de Shazer, S. (1985). *Keys to solution in brief therapy.* New York: Norton.

de Shazer, S. (1988). *Clues: Investigating solutions in brief therapy.* New York: Norton.

de Shazer, S. (1991). *Putting difference to work.* New York: Norton.

de Shazer, S. (1994). *Words were originally magic.* New York: Norton.

Gardner, H. (1991). *The unschooled mind.* New York: Basic.

Kohut, H. (1971). *The analysis of the self.* New York: International Universities.

Miller, W. R. (1985). Addictive behavior and the theory of psychological reversals. *Addictive Behaviors, 10,* 177–180.

O'Hanlon, W. H. (1987). *Taproots: Underlying principles of Milton Erickson's therapy and hypnosis.* New York: Norton.

Prochaska, J. O., Norcross, J. C., & DiClemente, C. C. (1994). *Changing for good.* New York: William Morrow.

Selekman, M. D. (1993). *Pathways to change: Brief therapy solutions with difficult adolescents.* New York: Guilford.

Selekman, M. D. (1997). *Solution-focused therapy with children: Harnessing family strengths for systemic change.* New York: Guilford.

Weiner-Davis, M., de Shazer, S., & Gingerich, W. (1987). Building on pretreatment change to construct the therapeutic solution: An exploratory study. *Journal of Marital and Family Therapy, 13*(4), 359–363.

White, M. (1988, Winter). The process of questioning: A therapy of literary merit? *Dulwich Centre Newsletter,* 8–14.

White, M. (1995). *Re-authoring lives: Interviews and essays.* Adelaide, South Australia: Dulwich Centre.

White, M., & Epston, D. (1990). *Narrative means to therapeutic ends.* New York: Norton.

2

Witnessing Bravery: Narrative Ideas for Working with Children and Families

Virginia A. Simons

Jill Freedman

The Barry Levinson film *Avalon* portrays the overlapping worlds of adults and children in an extended family. At one point Michael's father tells him: "When I was just a little younger than you, I thought the world was made up of just big people and little people. What I couldn't understand is why everything was made for the big people: the chairs and tables were too big, the sinks were too high, even the toilet bowl was too big."

Later in the film, after he fails to heed a warning to stop playing with matches, Michael frantically stomps the flames of a fire he and his cousin have set in the basement of his father's new store. After believing they have stifled the flames, they promise each other never to tell. That evening during a dinner celebrating the store's successful opening, Michael's world explodes. His father is called and told that the store is burning out of control. As the family reacts, Michael runs to his grandfather's house to seek comfort. There Michael confesses. His grandfather summons his father and tells Michael he must now tell his father about what he has done. The world stands still as the boy halt-ingly faces his father. We are amazed by his courage.

As family therapists working with and writing about children, we are aware that we are privileged recorders and coauthors of children's stories. This is both an honor and a challenge in work that aspires to honor children's voices and knowledge. When a child or family consults us, we try to keep in mind the restraints of dominant cultural beliefs and theories about children and to look at the actions and stories we are told in the context of children's limited power.

Depending upon one's perspective, Michael's facing his father and taking responsibility for the fire is either an ordinary, taken-for-granted act of a child "having" to tell a parent what he has done or an astonishing act of bravery.

From our perspective, children participate in acts of courage and trust daily, in families, at school, on playgrounds, and at childcare programs. These moments often go unnoticed in an adult-centered society. Since most children and their families enter therapy because of problems in their lives, we find it useful to bring events and family members' understanding of those events into a space to be questioned and reconsidered.

In this chapter we illustrate therapeutic work with children using narrative ideas. We discuss the collaboration with one child, Daniel, and his family. There are limitations in using a single example, since every situation is unique (a particular child, in a particular family, in a particular classroom, in a particular school, in a particular culture). However, the problems Daniel faces are familiar to most therapists seeing children and families. Through the interviews and examples of Daniel's developing a new lived narrative, we offer the reader a journey through this work. Our hope is that Daniel's story reflects the potency of narrative ideas and practices for creativity, collaboration, and celebration of children's strengths.

The Narrative Approach

Our work is based on social constructionist ideas (Berger & Luckmann, 1966; Gergen, 1985; Hoffman, 1990) and narrative practices (Anderson & Goolishian, 1988; Bruner, 1991; Freedman & Combs, 1996; Hoffman, 1991; Monk, Winslade, & Crocket, 1996; White, 1995; White & Epston, 1990; Zimmerman & Dickerson, 1996). Social constructionist ideas include: (1) a person's sense of self is constructed through interaction with others; (2) realities are socially constructed; (3) realities are constituted through language; (4) there are no essential truths; and (5) realities are organized and maintained through narrative (Freedman & Combs, 1996). We think of "story" instead of pattern or labeling; of "society" rather than system.

Any narrative is an act of bridging, connecting the teller, who in therapy is the person with intimate knowledge of the experience, and the listener, who is the therapist. The more narrative is studied, the more one realizes how very complex this bridging actually is, and how much our lives are shaped by such experiences, both for the teller and the listener. People come to therapy because of a problem that is bothersome and restraining to their life. The therapist tries to understand the influence of the restraints and provide an interaction with the teller where a co-construction of a preferred description can originate, take shape, and be acted upon.

As narrative therapists, we are concerned with meaning rather than generalizations or assumptions. We are interested in exceptions rather than similarities so we choose to look at specific contextualized details. We interview family members in the presence of each other (or about one another), seeking descriptions, beliefs, ideas, and perceptions of experiences. The perceptions of each person—therapist, interviewee, and listener—are relationally shaped by the presence of the others. It is more important to approach families with all of these ideas about therapy in mind, than to practice any particular narrative technique (Combs & Freedman, 1998). The culture each one of us lives in plays a tremendous role as a transmitter of ideas, expectations, and stories that people tend to experience as taken-for-granted realities.

As members of families, neighborhoods, and religious institutions, children are not exempt from these influences of the social world. Additionally, they are constantly exposed to the media. Outside of their families, schools are often the primary institutions where children are saturated in cultural narratives and witness cultural practices for extended periods of time each day. We do not suggest that teachers or schools "cause" problems for children, but we do think that exploration of school as part of a child's cultural context is fitting.*

When working with children and their families, it is also important to think about how dominant discourses affect our work. To name a few: the role of adults in relation to children is "instructional" (therefore interpretive and serious); children need to be "socialized" (so approaches need to be methodical); children are not old or wise enough to "know" things (so adults tell them what they should think or feel); and adult time is more "precious." If we as therapists

---

*For example, educators in Western cultures are socialized to see the formal curriculum as the core of what they do. While students may be attempting to study the curriculum, they are also engaged in life at school. Chris McClean (1995) points out how the educators' approach that considers underfed, poorly clothed, and inadequately supervised children as "unteachable" hides the reality that, for working-class and poor children, school can represent a hostile, class-based structure of authority and privilege to which they have no access. Education in these schools literally requires these students to become "class traitors." While this dilemma is very different than the one we describe in this chapter, it is illustrative of the way the dominant culture can create a context for problematic life stories to evolve.

get caught up in these assumptions we can unwittingly contribute to a child's experience of having little power in his or her own life.

Clearly we cannot change a child's culture in our office, but we can create a different kind of social interaction in which a child's knowledge is given greater value. We strive to stay mindful of our input and exercise responsibility regarding the weight of our influence in shaping children's lives and the narratives by which they describe their lives (Loptson & Stacey, 1995).

Opening Space for Preferred Stories

We are interested in helping people deconstruct the problematic stories they are experiencing and construct preferred stories. We use a number of practices to that end. We use questions to gain clarity of understanding and to offer linguistic options for expanding possible meanings (Stacey, 1995). We also name problems and have externalizing conversations about them (Doan & Clifton, 1990; Durrant, 1989; Epston, 1992; White, 1989). That is, we invite family members to join us in seeing problems as separate from people and to use therapy as a context in which to renegotiate the relationship with the problem. In so doing, we are turning a dominant cultural practice on its head. Rather than seeing the child as a problem we are inviting the family to join with the child in standing up to the problem. This helps eliminate blame and defensiveness and frees a child for more personal agency (Tomm, 1989). It helps family members unite with each other against problems instead of being torn apart by them or demonizing the child.

Once problems are exposed in this way, family members are free to recognize and construct preferred stories (Dickerson, 1996). It is useful to create an audience for these alternative stories and work to commemorate and celebrate change.

As we describe the example of our work with Daniel, we intersperse commentary about these ideas with descriptions of the work.

Case Illustration: Daniel's Story

Daniel's mother, Evelyn, called Virginia to request therapy for Daniel after psychological testing and a series of school meetings. Evelyn explained that Daniel was having difficulty with academics, as well as his behavior. Testing had revealed that Daniel had difficulty with verbal memory, verbal processing, and oral formulation skills. He had been engaged in speech and language intervention to learn techniques for enhancing processing of language and memory strategies. He was meeting with a resource teacher at school and had weekly tutoring after school. Evelyn expressed more concern about the anger and discouragement she saw in her son. Virginia arranged a meeting with Evelyn and Daniel. Daniel's father, Alex, traveled extensively as part of his work, and was unable to attend most of the therapy meetings.

At the time of the first meeting, Daniel was a nine-and-a-half-year-old boy who looked at least two years older. At first, he was cordial but not interested in talking, so initially the conversation was with Evelyn. She described her serious concern about the discouragement she saw in Daniel, the difficulty he was having in the classes, and the fights he was having at school. She said Daniel was "being teased and fighting back." He had gotten in trouble a number of times at school, most often on the playground or as school was letting out in the afternoon. However, the general discouragement about school had her deeply concerned. She began to experience helplessness and felt at a loss about what to do.

After Evelyn described her perceptions of the problem, Virginia hoped that Daniel might be ready to talk, so she began addressing questions to him.

WE LIKE TO BEGIN therapy by finding out about the life of family members separate from the problems that bring them to therapy. Hearing what they enjoy and are interested in helps all of us to avoid letting the problem color our ideas about family members. In this situation, Daniel declined to participate in this kind of conversation and Evelyn quickly began describing the problem. Rather than forcefully interrupt and redirect her, Virginia listened.

It is also our practice to ask children if there is a problem and how they would describe it. Virginia begins with the first of a cluster of problems described by the mother in order to understand Daniel's experience. In so doing, we acknowledge children as privileged authorities on their own experience. Thus, Virginia is interested in turning the conversation to Daniel as soon as he is willing to speak.

THERAPIST: Daniel, can I ask you some questions now? I remember you didn't want to talk when you first got here. I'm just not clear on some things, and would like to ask you. Would you talk now?

DANIEL: Yes, I guess so.

THERAPIST: How long has the problem of not understanding some things at school been giving you trouble?

DANIEL: A long time.

THERAPIST: Since kindergarten?

DANIEL: No, not *that* long. . . . I don't know.

THERAPIST: Since second grade? Do you remember second grade?

DANIEL: Yes, but it wasn't second grade.

THERAPIST: Not second grade either?

DANIEL: No, just before school was out last year.

THERAPIST: The end of third grade, then? (*At this point, Daniel is in the second month of fourth grade.*)

DANIEL: Yeah. (*Evelyn also nods yes.*)

THERAPIST: So tell me what happens. Is it just in certain classes?

DANIEL: Just sometimes, not all the time.

THERAPIST: So there are times you are free of the problems?

DANIEL: Yes.

THERAPIST: Really? Could I ask you some about this?

DANIEL: Yes.

THERAPIST: So Daniel, when are you free from them?

DANIEL: When I'm playing with my friends . . . when I'm playing hockey, and with my mom or my dad.

Since the mother had described a cluster of problems Virginia began with the first one, and then, rather than naming a specific problem, she quickly initiates an externalizing conversation by calling it "the problem" or "the problems."

THERAPIST: So you play hockey? What position do you play? Do you play on a team? (*They talk of hockey. Daniel loves hockey; he has been skating since an early age and has been playing team hockey since he was 7. Alex played hockey from childhood through college. Daniel talks about his favorite professional players. He and Evelyn educate Virginia, since she knows little about hockey.*)

The conversation about hockey helps to minimize the hierarchy inherent in therapy contexts (Cohen, Shulman, Lorimer, Combs, & Freedman, 1998). It reminds everyone that there are subjects in which Daniel is an expert and Virginia is not. It also reminds Daniel of happy stories in his life, which will undoubtedly be useful in changing his relationship with the problem.

THERAPIST: Daniel, what happens when the problem comes?

DANIEL: It's in math. I just have to ask questions and I don't get to, . . . because by the time I try and see if I can do it and I can't I just get mad. . . . Then the teacher doesn't want me interrupting . . . and then she says its time to do something else. I *really* get mad then. (*Then he blurts out*) I just have low confidence.

THERAPIST: (*Thoughtfully*) What does that mean, low confidence?

DANIEL: When I just don't want to try anymore.

THERAPIST: Did you think of this or did someone tell you? I mean is that the word that tells how you're feeling just then?

DANIEL: Yeah, for *that,* yeah.

THERAPIST: What about the anger, what happens to the anger then?

DANIEL: I don't know—I just get mad, and then when people tease, I fight.

THERAPIST: The other kids tease? Do they tease you about the schoolwork?

DANIEL: Yes, and other things too.

EVELYN: I think it's because he is big, and the other boys test that.

THERAPIST: How does the anger work? Does the anger come along with low confidence?

DANIEL: (*Dropping his head and speaking in a quieter voice*) Yeah, like a secret mission against me.

THERAPIST: A secret mission? So do you know when it's coming?

DANIEL: No.

In the externalizing conversation two candidate names are used for the problem: "anger" and "low confidence." As the work continues Daniel settles on "temper" and "low self-confidence." Virginia is interested in mapping the effects of the temper and low self-confidence in Daniel's life.

Deconstructing the Problem

In clarifying and writing down Daniel's words, Virginia thinks of her work as collaborating with Daniel in creating a document of his unique knowledge about the problems. It is this idea that becomes central in the document created. The "Temper's Secret Mission with Low Self-Confidence" document was developed over a number of sessions, with Evelyn in a listening position or with only Daniel and Virginia present when he requested time alone. The conversations through which the document was developed were playful and included a sense of struggling with a mystery. It was clear to everyone involved that personifying the problem and thinking about the problem as having a secret mission was Daniel's inspiration. The therapist joined in, asking questions to help Daniel fill in and expand his ideas (Griffith & Griffith, 1994). The document is written as if the problem is speaking. As Daniel examined the situation from the perspective of the problem, he gained ideas and descriptions of the mission that made the problem less confusing and overwhelming to him.

TEMPER'S SECRET MISSION WITH LOW SELF-CONFIDENCE AGAINST DANIEL

The mission of temper and low self-confidence: *To hide and sneak around Daniel Green for an invasion at any shaky moment.*

1. At the slightest quiver in Daniel, we move in closer, putting thoughts in Daniel's mind. We have him doubt his abilities; we have him think others don't look up to him, honor him, or care that much. We talk him into thinking he can't do something.
2. The biggest trick we pull is keeping Daniel thinking these thoughts, so he won't think about what he needs at the time. This is called the fake-it method.
3. Because we are so klutzy, we have to be careful, so he won't notice. We usually send frustration and irritation first. If Daniel falls for those we know we have a better chance to get him.[*]
4. We know when Daniel is not fully dedicated to the task. We can sense his weakest moments, when he feels the pressure of time or impatience creeping in.[†]

Through the process of creating this document, Daniel and Virginia deconstruct the problem (White & Epston, 1992) by illuminating its construction (Brooks, 1984). We assume that there are always counterplots or events that would not be predicted by problem-saturated stories. As the deconstruction was going on, Virginia was alert to any events or experiences that stood outside of the problem-saturated story.

A Possible Alternative Story

Virginia was interested in the times and ways Daniel had escaped from temper

---

[*]This was documented after Daniel really began to catch onto the methods temper was using in its mission.

[†]This was documented after a setback.

and low self-confidence. When asked about times when temper and low self-confidence were not around, Evelyn spontaneously announced that temper was completely absent during hockey. Virginia explored this further, asking Daniel for details about how he dealt with temper during hockey. She discovered that Daniel had no problems with temper during hockey practice or games or when playing with friends at home. Virginia asked him what made the difference in those situations. They discovered that although hockey was quite competitive, Daniel was confident and was enjoying the situation, and his favorite professional player never lost his temper.

Daniel also said his coach was a "fair person." This seemed important to Daniel, so Virginia asked about the meaning of this. Daniel meant not only that the coach followed a set of rules to determine consequences, but that he also had experienced the coach as having a fair and flexible way of addressing conflicts. Further comparative questions were then asked about his experience of school in order to understand what was troubling him about the situation. Although the playground was supposed to be a place to be with friends, forget academic struggles, and have fun, instead it had become a place where Daniel experienced fierce competition. Evelyn believed this was partly due to his size. Daniel told of three boys in his grade who regularly picked on other boys but rarely got into trouble because the playground monitor did not see them initiate it. More often the boy being taunted would get into trouble after defensively striking out. There was also the dilemma of a "no telling" code. ("Tattletales" are sometimes scorned in elementary schools, not just by other children, but by adults as well.)

Nevertheless, Daniel had proved that it was possible to get the best of temper. He had been able to do it in hockey and at home. An examination of how he did it in these two contexts was instrumental in developing the following "counterdocument."

DANIEL'S SECRET MISSION AGAINST TEMPER
AND LOW SELF-CONFIDENCE

Daniel knows to be watchful of the tentacles of temper and low self-confidence.

1. He says to himself, "This is just one thing" over and over and believes it. He reminds himself that whatever it is, "it won't kill you."[*]

---

[*]This second sentence was a later addition.

2. Daniel promises his mom and dad that he will hold their love and strength in his heart for tough moments. But more importantly, he remembers the promise to himself to hold love and strength in his heart and stay strongly committed to this for those times when he *really* has to fight temper and low self-confidence.

3. When someone trips him or teases him, Daniel asks, "Why did you do that?" This lets the person know he noticed but will *not* react back. Or he may say, "You had no reason to . . ." Other times Daniel makes himself not hear.[*]

4. Daniel has learned he cannot say "It won't work" and refuse to try with ALL his strength. He has to believe and say "I've *really* got to try this." Then when he believes, he starts feeling better. He reminds himself, "Don't get lazy, I have to do this every day."

5. Because temper is klutzy Daniel can sense when it is coming. He becomes irritated and frustrated, and he experiences more body movement, like jiggling and wiggling and he talks back. Then it's got him. Staying quiet helps Daniel deal with temper.

6. When kids are teasing, it's easy to get caught up in doing the same. Instead, he must not tease, because it comes back at him when he least expects it. The best thing to do is to stay quiet or stay away.

7. It is important to this mission to talk about what is making the jiggling and wiggling. He has to decide to speak with a caring person, either a trusted friend or concerned adult. Daniel cannot hide and must speak up, so others know.

Composing the counterdocument seemed to help generate hope and mastery for Daniel. The therapist works with the child's interest. If at some point the interest tangibly fades for the child, the therapist makes accommodations accordingly. Several ideas may be tried before one seems to fit. If the document or idea seems no longer useful, it is abandoned for new developments. When asked about his interest in the ideas described by the mission statements, Daniel said it helped him understand what was happening.

Circulating the New Story

Because Daniel's father, Alex, was not able to attend therapy sessions, some of

---

[*]This is an advanced skill that came after much practice.

the sessions were videotaped so that Alex could watch them. Daniel told Virginia that his dad was encouraging his secret mission project and had gone over the document with him. Daniel said this helped him know what he was up against and helped him know of his father's faith in him. Later in the therapy, Daniel talked about the significance of including his parents. He said that when his parents understood what he was up against and what he and they could do about it, they encouraged him rather than wondering what to do.

ALTHOUGH SOME MODELS of family therapy believe a parent is uninvolved or resistant if he or she does not attend therapy sessions, we do not make that assumption. We also do not necessarily focus on family relationships or assume that they are part of the problem. We do assume that the more people involved in the preferred story the better. For that reason we are very interested in people witnessing and participating in the development of the preferred story. Evelyn did this by being in a listening and reflecting position in the sessions. Alex did this by watching videotapes and talking with Daniel about them.

ALTHOUGH VIRGINIA MET with the school staff, the meeting was focused on academics. Daniel's grades and study skills were improving, and it was determined that he would continue with the part-time resource person. She had also become someone he liked talking with.

The school social worker was identified as an alternate person for Daniel to talk with as needed (this fit with point 7 in Daniel's secret mission). As Daniel experienced more positive changes in his life, he and his mom decided to share the secret mission document with the school social worker in an attempt to spread the news of his work. They thought this would help the project along at school. The social worker was supportive and had noticed positive changes in Daniel, but for unknown reasons she did not communicate with his teachers or principal.

Alternatives to the Problem-Saturated Story: A Step of Bravery

Daniel had been free of difficulty for well over a month when a problem erupted at school and Evelyn was called in to see the principal. Apparently Daniel had been pushed while standing in the line in the hallway. No one knew how or why this happened. For Daniel it had come out of nowhere, although the other boy was known for having problems with temper. Daniel pushed the boy back, on the leg, as the other boy tried to kick him. The other child started yelling curses and pushing others as well. As the other boy was taken to the office by the teacher, the other kids began snickering and laughing. Although

Daniel was not implicated, later, after the teacher returned, he asked to go down to the principal's office "because he felt bad for the other boy being taunted" and to take "responsibility for pushing back." This is an interview about Daniel's stand against temper and low self-confidence, about Daniel's own mission being practiced in a wider, more noticeable way. The following transcript is part of the therapy session two days later:

EVELYN: He asked to go down there (the principal's office), even when he didn't have to. He could have just gotten out of it. The teacher, the social worker, everybody knows that now, too. I'm glad I was called. I was kind of worried that this would be interpreted like the times before.

THERAPIST: I could see how it could be worrisome. Did you feel like going down to the office was a pretty brave thing for Daniel to do?

EVELYN: Yes. (*Quietly*) I was very proud, too.

THERAPIST: It could have been passed over, just kind of dropped there. And you were proud?

EVELYN: I was very impressed. But you can see there is some kind of readjustment going on around recess again, a different person is out there and it reached that time, that point, where kids were at each other.

THERAPIST: Yes, but you know, Daniel, I'm wondering if all of these times when kids are teasing are also opportunities for anger and temper to squeeze back into your life big-time? You know, to try to take over again? And you haven't let it so far, is that right?

DANIEL: Yeah, I didn't.

THERAPIST: Would you say going down to talk, downstairs in the school office, was a brave thing to do? . . . For you to try and reach out to somebody who was calling you names and curses?

DANIEL: Yeah, 'cause I know how it is . . . what it feels like to be so mad. . . . Yep. It was.

THERAPIST: So Daniel, do you know how you are able to be brave like that?

DANIEL: I just say it, like . . . I am part of it, because I did sort of push him back, on the leg. So I should go down to talk.

THERAPIST: Because you pushed him back, on the leg?

DANIEL: Yeah, I went down there. I was trying to help him feel better.

THERAPIST: So you went down and faced the adults who could have seen what you did as wrong?

DANIEL: (*Whispers*) I took responsibility.

THERAPIST: Yes, you did, and you also told the truth. You told them what you did, too.

DANIEL: Just to say . . . I pushed him on the leg. The teachers said he had two weeks to be in (meaning two weeks of staying in from recess or after school) because he got so mad. He said I kicked him but I didn't.

THERAPIST: And you went down to explain?

DANIEL: Just to say that I pushed him back. I tried to tell him I understood, that it isn't how it ought to be, teasing and all, . . . but, he tried to kick me again when I was down there. In a way, he deserves it.

THERAPIST: Yeah, but Daniel, you know what I'm saying? Instead of letting him tell a big whopper (lie) and not say anything because you were not in trouble, for you to go down to the office and tell them the truth about your reaction and also offer understanding to him, was that a pretty brave thing to do?

DANIEL: Yeah.

THERAPIST: What do you think makes it brave?

DANIEL: That I decided to go down. Because, I mean, I didn't really have to.

THERAPIST: You could take half responsibility on it?

DANIEL: Or none at all.

THERAPIST: Right.

DANIEL: But I just thought I'd have part of it.

THERAPIST: So you were willing to take the responsibility in that way?

DANIEL: Yeah.

THERAPIST: (To Evelyn) You know, you talked about this last time. His directness. What was it you said? I can't remember the exact words, where you said Daniel.

EVELYN: That he is very honest.

THERAPIST: Yes, and he didn't stay silent about this, that he said it outwardly at school. Earlier you said you really appreciated this about Daniel. That you felt good about his honesty and being able to trust him. It sounds like in this situation it was also a brave thing because it could have really backfired, right? Daniel, how did you stand your ground about this? How did you do it?

DANIEL: Well, when he said the "F" and "B" words, I just stood there. Everyone was laughing. I didn't laugh or anything.

THERAPIST: Really?

DANIEL: Just stood there.

THERAPIST: Now, was that the not-hearing strategy you talked about (looking at the mission list)? You know where you stop hearing?

DANIEL: Yeah. It was.

THERAPIST: Wow. Good for you. So, Daniel is there some way we need to add this not-hearing strategy to this list of the things for your mission? You remember this list?

DANIEL: Yeah.

THERAPIST: What do we add to this, do you think? Do you want me to read what we have?

DANIEL: Yeah.

THERAPIST: Say to yourself "this is just one thing" over and over again, until you believe it. You have to believe it.

DANIEL: And it won't kill you.

THERAPIST: Oh, and it won't kill you (*adding this to the first point in the mission document*).

THERAPIST: Was holding your parents' strength and love in your heart operating today, also?

DANIEL: I said, "Forget it." It just kind of came to me.

THERAPIST: Really? It just came from inside you?

DANIEL: Sure.

THERAPIST: So, do you think that's a good thing? That it just came from inside you?

DANIEL: Yeah. It was just there helping me with other people.

The story of this incident is an alternative to the problem-saturated story (de Shazer, 1991; Morgan, 1995). It speaks to Daniel's bravery (Radke-Yarrow, Zahn-Waxler, & Chapman, 1983), whereas the problem-saturated story was about temper and low self-confidence. The transcript illustrates questions asked to facilitate the retelling of this preferred story in detail and making meaning from it.

Later in the session Virginia became aware that she had made an assumption from her own response to hearing the story. The collaboration of narrative work includes the therapist openly questioning and correcting his or her own motivations or assumptions. She had introduced the word bravery and wondered if it was fitting for Daniel. Daniel responded, "I didn't go out and slay a dragon." Virginia then asked Evelyn about her ideas regarding bravery. She spoke of regular people who had shown some compassion for others. Virginia wondered if another term might be better, rather than imposing the term "bravery" on Daniel, but Daniel changed his mind, declaring, "It does count as a *step* of bravery."

As Dugan and Coles (1989), Freeman, Epston, and Lobovits (1997), Garbarino, Dubrow, Kostelny, and Pardo (1992), and others warn us, we do not want to romanticize young people or make them into heroes. Virginia's aim is to be respectfully attentive and to appreciate what Daniel is doing and thinking, but not overstate it. We do admit, however, there are times when we are astonished at what children think and how they are able to quickly redirect themselves. It is especially during these moments with children that we realize we are privileged to be speaking with them about their rediscovered personal agency.

Interviewing the Problem

Interviewing the problem is something that can be done at different points in the therapy. It can be done early on to expose the way the problem works or later to build motivation in the fight against the problem. Daniel had minor setbacks and then three weeks free of trouble. As a way of expanding Daniel's newfound freedom from the problem, Virginia asked if she could interview the problem. (Roth & Epston, 1996a, 1996b; Zimmerman & Dickerson, 1997). Pretending to be the problem offers the child a playful perspective about the experience of success.

In the following dialogue, Daniel is being interviewed alone; in the first part of the session Evelyn had told Virginia that the family would be moving and she wanted Daniel to have some time alone with her.

THERAPIST: This is just an idea. What if you pretend you're the temper? Would you be temper and low self-confidence?

DANIEL: What do you mean?

THERAPIST: You let me interview you. . . . You be temper and low self-confidence and let me interview you.

DANIEL: Do what?

THERAPIST: You be temper. As temper you have had a secret mission against Daniel, right?

DANIEL: Oh . . . yeah (*half smiling*).

THERAPIST: Along with low self-confidence, you have had this mission, right? Against Daniel?

DANIEL: Sure (*with more enthusiasm*).

THERAPIST: Okay, I'm going to be the interviewer. Temper, is Daniel right that you and low self-confidence decided to hide and sneak around him?

DANIEL: Yes, but now I'm dying (*gasping and holding his throat*).

THERAPIST: You're dying?

DANIEL: Yes (*slumping back in the chair*).

THERAPIST: Are you croaking for real? Okay, you're taking some of your last breaths, are you? Well listen, before you draw your last breath, can you just tell me one thing? Daniel has struggled with you for a while and then not. Would you say that you really put up a good fight with him?

DANIEL: Ahh, yeah, yes I did (*draping across one arm of the chair*).

THERAPIST: Did you or did you not try to take over his life?

DANIEL: Yeah, I did.

THERAPIST: And you're saying now he's won? Hmm, you're giving up?

DANIEL: Forfeiting (*raspy-voiced*).

THERAPIST: You're forfeiting! So you are going to forfeit and walk off, have I got this right?

Daniel: Uh-huh.

THERAPIST: Tell me (*trying to match some of his drama*), what strategy did Daniel use? I mean, what did he use to get you on the run? Was it some double moves? Or did he bring a lot of defensive action play against you? Or did he have some other kind of strategy to finally *get* you?

DANIEL: He . . . he . . . he had self-confidence.

THERAPIST: He had self-confidence, so he believed in himself. You decided that was enough for you! Temper, do you think you put up a good fight to get him? Do you think you've tried your lowest, sneakiest, and sleaziest ways with Daniel? Do you think you've practiced your most famous types of strategies against him?

DANIEL: (*Whispers*) This, this is the first time (*sigh*) I have *ever* lost.

THERAPIST: The first time you've ever lost! Unfortunate, uh-huh. Well, does it feel like some relief that you're going, that you're off, you're truly done?

DANIEL: Sort of (*whining*).

THERAPIST: Some relief about that for you?

DANIEL: Yeah.

THERAPIST: Is Daniel a pretty tough match?

DANIEL: Yeah. I do like a round of torture.

THERAPIST: You do like a round of torture, huh? You're not coming back for
               another round are you? Have you tortured Daniel enough?

DANIEL: Yeah, 'cause I'm dying, 'cause I screwed up.

THERAPIST: So you made a mess of it? Did you make a mess of it, or did
               Daniel outsmart you?

DANIEL: Yeah, he outsmarted me.

THERAPIST: Yeah, he outsmarted you. Can we switch back now? Will you be
               Daniel now?

Interviewing the problem helped highlight and thicken the story of the defeat of the problem. Virginia followed the interview of the problem with questions about Daniel's experience of being temper and low self-confidence. He said that he enjoyed this experience and decided that temper probably doesn't die, but forfeits. He realized in reflecting about it that he needed to be ready because it could try to return during his upcoming move to a new house and new school. They talked further about his family moving.

Circulating the Preferred Story Beyond the Family

As Daniel and his family prepared for the move to a new community, one concern was Daniel's new school and the importance of the problems not following him there. In that regard, Evelyn was very upset when she saw that the current school had prepared a report to accompany Daniel to his new school. Except for a letter from the resource teacher, the six-page report focused on Daniel's academic deficits and on previous behavior problems. Both Evelyn and Virginia thought the report did not reflect Daniel's great progress. In therapy Daniel was recounting more and more examples of his handling difficult playground and after-school situations well. These triumphs seemed to be at odds with the report.

This disparity discouraged Evelyn and Alex. Evelyn believed that even if they explained their current perceptions of Daniel to the school, the report could contribute to a negative start for him. For Virginia, the disparity highlighted the imbalance of power between the well-intentioned institution meant to serve children and the child and family being served. As therapists we do not see ourselves as neutral, but rather as on the side of preferred stories. We also strive to be aware of our own power. In this situation, Virginia decided to redress the power imbalance between Daniel and the school. She did this by creating a letter that could be offered to the new school as an alternative report.

AT THE FOLLOWING session, when Virginia told Daniel about the letter, he was very interested in knowing what it said. Together, they read the initial draft, sentence by sentence. He asked what different words meant, such as "socioemotional," and "inconsistent." He wanted to know why the letter sounded so "official." Evelyn explained that it should be formal because they hoped it would become part of his record—what his new school principal and teachers would read about him. The purpose of this letter was to offer alternative examples of some of the things cited by the school report. The following is the text of the letter:

Re: Daniel Green
To whom it may concern:

I have worked with Daniel over the past six months regarding his socioemotional adjustments to increased academic demands and often unpredictable educational methods. The school environment was inconsistent in structuring teaching and learning situations that would allow Daniel to use his skills consistently. There had been recommendations by the psychologist of how to set the structure by giving instruction at both the auditory and visual levels with follow-up and progressive steps for learning. These were not translated to the classroom or special classes in computer lab or in long-term classroom assignments.

The difficulties Daniel originally experienced led him to feel overwhelmed and desperate. These feelings brought his self-confidence down, and he did not feel safe asking for help at the school for fear of being criticized and ostracized (both of which had occurred). In addition, the school had not provided predictable emotional support for him when these difficulties became apparent.

I have found Daniel to be an eager child who responds well when encouraged and given tools to solve situations. Daniel has many strengths. He is empathic toward others, he is a good negotiator and leader when structures allow it, and he is usually diligent in his work. If he thinks something is beyond him, anxiety can come to haunt him, but if given encouragement and ideas to work with, he can pursue solutions independently, with follow-up.

Even with the obstacles in his educational environment, Daniel has progressed academically according to grade-level standards in all subjects, with exceptional strength in math, writing, and social studies. He does have some challenges when writing lengthy assignments, where the organization of thoughts and ideas converge with tedious writing skills. Once in more advanced grades, he can use spell-check and other computer aids to check his work.

As an only child he is sensitive to issues of belonging in peer relationships. This is understandable, because he depends on these relationships more than children with siblings or physically close kinship networks do. He tolerates competition well when he is confident in what he is attempting, but can become disappointed in himself when there is less self-confidence about what he is doing or no clear understanding of the task.

Daniel has made incredible advances over the last several months, and has perceptions beyond his age about emotional and moral issues, such as injustice, prejudice, acceptance of differences, honor, and honesty. He has had a number of pressures at home, including moving to a new place, the death of an uncle he was close to, and the absence of his father over the last three months. Given these stresses, he has accomplished incredible control of his anxiety, frustration, and fears. Daniel has a brave spirit and fortitude. It has been a great pleasure knowing him.

Sincerely,
Virginia Simons, M.S.W.

After hearing the letter, Daniel leaned back in his chair and took a deep breath. He said he liked the letter and did not want to change any of it. Evelyn smiled and said that now she felt more prepared for discussions in the new school situation. She was happy that the new school staff would learn of Daniel's efforts before he arrived. For the two of them, having an alternative letter in "official" language that could be read and re-read meant that the preferred version of Daniel's story could be circulated. Daniel would carry other convictions about himself to the new school within his heart and mind.

THIS IS AN EXAMPLE OF a letter that thickens a preferred story and circulates it beyond the family. Most often we write therapeutic letters (Freeman, Epston, & Lobovits, 1997; White & Epston, 1990) directly to the person or family we are seeing in therapy. This letter, instead, shifts the news to a more public arena, where documents about Daniel are on file. Daniel's knowledge and acceptance of this letter is also a significant therapeutic step because he had been rather private about his efforts until now. The letter signals his willingness to go public. Virginia hoped that this would lead the way for a community of acknowledgment in his new school.

Consulting the Consultant

As the work was drawing to an end, Virginia interviewed Daniel and Evelyn about therapy. This reinforced Daniel's status as an expert on his own experience in therapy (White & Epston, 1992). Along with his consultation about the therapy experience, Daniel agreed to be a reference for others who might come in with similar problems (Epston, 1992, pp.11–25). The following transcript is the section of the interview with Daniel.

THERAPIST: So, Daniel, would you tell me what it was like to come to counseling and being here, meeting and talking about all this?

DANIEL: Hell (*starts laughing, glancing over at his mom*).

EVELYN: (*Laughter*) "Hell?!" (*To Virginia*) And you've got the camera rolling?

THERAPIST: I've got the camera rolling.
(*Laughter; Daniel grins.*)

THERAPIST: So, Daniel, it was pretty hard, huh? What about it was hard?

DANIEL: It was hell the way I felt talking about the problem, figuring it out.

THERAPIST: Yeah, talking about the problem and what it was doing? What about the figuring it out? The mission? Daniel, if a kid were having difficulty would you advise him to come talk to somebody or not?

DANIEL: If they were having a problem everyday, yeah. If their parents don't know how to help, yes!

THERAPIST: So, if parents can't deal with it or can't seem to figure it out?

DANIEL: Yeah.

THERAPIST: Okay. So even though it was hard to talk, was it a good thing?

DANIEL: Oh, yeah. Tell them, once you start to know what is happening, it gets a little easier to come.

Reflecting on what happens in their world and facing and overcoming overwhelming odds may very well be hell for some children. Daniel's spontaneous summation of the experience holds wisdom for us all. Entering therapy can make children as well as adults feel at risk and vulnerable. When parents are present, perhaps it feels even more risky for children, who are in a less powerful position than adult clients.

Being in the role of consultant begins to redress the imbalance of power. This consultation acknowledges that the child has expertise about the experience. Daniel's interview thickened the narrative of him as a competent person (Seligman, Revick, Jaycox, & Gillham, 1995). It was not done as a strategy or technique, but rather as a way to recognize the wisdom he possesses about himself.

Rituals and Ceremonies

First introduced in narrative work by Michael White and David Epston (1990), celebrations and award- and prize-givings signal a shift of therapy's focus from the problematic relationships to the positive steps taken. This leads to future growth. The degree of focus on problems, and taking steps against them, compared to that on the preferred, alternative stories will vary according to the situation and motivations of the particular child and family. Marking out and highlighting accomplishments can be done through symbols.

As therapy was ending, Virginia mentioned the possibility of an award to honor his success (Freedman & Combs, 1996; Freeman, Epston, & Lobovits, 1997; White & Epston, 1992). Being a hockey fan, Daniel immediately began talking about the Stanley Cup. In the following transcript of the final session, Virginia followed up on the idea.

THERAPIST: We talked a little bit about this Stanley Cup idea last time. Do you think we can figure out how to do this? The Stanley Cup is *big*. We can create one, but it would have to be smaller.

DANIEL: Sure.

THERAPIST: Like a little Stanley Cup award?

DANIEL: Yes, out of candy?!

THERAPIST: Oh, a candy one? What kind of candy?

DANIEL: Chocolate.

EVELYN: Chocolate is his favorite.

THERAPIST: A chocolate Stanley Cup?

DANIEL: Yeah.

THERAPIST: Or something like that? Do you think it will be able to travel from here to your new house without melting? I'm thinking about that since you didn't want to get it until you are in school there, remember, so you know you have won, even in a new place. You said in two weeks?

DANIEL: I'll probably still be shy; wait more.

THERAPIST: Do you think we should wait longer than that? That you may still not be completely comfortable there?

DANIEL: Try three.

THERAPIST: Well, do you think anxiety could give temper a chance for a surprise visit?

DANIEL: Maybe.

EVELYN: We leave in a week, then settle in the new house, so it will be two weeks after starting at the new school.

THERAPIST: About three weeks then? We'll try for it to arrive after the beginning of going to the new school.

DANIEL: Maybe I could get it after the first week or two.

THERAPIST: Yes, if the post office cooperates.

EVELYN: Before you know the other kids that well.

DANIEL: Yeah, yeah.

THERAPIST: Okay. I'll try.

After the conversation about the Stanley Cup, Virginia presented Daniel with a copy of his certificate, since he preferred the original to be mailed with the Stanley Cup. To mark this time as a celebration, Virginia brought in a couple of balloons and a snack.

EVELYN: Wow (*responding to the balloons, soda, and a little package of "Yikes" pencils*).

DANIEL: Yes-s-s (*spontaneously raising his arms and clasping his hands in a victory motion over each shoulder*).
(*Virginia and Evelyn applaud.*)

This ended the sessions with Daniel. The day before the family moved, Evelyn left a message indicating that Daniel had been talking with her about his experience and thoughts about moving. His leave-taking at school and with friends had been sad. Evelyn said she was sometimes amazed by his insights. He had been helpful to her as she dealt with her own emotions.

Certificate of Bravery

This is to certify that

Daniel Green

has practiced numerous acts of personal bravery
in his fight for true, personal confidence in himself,
and that his story can be used
to give other children ideas about being brave.

Brave Persons Association of America

Dated this _____ day of_____, 20 _____

Signed: ___*Virginia A. Simons*___

Virginia A. Simons, Sponsor

Virginia checked nearby shops but was unable to find a cup made of chocolate. Instead she sent Daniel a small trophy cup filled with chocolates and engraved, "Stanley Cup of Bravery, Daniel."* She enclosed the original bravery certificate in the box.

In a letter that Evelyn sent after the box arrived, she wrote that the trophy sits among Daniel's hockey trophies and other treasures on his shelf, where he chose for it to be. Daniel was surprised and delighted to find it filled with chocolate. Evelyn saved the certificate for his memory book.

About six months later Virginia wrote to Daniel to ask if she could talk about his experience with a group of therapists who were meeting to discuss ways to help children. Evelyn wrote back giving permission. The main thing Daniel wanted therapists and other adults to know is how bad bullying and teasing is for kids. "It should not ever be allowed," Evelyn wrote. "It is not allowed in his new school, and he thinks that made a big difference for him. All kids want things to be good, because if they are not you're hurt and unhappy. Oh, and hockey is still terrific."

One year later, Evelyn wrote to say that after much soul-searching they were moving again to be near family. Both she and her husband had new jobs in the new community. Daniel had been on the B+ honor role for two grading periods and had been happy and doing well.

Conclusion

Using narrative ideas with children and families has repeatedly demonstrated that if we help people define problems, their experience can be the guide in authoring stories that stand outside the limits of those problems. Constructing preferred stories almost always goes hand in hand with the process of deconstruction. Once Daniel began to speculate and analyze the problem as external to himself, he could see places in life where he was already free of it. Acknowledging and concentrating upon these experiences that are exceptions to the problem can bring clarity, purpose, and direction to the therapeutic dialogues about the next steps to be taken. For Daniel this took the form of documents that both reveal the methods of the problem and declare his self-knowledge. The rest of the therapy included several narrative practices that allowed his story to be enriched, re-experienced, and shared.

---

*The total cost of this award, including postage, was less than $20.00, leading us to speculate on the benefits of including room for such expenditures in our practice budgets

Our hope in writing this chapter was to present a child's voice; Daniel's voice and his thinking, knowledge, and authorship of a preferred life story. Participating in Daniel's developments has made us aware that bravery does not have to speak in a loud voice or come from visibly grand demonstrations. His voice is one of many that reveal the abilities and knowledge accessible to us in children.

Virginia A. Simons, M.S.W., is Clinical Instructor, Case Western Reserve University, Family Medicine Department, Fairview Center for Family Medicine, Cleveland, Ohio.

Jill Freedman, M.S.W., is Co-Director of Evanston Family Therapy Center, Evanston, Illinois.

References

Anderson H., & Goolishian, H. (1988). Human Systems as linguistic systems: Preliminary and evolving ideas about the implications for clinical theory. *Family Process, 27,* 371–393.

Berger, P., & Luckmann, T. (1966). *The social construction of reality.* New York: Doubleday.

Brooks, P. (1984). *Reading for plot: Design and intention in narrative.* New York: Knopf.

Bruner, J. (1991). The narrative construction of reality. *Critical Inquiry, 18,* 1–21.

Cohen, S. M., Shulman, D., Lorimer, D., Combs, G., & Freedman, J. (1998). Minimizing hierarchy in therapeutic relationships: A reflecting team approach. In M. F. Hoyt (Ed.), *The handbook of constructive therapies: Innovative approaches from the leading practitioners,* (Vol. 2, pp. 276–292). New York: Guilford.

Combs, G., & Freedman, J. (1998). Tellings and retellings. *Journal of Marital and Family Therapy, 4,* 405–408.

Dickerson, V. (1996). On the client's voice. *AFTA Newsletter, 64,* 10.

Doan, R., & Clifton, D. (1990). The rules of problem lifestyles: Making externalizations more real. *Dulwich Centre Newsletter, 4,* 18.

Dugan, T., & Coles, R. (1989). *The child in our times: Studies in the development of resiliency.* New York: Brunner/Mazel.

Durrant, M. (1989, Autumn). Temper taming: An approach to children's temper problems, revisited. *Dulwich Centre Newsletter,* 3–11.

Durrant, M. (1995). *Creative strategies for school problems.* New York: Norton.

De Shazer, S. (1991). *Putting difference to work.* New York: Norton.

Epston, D. (1992). Temper tantrum parties: Saving face, losing face, or going off your face. In D. Epston & M. White, *Experience, contradiction, narrative, and imagination: Selected papers of David Epston and Michael White, 1989–1991.* Adelaide, Australia: Dulwich Centre.

Freedman, J., & Combs, G. (1996). *Narrative therapy: The social construction of preferred realities*. New York: Norton.

Freeman, J., Epston, D., & Lobovits, D. (1997). *Playful approaches to serious problems*. New York: Norton.

Garbarino, J., Dubrow, N., Kostelny, K., & Pardo, C. (1992). *Children in danger: Coping with the consequences of community violence*. San Francisco: Jossey-Bass.

Gergen, K. (1985). The social constructionsist movement in modern psychology. *American Psychologist, 40,* 266–275.

Griffith, J., & Griffith, M. (1994). *The body speaks*. New York: HarperCollins.

Hoffman, L. (1990). Constructing realities: An art of lenses. *Family Process, 29,* 1–12.

Hoffman, L. (1991). Foreword. In T. Andersen (Ed.), *The reflecting team: Dialogues and dialogues about the dialogues* (pp. ix–xiv). New York: Norton.

Loptson, C., & Stacey, K. (1995). Children should be seen and not heard? Questioning the unquestioned. *Journal of Systemic Therapies, 14*(4), 16–32.

McLean, C. (1995). Boys and education in Australia. *Dulwich Centre Newsletter, 1&2,* 29–42.

Monk, G., Winslade, J. & Crocket, K. (1997). *Narrative therapy in practice: The archaeology of hope*. San Francisco: Jossey-Bass.

Morgan, A. (1995). Taking responsibility: Working with teasing and bullying in schools. *Dulwich Centre Newsletter, 2&3,* 16–28.

Radke-Yarrow, M., Zahn-Waxler, C., & Chapman, M. (1983). Children's prosocial dispositions and behavior. In P. H. Mussen (Ed.), *Handbook of child psychology, Vol. IV: Socialization, personality, and social development* (4th ed.). New York: Wiley.

Roth, S., & Epston, D. (1996a). Consulting the problem about the problematic relationship: An exercise for experiencing a relationship with an externalized problem. In M. Hoyt (Ed.), *Constructive Therapies* (Vol. 2, pp. 148–162). New York: Guilford.

Roth, S., & Epston, D. (1996b). Developing externalizing conversations: An exercise. *Journal of Systemic Therapies, 15*(1), 5–12.

Seligman, M., Revick, K., Jaycox, L., & Gillham, J. (1995). *The optimistic child*. New York: Harper & Row.

Stacey, K. (1995). Language as an exclusive or inclusive concept: Reaching beyond the verbal. *Australian & New Zealand Journal of Family Therapy, 16*(3), 123–132.

Tomm, K. (1989). Externalizing the problem and internalizing personal agency. *Journal of Strategic and Systemic Therapies, 8*(1), 54–59.

White, M. (1989). Fear busting and monster taming: An approach to the fears of young children. In M. White, *Selected papers*. Adelaide, Australia: Dulwich Centre.

White, M. (1995). *Re-authoring lives: Interviews and essays*. Adelaide, Australia: Dulwich Centre.

White, M., & Epston, D. (1990). *Narrative means to therapeutic ends*. New York: Norton.

White, M., & Epston, D. (1992). *Experience, contradiction, narrative, and imagination*. Adelaide, Australia: Dulwich Centre.

Zimmerman, J., & Dickerson, V. (1996). *If problems talked: Narrative therapy in action*. New York: Guilford.

3

Collaborating Beyond the Family System

Sally St. George

Dan Wulff

What do we say to a 6-year-old boy who earnestly and sadly tells us, "I'm afraid my mama is gonna die"? He constantly begs to stay by her side and does poorly in school. He isolates himself from his classmates and has difficulty concentrating on his studies. His parents are worried about his all-consuming fear and have requested that he be seen for therapy. There are various ways to conceptualize this situation. It could be viewed as an example of irrational or unreasonable behavior on the part of this boy, an indication of a marital problem represented by this symptomatic behavior, an effort to manipulate parents, or a manifestation of unresolved family grief. A therapist's interpretation of what is occurring will determine who is seen and what the focus of therapy will be. Our preferred approach is to assemble the various understandings of what is transpiring from those most knowledgeable and concerned about the boy—this could include, but not be limited to, his mother, father, teachers, grandparents, and the boy himself. Their viewpoints form the bedrock of how we need to proceed. We believe these significant people in the boy's life have the seeds of the resolution to this dilemma.

When a child evidences alarming behavior, we may find parents, siblings, grandparents, teachers, therapists, ministers, neighbors, friends, doctors, lawyers, or juvenile court officials each playing a part in trying to help that child. We can work with these individuals to create a set of coherent and focused responses that can help the situation. Responding in fragmented and contradictory ways may unintentionally sabotage improvement. The focus of this chapter is to illustrate how collaborative language systems (CLS) can be an effective approach in coordinating treatment for children.

Speaking of Theory

CLS (Anderson, 1995, 1997; Anderson & Goolishian, 1988) is a perspective from which to conceptualize and relate to troublesome issues and relationships by explicitly appreciating the multiple views simultaneously held by various participants about a given issue or event. We understand people's behaviors as shaped by a set of varied, unique, coexisting, and changing factors.

CLS is grounded within the following social constructionist ideas (Gergen, 1985). First, what we come to know is relationally constructed—human relationships are the contexts in which we assemble our views about truth, knowledge, and identity. Second, language is the medium through which such constructions are made. Rather than searching for a pre-existing set of certainties or essences about the world, those who work from a relational perspective create, design, and refine their own realities with one another through language. *Language* refers not only to our words, but also to nonverbal communications and actions, all of which lead to meaning-making. Language, the medium through which we build (and rebuild) meaning, is the "stuff" of our work with clients. Our job is the art of helping clients to articulate the meanings they hold about the important events and interactions in their lives. Likewise, with clients we create meanings that emanate from our interactions with them and that guide our movement in therapy. We are neither objective nor neutral influences—we affect and are affected by our clients.

CLS represents a set of ideas that allows a therapist (in his or her role with clients) to appreciate the complexity of life and the relational nature of our existence. CLS does not attempt to capture the *totality* of another's world, as if "truth" were clearly definable, objective, singular, fixed, tangible, and comprehensive. In using social constructionist ideas, we, as therapists, relate to our clients' worlds without streamlining them to fit our expertise or our own comfort level. As therapists we do not believe it is necessary to impose predetermined treatment protocols or professional jargon upon our clients in our efforts to help them. We recognize that our views of the world and our views of clients' predicaments are grounded in our own unique experiences. Similarly, our clients see the world and their predicaments from their own vantage points. We do not assume that we know more about our clients than our clients do themselves. They are considered to be the experts on their own lived experience (Anderson & Goolishian, 1992).

A CLS therapist conceptualizes the situation from a range of positions held by the various individuals involved. Anderson and Goolishian (1988) have articulated this stance as a position of "multipartiality." Each view of a problem, no matter how discrepant from others' views, is considered credible and understandable. The therapist does not try to reframe or revise what the participants already "know" to be true. "Each person involved in a dilemma has his or her own story about how the dilemma evolved, what it is about, whose fault it is, and what should be done. This includes the therapist" (Anderson, 1995, p. 33).

Some critics of collaborative approaches suggest that a therapist from this perspective would be unable to say or initiate anything. This is not the case. The therapist does have a voice but deliberate care is taken to avoid giving the therapist's voice a preeminent or defining role. The therapist uses a tentative language that carefully situates his or her comments as no more (or less) useful than anyone else's (Anderson, 1995). The therapist is sincere in his or her views but does not dogmatize those views or denigrate the client's differing view(s).

In collaborative therapy therapists and clients together determine the nature of their relationship and how they will proceed during their time together. This allows for clients to say how they can best be helped. Clients are invited to express not only their thoughts and feelings, but also their views about the structure of the therapy process. This approach is described as nonhierarchical. The term does not mean that no differences exist between therapists and clients; significant power and influence differences are often factors in the process of therapy. Society affords therapists a professional position, and in turn therapists have responsibilities and privileges vis-à-vis their clients. Therefore, we must make sure our professional "dominant" discourse does not negate other discourses that may be marginal or less appreciated.

CLS therapists work with "problem-determined" systems, which Anderson, Goolishian, and Winderman (1986) describe as those persons affected by the identified problem. The CLS approach does not originate from a preconceived set of notions about what constitutes a problem or which social group should be addressed in therapy. Persons involved in any capacity (no matter how peripheral) with the events or situations that led to the therapist's inclusion belong to the collective set of partners invested in the situation. Madigan and Epston (1995) use the term "community of concern" to refer to individuals involved with one another because they share similar struggles. We expand this definition to encompass all people affected by the individual manifesting the troublesome behaviors. The belief is that problems exist as long as those who are affected by them stay connected (positively or negatively) to one another via the problem.

When attending to this set of persons, "the problem presented to the therapist is the multiple, discrepant ideas members of the problem system hold about the problem" (Goolishian & Anderson, 1987, p. 534). As noted earlier, all participants' perspectives are considered valid, and no single participant possesses a comprehensive view that encompasses all views. According to Goolishian and Anderson (1987), "the members of a problem system are the experts in that problem; the therapist is simply an expert in maintaining conversation about it" (p. 536). As the "expert conversationalist," the therapist assists all involved in coordinating their actions to work on the problem. As the meanings of the problems and their influences on the participants are revealed and discussed, new ways of relating to the problem and to those individuals associated with it emerge.

Speaking of Therapy

What techniques do CLS therapists use? How do they decide when to use them? These are two questions about therapy process that we frequently hear from students or other professionals who are new to CLS. Basically, there are no specialized techniques—there are only relational processes, that is, how people speak with each other about their difficulties. Thus, our main approach is to listen and speak to people such that their views are validated and understood in their context and that the conversation should continue. We accomplish this by asking questions that encourage people to think about their dilemmas from positions other than the predictable and customary. We cannot tell in advance what these questions are because they fit within the ongoing conversation of therapy. Our questions have no preconceived answers or an a priori destination.

Given all the persons involved in or affected by a problem, we rely on our clients to describe who is most relevant to include in therapy. They may include some individuals we might consider less important and they may leave out some individuals that we might believe to be necessary. We explicitly discuss who to include (and who not to include) and come to a plan on how to proceed. Sometimes people invited to participate will not or are reluctant to, so modifications may need to be made. Once the meeting occurs, we decide as a group about how often to meet (or even whether to meet again). This "problem-determined system" charts this course.

In an interview, the way in which we converse is critical. We believe in making space for all the talk that needs to become public. Our role is that of facilitator—we are not the central figure. If we begin the interview we retreat from that central position to allow others' voices equal opportunity to speak and be heard. In the event that someone "takes over" the conversational space, we might say, "You have given us so much information that is important; what is the one thing that you want us to know—that we absolutely should not miss" or "It might be important to find out what others are thinking at this time." Sometimes the opposite happens when a member is silent. We might ask, "What thoughts, reactions, or conversations are you having inside right now?" We also respect the right to be silent and do not interpret silence as bad or undesirable.

It is important to use simple language when asking questions of all members in the group. Questions and statements should be understandable by everyone, including children. In this way all participants are included equally.

This chapter's case study illustrates how a CLS perspective guided our work involving an 8-year-old child who had just entered the juvenile justice system. The ideas we used and the specific ways they were enacted were linked to our preferred ways of working, the client family's circumstances and viewpoints, and the conditions of time and place. Our example is only one way of proceeding. Others operating out of a CLS perspective could proceed differently, and we would probably respond differently at another point in time.

Case Illustration: From Breaking Windows to Opening Windows

Benny was 8 years old when he came before juvenile court. He had threatened some neighborhood kids and was charged with destruction of property for throwing rocks through his neighbor's windows. This was the first occasion where the police and the juvenile court formally identified him. Sally was working as an in-home family therapist in a program designed to work with families who had a child in legal trouble for the first time. Dan was the supervisor of this new program, which was housed within a large social service agency. The program was developed by the local juvenile probation department to provide intensive, comprehensive counseling services to families of pre-delinquent kids in order to avert any future run-ins with the law.

Therapists in this program went into families' homes, spent as many as 10 hours per week with each family, and had the programmatic freedom to address any and all issues contributing to the child's troublesome behaviors. This program was not restricted to counseling or "talk therapy." Because the families referred to this program had multiple problems on many fronts, the therapists needed to be able to assist with issues such as utility bill payments, transportation problems, marital strife, job searches, school problems, parenting, securing food, neighborhood disputes, and so on.

Sally received the referral of Benny and his family from juvenile court. Benny, his mother, Kendra, and his 6-year-old brother, Marcus, were given the opportunity to work with a therapist in lieu of the formal juvenile court process. Sally met the family at the probation office. The probation officer introduced Sally to the family and explained the reasons why she had referred the family to Sally's agency, articulating the specific incidents and conditions she felt were problematic. This was basically a list of bad things centering around the police report.

SALLY:	What do you know about my program?
KENDRA:	I only know what I have been told. We can have family counseling and then we don't have to work with the probation officer or go to court.
SALLY:	So what do each of you think about the idea of family counseling?
KENDRA:	I would like to learn how to get Benny to mind me better.
SALLY:	And you, Benny?
BENNY:	I think it might be good for my mom because she has a lot of stress.
SALLY:	Marcus, how about you?
MARCUS:	(*Shrugging*) I want my family to be happy.
SALLY:	Benny, what kind of stress do you think your mom is experiencing?
BENNY:	She has to worry about me because I'm always getting into trouble, she has to worry about money because she doesn't have a job, and she has to take care of my brother who is sick a lot.
SALLY:	Marcus, do you agree with the things Benny is saying?
MARCUS:	Yeah.
SALLY:	Would you like to add anything?
MARCUS:	(*Shrugging*) No.
KENDRA:	I know Benny worries about me too much and he shouldn't have to. He's just a little boy.

To understand all of the opinions that have a bearing on therapy, it is important to invite into conversation all the persons who are involved with, and possess ideas about, the child's problematic situation. To prevent misunderstandings and the possibility of professional secrets, the probation officer was invited to speak in front of the family.

SALLY: What are your ideas about how counseling could be useful for this family?

OFFICER: Benny needs more consistency and structure at home.

SALLY: What picture do you have of this family—what should they look like, so that they no longer would be a concern to the court?

OFFICER: Benny needs to be a good student in school, he needs to understand that what he did was wrong, and Kendra needs to be more firm in disciplining Benny.

SALLY: How could I best relate to this family to be helpful?

OFFICER: They need somebody who will give them more than just the one hour a week I can. A program like this will hopefully support the whole family, not just Benny.

SALLY: Kendra, you've been listening to the conversation and I'm wondering what you would like to add—like what have you been thinking?

KENDRA: What Benny did was wrong, and we have to keep him off the streets. Plus nothing ever gets better when the police are in on it, and I don't want my kids being harassed by the police. I want him to be helped at school. He needs encouragement—not punishment—or he'll end up in a gang.

SALLY: You all have said many important things. Each of you seems to have some definite thoughts on this situation and I like to take time to really get the best picture of how everyone involved sees what's going on because each view is special and useful—this is how I like to work with families. So, I am willing to talk about all of it with you and see what we can do together so that you don't have to have these worries.

KENDRA: I'm willing to give it a try because I love my kids and I want them to have a better life than I have. I just don't want them involved with the police. I don't know you at all, but I would rather have any counselor work with us than a probation officer—or anyone from the court.

SALLY: I can't guarantee what's going to happen. This is a new program and I'm new to this agency, but I've been around the block a few times. We can keep a close watch on how we are doing to make sure our working together is a good idea. Let's give it our best shot.

Acknowledging the family's right to decide to accept or refuse the invitation of counseling was an important first step toward working collaboratively with this family. Coercion to work with a counselor sends a message to clients that someone else runs their lives. Such coercion by the courts is occasionally present in counseling (as it was in this situation) and if it is an element of the counseling context, open discussion of such duress is wisely included in the initial talks. In this case, failure to work with this program would have prompted formal legal action, so Kendra chose to accept counseling as the "lesser of two evils." Speaking openly about the forced choice given to Kendra and her family placed it on the table as a discussable point rather than allowing it to remain a dark shadow that influenced counseling but could not be mentioned.

The issue of coercion can emerge in other ways, particularly in work with children, who typically do not get to decide whether or not they participate in counseling. Putting a child in counseling may be a benevolent decision made by adults, but children often feel imposed upon or controlled nonetheless. Comments that it is for their "own good" do little, if anything, to diminish their feelings of being pushed around. Some children respond by reserving the right to not invest themselves significantly in the process. With this family, Sally specifically asked each child about what he hoped would happen in counseling. This reinforced the notion that they had a right to an opinion and that what they said mattered (Anderson & Levin, 1997).

Allowing children to see and hear how therapy decisions are made is often beneficial for them; they can be privy to what they earlier might have only wondered (and perhaps worried) about. Making such conversations public is an education for children. It also puts pressure on the adults present to be efficient and appropriate; they are put on display, so to speak, which encourages them to perform in constructive ways.

Sally did not assume that this family would see counseling as the most effective way of weathering the storm they faced, even though the program afforded them the opportunity to bypass legal ramifications. Therefore, in this first meeting Sally joined with the family and the probation officer by discussing how counseling might fit into this family's situation. Sally explained her stance of valuing all viewpoints and not siding with one person over another.

The second meeting with the family took place in their home. As Sally entered the family's apartment, Kendra, who was visibly upset, announced that they had just received notice that they were being evicted within the next week and that the utility company had already turned off their power.

SALLY: How can I be helpful?

BENNY: Please protect our mom from her boyfriend and his brother.

SALLY: What's going on here?

KENDRA: I am so mad—I was arguing with police all night, picked up my kids from my sister's, was met by the landlord, who said we're being evicted, and came in to find our electricity shut off. How will I feed my kids?

SALLY: Let's think a minute. Which of these issues is most critical—do we have to worry about your safety?

KENDRA: We don't have to worry about him [the boyfriend] because he's in jail and he's never coming back here.

Kendra then sent her boys out of the room so that she could speak privately with Sally. She explained that she, her boyfriend, his brother, and another friend had become intoxicated the night before. They got rowdy, and their neighbors called the police. Kendra and her boyfriend then argued with the police and all four were taken to jail. She explained that she didn't want her kids to know about this—they had been staying at her sister's during the incident. Kendra expressed concern about discussing this in front of them because they had a tendency "to worry too much anyway." She then brought up another problem facing the family.

KENDRA: By the way, there's one more thing. Benny's school principal called yesterday because Benny's been threatening other kids and they want to test him for a special ed class.

SALLY: (*Feeling overwhelmed and worried about the boys feeling overwhelmed as well*) Boy, there's a lot going on—and I wonder what Benny and Marcus are thinking right now.

KENDRA: They're in there worrying about me.

SALLY: Is there some way we can talk about this with them to help them too?

KENDRA: Yeah, but I don't want them to know about the jail stuff.
            (*Benny and Marcus rejoin Kendra and Sally.*)

SALLY: Who is most worried about what's going on right now?

KENDRA:	Benny is most worried because he constantly worries about my safety and is anxious about what's going to happen at school.
BENNY:	I think it is my mom because she has so much stress in her life. Right, Marcus?
MARCUS:	Uh huh.
SALLY:	(*Trying to open the conversation further*) Who in the family needs the most encouragement at this moment?
KENDRA:	For sure it is Benny because he has both home and school worries. (*Both boys nod yes and look down.*)
SALLY:	How would you like to use the time we have today?
KENDRA:	Could we talk about what can be done with the problems at school?
BENNY:	(*With all eyes on him, Benny shrugs and looks sheepish*) Okay.

Some therapists might have chosen to focus on the issues of domestic violence, inadequate housing, Benny's aggressive behaviors, and Kendra's alcoholism and lack of parental supervision. Their efforts might have centered on their conceptualizations of the situation or dilemma and would have been informed by their experience, education, and the protocols or templates that prescribe specific actions for therapy. But if we assume that clients know what is best for them and are capable of prioritizing or determining where they can benefit the most from assistance, it would be disingenuous for us to override their priorities in order to pursue our own agendas.

This is crucial because we believe that our clients quickly become aware of the importance we place on their views in the process of structuring therapy. Downplaying a client's suggestions about what needs to be done and how it should be done puts him or her in the backseat of the therapeutic process. Clients often rank their problems according to their urgency. They are in the best position to decide which problem ought to be tackled first, second, and so on. They also have a sense of what approach would be most successful. When clients play a significant part in decision-making in therapy, their commitment to and involvement in the implemented plan increases the likelihood that progress will occur.

This family presented Sally with multiple areas of concern—the avenues to pursue in therapy were numerous. Sally followed Kendra's lead and began with Benny's school difficulties, even though the issues of Kendra's jail experience and danger to the children might have seemed more pressing. It requires courage and commitment on the part of the therapist to maintain confidence in following the direction of the client.

SALLY: Please tell me more about what is going on with Benny's problems at school.

BENNY: The teachers won't help me with my worksheets and the other kids make fun of me. They call me "tubby" and laugh when it's my turn to read out loud.

KENDRA: Benny's teacher told me on the phone that Benny is failing every subject and is not putting any effort into his studies. He reads and writes at the first grade level and, worst of all, Benny bullies his classmates.

SALLY: Can you think of anything else that might be important for me to know so that I would better understand the situation with Benny and his school?

KENDRA: I know what is going on with my boys. I like to read myself and I regularly read with both Benny and Marcus and occasionally check their writing. I can tell where Benny has some difficulty— it is when he tries to read "advanced" words. Plus spelling is hard for him. I am no teacher, but these few things are nowhere near as bad as what that teacher said. My son is not an angel but he can be sweet and gentle.

SALLY: Okay.

KENDRA: (*With passion*) My boys have to get their education. They are not geniuses and neither am I, but we all know what goes on in the streets. I don't want my boys to have worries about where the money is coming from and I definitely don't want them having to mess with the police. I want them to be able to get jobs and be happy and do good in this world. . . . Sometimes I just don't know what to think. I want to believe that Benny is not to blame for the school trouble but I know him well. He probably could do better. I think the school does pick on Benny but I know in my heart that he needs to be responsible, too—Benny's no angel.

SALLY: Kendra, please tell me about previous meetings that you have had with school personnel.

KENDRA: The only time I talk with them is when the teacher or the principal calls to complain about what Benny has done.

At this point, the conversation seemed to have a familiar, repetitive quality to it. A CLS therapist tries to facilitate conversations that have some newness or differentness to them. So Sally was motivated to shift the talk to make room for more than negativity and complaining, though she did not have a specific detailed strategy in mind.

SALLY: Kendra, are there things you think would be useful for the school to know or understand about Benny that you don't think they know?

KENDRA: (*Grimacing*) What makes you think they would be interested?

SALLY: From what I am learning about Benny by talking with you and Benny, there are some qualities that are pretty special about him. Maybe school people just don't see these qualities and get overly focused on the bad stuff. Maybe if they knew him in other ways, they would be less likely to be down on him. It might be helpful for you to know that I was a middle school teacher for many years and know how easy it is for teachers to become overwhelmed when they don't see the progress that they would like to see.

KENDRA: Oh boy! You don't seem like a school teacher—maybe it would be handy to have one on our side. How about that Benny! Maybe you could help us—I don't want to talk to those other school people.

SALLY: (*Smiling*) Did I blow it? Am I going to be suspected of being a bad guy now that you know?

KENDRA: (*Laughing nervously*) Uh, well, no.

SALLY: Please, tell me more about your not wanting to talk to the school people.

KENDRA: Because you were once a teacher, I, well, um . . .

SALLY: (*Offering a thought to see if she understands what Kendra is thinking*) Do you mean that I might not understand your situation from a parent's point-of-view, that I would take up for the school?

KENDRA: Well, yeah. Oh, but I don't mean to offend you, put you down.

SALLY: (*Not offended*) I have some ideas about how parent-teacher conferences could be different than they usually are, so that nobody has to leave feeling frustrated or like nothing had been accomplished.

KENDRA: (*Remains silent*)

SALLY: Sometimes people need to think about things for a while before they make a plan. Let's both sleep on it and then talk tomorrow. We'll probably have better ideas then.

This ended the conversation for that day and Sally returned the next day. Kendra was home alone and the kids were at school. Sally opened the conversation.

SALLY: Have you had any more thoughts about what we discussed yester-
            day?
KENDRA: Well, the school called again, so we have to do something. They
            want to meet with me. I told them I would call them back. I said
            that I have a counselor now and I would call them back after we
            met. So, I was thinking, since you were a teacher, you could go to
            school and talk to them and set things straight. You would do a
            better job than I could.

   At this point, Sally wants to assist Kendra, but not take over for her. Though
we tend to follow a client's lead and judgment, we remain in a collaborative
effort and therapists have a voice in how therapy will proceed. Therefore, Sally
also has the right to outline how she can participate in her best judgment.
Kendra suggests that Sally be the spokesperson for her with the school; Sally
presents her view that it would be more productive if they went together. This
keeps the family involved and allows the school to interact more significantly
with Kendra than when phone calls are made to report Benny's latest behavior
problems.

SALLY: Tell me again what is so distressing to you about talking to school
            people.
KENDRA: (Upset) They do all the talking. All they say is how awful Benny
            is and how I should do more. I already feel bad enough and I don't
            want to hear it! And besides, they would listen to you because
            you're smart and you were a teacher.
SALLY: I'm hesitant to speak for you. Your ideas about your son are very
            important. And you can shine some light on the school situation
            that no teacher, counselor, or principal can—you are his mother,
            and I'm afraid I couldn't do as good a job as you. You are the
            expert on Benny. And furthermore, Benny probably has some
            ideas that would help too—things that we haven't given him a
            chance to say yet. What if we all went to talk to the school peo-
            ple—you, Benny, and me, as a team?
KENDRA: I'm really not wild about going but I suppose I can't let Benny
            down. Will you call the school to set it up?
SALLY: Yes, I will. Who do you think should be at this meeting—I mean,
            what school people? Think about those who you have talked with
            before or those who you would like to have a chance to talk with.

KENDRA: I suppose Benny's teacher and the principal—because he's the one that calls me.

SALLY: Is there anyone else who is, or has been, involved with Benny?

KENDRA: (*Thinking aloud*) The principal mentioned something about a special ed teacher.

SALLY: Okay, the teacher, the principal, the special ed teacher. Is there a school counselor at Benny's school?

KENDRA: Not that I ever heard of.

SALLY: (*Offering*) How about if I set up a meeting including all of these people so we can find out who is thinking what things? Then we don't have to guess. We will have a clearer picture and so will the school personnel, and we will all have a much better chance of doing what is best for Benny.

KENDRA: (*Nods*)

SALLY: I feel very good about this plan. I think we'll get somewhere.

As Kendra's comments reveal, a conference with professionals in attendance can create anxiety for those participants (e.g., parents, children) who feel powerless in the company of the professionals involved. Sally used her experience as a former school teacher together with the supportive offer to accompany Kendra and Benny to help set up a positive, helpful meeting that would maximize the family's participation. Everyone who had a vested interest in Benny (including Benny himself) was invited to the school conference so that each could shed light on the situation.

CLS meetings ideally include all those persons who are "in language" (Anderson & Goolishian, 1988) about the condition that has caused concern or alarm—that is, those who are affected by the defined problem. In this case, Benny's behavior affects and is affected by his personal relationships with family and friends as well as the professionals working with him. The teacher's life may be made more difficult because of how she is relating to Benny and his life may also be made more difficult by the ways she relates to him. Shifting the ways we see relationships and how we attribute meanings to one another's behavior is a valuable way to envision possibilities in changing unsatisfying relationships or troublesome behaviors.

When the boys came home from school that day, Sally had a meeting with Kendra, Benny, and Marcus. The discussion centered on the school situation and the plan to have a joint meeting with the school. Kendra told Benny that she and Sally had talked about this and thought it would be important to have him present at the meeting. Benny made it clear that he did not want to be a part of the meeting. Kendra explained that she didn't particularly want to go either, but it must be done, and Sally would go with them so that their thoughts and ideas would be represented along with the voices of the school personnel. Benny shrugged but agreed to go. Sally returned the principal's call and asked about the possibility of scheduling a joint meeting with Benny's teacher, the principal, special education teacher, Sally, Benny, and Kendra. Here is an excerpt from that phone call.

SALLY: Kendra, Benny, and I have been talking about the seriousness of Benny's difficulties and performance at school. We have discussed some ways that we might proceed to change the situation and we were wondering if it was possible to have a combined meeting of all those who are involved or might be involved with Benny. I realize that scheduling is often difficult, but I believe that if everyone's voice is represented and viewed as part of the whole picture that we will be able to make some changes that could be immediate and that could last longer.

PRINCIPAL: (*Without much confidence*) We've set up this kind of meeting before, only to have Kendra cancel it. Do you think that she will follow through this time?

SALLY: (*Responding positively*) Yes, I will be accompanying them—I will pick them up and take them there. And we are very anxious to talk this out and understand everyone's view so we can get Benny on a good track.

PRINCIPAL: I guess we could try again. Maybe now that Kendra and Benny have a counselor it will help. You know it has not been easy or fruitful before. I will make the arrangements for us to meet tomorrow. Should we make a plan—do you want me to start the meeting? What will you do?

SALLY: I am so glad to hear your willingness to have everyone meet together. I am really optimistic about tomorrow. If you would like to start the meeting, that will be fine, that seems appropriate. If it is all right with you I would like to listen and ask questions of the group or of certain members as they occur to me. This is pretty typical of how I view my role when I work with families. I try to ask questions that will allow us to talk about things in some new ways so that we can proceed with hope and interest. I cannot tell

you in advance what those questions will be because they come
from our conversation. Do you think this can be useful?

PRINCIPAL: I hope so. I have never done this before, but we sure do need
something. We are all getting pretty drained. Now who should
come to this meeting?

CLS therapists believe what clients say to them, even if what is said appears
contradictory, unusual, or illogical. In fact, all participants involved with the
problem are considered credible reporters of what's going on from their vantage points. The point is to understand the client system from the various
descriptions given by each of the participants. Sally's position involves coming
to understand Kendra and the school personnel in relation to the dilemma that
join them. How they organize around Benny's misbehavior and poor school
performance along with their appraisals of one another's commitment to be
helpful is often the locus of our therapeutic work.

We do not try to ascertain the historical or literal truth about a situation, but
rather the participants' understandings about it. It is clear to Sally that the principal and Kendra have a conflicted history where each party thinks the other is
at fault. Neither tale is the final and only version; it is the therapist's task to find
ways to appreciate and validate each person's rendition on the journey to finding another narrative that each participant can value. If what we are told by the
participants sounds confusing or unreasonable, we take this to mean that we do
not yet have sufficient understanding of the participant's life or situation—the
client's logic is still hidden from us. We are prompted to continue to ask questions and listen to achieve understanding.

We consider relevant all the voices of those with a stake in the presenting
problem. Including all voices and positions surrounding a stressful issue
requires a deliberate and concerted effort given the traditional therapeutic view
that designates individual problem bearers or their families to be the only pertinent voices. A voice that differs from a dominant story line is welcomed as
much as one that confirms the story line. In fact, in our view, the difference in
various individuals' perspectives creates a crucial combination of ideas or a
"critical mass" that opens the window to new synthesized strategies that would
not be there without such initial diversity of understandings. Anderson (1995)
explains:

We were fascinated by the differences in the clients' experiences and
explanations of the same event, and we somehow sensed that these dif-

ferences were valuable and could be fruitful. We no longer wanted to negotiate, blur, or strive for consensus (that is, in problem definitions) but wanted to maintain the richness of differences. (p. 28)

Children's ideas about what is happening to them are vital to this process. These viewpoints add unique perspectives that substantively shape the solutions attempted (Anderson & Levin, 1997). Including children's voices also sends the message that they are considered a genuine part of the team that is solving the problem at hand. For these reasons, Sally asked Kendra if they could bring the boys back into the talk that concerned them and if Benny could attend the school conference.

The school meeting took place as planned the next day. In attendance were the principal, Benny's teacher, the special education teacher, Kendra, Benny, and Sally. The principal began by thanking everyone for coming together on such short notice. He expressed a wish that the group could have come together for more positive reasons but said he was pleased that the attendees were there to tackle the "tough problem" posed by Benny's behavior. The principal began the discussion by referring to a computer printout.

PRINCIPAL: Just to summarize, Benny has been referred to my office for disciplinary action on six occasions in the last four weeks. I wish I could say they were not for serious reasons, but I can't. These referrals have been for repeated occurrences of verbal and physical aggression with other students. In my opinion, Benny's behavior is disrupting learning in the classroom. Perhaps you (*indicating Benny's teacher*) should outline your concerns.

TEACHER: Benny does not stay seated, he wanders around the classroom at will regardless of what the other children and I are doing. When I ask him to sit down, he does but only for a few minutes. He also does not finish his assignments, whether it is classroom work or assigned homework. And what concerns me the most is that the other children complain that he harasses them and threatens them.

KENDRA: I am worried that my son will have to take third grade over again and I'd like to know why you [Benny's teacher] refuse to help him with his worksheets. Benny told me that the other kids harass him.

SALLY: (*Observing that the meeting was becoming a series of accusations and rebuttals*) Because I am the newest member here, may I ask all of you a few questions so that I might get a better picture of what is going on? (*No one really gave approval or disapproval so she continued to speak.*) I am wondering how all you guys have gotten along with each other. Is it a friendly relationship or more business-like? What has the communication between the school and the home front been like?

PRINCIPAL: We certainly have wanted to be friendly and helpful but our contacts have been limited to phone calls because Kendra has never come to any of the meetings we've set up.

TEACHER: My contacts have also been only by phone or by notes that I give to Benny. I never got responses back from these notes and frankly I'm not sure if Benny got them to his mother.

KENDRA: I don't think you know how hard it is to be a single mom. I wanted to be cooperative but you don't make it easy.

SALLY: Benny, what do you think?

BENNY: (*Quietly and looking down*) Sometimes I really get along with my teacher and sometimes it's awful.

Sally heard this conversation as a struggle between the family and the school, with both sides thinking that the other was to blame. She wanted to help everyone get to a place where they could interact and speak freely about their own experiences without fearing an accusatory backlash. Once again Sally approached the group as a whole.

SALLY: If you don't mind, I have some thoughts that might seem odd for now, but I think they will be very helpful to my work with Benny and Kendra. Please reflect on your relationships with each other and think about the times that are characterized by smoothness, success, or a feeling of accomplishment.

TEACHER: I must say that Benny is charming at times.

SALLY: Could you please describe those times more specifically for us?

TEACHER: During the less structured activities such as a group discussion about a news event or a brainstorming session, I notice that Benny participates in a positive way; he shows us that he has a good sense of humor and asks good questions.

PRINCIPAL: Benny has always been respectful to me, always answers my questions politely and usually refers to me as "sir."

KENDRA: When my boys and I read at home, Benny is always attentive.

BENNY: (*After Sally nods to him*) When I do what I am told, class always goes better for me.

SALLY: (*Noticing that the talk seemed more positive and wanting to orient it more toward understanding the meanings that the participants attach to their interactions among one another*) Again, if you don't mind, this is so valuable and eye-opening. What does it mean when dealings with each other are smooth and when times are rocky?

PRINCIPAL: Smooth times occur when Benny's teacher and Kendra are creative and resourceful, such as the time when they coordinated giving rewards to Benny for doing well in class—you know, finishing a project or getting real involved in a class activity. On the other hand, the rockier times occur when Benny misbehaves in class and we can't reach Kendra.

TEACHER: Smooth going with Benny is when he acts appropriately in class and gets his work done on time. At these times, I am pleased, encouraged, and feel like I am successful and doing some good for Benny. When Benny has troubles in class or with his homework, especially when I had tried some special strategies, I feel that I am a failure, like we are all failures, and I can't come up with any ideas that would even begin to work. I can't believe I'm saying this—it must really make me look bad. Also, when I had to contact Kendra for a bad reason and the conversation with her was unpleasant, I thought that Benny and Kendra did not appreciate my hard work and extra efforts. It made me feel pretty washed out.

KENDRA: When the school called me or sent me a note telling me that Benny had another problem and that I needed to come in to do something about it, I thought the school people figured I was a bad mother. I thought that the school pegged my son as dumb and that they gave up on him. I didn't want to hear that even they didn't know what to do with us.

BENNY: I thought that my teacher and principal were mad at me when I had trouble with my worksheets or when I got in a fight with another kid. When things were okay with my schoolwork and I wasn't getting into fights, I thought that maybe they liked me a little bit.

SALLY: (*Realizing that she had moved into a facilitative role, a role she was comfortable with*) From your places as Benny's mom and Benny's teacher (*nodding to each*), could you two comment on what it is like to listen to each other here?

KENDRA: (*Jumping in quickly*) I was surprised to find out that Benny's teacher feels bad when things don't go well with Benny. I thought she could care less one way or another. I'm beginning to think she really cares for Benny.

TEACHER: (*Responding in kind*) Kendra really seems like a good mother—she helps her son read and I can see that she obviously loves him dearly. I think that my frustration with Benny in class and when I couldn't get Kendra in for a conference led me to think that she didn't care what happened to her son. I now believe that I was off base on this.

SALLY: I am curious about what everyone else is thinking at this time.

PRINCIPAL: I have never been to a meeting quite like this one, and that even though it took an hour and a half, the atmosphere is much better and I can see myself leaving more and more of the decisions about Benny to his teacher and his mother—I can give up the role of being the tough enforcer of the rules. I don't think that Benny was responding positively to my discipline anyway. Just maybe we have opened up a window of opportunity to work together to help Benny.

BENNY: (*Barely audible*) The meeting has become so friendly-like. If my mom and my teacher are friends, then maybe my teacher will like me more.

SALLY: (*Addressing the special education teacher*) You have sat here quietly and patiently and have not yet had any interaction with Benny in a classroom setting and I certainly don't want to exclude anyone from voicing their thoughts. What thoughts or reflections on this conversation can you offer our group?

SPECIAL ED TEACHER: I think it is so important for parents and teachers to work together to ensure student success, and I am willing to join with Kendra and the faculty to help Benny's situation in any way that I can.

SALLY: I would like to thank all of you for investing your time and speaking honestly and openly about your ideas about Benny and his situation. I hope that we can continue the strides we made today, that is, the talking and listening so that things improve and move forward to better help Benny.

The role of the therapist entails creating and nurturing a safety zone for conversation. When the school conference became an exchange of accusations,

with each participant blaming someone or something else for Benny's problems, Sally interjected a different set of questions that were designed to change
the nature of the ongoing conversation from blaming to descriptions of relationships (e.g., "I am wondering how all you guys have gotten along with each
other? Is it a friendly relationship or more businesslike? What has the communication between the school and the home front been like?"). Participants need
to have confidence that their views will be respected if they are to feel comfortable talking about things in new ways. If people think that they will not be
heard, the odds of getting them to openly express their views (and especially
their doubts or fears) are very remote. The special education teacher was
included in this meeting because of the proposal to test Benny for special education suitability. His views were valuable too.

A CLS approach values reflective questions and conversation that are more
positively constructed and less loaded with evaluative components (e.g.,
"Please reflect on your relationships with each other and think about the times
that are characterized by smoothness, success, or a feeling of accomplishment.
What does it mean when dealings with each other are smooth and when times
are rocky?"). Problems are discussed in nonpathologizing ways, including language that is more commonplace (e.g., *rocky* rather than dysfunctional, *smooth*
rather than functional). Sally also described effective therapy in the initial
meeting as "*a good idea.*" Assessing progress was described as "*a close watch
on how we are doing.*" These everyday phrases include all participants in the
discussion and emphasize the joint venture quality of working as a therapist in
this manner. This process can be considered an "interactive reflecting process,"
utilizing Andersen's (1987) notion of a "reflecting team" and allowing the participants to directly interact with one another by talking about their own experiences and then about the reflections of others. The therapist encourages a
variety of different viewpoints by being curious about what each person is
thinking or how each is interpreting the talk, and making sure that all participants feel safe to express themselves. This requires a genuine appreciation for
what each participant is expressing. In order to appreciate another's view, we
find it helpful to adopt a position of "not knowing" (Anderson & Goolishian,
1992). This means we do not interpret or try to figure out clients by certain
cues—we let them tell us their story in their own words, in their own way. We
have patience to listen. The therapist must be multilingual in the sense of
understanding and being able to converse within different frames of reference.
Sally made sure that all participants had time and an opportunity to talk. No
one was allowed to dominate the conversation, herself included.

Speaking of the Future

The school meeting was only one part of the work that Sally, Kendra, Benny, and Marcus did together. Those who were involved in Benny's life at school required ongoing encouragment and validation to continue their commitment to making the changes that would lead to success with Benny. Benny met the criteria for inclusion in a behavior and learning disabilities program and worked with the special education teacher who had been present at the meeting. As time went on, most of the interactions at school were between this new teacher, Kendra, Benny, and Sally.

The school conference set a tone of collaboration and partnering between the family and the therapist that carried over into working on the family's other issues. When the mother's boyfriend reentered the scene, Kendra requested Sally's help in changing her relationship with him to make it happier and more secure. When Benny was taken in by the police for another neighborhood rock-throwing incident, the family, Sally, and the probation officer joined together and focused on this identified issue. The neighbors who had their windows broken were included in this process of "straightening things out," very similar to the process outlined with the school situation.

Because life consists of many concerns, the successful handling of a troublesome situation is not the end of the story. Resolution of an issue may open the door for a new issue or problem and its surrounding areas of concern. Benny's family was no exception; there were numerous issues that they faced and negotiated. The success on the school front allowed them to reallocate energy to other issues. Those other concerns, such as the problems in the neighborhood, were addressed in a manner similar to the way in which the school problems were addressed—Sally first discussed with the family their desired approaches to the issues and, when they committed to an issue, the relevant persons were identified, discussion ensued, and a coordination of efforts was set in motion.

Benny's story illustrates how a collaborative language systems approach can facilitate movement in positive directions. However, much was left to do with this family. We like this example because it helps to make the point that work with clients is ongoing and usually not "curative." When Sally left her working relationship with Benny's family, she could not pronounce them "well" or consider them no longer a concern of the court, but she could say they had faced some tough issues and created some resourceful ways to talk about those issues and respond to them. This way of working with clients fits the ethical and moral standards of how we want to help our clients. Of course, we hope to be effective—useful in helping people—but we could not engage in a style of work that was considered effective but not respectful. CLS embodies a democratic attitude that stands resolutely for fair representation and involvement of all individuals in events that have an impact on them. The process of inclusion carries the day. We can deal with all outcomes that emanate from a process that includes all relevant voices.

Reflections on Collaboration Beyond the Family System
Harlene Anderson

I approached this chapter with anticipation and curiosity, wondering how St. George and Wulff would understand, personalize, and put a collaborative approach into action. I wondered how ideas and practices that developed with passion from a multiplicity of experiences over time and that were based in a foundational ethics peculiar to my own history would be translated, as interpretation inherently and simultaneously continues, expands, and alters the original. The chapter read like a good story. The plot was engaging, the language was clear, and I was invited into an imaginary dialogue with St. George and Wulff. Here I offer some of the thoughts that I had while reading this refreshing chapter.

Philosophical Stance

What comes to mind as St. George and Wulff tell their therapy story is the notion of *philosophical stance,* how St. George positioned herself with the family. Philosophical stance refers to certain beliefs about the way that we think, talk to, and act with the people we meet in therapy (Anderson, 1997). This includes the beliefs delineated by the authors throughout the chapter: All voices are valued, respected, and invited; the realities brought into and created in therapy are mutually constructed; and each member of a therapy system, including client and therapist, brings his or her own expertise and wisdom. St. George and Wulff show that when a therapist assumes the CLS philosophical stance, generative conversations and relationships develop and the pragmatics of therapy take care of themselves.

One belief inherent in the philosophical stance is that paying careful attention to how we first meet—and continue to meet—the people we work with in therapy can help dissolve the tensions, misunderstandings, and polarized expectations often embedded in mandated referrals. A reader might overlook the importance of the collaborative philosophy associated with the authors' home-based therapy. Meeting the people in their environments—including home, school, and other settings—rather than in the therapist's environment allows therapists to have a different sense of people and to include people in the therapy that might not otherwise have been included. Home-based therapy is one way a collaborative approach embraces doing what the occasion calls for at any moment in time.

As the authors suggest, another value is the use of ordinary language. Like in their therapy, the authors use everyday, ordinary language in the telling of the story. Such language helps the characters in the story come alive on these pages and be more than just another family with a child on the fringe of a juvenile justice system. The dialogue allows the characters to present themselves rather than to be seen solely through the therapist's or narrator's eyes. In the therapy room, using ordinary language contributes to mutuality and equality. I am often asked, "Don't therapists have expertise?" or "Aren't therapists in hierarchical, authoritative positions?" I would answer "Yes" to both questions. However, as St. George and Wulff so aptly demonstrate, in the CLS approach the therapist is an expert on the process of creating a space for and facilitating generative conversation. The client is the expert on his or her own life, as illustrated from the beginning of the therapy when the therapist acknowledges the family's right to accept or refuse therapy. And, a therapist has choices and options about how to use his or her culturally and professionally deemed authority.

St. George and Wulff also aptly illustrate the value of their belief of being "public," that is, "speaking openly," sharing one's inner ideas and offering them food for thought and dialogue. In being public, the therapist invites the same in others.

Speaking of believing, St. George and Wulff say that "CLS therapists believe what clients say to them." This therapist value has been pointed out and elaborated on by clients I have interviewed over the years about their experiences of successful and unsuccessful therapy. Clients talked about the significance of therapists believing them (Anderson, 1997). Being believed is part of feeling as if they belong to the conversation.

Conversations and Relationships

The therapy amply illustrates the notion of the generative and relational nature of language and knowledge. And, it particularly brings to life the notion that the kinds of conversation we have with others inform, form, allow, and limit the kinds of relationships we can have with them and vice versa. Each conversation is part of past and future conversations. The therapist hopes that each conversation will invite, lead to, and open up others that might not have been possible in the past. Certainly, St. George and Wulff's case illustration shows the twists and turns that a conversation can take. How a therapist invites and participates in therapy talk can allow for or discourage openings for generative conversation and mutual, fruitful relationships. The conversation includes asking questions, making comments, offering thoughts, and listening responsively—all aimed toward understanding the client and clarifying, expanding, and creating meanings.

St. George wisely understood that most likely Benny's family members would see her as a representative of a hierarchical and authoritarian institution with its associated reputation. She, therefore, from the first meeting took care to give them the opportunity to know her uniquely. Thus, the relationship and conversations that she began to have with them slowly dissolved the often embedded tensions and polarized opinions in mandated therapy and lessened the opportunity for therapist drop-out.

Perhaps I can add to the authors' comment "We have patience to listen." It seems to me to be more than patience. Listening requires valuing, being interested in, and believing that the other person has something worthy to say. When listening from this position, listening is spontaneous and genuine. Listening places the therapist in a position more alongside the other rather than nudging him or her from behind, leading from ahead, or waiting patiently. Listening is part of the interactive process of the generation of meaning.

One Illustration

From a CLS approach the outcome of Benny's therapy could not have been designed or predicted ahead of time. Here the story pauses as one aspect of the problem dissolved. Situations and relationships that could have led to a stalemate instead led to, in Benny's words, "The meeting has become so friendly-like. If my mom and my teacher are friends, then maybe my teacher will like me more." The story leaves the reader with a sense of hope that the overall outcome will be successful, and that the people involved will continue to feel that they belonged to the conversation, had participated in its direction, and felt ownership of its products.

Hopefully, readers will not leave this chapter frustrated because they do not have a new set of techniques about how to be collaborative or how to work with child, family, school, juvenile justice system, or larger system problems. Hopefully, instead, the reader will leave with a sense of a collaborative philosophy and one view of how it can translate into action. Each clinical situation is unique; each therapist is unique; and the combination of the two at any one point in time is unique.

Sally St. George, Ph.D., is Associate Professor, Counseling and Human Development, Lindsey Wilson College, Columbia, Kentucky.

Dan Wulff, Ph.D., is Assistant Professor, Kent School of Social Work, University of Louisville, Louisville, Kentucky.

Harlene Anderson, Ph.D., is a founding member of Houston Galveston Institute and Taos Institute, Houston, Texas.

References

Andersen, T. (1987). The reflecting team: Dialogue and meta-dialogue in clinical work. *Family Process, 26,* 415–428.

Anderson, H. D. (1995). Collaborative language systems: Toward a postmodern therapy. In R. H. Mikesell, D. Lusterman, & S. H. McDaniel (Eds.), *Integrating family therapy: Handbook of family psychology and systems theory* (pp. 27–42). Washington, DC: American Psychological Association.

Anderson, H. (1997). *Conversation, language, and possibilities: A postmodern approach to therapy.* New York: Basic.

Anderson, H., & Goolishian, H. (1988). Human systems as linguistic systems: Evolving ideas about the implications for theory and practice. *Family Process, 27,* 371–393.

Anderson, H., & Goolishian, H. (1992). The client is the expert: A not-knowing approach to therapy. In S. McNamee & K. J. Gergen (Eds.), *Therapy as social construction* (pp. 25–39). Newbury Park, CA: Sage.

Anderson, H., Goolishian, H., & Winderman, L. (1986). Problem determined systems: Towards transformation in family therapy. *Journal of Strategic and Systemic Therapies, 5,* 1–13.

Anderson, H., & Levin, S. (1997). Collaborative conversations with children: Country clothes and city clothes. In C. Smith & D. Nylund (Eds.), *Narrative therapies with children and adolescents* (pp. 255–281). New York: Guilford.

Gergen, K. J. (1985). The social constructionist movement in modern psychology. *American Psychologist, 40,* 266–275.

Goolishian, H., & Anderson, H. (1987). Language systems and therapy: An evolving idea. *Psychotherapy, 24*(3S), 529–538.

Madigan, S., & Epston, D. (1995). From "spy-chiatric" gaze to communities of concern. In S. Friedman (Ed.), *The reflecting team in action: Collaborative practice in family therapy* (pp. 257–276). New York: Guilford.

4
Internal Family Systems Work with Children and Families
Laura M. Johnson

Richard C. Schwartz

Cathy and Tom, a white, middle-class couple in their mid forties, sought therapy for their 8-year-old son, Jimmy. Jimmy was having difficulty both socially and academically and was described by his teachers as a "behavioral problem." He was easily upset and tended to lash out in physical violence at other children. Cathy and Tom described their other child, 14-year-old Carla, as "perfectly behaved." She maintained excellent grades and was involved in many school activities. They were surprised when the therapist suggested that they all come to the first session.

In this initial session, Cathy described her constant struggle with Jimmy. "He just infuriates me with his childishness. Sometimes I lash out at him with an anger that I don't understand. A part of me is so repulsed at his childishness, but he *is* a child—I know he can't, and shouldn't, act like an adult." Jimmy's father wanted to be able to set better limits on his son's behavior. "I try to be firm with him, and most of me really wants to, but a part of me says that if I'm firm, then I am just like my own father."

Jimmy said little in therapy, withdrawing into silence, occasionally moving around the room. Like his parents, Jimmy also demonstrated different sides of himself in session. At times, he would cuddle on his mother's lap and at other times he would insist that he was "too big" for such behavior. His parents seemed to like Jimmy's younger actions, while giving him subtle cues that his "big boy" behaviors were not as acceptable. In part they wanted him to act older, but at the same time they seemed to discourage his competency.

Carla said little throughout the initial session. When asked her opinion of the situation, she said, "I don't know. I shouldn't even be here." The therapist explored this further, "So you don't want to be here and yet you are here?" "My mom made me come," she replied. "So the part of you that cares what your mom wants won out over the part of you that doesn't want to be here?" the therapist asked. "Yeah, I guess so. I'm always doing things I don't really want to do. That part usually wins out. I should just break out and do crazy things like Jimmy—he's got the idea."

The therapist took a little time to be aware of her own thoughts and feelings. She recognized that she was feeling some pressure to "do something to help," since Jimmy's school was threatening suspension. However, the therapist knew that this part of her was connected to more than just wanting to help. She knew that it also came from a need to succeed. And though the therapist knew that Jimmy's behavior made sense in the context of his family, she was aware that a part of her wanted to "shape him up" like his parents sometimes wanted. The therapist knew that over the course of this family's therapy she would need to work with these parts of herself to help them to step back and let her be fully present with her clients.

THE CONVERSATION THAT began in this family's initial session was partly shaped by the therapist; yet clients frequently describe their internal struggles in this language of parts. Using the internal family systems (IFS) approach, the therapist applies systemic principles to both the interpersonal and the internal relationships and assumes that all of the various feelings, thoughts, and actions of each family member are serving a function in the family system.

The IFS model (Breunlin, Schwartz, & Mac Kune-Karrer, 1992; Goulding & Schwartz, 1995; Nichols & Schwartz, 1997; Schwartz, 1987, 1988, 1992, 1995, 1997) synthesizes two already existing paradigms: systems thinking and the multiplicity of the mind. It brings concepts and methods from the structural, strategic, narrative, Bowenian, and experiential schools of family therapy to the world of subpersonalities. This synthesis came about when the second author, as a young, fervent family therapist, began hearing about his clients' inner lives. After setting aside preconceived notions about therapy and the mind and listening closely to what clients were saying, he recognized an emerging theme. Clients consistently provided descriptions of what they often called their "parts"—the conflicted voices or subpersonalities residing within them.

This was not a new discovery. Many theorists have described a similar inner phenomenon, beginning with Freud's id, ego, and superego, and more recently seen in the object relations conceptions of internal objects; it is at the core of less mainstream approaches like transactional analysis (ego states) and psychosynthesis (subpersonalities), and is even manifested in cognitive-behavioral approaches under the term schemata. Prior to IFS, however, little attention has been given to how these inner entities function together.

With a background in systems thinking, it was second nature to begin tracking sequences of internal interaction the same way one tracks interactions among family members. Certain themes surfaced. For example, many people's parts seemed to take on similar roles and inner relationships; these inner roles and relationships were not static and could be changed by careful and respectful intervention. Conceiving of the mind as an inner family provided a way to apply family therapy theory and techniques to the internal world of the individual.

Since its conception, IFS therapy has focused primarily on adult individuals, with little attention given to working with children and families. This chapter explores the use of IFS therapy with children and families, covering the theoretical and practical issues associated with this work.

Introduction to the Internal Family Systems Model

The IFS model sees a person as containing an ecology of relatively discrete subminds, each one intrinsically valuable and seeking a positive role within the internal system. Life experiences force these subminds, or parts, out of their valuable roles, which can reorganize the system in unhealthy ways. This process is similar to the way children in an alcoholic family are forced into protective and stereotypic roles by the extreme dynamics of their family. While a common pattern of sibling roles is evident across alcoholic families (e.g., the scapegoat, mascot, hero, lost child), those roles do not represent the essence of those children. Instead, each child, once released from his or her role by intervention, can find interests and talents separate from the demands of his or her chaotic family. The same process holds for internal families—parts are forced into extreme roles by external circumstances and, once it seems safe, they gladly transform into valuable members.

What circumstances force these parts into extreme and sometimes destructive roles? The effects of childhood sexual abuse, which have been discussed elsewhere (Goulding & Schwartz, 1995), and other types of trauma are factors. But more often the values and interactional patterns of a person's family create internal polarizations that escalate over time and are played out in other relationships. This also is not a novel observation; indeed, it is a central tenet of object relations and self psychology. What is novel to IFS is the attempt to understand all levels of human organization—intrapsychic, familial, and cultural—through the same systemic principles, and to intervene at each level with the same ecological techniques.

Most clients have parts focused on keeping them functional and safe; they try to maintain control of individuals' inner and outer environments by, for example, preventing the client from getting too close or dependent on others, criticizing the client's appearance or performance in order to make him or her look or act better, or focusing on taking care of others rather than on his or her own needs in order to ensure acceptance. Because these parts are in protective, managerial roles, they are called *managers.*

When a person has been hurt, humiliated, frightened, or shamed in the past, he or she will have young parts that carry the emotions, memories, and sensations from those experiences. We've all experienced childlike fears of aloneness, shame, vulnerability, or pain. Managers often want to keep those feelings out of consciousness and consequently lock vulnerable and needy parts in inner closets. Those incarcerated parts are known as *exiles.*

The third and final group comprises the parts that go into action when a young exiled part floods the person with extreme feelings or makes the person vulnerable to being hurt again. This group tries to extinguish the inner flames of feeling as quickly as possible, so they are called *firefighters.* They tend to be highly impulsive and seek stimulation that will override or dissociate the person from the exile's feelings. Bingeing on drugs, alcohol, food, sex, or work are common firefighter activities.

The most crucial aspect of the IFS model is the belief that everyone has, in addition to these parts, a core Self that contains many valuable leadership qualities like perspective, confidence, compassion, and acceptance. Working with hundreds of clients over the past decade, some of whom were severely abused and suffer severe symptoms, has convinced us that everyone has this Self, despite the fact that many people initially have little access to it.

The goal of IFS is to release the Self's resources by differentiating it from the parts, and then to enable the person, in the state of Self, to help his or her parts realize it is safe to leave their extreme roles. With adults, this is accomplished by talking about parts, identifying their extreme roles, and helping the client access the Self (or the central "I") in order to restore its leadership role. Once in a leadership role, the Self can bring parts out of extreme roles and depolarize the internal system. The following list summarizes the basic assumptions of the IFS approach:

1. The mind consists of distinct parts. These parts are personified as having complex aspects to each. Personification leads to the view that parts deserve to be valued and treated with respect.
2. Though the nature of each part is unique, parts take on the common roles of managers, exiles, and firefighters.
3. Many problems stem from the tension between the needs of the exiles and the needs of the managers; exiles want to let the person feel pain, managers want to keep those feelings at bay.
4. Each person also has a Self—a curious, compassionate, calm center that can and should lead the parts.
5. When the Self is in charge, it is possible to bring healing to the exiles and to create harmony in the internal system.
6. Health is defined as the Self having a positive leadership role with all the parts, valuing the intent of each, and creating teamwork among them.

Working with children and families introduces a complex set of issues. It is important to examine the development of children's internal systems, the differences in adults' and children's internal systems (considering the development of children's parts), the interactions between children's and parents' parts, and specific techniques based on children's unique ways of processing information.

The Development of Children's Internal Systems

The makeup of parents' internal systems strongly influences the development of children's parts. Object relations theory (see Scharff & Scharff, 1991) describes the process of introjection during which children internalize important people in their lives (parents, siblings, and other significant people) who then become parts of them. When a child considers taking a cookie before dinner, she may hear the voice of her mother telling her that she will ruin her appetite and get into trouble if she takes it. Although she wants the cookie, this voice may convince her that the cost of taking the cookie is greater than the pleasure of it, so she leaves it alone. While initially the voice was actually her mother's voice, the child has now created an internal introject of her mother that may, over time, resemble her actual mother less and less as it is modified by her own needs and temperament. Over time, the introject (or part) becomes a stable part of her psyche that helps to direct her behavior.

This is a highly complex process, given that each significant person in the child's life also has many parts. Children internalize various parental voices, which may then become distinct parts of their inner systems. For example, a child may internalize the critical, exacting part of the father as well as the fun-loving, relaxed part of him.

However, parts are not solely the introjected voices of significant care-givers. Parts also develop in response to life situations in order to help individuals to cope with their surroundings. Parts of children are also sent into exile as a way of coping with life's stresses. Examples of this can be found in abuse cases, but it also occurs in response to daily stressors. For example, a child who is punished for showing anger will likely exile her angry part and develop an internal critical part that parallels the parent's criticism of the child's anger. This ongoing process shapes the development of the child's personality and the nature of her interactions with others.

Furthermore, the development of parts interactions is a patterned, intergenerational process. It is an IFS axiom that children relate to their parts in much the same way that the adults on whom they depend relate to their own parts. For example, a father's manager parts may be triggered by his son's crying because he cannot stand his own sad parts. The father will then shame the boy just as he shames himself internally. The boy's parts that are desperate for Dad's approval will begin shaming and exiling his sad parts in the same way that his father exiles his own. In this way, families transmit the same internal organization over generations.

How Children's and Adults' Internal Systems Differ

Many of the differences between children's and adults' internal systems are intertwined with the developmental issues just outlined. This section examines four ways that adults' and childrens' internal systems differ.

Children's Parts are Less Fixed in their Roles

Because children are easily influenced by the significant people in their lives, their internal systems fluctuate more than those of adults. While adults' parts generally have distinct roles (e.g., manager, firefighter, exile), children's parts do not—though certainly parts of children can become extreme. For example, a part may take a managerial role to protect the child by taking an "I don't care" stance against the world. Yet with children, more than with adults, this part is likely to abandon its mask of indifference and show its other facets. Therapy can quickly reveal that the child's "I don't care" part is also worried about what others think. For adults, this awareness may take more time.

Change can occur quickly with children, but positive changes can be undone quickly as well. A very self-critical child can be taught to soothe, accept, and allow the Self to take leadership of that critical part. However, a critical parent can undo that work in a very short time. For this reason, family involvement in children's therapy is absolutely crucial.

A Child's Self is More Easily Accessible

It is our observation that, like adults, even very young children have a fully intact Self. In the IFS model, the Self is not analogous to the ego as it has been traditionally defined, but rather is more like the soul described in many religious and spiritual practices. It is the core and essence of the person in which exists love, compassion, curiosity, and real connection to others. The Self emerges as a person's protective, hurt, or angry parts step out of the way.

In fact, the Self seems to be more accessible in children than in adults. Adults have sophisticated managers who know how to imitate the Self, whereas children, who have not lived as long as adults, have not had as many years of practice in hiding their true selves. Children are quick to forgive, to let down their walls and connect on a real level with those who are real with them.

Children Do not Manage their Parts as Well

While children's Selves are easily accessible, they are not likely to maintain leadership for long periods of time. Because their parts have not become locked into extreme roles, children are more likely than adults to react impulsively. Their hurt, angry, vulnerable parts have not been exiled, and their managerial parts are not practiced at covering extreme emotion. Parents play a critical role in modeling Self leadership for children and must at times act as the substitute Self for a child leading with an extreme part. Loving, centered discipline involves setting limits on the child's extreme behaviors from the context of the parent's Self. The child should eventually be able to do this consistently for herself.

Children are More Accepting of their Parts

Although children do not exercise Self leadership as well as most adults do, they usually are more accepting of their parts. While an adult may try to hide the fact that she feels jealous or angry, children tend to gladly demonstrate those feelings. Kids haven't learned to hate their parts—adults teach them this. So, while adults can learn from children how to accept their parts, they can teach children to manage them.

Goals of Therapy

Because it is an integrative approach, IFS therapy works well in conjunction with other family therapy models. Many of its goals overlap with those of the structural, strategic, Bowenian, and experiential schools. At its core, IFS provides a way of conceptualizing the internal differentiation process introduced by Bowen (1972). It describes the process in terms of the Self becoming an active, valuing leader of all the parts. The basic goal is to help this internal differentiation take place for each family member, thus promoting interpersonal differentiation and problem-solving.

At its most basic level, the goals of IFS are to differentiate the parts in order to access the Self of each family member, to promote Self-to-Self interactions by increasing Self-leadership within each family member, to help parts to release their burdens so that they can trust the Self to lead, and to work toward the depolarization of polarized parts both within and between family members. The desired outcome of this differentiation and depolarization is harmony in the internal and relational systems. IFS theory assumes that families can find solutions to seemingly insurmountable problems when each family member can remain in the Self in the face of interpersonal stress.

Different families create very different interactional styles, but patterns of parts' interactions exist across families. This section considers those patterns in the context of exploring the goals of IFS therapy with families.

Differentiate the Self from the Parts

An initial goal of therapy is to differentiate each family member's Self from his or her parts. When a part is fused (or blended) with the Self, the person generally leads with that part, experiences it as "me," and has difficulty seeing other aspects of him- or herself. For example, one child may lead with a part of himself that feels entitled; another may lead with a part that feels indebted. Early in therapy sessions, the therapist's goal is to frame the conversation in a way that assumes that the entitlement or the indebtedness are only pieces of these children.

Differentiation of parts is not equivalent to externalizing the problem. The goal is not to separate the problem from the people, instead, it is to separate all of the thoughts, feelings, and beliefs about the problem from the core Self of each individual in the family. This automatically creates teamwork. When the core Self of each family member is working with the others, then all attitudes, behaviors, thoughts, and reactions are seen as separate from the people themselves. This sets the stage for compassionate interactions.

For example, a mother is fed up with her daughter's rebelliousness, and the daughter can't stand her mother's angry outbursts. The therapist, through careful reflection of their feelings and experiences, helps each to describe her feelings as a part of herself (e.g., the rebellious part of the daughter) which reacts to a part of the other person (e.g., the critical/rageful part of the mother). This description creates space for them (the two core Selves) to team up to find ways to manage their reactions to one another.

Promote Self-to-Self Interactions by Establishing Self Leadership

Differentiation of the Self from the parts is the first step toward helping the Self take leadership of the internal system. One of therapy's primary goals is to help family members relate to one another from the Self, which requires that individuals in the family exercise Self leadership. The therapist's job is to help the parts trust that it is safe to let the Self lead, so that more of this relating can happen and basic needs for connection can be met.

In order to produce and maintain Self-led discussions, IFS therapists follow a basic conversational rule. The content of a complaint or discussion can be addressed only when the conversation is Self-led. When someone's part takes the lead, the therapist turns to the person and addresses this, asking the person to find out more about that part and to ask it to step back and allow the Self to lead. A variety of techniques are examined in the next two sections, which can help family members accomplish this. These include talking about parts, interviewing parts, finding the valuable intention of the parts, and using a variety of imagery techniques. With young children (under age 7) it is helpful to use concrete methods such as play, drawing, puppets, and other expressive techniques to promote Self leadership.

Though it is important to work with all family members to promote Self leadership, it is essential that parents/caretakers learn to relate from the Self with each other and with the child(ren). When parents act from the Self, the child is much more likely to do the same. The therapist, then, must focus on helping the parents to have Self-led discussions with both the child and each other.

For example, a parent who screams, cajoles, or begs a child to behave is allowing a part to take over and lead his or her actions. In a Self-led discussion, the parent allows the part to have input but does not let it do the talking. For example, a parent may say to a child, "You know, I get so frustrated with you when you don't do as I tell you. Sometimes I just want to scream." This has a far better result than allowing that frustrated part to take over and do the screaming.

Though relating to children from the Self should be the parents' obligation, some parents try to get the therapist to place that responsibility on the child. Such parents may complain that they do not get respect and that until they do, they will not show respect for the child. The therapist must remain aware that this type of statement comes from an extreme part of the parent and not from the Self.

The therapist can say to the parent, "I'd like to understand more about the part of you that believes you cannot show someone else respect unless that person shows it to you." This initiates a Self-to-Self interaction between the therapist and the parent in which the therapist is curious and compassionate toward this part. The parent is likely to describe past injustices that have made this part feel hardened and unwilling to be mistreated. The therapist empathizes and requests that the parent have that part step back. Once the therapist accesses the parent's Self, he will find that the parent is curious and concerned about the child's behavior and is willing to set appropriate consequences without much anger.

As the therapist continues to work with all members of the system (both internal and relational), family members can begin to acknowledge the needs of their parts and will be able to unload the feelings and beliefs from the past that make their parts so easily hurt, angered, and reactive to each other.

Help Parts to Release their Burdens

IFS refers to this unloading as "unburdening." The IFS model assumes that one reason parts do not trust the Self to lead is that the parts carry burdens. For example, an abused child may have a part that believes she must never talk about the abuse. Instead of trying to get her to "overcome" this belief, a goal of therapy is to explore the history of the part that holds that belief. In the process of this exploration, the therapist helps her to discover and unload the burdens the part is carrying.

Therapy involves talking about and to that part as though it were a person, and letting that part describe its history, its beliefs, and the fears that keep it locked in its extreme role. The therapist guides the process and, through a variety of techniques, helps that part to release its burdens and feel safe enough to trust the Self to lead and protect it. The next section explores specific techniques for helping to soothe and heal these hurt parts.

Depolarize the Parts

The internal and interpersonal polarization of parts is a barrier to Self-leadership. Hence, the therapist must work with family members to depolarize both their internal and interpersonal systems.

Rather than seeing polarization as occurring simply between individuals, the IFS model suggests that it occurs between parts, both internally and relationally. That is, the parts of the parents and children, rather then their whole personalities, may become polarized. For example, a mother who insists that the child be "fixed" by the therapist is leading with a panicky, perhaps controlling part who wants the child's behaviors to "improve or else." That part is likely polarized with the child's "out of control" part. That is, the more the mom's insistent part leads, the more the child leads with the negative behaviors. As therapy continues the mother refuses to follow through on assignments and fails to enforce consequences with the child; thus, it becomes clear that another part of her is inadvertently supporting the child's behavior, perhaps a part that depends on the child for comfort. So there exist in this case both internal polarizations (between the parts of the mom that support and resist behavior change) and interpersonal polarizations (between the controlling part of the mom and the rebelling part of the child).

The unhealthy result of the polarization process is that each part becomes more extreme as the cycle continues. Additionally, the parts have reduced options for action, since they believe that if they do not remain extreme, the other part will take over and threaten the stability of the system. Self-leadership is threatened by this process because the extreme parts of one family member activate the extremes in other family members.

In families, polarizations take many forms, and therapists need to be aware of these various types of familial polarizations and their implications for treatment. One type of polarization occurs when children demonstrate their loyalty to a parent by acting out an exiled part of the parent. The result is that the parent may simultaneously hate and like the child's behaviors, setting up internal and interpersonal polarizations. This love-hate relationship with the child's behaviors can bee seen in the parents' smiling complaints or refusal to enforce consequences.

This results in parents giving children double messages regarding their behavior. A father tells his son that he must not "talk back" to the teacher (the view of one of his manager parts) yet he smiles while he says this. The smile represents the viewpoint of one of his exiles, in this case, a child part of himself that longs to "tell off" his own boss. Therapeutically, it is important to see both of these views as legitimate. Dad really does feel both ways, although he has not consciously acknowledged the feelings of the exile. The child is unconsciously aware of his father's conflict, and "helps" him psychologically by living out the needs of his father's exile. When dad is able to address his own exile, accepting it and allowing it to have appropriate input in his life, his son will be better able to change his interactions at school.

Another example involves the tendency of children to side with the perceived "weaker" parent by protectively acting out their exiles against the "stronger" parent. For instance, a mother who allows her husband to make all her decisions, even when she is harmed by his decisions, is likely to have a child who stands up to the father loudly, acting out the mother's more assertive exile. In this way, the mother's acquiescent part is able to remain in the lead, as it polarizes with the assertive part played out in the child. The child, then, is likely to carry this internal imbalance into other relationships.

A subgoal of therapy, then, is to help the parents meet the needs of their exiles so that the children do not try to do this for them, and to help parents become aware of the roles their children are playing by aligning with and giving voice to the parents' exiles. In this case, one goal would be to help Mom to become aware of her own assertive exiled part, accept it, and let it have a voice, taking into account the parts of Dad it may activate. If this discussion can take place with all family members relating from the Self (see next section) then polarizations can be addressed safely. When any one family member cannot access and reaccess the Self, the therapist needs to work with that member alone or explore other safety measures.

A second type of familial polarization is that of siblings' parts. It is our view that sibling constellation is very important in the family system. We have observed that children seek recognition and establish a place in the family by showing parts of themselves that other siblings do not show. A child who leads with a timid part will probably have a sibling who leads with a more gregarious part. As parents notice and positively reinforce (even inadvertently) certain aspects of a child's behavior, that child will likely increase those behaviors and form her identity around them. Other siblings in the system may avoid those behaviors in order to be noticed by their parents for something unique.

While this can result in positive identity formation in children, it can also have the opposite effect. Parents inadvertently reinforce behaviors that are not productive for the child. It is a well-known structural systems concept that when parents regard a child as "bad in school" or "aggressive," the child will fulfill the parents' expectations. Therefore, another goal of therapy is to help parents to acknowledge children individually in a way that does not polarize their parts or encourage unacceptable behaviors.

A third type of familial polarization is that between spouses, which is often reflected in internal polarizations in children. That is, if parents reject parts of each other, children will reject those corresponding parts within themselves. Depolarizing the parental system will help parents openly value the various parts of each other and model for their children a respect for difference. This involves therapists helping parents to disagree in healthy ways in front of their children.

While rejection of parts feeds polarization, acceptance reduces it. Therefore, another goal of therapy is to help family members to accept and value all their parts, though not all the parts' behaviors. Many people try to depolarize by eliminating the "bad" part of the system (bad kid, bad uncle, bad part of him- or herself). Acceptance involves helping people to see even their extreme parts as having a positive intention for the individual and for the family system. The recursive process of acceptance of parts reduces polarization, enhances Self-leadership, and promotes healthy interpersonal connection, which results in parts finding positive, less extreme roles in the family.

General Techniques for Producing Change

This section reviews the general process of IFS work with families. Because they are talking interventions, most of the techniques in this section work well for all children above the age of 7. However, with younger children, verbal discussions are less effective. The following section highlights some concrete, interactive techniques that engage family members of all ages.

For the sake of illustration, one family will be used as an example throughout this section. This family consists of Mom (Rose, 35), Dad (Cameron, 41), and Gina (11). Gina is the identified patient. She has lost a significant amount of weight and recently was discovered inducing vomiting. The parents are concerned, though Dad is also angry that Gina has "put them up to this." Gina is sullen and withdrawn.

The Therapist's Role in Producing Change

IFS therapy requires that the therapist know how to be in the Self. The Self is by nature compassionate, valuing, and open, and therefore produces an atmosphere of warm acceptance. This means that the therapist is committed to valuing all of the clients with whom she works. The assumptions of the model make this possible, because no matter what sort of hateful or difficult parts the therapist sees, she is committed to the belief that this part is not all of the person. Therapists also commit to valuing all parts of all clients. Certainly, all behaviors are not sanctioned, but the model assumes that all parts have a positive intent.

Safety in the relationship is defined primarily by the ability of the therapist to remain centered in the Self. The therapist must be tuned into her own internal system and be able to calm and manage the parts of herself that tend to take charge in the therapy room. In other words, she should not allow a part of herself (e.g., a part that needs the client's approval, a part that needs to be the expert, or a part that dislikes the client) to take over and threaten the balance of the therapeutic relationship. Neither, however, should the therapist ignore the messages of her own parts. These messages usually have valuable input for the therapy. Yet, it is only from the state of the Self that the therapist can provide the genuine curiosity, compassion, and perspective that creates good therapy.

It takes time, experience, and personal awareness for therapists to consistently recognize the difference between the parts and the Selves of their clients. The development of this "parts detector" is a key to doing effective IFS therapy. By immediately noticing, valuing, and differentiating parts from Selves, therapists help families emerge from polarized, destructive patterns of behavior into differentiated relating. It is in differentiated relating that problems find their own solutions, and where people can find ways to live in peace with those that may be unsolvable.

Introduce and Normalize IFS Language

Dialoguing with the family in the initial interview sets the stage for effective parts work. The therapist should begin to frame the family's discussion in IFS terms. Dad initiates the discussion by sharing his view of Gina's bulimia: "I'll do what I can to help her, but I think this is ridiculous that she's forcing us to have to come here." The therapist reflects his feelings in parts language: "So it sounds like you're saying that one part of you sympathizes with your daughter and agrees that she needs help, but there's another part that is angry at her for bringing the family to therapy at great cost to all of you." Often family members are already speaking this way and such statements affirm their own language. Introduced gently and offhandedly, most clients quickly adopt the terms and use them throughout therapy.

At times, however, someone may react negatively to this language, fearing that the therapist thinks they have multiple personality disorder. In those cases, the therapist needs to normalize the language with a brief statement such as, "Oh, I don't mean like Sybil, I just mean the normal parts that we all have." The briefer the explanation, the more readily it is accepted by the family. Above all, therapists must believe in the model if they want families to feel comfortable with it. Giving a quick personal example may help to normalize the language. For instance, a therapist may comment, "Sometimes part of me wants me to do some important task, while another part just wants to relax in front of the television." Most people can identify with this sort of situation and quickly translate it to their own experiences.

In the initial session, it is important to introduce the concept of the Self and distinguish it from the parts. The therapist can simply refer to the Self as "you." "So, the angry part of you wanted to yell at her; what did you think about that?" This also begins the process of differentiating parts from the Self. If the therapist has developed a keen "parts detector," she will know when the person is describing a part rather than the Self. If Dad says, "Yeah, part of me wanted to tear into her, but I didn't because I was certain that would push her over the edge again," the therapist can respond with, "So, part of you was worried and felt like you should step lightly and be protective of her. What do you think about that?" The therapist thus continues to peel back layers of parts until the person describes the viewpoint of the Self, which is always compassionate, centered, and curious.

As this discussion continues, the therapist takes the opportunity to address all the family members in this way. After asking Gina what she wants to have happen in the session, she replies, "Nothing. I just want to be left alone." The therapist responds, "Sounds like part of you doesn't like all this attention. I believe that there are also other sides to you, too. I will not push you to talk, but I know that some parts of you would really love to have their say, so I hope you don't keep them from being heard." Gina shifts in her seat but gives the therapist a moment of clear eye contact. The therapist does not push Gina to open up or to share any of her thoughts. She knows that would come from a part of her and not from her Self.

This initial discussion is aimed at helping all family members to recognize their multiple perspectives. Reflecting in parts language and explaining (if necessary) may be all that is needed to get this sort of discussion going. For those individuals who do not adopt the language or who remain blended with one extreme part, certain questions can help to draw out parts dialogue. Here are some examples:

- So, I hear that you are very frustrated with her. What else do you feel?
- So, a big part of you doesn't want to go to school. Can you tell me about the other parts of you? The parts that want to be there?
- When your teacher did something you liked this week, how did you feel toward her then?

Continue Interpersonal Discussions Only
When Selves Are In the Lead

After general introductions and joining, in which the language of parts is introduced, the aim is to have family members begin to talk with each other about their situation. As family members share their views with each other, the therapist acts as a referee or coach, by listening for parts and stopping discussions that are not Self-led.

For example, as Dad is describing his anger to Gina, Mom interjects, "Don't be angry at her, Cameron. She can't help herself." Recognizing this as a part of Mom, the therapist turns to her and addresses the part, "I notice that you're uncomfortable with Dad expressing his anger to Gina. What's that about for you?" Mom responds, "Well, I feel like a referee for these two. Someone's got to protect Gina." This turns the conversation to a part of Mom that fears not only her husband's anger, but also anger in general. Once this part has been addressed, Mom is able to resume hearing Dad share his anger without feeling the need to intervene.

As long as Dad can talk with Gina about his anger and Mom can talk with Dad about her fear of him and her need to referee, then the therapist allows the family to focus on the content of the discussion. However, when a family member's part begins to take charge, the therapist turns to that person to begin dialogue about the part. Parts should not be allowed to take over in session, as people can harm each other and jeopardize the safety of therapy. If the therapist allows parts to lead the discussion, therapy begins to replicate the clients' home interactions and the family members lose faith in the process.

Ask about Parts Interactions

There are a number of ways to help family members work with parts that are interfering with Self-led discussions. The simplest way is to ask about the part and its interactions with the parts of other family members. For this family, some obvious questions are:

- So what happens, Dad, when the angry part takes charge of you?
- How do others react when you let this happen?
- What parts of you, Gina, are activated by this part of Dad? Mom?
- How does the part of you, Dad, that sympathizes with Gina feel when your angry part takes over? (*Tracks parts' interactions*)
- Mom, how do you take care of the part of you that works so hard to take care of Gina? (*Encourages self-soothing*)
- What do you like about Gina's angry part? (*Presumes that the person can find a positive aspect of the part*)
- Gina, what's one thing that Dad does that makes it easier for you to keep your "Leave me alone" part from taking over? (*Targets behaviors that promote Self-led discussions*)

Asking these questions automatically acts to externalize the problem (a goal in narrative therapy), allowing all family members to be seen as inherently good and working together to deal with the out-of-control parts. It is important, though, to ask these questions in a way that presumes that each individual has full responsibility for managing their parts. Externalization is helpful only if it also maintains the individual's responsibility for his or her actions.

The therapist can also ask questions that help family members to describe their parts to one another. For example, after a discussion between Mom and Dad regarding their disagreement about how to react to Gina's bulimia, Gina begins to cry. The therapist tells Gina that she sees her sadness. Gina then describes feeling "lost" when her parents disagree. The therapist asks her to describe this "lostness" by asking what it looks, sounds, and feels like. Here the therapist has opened up room for exploration of Gina's visual, auditory, and kinesthetic experience. Her response to this question will guide the therapist in future work with Gina. She responds, "I feel so sad when they argue. I feel it like an ache in my stomach." She shows her tendency to feel her parts kinesthetically. In the future the therapist should ask her feeling-based questions.

After the first session, it can be helpful to give homework assignments that encourage the whole family to continue thinking about their parts and their parts' interactions. Assignments should, however, encourage individuals to examine themselves, not other family members. Analyzing one another's internal systems can result in a disastrous blurring of boundaries between family members.

Family members can be asked to think of ways that they can get to know their own parts. Some clients decide to journal, others choose to spend quiet time thinking about it or asking questions of themselves. Most people quickly adopt this model and return to therapy ready to describe the characters in their inner world.

Ask Individuals in the Family to Interview Parts

As discussions continue across sessions, family members will begin to see how difficult it is to speak from the Self and how easily their parts interrupt and take charge. If they have adopted the language, it is an easy next step to ask each person to interview his or her parts. The goal of the interview is to have people move toward themselves, rather than to move away, which is the natural tendency. As people go toward their parts with acceptance and curiosity, the parts share a great deal of information that previously may have been outside the individual's conscious awareness.

Family members can do such exploration internally and then report their findings to the group. In one family session, for example, the mother describes a part of her that feels she must referee the battle between Cameron and Gina. The therapist might suggest, "Why don't you try to go inside yourself and interview this part of you. Stay with it for a minute or so and then let us know more about it." The interview is a quiet, internal process conducted by the individual. Again, the therapist should believe in and be comfortable with the model. As a rule, the more casually the therapist makes this suggestion, the more readily it is accepted.

If clients respond with confusion to this suggestion, the therapist should empathize with her and gently explain the purpose of the interview. For example, Mom says, "What do you mean, 'interview the referee?' I don't know how to do that." The therapist responds, "Yes, this is a different way of interacting than many of us are accustomed to. I mean for you to try to learn more about that part of you that feels so pulled between Dad and Gina. You can take your time, and even close your eyes if you choose. See what this part looks like, how you feel it in your body, what it tells you to do. Don't try to change it, just get to know it."

This type of suggestion slows family discussions and teaches introspection as a way of managing the stress of difficult topics. It also moves individuals toward internal differentiation. If Mom is able to talk to the referee, then during that time period she will experience her Self as separate from it. As she learns about the needs of the referee, she will begin to take more responsibility for her reactions to Cameron and Gina. Internal differentiation leads to interpersonal differentiation.

In family sessions, it is common for family members to react negatively to such suggestions. If the mother is highly blended with her referee part, the presence of Dad and Gina may threaten her ability to separate from it enough to interview it. The therapist should not, however, stop such questioning due to reactivity.

A person's inability to interview a part in the presence of a family member may be evidence of yet another part that the individual has not acknowledged. For example, Mom may respond to this request with, "I just can't interview this part in here. All I keep thinking is that Cameron won't agree with me; he doesn't think I need to referee at all, but I do." This is excellent information about yet another part, to which the therapist can respond, "So you've found that you have a very valuable part of you that monitors your reactions based on what Cameron might think of you. Sounds like an important part that would be worth exploring."

The principle that the therapist should consistently follow is to value and explore all thoughts, feelings, and reactions of each family member. Parts are intricately woven into and layered upon each other. If a person has difficulty interviewing one part, she can be asked to interview the part that prefers that she not interview the first one. Such work increases empathy between family members and provides tools for the family to solve their problems on their own.

As a way of including other family members in the process, the therapist may ask one or more of the others to pay attention to their own reactions while the individual is interviewing and discussing their parts with the therapist. Depending on the safety level, it may be possible to have the others share their reactions directly with the individual, although in highly volatile families, the therapist needs to monitor reactions closely.

In cases of extreme interpersonal reactivity, the therapist may choose to schedule a session with an individual in order to explore his or her internal process. One individual session may greatly reduce interpersonal reactivity in subsequent family sessions.

During the individual's interview, the therapist guides the person to ask certain questions of her part. Some examples of commonly asked questions are:

- How do you feel toward the part? (*Ensures that the Self is present with the part*) If the person says, "I hate it" then the therapist would ask the person to have the part that hates it to step back. If it is unwilling to do so, then the interview shifts to the part of the person that feels hate. When in the Self, the person will respond in a way that shows compassion and curiosity.
- What does the part want for you and from you? (*Identifies positive intentions of parts*)
- What can you do to help it to trust you? (*Sets the groundwork for Self leadership*)
- What other parts make it nervous? (*Identifies polarizations, coalitions of parts*)
- When does it feel like it needs to take over? (*Explores internal and interpersonal polarizations*)
- What would it rather be doing instead of its current job? (*Suggests that the part can fulfill an important role without becoming extreme*)

Having individuals interview their own parts (rather than the therapist interviewing them) encourages Self leadership. In some cases, such as those in which severe abuse has been an issue, the Self is not readily accessible and is greatly distrusted by the parts. In these cases, the therapist may choose to directly access a part and ask it questions. This work, however, is seldom necessary with families. (For more information on direct access, see Schwartz, 1995.)

Individual IFS work is easier to keep up with than whole family work because the therapist usually finds complex sets of polarized parts and resultant interactional sequences. She may decide to take notes on the clients' various parts in order to remember and study them.

Find the Valuable Intention of the Part

The therapist makes the assumption that all parts have positive intentions, even when they play a negative (extreme) role in the internal and interpersonal systems. The question "What does the part want for you?" helps to reveal this positive intention. Most people want to get rid of parts; the therapist's role is to help people accept and guide the behaviors of their parts.

It is important to model acceptance of parts, but not necessarily of the parts' behaviors. The therapist should communicate an acceptance of the value of all parts (and all people) in the room, while holding them fully responsible for managing their actions. Through the process of finding the valuable intention of parts, they should begin to feel understood, relax, and become less extreme. This allows other polarized parts to become less extreme, as well, facilitating the goal of depolarization.

For example, the therapist helps Gina to find the positive intention of her "stomach ache part" by having her interview it. She reports that the ache in her stomach wants her to be happy. She describes it as "a big pain that makes her forget her problems." "So," the therapist responds, "this ache in your stomach is trying to help you out. I wonder if it may be trying to help your parents, too, by keeping them from talking about their disagreements." "I don't know," Gina answers, "but I know that this ache hurts a lot and makes it hard to eat. Then sometimes I can't stop eating." "Oh," the therapist says, "there's another part that tries to help you by getting you to eat. Sounds like a good part that is just going overboard with its good intentions." "Yeah," Gina laughs.

The therapist also helps Dad interview his angry part. He discovers that it is acting extreme because it wants to protect the family and keep Gina healthy, which he believes he should be able to do. When asked what how he feels toward this part (attempt to access the Self) Cameron states that he hates that part because it blows up and hurts people, making him just like his abusive father. Clearly, this is not the Self talking, so the therapist responds, "So there's a part of you that hates the angry part and wants to get rid of it, which is understandable, but scary, too. It sounds to me like the angry part is trying very hard to do something valuable but is going about it in a terrible way. I wonder how you could help it to express itself in a less hurtful way." Thus, the therapist values the part, but not the part's behavior, and also highlights the internal polarization reflected in the interpersonal polarization between Mom and Dad.

Help Clients Nurture and Soothe their Parts

One aspect of interpersonal differentiation is the ability to self-soothe. IFS therapists help clients to soothe and nurture their parts, which reduces reactivity and increases the family's capacity to tolerate anxiety.

As Gina interviews her stomach ache part, the therapist asks her to find out what that part needs from her. This suggests that Gina has the ability to respect, value, and meet the needs of her internal pain. Gina goes to the chalkboard and begins to draw a set of circles inside of each other. "This is the pain way down in the middle," she says. "I can't get to it because it is inside of so many other circles." "So it needs you to go and be with it," the therapist responds, "but it's hard to get there when other parts of you keep you out. Maybe we can go be with those other parts first and help them to let you in. Can you tell that inside circle that you care about it and that you are working to get there?" She moves to the toy box and finds the baby doll, holding it to her chest. "This will be the stomach ache for now. I can hold it for a while to help it calm down."

The IFS personification of parts leads discussions in this self-nurturing direction. If mere feelings or attitudes are at issue, they may be viewed as disposable. The construct of humanness leads clients to value and nurture their parts. It is a way of viewing the mind that requires continual self-care.

Ask Clients to Have their Parts Step Back

When a part is fused (or blended) with the Self, additional techniques may be needed to separate the part from the Self. For example, when asking a teenager to interview a rebellious part, she replies, "What do you mean? That's me! I hate my parents for the box they put me in!!!" Even when she is able to interview the part, it is so extreme that she cannot let her Self take a leadership role. In this case, it may be helpful to have her ask the part what it would take for it to step back and let her learn more about it. This can be done by having her visualize a room for the part to step into or any place that would provide a boundary between herself and the part (e.g., across a stream, in a field). From this perspective, it is much easier for the individual to interview the part, and it is more likely that the part will not take over in sessions and become extreme.

Specific Techniques for Children and Families

In families with young children, much of the work involves verbal discussions aimed at helping parents to exercise Self leadership. Such work is directly beneficial to the children in the family, since parents are responsible for modeling behaviors for children and since children tend to lead with the Self to the extent that the parents do.

However, verbal discussions can leave young children out of the process. This section reviews a variety of action-oriented techniques that can help to involve children actively in the therapy process. It is not enough to work with parents and assume that the kids will improve. Children have issues of their own that need to be addressed both during family sessions and individually.

Play

Talk therapy may be helpful for families with older children and teens, but young children use play as their primary mode of communication. Therapists working with families with young children need to provide resources for play. (For information on appropriate toys for play therapy see Landreth, 1991, and Johnson, 1995.) Preoperational children and concrete operational children need to be able to act out their feelings in order to understand and respond to them.

Parts will act themselves out in play and the therapist can model acceptance of the part without allowing it to behave in harmful ways. Play also helps parts to experiment with alternative roles, and fantasy play can allow this to happen in a safe environment. For example, one child pretended in session to flush a baby doll down a play toilet and thus worked with a part of himself that was jealous and rageful. Because it was fantasy play and not reality, he could play out his feelings in safety, knowing that the baby was not really hurt. The therapist facilitated a play interview of that part in which the child experimented with alternative behaviors and showed the jealous part acceptance and understanding.

It can also be helpful to involve all of the family members in fantasy play, led by the child. If the adults in the room are willing to follow the child's lead, the child will create elaborate fantasies that illustrate his or her parts concretely. One little girl (age 5) continually pretended to be an ambulance by running across the room making siren noises. At first, her mother tried to stop her, but the therapist encouraged the mother to reflect her daughter's behavior. "You're being an ambulance," Mom said to her. "I'm coming to rescue the people from the burning house!" the girl exclaimed.

The therapist responded, "The house is burning! I wonder if you can talk to the ambulance about that. Will it tell you how it feels to be in such a loud hurry to help?" "It says it has to save everybody, but it gets tired sometimes, too," she replied. At this point, the girl was sitting on the floor, holding a small toy car. The therapist sat down beside her. "You have a car," the therapist said. "This is the ambulance," the girl responded. "It's resting." "You are helping it rest," the therapist commented, "I wonder if you can find out more about the ambulance." "It runs over people sometimes," she said. "It's scared when people yell."

In such a dialogue, children's play can facilitate the expression of feelings and attitudes. In this case, the mother noted that her daughter was a big "helper" at home, and she wondered out loud if her "helper part" was trying to put out fires. Though the girl was not able to verbalize this process, she was quite capable of playing it out in session.

Drawing

There are a variety of ways to use drawing to help children and families learn to manage their parts' interactions. A benefit of drawing is that the product is tangible. It can be talked to, shown to family members, and brought to future sessions. If a family member is not present, a drawing of that person can be made and placed in a chair to represent him. Drawing also concretely externalizes parts. Oaklander (1988) generally assumed that the different parts of a drawing represent the different parts of the individual. This assumption, whether true in any objective sense, does stimulate productive parts discussions.

In general, drawing techniques can be divided into free drawing and structured drawing tasks. For any drawing activity, therapists should have paper, crayons, colored pencils, a chalkboard, easel, and/or a dry-erase board in an accessible place in the therapy room. Free drawing happens frequently in therapy rooms that have art materials available; how those drawings are used depends upon the orientation of the therapist. The following case illustrates the application of IFS language to a child's free drawing in a family session.

In a stressful discussion between parents, one 6-year-old child wandered to the dry-erase board and began drawing with the black and red markers. The therapist asked the child, "Which part of you drew that?" The child responded, "My mad part." "Your mad part drew that picture," the therapist said. "It seems to me that when Mommy and Daddy talk about hard things, your mad part has a lot to say."

Because behavioral problems were an issue with this child, the therapist decided to use the drawing to have Mom and Dad model positive interaction with this mad part. "Mom, what can you say to that picture to let it know that you understand what it's like to be mad?" the therapist asked. Mom tentatively turned to the picture and said, "I like your colors. I'm mad sometimes, too, and it helps me say what I think to other people." The therapist turned to Dad, who said to the picture, "I don't like some of the things you do, but I get mad, too. Everybody does."

At this point, the child was laughing uncontrollably. "It feels good to know that this mad part is good," the therapist said to the child. "What would you like to say to it?" The child turned to the picture and said, "I like you too. But I'm also scared of you. You hurt people sometimes!" This led to an important family discussion about ways to express anger appropriately. The use of the drawing to embody the anger allowed the child to differentiate from it and the family to externalize her behavioral problems.

At other times, therapists choose to structure a drawing task. Oaklander (1988) describes a variety of structured methods, some of which are reviewed here. The therapist can ask a child to draw a picture and then ask the child to pretend to be some part of the picture and speak to another part of the picture. The assumption is that the parts of the picture represent parts of the child, and the goal is to help the child to connect with and value all of her parts.

In a family session, the therapist can ask each family member to draw the family in symbols. The symbols often represent the role each person plays in the group. After each family member shares the meaning of the symbols he or she has chosen, the therapist can ask each family member to share how it feels to be seen as fitting these symbols. The discussions which follow this activity are rich with IFS dialogue. For example, the therapist said to Mary, a teenager, "I notice that you are seen as a trumpet, a ball of fire, and a cat. How does this feel to you?" Mary responded, "I know that my family sees me as 'out there,' kind of feisty and confident. Inside, though, I don't feel that way. I don't think they know how scared I am a lot of the time." This led to a discussion of her exiled fear and how she could show it in the family. The revealing of this hidden part created a new sense of intimacy between Mary and her mother as she shared similar high-school experiences.

The IFS therapist can do many creative things with drawing and painting, involving whole families in the process. Such work can directly access parts while providing a container for the exploration. The result is often a deepening of family relationships as individuals become aware of each others' internal struggles.

Parts Genograms

Drawing a parts genogram can help to increase awareness of intergenerational parts patterns, instill hope for different future behavior, relax parents' anxious parts, and make children feel connected with their parents. After helping the family to draw a genogram, the therapist asks questions about parts. For example:

- Which parts of parents were most in charge while living at home with their parents?
- Which parts did they not show to their parents, and why?
- Do the children see any similarities in the parts that they show and do not show to their parents?

The parent who is showing the child the "you'd better shape up" part and hiding the parts of himself that sympathize with the child will often find that his parent did the same with him. He may also notice that his mother's actions activated in him a part similar to the part that is being activated in the child.

Even young children can be involved in creating the parts genogram. In their candidness, they are frequently the source of rich personality details. While an adult may focus on the "polite" aspects of Grandma, a child will more readily share her other parts. For example, while one father told about his loving, big-hearted mother, his 5-year-old son said, "Tell him what a clean-freak she is!" This comment initiated a conversation about the positive and negative aspects of this part and the way this part was also an extreme managerial part of Dad. Though he was very exacting about the cleanliness of the home, Dad did not like this side of himself. Another part of him felt that he should relax and "be okay with things," and these two took turns determining his attitude at home. The parts genogram provided an intergenerational illustration of this pattern.

Role Switching

The role-switching technique is most useful when it is clear that the family members have become stuck in particular roles. For example, a mother who worries constantly about her son's grades may be polarized both with her son, whose role is to ignore her, and with her husband, whose role is to belittle her fears. The IFS assumption is that these roles represent the extreme behaviors of parts of these people. The therapist can direct family members to switch roles in session and act out a familiar scenario. Then, each can report what felt good about taking on the new role, letting the other person's part be in charge.

The purpose of this task is to highlight these polarizations and increase empathy for each other. Family members act as a mirror for each other; parents see that children have the ability to access parts of themselves other than the ones parents deem "irresponsible" and children see the "childlike" parts of the parents. Family members begin to empathize with each other. Role switching also creates a humorous atmosphere, which lightens the session and encourages the enthusiastic involvement of the children.

A homework assignment based on the role-switching technique is to have parents play a game with kids in which they take on the disliked behaviors of the child for a limited period of time. This activity aids parents in acknowledging parts of themselves that enjoy the child's behavior. For example, when the above mother switched roles with her son at home, she found that she thoroughly enjoyed ignoring him at times. When the therapist explored this in session, she found that she had accessed a part of her that wanted to focus on herself and tune others out. Interestingly, the mother also noticed that when she ignored her son, he worried about her (he had automatically switched roles with her). The therapist used this information to explore other worries and found that the boy worried about his grades, too. As long as Mom worried for him, he had exiled the worry. When she ignored him, it sparked this and a range of other fears that now could be addressed in session.

Puppet Shows

In this activity, the therapist asks each family member to pick puppets that represent their various parts and to act out a familiar family argument with the puppets. For example, Mom may pick two puppets, one that represents her angry, "shape up" part, the other, her guilty, "I'm being too hard on him" part. The child picks one puppet to represent his rebellious part and another his scared part. They would then begin to have a conversation about the child cleaning his room, changing puppets when another part wants to talk. In this case, only two family members are in session. Certainly, the more family members present, the more complex the puppet show becomes.

The role of the therapist is to watch the interaction, noticing how each part influences the behavior of the others. Because it is an enactment of interactions at home, much can be learned from it, so it is best not to interrupt it prematurely. However, it is also important not to allow parts to become harmful to others. Usually, the scene runs its course and the individuals either begin to laugh or turn to the therapist for guidance. To process the activity, the therapist can ask:

- What did each of you learn about yourself? The other?
- What do you like about each of your puppets? Each of the other's puppets? (*Helps promote valuing all parts*)
- What happens when these parts take over and attack each other?

This activity highlights which parts are in charge in certain situations and can prompt a discussion about how family members can have the same argument from the context of the Self.

A follow-up activity is to have family members choose the same puppets, but to instruct them to have the puppets speak to the holder, rather than to the other person's puppet. The only interpersonal speaking should be between the people, who speak in the Self. For example, Mom picks up her "shape up" puppet and has it to say (to herself), "Tell him to act better. He's getting in trouble all the time." Then, she holds up her "I'm being too hard on him" puppet, who says, "Leave him alone, you're such a nag!" The therapist then asks her to have a conversation with them, as a team, to discuss what she should say to the son. She says to them, "I know you both want to tell me what to do, and I appreciate what each of you is trying to do. I'm going to take both of your views seriously, but I have to talk to him, not you two." She then says to her son, "Andy, I want to understand what is going on for you. I want you to stop getting in trouble, and I can't leave you alone about it because I care about you." Andy then either responds to her verbally (in the Self) or chooses one of his parts' puppets to speak to himself.

The therapist can get involved in the Self-to-Self puppet show, which works well with very young children. For example, one therapist asked a 4-year-old child a question and got no response. So, the therapist chose a puppet and had it talk to himself. "Oh no," the puppet said, "this little boy doesn't want to talk to you! I think you scared him!" The boy became quite attentive as the therapist chose yet another puppet. "He's not scared," the other puppet said to the therapist, "he just doesn't like to talk unless he knows he's safe." "Oh," said the therapist to the second puppet, "then I should make sure he knows that he's safe in here." And, turning to the first puppet, "I'll make sure he knows that even if he's scared, that's okay." The boy then ran to the box to pick out some puppets for himself, and he used them frequently thereafter to share his feelings and opinions. This therapist built instant rapport and modeled acceptance of his own, and the child's, parts.

Rules and Consequences Poster

Particularly helpful for children with conduct problems and parents who overreact to children's behaviors, this activity involves having parents and children develop, either at home or in the office, a list of target behaviors and appropriate consequences for them. It is also helpful to list positive behaviors and rewards. The therapist helps parents to set appropriate, logical consequences. The poster is hung in the house, and parents can refer to it when a child breaks a rule, ensuring that the Self has leadership of the disciplinary action.

This activity can spark parts discussions in session. For example, when a parent does not enforce the consequence, the therapist can ask, "Which part took over and told you to go ahead and give her the car keys anyway?" or "Which part jumped in and yelled when you had already decided that you would use time out?"

This activity often reveals parts of kids that parents didn't know existed. In one session, the therapist asked the child what he thought of the consequences and the child responded, "They're really not tough enough. Sending me to my room is no punishment with the TV in there." The Self-to-Self conversation between the father and son that ensued demonstrated a kind of connection they had not previously had.

Case Illustration*

The family introduced in the beginning of the chapter consists of Tom (47) and Cathy (44) and their two children, Jimmy (8) and Carla (14). Cathy had made the initial phone call to the therapist, seeking help for Jimmy. "He's only 8," Cathy told her, "so I don't see how behavioral problems could be such a big issue—but the principal is threatening to suspend him! I don't know what his teacher is expecting. Maybe we haven't done the best job with him, I don't know. . . . I guess therapy is our only hope of keeping him in this school."

Already the therapist could hear various attitudes in Cathy's description of the problem, and she wondered how they were interacting with each other and with the others involved. "Sounds like you're confused and angry about how the school is handling Jimmy," the therapist said, "and you also sound worried about him and about your role as a parent." The therapist arranged for the entire family to come to the first session.

Session 1

Goals: To join with all family members; to introduce the language of parts; to value every aspect of each person in the room (helps the managers relax and show more of the person); and to begin noticing the interaction and polarization of parts.

Mom and Jimmy came to the first session on time, but Dad, who was picking Carla up from school, was late. In fact, they did not arrive until 20 minutes after the session was to begin. When the therapist invited the four of them into the office, Cathy seemed upset. The therapist asked the family members to introduce themselves and to share their view of what they wanted out of therapy. Cathy spoke first.

---

* This case does not portray therapy with an actual family, nor are the dialogues from actual sessions; rather, the case has been created to illustrate the use of IFS with a family group.

CATHY: I want to get relief. This is just getting out of hand.

THERAPIST: Relief . . .

CATHY: From handling everything myself! Jimmy is out of control, he needs therapy, and it's impossible for his Dad to get here on time!

TOM: Cathy, don't start.

THERAPIST: Cathy, sounds like you're feeling overwhelmed. (*Leans toward her*) I'd guess there's a lot that's led up to that feeling getting so strong. It matters that you're angry. Can you tell Tom in a way he can hear it?

TOM: Give me a break. I hear it all the time. What else is new?

THERAPIST: (*To Tom*) You sound like you feel blamed a lot.

TOM: I know you think we're the problem, coming in here fighting right off the bat.

THERAPIST: I know that when families come to therapy there is a feeling of having messed up somehow. I don't think that, though. I think you all care a great deal about getting help for Jimmy.

Both Tom and Cathy relaxed at this comment. The therapist's intent in this exchange was to show the family that all feelings are valued, with the suggestion that how they are expressed is important. In order to remain in her Self, the therapist had to work with her own anxiety. To do this, she noticed it, validated it, and asked it to step back. This allowed her to communicate unconditional acceptance to the angry and sarcastic parts of Cathy and Tom.

CATHY: (*To the therapist*) We really don't fight like this all the time. I'm just feeling a lot of pressure to get some help for Jimmy. I want to be supported. (*The therapist's response from the Self helped Cathy to speak from the Self, as well.*)

TOM: (*To Cathy*) I support you, Cathy. I got away from work late.

CATHY: What else is new?

THERAPIST: Cathy, I hear you saying that what you want from therapy is get help for Jimmy and to find a way to feel more support than you do now.

The therapist noticed that parts of Cathy and Tom were highly reactive to and polarized with each other. She assumed that the stress of Jimmy's situation intensified the polarization, just as the polarization probably affected his behavior. She noted this cycle to return to it later.

CATHY: Yeah, that's pretty much it. I don't really know what Jimmy needs, though. He's only 8. I don't know what all the fuss is about, really.

THERAPIST: (*To Cathy*) So there's a part of you that worries about Jimmy and thinks he needs help. Then, it sounds like there's another part that believes he's fine—that the school is making a big deal out of nothing.

CATHY: I guess you could say it that way. He is only 8. Isn't that young to have problems?

THERAPIST: It's hard to think about a child having difficulties.

CATHY: Like, did I do something wrong?
            (*Jimmy crawls in his mother's lap and begins playing with her coat buttons. Cathy hugs him and he cuddles up to her.*)

The therapist noted that mom's belief that the school was to blame (a manager) was protecting her from the guilt she alluded to. When this exile showed up, it activated a protective part of Jimmy.

THERAPIST: Jimmy, it seems like you try to take care of your mom when she worries about things. I bet this part of you that takes care of people does a lot of good for your family. What do you want to have happen here?

JIMMY: I don't know.

THERAPIST: It's hard to be somewhere like this when you're not sure what you want.

JIMMY: No it's not.

THERAPIST: So you're not sure what you want but you like being here.

JIMMY: I didn't say I like it here.

THERAPIST: Sounds like you just aren't sure about me asking you questions. I like to see that. You're someone who doesn't trust just anybody. It's good to be careful.

Jimmy smiled a little and made eye contact with the therapist. The therapist was aware that Jimmy was leading with a protective manager, so her goal was to let him know that she valued the job it was doing. She wondered if his protection of his mother and of himself was the work of the same part that got him into trouble at school. She noted this for later.

THERAPIST: (*To Tom*) What would you like to get out of coming here?

TOM: Well, I'd like Jimmy to straighten up. He knows better. He's been taught how to act.

THERAPIST: You've taught him how to act, so it makes you mad that he's not doing that.

TOM: Well, that doesn't sound very concerned, the way you say it. I guess I am mad at him for putting us in this bind with his school. I also realize that I'm too easy on him a lot of the time.

THERAPIST: So one part of you really tries to "keep him in line" while another part of you lets him get away with stuff.

TOM: That's a pretty accurate way to say it. I get really tough on him and then I feel bad about it and let him have his way. I hate that I do that! I know how important it is to be consistent.

THERAPIST: I'm hearing another part, too. Sounds like there's a critical part that tells you how you ought to do things.

TOM: Oh, that's the same one that's hard on Jimmy. It's hard on me, too. It sees what a fool I am for being so easy on him.

The therapist noted that Dad had an internal polarization between these managers and that he was more sympathetic to the critical part. This probably explained how the "easy one" had to take over in order to have input.

THERAPIST: I think that these three sides of you are trying to do a good job raising Jimmy. I bet they all have good ideas. Maybe they just get out of hand.

CARLA: Like that lady on TV with multiple personalities.

TOM: (*To the therapist*) You're saying it's good to be easy on him?

Therapist: Well, it sounds like that part is working hard to keep the tough guy in check.

TOM: Maybe so.

THERAPIST: (*To Carla*) Glad to hear your voice. You've been quiet up 'til now.

CARLA: I'm always quiet. I don't get in trouble that way.

THERAPIST: So you keep all your thoughts and feelings to yourself so you won't get in trouble. I bet that's a lot of work.

CARLA: Not really. I'm used to it.

THERAPIST: What would you like to get out of coming here?

CARLA: I have no idea. I shouldn't even be here. Jimmy is the one with the problem.

THERAPIST: So you don't want to be here and yet you are here.

CARLA: My mom made me come.

THERAPIST: So the part of you that cares what your mom wants won out over the part of you that doesn't want to be here?

CARLA: What? Yeah, I guess so. I'm always doing things I don't really want to do. That part usually wins out. I should just break out and do crazy things like Jimmy—he's got the idea.

THERAPIST: So is it safe to say that you'd like to figure out a way to get to do more of the things you want to do?

CARLA: Sure, I guess.

THERAPIST: Sounds like a good goal. It's a tough job to give up what you want for a long time. I bet that part of you gets tired.

TOM: Carla, don't be ridiculous. We give you lots of freedom.

THERAPIST: (*To Carla*) Is that what you mean, that you don't have freedom?

CARLA: No. I mean that I don't say the things I want to say a lot of the time.

THERAPIST: You said that pretty clearly, Carla. You've already made a good start.

MOM: Carla, I can't believe I'm hearing this! (*To the therapist*) She's at the head of her class and doesn't ever get in trouble.

THERAPIST: (*To Mom*) It's hard to know that Carla has her own things to worry about. Sounds like worrying about Jimmy takes about all the strength you've got right now.

MOM: I'm very tired of holding all this. If I felt more support I'd have more sympathy.

The therapist had begun to see a pattern of the parts' interactions in this family. Cathy and Tom seem to show one another only one part of themselves. In relationship to Tom, Cathy leads with a tired, overwhelmed part that demands help from him. In relation to Cathy, Tom leads with a sarcastic manager that belittles her needs. The therapist realized that these parts are stuck in a no-win situation. Neither could back off because each believed that they were needed for protection. The therapist assumed that this was not the only interaction between Cathy and Tom. She assumed that other parts of each would interact with each other quite differently.

The therapist saw that Jimmy acted as Mom's protector by cuddling up to her at the moment she expressed guilt. She wondered if his problems at school were related to protection of others or of himself. She recognized that Tom's internal polarization between the tough guy and the easy one likely fed

Jimmy's problem, too. She noticed that Carla had allowed her own needs to get shuffled to the background by being the "good girl." The therapist wondered how she expresses anger and jealousy in her family and noted that Carla may need some individual attention to find out how she is handling adolescence— a time of life that is full of extreme emotions.

Structurally, the therapist could see the need to help Tom and Cathy work out their marital issues, which likely have an impact on the way they parent Jimmy and Carla. She knew, also, that Jimmy and Carla had issues of their own. The therapist was aware that the pressure to "be tough" is strong for males in Jimmy's age group. And because adolescence is naturally a difficult time, Carla was likely struggling with issues of her own, as well. Her tendency to not say what she wants would make this struggle even harder. Because the presenting issue was Jimmy's aggression at school, she decided to center the family system around this issue, though she believed that wherever she started, the changes would reverberate throughout the system.

The therapist ended the first session by summarizing each person's needs for therapy and thanking each one for being willing to share themselves with her and with each other.

Session 2

Goals: To help the family discuss the issue of Jimmy's aggression in the Self, stopping the conversation to address any parts that become extreme. Because the family had adopted the language fairly easily, there should be a smooth transition to this individual work.

The family came to the session reporting that Jimmy had yelled a curse word at his teacher this week and was on a two-day suspension.

CATHY: I have to tell you that Jimmy went over the line this time. You just can't curse out the teacher.

TOM: Jimmy, what were you thinking? You know you can't do that kind of thing, even if you can't stand her.
            (*Jimmy is sullen and unresponsive.*)

THERAPIST: (*To both parents*) You both seem very upset with Jimmy. I agree that his behavior was unacceptable; I'm wondering if you both could check inside to find out about your anger. Can we start with you Tom?

(The therapist chooses Tom because his anger seems more extreme and his hint about not being able to stand the teacher suggests a hidden internal polarization.)

TOM: What do you mean?

THERAPIST: Well, I mean to go be with the part of you that is the most upset about Jimmy's behavior and find out more about it. Maybe if you understand it more, then you will be able to get it to step back so you can talk with Jimmy instead of at him.

TOM: I guess I'm angry because I want him to succeed and he's sabotaging that.

THERAPIST: So the angry part is trying to protect him from failure. Can you find out more about that? Where do you feel the anger? Or do you hear it or see it?

CARLA: I told you, Dad, she thinks you're like Sybil!

THERAPIST: *(Laughing)* No, not at all. I don't mean that you have multiple personalities, but I do believe that the parts of us sometimes act without our permission, almost. Like, have you ever wanted to have a calm conversation but found yourself yelling, even when you told yourself not to?

CATHY: *(Smiling)* All the time!

TOM: Well, I feel the anger in my head, like a pounding headache sometimes.

THERAPIST: Can you go be with it now? You can close your eyes if you like, or keep them open—any way that is helpful.

TOM: *(Eyes open)* It's like a pressure—a pressure to make things right for Jimmy. I'd hate to see him screw up his life.

THERAPIST: How do you feel toward that part of you?

TOM: Well, I see that it wants me to help out, but I think it gets out of control.

In later sessions, Tom explored this part further and found that this angry part mirrors a part of his own father. The side that "goes easy" on Jimmy is trying to help Tom to avoid mistreating Jimmy, as he felt his father had done to him.

THERAPIST: Can you tell it that you know it's trying to be helpful, but ask it to step back while you talk to Jimmy?

TOM: Yes, okay It's alright with that.

THERAPIST: Now can you tell Jimmy how you feel?

TOM: (*To Jimmy*) I'm really afraid that you're going to mess up your chances for a good future if you keep on getting in so much trouble all the time.

JIMMY: I'm only 8!

            (*Jimmy goes to the toy box and starts rifling through the toys.*)

TOM: Jimmy, I'm talking to you!

THERAPIST: Tom, could you go over and sit down beside Jimmy? Maybe he can talk better with toys.

Tom moves toward Jimmy and the therapist joins them on the floor. Mom and Carla remain seated, but watch closely. Jimmy begins to bang two cars together, slowly at first, and then with more anger.

THERAPIST: You're really banging those cars together!

JIMMY: This one's going to kill that one!

THERAPIST: You want us to see how mad that one car is at the other one. So mad it wants to kill it.

JIMMY: I get mad like that. I hate my teacher.

THERAPIST: Part of you hates your teacher. I wonder if you and your dad could figure out together what would be a good way to express those feelings. Dad, do you know how it feels to not like someone in charge of you?

TOM: Oh yes! But I don't cuss them out.

THERAPIST: A good thing you don't, but do you ever want to?

TOM: Sure, sometimes I'd like to say a few things to my boss.

THERAPIST: So you know how to help those mad parts of you express themselves in constructive ways.

TOM: No, I usually just keep it in. I just blow it off.

A discussion develops in which Dad notices that part of him is proud of Jimmy for expressing himself. The part of Dad that goes easy on Jimmy felt that it was about time that Jimmy told that teacher what he thought. Jimmy perked up considerably and listened intently as Dad talked about ways he could express anger appropriately to his boss.

THERAPIST: So, Jimmy, you've been helping your dad by showing him how to be mad. Dad, I wonder if you could help Jimmy figure out how to do it more appropriately?

Dad began to describe the trouble that he had been in as a child. His parents had divorced when he was in grade school, and he had begun to act out shortly thereafter. He had tears in his eyes as he described the pain of those years. The therapist helped him to stay with the part of himself that was in so much pain and to soothe it. "That's going to take a lot of work," Dad said. The therapist agreed, and suggested that soothing that part would involve getting to know it, like a person. Jimmy reached out to his dad and put his hand on his shoulder.

THERAPIST: You like to be close to your Dad.
JIMMY: Yeah, I do. We never get to do much together, though.
TOM: I work a lot, I know.
THERAPIST: (*To Jimmy*) Sounds like that makes you sad. Can you find out more about that?

Cathy had moved over beside Jimmy. The therapist gently asked her to move over beside Dad so that Jimmy and Dad could remain in conversation.

JIMMY: I'm scared of Billy Waterson and his friends.
TOM: It's okay to be afraid, but not to hit people.
THERAPIST: Sounds like a tough time, with lots to figure out at school. Can you and your Dad spend some time together this week trying to figure out what you can do?
THERAPIST: (*To Cathy and Carla*) You two haven't been as involved today. What's going on for you two?
CATHY: I'm not really sure. For a while I wanted to make it all better for Jimmy, and it made me mad when Jimmy said that he doesn't spend time with his Dad.

The therapist was able to help Cathy explore her anger, too, which was connected to the part of her that feels unsupported by Tom. She was able to see that her rescuing Jimmy keeps him from connecting with Dad, and it also lets Dad off the hook. She discovered that though she complains a lot about being unsupported, she also takes up the slack at home. She found that her behaviors are led primarily by this other part of her that relentlessly works to keep everyone happy. She was blended with that part, not even realizing that it was not her Self. She realized that her anger at Tom was really anger at herself for allowing this tireless, selfless part to take over all the time.

She and Carla began to notice the connection between them in this internal pattern. Like her mother, Carla works hard to please others, and rejects her "selfish" side. The therapist suggested that Mom would be a good one to show Carla how to begin to value this side more—to listen to its suggestions and allow it to have more input in guiding her decisions and behaviors. She also suggested that when the "selfish" part had more input, it wouldn't have to complain to Tom or Jimmy. At that point Cathy would be able to follow through on consequences without a lot of anger.

After session two, the therapist assigned homework to Cathy and Tom. Tom was to spend an hour this week with Jimmy—just playing, not trying to get him to act right. And Cathy was to spend an hour with Carla, helping her to find ways to be appropriately "selfish."

Therapy continued with this family for 15 sessions. After the third session, Jimmy's behavioral problems had dramatically reduced, but the family had really only begun to work with the parts of them that kept them from Self-to-Self relating. Cathy and Tom requested to come in alone for several sessions. Cathy's new "selfishness" had induced a marital crisis. She had begun to take dance classes and was out of the home three to four evenings a week. Their marital work helped them to clarify with each other their expectations and hopes for the relationship.

Carla reported feeling less pressure to accomplish so much. She also developed a romantic relationship which activated anxiety for her parents. They had learned to soothe themselves enough at that point, however, that they had little difficulty setting limits on her behavior (curfew, number of dates per month, etc.) and then following through with appropriate consequences.

This case illustrates the complexity of IFS work with families. The goal of IFS is to help each family member to access his or her Self in order to relate to the others in an authentic, loving way.

Laura M. Johnson, Ph.D., L.M.F.T., is Assistant Professor, Marriage and Family Therapy Program, Appalachian State University, Boone, North Carolina.

Richard C. Schwartz, Ph.D., L.M.F.T., is Senior Staff Therapist, The Family Institute, Northwestern University, Evanston, Illinois.

References

Bowen, M. (1972). On the differentiation of self. In J. Framo (Ed.), *Family interaction: A dialogue between family researchers and family therapists*. New York: Springer.

Breunlin, D. C., Schwartz, R. C., & Mac Kune-Karrer, B. (1992). *Metaframeworks: Transcending the models of family therapy*. San Francisco: Jossey-Bass.

Goulding, R. A., & Schwartz, R. C. (1995). *Mosaic mind: Empowering the tormented selves of child abuse survivors*. New York: Norton.

Johnson, L. (1995). Filial therapy: A bridge between individual child therapy and family therapy. *Journal of Family Psychotherapy, 6*(3), 55–70.

Landreth, G. (1991). *Play therapy: The art of the relationship*. Muncie, IN: Accelerated Development.

Nichols, M. P., & Schwartz, R. C. (1997). *Family therapy: Concepts and methods* (4th Ed.). Cambridge, MA: Allyn & Bacon.

Oaklander, V. (1988). *Windows to our children : A Gestalt therapy approach to children and adolescents*. Highland, NY: Center for Gestalt Development.

Scharff, D., & Scharff, J. (Eds.). (1991). *Object relations family therapy*. Northvale, NJ: Jason Aronson.

Schwartz, R. (1987). Our multiple selves. *Family Therapy Networker, 11,* 24–31.

Schwartz, R. (1988). Know thy selves. *Family Therapy Networker, 12,* 21–29.

Schwartz, R. (1992, May/June). Rescuing the exiles. *Family Therapy Networker,* 33–37, 75.

Schwartz, R. (1995). *Internal family systems therapy*. New York: Guilford.

Schwartz, R. (1997, March/April). Don't look back. *Family Therapy Networker,* 40–45.

5

Emotionally Focused Family Therapy: Restructuring Attachment

Susan M. Johnson

Alison C. Lee

As a field, family therapy has been accused of becoming impersonal and mechanistic. Perhaps when we focus on the family "game," individual players and the compelling emotions that link them to others become almost invisible. We then lose touch with the "exquisitely elemental" (Liddle, 1991). For the emotionally focused family therapist, the elemental, the core of close relationships, is the attachment bond between family members and the compelling emotions that define that bond (Johnson, 1996; Johnson, Maddeaux, & Blouin, 1998). The goal of emotionally focused family therapy (EFFT) is to foster the secure emotional connectedness that then allows for open communication and effective problem solving. A process study of change in family therapy found that this kind of connectedness facilitates successful problem solving (Friedlander, Heatherington, Johnson, & Skowron, 1994). Emotionally focused therapy is best known as a brief, empirically validated couples therapy (Johnson, Hunsley, Greenberg, & Schindler, 1999). It is also used as a family intervention (Johnson, 1996, 1998) and preliminary research has documented positive outcomes with families where adolescents are struggling with eating disorders (Johnson et al., 1998).

Emotionally focused couple (EFT) and family (EFFT) therapies combine experiential interventions that expand and reshape inner experience with structural systemic interventions that change interaction patterns. An EFFT therapist might focus on the recurring cycle of *parent criticize/child withdraw and act out* that characterizes the relationship between a father and daughter. The therapist might heighten the defeat and hopelessness implicit in the young daughter's angry outbursts and help her formulate her lack of connection with her father and her need for his reassurance. The therapist would then support the father to respond in ways that redefine the security of the bond between him and his daughter.

The EFFT therapist assumes the following:

- Family members are caught in negative interactional cycles that maintain powerful emotional states of fear, anger, and grief. These emotional states and interaction patterns mesh to form family dramas that narrow communication and maintain attachment insecurity.
- Family conflicts that elicit symptomatic behavior are most usefully viewed as attachment dilemmas resulting in separation distress. Attachment needs for security, protection, and comfort are seen as healthy and adaptive (Bowlby, 1969). It is how such needs are expressed or denied in an atmosphere of perceived insecurity that becomes problematic. Attachment needs are naturally most intense at times of transition and crisis when the responsiveness of others is most needed.
- Accessing and reorganizing key emotional experiences is the most powerful route to shaping new responses to the ones we love. Emotion plays a key role in interactions with those we depend on, focusing us on our most salient needs and bringing the core schemas or models that we use to define ourselves and others to the fore. Emotion may be seen as what Bertalanffy (1968), the father of systems theory, would call a leading or organizing element in system (Johnson, 1998). Emotion is the music of the attachment dance. Reshaping key emotional responses helps clients reconstruct their inner worlds and how they communicate with and define relationships with those they love.

The Attachment Perspective: A New Model for Family Therapy

The field of family therapy has taken an ambivalent view of emotional connectedness. It has most often focused on boundaries and viewed connectedness as enmeshment and as constricting individual development and autonomy. Traditional concepts such as enmeshment are now being criticized for confusing coercion with closeness and caregiving (Green & Werner, 1996). In general, as family therapists, we seem to have pathologized dependency and neglected nurturance as a crucial dimension of family life (Bowlby, 1988; Mackay,1996). Feminist writers also suggest that "despair over disconnection" (Gilligan, 1987, p. 66) is a core and neglected issue in unhappy families.

EFFT is one of several recently emerging treatment models that use an attachment perspective to understand and guide intervention in families (Byng-Hall,1995; Diamond & Siqueland, 1995; Kobak, Duemmler, Burland, & Youngstrom, 1998; Liddle, 1994) and that recognize the power of emotion to organize attachment responses. The attachment perspective views optimal development and autonomy as arising out of secure connectedness with others. Such connectedness offers us a secure base from which to explore and grow and a safe haven in times of trouble that fosters resilience (Walsh, 1996).

An attachment bond, as defined by John Bowlby (1969), is a set of behaviors that maximizes proximity with irreplaceable others and so creates a felt sense of security. These behaviors are shaped by emotional responses and by sets of schemas concerning the reliability of others and the acceptability of self. This perspective has been used to understand and to address psychopathology in adolescence and adulthood (Atkinson & Zucker, 1997; Bartholomew & Perlman, 1994). The quality of attachment between parents and children has been specifically related to depressive symptoms and anxiety and to aggressive behavior (Adam, 1994; Kobak, Sudler, & Gamble, 1991; Lyons-Ruth, 1996). Empirical evidence is beginning to suggest that, even in adolescence, the challenge is to realign and refine secure connectedness with parents, rather than to promote separation (Grotevant & Cooper, 1984).

The central tenets of attachment theory are as follows:

- Seeking and maintaining contact with others is a primary motivating principle in human beings. Dependency is an innate part of being human rather than a childhood trait that we outgrow.
- Such contact is an innate survival mechanism. The presence of an attachment figure provides comfort and security, while the perceived inaccessibility of such a figure creates distress. Positive attachments create a *secure base* from which individuals can operate and most adaptively respond to their environment. Positive attachments also create a *safe haven* and provide a buffer against stress and an optimal context for the continuing development of the personality. In this model, separation from attachment figures or a lack of confidence in their availability and responsiveness is considered a potential lifelong trauma.

- The building blocks of secure family bonds are emotional accessibility and responsiveness, whether the relationship is between child and parent or between two adult partners.
- When the security of the bond is threatened, powerful affect arises and attachment behaviors are activated. If these behaviors fail to provoke responsiveness from the attachment figure, a prototypical process of separation distress occurs. This process involves angry protest, clinging, depression and despair, and finally, detachment.
- The number of ways that human beings have to deal with the unresponsiveness of attachment figures is limited. There are only so many ways of dealing with negative answers to the central question: "Can I count and depend on you when I need you?" When attachment or connection with a valued and irreplaceable other is threatened but still hoped for, the attachment system may go into overdrive. Attachment behaviors become heightened and manifest as anxious clinging and constant pursuit of the attachment figure or as aggressive attempts to control the way the attachment figure behaves. The second strategy for dealing with loss of safe emotional engagement, particularly when hope of responsiveness from the attachment figure has been lost, appears as avoidant or seemingly disinterested behavior and as hostile anger, which Bowlby (1973) calls the "anger of despair."

An EFFT therapist might see a child's angry, coercive behavior as attachment protest—an attempt to get a parent to respond to the child's attachment needs. If children feel securely connected with their parents, they experience others as responsive and see themselves as worthy of care and love. They are then more resilient in times of transition and stress. The quality of attachment in the family will then make all the difference in how children deal with difficult times and crises (as the case presented in the following pages illustrates). Attachment theory offers the therapist a map of family relationships. It specifies how habitual forms of engagement with those we depend on defines our world and our sense of who we are.

Goals of EFFT

EFFT is concerned with modifying the distressing cycles of interaction that maintain attachment insecurity in family members while also fostering positive cycles of accessibility and responsiveness (Johnson 1996; Johnson et al.,

1998). The goal of EFFT is to foster alternative formulations of emotional experience that create new points of contact with significant others. For example, a therapist might help Todd, an angry 9-year-old, explore how left out he felt in his new stepfamily and how he had "lost" his mom to his new stepdad. As he shares this with his new dad, his dad is able to respond with concern and reassurance and perhaps share some of his own fears about being rejected by Todd. This kind of new interaction is in sharp contrast to the *stepparent lecture from a distance* followed by a *child simmer-and-explode* pattern that had evolved in this family. This new interaction has the potential to change:

- How Todd regulates his emotions in the family. He could talk to his new dad rather than acting out.
- How Todd processes information. Safety promotes curiosity, openness to new information, and tolerance of ambiguity. Todd may start to see his dad as a resource and a source of comfort, rather than a threat. Todd may also start to see himself as a kid that his new dad might want to comfort and protect. He can perhaps listen to his parents' concerns about his behavior without an overlay of resentment and fear.
- How Todd communicates with both his parents. He is able to disclose his fears and concerns in a way that pulls for his parents to comfort and reassure him.
- How Todd's parents see him and how responsive they are able to be to him when they see his vulnerability.

Nichols (1987) suggests that therapists need "dynamite" to change emotionally loaded family interactions. The EFFT therapist uses the dynamite of newly formulated emotions and interactions to create a new family drama. Insight and behavioral solutions are often not enough to change the plot. A new experience of emotional connection is needed to change perceptions or models of self and other and attachment behaviors.

In sum, the goal of EFFT is to increase accessibility and responsiveness in family relationships, and thus help the parents to create a secure base and safe haven for their children while feeling confidant and competent as parents.

The Process of Therapy

Session Structure

In this form of family therapy the family is usually seen as a group for the first one or two sessions, even if the parents identify the child as the patient. In these sessions the therapist assesses interactional positions and patterns and identifies problematic relationships and family cycles that appear to be related to the identified patient's problems. After these initial sessions, family subsystems are invited to individual meetings. Typically, for example, the parents are invited to come in and talk about their relationship and their parenting role; the sibling subsystem is invited to a different session; and the identified patient and each parent, or both parents, also meet. This treatment involves a flexible combination of dyadic, triadic, and family group sessions. The essential treatment process of using the expression of newly processed emotions to create new interactions is the same whether the session involves a client dyad or triad. Dyad sessions, in particular, encourage a sense of safety and focus that allows for increased emotional engagement. Sessions are one to one and one-quarter hours in length and are usually conducted weekly. Treatment usually takes ten to twelve sessions and is implemented by a single therapist or two cotherapists. Treatment ends with a session where all family members attend to ensure that specific changes are integrated into the system as a whole. Regardless of the number of people in the session, the process of therapy still involves accessing new emotions to create new interactions between family members.

The EFFT therapist must be able to gain the family's trust and confidence so that members actively engage in the therapy process. As with emotionally focused couple therapy, this kind of intervention is deemed inappropriate for abusive or violent families, since the expression of vulnerability and openness is part of the treatment process. Not only is this openness difficult to achieve in violent relationships, but it may also put family members at physical risk. This kind of treatment is also inappropriate for family members who wish to live very separate lives and do not want to examine or improve family contact.

The Therapist's Tasks

An EFFT session should help children and parents to reconstruct and articulate their experiences in a way that changes the interaction between them. For example, an EFFT therapist might help a child share with her father how despairing she is when he gives her advice, hearing in his advice that she has already disappointed him and will never please him. The therapist will then direct her in an interactional task where she shares this hurt with her father in a way that allows him to hear her and move closer to her. The therapist will then reframe her defiance of her father in terms of this hurt and hopelessness. In this interaction the therapist also provides a holding environment for the father so that he can listen to his daughter and understand the impact that he has on her.

The three basic tasks for the emotionally focused family therapist are:

• to actively create and maintain a positive alliance that offers a secure base to family members to explore their relationships;
• to explore and reformulate key emotional responses, so that peripheral or unformulated emotions become more central in awareness and dialogue; and
• to create new interactions based on these reformulations that foster secure bonding.

In every session, the therapist becomes part of the family members' interactional dance and uses shifts in experience to generate new moves in the dance and vice versa. For example, a son accesses his need for attention from his mother, a need that is usually hidden under bravado and cynical remarks; as he tells his mother this, a new kind of interaction begins, which then begins to have an impact on his mother's emotional experience of and response to her son.

The three tasks outlined above continue throughout therapy, although a particular task may be more central at particular times during the therapy process. When accessing emotions the therapist uses reflection and asks evocative questions such as, "What is that like for you?" or "How do you feel when . . . ?" The therapist also uses heightening and makes experience more vivid by repetition or imagery, as well as making empathic conjectures that add to the way a response is understood. For example, the therapist might frame acting-out behaviors as a form of attachment protest designed to force parents to engage and make contact. When creating new interactions, the therapist tracks and reflects interactional sequences and cycles, reframes responses in the context of the cycle and in terms of underlying vulnerabilities and attachment needs, and shapes present interactions. He or she does this by encouraging family members to speak from new, more emotionally explicit places (as in, "I shut you out, I'm so afraid of your judgments"), choreographing new kinds of interactions characterized by emotional engagement, and supporting members to take new positions with each other. At the end of the second stage in therapy the therapist will foster bonding interactions where family members express their attachment needs and other members are able to respond empathically.

Other techniques used in therapeutic impasses such as painting diagnostic pictures of the impasse or mirroring the impasses in narratives called disquisitions are outlined elsewhere (Johnson, 1996; Milliken & Johnson, in press)

Assessment

The task of creating a positive therapeutic alliance with each member of the family is the first priority in EFFT. To accomplish this, the therapist must make a deliberate and constant attempt to validate each person's experience without invalidating the experience of other family members. The therapist might say: "I understand that you feel your parents are being unfair, Sarah, and I hear from your perspective, Mom and Dad, that you feel that you are struggling to be responsible parents."

At the beginning of therapy the Rogerian origins of EFFT are particularly apparent. The EFFT therapist follows Rogers's (1951) prescription of genuineness, empathy, and acceptance or positive regard. A belief in the "brilliance of ordinary people" and their ability to grow is an essential part of the therapist's stance. This collaborative, respectful stance is also advocated by recent postmodern theorists such as Anderson (1997). It is essential that the therapist empathetically attune to all family members and connect with each on a personal level while maintaining a nonjudgmental stance and creating a safe context in which change can take place. Although particularly essential during the first part of therapy, the monitoring of the therapeutic relationship should also continue throughout the entire process.

The initial assessment phase of EFT is completed in the first and second sessions. The therapist observes the organization of family interactions, the various family alliances, the predictability and rigidity of interactional patterns, the strategies used to deal with conflict and frustration, and how family members support and comfort each other. Questions such as "If you have a worry or a problem, who do you confide in?" or "Who do you go to when you are feeling sad and you need a hug?" help to assess alliances and family ability to provide comfort and support. Family members are encouraged to talk about recent events or crises that typify the way they interact. The therapist also notices the emotional tone of the family (sad? depressed?), how family members respond to each other, and patterns of accessibility (do family members listen to each other or dismiss problems with jokes and laughter?). Additionally, the therapist asks how family members view these patterns. By the end of the assessment phase the therapist should be able to identify key cycles of negative interactions and formulate with the family how these cycles might help to maintain the symptoms of the identified patient. To obtain a picture of an interactional cycle, the EFFT therapist might ask sequence questions, such as "What do you do when your husband shouts at your daughter? How do you respond to that? What happens next? If I were a fly on the wall in your kitchen what would I see happen then? How do you see it, Sarah? What do you do when this happens?" The therapist then draws a picture of the family drama and how cycles such as *criticize/distance* seem to control family interactions and to be self-perpetuating, as well as priming negative symptoms in the most vulnerable family members.

The Steps of Therapy

The process of change in EFFT has been outlined in three stages and nine steps. The first four steps are concerned with assessment and de-escalation of negative cycles, and are accomplished in the first two to four sessions. After the initial assessment, the next three steps are: to formulate and clarify problematic cycles (step 2), to help the family members identify the emotions underlying their positions in the cycle (step 3), and to frame a shared version of a problem that validates all and blames no one (step 4). The middle stage of therapy, where interactional patterns evolve and change, occurs in steps 5 to 7. This stage involves accessing and exploring disowned or unformulated attachment needs and emotions and creating new interactions that address these needs and emotions. At the end of this stage of therapy new kinds of interaction occur that redefine the bond between family members. For example, a distant, depressed parent might express regret and ask for understanding and a child might then offer acceptance and assert a need for caring in a manner that evokes a reassuring response from the parent. In the last stage of therapy, steps 8 and 9, the therapist helps the family to consolidate new interactions, integrate them into the family system, and develop new problem-solving processes. The steps are outlined below and demonstrated in the case study that follows.

Stage 1: De-escalation

Step 1: Delineate the conflict issues and attachment struggles in the family. The therapist focuses on each family member's experience in the family, in particular on how members interact and how their responses mediate the closeness or the separateness of the bond between them. The assessment process, described above, is also part of this step.

Step 2: Identify and clarify negative interactional cycles that maintain insecure attachment. The therapist might describe a cycle as follows: "So Dad, when you attempt to help Helen, you experience her as rejecting and rebellious. This worries you, and you find yourself getting angry. Then if he gets to the point of shouting, Mom, you feel compelled to come in and protect your daughter. Is that it? Then Dad usually withdraws for a few days, feeling like there is nothing he can do, and Helen, you go off with your friends, the ones you told me were 'dangerous' but not 'critical' like your Dad, yes? And Mom, you get depressed and end up telling Helen that she is killing you all (everyone nods). Everyone ends up feeling upset and alone. Is that it?"

Step 3: Access unacknowledged emotions underlying interactional positions in the family. As significant events (fights, misunderstandings) occur, whether in or between sessions, the therapist focuses on them and heightens the experience.

THERAPIST: So when Helen acts rebellious you feel worried? Kind of helpless?
DAD: Yes, I feel like I am screwing up somehow because my kid isn't doing her schoolwork. I don't know what to do next. I feel like I'm failing as a parent.
THERAPIST: And Helen, is that when you begin to feel like you can never please your dad, never get his praise, so you might as well be as bad as he thinks you are? What's that like for you to feel like you can never meet your dad's expectations?"

Step 4. Redefine the problem. Once the underlying feelings have been accessed, the problem is redefined in terms of the negative cycle that the family is caught in and the powerful emotions associated with that cycle. So, for example, the father who appears punitive and controlling is, with more emotional information, framed as worried and feeling helpless. This reframe is highly credible because it is based on information that is vividly experienced in the session as the father speaks to his daughter about his sense of failure as a parent.

Stage 2: Interactional Shifts

Step 5. Promote identification with disowned needs and aspects of self. In this step the clients are first helped to explore and identify fully with their positions in respect to other family members and any implicit attachment needs. They are encouraged to encounter, embrace, and accept the emotions underlying their position in the family dance. For example, a usually defiant daughter might be able to formulate and talk to her mother about her sense of despair when she feels her mother withdraw from her. She might also talk about how her mother's support is a touchstone for her in a changing world where growing up is scary and overwhelming.

Step 6. Foster the acceptance of each person's experience and new interactional responses. Here the therapist helps the other family members to hear, understand, and accept the emotions and needs expressed in step 5. So the mother, in the scenario described above, will be encouraged to see her daughter's defiance as desperation and accept her need for closeness and support.

Step 7. Facilitate the expression of needs and wants to restructure interactions. The therapist helps withdrawn and distant family members to become more engaged and more available. More aggressive or critical family members are supported to talk about their attachment emotions and needs in a way that evokes responsiveness from others and creates a sense of trust and secure connection. In this stage of therapy a child may be able to confront her now more engaged mother and ask for her respect and caring in a way that pulls for a supportive emotional response from her.

Stage 3: Consolidation of Change

Step 8. Establish the emergence of new solutions to previously problematic situations. Problem solving and negotiation are much easier when they are no longer contaminated by powerful negative affect and emotional agendas concerning the definition of the relationship. Research in couple therapy suggests this change process, in particular the occurrence of a change event called a softening, where a previously critical or aggressive person is able to turn to an attachment figure and ask for their needs to be met from a position of vulnerability, makes success in therapy more likely (Johnson & Greenberg, 1988). This kind of safe emotional engagement between family members has also been shown to facilitate successful problem solving in family therapy (Friedlander et al., 1994).

Step 9. Consolidate new positions. The last step of EFFT is concerned with strengthening and integrating the changes that have taken place in therapy. Family members are asked to clearly differentiate between old and new patterns of interaction and to take a meta-perspective on their problems and how they found new solutions for them. The therapist validates their struggle and summarizes the journey of change for them.

Case Illustration: Reach for Us and We'll Be There

Captain Bert Fuller ushered his family into the office, sat heavily in an arm-chair, and introduced the therapist (ACL) to everyone. His tall wife, Michelle, sat on the couch, avoiding eye contact with everyone in the room. Penny, whose punk haircut glinted a magenta hue, had a direct, disarming smile. She had just had her twelfth birthday. She nestled beside her mother, lifting her mother's arm and placing it around her own shoulders. Adrian, tall, thin, with the blotchy skin of a 15-year-old, sat apart from the family, his shoulders hunched forward.

"I simply told them we were coming in and here we are," began Captain Fuller. "I mean to get this problem sorted out." In fact, it was thanks to Penny's efforts that the family was referred to me. She had disclosed her frightening symptoms to their family physician: periods of dissociation, self-mutilation, binge eating with purging, and suicidal thoughts. After three visits with a psychologist colleague she was described as markedly depressed, with a notable sense of nonacceptance by her family and a high sense of acceptance by her peers.

The parents started the session by talking about Penny's new friends, a large group of youngsters who "hung out" at shopping malls where they were intimidating to local shoppers. Penny had just been banned from the local mall for shoplifting and had recently been suspended from school. Penny's friends streamed into the Fuller's home after school most nights, where they smoked, left burns in the carpet, and took over the household. The Fullers were unsure how to deal with this intrusion, because on one hand they wanted their children to bring their friends into the home, but on the other hand they found Penny's friends to be too much and too many. Captain Fuller was worried about Penny because she had a bright future ahead but was "derailing herself." She had been on the honor roll at school, but this term her grades had dropped drastically.

Captain and Mrs. Fuller did not know how to stop Penny from getting into trouble with her friends. They had tried grounding her and stopping her allowance. When these efforts to set limits proved unsuccessful, they began shouting and threatening, which now occurred frequently in their home. They were thinking of canceling their summer vacation in Hawaii.

Captain and Mrs. Fuller then moved on to discuss the constant fighting between Penny, whom they labeled as their "brainy child," and Adrian "the computer whiz." Adrian admitted that he provoked everyone in the family, and

Penny owned that she reacted to his provocation in a negative way. The fights frequently escalated to violence, resulting in cuts and bruises.

My goal in this initial step of therapy was to form a therapeutic alliance, maintain a nonjudgmental stance, and gain a picture of their conflict issues, attachment struggles, and negative interactions at home. So I followed what they said to me, asking questions such as: "So what happens, Adrian, when you say that to Penny? What does she do then?"

I then moved into step 2, and described to the family the negative cycle that I saw occurring in the session and heard described in their family life. "I'm going to rely on you to correct me if I get this wrong, okay? Penny, it sounds to me like you are somehow acting out, and your mom and dad sound like they're very worried about you. So you, Bert and Michelle, try to talk to Penny and protect her by trying to set limits, for example, by grounding her and stopping her allowance. Is that right? And as your parents pursue you in this way, Penny, you seem to withdraw. You are polite to them, but you just go to your room. Is that what it's like?"

"It's like talking to a brick wall," said Captain Fuller. "I think she's listening but she isn't. She goes up to her room and ignores us."

Adrian's role was also described. It seemed that he withdrew from everybody and spent his time on the Internet or watching television. He seemed to want some contact with his family but appeared to reach out in a negative way, sparking off fights. The main elements in the formulation of the cycle were the father's criticism of his daughter, Penny's withdrawal or outbursts of anger, the parents' continued anxiety and attempts to change their daughter, and the son's withdrawal. As we talked about this cycle, Penny told us that when she went to her room, she felt very bad because she was disappointing her father.

I explored the negative cycle in further sessions, accessing the underlying feelings (step 3). In session 2, I had a single session with Penny in order to strengthen our alliance. In this session, I found out more about Penny's part of the cycle. To access her underlying feelings I asked, "So what happens for you, Penny, when your mom and dad are angry with you and you go to your room?" She told me she felt upset because she was a "bad person." I simply reflected back to her, "You feel like a bad person?" Penny then described feeling herself go numb, everything becoming pink and then black. She would find herself up on the ceiling watching herself screaming, throwing her possessions around her room, and cutting herself. She rolled up her sleeves and showed me her arms. There were numerous cuts in various stages of healing. She also used food to soothe herself. She told me: "I often sneak down to the kitchen when they are in bed and eat everything I can find, and then I throw up in the bathroom."

I explored with Penny what triggered these self-destructive behaviors. She told me of her feelings of depression, and how she longed to go to her father for support, but felt he was disappointed with her because of her performance in school. She was glad that he thought she was smart but thought it unfair that if Adrian achieved 75% at school he was applauded by their parents, while she was only told to work harder if her marks were as low as 75%. For the last 18 months she had been feeling very angry with her father because of this. She had always been very close to her father but she now experienced him as critical and distant. She was never very close to her mother, but had always been able to tell her dad anything. Now I knew that underlying Penny's position in the cycle was despair that her father was disappointed in her and this was occurring at a time when she was in critical need of his support.

I saw Captain and Mrs. Fuller together in session 3. Here, I was again trying to strengthen our alliance, and also assessing the marital relationship to see if the couple supported each other. Mrs. Fuller presented as a cool and detached woman. She was very successful in her career as a lawyer, and she commented that people need to cope with their own problems rather than come for psychotherapy. In contrast, her husband was very engaged, telling me how worried he was about his daughter, who was "extremely intelligent with great potential." He had been worrying since long before Penny reached her eleventh birthday that she would "go off the tracks" and spoil her whole life. He disclosed that he had "wasted his own youth" by drinking to excess and failing in school. This helped me to better understand his worry for his daughter. He told me that his son did not have the same potential as Penny, and acknowledged that he put a great deal of pressure on Penny to "maximize her potential."

In session 4, I decided to have a second session alone with Penny because I was concerned about her symptoms of distress. Penny felt safe enough to describe the events that led to her first "blackout." She had nearly been raped one year ago. She had been cutting through a back street, after a party, to a friend's house where she was staying the night, when she was attacked and dragged into a yard by an older teenager. She was lucky to get away unharmed, but later at her friend's house, she felt "dirty" and "bad." That night, she found herself up on the bedroom ceiling looking down and watching herself screaming. Penny was very frightened by this episode but did not dare to tell her parents about it. She believed that her father would be angry that she had been out late alone, and that her mother would say that she was at fault—she never confided in her mother.

It became clear that Penny had become depressed after the attack. She longed to tell her father, but believed he would be critical of her for putting herself at risk. Where she had previously experienced him as the person on whom she could depend if she needed help, she now found her connection with him was threatened. I suggested to Penny that her acting out behaviors might stem from feeling lonely, unprotected, and despairing, and she thought this might be so.

Penny went on to describe how over the last year she had begun to leave her former friends, who were "goody-good" and lean more toward a new group of friends who "had problems too." When she got into trouble at home as a consequence of her behavior with her new friends, she felt very bad, and frequently dissociated in her bedroom when she would wreck her possessions or cut her arms. She was so distressed by these episodes that she often felt that she might kill herself.

As Penny told the story of the attempted rape, she became flushed, breathless, and sweaty. She said her heart was thumping in her chest. I validated how hard it was to tell and how brave she was. I also began to reprocess the event she had described, to help her see that she was not a "bad girl," but a victim. At the end of the session Penny said it felt good to finally share this secret.

Because I was concerned about her symptoms, I asked Penny if she felt that I could support her so that she could tell her parents this story. In addition, this disclosure would enable the parents to understand the emotions underlying Penny's position in the negative cycle. She agreed to try. Consequently, in session 5, I met with Bert, Michelle, and Penny, having promised Penny that I would give her as much support as she needed. In the following excerpt from the session, I am working on steps 3, 4, 5, and 6.

Penny began by taking a deep breath, rolling up her sleeves and telling her parents that she was cutting her arms:

MICHELLE: (*In an angry tone*) I knew you were lying to me about that. I knew that already. All your friends do it. It's a stupid craze.

PENNY: Mom, it's not a craze. I do it when I have a blackout.

MICHELLE: (*In a controlled and quiet voice*) It's so stupid. It breaks my heart to see you do that to yourself. Why do you do it?

THERAPIST: (*Reflects emotional experience of the child*) Michelle, I think Penny is trying to tell you about how badly she has been feeling inside. She's been holding it all in and it's been hard for her. (*Sets up a therapeutic task*) Penny, can you help your Mom understand?

PENNY: (*Puts her head down and fiddles with her watchstrap*) Mom, something happened, and I wanted to tell you but I was scared you and Dad would be angry (*begins to cry*). Last year a boy grabbed me and tried to rape me. He didn't. I got away. But I was so scared. . . . I thought you'd be so mad at me.

MICHELLE: (*Looks down at her interlocked fingers, a faint blush creeps over her cheeks*) That happened to me once. I never told anyone about it. It's best to keep these things to yourself (*Glances at her daughter and then out the window*).

BERT: (*Leans forward and puts his elbows on his knees; he looks worried*) Penny, why didn't you tell me about this?

PENNY: (*Sobbing*) You're angry with me. You think I'm screwing up my life.

THERAPIST: (*Reflects child's underlying fear that restricts connection with her father*) You are telling your Dad you were too scared to come and tell him?

PENNY: (*Nods, still crying and looking into her lap*) I thought you'd be mad at me. I'm screwing up. I felt dirty.

THERAPIST: (*Reflects underlying attachment-related fears that keep Penny in a disengaged position with her father*) It's kind of like you were afraid he'd be disappointed in you?

PENNY: Yes, and he gets mad if I screw up. He used to be proud of me. But he's not now.

THERAPIST: You sometimes worry your Dad isn't proud of you any more, right?

PENNY: (*Lifts her head and looks at the therapist tearfully*) Yes, he thinks I'm a lost cause. He thinks I'm no good now.

THERAPIST: (*Reflects the shame that has infused Penny's sense of self and evokes her need to hide and withdraw from her father*) And this happening—the attack—that really made you feel bad—dirty somehow—like you were no good. This made it even harder to believe you were okay and your dad might be proud of you? (*Penny nods and cries*) Can you let your Dad know what that's like for you, Penny?

PENNY: (*Crying*) I feel alone . . . bad . . . dirty.

BERT: (*Visibly upset*) Penny, it hurts me to hear that you were scared to tell me. I want to protect you—that's my job. If I could get my hands on that little creep I'd . . .

THERAPIST: (*Underscores father's availability to hear his daughter's pain*) You're feeling very upset that your little girl was hurt.

BERT: Too damn right. (*Turns to Penny and puts his hand on her knee*)
              Penny, I love you. I want to protect you. I feel so sorry that you
              could not come and tell me (*Bert has tears in his eyes*).

THERAPIST: When you put pressure on Penny and tell her to work harder,
              you're trying to protect her—make sure she does well—make sure
              she doesn't make the mistakes that you made. It's sad for you to
              hear that your efforts to keep her on track have backfired, and
              she's been feeling lonely and bad, like she's a disappointment. So
              when this attack happened she couldn't come to you.

BERT: (*Leans over to Penny and puts his hand on her knee again*) I never
              meant for you to feel so pressured. I guess I've screwed up. I just
              feel so awful that you couldn't come to me with this.

PENNY: (*Looks up at her father and wipes her eyes with a tissue*)

BERT: (*Turns to therapist*) It's so critical when they get into their teens.
              It's so important that they don't get off track. She's going to spoil
              everything for her future.

THERAPIST: (*Again, accessing emotions underlying the negative cycle, as well
              as fostering the acceptance of each person's experience, step 6*)
              You worry for Penny. You want to protect her. Yet when you try to
              help Penny take care of her life, she somehow hears that you are
              disappointed in her and when she hears this she feels kind of des-
              perate.

BERT: (*Turns back to his daughter and takes both of her hands in his*)
              Sweetie, I don't mean you to think you're screwing up. I want to
              help you not to make the mistakes that I made when I was grow-
              ing up. You've been scaring me.

PENNY: So you're not mad at me about that, the attack?

BERT: I'm not mad at you, no. If I could get my hands on that jerk I'd kill
              him. (*Bert turns to therapist*) What can I do to help our relation-
              ship?

THERAPIST: You'd like to help Penny to feel safe and to know she can come to
              you if she is scared or hurt?

BERT: Yes, I would.

THERAPIST: (*Facilitates the expression of needs and wants to restructure inter-
              action, step 7*) Can you ask her how you can make it safe for her?

BERT: (*Turns back to Penny*) How can I help our relationship?

PENNY: I need you to trust me that I'll do a good job. I'm really trying at
              school. I want you to be proud of me and see I'm trying.

THERAPIST: (*Sees that Michelle is looking out the window and not joining her husband and her daughter as they speak*) Michelle, what's happening for you right now?

MICHELLE: (*Turns to the therapist, biting her lower lip*) I'm angry.

PENNY: (*Puts her head down again*) Mom, it wasn't my fault.

MICHELLE: (*To Penny*) I'm not angry at you. I'm angry with that boy—if I could get my hands on him . . .

THERAPIST: You are angry that someone hurt your child? (*Michelle nods silently*) Can you tell Penny this?

MICHELLE: (*Looks down at her hands*) I guess I'm angry at myself. . . . I've been so caught up in my work—I guess I've left you to fend for yourself. (*Michelle begins to cry*) It happened to me you know. I was attacked when I was fifteen.

In a flat voice, Michelle then described her family home. Her father used to drink heavily. They were a large family, with very little money. Her mother was always exhausted and her father hit her mother when he was very drunk. Michelle could never share with her mother any of her fears, concerns, or hurts. Her mother had enough on her plate. One day, Michelle was raped by a young man on her way home from a school concert. She never told anyone. During the telling of her story, Michelle turned away from us and looked out the window.

MICHELLE: (*Suddenly leans forward toward her daughter and touches the arm of her chair*) I don't want to be the kind of parent you can't tell things to. I guess I've always assumed that you were so close to your dad that you didn't really need me anymore. I'm so sorry. (*Penny leaves her chair and sits on the loveseat beside her mother. She snuggles up close to her mother, who puts an arm protectively around her shoulders.*)

THERAPIST: (*Moves to support Penny's asking for help with her fears. This new kind of interaction is a key part of change [step 7] in EFFT*) Penny, how could your mom and dad help you to come to them when you feel upset or scared or when you have a memory of the attack? Can you tell them how to help?

PENNY: (*Much brighter now*) It helps to say all this here. And when Mommy holds me, it's easier to talk then.

THERAPIST: Your Mom helps you by holding and comforting you. Maybe you need lots of hugs right now. Is that it? (*She beams and nods*) Could

> you come downstairs and tell Mom and Dad if you had one of
> those times when you space out and go up to the ceiling?
>
> PENNY: (*Nods*) I think so. I'll try.
>
> BERT: (*Reaches out to Penny*) We'll be there. Reach for us—we'll be
>   there.

We followed up on this in session 6, again with Penny and her parents. Penny did have another blackout, and was able to tell her parents, who comforted her and talked with her about the attempted rape, assuring her that it was not her fault. In this session the Fullers also brought up the ongoing fights between Penny and Adrian. They asked me to see the children alone.

In session 7, Adrian and Penny were glad for the chance to discuss their fighting. Adrian told Penny about how excruciating it was for him that she and her friends got into such trouble at school and in the shopping malls. He was embarrassed and humiliated about the way she behaved on the school bus. "People will think that we are a bad family. I feel so ashamed. I get really mad at you. That's why I bug you a lot." Penny told Adrian that she understood. I then asked Adrian what it was like for him at home when Penny's friends came to the house. He described himself being taunted by Penny's friends and shutting himself in his room. He did not feel safe in his own home and was very angry.

Adrian also told Penny about his fear that Michelle liked her better than she liked him. Penny responded: "That's funny—she and Dad always clap when you get 75% at school but rag me out if I get 75%—who's the one they like best then?" They laughed together. We talked about how they had been good friends when they were younger. To facilitate the emergence of new solutions (step 8), I asked them what would need to happen for them to regain this friendship. I helped Adrian to tell Penny how he needed his home to be a safe place for himself (step 7). Penny understood this, and agreed to have only two friends visit at a time. She also volunteered to talk to her friends and tell them she expected them to respect her brother.

Three weeks after this session I met with the entire family again. They reported that the family atmosphere was much improved. Penny had kept her word about her friends and she and Adrian had stopped fighting. Penny had experienced only one more blackout, after which she went to her mother, who hugged and soothed her. She proudly showed her arms, which had begun to heal. She also told me that she had stopped binge eating and no longer vomited. Together we examined the changes that the family had made. Penny told us that she felt her parents now understood her and was glad they were more responsive to her. Thus, she was less withdrawn. Bert and Michelle told us that they were less worried because they understood what had happened to their daughter. Bert was trying hard not to pressure Penny over her schoolwork. Adrian told Penny that he noticed that she had kept her word about inviting fewer of her friends in the house in the evenings, and the siblings agreed that they were glad they did not fight so often. This is how we worked on consolidating new family interactions (step 9). I validated the changes the family had made, and also described how, because they are human, inevitably they would not be perfect from then on. Fights and difficulties would occur again, and it would be important for them to be able to talk to each other about their needs and their feelings (preparation for termination).

We had a ninth session as a follow-up three months later. Captain Fuller told his family that the person who had changed most was himself: He was working very hard not to put pressure on his children, and he was proud of them. Penny's periods of dissociation had stopped altogether, her arms were now healed, and she had stopped bingeing and purging. Moreover, she was spending less time with "the gang" and had begun to spend time with her former friends. Her fights with Adrian were now infrequent, and she and her mother were now closer and better able to confide in each other. We spent more time in this session consolidating the new positions in the family interaction (step 9). In particular, we explored the difference in the pursue-withdraw cycle between Penny and her parents.

In this case study, a family had become disengaged just at a time when a traumatic incident occurred, making Penny, the identified patient, particularly sensitive and increasing her need for a safe connection. Penny felt distanced from her father and her mother, and had withdrawn. As she became more and more isolated, the ways she found of soothing herself became more and more dangerous, and her image of herself became more and more negative. The intervention helped the family to step aside from the negative cycle (punishment, threats, withdrawal, escalation) that was priming and exacerbating Penny's symptoms, and learn new cycles of confiding, open communication, and secure attachment.

Transitions, such as reaching adolescence, evoke attachment issues, and the experience of trauma intensifies the need for secure attachment (Herman, 1992; Johnson & Williams-Keeler, 1998). This family illustrates the point made by trauma theorists (van der Kolk, McFarlane, & Weisaeth, 1996) that the outcome of trauma is best predicted from the survivor's ability to seek comfort from significant others, and, in this case, by the family's ability to respond and provide a safe haven for their child.

Susan M. Johnson, Ed.D., is Professor of Psychology and Psychiatry, University of Ottawa, and Director of the Couple and Family Therapy Clinic and Ottawa Couple & Family Institute, Ottawa, Ontario, Canada.

Alison C. Lee, Ph.D., is a Registered Psychologist and Vice President, Ottawa Couple and Family Institute, Ottawa, Ontario, Canada.

References

Adam, K. S. (1994). Suicidal behavior and attachment. In M. B. Sperling & W. H. Berman (Eds.), *Attachment in adults: Clinical and developmental perspectives* (pp. 275–347). New York: Guilford.

Anderson, H. (1997). *Conversation, language and possibilities.* New York: Basic.

Atkinson, L., & Zucker, K. J. (1997). *Attachment and psychopathology.* New York: Guilford.

Bartholomew, K., & Perlman, D. (1994). (Eds.). *Advances in personal relationships: Attachment processes in adulthood.* Bristol, PA: Jessica Kingsley.

Bertalanffy, L. (1968). *General system theory.* New York: George Braziller.

Bowlby, J. (1969). *Attachment and loss: Vol 1. Attachment.* New York: Basic.

Bowlby, J. (1973). *Attachment and loss: Vol 2. Separation.* New York. Basic.

Bowlby, J. (1988). *A secure base.* New York: Basic.

Byng-Hall, J. (1995). Creating a secure family base: Some implications of attachment theory for family therapy. *Family Process, 34,* 45–58.

Diamond, G., & Siqueland, L. (1995). Family therapy for the treatment of depressed adolescents. *Psychotherapy: Theory, Research and Practice, 32,* 77–90.

Friedlander, M. L., Heatherington, L., Johnson, B., & Skowron, E. A. (1994). Sustaining engagement: A change event in family therapy. *Journal of Counseling,* 438–448.

Gilligan, C. (1987). Adolescent development reconsidered. In C. E. Irwin (Ed.), *Adolescent social behavior and health.* San Francisco: Jossey-Bass.

Green, R. J., & Werner, P. D. (1996). Intrusiveness and closeness-caregiving: Rethinking the concept of family enmeshment. *Family Process, 35,* 115–153.

Grotevant, H. D., & Cooper, C. R. (Eds.). (1984). *Adolescent development in the family.* San Francisco: Jossey-Bass.

Herman, J. L. (1992). *Trauma and Recovery.* New York: Basic.

Johnson, S. (1996). *The practice of emotionally focused marital therapy: Creating connection.* New York: Brunner/Mazel.

Johnson, S. (1998). Listening to the music: Emotion as a natural part of systems theory. *Journal of Systemic Therapies, 17,* 1–17.

Johnson, S., & Greenberg, L. (1988). Relating process to outcome in marital therapy. *Journal of Marital and Family Therapy, 14,* 175–184.

Johnson, S., Hunsley, J., Greenberg, L., & Schlinder, D. (1999). Emotionally focused couples therapy: Status and challenges. *Clinical Psychology: Science and Practice, 6,* 67–79.

Johnson, S. M., Maddeaux, C., & Blouin, J. (1998). Emotionally focused family therapy for bulimia: Changing attachment patterns. *Psychotherapy, 35,* 238–247.

Johnson, S., & Williams-Keeler, L. (1998). Creating healing relationships for couples dealing with trauma: The use of emotionally focused marital therapy. *Journal of Marital and Family Therapy, 24,* 227–236.

Kobak, R., Duemmler, S., Burland, A., & Youngstrom, E. (1998). Attachment and negative absorption states: Implications for treating distressed families. *Journal of Systemic Therapies, 17,* 80–92.

Kobak, R., Sudler, N., & Gamble, W. (1991). Attachment and depressive symptoms during adolescence: A developmental pathways analysis. *Development and Psychopathology, 3,* 461–474.

Liddle, H. (1991). Empirical values and the culture of family therapy. *Journal of Marital and Family Therapy, 17,* 327–348.

Liddle, H. (1994). The anatomy of emotions in family therapy with adolescents. *Journal of Adolescent Research, 9,* 120–157.

Lyons-Ruth, K. (1996). Attachment relationships among children with aggressive behavior problems: The role of disorganized early attachment patterns. *Journal of Consulting and Clinical Psychology, 64,* 64–73.

MacKay, S. K. (1996). Nurturance: A neglected dimension in family therapy with adolescents. *Journal of Marital and Family Therapy, 22,* 489–508.

Milliken, J., & Johnson, S. (in press). Telling tales: Disquisitions in emotionally focused therapy. *Journal of Family Psychotherapy.*

Nichols, M. (1987). *The self in the system.* New York: Brunner/Mazel.

Rogers, C. (1951). *Client-centered therapy.* Boston: Houghton/Mifflin.

Van der Kolk, B., McFarlane, A., & Weisaeth, L. (Eds.). (1996). *Traumatic stress.* New York: Guilford.

Walsh, F. (1996). The concept of family resilience: Crisis and Challenge. *Family Process, 35,* 261–281.

II
CONTENT AREAS

6

Treatment of the Sexually Abused Child

Mary Jo Barrett

Joseph Cortese

Kristen Marzolf

When the call came in, an overwhelming feeling flushed over the practitioner. He heard the panic in the woman's voice, caught between her suspicions that her daughter may have been sexually abused and a desire not to traumatize her daughter any further by peppering her with probing questions. Would this permanently damage her daughter? How could it have happened? Where should they start? And how could they balance their fears as parents with the child's needs? The therapist needed a clear plan for proceeding so that he did not get swept up in the family's anxiety.

Childhood sexual abuse is a devastating trauma that should not occur, but the hard reality is that it does. Some sources report that child sexual abuse occurs at the alarming rate of one out of four girls before age 18 (Russell, 1984). While estimates vary with regard to both males and females, it is commonly reported that one of five children may be sexually abused prior to age 18 (Freeman-Longo & Blanchard, 1998). The therapist's struggle for clarity feels familiar to many clinicians. In learning how to provide the best treatment for families affected by sexual abuse, we have developed a systemic framework to give us clear guidance in the face of our client's anxiety and overwhelming needs. This chapter specifically explores integrating children in our existing framework for treating incestuous families.

The basis for treatment is an organizational model first described by Trepper and Barrett (1985). It is a multiple systems perspective that divides the therapeutic process into stages. The reader must bear in mind that this model calls for the treatment of victims, nonoffending parents, nonabused siblings, and perpetrators. We believe that when child sexual abuse happens in a family, the entire family is affected. Everyone's development, as well as the development of the family as a whole, is interrupted by the traumatic event and its discovery. Consequently, it is our belief that the entire family system must receive treatment. The type of intervention (individual, family, or group) and the frequency of the sessions are determined both by the needs of the client and the assessment of the clinician. For the purposes of this chapter, however, we will focus on the treatment of the child victim within the multiple systems framework, exploring assessment, play therapy, children within family therapy, and larger systems intervention (i.e., departments of social service, judicial and legal systems).

Definition of Child Sexual Abuse

We use the following definition of child sexual abuse (Finkelhor, 1980; Russell, 1984; Trepper & Barrett, 1989).

1. Any sexual contact, defined as:
   a. touching, with the intention of sexually arousing the child or providing sexual arousal for the offending adult
   b. kissing, in a prolonged manner, or by one whose purpose is similar to touching
   c. fondling of genitals or other parts of the body in a sexual or prolonged manner
   d. overt sexual contact, such as oral-genital contact, manual stimulation of genitals, or intercourse
2. Any behavior that is intended to stimulate the child sexually, or to sexually stimulate the offending adult through the use of the child, including showing the child erotic materials, photographing the child in a sexual manner, or talking sexually to the child.
3. Sexual contact by an adult or adolescent who is older than the child or who is in an older developmental stage than the child. Even children in the same developmental stage can experience the act as abuse if physical or emotional harm is inflicted or threatened.

Overview of the Multiple Systems Model

Maddock and Larson (1995) propose as the most desirable treatment for child sexual abuse a meta-model to be incorporated by clinicians and integrated with their own personal style and therapeutic interventions. The multiple systems model we utilize is organized into three stages, although we, like Maddock and Larson, realize that treatment does not always proceed linearly. We find it helpful to maintain an awareness of the stage of treatment with a family in order to set reasonable goals and expectations.

Stage 1: Creating a context for change. This stage creates safety for the family and the victim within the context of treatment. The clinician attempts to assess safety both inside and outside of the treatment. Fluid assessment of individual and familial strengths, interactions, and difficulties takes place. An ongoing treatment plan and goals are then designed and agreed upon with the entire community team and the family.

Stage 2: Challenging patterns and expanding realities. In this stage, the team helps both individuals and families explore the patterns that have created and maintained the sexual abuse, encouraging them to create alternative behaviors, thoughts, and feelings. This is accomplished through a combination of individual, family, and group therapy with both children and adults.

Stage 3: Consolidation. This is the relapse prevention stage. The family and the team review what they have learned, reinforce what has changed, and look to the future. Together they predict where they might have difficulties in the future and, based on the current strengths, design a plan to help themselves with future difficulties and to prevent relapse.

Goals for Treatment

In follow-up interviews with both adult and child clients from families where sexual abuse had occurred, clients were asked what they experienced as the most significant elements of the therapeutic process. Their answers, indicating what had been the most helpful, became our generic goals for treatment. Clinicians can design their treatment plans and specific interventions with these ends in mind.

Therapeutic Team Approach

The clinician should continually strive to build a team with the family, including the child, and other involved professionals. Doing so helps clients rebuild a sense of power and control in their lives. Team relationships must emphasize the value of all members of the community. Interactions need to represent healthy and meaningful relationships (i.e., respectful and articulate communication and appropriate problem-solving skills). The family needs to be a part of this team and learn that positive, non-abusive relationships can and do exist.

Recognition of Patterns

It is important for the family and child to recognize the repetitious patterns of behavior, thoughts, and feelings that contribute to and maintain the symptoms. For example, families should be aware of the pattern surrounding a sexually acting out episode or a victim behavior. Recognition of these predictable patterns can be discussed during assessment (stage 1), and interventions designed and implemented with the understanding of the entire treatment team (stage 2).

Recognition of Exceptions

It is important to help family members recognize that they possess inherent strengths that can help them alter problematic behaviors (Wolin & Wolin, 1993). Exceptions to the problem—times when things are going well and there is no abuse—should be highlighted. Such recognition is a step in the direction of empowering families and maintaining hopefulness.

Boundaries and Safety

When working with children who have been abused, it is imperative to focus in each session on building safety and helping them understand and design appropriate boundaries. Child sexual abuse is an incredible boundary violation, which disrupts a child's sense of safety. The therapeutic process must help abused children re-establish their sense of safety and define boundaries for themselves that will not only keep them safe but also assure they will not hurt anyone else. In order to keep the child safe, clinicians must also be continually aware of their own boundaries. Interventions can be designed through play to highlight the creation and maintenance of boundaries (Scott, 1992).

Creating and Maintaining Hope

The process of discovery of and recovery from sexual abuse is painful, frustrating, complicated, and often confusing for both the client and the clinician. In our follow-up interviews clients were unanimous in saying that the *hope* of the team members was crucial in helping them through the treatment maze. It is imperative that the team members communicate openly and that clinicians receive ongoing supervision and consultation so that all helping professionals involved with the family will be able to maintain an ethical, well informed, and hopeful perspective on each and every case.

Stage 1: Creating a Context for Change

The main components of stage 1 include pretreatment planning, assessment (especially understanding the child's individual responses to the trauma), and creating a place of safety. We find it absolutely essential to attend well to stage 1 activities, as these form the basis for healthy, empowering treatment. Stage 1 tasks are never accomplished within the first session; rather, they are dealt with throughout the first segment of treatment.

Pretreatment Planning

Pretreatment planning usually begins with the initial contact with a family and is well underway before the child's first therapeutic contact. From the very start, the five goals of treatment drive the assessment planning stage. Pretreatment planning involves the creation of a healthy treatment team, including the therapist, the family, and any other professionals involved. Active, respectful communication among the professionals and with family members models appropriate interactions and contributes to the therapeutic intervention. In addition, it is well worth the clinician's time to form relationships with child protective, educational, and legal professionals in a child's life before painful decisions have to be discussed or problematic patterns are created.

Child Protective Services

Involvement of child protective services (CPS) in the life of a family indicates that there have been concerns about the family's ability to protect the children. If the family becomes involved with CPS after entering therapy, the therapist may be in a unique position to create a therapeutic system, having already established a trusting relationship with the family and also hopefully having the respect of CPS. The family may look to the therapist for guidance and protection, and the therapist can use his or her expertise and experience to take an active role in any investigative or follow-up services. Again, healthy relationships with other professionals are important. By keeping in mind the family's typical problematic patterns (i.e., keeping secrets, triangulation, structural issues), the therapist can help prevent repetition of abuses within the larger system. For example, a parent who tends to drop to the lower level of the family hierarchy when unsure of him- or herself can be helped to counter those self-deprecating voices and assert his or her right to have input into decisions.

Schools

School systems clearly play an important role in the life of the child and can help by alerting the team to problematic patterns, giving feedback to therapists about behavior of family members outside of treatment, and becoming allies in planning behavioral interventions. Developing a relationship with teachers and principals before problems develop increases the likelihood of successful intervention in stage 2.

Legal System

A determination can often be made early on as to whether the case will enter the legal system. Some cases clearly have legal complications; others have a potential for disclosure of abuse, foreshadowing involvement in the child protective and legal systems. The court system can be used as a tool for power and control, so therapists are wise to learn the workings of their particular legal system. Criminal, family, and child protective court have different processes and goals. Well-timed clarification of the legal process and a consideration of legal strategy can help a family feel safer within the therapeutic context. Some kinds of common legal issues that arise with sexually abusive families are discussed below.

- Custody: A clinician may be asked to assess for abuse or to render an opinion as to how the child's needs are best served given a pending divorce. Keeping in mind the vulnerability model (discussed below) and offering the court an assessment of the family's vulnerability factors rather than duplicating the family's tendency to split, the therapist may be able to bring the family together over the interests of the child. We often take on the role of mediator to help the parents make healthy choices on behalf of their children.
- Criminal prosecutions: Children who have offended may be adjudicated in the legal system. A therapist who repeatedly reminds the court of the importance of rehabilitation (rather than punishment) can be a true asset. Child victims may also be asked to testify and may need the protection of

the family and the therapist to minimize secondary traumatization due to the court proceedings. Perhaps the therapist will be allowed to reveal the child's disclosures, or the therapist may assist the court in taking and videotaping testimony in a way that is child-sensitive.

• Child welfare court: If there is an allegation of abuse or neglect and the family is being monitored by child protective systems to ensure a safe environment for the child, the therapist may be called on to give an opinion regarding placement decisions, to assess safety within the family, or to discuss attendance and progress in therapy. Careful consideration of the sometimes competing principles of child safety and confidentiality is important in maintaining both the safety of the child and the trust of the family. Consultation with peers regarding strategic alliance and trust issues may prove helpful, as the therapist should carefully consider the ramifications before acting in such a public forum.

Assessment

Success in stage 1 depends on using assessment first to create a context for understanding for therapist, child, and family and then to communicate that understanding to the rest of the treatment team. Assessment is based on the vulnerability model (Trepper & Barrett, 1986, 1989), which calls upon the clinician to understand the family's story within its social/environmental, familial, and individual contexts. In addition, understanding the precipitating factors to abusive episodes and the child and family's coping skills is important. During assessment we do not attempt to isolate one particular cause of a problem; rather, we identify the many factors that made the child and /or family vulnerable to a problem. This kind of systemic assessment recognizes that childhood sexual abuse, as one in a category of childhood traumatizing events, can affect all levels of a family's and child's life. James (1994) described chronic traumatizing experiences in childhood as having the potential to disrupt all levels of childhood development, including identity formation, cognitive processing, experience of body integrity, ability to manage behavior, affect tolerance, spiritual and moral development, and the ability to trust self and others.

Social/environmental factors contribute to who we are by developing our values, organizing our beliefs, and shaping many of our behaviors. In order to understand how the sexual abuse began and its consequent impact on the child, we must explore the following variables: age, race, gender, culture, education, religion, sexual orientation, and socioeconomic status.

Familial factors not only influence a child's vulnerability to abuse but also determine how the family will function after the abuse. The factors we assess during stage 1 include rules, roles, hierarchy, adaptability, boundaries, communication patterns, style of interaction, and degree of isolation.

The individuals' psychological and biological functioning is also assessed and, in the case of a child, we explore impulse control, ability to learn, ability to self-soothe, coping mechanisms, patterns of behaviors, patterns of disassociation, patterns of attachment, toleration of strong affect, and degree of anxiety and/or depression. Below we discuss typical childhood responses to trauma—important information not only to include in the assessment puzzle but also to use in educating parents about their child's responses.

Response to Trauma

Van der Kolk (1987) identified many factors that can influence and/or mediate the child's response to trauma. These factors include prior trauma, personality, genetic predisposition, stage of development, the severity of the abusive incident, and strength and appropriateness of the social support system. Van der Kolk also pointed out that children are at greater risk for traumatization due to their formative stage of development and limited array of coping mechanisms. Assessing the impact of sexual abuse involves determining not only the nature of the event, but also the context of the abuse and the meaning given to the event(s) by the child. Family therapists need to integrate trauma and attachment theory with an extensive working knowledge of the continuum of childhood sexual behaviors (see Gil & Johnson, 1993).

Finkelhor and Browne (1986) conceptualized a four-factor model of the traumatogenic dynamics of childhood sexual abuse. The four factors are betrayal, powerlessness, stigmatization, and traumatic sexualization. After analyzing data on the short-term effects of sexual abuse, Finkelhor and Browne (1986) found that sexually abused children regularly exhibited the following indicators: depression, fear or anxiety, anger and/or hostility, difficulties in school, problematic sexualized behavior, and severe oppositional or delinquent behaviors.

In addition, sexual abuse has unique physical and emotional reinforcers and conditioners that differ from other forms of trauma, creating ambivalence and confusion. Children may develop very confusing approach-avoidance behaviors with attachment figures. Their capacity to develop healthy, sustaining attachments may be impaired, both in childhood and later in life. Ryan (1989) described the experience of sexual victimization as being both the same and different from other abusive experiences, pointing out that, while sexual abuse entails emotional betrayal and psychological distress, the abusive interactions may also meet the child's needs for attention and nurturing.

Abuse of all types and traumatogenic reactions also have strong physiological components. Perry (1993) reported that, if a stressful event is sufficient in terms of duration, intensity, or frequency, the child's brain may be altered. He characterized the experience of the traumatized child as embodying fear, threat, pain, chaos, hunger, frustration, and unpredictability. The template for the brain's organization then becomes the stress response.

James (1994) described the stress response as an automatic survival response to acute trauma comprised of flight, fight, or freeze behaviors. In children, the fight response may be characterized by regressive tantrums or aggressive behaviors; the flight response is very often characterized by dissociative behaviors, since physical flight is often not an option; freezing can be exhibited by oppositional-defiant behaviors. These fight, flight, or freeze behaviors are primitive, automatic brain responses that can be stimulated by reminders of the traumatizing event.

Therapists also need to assess the unique physiological reinforcers present. Berliner and Rawlings (1991) reported that the child may respond to sexual abuse with aversive feelings and thoughts that become associated with the memories of the abuse or certain evocative stimuli. The child may then experience intrusive thoughts, nightmares, flashbacks, hypervigilance, exaggerated startle response, heightened physiological arousal, and fear upon presentation of the stimuli. Ryan, Lane, Davis, and Isaac (1987) explained the physiological impact of sexual abuse by noting that sexual behavior, even when coerced, may be reinforced by a physiological reward, that is, sexual arousal. During abuse, the child experiences sexual arousal along with pain, fear, anger, anxiety, helplessness, and/or aggression, so that the physical sensation is paired with these psychological and behavioral responses to abuse. Later, when the child experiences similar feelings of fear or anxiety, he or she may also feel sexual arousal, so that the reinforcement of the associations linking these powerful negative affects occurs. Berliner and Rawlings (1991) also reported that the child usually experiences distress during the abuse and is then conditioned to associations with the abuse. Finally, Ryan (1989) described the possible conflict for the child, in that she may experience both physical pain or injury, and pleasure and/or sexual arousal.

Safety

Developing an environment of safety both in and out of the office is paramount to the success of any intervention. Safety means that the child both feels personally safe and is also kept safe from further emotional damage in his/her interactions with others. While the concept of safety appears simple and elemental, *therapists cannot allow their attention to be diverted from this goal. It is essential never to proceed too quickly.* Proceeding at a pace that neither the child nor family can tolerate will result in resistance to the assessment and treatment and possible failure to engage. The therapist will at times be tempted to press the pace of assessment as others (parents, child protection, legal authorities) want either information or the immediate cessation of certain behaviors. Resisting such pressures to maintain a calm, child-centered environment is crucial to the success of treatment. Enlisting others in the child's social context as part of the team and facilitating their understanding of the process often helps the therapist maintain a pace suitable for the child. In order to achieve safety outside of the therapy office, emphasis should be placed on helping family members develop both their own feelings of safety and their capacity to support the child as they proceed through the emotionally demanding assessment process. This task is tackled at a pretreatment meeting with the significant family members, where the importance of keeping the family's (thus the child's) safety concerns paramount is emphasized.

Another aspect of creating safety is the coordination of services with all of the professionals involved. Having the professionals in active, healthy communication with one another and the family members models appropriate patterns and contributes to the therapeutic intervention. Finally, good boundaries, respectful, open interest in the child, and a gentle, nonjudgmental manner will all aid in the process of creating and maintaining safety.

First Clinical Sessions

As described above, child victims present a wide array of behaviors and affect. In fact, James (1994) described children as exhibiting a "storm of affect." The storm of affect and the related behaviors can create feelings of confusion, fear, and even anger in parents, caregivers, teachers, and professionals involved with the family. Parents and caregivers typically have many concerns about the child and themselves. Identifying their many concerns is very important in the assessment planning stage.

When the therapist first meets with the child and family, the therapist should thoroughly address their concerns and facilitate their understanding of these confusing and alarming behaviors. This creates a context for understanding. Thus, a clinician needs to be somewhat educated in the individual, traumatogenic dynamics of sexualized children. The first clinical sessions (pre-assessment planning) should accomplish the following tasks:

- Obtain and review all relevant discovery materials, including prior social assessments, psychological and psychiatric reports, reports of prior hospitalizations, child's history in substitute care, child's abuse history, previous diagnoses, and all reports of unusual incidents.
- Determine the constellation of the family, that is, biological, family foster, or traditional foster. Phone and face-to-face contact with all important collaterals, especially with any significant attachment figures, is essential. Elicit their concerns and the strength of their connection to the child.
- Identify past and present functioning and begin identification of behavioral patterns, possible attachment disturbances, and posttraumatic behaviors and reactions, such as self-blame, powerlessness, loss and betrayal, eroticization, destructiveness, dissociative behaviors, issues of body integrity, and difficulty in regulating affect. Develop an early hypothesis of how sexual behaviors may be connected to these states. Not all of this information will be readily available, but questioning primary caregivers about these issues will help the clinician build an early theory of how the abusive episodes developed.
- Begin to identify the child's stress response, including fight, flight, or numbing responses, the antecedents (triggers), and the sexual contexts of the affective arousal.
- Identify who should be included in the initial assessment session and select a "bridge person" (i.e., the individual in the child's family or social support system who can be most supportive and who can help the child develop and maintain safety and security).
- Preparation of the bridge person and other key members prior to initial meeting. Ensure that the bridge person is not a perpetrator of the sexual abuse or of any other type of abusive behavior. Explain the evaluation process and provide education on trauma, sexualized children, and attachment disturbances.
- Determine whether the child is exhibiting and/or engaging in sexual behaviors that are causing concern to caregivers and family and if other children may be at risk.

Much of the above can be accomplished without the child present. The goal throughout stage 1 is to communicate to all in the family system their value and to emphasize the importance of their role in the evaluative process. This empowers them to create and maintain a safe and secure environment and reduce intrusiveness of the evaluation. Finally, develop a safety plan to prevent any further episodes of abuse during early sessions.

Creating a context for understanding provides the child with a voice in therapy and facilitates all later clinical efforts. It is dependent upon developing a bridge to the child's experience. Understanding a child's response to sexual abuse includes helping the child communicate the meaning that he or she has given to the abuse and his/her idiosyncratic victim/survivor patterns of behavior, including his/her unique stress response. For a child to find his or her voice in the assessment and treatment process, a *child-centered medium of communication* must be used. The therapist should approach the child in a gentle and low-key, straightforward and matter-of-fact way. The child should have been prepared by the bridge person prior to the first session. The therapist should also directly communicate to the child the purpose of the session. The bridge person is incorporated into the dialogue from the very beginning and helps the clinician understand past experiences and concerns with the child.

An interactional expressive play medium is employed with the child, and the bridge person is incorporated into the play. The therapist sets boundaries and explains that the session will include both play and talk. The child is allowed to explore the selected expressive toys. As the toys are explored, the therapist begins to introduce metaphors (Bray, 1991) related to the feelings and behavioral states associated with physical and sexual abuse and neglect. The toys have all been selected to evoke the feelings that are part of the storm of affect, and the metaphors bring these feelings into verbal realm.

Our toy selection includes some of the following: the Sad Dinosaur, the Tricking Plant, the Wise Tiger, the Hungry, Hungry Monster, the Sleep Time Bear, the Bunny Who Goes Inside Herself, the Man with Scared Feelings Inside, the Man with Angry Monster Feelings Inside, and the Strong Man. The child is told that the Sad Dinosaur, for example, emits a very sorrowful noise; this can evoke experiences of sadness for the child. The Wise Tiger stuffed animal knows a lot about children with hurt feelings. Many children use the Wise Tiger both as a vehicle to disclose their own hurts and also as a soothing figure. The Bunny Who Goes Inside Herself has a head that folds into her body, which can evoke withdrawal and/or dissociation. The Man with Scared Feelings Inside is a puppet whose face can change into a fearful expression, reflecting the child's own inner fears. The Man with Angry Monster Feelings Inside is a figure of a football player whose back opens up to display the face

of an angry monster. Children often disclose their own angry feelings or experiences to him. The Strong Man becomes a symbol of resilience and safety, and
children are told that he likes to loan his strength to kids to help them talk about
their feelings.

The selection of toys is limited only by imagination and space. Ones that
are chosen should evoke a reaction on the part of the therapist. This connection
with the toys will be reflected in the clinician's enthusiasm during the play.
There should be a wide range of toys that address the full spectrum of affect,
from happiness, contentment, and excitement to anxiety and overstimulation,
as well as from boredom and sadness to strong negative affects such as fear and
anger. The toys can be used to stock the playroom. Alternatively, they can be
packed into bags or bins, allowing the therapist to meet the child in the most
stable, secure environment available. The child is exposed only to specific,
selected diagnostic toys. The toys thus become a medium for the child to verbally communicate feelings and experiences, many of which have previously
been stored only in sensory or somatic memory. As the toys provide a bridge
to the experiences, the child begins to progress to more direct verbal exchange.
Younger children usually require more play interaction, while older children
can engage in more direct inquiry.

Case Illustration—Stage 1

Susan is 7 years old and is living with her mother, father, Aunt Eileen, grandmother, and two younger cousins. She exhibits many sexualized behaviors,
including openly masturbating, simulating intercourse with toys, and, of greater
concern, having been found fondling the genitals of other children both at home
and at school. There has been no disclosure by Susan of sexual abuse. There is
a secure attachment with both parents and, with help, the mother has been developing the capacity to be firm but not punitive in her response to Susan. Susan
had been referred by her school because of her sexualized behaviors.

Susan's mother, Mary, and father, Pat, are seen in a separate session prior to
Susan's scheduled appointment. The parents are informed about the details of
the assessment process and their concerns and worries are addressed. This meeting also allows the therapist to provide education about children with problematic sexual behaviors and to help normalize the feelings of the parents. The
therapist helps the parents think through necessary steps to ensure that Susan
will remain both personally safe and safe in her interactions with other children.
At this meeting the therapist and parents decide that Mary will function as the
bridge person, based on her strong and nurturing attachment with Susan.

The parents and therapist also decide it will be best to prepare Susan by calmly sharing their worries about her touching behaviors and their desire to help her learn to be safe with herself and with others. The therapist shares with the parents the language that will be used in the assessment with Susan. The parents explore how best to inform Susan of the first appointment. They agree that they will tell her that they have found a person who "has talked to many children who have touching problems, and has learned how to help them be safe." Mary will also describe to Susan that the meeting will be in part to talk, but that the therapist has many really interesting toys with which she can play.

Susan is a tall, slim child who is reading a book while sitting close to her mother in the waiting room. Her face is sad and serious. She continues to look at the book after quickly glancing at the therapist. The therapist says hello to Mary and then greets Susan in a very gentle manner. Mother and child are invited into the playroom. Susan again sits close to her mother with her arms folded around her body. The therapist takes a seat at a comfortable distance and sits with a relaxed posture. The therapist addresses both Mother and Susan with an expressive, yet very calm and soft conversational voice. The first goal is to establish safe rapport with Susan.

THERAPIST: Hello, Susan, I am Joe Jones and I am a social worker. I guess you have met other social workers. Can you tell me about some of the other social workers you have met?

SUSAN: (*She slowly nods her head, acknowledging that she has, and speaks tentatively.*) I see Mrs. Grey at my school 'cause I get in trouble with my teacher.

THERAPIST: Oh, you've been getting into trouble at school? Is that why you are here to see me?

SUSAN: No, ah, maybe, ah, I don't really know why.

THERAPIST: (*Turning toward Mother*) Well, Mom, is that why you and Susan have come to see me? Are you worried about school? (*At this point, Susan nestles closely into her mother and looks very sad.*)

MOTHER: (*Putting her arm around Susan to comfort her*) Well, that is part of our worries. Susan has been getting mad at school and then has been hitting other children at school, but that is not all. Susan has been touching children at school and around the house.

THERAPIST: (*Turning to Susan, who looks very sad and tense*) Susan, do you know what your mom means by "touching other kids"?

SUSAN: (*Nods her head yes and slowly points to her genital area*) Here.

THERAPIST: That's right, Susan. Remember, I said that I am a social worker, but I am a very special type of social worker. I talk to lots and lots of kids who do touching to other kids and also kids who have been touched by other kids or maybe adults. Talking to so many kids has helped me understand the feelings and thoughts that kids have when they do touching. Understanding the feelings and thoughts helps me help kids learn how to be safe and to be safe with other kids. Mom, isn't that your worry?

MOTHER: Well, ah, yes, both her dad and myself have lots of worries about Susan not being safe with herself or with other kids.

THERAPIST: Susan, I have learned from the other children that it is really boring to just sit and talk to adults. So we will spend some of the time talking and some of the time playing. Other children have told me that it can be real hard to talk about touching so we have figured out that taking a break can help when the feelings get real strong. Playing with the toys is one way to have a break from the talking, but each time we meet we will talk about touching. (*As the therapist speaks, Susan looks at the toys assembled in a corner of the room.*) I know that the other children who come to see me have found many of the toys lots of fun.

Susan continues to sit close to her mother. Mary indicates that Susan likes to draw and the therapist supplies paper and markers. Susan becomes less tense, separates from her mother and starts to draw. Susan begins to print the alphabet in very ordered and straight lines. She continues to print as we talk about the neatness of her printing, which leads to talking about her favorite activities. This conversation allows both her mother and the therapist comment on her strengths and skills. She relaxes as we talk. Susan begins to initiate contact with the therapist as well as her mother. As we talk about favorite school activities, the therapist asks about the touching at school. Susan can only nod her head in response to questions about having touched children at school. Susan has great difficulty in talking about the touching behaviors.

In order to establish a baseline of behavior, the therapist asks Susan to describe her worries in detail. As Susan describes the problematic sexual behaviors, her printing becomes messy and quickly she begins to scribble all over the paper until it is covered with overlapping lines. As she marks the paper, Susan becomes more and more anxious and fidgety. She begins to walk around the room, going to the white board. She picks up the marker and begins to scribble on the board. As Susan's drawing becomes more intense, the therapist comments to Mary about Susan appearing to be feeling many "jumbled up and excited feelings." Mary describes sometimes seeing these same types of behaviors and feelings at home and with other children. While Susan continues to draw, she is very obviously listening to the conversation, making comments about her mother's statements. As the board becomes covered, she begins to calm down. Once the board is completely covered and Susan has sufficiently quieted herself, she asks if she can play with the toys.

Susan slowly approaches the toys and begins to examine each toy. She is especially attracted to those toys with prominent mouths and tongues and explores each with her fingers. Her affect is now tense and serious. As Susan explores each toy, the therapist tells the toy's story. Susan begins to approach the therapist and initiate direct interactions. As she realizes that each toy has its own story, she begins to ask the therapist, "What's special about this one?" She becomes more interested in some of the toys, reexamining each unique feature over and over, as the therapist relates to her and the toy.

THERAPIST: (*As Susan explores the Sad Dinosaur, it emits a very low, mournful sound.*) My! Is that a sad, sad sound. I wonder what has made the little dinosaur so very sad.

SUSAN: I guess it gets sad when its parents aren't home.

THERAPIST: Gee! What causes the little Dinosaur to be so sad when its parents are not home?

SUSAN: It misses its parents and gets scared! (*Susan continues to squeeze the toy as she talks.*)

MOTHER: (*Who has been watching her daughter very intently*) Susan, what happens to make the Little Dinosaur scared?

SUSAN: (*She stares at the toy while still squeezing it*) It gets bad dreams. (*Susan has been having nightmares for several months prior to the family contacting the agency.*)

THERAPIST: (*Picking up a teddy bear dressed in pajamas*) Well, Susan, teddy bear here is dressed for bed, and it too has bad dreams. It knows all about bad dreams and likes to help children talk about their scary dreams. It even has a special place for children to put pictures of their scary dreams. (*The therapist reveals to Susan a hidden pocket in the side of the bear, and she explores the toy and the pocket.*) Maybe for next time you could draw a picture of your scary dream?

SUSAN: (*Nods her head as she still explores the toy*)
MOTHER: Susan, that does sound like a good idea! Maybe we can do it together if you have a bad dream again?

Susan continues to explore all of the toys. She reacted to the Man with Scared Feelings Inside, the Man with Angry Monster Feelings Inside, the Chameleon Who Changes Color to Show Feelings, the Snake Puppet, and the Tricking Plant. Susan reports that the man is scared because "somebody did mean things to him." She reacts strongly to the Snake Puppet and decides it has to stay in the corner. When asked about angry feelings, she says that they cause confused, mixed-up feelings. With the plant puppet, she enacts a scenario, having the therapist use the plant to perform several different types of "tricking" games. The plant tells the fly to come see its pretty colors and Susan has the plant then eat the fly. The plant also tricks the bee by telling it to "come try its sweet juice" and then eats the bee.

During the next three sessions, Susan returns to these same themes with the toys. A portion of each session is spent talking about the "touching feelings, thoughts, and behaviors." Then, as in the first session, she returns to the play. She continues to become agitated, as in the first session, while talking about the touching, returning to the white board and covering the surface with marker. The therapist continues to talk about the excited feelings returning as she engages in drawing with the marker. In later sessions, Susan begins to talk about her excited or nervous feelings. Toward the end of the evaluation she is able to describe wanting to touch other children when she has nervous feelings.

Her mother remains a vital participant, becoming more verbally active as she gains comfort and familiarity with the thematic communication. In fact, she becomes very effective at clarifying some of Susan's statements.

In the third session, Susan brings a drawing of her latest nightmare. The picture depicts several snakes around the figure of a female child. Two of the snakes are kissing the child on the lips. After telling the therapist about the nightmare, she places the paper in the pocket of the bear and turns to play with other puppets to which she had been attracted earlier. As she plays, she explores the feelings each toy evokes.

In the fifth session, Mrs. Smith reveals that Susan has been talking about the touching feelings and thoughts and has said that she wants to tell the therapist about where she learned about the touching behaviors. The therapist introduced this concept in the second session.

THERAPIST: (*Observing that Susan had immediately started exploring the toys*)
             Well, it looks like you want to play and talk at the same time
             today.
SUSAN: (*Nodding her head yes*) Yeah! Please!
THERAPIST: Okay! (*Susan picks up the Strong Man's belt and puts it around
             her.*) Gee! It looks like you want to borrow some of the Strong
             Man's strength today. (*Susan just nods yes and continues to
             explore the same toys, throwing the Snake Puppet across the room.
             She returns again and again to the Sad Dinosaur*) The little
             dinosaur sure seems sad. I wonder why?
SUSAN: It's sad because somebody has been doing touching to it.
THERAPIST: My, that would make a little dinosaur sad. As other children have
             told me, it also makes boys and girls sad, too.
SUSAN: (*She stares at the Sad Dinosaur. The therapist and her mother sit
             silently with her. She then picks up the Wise Tiger puppet, who
             likes to help children talk about their sad, touching, or mad feel-
             ings. Speaking in an altered voice and manipulating the tiger's
             mouth, Susan speaks.*) Susan wants to talk about where she
             learned about the touching.
THERAPIST: Well, Tiger, where did Susan learn about the touching?

Using the Wise Tiger puppet, Susan discloses multiple instances of abuse
by a male babysitter. The babysitter is a next door neighbor, who has known
the family for many years. In fact, the families are very close and the children
have freely gone between houses. While her mother is distressed, she remains
calm and helps to also question Wise Tiger. (The importance of remaining calm
in the moment of a disclosure has already been discussed in pretreatment planning sessions.) After the session, Mrs. Smith contacts the therapist at a pre-
arranged time to help process her feelings and to plan future action, including
calling a report into Child Protective Services. At the end of the session, Susan
was prepared to talk to the Child Protective Services worker. She was informed
that these were also people who really want to make sure that kids stay safe and
will need to talk to her to help figure out how to keep her safe from the babysitter and to make sure he stays safe with other children.

Once Susan disclosed, the therapist was able to finish the evaluation and
move into the active treatment phase of stage 1, beginning to develop a treatment plan. The treatment plan addressed both the victim experience and the
touching behaviors with other children. Treatment combined individual, fam-

ily, and group therapies. The therapist collaborated with Child Protective Services to ensure effective coordination of services.

Stage 2: Challenging Patterns and Expanding Alternatives

In stage 1, strengths and problematic patterns are identified and a safe connection established. In stage 2, the clinician helps the child and family interrupt patterns that are not functional and utilize the child's strength to create new behaviors and beliefs. Healthy progress in stage 2 can be accomplished only after stage 1 work has been carefully and thoroughly completed. Stage 2 is when therapists are often the most comfortable and creative, using their unique training, experiences, and creativity to challenge thought, behavioral, and interactional patterns that have become blocks to a child's healthy development.

An important part of stage 1 is to create a trusting, workable relationship with the parents. This relationship will be essential in creating lasting, positive change in stage 2. We often spend a portion of each session talking with parents, to hear about the challenges the child has faced during the past week, to interpret their meaning based on the family's vulnerability factors, and to problem-solve intervention strategies. Sometimes the overt issue of sexual abuse is discussed; other times the family's other vulnerabilities are worked on.

As therapy proceeds, the clinician and caregivers intervene actively around themes of safety, control, attachment, and powerlessness that have been identified in the assessment phase of stage 1. Therapists can help children role play with toys, express themselves assertively through letters, plan new self-care strategies, or play games that create options to change internalized beliefs (such as "I am powerless" or "I am not loveable"). Again, it is important that active interventions to change oppressing beliefs not occur until a thorough connection and assessment have been accomplished. The therapist-parent team also uses systemic supports to change the child's environment in a way that reflects new messages of connection and empowerment. By this stage, parents have usually been empowered enough to be creative, active participants in their child's treatment.

Resistance will almost certainly be encountered during stage 2. Typically, the child becomes bored with treatment, the family or child enters a short, stable period free from problematic symptoms, or the child encounters anxieties that prohibit openness. Safety concerns may surface around each step of disclosure (whether of facts or feelings). A therapist working with children has a responsibility to keep treatment techniques and modes varied and creatively stimulating so that children will stay engaged. See Oaklander (1988), Gil (1991), and James (1994) for ideas for creative, playful interventions with children and families. Creating lasting change in families does, however, require repetition, as the same interactions have to be challenged repeatedly and consistently.

As the family changes in stage 2, the child's assumptions, previously needed as protections, may no longer be valid or necessary. If the assumption and related behavior pattern have served the child well and are chronic, the team can expect regression and testing of the family's new patterns. Familiar routines, structure, and limits, balanced with some gentle reassurances, will prove important to ensure safety at this time. Predicting this with the caregivers, then outlining behavior management strategies will both help adults remain in the parental position of the structural hierarchy and keep the child safe.

Utilizing a variety of modalities to take a broader, more contextual view of the problem helps create faster, more lasting change. More than one therapist may be employed on a case, and information from one modality should be used to inform another.

• Individual child sessions help a child to separate from parents and other family members still in denial. They also are important for teaching new problem-solving techniques and protective and social skills and for working on individual reactions to the original trauma.
• Individual adult sessions can help parents understand their responsibility in supporting repetition of abusive patterns (and its roots in their families of origin), to elevate the parents in the family hierarchy, to gain empathy for other family members, and to encourage responsible problem solving. These continue to be very important while a parent struggles with taking responsibility.
• Sibling sessions can center on exchanging validation regarding members' views of the family, creating a strong sibling alliance, and altering the various family roles of each child. Involving siblings begins a lifetime of openness in discussing problematic familial patterns, an important support during adulthood.
• Whole family treatment is important to make problematic patterns in the family overt, to discover the role each member takes in maintaining the

pattern, and then to find new ways to get the family's intimacy needs met without victimization.

• Parent/child or other dyad sessions encourage better attachment and relationships without triangulation.

• Group therapies, a highly effective mode, help individuals gain support for their role, receive feedback on their behavior, be confronted or validated on their thought process, practice appropriate boundaries, and learn new social skills. Scott (1992) and Gil and Johnson (1993) discuss forming and leading group therapies for children.

Occasionally, a child will proceed through stage 2 and form a trusting individual relationship with the therapist, even though the parents continue to see the child as the identified problem. For instance, this would occur if parents refused to engage in couples or family sessions. This stance may keep the parents from both taking responsibility for examining their own contributions to the vulnerabilities and accepting their power to affect the child's development positively. Keeping children and parents separate in sessions would then be indicated, both to help the parents move more quickly through stage 1 and to help the child separate from his/her parents and their problematic patterns.

Stage 2 tends to be fun, creative, and fulfilling work for the therapist, who may find him- or herself limited only by his or her own inhibitions. An aversion to sitting on the floor, talking about sexuality, or playing giggly scenarios with puppets will not only be noted and interpreted by a child, but also taken in and unintentionally modeled for the parents. Even in stage 2, children may still test the therapeutic relationship by behaving to recreate the abusive episode. Therapists need to be vigilant to ways in which he or she is reacting to the child in a similar way to the environment as a result of being too closely identified with the adults around the child. An example of this might be if the therapist unconsciously emphasized play centered around learning about visits with the child's father in order to gain information for the anxious, divorced mother. The therapist will want to be aware of any transference reactions that arise and to receive consultation when appropriate.

The end of stage 2 and transition into stage 3 is likely to be gradual. Signs of movement into consolidation include fewer problematic symptoms being reported, a clear ability to problem-solve independently on the part of caregivers, and fewer power, control, safety, and attachment themes in the child's play.

Case Illustration—Stage 2

MOTHER: (*Meeting first with the therapist at the start of a planned individual session with the child*) I'm getting reports from Susan's teacher that she is fighting with another child, Jennifer, at school, and is defiant with the teacher. Mrs. Cortez said that she is almost unmanageable in the afternoons.

THERAPIST: What does Susan say about it?

MOTHER: She's told me that she doesn't like Jennifer, that Jennifer takes the ball away from her and teases her during lunch. And I almost forgot . . . her masturbation has started again the minute she gets home from school.

THERAPIST: What's your theory about what's going on?

MOTHER: I think she's mad at Jennifer. She doesn't say anything when it happens, but is mad in class all afternoon. She'll need to learn to handle being teased better. I remember it happening to me. She may as well get used to it.

THERAPIST: It sounds to me like Susan feels pretty powerless around Jennifer and isn't sure how to handle the situation. What did you learn to do about teasing when you were a kid?

MOTHER: I would just go play with other kids, but sometimes it got to me and I would cry. After I got caught crying and teased by my older brother, though, I learned to tough it out and not say anything.

THERAPIST: It sounds like Susan is doing the same thing . . . finding her own way to handle it. She seems to try to not get angry with Jennifer for making her feel so powerless, but sometimes it gets too hard to keep a lid on such strong feelings, just as you must have felt when you cried as a child. Her feelings are coming out in the classroom at a safe target such as the teacher. She's also beginning to need the self-soothing behavior of masturbation to take care of herself again, similar to the situation last fall when she felt powerless to tell you that she was afraid to walk to school alone. I'm afraid that if we don't teach Susan to speak up when she's being victimized, we'll be allowing the same abusive pattern to repeat. And we all know now that her difficulty speaking up when she's powerless is one of her vulnerabilities to being re-abused.

Mary and the therapist then discuss her reluctance to talk with Mrs. Cortez about the situation ("What could she do about it anyway?") and how Mary is modeling powerlessness to Susan. They do some concrete problem-solving to help Mrs. Smith feel more hopeful and empowered. Then, they make a plan to discuss the situation with Susan together in the remainder of the session.

THERAPIST: Susan, your mom tells me that you've been having trouble with Jennifer at school.

SUSAN: I don't like her. She's mean to me. But I don't let her bother me. I just go play by myself.

MOTHER: Honey, I wonder if it bothers you more than you think. . . . I hear that you get really angry with Mrs. Cortez sometimes after lunch, and I see you needing to feel better by touching yourself again, like before.

SUSAN: (*Escalating in emotion*) I don't want to talk about it!!

THERAPIST: It sounds like this is tough to talk about. I wonder if the Wise Tiger might be able to help again. (*Susan nods and pets the tiger affectionately.*)

MOTHER: (*As planned in first part of session*) Susan, I got teased when I was a kid too.

SUSAN: (*Wide-eyed*) You did??

MOTHER: Uh-huh. And I never said anything about it to anyone. And it just kept on happening. It didn't help not to talk about it.

THERAPIST: Susan, your mom and I don't ever want you to be hurt again, like you were with Tommy. So part of our job is to help you learn the words to say to speak up and to practice saying them so that everyone hears you. I know you can do it, but it's harder for some people, especially kids who have already been hurt like you have. (*Turning to puppet*) Wise Tiger, what do you think would happen if Susan told somebody that Jennifer was taking your ball? (*pause*) What did he say?

SUSAN: That Jennifer wouldn't like me anymore.

THERAPIST: It sounds like you feel really stuck, then. If you say something, it feels like she might not like you. If you don't say something, the angry monster we drew last week comes out and makes you feel bad about yourself. (*Susan nods, looks sad.*) Mary, I wonder if Susan needs a hug and some reassurance that we'll help her with this?

MOTHER: (*To therapist*) Now? (*Therapist nods, moves so parent and child can sit closer.*) I'm sure we'll figure something out, honey. We won't let Jennifer keep picking on you like that.

The rest of the session is spent playing dolls, where Mary, Susan, and the therapist all assume the role of a friend to Susan's doll. The therapist takes a strong lead in the play, initiating enactments of problematic peer situations, then teaching social skills to resolve the conflict positively.

In the next session, Susan reveals both verbally and with puppets that she feels "frozen" when Jennifer approaches her. She is helped to create a shield and an oxygen tank (like in diving) to protect herself and to breathe if she feels immobilized. Susan and the therapist practice using the shield and the tank, with the therapist playing the role of Jennifer. Mary is invited into the room partway through so that she can learn to play this "game" with Susan at home. Future sessions help Susan make the overt connection between the immobilized, powerless feeling followed by explosive anger and her reactions to the abusive episodes with her perpetrator.

Mary is also coached on how to interface with school personnel so that they are more aware of the problem and intervene more actively. Mary and the therapist then review the guidelines for handling masturbation that were outlined in the pretreatment planning phase. These often include a way to validate the right of the child to touch herself, but to restrict that activity to a safe, private place with masturbating to be done without the use of objects that could physically harm her. Since Susan has had a history of victimizing other children or sexually acting out with peers, both the school and all caregivers need to be aware of her vulnerability to abuse at these times, possibly increasing supervision during interactions with other vulnerable children. This theme can also be made overt to Susan and discussed both playfully and verbally in terms of safety. Mary and the therapist also discuss ways in which Mary continues to be reluctant to speak up to her husband when she is being victimized, modeling powerlessness to Susan. That conversation then leads to a couple session in which the power imbalance in the marital relationship is discussed and its influence on Susan highlighted. Familial patterns of handling anger are also discussed, first with parents, then in a whole family session.

Stage 3: Consolidation

The message sent to the child during consolidation is one of hope and strength. The child understands that there are adults in her life who she can count on and that she will be able to use these resources in the future. Sessions are spaced further apart during this stage and eventually are reduced to a checking-in type of meeting where the clinician is updated on current events.

Rituals for saying good-bye to people and toys are utilized. Parties are planned, good-bye messages are sent, and pictures are taken. The child is an active participant in the planning and execution of these activities in the consolidation phase.

Relapse prevention is accomplished by summarizing with the family and child all the stages of treatment. They explore what brought them into treatment, how the sexual abuse happened, what changes they have made, and how they plan to maintain those changes. By looking into a beautiful crystal ball we can see and imagine some of the trouble spots that may occur in the future. The clinician can guide this exercise by predicting potential danger at certain individual and family developmental stages. Times of transition pose difficulties for children and their families, leading them to resort to old, problematic thinking and behaviors.

After imagining future problem areas together, family and therapist design a very specific relapse plan. The plan should include: the thoughts and behaviors that will alert them that either they or someone else is in trouble, how they plan to communicate about the difficulty, who they will include in their problem-solving, how they can monitor one another, and how they will recognize that they are back on track. Often the clinician is involved in the plan, implying a potential for a future relationship.

Case Illustration—Stage 3

After 28 months of treatment, Susan is presenting as a more playful, outgoing child who has appropriate peer relationships, is developing well academically, and can talk easily about the abuse that occurred. Her parents report few difficulties at home or school and are able to resolve any problems that arise.

In individual sessions, the therapist and Susan remember how she felt when she first entered treatment. The two make clear plans for how she will express herself when she is feeling her old stress reactions (i.e., frozen, disconnected, powerless, then angry). She understands the importance of not touching other children but is no longer internalizing the shame of her previous behavior. They draw the "old" Susan vs. the "new" Susan. Finally, she finishes the relationship with the puppets that she has found so helpful, throwing them a little thank-you party.

In couple sessions, Susan's parents review what they have learned about both their parenting behaviors and couple interactions that have helped to create and maintain change. They discuss warning signs signaling the return of their previous patterns and formulate a plan for staying connected with each other enough to consciously create different ways of parenting. The adults also review together upcoming events in Susan's life that might cause a reversion to previous feelings and behaviors (e.g., a change in schools, the onset of adolescence).

Finally, in a whole family session, the family and the therapist together create and enact a ritual that helps them end this process in a complete, joyful way. Susan's family chose to do a puppet show, telling the story of their process. Symbolic gifts, along with a letter of affirmation and support, were given to them by the therapist, and a whole family outing was discussed as a way to celebrate their changes. Finally, the family was invited to call or return for a check-up if they found it necessary.

The treatment for child sexual abuse is a complex process, but if managed properly that complexity need not become overwhelming. Therapists need support from their peers, patience, and a clear, multisystemic model in order accomplish permanent change on many levels. From such a place of healthy attachment and clarity, the clinician can create an empowering, hopeful team with the family to make successful rebuilding after a devastating trauma a reality.

Mary Jo Barrett, M.S.W., is Director of Training and Consultation, Center for Contextual Change, Skokie, Illinois. Joseph Cortese, L.C.S.W., and Kristen Marzolf, L.C.S.W., are Co-Clinical Directors, Center for Contextual Change, Skokie, Illinois.

References

Berliner, L., & Rawlings, L. (1991). *A treatment manual: Children with sexual behavior problems.* Seattle: Harborview Sexual Assault Center.

Bray, M. (1991). *Poppies on the rubbish heap.* London, England: Cannongate.

Finkelhor, D. (1980). *Sexually victimized children.* New York: Free.

Finkelhor, D., & Browne, A. (1986). Initial and long-term effects: A conceptual framework. In D. Finkelhor & S. Araji (Eds.), *A sourcebook on child sexual abuse.* Newbury Park, CA: Sage.

Freeman-Longo, R., & Blanchard, G. (1998). *Sexual abuse in America: Epidemic of the 21st century.* Brandon, VT: Safer Society.

Gil, E. (1991). *The healing power of play: Working with abused children.* New York: Guilford.

Gil, E., & Johnson, T. C. (1993). *Sexualized children: Assessment and treatment of sexualized children and children who molest.* Rockville, MD: Launch.

James, B. (1989). *Treating traumatized children.* Boston, MA: Lexington.

James, B. (1994). *Handbook for treatment of attachment-trauma problems in children.* New York: Free.

Maddock, J., & Larson, N. (1995). *Incestuous families: An ecological approach to understanding.* New York: Norton.

Oaklander, V. (1988). *Windows to our children.* Highland, NY: Gestalt Journal.

Perry, B. D. (1993). Medicine and psychotherapy: Neurodevelopment and the neurophysiology of trauma. *The Advisor, 6,* 1–18.

Russell, D. E. H. (1984). The prevalence and seriousness of incestuous abuse: Stepfathers vs. biological fathers. *Child Abuse and Neglect, 8,* 15–22.

Ryan, G., Lane, S., Davis, J., & Isaac, C. (1987). Juvenile sex offenders: Development and correction. *Child Abuse and Neglect, 3*(3), 385–395.

Ryan, G. (1989). Victim to victimizer: Rethinking victim treatment. *Journal of Interpersonal Violence, 4,* 325–341.

Scott, R. L., & Stone, D. A. (1986). MMPI measures of psychological disturbance in adolescent and adult victims of father-daughter incest. *Journal of Clinical Psychology, 42,* 251–259.

Scott, W. (1992, Winter). Group therapy with sexually abused boys: Notes toward managing behavior. *Clinical Social Work Journal, 20*(4).

Scott, W. (1994). Group therapy for male sex offenders: Strategic interventions. *Journal of Family Psychotherapy, 5*(2), 1–20.

Trepper, T. S., & Barrett, M. J. (1986). Vulnerability to incest: A framework for assessment. In T. S. Trepper & M. J. Barrett (Eds.), *Treating incest: A multiple systems perspective.* New York: Haworth.

Trepper, T. S., & Barrett, M. J. (1989). *Systemic treatment of incest: A therapeutic handbook.* New York: Brunner/Mazel.

Uherek, A. (1991). Treatment of a ritually abused preschooler. In W. Friedreich (Ed.), *Casebook of sexual abuse treatment.* New York: Norton.

Van der Kolk, B. A. (Ed.). (1987). *Psychological trauma.* Washington, DC: American Psychiatric.

Wolin, S. J., & Wolin, S. (1993). *The resilient self.* New York: Villard.

7
Family Therapy with Children Who are Victims of Physical Violence

Dean M. Busby

Geoffrey L. Smith

"I remember feeling terror when I heard his voice crescendo in anger. I desperately wanted to disappear into the walls, hoping that he wouldn't find me or that, selfishly, one of my siblings would be the target of his rage. Inevitably he would stomp up the stairs and smash open my door yelling about some tool or other thing I had lost. I would cower, waiting for the blows to strike. Sometimes it was a kick in the side, other times it was a punch in the head or a yanking of the hair. I never knew where he would injure me. When the blows came it was almost a relief, at least the terror would subside for awhile. The terror was worse than the physical pain."

—Recollections of a victim of child abuse

It is not uncommon for therapists to find themselves working with a family in which terror is like another person in the session. This invisible entity is often more powerful than anyone else in the room, stifling openness, constricting affect, and impeding rapport. Although the terror is usually sitting closest to the most vulnerable members of the family, it accompanies even the perpetrators of violence; they are terrified that the truth will come out and the monster that dwells within them will be exposed. For many therapists, the terror overpowers them also and successfully keeps the secrets hidden in the walls.

Perhaps the most challenging aspect of working with families where physical violence is present is creating an environment where it is safe to disclose

164

the abuse. It is particularly difficult when all parties recognize that the costs of disclosure are often high, ranging from monitoring by state agencies to prison sentences. However, the only path to healing, whatever the cost, is through the door of honesty. This is true with all presenting problems but is especially crucial in cases of violence.

Violent tendencies are present in all of us, though few are willing to admit this. These tendencies represent the darkest side of our souls and remind us that we are all on the edge of horrible actions if we are not careful. Because violence reminds us of aspects of our personalities we would prefer to forget, we all hold a corner of the blanket of denial that shrouds this all too common problem.

One of the most liberating and healing experiences for each participant in therapy, including the therapist, is the disclosure that violence is a problem in the family. Through the disclosure, the wind that fills the sails of abuse is blocked and the family has a chance to travel a different course; without secrecy it is much more difficult to continue abusive behaviors or stay in a relationship that continues to be abusive.

Although many family members feel a great sense of relief and hope after disclosure, the resulting crises that emerge chase these positive feelings away as quickly as they came. The first few months after disclosure are often the most tumultuous months for families. It is a time when decisions are made for them by those who have the families' "best interests" in mind. As sadness and despair replace hope, it is the first of many reminders that the pathway back from trauma is slow and arduous. Sometimes it seems that just as progress begins, clients drop out of therapy or return to violent relationships.

Why would a therapist choose to work with such difficult problems? Wouldn't it be much easier and enjoyable to concentrate on "regular" parenting problems or marital difficulties, where the success rate is higher? Unfortunately, each time we have monitored the assessment files of our family therapy clinic, more than 70 percent of the clients were victims of physical or sexual violence. As was reported a few years ago, it is likely that the majority of clients seen by therapists are victims of either physical or sexual abuse (Busby, 1996). There really seems to be little choice in the matter. When a person embarks on a professional career in a helping profession, he or she implicitly agrees to spend a considerable amount of time confronting the effects of violence in families. Violence is a "regular" parenting problem or marital difficulty.

In our work as supervisors we repeatedly have the astonishing experience of hearing therapists assume that the parents they are currently working with are not violent. No questions are asked about violence. There is a persistent denial of the likelihood that, if most adult clients are victims of violence, many of the family members who are in therapy are probably violent with one another.

It is not that we must automatically presume that the parents we see in therapy are violent. Surely this would be an error as egregious as assuming that violence is very rare. It is simply important to consistently remind ourselves that violence surrounds us and is more common than we would like to admit. We must ask questions about it, we must be aware of the signs and effects that follow violence, and we must be willing to probe a bit when problems don't make sense.

Assessment of Childhood Physical Abuse

There is no uniform effect on a child or family when violence is part of the home environment. Some children appear to be tremendously resilient while others can become suicidal or severely aggressive after what some might consider "mild" abuse. This should not surprise us. Immune systems are quite variable from person to person and there is no reason to believe that our psychological immune systems are any less variable.

Since childhood physical abuse can have such a damaging effect on the child, therapists should pay particular attention to cases where there is evidence of abuse and know how to handle these situations. This is especially important since therapists are mandated reporters (Busby & Norton, 1996). Therapists not only have a responsibility to the child, but there are also negative legal implications for a therapist who ignores signs of potential abuse. The philosophy behind mandated reporting is that there are people in our society who are powerless and need extra protection. Therefore, mandated reporting has been set up to protect children from abuse. This can be important because often in family therapy the child is ignored or given minimal attention. Many family therapists believe that if problems in the couple relationship are resolved then problems with the children will improve on their own. Even if that theory is correct, in some instances it ignores the fact that childhood physical abuse should be considered a "crisis" situation and should take precedence over other issues. The damage that is done to children while the couple is working on their relationship may be irreparable.

To date, the vast majority of articles written about assessment of childhood physical abuse have focused on various instruments that families could complete to reveal any indication of physical abuse (Fantuzzo & McDermott, 1992; Hansen & Warner, 1992; Milner, 1995). Although these kinds of measures may be helpful, in most instances a marriage and family therapist will facilitate disclosure of abuse during therapy sessions rather than through paper and pencil instruments.

Indicators of Childhood Physical Abuse

This section is divided into four areas: clear signs of childhood physical abuse, developmental characteristics of physically abused children, characteristics of physically abusive parents, and interactional characteristics of abusive families. Although the indicators in these areas are more common in families where children are physically abused, it should be understood that just because a child, parent, or family has some of these characteristics, it does not necessarily mean that child abuse exists in that particular family. An abusive family may have few of the indicators mentioned in the following sections, and a family that is not abusive may have most or all of the indicators mentioned in these sections. Therapists need to be skillful and tactful when interviewing families, because reporting a family for suspected violence has several implications. If there is abuse, then there should be a report, not only because it is mandated, but also because it can set the family on a path to nonviolence. However, making a report on a family that is not abusive could lead to many problems such as loss of trust in the therapeutic relationship, the stigma of being reported, and unnecessary complications with state agencies.

Clear Signs of Childhood Physical Abuse

The most obvious way for a clinician to be alerted to a case of childhood physical abuse is to witness a situation where the child is hit or slapped. Although such instances are somewhat rare, the therapist should be particularly concerned about such an event because parents who hit their child in front of the therapist, despite clear social pressure not to do so, may be abusing the child more severely at home.

Tokarski (1988) gives other indicators of more obvious signs of childhood physical abuse. One of the most prevalent is skin injuries. A child may have burns, bruises, scratches, bite marks, and/or lacerations. Routine childhood injuries are usually different from abuse injuries. Normal injuries will often appear on knees, elbows, or the forehead. Injuries from abuse will more likely be on cheeks, abdomen, arms, or legs. If a child has many of these marks and they are at different stages of healing it may be an initial indicator that the child is a victim of physical abuse.

Another clear indicator that the child is suffering from physical abuse is to have the child or parent admit to the abuse in therapy. Young children may simply reveal their abuse when asked by the therapist. They are often too young to know that they are supposed to lie about it.

Child disclosure of abuse may be tricky for therapists to handle. In some cases children do lie, though this is not common, especially in young children. They may lie because of the embarrassing nature of the abuse, to stay with a noncustodial parent, or because lying has become habitual. In other situations the child may truly be experiencing abuse, but may not be believed. If this is the case, it can be particularly damaging for the child if the therapist does not intervene in some way. This leaves the therapist in a precarious situation: to report or not to report. Our experience has been that very few children lie about abuse. Our philosophy is that unless there are compelling reasons to disbelieve someone (e.g., history of lying, a strong motive other than violence to change his or her current living arrangements), we would report the allegations and let the state agency do the investigatory work.

Developmental Characteristics of Physically Abused Children

Children who suffer from physical abuse often have some characteristics that differentiate them from children who are not abused (Green, 1988; Kelly, 1983). Researchers have shown that some children are more prone to being abused than others. Premature infants, colicky infants, or babies who are especially unresponsive are more difficult for parents to care for, so they are more likely to be abused. Also, mentally retarded children or children with a physical defect or chronic illness may be more challenging to care for and may strain the parent's patience (Hullings-Catalano, 1996).

The general effects of violence on children are well documented and read like a shopping list from hell (Fatout, 1990, Hullings-Catalano, 1996; Jaffe, Wolfe, Wilson, & Zak, 1986; Ney, 1987; Widom, 1989). Common items on the list include acting-out behaviors such as aggression, defiance, or delinquency, and internalized responses such as depression, anxiety, or withdrawal.

Children who have not been physically abused may also exhibit the very same behaviors as those who are victimized. Violence is only one source of distressing symptoms in children. However, even though each victim of violence will have unique symptoms, or no symptoms at all, each will carry a world view that is different from someone who is not victimized. Once a child is physically abused the world becomes a place that is not safe. This perspective emerges because those who were supposed to be the most loving and protective have become perpetrators of terror and pain.

The lack of safety in a child's home environment can lead to one of three behavioral styles. The first is a hypercompliant style of interacting. The child wants to do everything possible to avoid upsetting others. In simple tasks the child may consistently defer to the preferences of others and may seem to be carefully watching others so as to predict their reactions. The second style is withdrawal. Behavioral manifestations of this style might be excessive shyness, clinging to the nondominant parent, and almost exclusively engaging in solitary play. The third style is anger. The angry child is trying to control the environment and other people by using anger. It may be that the child is severely punished for his anger but at least this is predictable rage from the parents rather than the "out of the blue" type that can be so terrifying to children. The anger will often be expressed when the child does not get his way with others and may often be used to victimize the most vulnerable siblings. Although one behavioral style may be the child's preferred way of interacting, it is not uncommon for a child to alternate between the three styles depending on his or her age or circumstances in the home.

In addition to the characteristics just mentioned, there are many developmental markers that may indicate the presence of childhood physical abuse (Green, 1988). Infants and toddlers who are abused may not be as securely attached to a primary caregiver as are other children. In session they may be particularly unresponsive, or even scared of the parent. Abused children are also more likely to be depressed. There may even be suicidal thoughts or a suicide attempt. For children who are older, there will likely be indications of trouble in school. Abused children may have a shorter attention span than other children and this will likely be manifested by poor grades, language difficulties, and aggressive behavior toward other children. A sudden change in the child's attitude from positive to more troubled could be an indicator of recent abuse. In some cases, the therapist may want to contact school officials to see how the child behaves at school.

Characteristics of Physically Abusive Parents

Although there is no single indicator of a physically abusive parent, there are several common characteristics (Kelly, 1983; Milner, 1995; Milner & Chilamkurti, 1991). Again, it should be stressed that a parent who possesses some or all of these characteristics is not necessarily abusive.

One of the primary indicators of physically abusive parents is a personal history of having been abused as a child. These parents may have learned to discipline in an abusive manner and may not be aware of other disciplinary choices (Ney, 1987). They might come from a culture that is accepting of physical violence as a means to raising children and see no problem with their manner of discipline.

There are also biological considerations to take into account. Parents who have a mental illness are more likely to physically abuse their children (Kaplan, Pelcovitz, Salzinger, & Ganeles, 1983). Parents who are depressed may be particularly susceptible to physically abusing their child.

Some characteristics specific to the parent's behavior may increase the likelihood of physical abuse in their household (Hullings-Catalano, 1996). Parents who are using drugs or alcohol are more likely to abuse their child than parents who are not using these substances. Additionally, parents who lack social support will more easily become overwhelmed with child care and eventually may hit the child. Other stressors will also increase the likelihood of childhood physical abuse. A recent divorce, loss of a job, or any major life change may produce enough stress that the parent becomes less patient and more abusive with his or her children.

Another problem that abusive parents might have is unrealistic expectations of the child. Parents who have little understanding of child development may expect a child to behave in a manner that is beyond his or her abilities. In such cases, the parent may become abusive. Also, a parent may have insufficient knowledge about other forms of disciplining children. For some abusive parents, parental skills education may be sufficient to break the cycle of abuse (Kelly, 1983).

Milner and Chilamkurti (1991) also report some personality characteristics of adults who are more likely to physically abuse their children. These adults are more angry, anxious, and rigid, less assertive and empathic, and are often unable to form attachments with other people. Many of these personality traits undoubtedly interact with some of the aforementioned characteristics of physically abusive parents. When a combination of these traits are noticed, the therapist should look for signs of physical abuse in the child.

Interactional Characteristics of Abusive Families

In a review of the literature regarding childhood physical abuse, Hullings-Catalano (1996) describes some of the characteristics common to families where there is childhood physical abuse. The five things that she mentions are isolation from the community, few social supports, noninvolvement in school affairs, children's friends not allowed in the home, and poor medical care for the children. The common factor in all of these instances is a sense of isolation from family, school, and community. If a family seems to be isolated and secretive, this could be an indication that the family is at increased risk for childhood physical abuse.

Additionally, a child's apparent fear of his or her parents could be taken as a possible indicator of physical abuse. For example, if the child often looks at his or her father or mother before speaking, playing, or even moving, it could be a sign that there is physical abuse. This "checking-out" behavior is common for children who are fearful of their parents.

Another family indicator that there is physical abuse is the "confused family." This family comes to therapy, but is noncommittal about why they are there. When pressed on the matter, they are unable to be specific about any relevant problem. This family may be guarding the secret of physical abuse. Seeing family members in individual sessions could provide an avenue for family members to speak openly, or it could lead the perpetrator to discontinue therapy for the whole family.

In the end, violence represents the breakdown of a relationship. Relationships need love, trust, compassion, and commitment to flourish. Violent relationships consist of anger, fear, force, and pain mixed with moments of love and compassion. This stream of mixed messages can be the most damaging process that occurs in violent homes. It might be much easier to recover from violence if the parent were tyrannical all the time. This would allow the child to contrast the parent with other people who are not tyrannical and eventually locate the problem in the parent rather than the self. It is never so simple. Because love and hate combine almost on a daily basis, the resulting relationships develop into a situation where neither love nor hate is trusted in or outside the home. This creates a difficulty in connecting with others. The child begins to experience the same feelings as the adults: strong feelings of love mixed with feelings of hate and loneliness. As these contrasting feelings dominate the child's emotional landscape, and inconsistent actions result, it is more and more common for the child to blame him- or herself for the violence. This is an especially pervasive problem because violent outbursts from parents are blamed on childhood behaviors and called "discipline."

Even if only one child is physically abused by one parent, all family relationships are changed. It is not uncommon for the abused child to have the strongest feelings of anger toward the nonabusing parent or sibling for failing to protect the victim (Pardeck, 1989). Marital relationships are severely strained when one spouse is violent toward a child. If there is a nonoffending parent, she or he is asked to continue to be intimate with a perpetrator of violence and to continue to be a loving parent to the victim. Most of us cannot imagine being forced to live next door to someone who has been very hurtful to our child, let alone sleep in the same bed with that person. This double bind can be devastating to the emotional stability of the parent who has the greatest chance of helping the victim heal. In addition, the whole family develops a layer of secrecy and shame. This shame increases the isolation of the family and the likelihood of more abuse. Finally, it is rare, when a parent has elected to be violent toward a child, that others in the family do not also perpetrate violence. The resulting system is one where most people regularly exchange the roles of victim and perpetrator, further impeding trust and connection in the family.

Clinical Interventions for Uncovering Suspected Abuse

Before seeing any family members, the therapist should ask the clients to complete an informed consent document. An important issue to cover in the informed consent is the therapist's obligation to report childhood physical abuse. It is essential to the client-therapist relationship for this to have been agreed upon before any parental disclosure of abuse. It models the appropriate limitations of loyalty as well as consequences that will result from the misuse of power, crucial processes that must be learned by violent and nonviolent parents. While it is true that informed consent might increase the likelihood of denial, we find that usually it is not a problem for two primary reasons. First, informed consent is obtained in the first interview and disclosures of violence usually come later, after trust has been established. This reduces the possibility of denial because of feared consequences. The second reason is that most clients will talk openly to a trusted therapist, even when there may be negative consequences. We have found that most parents want to do what is best for their child.

As previously mentioned, the best way for a therapist to know if there is childhood physical abuse in a family is to witness it. Because this rarely happens, the next best way to tell if there is abuse is to have one or all of the family members admit to the abuse in session. The following three sections of this chapter will give recommendations for interviewing children, interviewing parents, and interviewing families.

Interviewing Children

In some cases, the clinician may prefer to meet with the child alone. This would be especially appropriate if the therapist believes that the child would not be able to be completely honest about his or her situation if the parents were present. It would also be appropriate if the therapist has a strong indication that there is physical or sexual abuse.

An excellent method for interviewing children is using the "Typical Day Interview" (Gil, 1994; Smith, in press). The therapist should have a doll house with dolls to administer this interview appropriately. The child is asked to choose some dolls that represent people who live in her house and then pick a day of the week that she would like to explain. The therapist asks the child to start in the morning when everybody is waking up. The therapist takes the child through the day, asking questions that are relevant to learning the nature of the child's life. Gil (1994) suggests six primary areas that therapists should attend to in their questioning: television watching, eating habits, sleeping habits, hygiene, anger, and affection. Questions about what people in the house do when they are angry is a good way to check for possible physical abuse. Additionally, the counselor should ask the child what happens when she misbehaves. For cases of physical abuse, the therapist should have a good idea of how the child is disciplined by every person that lives in the house. The therapist should also be aware of the possibility of sexual abuse, which may be revealed during the parts of the interview that include television watching, sleeping habits, and affection.

Interviewing Parents

An effective way to help parents divulge that they have been physically abusive to their children is to let them know that you are on their side and are there to help them regardless of how awful their behavior might have been. The best way to do this is to join with them by showing them empathy (Rogers, 1980). Trust and empathy are the key building blocks for any therapeutic relationship. They are especially important when the therapist is helping clients share something that will be difficult for them to divulge. Parents who are abusive to their children often feel guilty that they are not providing an appropriate home environment for their child, but they may fear that if they tell anyone about the abuse state agencies will take the child. If the parents truly believe that the therapist is on their side and that he or she is willing to help them through any situation, then they will be more likely to seek help from the therapist by sharing abusive experiences.

Most therapists should not have a difficult time finding areas where they can effectively show empathy to an abusive parent. As discussed previously in this chapter, most abusive parents are under stressful life situations. Empathizing with the parents about their personal history of abuse, the difficulty of raising children in today's society, their particular life stressors, or whatever seems most relevant for them will help the parents gain trust in the therapist. For example, a mother who has separated from an abusive spouse and does not receive child support payments from him will no doubt be coping with extreme financial and emotional stress. If the increased stress has contributed to her physically abusive behavior, she will feel guilty and depressed. If the therapist is able to show that he or she truly cares about the client and is willing to help her through her situation, then the client will be more likely to seek the help that she needs.

The primary mechanism that therapists have to elicit disclosure from clients regarding their abusive behavior is the same mechanism they have to elicit disclosures about any other sensitive topic: a belief that the therapist is genuinely concerned for them and will be helpful. Probably the best way to develop this belief is to consistently help clients understand themselves more clearly and to provide support when intense emotions arise. Clients will often feel more clarity about their problems when the therapist picks up on cues regarding unspoken feelings or thoughts and encourages discussion. This disclosure will provide a sense of relief because the feelings are expressed and no longer need to be maintained. In addition, if the therapist can assist clients in coping with feelings in more helpful ways rather than through addictive or injurious behaviors, they will feel more trust.

Marital and family therapists have the added advantage of assisting family members to more clearly understand and support one another. Hence, through improvements in relational patterns and support, trust will build between family members as well as between family members and the therapist. Typical marital and family interventions that improve relationships are beyond the scope of this paper but one excellent method that is empirically validated is emotionally focused therapy (EFT; Johnson, 1996). While this method has not been validated with violent couples or families, it is rare that the family presents with violence at the beginning of treatment. With some EFT sessions and moderate improvements, clients will often feel sufficient trust to disclose more serious problems.

Interviewing Families

Many therapists will include as many family members as possible in the first sessions with a new case. This is the primary way to begin to see what the interactional patterns are and who holds what roles and responsibilities in the family. Obviously, if abuse has already been disclosed it may not be appropriate to see all family members in the same session.

Therapists need to evaluate the patterns of discipline in every family. Discipline is such a crucial and potentially harmful component of all families that it would be negligent not to ask detailed questions about this process. An appropriate way to discover parental disciplining techniques is through enactment (Minuchin & Fishman, 1981), a family therapy technique by which the therapist invites the family to "dance their dance" in the therapy room. By doing so, the therapist can see how the family interacts with each other.

To do an enactment around discipline, the therapist prepares a situation where the parents will have to discipline the child at some point during the interview. A simple way to do this is to provide some toys for the child to play with during therapy. Often, the therapist will get some idea of the parent-child interactions throughout the session because many parents will make occasional comments to the child concerning their behavior. Near the end of the session the therapist should ask the parents to tell the child to clean up the mess. If a parent begins to clean up for the child, the therapist should tell the parent that the child needs to clean up the mess and the parent needs to have the child do it. By observing their interactions, the therapist can glean some insight into how discipline works (or doesn't work) with the family. Depending upon the age of the child and if the therapist is feeling creative, she may ask the child and parent to switch places; the child plays the part of the parent and the parent plays the part of the child. In such role changes, the actors usually will exaggerate the role of the person that they are playing and choose to illustrate less successful instances of discipline.

While doing the enactment, the therapist must create a safe environment. The therapist needs to control the situation so that there is no violence during therapy. Also, the therapist needs to consider what may happen after the session if a child reveals, in the parents' presence, that she has been physically abused. Such a revelation may enrage the parents and result in more physical abuse when the session is over. Enactment is a powerful tool in the therapist's repertoire, but in cases of childhood physical abuse the therapist must seriously consider all possible consequences before utilizing it and design appropriate emergency procedures if the child appears to be in immediate danger. This usually includes calling the police and child protective services before the family leaves the therapy room.

Another interviewing technique that may be used in a family session or in an individual session with parent or child is having a discussion about discipline and anger. The therapist may ask a child simple questions like, "When was the last time you really got in trouble?" and "What happened to you when you did that?" Parents can be quizzed about what happens when they get angry, their methods of disciplining the child, or the last time they really "lost it" around their kids. Simple, straightforward questioning is often all that is needed to facilitate a disclosure.

Reporting Abuse to State Agencies

Once the therapist has decided that there is physical abuse and a report must be made to appropriate agencies, the best way to maintain the therapist-client relationship is to have the client be a part of the reporting process. The therapist can invite the client to make the phone call in the therapist's presence. Reporting can be difficult, but if handled well it can actually be helpful to the long-term relationship between therapist and client. It is rare, when a client self-reports and shows consistency in treatment, for state agencies to take dramatic steps like removing a parent or child permanently from the home. This fact can be shared with clients to help them understand the importance of cooperating during the reporting process and to relieve some of their anxiety. It is also helpful to envision with them what it will feel like to have agency workers in their home asking sensitive questions of all the family members. If the therapist can help them predict their own anger and vulnerability, they can make decisions about how to keep these feelings from making the situation worse.

Self-reporting is appropriate only when the source of the disclosure is the parent rather than the child. When the disclosure comes from the child, in most instances it would not be advisable to try to get the parents to self-report. Upon hearing that their child has disclosed, parents will often exert pressure on the child to recant, which has implications for harming the child even more and for interfering with the state investigation. (For a thorough consideration of therapists and mandated reporting, please see Busby and Norton, 1996.)

In instances where it appears that a parent has been violent enough to be removed from the home, it can be helpful for the therapist to encourage the parent to move out immediately on the day of the disclosure, thereby showing that he or she is willing to do whatever is necessary to repair the damage that has been done. It is our belief and practice that whenever possible the offending parent, rather than the child, should leave the home. We encourage the parents and state investigators to make this choice. This sends the appropriate message to the child that he or she has not done something wrong. In cases where there is only one parent, the child can be gently helped to understand that the separation is occurring to protect her, not because he or she is at fault.

Once the state has made a decision to intervene in the family, it is not uncommon for everyone in the family to wish that the disclosure of abuse had never happened. During this time, it is crucial for therapists to stay closely connected to all family members, including the offending parent. Initial sessions may need to include permission to express anger toward the therapist for insisting that a report was made. In this way family members are given space to express their frustrations in a safe environment and to be gently reminded that it must get worse in the short term so that they can learn to live without violence in the long term. Also, it is crucial that the frustrations of family members be centered on the abusive behaviors and the perpetrator rather than on the children who were victimized.

Sometimes families will drop out of treatment after a report is made. Although in our experience this is rare because the courts and child-protective agencies exert pressure on family members to stay in treatment, it is still a frustrating reality at times.

Treatment

Researchers indicate that one of the most important factors influencing a child's recovery from violence is the existence of supportive relationships (Sumner, 1996; Werner & Smith, 1982). This is not a profound or unexpected finding, but it is an important one to remember. If there is one person in the life of a victim who is trustworthy and nonviolent, a lifeline for recovery exists. As a result, it is natural to think of therapy, especially relationally oriented therapy, as a place where healing can begin to occur.

As family therapists, we see the family as the unit of treatment. This does not mean that all family members are in every session, or even that they are in most sessions. It means that we are always trying to consider how treatment is helping all family members and how we are helping relationships between family members improve. It is common for the treatment of violent families to revolve primarily around the victimized child and the parental subsystem, but it is a mistake to make these two subsystems the sole focus of therapy. Typically all members of a family are in pain, whether they are witnesses, victims, or perpetrators of violence. Therefore, it is important for therapists to consistently find ways to help all family members heal and to help all family relationships improve.

Assuming that disclosure has already occurred, there is much to be done in order to initiate reparative processes in violent families. The sequence of treatment will be presented as follows: philosophy of treatment, alternatives to violence, improving connections, letting go of the past, making space for uniqueness, strengthening support systems, more play, and self of the therapist.

Throughout the treatment section a case example will be used. In this case the father (James) had been violent with the children (Joshua, age 10; Matt, age 6; and Cindy, age 3) and his wife (Betty). His primary method of discipline was to yell and hit the children, sometimes to the point where he would injure them physically with harsh kicks and punches. His primary victim was Joshua, a stepson from Betty's previous relationship, though sometimes Matt would also be hit and, on rare occasions, Cindy too. He was also violent with his wife and would harass and force her to participate in sexual behaviors she found repulsive. Although Betty initially was never violent with the children, over the last several years she had begun to yell and hit the kids.

At the time this family entered treatment, Betty had just separated from James. Joshua, after an episode where his father repeatedly kicked and hit him, retreated from the outside world and began hallucinating about aliens and other imaginary beings to the point where his school insisted that he get inpatient treatment. As the therapists in the inpatient unit interviewed Joshua, it became clear that the children were being abused. Betty, under pressure from child protective workers, obtained an order of protection against James and moved into a new apartment.

Philosophy of Treatment

There are two primary forces working in families: the need to belong and the need to be unique. This striving for connectedness, the need to belong, pushes us toward people and significant relationships. When we act from the place of connection we try to fulfill the needs of the bigger whole, whether it be the family, the culture, or the earth. The end result of this striving is that we become part of meaningful relationships. If the striving for connection is not balanced with the striving for uniqueness, the sense of self is lost and terms such as "diffuse boundaries" and "enmeshment" apply.

In contrast, the need to be unique encourages individuation and mastery. It is this striving that helps us explore our universe, become creative, and develop diverse personalities. When the need to be unique is not balanced with the need to belong, selfishness and greed result and terms such as "disengaged" or "rigid" apply.

There is a dynamic tension between the need to be unique and the need to belong. Growth can be a result of this tension if individuals struggle with each other's differences and learn to negotiate belonging in a way that allows each individual to be unique. This process is known as celebrating differences.

Conflict can also be a result of the tension between the need to be unique and the need to belong. If individuals seek to impose sameness at the expense of differences, the cost will be the self-identity of those who remain in the group and alienation of those who leave the group. The negotiation of differences is one of the main forces in life that produces flexibility and growth. If differences cannot be negotiated, rigidity and stagnation are the outcome.

Individual systems are notoriously incompetent at perceiving their weaknesses and growing beyond them. Within supportive relationships there is enough leverage for partners to provide feedback to each other to help compensate for their inaccurate individual perceptions. Thus, relationships help individuals know where to grow and change, and they provide the necessary support to maintain change. In sum, supportive relationships are necessary to reach optimal levels of growth and happiness.

Conversely, nonsupportive or destructive relationships polarize individuals, thereby reinforcing inaccurate perceptions and dysfunctional behaviors. Dysfunctional behaviors can originate from many sources, but are often a result of: (1) current or past relationships in which differences cannot be negotiated and sameness is imposed (oppression) and (2) the absence of intimate relationships (deprivation). Violence is one of the most common types of dysfunctional behaviors.

In the ideal world children are raised in a nurturing environment where their connections help them feel safe to explore their uniqueness through creativity, learning, and daily experiences. Parents connected to children with a strong bond have the necessary leverage to set and enforce boundaries in ways that are not destructive to esteem. Children are compliant when they are motivated to please and stay connected with parents. The primary mechanisms for connection with children are physical touch and play. Play is also the primary mechanism for discovering uniqueness.

When the nurturing environment is weak a child develops insecurity, instead of trust and confidence, and seeks connection through whatever means possible, even destructive behaviors. Parents who have not bonded to their children do not have sufficient leverage to compel children to respect the boundaries and rules in the families. Parents then must either relinquish authority or resort to more coercive and destructive forms of discipline, such as violence.

As a result, children feel more insecure and less connected, so their acting out accelerates.

Alternatives to Violence

Two important cognitive changes need to occur before parents can be consistently capable of restraining violent tendencies. If these changes cannot occur it is doubtful whether a nonviolent environment can be sustained. While these cognitive changes are essential, they are only the first step in a larger program of treatment.

The first cognitive change is the awareness that the child must take center stage in family life. In most instances we encounter parents who see the child as important, but adult problems and interests take precedence. This means that often, when the parent is trying to get something done, the child is perceived as a nuisance and an impediment to the "important things" in life. Many violent instances revolve around times when a parent is under stress to accomplish something, to go somewhere, to talk to someone on the phone, or to take care of another adult concern. The child interferes in typical child ways to get his or her needs met and the parent becomes irritated. The child persists and becomes more disruptive and then the parent, often after yelling or using some other type of coercive behavior, resorts to violence.

Most parents, at some level, understand that their children are more important than anything else in their lives, but responsibilities get in the way of this value and it is easily forgotten. Beginning therapy by helping parents reconnect to this belief and hold it in the front of their minds is a crucial first step. Sometimes after a report has been made and parents are at risk of losing their children, they are more contrite than ever before. This contriteness makes them more open for cognitive restructuring. It is an ideal time to help them consider how their belief in the importance of their children was sublimated by less important concerns. It is also an ideal time to encourage them to consider times and ways they were taught to consider children as second class citizens. As therapists help parents touch on their own victimization, the motivation for change increases. Simple cognitive rehearsals, such as "I'd really like to finish this book, but my child is more important," can be useful. Therapists can help parents develop a list of these statements around common experiences where frustration is most likely. Initially it may be necessary to encourage daily rehearsals of the new cognitions so that these thoughts become embedded in the parents' minds.

In the case of Betty and James this cognitive shift came from different sources. Betty was in a "shell-shocked" frame of mind as she was dealing with the difficulties of leaving her husband, surviving on her own, and trying to cope with her children's disruptive behaviors. To help her survive this stressful time, she was encouraged to connect with social service systems who could provide additional financial assistance and to attend a parenting course. In conjunction with the messages from the parenting course, a dominant theme of the early sessions of therapy was that she was courageous to step out on her own and declare that her children's safety was the most important thing in her life. When she initially heard this message she grew tearful and stated how she should have left her husband much earlier. Hence, it was not difficult to help her recapture the thought and feeling that she would do anything to put her children first in her life. When she considered moving back in with James as finances became limited, and his harassment increased, she was encouraged to ask herself if she thought this is what would be best for the children and for her. Her answer was always a resounding "No."

James had a much more difficult time making the cognitive shift regarding the importance of his children. Initially he was livid with both Joshua and Betty for telling "lies." Because he was not taking responsibility for his behavior, he was mandated by the family court to attend a group for perpetrators. After attending this group for approximately six months, and seeing that he was not capable of manipulating his wife to return to him, his attitude slowly started to change. He became overwhelming lonely and aware that his life was falling apart because he was treating his family so poorly. At this point it became possible for him to take responsibility for his behavior and consider how he could see his children's needs as more important than his own.

The second cognitive shift, or reframe, is to help parents understand that compliance in their children is based on connection rather than discipline and fear. Instead of viewing acting out as needing more force and discipline, they can see it as a sign that more connection needs to occur.

The second cognitive shift can often be simply illustrated by drawing analogies between relationships that the parents have with employers or other authority figures. By helping them understand how much more willing they are to be compliant because they know their boss cares about them and is on their side (rather than because they are afraid of losing their job), they can see the importance of building connections, rather than fear.

An additional mechanism for helping parents see the power of connection in earning compliance in children, is to help them enact connective experiences in the therapy room. These experiences can include playing games together, reading stories, expressing feelings of love, and so on. The therapist may need to model these experiences with the child and then coach the parents during the session. It is important to emphasize that critical or punitive statements during these activities must be avoided so that the child and parents learn that play time is safe and nonjudgmental time. If the parents ask the child to do something, such as cleaning up the therapy room, after sharing a connective experience, the child will usually comply. This can be pointed out to the parent as evidence for the effectiveness of this approach.

In Betty and James's case it was challenging to help them believe that connection would bring the positive results that they saw from their use of fear and threats. Neither parent was raised in a family where positive support and love were expressed. While Betty and James were both helped by parenting classes, which gave them alternatives to violence, it seemed that they were not fully on board with the idea that connection would bring compliance rather than punishment. Fortunately, all three children were still naturally loving. It was easy to encourage and engage the children in expressions of love toward Betty during session. In addition, the children expressed a desire to see their father, and although this was not possible in the early stage of treatment, they were given opportunities to write letters and make phone calls to him expressing their feelings. These experiences were powerful for both parents. As both parents were encouraged to express their love to their children, there was a marked difference in the children's willingness to cooperate both in session and at home.

As these cognitive shifts occur it is essential to help family members make a nonviolent contract with each other. This contract helps each person explicitly state that they do not believe in using violence to get their way and they will not do so in the future. Obviously if this contract cannot be made by the parents it is doubtful whether the rest of treatment will be successful. It is preferable to make this contract as soon after the disclosure of abuse as possible.

The contract is only the beginning and must not be made without helping parents learn alternative disciplinary techniques. Without alternative approaches to setting boundaries and monitoring children, the nonviolence contract is doomed to fail. There are many good parenting programs from a variety of orientations that can be used to teach parents to reward positive behaviors, to ignore or extinguish negative behaviors, to establish time-out procedures, and to manage anger. Several programs include excellent videotapes with exercises and workbooks that can be done in the therapy room or at home. Many of these programs have demonstrated success rates and research supporting their use with a variety of families (see Estrada & Pinsof, 1995, for details on these programs).

Improving Connections

Since connection is the key to compliance in children and bonding is the strongest impediment to violence, a considerable amount of time must be invested in helping family members improve their relationships through play and other activities.

In many families the ability to play in connective ways has been lost. The typical activities that families engage in during free time involve interacting with a machine: watching television or videos, surfing the Internet, talking on the phone, or playing video/computer games. These activities have little value in improving connections, especially considering the violent content of so many programs and video games. In other instances siblings play with each other in more connective ways but parents do not participate.

The structure of play therapy varies depending on the severity of the abuse and the symptoms that result from the violence. In cases of mild abuse it is possible to start with family play therapy. When the child has been severely traumatized, at least some initial sessions of individual therapy may be necessary for the children and the parents.

In cases where families have experienced severe violence and the connections between parent and child are very weak, it is useful to start with child-centered nondirective play in the therapy room. This approach, originally introduced by Axiline (1969), is designed to create an environment where criticism and punishment are nonexistent so the child can freely express him- or herself through the use of play materials, such as dolls, puppets, drawing tools, clay. Initially the therapist can have the parent observe unobtrusively while the therapist models nondirective, clarifying remarks that help the child feel understood. Often, after only a session or two of this modeling, the parent can take over the role of the therapist and the therapist need only intervene when the parent resumes a nagging or punitive stance with the child.

We have found that this type of nondirective play is an excellent beginning with severely traumatized children and often is the first time they are able to experience their parent as being nonjudgmental. Once the therapy room is seen as a safe place to explore feelings and thoughts and the parent is seen as an ally, the therapist can begin to help them create this environment at home for short periods of time. It is then possible to move on to more directive play experiences in the therapy room.

When the trauma has not been as severe or is distant enough in the past that it is apparent that the parent and child have a moderate level of connection, as observed in the therapy room, it is possible to skip the nondirected play sessions. The therapist can move directly to helping the family structure a regularly scheduled playtime where the child is the center of attention and the parent offers as few structuring interventions as possible.

Joshua's retreat from reality suggested that he needed some individual sessions to help him integrate the trauma more successfully. He was seen regularly for a few months through a nondirected play approach. Joshua seemed to quickly recover from his difficulties and his psychotic symptoms receded within a few weeks of his release from the inpatient unit. He appeared to be comfortable with the therapist, so within six sessions Betty was brought into the play experiences and taught how to participate in a nondirective way.

Betty was able to participate in playful activities with Joshua and his siblings during session with some assistance from the therapist. At first she was very uncomfortable with play and kept trying to direct the children and speak to the therapist. After coaching she gave up this role and joined in the playing activities, though not very enthusiastically. We were not able to fully engage Betty in play with the children until we discovered she had been somewhat of an artist in her younger days and had let this passion die after getting married. We helped her reconnect with this talent and provided her with many opportunities to teach it to her children. This ended up being a very connective experience for them. Still, it never became easy for Betty to play with the kids. To her credit she pushed herself to do so anyway and learned to find ways that were more tolerable to her such as art and music.

James was actually more natural than Betty at playing with the kids. He had experience in athletic events and games and enjoyed playing with the children. Once supervised contact with the children began, they regularly played together. His only problem was a tendency to be too directive and demanding in his approach to games. With help he was able to recognize this as a part of his competitive upbringing and he learned to let the children lead the process.

Letting Go of the Past

Given a safe environment, children will often initiate healing processes on their own. These processes may include more physical touch with the parent, expressions of love, and a future orientation. Children are natural healers in that they do not hold grudges, they are usually optimistic, and they seek connection. If therapists are successful in changing cognitions, introducing new parenting approaches and establishing nonjudgmental play times, most of the important processes are in place to promote long-term healing.

However, we have found that in some instances parents have a hard time letting go of their guilt and pain surrounding the abusive experiences. On occasion children have unresolved feelings and thoughts about the abuse as well. It is sometimes helpful to use the concept of a forgiveness session to allow all members of the family to openly talk about what happened and express their forgiveness for past wrongs (Madanes, 1990; Trepper & Barrett, 1989). These are often very powerful sessions where rituals around letting go of the past can be initiated. Some families, especially with younger children, have created elaborate puppet-plays to act out how the old family was and then to leave this family behind for the new one they have been experiencing. With older children it is sometimes possible to create funeral-type rituals for the old ways and old pain and then to have a birthday party for the new way of being together. Families can be encouraged to repeat this party at regular intervals to celebrate their new beginning.

Both James and Betty took the opportunity to ask forgiveness of their children. The children were very touched by this experience and freely expressed their acceptance of each parent. When James apologized to his children it was particularly powerful for Joshua who never before felt like a real son. James acknowledged that he was too hard on Joshua and that it didn't have anything to do with Joshua, but was a result of his weakness. They hugged and James cried openly. After this session it was only a matter of a few weeks before Joshua decided on his own that he wanted to be a part of the supervised visitations that his siblings had been participating in for months.

Making Space for Uniqueness

As the connections improve and the family continues on the path of nonviolence it is crucial to discuss the idea of allowing space for the unique personalities and world views of each family member. It is common in violent families for parents to try and apply a singular approach to discipline and not to adjust their parenting to the different developmental stages of the children.

Discussing children in a strength-oriented perspective can be a useful way to help parents discover the different styles that work best for each child. It is also important to help parents give older children more room to lead self-directed lives where they learn from their own experiences what works and what doesn't. This is not a permissive approach to parenting as much as it is a recognition of the expanding capacities of older children. After the preschool years the worst violence often occurs during the teenage years, when the parents expect children to respond as they did when they were younger and the parents use disciplinary techniques more appropriate for preteen children. Teenagers often respond to this overcontrol and protectiveness with increasing levels of belligerence.

In order to avoid more rebellious teenage experiences it is essential for parents and children to discover at the youngest age possible the unique talents and passions of each child. This is often facilitated by experimenting with a variety of activities such as music, art, sports, and other hobbies together. Eventually each child learns what they love to do and what they are good at. With this self-confidence, more destructive forms of experimentation, such as using drugs and promiscuity, are less attractive. While this may seem impossible with multiproblem families, any success in getting children involved in community activities will benefit the whole family.

Betty was able to support Joshua, a very active child, by becoming involved in karate. This was a great benefit to both Betty and Joshua as this gave her a chance to spend more individual time with the younger children and it helped Joshua make friends outside the family. James was willing to assist with the financial burden of the classes and later supported Matt in his desire to play baseball in the local league.

Both Betty and James were encouraged to explore with each child the different talents they seemed to possess. Joshua was scientifically oriented and enjoyed the time his parents spent reading science fiction stories with him. Matt and Cindy seemed to be more artistically oriented and were given the chance to explore these talents in and out of therapy.

Strengthening Support Systems

An important side effect of helping family members develop their unique skills and talents is the broadening of support systems. Coaches, music teachers, and other community members can help children and parents expand their significant relationships. Isolation is a necessary condition for violence to continue, so any endeavors that therapists and families can engage in involving other people are beneficial.

It is not unusual for violent families to have many children and only one parent, greatly increasing the stress on the parental system. In these instances inviting extended family members or even neighbors and baby-sitters to sessions can be helpful. Developing a schedule where the parent has a few hours away from the kids during the week can assist a great deal in lowering stress levels in the home. Support groups for parents can be very helpful in developing a broader system of help and expanding friendships.

More Play

Throughout treatment and family life it is important for therapists to consistently encourage families to play. Especially when natural problems or conflicts arise, play time can do much to initiate new feelings and behaviors in families.

Scheduling special play nights or family nights can be helpful for ensuring that there is space in busy lives to reconnect through activities. Often the only thing that is needed to find time in "no time" families is to have them participate in a media fast, when they shut down the TVs and other electronic devices that are swallowing up most of the free time in family life. Additional rituals, such as storytime, walktime, or talktime can be built into family schedules. The best activities include those that encourage conversation, physical movement, and connection to the natural world. Several books provide excellent guides to activities and rituals that help families stay connected. Some examples include *The Shelter of Each Other* (Pipher, 1996), *Silver Bullets* (Rohnke, 1984), and *Quicksilver* (Rohnke & Butler, 1995).

Betty and James eventually divorced. Through the process of the divorce, stress increased and setbacks occurred. Still, both parents maintained improved relationships with their children. Although at times they would revert to anger and yelling, they did not become physically violent. They came back to therapy about once every three or four months, or when life seemed to be getting difficult. Neither parent had a background that provided a clear sense of "normal" child development, so these sessions helped them adjust their parenting and reconnect to their children until relationships improved.

Self of the Therapist

It is our experience that therapists' personal issues are often the primary impediment to successful treatment. There are three common responses to abuse that may interfere with therapists' work: denial, anger, and protectiveness. While it may be that a particular therapist experiences one response almost exclusively, others may have all three responses during the course of treatment with a family.

Some therapists cannot see around their own denial about violence, hence they don't recognize it and ignore the implicit cries of help from victims. As was stated earlier, it is likely that the majority of clients who seek help from therapists are suffering from the effects of violence (Busby, 1996). The primary reason some therapists do not know about the violence in clients' lives is because they do not want to know. This denial can be a result of many factors in the therapist's experience: poor training, naiveté, or personal experiences with violence that are still unresolved. Denial on the part of the therapist is the most serious detriment to helpful treatment because it is common for clients to give only subtle hints regarding their abuse. If therapists are not looking for these hints, clients will experience therapy as another place where they can't get the help they need. Therapy is often a last resort. As a result, when treatment is ineffective, hopelessness can overwhelm the victims of violence.

While many therapists were not abused as children, many have had negative experiences with authority figures who misused their power and created anger and resentment in the therapist. These past experiences may trigger similar feelings of anger toward perpetrators, who misuse their power over their families and children. Anger is a frightening, paralyzing feeling for victims of violence, so when they sense anger in the therapist it may result in premature termination from therapy. If therapists are consistently feeling strong anger toward violent family members, it is necessary for them to seek their own personal therapy to help them become less reactive. It is our belief that to be successful with families where violence is occurring, therapists must feel the same concern and caring for the perpetrators as they do for the victims. It is necessary to feel this care for the perpetrators in order to help victims work through their ambivalent feelings of love and hate.

Another common response from therapists that can impede treatment is a strong feeling of protectiveness. While it is natural to want to protect people who are being injured, it is not helpful to the therapy process if this is the therapist's dominant feeling. It will result in alienation of the perpetrator, which will usually engage strong feelings of loyalty in the family. The partners then return to violent relationships and family members refuse to testify in court. Again, to be helpful it is necessary for therapists to contain their reactivity and allow family members to feel and express their own feelings of anger and protectiveness. When the therapist's feelings begin to dominate the decisions and therapeutic experience, it is a replication of the client family's experience of someone in power deciding for others what needs to be done.

Sometimes professionals are simply paralyzed by fear and cannot stay connected with violent parents. The intrapersonal issues interfering with the powerful connection between people that gives healing a chance are as likely to exist between therapist and client as they are to exist between parent and child. Supervision, consultation, and personal growth experiences for therapists are crucial antidotes to the breakdown of the client/therapist relationship.

Conclusion

It is often the case that chapters on treatment approaches to difficult problems seem to imply that families progress on a smooth process of healing until they live happily ever after. Families who are violent are as varied as any other type of family: Some are very cooperative and change quickly, while others take years to even decide that help is necessary. There is more pressure with violent families, as the potential for permanent damage is ever-present. Yet families can rarely be forced to improve, just like children cannot be forced to behave.

Violence against children by their family members is one of the saddest epidemics that occurs in our society. Most of us think of the family as a place where children can be nurtured and brought up to reach their full potential. Physical abuse can have a devastating effect on children because parents are the ones who teach them what to expect from the world and give them a sense of how trusting relationships are to be managed.

Because childhood physical abuse can have such a negative influence on a child and is not an uncommon phenomenon, we must all be engaged in the process of learning about assessment, treatment, and prevention of this problem. Each time terror has left the family, a chair sits empty, ready to be occupied by more inviting entities such as empathy or compassion. With these new entities sitting next to parents and children, the youngest generation can be raised free from trauma. If we help only a few people achieve this liberation, our careers are of value to our communities.

Dean M. Busby, Ph.D., is Professor and Chair of the Human Development and Family Studies Department at Texas Tech University, Lubbock, Texas.

Geoffrey L. Smith, M.A., is Marriage and Family Therapist, Sex Abuse Treatment Program, Tulare Youth Service Bureau, Tulare, California.

References

Axiline, V. M. (1969). *Play therapy.* New York: Ballantine.

Busby, D. M. (1996). Symptoms of survivors of physical and sexual abuse. In D. M. Busby (Ed.), *The impact of violence on the family: Treatment approaches for therapists and other professionals* (pp. 213–228). Boston: Allyn & Bacon

Busby, D. M., & Norton, J. R. (1996). Therapists and mandated reporting. In D. M. Busby (Ed.), *The impact of violence on the family: Treatment approaches for therapists and other professionals* (pp. 325–342). Boston: Allyn & Bacon.

Estrada, A. U., & Pinsof, W. M. (1995). The effectiveness of family therapies for selected behavioral disorders of childhood. *Journal of Marital and Family Therapy, 21,* 403–440.

Fantuzzo, J. W., & McDermott, P. (1992). Clinical issues in the assessment of family violence involving children. In R. T. Ammerman & M. Hersen (Eds.), *Assessment of family violence: A clinical and legal sourcebook.* New York: Wiley.

Fatout, M. F. (1990). Consequences of abuse on the relationships of children. *Families in Society, 71,* 76–81.

Gil, E. (1994). *Play in family therapy.* New York: Guilford.

Green, A. H. (1988). The abused child and adolescent. In C. J. Kestenbaum & D. T. Williams (Eds.), *Handbook of clinical assessment of children and adolescents* (Vol. II). New York: New York University.

Hansen, D. J., & Warner, J. E. (1992). Child physical abuse and neglect. In R. T. Ammerman & M. Hersen (Eds.), *Assessment of family violence: A clinical and legal sourcebook* (pp. 48–85). New York: Wiley.

Hullings-Catalano, V. (1996). Physical abuse of children by parents. In D. M. Busby (Ed.), *The impact of violence on the family: Treatment approaches for therapists and other professionals* (pp. 43–74). Boston: Allyn & Bacon.

Jaffe, P., Wolfe, D., Wilson, S. K., & Zak, L. (1986). Family violence and child adjustment: A comparative analysis of girls' and boys' behaviors symptoms. *The American Journal of Psychiatry, 143,* 74–77.

Johnson, S. M. (1996). *The practice of emotionally focused marital therapy: Creating connection.* New York: Brunner/Mazel.

Kaplan, S., Pelcovitz, D., Salzinger, S., & Ganeles, D. (1983). Psychopathology of parents of abused and neglected children and adolescents. *Journal of the American Academy of Child Psychiatry, 22,* 328–344.

Kelly, J. A. (1983). *Treating child-abusive families: Intervention based on skills-training principles.* New York: Plenum.

Madanes, C. (1990). *Sex, love, and violence: Strategies for transformation.* New York: Norton.

Milner, J. S. (1995). Physical child abuse assessment: Perpetrator evaluation. In J. C. Campbell (Ed.), *Assessing dangerousness: Violence by sexual offenders, batterers, and child abusers* (pp. 161–194). Thousand Oaks: Sage.

Milner, J. S., & Chilamkurti, C. (1991). Physical child abuse perpetrator characteristics: A review of the literature. *Journal of Interpersonal Violence, 6,* 345–366.

Minuchin, S., & Fishman, C. (1981). *Family therapy techniques.* Cambridge, MA: Harvard.

Ney, P. G. (1987). The treatment of abused children: The natural sequence of events. *American Journal of Psychotherapy, XLI,* 391–401.

Pardeck, J. T. (1989). Family therapy as a treatment approach to child abuse. *Family Therapy, XVI,* 113–120.

Pipher, M. (1996). *The shelter of each other: Rebuilding our families.* New York: Grosset/Putnam.

Rogers, C. (1980). *A way of being.* New York: Houghton Mifflin.

Rohnke, C. (1984). *Silver bullets.* Beverly, MA: Project Adventure.

Rohnke, C., & Butler, S. (1995). *Quicksilver.* Dubuque, IA: Kendall & Hunt.

Smith, G. L. (in press). The typical day interview: A play therapy intervention. In T. S. Nelson & T. S. Trepper (Eds.), *101 interventions in family therapy* (Vol. II). New York: Haworth.

Sumner, K. L. (1996). Adult survivors of childhood physical abuse. In D. M. Busby (Ed.), *The impact of violence on the family: Treatment approaches for therapists and other professionals* (pp. 149–184). Boston: Allyn & Bacon.

Tokarski, P. (1988). Child physical abuse: Assessment and reporting guidelines. In A. L. Horton & J. A. Williamson (Eds.), *Abuse and religion: When praying isn't enough.* Toronto: Lexington.

Trepper, T. S., & Barrett, M. J. (1989). *Systemic treatment of incest: A therapeutic handbook.* New York: Brunner/Mazel.

Werner, E. E., & Smith, R. S. (1982). *Vulnerable but invincible: A study of resilient children.* New York: McGraw-Hill.

Widom, C. S. (1989). Does violence beget violence? A critical examination of the literature. *Psychological Bulletin, 106*(1), 3–28.

8
Anxious Children and Their Families: Affirming Courageous Alternatives

Linda Stone Fish

Michelle Jensen

Tracey Reichert

Jennifer Wainman-Sauda

Billy was 9 years old and frightened. He was afraid to go to bed because he could never fall asleep. He lay awake instead and thought about his mother dying or robbers coming into the house and killing his younger sister. He was afraid to go to school because there were some boys who picked on him and occasionally beat him up. He was afraid to eat because his food might be infected with too many chemicals, and he was afraid to go outside because there were dogs in his neighborhood that might get loose and bite him. Anxiety was organizing Billy, and it wasn't a pretty picture.

Children with anxiety that overwhelms their lives can benefit from family therapy. When children present for therapy it is important to have a thorough understanding of the anxiety and how it is organizing the child and the family. It is equally important to understand the context in which the anxiety festers. This can best be accomplished in family therapy. In this chapter, we present a three-phase treatment plan of family therapy for children with anxiety. Therapy begins by developing a therapeutic contract with both the child and the family. The second phase of therapy affirms courageous alternatives to the anxiety. In the third phase, treatment focuses on contextual variables that aid the anxiety and help the child and the family increase complexity in their lives. Complexity then gets consolidated as a way of life and takes over for anxiety.

Although we recommend family therapy for the treatment of children with anxiety, we recommend it as part of a multimodal approach, meaning that other methods of treatment may be incorporated into the healing process. Studies have shown efficacious treatment outcomes with children with anxiety disorders, utilizing a multimodal approach. Barrett (1998) evaluated a cognitive behavioral group treatment approach and found high success rates for those who received the group treatment. At one-year follow-up, the success remained and those who had received a family component to the treatment had higher success rates at follow-up. Other researchers have also shown significant improvements using family-based cognitive-behavioral treatment and cognitive-behavioral therapy (Howard & Kendall, 1997; Kendall, Flannery-Schroeder, Panichelli-Mindel, & Southam-Gerow, 1997).

Bernstein, Borchardt, and Perwien (1996) have developed practice parameters for the assessment and treatment of anxiety disorders. These include parent education, consultation to primary care physicians and school personnel, cognitive-behavioral interventions, psychodynamic psychotherapy, family therapy, and pharmacotherapy. Our general belief is that drug therapy for children should be considered only under extreme circumstances and should not be the crux of treatment. If a therapist believes that the anxiety is too serious to be effectively treated through therapy alone, then a physician should be consulted so that the child and his or her family can be assessed and evaluated for pharmacological treatment. Although there has been adequate research done on the pharmacological treatment of anxiety problems for adults, there have been few studies done regarding adequate medication for anxiety problems in children. With the exception of obsessive-compulsive disorder (Leonard, Lenane, & Swedo, 1993; Piacentini, Jaffer, & Gitow, 1992), effective medication for the treatment of childhood anxiety disorders is not well documented or supported. Birmaher and colleagues (1994) found that children with anxiety disorders improved using fluoxetine. Other common medical treatments for children include benzodiazepines and other tricyclic antidepressants. For a good review of the work that has been done on the medications for anxiety disorders see Allen, Leonard, and Swedo (1995), Kutcher, Reiter, and Gardner (1995), and Reiter, Kutcher, and Gardner (1992). Given the limited amount of established research on the effectiveness and efficacy of pediatric drug therapy for anxiety, we recommend that ongoing family therapy occur if pharmacological treatment is indeed incorporated.

Developing a Therapeutic Contract

To begin helping children and their families with anxiety, it is important to start with a thorough assessment of the child, the anxiety, and family and contextual variables. As therapists working with children, our focus is on their strengths, flexibilities, and competencies. In the initial phase of treatment, however, their struggles must also be explored. In many settings, it is necessary to diagnose children who are referred to therapy. In order to communicate with other professionals and properly serve children and their families, it is helpful to know how to assess for various childhood disorders.

The *Diagnostic and Statistical Manual, Fourth Edition* (*DSM-IV*; American Psychiatric Association, 1994), lists separation anxiety as the only childhood anxiety disorder. However, there are numerous anxiety disorders, including specific phobias, social phobias, and general anxiety disorders, that afflict children. In addition, some children in therapy may have obsessive-compulsive disorder, posttraumatic stress disorder, or acute stress disorder. These are all forms of childhood anxiety. Some of the general behavioral symptoms for anxiety disorders that are described in the *DSM-IV* include restlessness, distractibility, being compulsive, inattentive, or shy, and/or having academic problems. Unfortunately, parents present these behavioral symptoms as complaints about their children for all sorts of problems.

We are often referred children who have already had a thorough assessment done by a team of professionals. Often, parents or school systems request evaluations for possible learning disabilities and/or attention-deficit/hyperactivity disorder (ADHD). Children are referred for family therapy because they are diagnosed with anxiety. They may or may not have also been diagnosed with major or minor learning disabilities or ADHD. Sometimes, families are referred to us because the children are so anxious that therapists are unable to assess whether other developmental or biological concerns are present. Parents are often concerned and confused by the summaries they receive from professionals. Some parents focus on one or two lines and worry incessantly. To help organize our therapeutic contract, we ask for, and read carefully, the evaluations done on the child. It is important for the therapist to have a working knowledge of the assessment instruments administered, both to understand the child more thoroughly and to help parents with questions and clarifications.

Assessment

Various methods and tools have been developed to assess anxiety in children. The type used may depend on the therapist or the ultimate purpose for the assessment (Silverman, 1994). For example, some methods assess children for all disorders, while others specifically screen for anxiety. Some formats may be solely for evaluative purposes, while others may be a part of building rapport with children and families. Some professionals may simply need to administer an initial screening for disorders, while others need to pinpoint the problem and the effect it has on the child and family.

There are structured interviews that assess anxiety in children. Some assess children for a range of disorders and contain anxiety scales. These include the Diagnostic Interview Schedule for Children (DISC; Costello, Edelbrock, Dulcan, Kalas, & Klaric, 1984), the Diagnostic Interview Schedule for Children and Adolescents-Revised (DISCA-R; Welner, Reich, Herjanic, Jung, & Amado, 1987) and the Child Assessment Scale (CAS; Hodges, McKnew, Cytryn, Stern, & Kline, 1982). One structured interview that focuses solely on anxiety is the Anxiety Disorders Interview Schedule for Children (ADIS-C; Silverman & Nelles, 1988).

There are also self-report questionnaires that allow children to provide information about their anxiety. Those that contain anxiety scales and are most often used to assess a wide range of disorders are the Minnesota Multiphasic Personality Inventory (MMPI; Hathaway & McKinley, 1967) and the Behavior Assessment System for Children (BASC; Sandoval & Echandia, 1994). Two self-report instruments designed to specifically assess anxiety in children are the State-Trait Anxiety Inventory for Children (STAIC; Speilberger, 1973) and the Revised Children's Manifest Anxiety Scale (RCMAS; Reynolds & Richmond, 1985).

Other ways to assess anxiety in children are through standardized behavior checklists and behavioral observations. Two widely used checklists that have dimensions to measure anxiety are the Conners' Teacher and Parent Rating Scales (Conners, 1969, 1990) and the Child Behavior Checklist (Achenbach & Edelbrock, 1983). Both are global measures that contain subscales to identify anxiety in children. Behavioral observations of anxiety are not administered as often as checklists. While there are specific observational methods for assessing anxiety, like the Behavioral Avoidance Test (BAT; Lang & Lazovik, 1963), and recording the mannerisms of an anxious child (Dadds, Rapee, & Barrett, 1994; Strauss, 1991), these are not widely used. Instruments, checklists, and observations are all helpful assessment measures and their use depends on the context and purpose of the assessment.

Assessing children for anxiety is helpful in ruling out other biological or developmental concerns. Some symptoms of anxiety can be mistaken for other childhood problems, and vice versa. In our work, for example, children are often referred by schools or parents for a suspected attention-deficit disorder. After a thorough assessment done by a team of psychologists, social workers, psychiatrists, and family therapists, many of the children are diagnosed instead with some type of anxiety. This same type of confusion can also be found with other types of acting-out disorders. For example, children who refuse to go to school are often labeled as truant when they are really experiencing anxiety and fear of school. Some parents complain about oppositional children who have tantrums and refuse to go places, but the child may actually have some specific anxiety about what is being asked (Strauss, 1991).

Comorbidity

Apart from having behavioral characteristics similar to those of other disorders, anxiety has a high rate of comorbidity with other problems. In one study, the comorbidity rate of anxiety with other childhood disorders was 44% (McGee, Feehan, & Williams, 1995). Other issues children with anxiety often struggle with include peer deficits (Strauss, 1991), depression (Bernstein & Grafinkel, 1986; Kolvin, Berney, & Bhate, 1984; Strauss, Last, Hersen, & Kazdin, 1988), attention-deficit disorders, and oppositional behaviors (Last, Hersen, Kazdin, Finkelstein, & Strauss, 1987).

These comorbid factors may be intricately linked to one another. For example, a child who is anxious is less likely to have friends or even be able to develop relationships with peers (Strauss, 1991). It also makes sense that children who live with anxiety are depressed. Perhaps the situation that causes fear also leads to depressive symptoms. It is highly possible that being anxious and feeling alone lead to depression. Some behaviors of anxious children, such as fidgeting and distractibility, are also criteria for attention-deficit disorder. Clinicians need to assess carefully; it is possible for a child to have both types of problems. Similar to the comorbidity of attention problems are oppositional issues. Anxious children may cry, have tantrums, refuse to do things, and argue with authority. When this pattern continues out of anxiety or fear, it certainly may develop into an oppositional disorder.

Issues in the Early Stages of Treatment

When children are diagnosed with anxiety, parents are often quite dissatisfied with the label. They wonder what their children are anxious about and may continue to look for developmental or biological reasons for the anxiety. However, it is far more important to learn whether the anxiety is masking or being organized by another disorder. For instance, is a child anxious about going to school because an undetected learning disability prevents him or her from keeping up with classmates and makes him or her anxious?

Children's behavior always makes sense. In developing a therapeutic contract, we never rule out other diagnoses and continue to support parents in their search for "the truth." We think of ourselves as members of a team of imperfect professionals. We let parents know that we are convinced that at this point the mental health profession is in its infancy in terms of its understanding of the connection between biology, development, and contextual variables, although each of us has our own particular expertise. With their expertise as parents, ours as family therapists, and an open connection with other mental health professionals, together we can provide the best help available to their children. A therapeutic contract is then negotiated that leaves room for multiple truths about a child's label or diagnosis. Whether or not the child is labeled (some families want a label, others do not), we develop a contract to help ease the child's anxiety. Part of easing the anxiety is understanding how it makes sense in a child's life.

The therapeutic contract negotiates the rules and the goals of therapy. The negotiation around rules includes scheduling, payment, who is involved in therapy, and modes of interacting. Since some of our therapy techniques are nontraditional play therapy techniques, we often talk with families about using these techniques as part of the contract negotiation. We talk with families about goals, suggesting that they will be negotiated together and that they may change over time.

This first phase of contract negotiation and goal setting takes two to three sessions and is centered around gathering as much information as possible. The whole family is asked to come to therapy so that each person's viewpoint is understood. If there are other members who are important in the child's life, we ask that they attend as well. Sometimes parents want to come and talk to us before we see the child; often they would like to share information about the child without the child present, and we respect this boundary. We always encourage parents to talk with us alone at first if it makes them more comfortable. The child is never seen alone on the first visit. Parents who do not want to be involved in treatment are encouraged to seek help elsewhere.

Once the therapist and the family determine that it is indeed the child's anxiety that should be the focus of treatment, the central goal for this phase of therapy should be to understand the context of the anxiety. This includes gathering information about when the anxiety began, what the feared objects or situations are, when and where anxiety occurs, who is present when the child is most anxious, and patterns around time, frequency, and duration. An important part of comprehending the anxiety context is understanding the role that other family members play in the child's anxiety and, more specifically, how other people react to the child's anxiety. Who accommodates the child, praises the child, encourages the child to change, ridicules the child, or identifies with the child's fears and anxieties? Each member of the family is asked how he or she makes sense of the anxiety, who else in the family and in the extended family is anxious, and whether there is any connection with the child's anxiety.

It is important to gather as much information as possible from the identified child and to avoid letting other family members define the child's experience. Although we emphasize this primarily in the first phase of treatment, it should be emphasized throughout therapy. Gathering information from the child not only gives the therapist the opportunity to assess the child's abilities to think and communicate about the anxiety, it also begins the process of encouraging the child to communicate about his or her experience, which will be a vital part of the treatment. Accessing information from children always involves both direct and indirect means of expression. We incorporate Gil's (1994) play therapy techniques in all of our therapy sessions (see chapter 13). These often involve drawing, role playing, telling a story with puppets, or metaphoric story telling. We find that children are best able to express themselves using multiple mediums of expression.

Inviting family members to dialogue with the child about the anxiety is another important part of teaching the child to express his or her experience. This should not involve the parents' pressuring the child to change, but rather opportunities for the child to hear the parents say that it is important to them that the child overcome his or her fears, and that they believe in the child's abilities to do so. This is therapeutic for both the parents and the child and will help the therapist learn more about how the family communicates. Sometimes this process is difficult because the family may not be used to interacting this way—their children are not used to the parents speaking openly about their concerns, while the parents may not be accustomed to helping children identify their feelings and communicate about their experience. The therapist may be required to act as a coach and help the parents gather information from the child in as safe and nonanxious a way as possible. The goal of this process is to demonstrate to the child the importance of communicating his or her anxiety to others who can help him or her get through it. Talking about the anxiety and identifying it when it is happening is often the first step in trying to manage it.

Children with anxiety are anxious for a reason. It may be that they are biologically disposed to manifest anxiety in ways that impede their functioning. It may be that their lives are stressful. School may be painful. Learning may be difficult. Their homes may be intense and uncomfortable environments embedded in other highly anxious environments.

Family Dynamics

In studying the families of anxious children, Snyman and Rensburg (1992) found that there is a significant relationship between family functioning and children's anxiety. Overall, the families of anxious children did not communicate as well as other families. Specifically, they had more difficulty with problem solving, behavior control, family roles, affective responsiveness, and involvement. Families without anxious children reported more confidence and demonstrated better ability in coping with stressful life events. Essentially, the families without anxious children had a more optimistic outlook on problems because they had more success determining, defining, and reframing stressful events.

Some research suggests that parenting style and overall family milieu are related to anxiety levels in children. In a large cross-cultural study, Scott, Scott, and McCabe (1991) found that familial harmony and parental nurturance were associated with low anxiety and high self-esteem in children, independent of cultural type. Krohne and Hock (1991) found restrictive mother-child interactions and consistent negative feedback from a mother to her child to be significantly related to anxiety in children. Last and Strauss (1990) found that school-phobic children's mothers were more overprotective than nonanxious children's mothers. (Neither Krohne and Hock nor Last and Strauss looked at fathers.) Finally, children who have parents with mental health problems are considered to be at risk for pathology themselves. Children who are anxious are more likely to have parents with anxiety disorders or other psychiatric symptomatology (Bandura & Menlove, 1968; Bondi, Sheslow, & Garcia, 1985; Last & Strauss, 1990; Rutter et al., 1990).

In our work with anxious children we have found two common family dynamics. First, a finding that is well documented in the literature (e.g., Klein & Last, 1989; Silverman, Cerny, & Nelles, 1988) and alluded to in the paragraph above is that anxious children often have one or two anxious parents. Second, we have found that parents are deeply concerned about their anxious children but confused about how to be helpful. Parents with anxious children are some of the most willing parents we have encountered in therapy. They are often hypersensitive to the therapist's questions and feedback. Even the most nonjudgmental stance toward a family can engender guilty feelings in concerned and overwhelmed parents. Parents whose children have been diagnosed with anxiety often feel blamed, inadequate, and entirely incompetent.

When assessing children's anxiety, an assessment of other family members' anxiety is helpful. If other family members' anxiety is not addressed it may be a stumbling block for successful change in the child's anxiety. If other family members are displaying intense anxiety, they may be unable to help the child become less fearful, especially if they believe that the child's fears are warranted (Ginsburg, Silverman, & Kurtines, 1995). Often a parent can act as a powerful role model for the child around challenging fears. If a child sees a parent challenge a fear that has organized his or her life, it creates space for the child to hope for his or her own change. If other family members present with anxiety, it is helpful if the treatment goal also incorporates behavior change in those family members.

Treatment Goals

A therapeutic contract is established when people can comfortably commit to working as a family to reorganize their lives so that the anxiety is not organizing them. We listen carefully to the ways in which family members have become preoccupied by concerns around the child's anxiety. This preoccupation may take the form of wanting a definitive causal explanation for the anxiety or it may take the form of such concern that they are not able to feel satisfaction with family life. We often suggest that causal explanations are not as helpful to the cessation of anxiety as are current changes in the anxiety. We may also suggest that families begin to understand the anxiety better once changes occur in behavior. The process of committing to therapeutic goals in and of itself is often helpful in beginning the process of feeling more satisfied with family life. Families are able either to take a wait-and-see attitude about the need for further physiological evaluation or pharmacological prescription or to work on other areas as well as family therapy, for example, school consultations. They have all agreed that they can be part of the solution whether or not they are part of the problem and they have all come to recognize that they are committed to change.

Oftentimes, a child dealing with general anxiety will manifest anxiety across several different situations. The anxiety may not just be about going to school, but also about leaving the house, being left alone, going certain places, or being separated from a parent. At this stage of therapy, the first step is to determine the contract for therapy or rather, the goal for change. It is important that the treatment goal be as specific and concrete as possible. Children with anxiety will give voice to their treatment goals. They do not like feeling afraid and anxious, and their desire to make it better will allow them to talk about what they want to change. This is important not only in that it gives the child a voice of power in his or her treatment, but also because, if the information does not come from the child, it will be that much more difficult for the child to confront. If children have the power to determine the goals of their therapy, then they will have the power to take away the anxiety that is controlling their lives.

An example of a reachable treatment goal for anxiety may be for the child to stay at home with a sitter one afternoon out of the week, or attend school for the whole day without the parent. An example of an ineffective treatment goal would be that the child not get upset every time the parent leaves the house, or that the child enjoy going to school. While determining a treatment goal, therapists should be cognizant of how realistic a goal is, given the child's age and cognitive ability. When children are anxious, parents often lose perspective around typical developmental fears. It is often helpful for therapists to point out typical developmental fears. For instance, most latency-aged children do not like to be left alone, most children go through periods in which they are afraid at night, afraid of the dark, afraid of babysitters, afraid of animals, afraid of their fathers, afraid of burglars, afraid to get hurt, dirty, etc., hate school, don't want to play with friends, and prefer one parent over another. In addition, therapists should start off with one goal, and then change the therapeutic contract as therapy proceeds. If the family has too many goals it becomes difficult to focus, difficult for the child to understand what he or she is working on, and difficult to build upon small successes. Therapy that loses focus loses families.

Affirming Courageous Alternatives

The second phase of therapy begins once the therapeutic contract has been negotiated. The second phase entails working toward decreasing the hold that anxiety has on the family's life by finding ways in which the family and particularly the child have already found courageous alternatives. Our job, then, is to build on those alternatives. Children, parents, and siblings can often find times in which the child has not been organized by anxiety. By focusing on those times, dissecting them in minute details, we can discover the ingredients for other anxious moments to be negotiated more successfully.

Affirming courageous alternatives is the stage of treatment in which we challenge both the child's anxiety and the family dynamics closely associated with the anxiety. Sometimes this is done while focusing solely on the child's anxiety and other times it is done after the child has taken control of his or her anxiety. It may be easier for parents to begin to focus on other concerns at that time. During this stage we help parents encourage the child to achieve a goal, praise the child for good work, and help the child talk about his or her feelings (which often means helping the child identify feelings). This is the stage in which the family addresses the child's use of anxiety as a coping strategy. If the child and the family can learn to communicate about the feelings that the child is having, the feelings become the coping strategies rather than the anxiety. We may ask the parent to guess what the child is feeling or we may say how we would be feeling if we were in the same situation. The child learns that having feelings is part of being alive and that expressing them is encouraged. When this begins to happen, parents begin to acknowledge their own feelings, which have been overshadowed by the anxiety.

Another effective way to affirm courageous alternatives is to separate the fearful part of the child from the calm and nonanxious part of the child (Breunlin, Schwartz, & Karrer, 1992). Because children have images of themselves as constantly fearful, they are often unable to immediately label the parts of themselves that are successful, brave, and able to conquer. Parents, caught in anxiety's organizing web, are also often at a loss to describe the ways in which their children are competent. When discussing their anxiety, however, children are often able to give calm explanations of their difficulties through play, metaphor, drawing, or direct verbal communication. They show tremendous courage in the therapist's office and are often calm and nonanxious even though the situation warrants some anxiety. It is helpful at this time to identify the strength in this part of the child and help other family members to do the same. We often label the calm and nonanxious part of the child with the child's name, referring to his or her core self (Breunlin et al., 1992), and encourage the child to give us a name for the anxious part. Children have used such labels as "butterflies in my tummy," "the heebie-geebies," "the scarey place," and "the worries."

Courageous alternatives are present in the child and the family's life but the anxiety overshadows their helpful power. We think of courageous alternatives similar to the way in which White and Epston (1990) describe unique outcomes in narrative therapy. We look for situations in the family's current life that warranted anxiety and we focus on the ways in which the family coped with the anxiety rather than let the anxiety overwhelm them so that they were unable to cope. Therapy, for example, is an anxiety-producing situation. We may spend a great deal of time looking carefully at the ways in which each member in the family found the courage to come to therapy and be open and honest about their experiences. Families will be quick to tell you all the ways they were unsuccessful and the therapist must gently persist in finding the courageous alternatives that were apart of their experiences. We may say things like, "Most of the families in the world who are struggling with the same problems you encounter are too fearful to come to therapy. What did you do to conquer that fear?" They may resist this idea as a courageous act, but they cannot deny that they have successfully come to therapy. This begins the process of identifying themselves as brave human beings.

Cognitive-behavioral techniques have also been well established as effective in treating children with anxiety (Francis & Beidel, 1995; Hagopian & Slifer, 1993; Kendall, 1994; Ronen, 1996; Treadwell & Kendall, 1996). These include exposure-based techniques, systematic desensitization, contingency management, modeling, and cognitive-strategies such as self-instruction training, problem solving, and changing maladaptive self-talk about not being able to handle the anxiety-provoking situation. Cognitive-behavioral therapy techniques have much in common with the family therapy techniques we employ. The child learns to ask for and seek support, the child imagines him- or herself doing the feared activity, the child plans out how he or she is going to deal with it, and connects the activity to something else that the child already does successfully.

JODY WAS AN 8-year-old girl who presented with anxiety about leaving her mother. She had such bad stomachaches before going to school (with no physical cause) that she had missed more days than she had attended. The school was threatening to have her held back, so her mother was fighting the threat by tutoring Jody and making sure she did all assigned schoolwork. Jody was also deeply afraid when her parents went out and left her at home even though she was always left with either her grandmother or her aunt, both of whom she adored. She was afraid because she was convinced that her parents would not return. She was afraid to play in the neighborhood because there were dogs a few houses down the street. Although they were leashed or locked in the yard, she was fearful that they would escape. Jody wanted to play with her cousin who lived around the corner, but she was afraid to walk to the cousin's by herself. She had many other fears that she was afraid to tell us.

Jody's father, Bill, 30, left the family when Jody was 3 months old and returned when she was 3 years old. It was upon his return that Jody's mother, Sally, 27, developed her symptoms. Sally also had major anxiety problems that organized her life. She was afraid to leave home because she was afraid to use the bathroom in a public place. She would only go out if she had not eaten or had anything to drink for five hours before she left. Sally was also afraid to leave her home unless it was in perfect order, so she spent an inordinate amount of time cleaning and organizing. While she would walk with Jody to her cousin's house (where she was comfortable going to the bathroom), she was not always ready to go with Jody when Jody wanted to go. Because therapy began at the end of the school year, we decided to first contract on Jody's anxiety around walking to her cousin's house and leave the school problems until the fall.

Between the third and fourth sessions the family took a week's vacation in which they had to take an unplanned plane ride on a little commuter jet. They began the fourth session telling us how anxious both Jody and Sally had been about flying, describing a new anxiety that they both shared. The therapist took this opportunity, instead, to focus on affirming a courageous alternative. She said to Jody, "So Jody, you were incredibly anxious getting on that plane, but you got on it, didn't you? Tell me, did your parents knock you out and drag you on the plane?"

"No," Jody replied.

"Did they drug you and put a paper bag over your head and lead you on the plane?"

"NO," Jody chuckled.

"Did they rope you and attach you onto the wing of the plane so you could never fall off?"

"NO, NO, NO!!" Jody said. By now the parents were chuckling too.

"So how did you manage to be brave enough to get on that plane?"

"Well," Jody thoughtfully replied, "I held on tight to my mother and I pictured the plane as just like a big white box."

"You held on tight to your mother and thought the plane was just like a big white box. You got support from your mother and you found something you weren't afraid to walk into as you were getting on the plane. You know, Jody, I was going to use this session to explain to you some of the ways the experts know about conquering fears, but you already showed me that you have the knowledge that you need." The therapist looked at the parents and said, "What Jody did shows incredible sophistication. Leave it to a kid, right? She did the two things that she is supposed to do when anxiety takes over: she gets support and she conquers the fear by giving it less power. She is unbelievable. Let's go over this again."

The therapist spent about 30 minutes highlighting this sequence. The parents were quick to dismiss this as a chance event, as a temporary solution, but the therapist kept coming back to the way Jody had found a courageous alternative to this anxious event. Jody was able to relate two other instances during the vacation when she had come up with a courageous alternative, and the therapist was equally impressed. Using cognitive-behavioral techniques, the therapist continued to affirm the ways in which Jody could use knowledge she already had to deal courageously with the next anxiety-producing situation. The key to highlighting courageous alternatives is not to look for times when the child was not afraid, but to find times when the child was afraid and did something anyway. Courageous alternatives are not the absence of anxiety; they are alternatives to being overwhelmed by anxiety that stops one from living. As we affirm courageous alternatives, families recognize that it is not the anxiety that is the problem, but the way they have let the anxiety organize their lives.

MICHAEL, 7, WAS REFERRED to therapy because he was so anxious about going to sleep that it took his mother (Jessie, 30) and her boyfriend (Ryan, 34) three hours every night to get him into bed. When he finally got into bed, he would toss and turn until midnight and eventually fall asleep either on his mother's bed or lying near her bedroom door. Michael was battling real fears. When he was 2 his mother went into a drug rehabilitation center and left Michael with his dad and grandfather. His grandfather sexually molested him, so he was sent into foster care where another foster child sexually molested him. When Michael was 6, his mother felt capable of mothering him and took him from foster care. She worked hard on herself, and went to AA and NA meetings religiously. She had also been sexually abused and continued to be in a survivors group while undergoing intensive individual therapy. Ryan was also in recovery and they were both working hard to make a good life with Michael.

During the second session with Michael, Jessie, and Ryan, the family was asked to put on a puppet show. Utilizing Gil's (1994) puppet interview, the therapist told the family that she wanted them to put on a puppet show for her, and there were only two rules. First, the puppet show had to be made up, it couldn't be a story they already knew, like Cinderella or Goldilocks and the Three Bears, and second, it had to have a beginning, a middle, and an end. The therapist gave them about ten minutes to design their show while she sat behind the one-way mirror and watched the planning. When the therapist went back into the room she asked that the puppets introduce themselves, and then she watched the show. (We rarely comment on a show, but instead use it to help us explore family dynamics and intervene in future sessions using some of the puppet metaphors.) Michael orchestrated this puppet show and Jessie and Ryan went along. Most important in this puppet show was one of the characters that Michael chose to use. Michael chose a fish who had magic power and could do anything he wanted. The fish became the spokesperson for courageous alternatives, having already provided a unique outcome within the family puppet show.

In the third session the therapist had the family act out in detail their nighttime ritual in which they all attempted to get Michael to sleep. Michael confessed that the reason he could not sleep in his room was because he had monsters under his bed. "Lions and tigers and bears," he explained. The therapist asked him to pick puppets that looked like the monsters and to put them under his bed (which they had set up with pillows on the floor) while he was detailing the story. "The thing is," he said, "the monsters only come out when no one else is in the room. When my mom is lying in bed with me, they don't come out." After the family had given great details about the nighttime traumas, the therapist asked Michael to consult with the fish as to what could be done about the monsters. The therapist played the fish and coaxed Michael to talk about how to get rid of the monsters. With the therapist's encouragement, Michael was able to help the fish come up with an idea to trick the monsters into thinking that Michael's mom was still in the room after she had said good night. Together they decided that they would put a very large stuffed bear wearing mom's blonde wig and her earrings under the bed. This courageous alternative was encouraged by the therapist and by Jessie and Ryan.

Jessie had not talked to Michael about their family trauma. She had not talked to him about the physical and sexual violation that had been perpetrated upon him and she had not talked about the trauma of her leaving him. She was afraid that talking about it would stir him up and she wanted him to settle down. She was afraid to talk about it because she didn't know if she could handle it. The therapist respected her fear and also used this opportunity to affirm her courageous alternatives. Jessie and Ryan were excited about their new nighttime ritual, and the therapist suggested this excitement had, in part to do with their knowledge that Michael's monsters were real. They both wholeheartedly agreed. This was the first time that Michael had talked about the monsters and Jessie and Ryan recognized that this was a golden opportunity to open the door to the possibility of beginning to talk about the trauma. The therapist and mom then added another nighttime ritual to Michael's courageous alternative. Every night mom was to put Michael in bed and tell him that the monsters were not to come tonight because she was here to protect him. She was to apologize for not being there to protect him before when he needed protection, but state that she was here now, and there was absolutely no reason for the monsters to come back. She told the monsters that she would be sleeping under Michaels' bed to protect him. They practiced this ritual in the therapy session and the family left excited to try out this new idea. It worked. Then began the process of Jessie and Michael talking about why she had left and what had happened to him in her absence.

Consolidating Complexity

Most children are flexible and adaptive. When encouraged to talk about their anxiety, affirmed for courageous alternatives, and praised for using the calm and nonanxious parts of themselves, children are quick to change. Families and larger contexts in which the children are embedded, however, are not as quick to change. Children must learn how to cope in imperfect settings while the settings are challenged to be different. This is consolidating complexity, the task of the final phase of therapy. Anxious children are often hypersensitive to their environment. They have a keen and deep understanding of familial dynamics, when their world is threatened or threatening, and how the people they depend on are feeling. Once the self-absorbing cloud of anxiety is lifted, children are still gifted with this special sense.

Consolidating complexity is the phase of therapy when the family recognizes threatening aspects of their environments. This is a time when families decide whether they want to continue their work in therapy, change the focus on individual or couple concerns, or terminate with this initial success. They have come to recognize that they all have coping strategies for anxiety that they weren't using previously and are now able to utilize, and they have come to recognize that there are environmental as well as physiological factors that have contributed to anxiety taking over their lives in the past.

This phase of therapy focuses on helping families successfully manage the complex struggles that exist in their worlds. We help families come to terms with the fact that there are no simple solutions to their complex situations, but how they choose to cope with this complexity can make a difference in their satisfaction with their day-to-day struggles. A mother, for example, may be feeling a loyalty conflict between a child and a new partner. She may deny the conflict because she believes either that it should not exist or she is a bad person for having this experience. We, as therapists, embrace the conflict by recognizing its existence, helping clients expand alternatives to denial, and walk through the challenge to successful resolution. Consolidating complexity means learning to live with ambivalence, expanding both cognitive and behavioral alternatives, and acknowledging that life's challenges strengthen us.

Consolidating complexity is the phase in therapy when children and their families recognize that anxiety will always be a part of their lives but that it need not organize them in the same way it did when therapy began. Life after therapy is not about living without anxiety but about learning to live with it. Anxiety no longer organizes the child and the family, they instead have an unlimited capacity to organize it.

NINE-YEAR-OLD BILLY (mentioned at the beginning of this chapter) came to therapy organized by anxiety. Billy's father, a violent alcoholic who had been out of Billy's life for two years, had recently contacted his lawyer for visitation rights to see his children. Billy's mother (Darlene, 30), who had been abused by her ex-husband, was quite anxious about his reentry into their lives. She had had no contact with him and no indication whatsoever that he had changed. When she and her children entered therapy, she also had no indication that Billy knew anything about her fears or her phone conversations with her lawyer, her sister, and her mother about the situation. Billy, of course, being the smart, intuitive, and highly engaged 9-year-old that he was, knew everything.

Darlene was very concerned about Billy and took him for a psychological evaluation. Her ex-husband's mother was psychotic and she was convinced that Billy was beginning to show some of the same signs as her mother-in-law. Billy was diagnosed with anxiety and referred for family therapy. Because Darlene had explained over the phone that she was still convinced that Billy had dormant psychosis, the therapist decided to see Darlene alone for the first session. The second session was a family session with Darlene, Billy, and his sister, Amelia (5). For the third session, the therapist decided to see Billy alone. Billy was an engaged, forthright boy who was protective of his mother. Billy was seen alone so that the therapist could get an accurate sense of how much Billy knew about his father. Billy was also seen alone because Darlene wanted the therapist to assess his psychological state as accurately as possible. Darlene felt that Billy was more honest with the therapist than he had been with the evaluator and that the therapist could really tell whether he was psychotic.

Through play in the family session and through direct verbal contact in the individual session, Billy shared his knowledge about his dad. Billy and his sister did a puppet show in which a dog and a bear were having a picnic with their dad, a dinosaur. During the picnic, the dinosaur gave the dog and the bear everything they wanted to eat and played all sorts of wonderful games with them. Darlene was visibly upset during the puppet play. After the puppet play, the therapist encouraged Darlene to talk with her children about their father, their memories of him, and their hopes and dreams. They remembered only good times, did not acknowledge ever being beaten (although they had been on numerous occasions), and talked about "sort of" wanting to see him again, but being afraid to because he was not very nice to their mother. In the individual session, Billy talked about longing to reengage with his dad and gave many reasons he had come up with as to why his father had not contacted him in two years. He knew his dad had recently contacted his mother and that he would be seeing him soon.

The next four sessions focused on affirming courageous alternatives with Billy around his anxiety and doing the same with Darlene around her feelings about Billy's psychological state. Billy found access to wonderful alternatives to his anxiety. He had a favorite stuffed animal that guarded him at night, and he and his mother went over emergency plans for bad guys attacking. The therapist opened the flood gates around talking about Billy's dad and Darlene remembered a time when Billy had held his ground against his father. The therapist used this piece of information to help him with a mean boy at school. The therapist talked with Darlene about the difference between anxiety and psychosis, which seemed to help with her fears around Billy's psychological state. Darlene came to recognize that she had become part of the problem by overreacting when Billy expressed typical developmental fears. Her concern about his "hereditary psychosis" made her anxious, which just made Billy more anxious, which made her more anxious, etc. We also made connections for everyone in the family around worried feelings and the lack of stability in their lives. Billy and Amelia started asking more questions about their father outside of session and Darlene began to talk about him as well. Darlene, Billy, and Amelia acquainted themselves with their mixed feelings about Dad not being around and about his possible return. They all came to recognize that it was okay to long to see their dad and also be angry with him for his behavior and his disappearance.

Billy's anxiety was quite manageable, so the therapist asked the family whether they wanted to do anything else in therapy or think about termination. Darlene recognized that much of Billy's anxiety was fueled by the lack of stability in their lives, coupled with his intuitive nature and her own anxiety. We spoke about alternatives and Darlene decided that she wanted some sessions with her mother and sister to discuss her husband and his possible visitation. Family therapy then focused on ways in which Darlene's extended family could help her make decisions that would be in the best interest of herself and her children. Limited, supervised visitation with dad began and went very well. Dad had stopped drinking and was taking an active, yet guarded, interest in the children. Billy was doing well and therapy terminated. When asked how therapy was helpful, Billy said, "You taught me that everyone worries. Jimmy (a mean boy) worries, that's why he hits, Amelia worries, that's why she whines. Mama worries, that's why she gets that look on her face. I don't have to let my worries keep me young. I have places to go and people in my heart." Three years later Darlene recontacted the therapist for couple therapy with a new boyfriend. She reported that Billy was doing great and was no longer organized by his anxiety.

Billy successfully gained control over his anxiety as both he and his mother recognized that he had much to be anxious about and that he had courageous ways to handle his anxiety. Those courageous alternatives were activated when Billy could focus on times he had used them successfully before. Successful use of courageous alternatives breeds more successful use of them. By the end of therapy, Billy was able to spontaneously share with us many new ways in which he controlled his anxiety in situations that were threatening. Therapy was also successful because it helped facilitate space for the family to talk about and manage anxiety-provoking situations. By talking about the complexity in their lives, family members' feelings were affirmed, worries acknowledged, and alternatives to anxiety explored. Rather than running from her anxiety (which only fueled its power), Darlene was able to gather support from her extended family by embracing the complexity of visits from her ex-husband.

WHILE THIS CHAPTER has focused on concrete phases of family therapy with anxious children, these phases often merge in the real practice of therapy. Throughout the therapy process, we find ourselves redefining the therapeutic contract, affirming courageous alternatives, and consolidating complexity. While each therapeutic encounter is different, we have found that when we listen to children in a family setting, affirm their courage, embrace complexity, and maintain direction toward specific goals, the family therapy process is helpful in alleviating the devastating effects of anxiety.

Linda Stone Fish, Ph.D., is Associate Professor and Program Director, Marriage and Family Therapy Program, Syracuse University, Syracuse, New York.

Michelle Jensen, M.A., is Director of Residential Services, Northern Tier Children's Home Residential Services, Inc., Harrison Valley, Pennsylvania.

Tracey Reichert, M.A., is a family therapist and doctoral student at Syracuse University, Syracuse, New York.

Jennifer Wainman-Sauda, M.A., is a family therapist at UNIVERA, Baldwinsville, New York.

References

Achenbach, T. M., & Edelbrock, C. S. (1983). *Manual for the Child Behavior Checklist and Revised Child Behavior Profile.* Burlington, VT: University of Vermont.

Allen, A. J., Leonard, H., & Swedo, S. E. (1995). Current knowledge of medications for the treatment of childhood anxiety disorders. *Journal of the American Academy of Child and Adolescent Psychiatry, 34,* 976–986.

American Psychiatric Association. (1994). *Diagnostic and statistical manual* (4th ed.) Washington, DC: Author.

Bandura, A., & Menlove, F. (1968). Factors determining vicarious extinction of avoidance behavior through symbolic modeling. *Journal of Personality and Social Psychology, 8,* 99–108.

Barrett, P. M. (1998). Evaluation of cognitive-behavioral group treatments for childhood anxiety disorders. *Journal of Clinical Child Psychology, 17*(4), 459–468.

Bernstein, G. A., Borchardt, C. M., & Perwien, A. R. (1996). Anxiety disorders in children and adolescents: A review of the past 10 years. *Journal of the American Academy of Child and Adolescent Psychiatry, 35,* 1110–1119.

Bernstein, G. A., & Grafinkel, B. D. (1986). School phobia: The overlap of affective and anxiety disorders. *Journal of the American Academy of Child Psychiatry, 25,* 235–241.

Birmaher, B., Waterman, G. S., Ryan, N., Cully, M., Balach, L., Ingram, J., & Brodsky, M. (1994). Fluoxetine for childhood anxiety disorders. *Journal of the American Academy of Children and Adolescent Psychiatry, 33*(7), 993–999.

Bondi, A., Sheslow, D., & Garcia, L. T. (1985). An investigation of children's fears and their mothers fears. *Journal of Psychopathology and Behavioral Assessment, 7,* 1–12.

Breunlin, D., Schwartz, R., & Karrer, B. (1992). *Metaframeworks: Transcending the models of family therapy.* San Francisco: Jossey-Bass.

Conners, C. K. (1969). A teacher rating scale for use in drug studies in children. *American Journal of Psychiatry, 126,* 884–888.

Conners, C. K. (1990). *Conners' rating scales manual.* North Tonawanda, NY: Multi-Health Systems.

Costello, E. J., Edelbrock, C. S., Dulcan, M. K., Kalas, R., & Klaric, S. H. (1984). *Report to NIMH on the NIMH diagnostic interview schedule for children (DISC).* Washington, DC: National Institute of Mental Health.

Dadds, M. R., Rapee, R. M., & Barrett, P. M. (1994). In T. H. Ollendick, N. J. King, & W. Yule (Eds.), *International handbook of phobic and anxiety disorders in children and adolescents.* New York: Plenum.

Francis, G., & Beidel, D. (1995). Cognitive-behavioral psychotherapy. In J. S. March (Ed.), *Anxiety disorders in children and adolescents.* New York: Guilford.

Gil, E. (1994). Play in family therapy. New York: Guilford.

Ginsburg, G. S., Silverman, W. K., & Kurtines, W. K. (1995). Family involvement in treating children with phobic and anxiety disorders: A look ahead. *Clinical Psychology Review, 15,* 457–473.

Hagopian, L. P., & Slifer, K. J. (1993). Treatment of separation anxiety disorder with graduated exposure and reinforcement targeting school attendance: A controlled case study. *Journal of Anxiety Disorders, 7,* 271–280.

Hathaway, F. R., & McKinley, J. C. (1967). *Minnesota multiphasic personality inventory manual.* New York: Psychological Corporation.

Hodges, K., McKnew, D., Cytryn, L., Stern, L., & Kline, J. (1982). The child assessment scale (CAS) diagnostic interview: A report on reliability and validity. *Journal of the American Academy of Child Psychiatry, 24,* 437–441.

Howard, B. L., & Kendall, P. C. (1997). Cognitive-behavioral family therapy for anxiety-disordered children: A multiple-baseline evaluation. *Cognitive therapy and Research, 20*(5), 423–443.

Kendall, P. C. (1994). Treating anxiety disorders in children: Results of a randomized clinical trial. *Journal of Consulting and Clinical Psychology, 62,* 100–110.

Kendall, P. C., Flannery-Schroeder, E., Panichelli-Mindel, S. M., & Southam-Gerow, M. (1997). Therapy for youths with anxiety disorders: A second randomized clinical trial. *Journal of Consulting and Clinical Psychology, 65*(3), 366–380.

Klein, R. G., & Last, C. G. (1989). *Anxiety disorders in children.* Newbury Park, CA: Sage.

Kolvin, I., Berney, P., & Bhate, S. R. (1984). Classification and diagnosis of depression in school phobia. *British Journal of Psychiatry, 145,* 347–357.

Krohne, H., & Hock, M. (1991). Relationships between restrictive mother-child interactions and anxiety of the child. *Anxiety Research, 4,* 109–124.

Kutcher, S., Reiter, S., & Gardner, D. (1995). Pharmacotherapy: Approaches and applications. In J. S. March (Ed.), *Anxiety disorders in children and adolescents.* New York: Guilford.

Lang, P. J., & Lazovik, A. D. (1963). Experimental desensitization of a phobia. *Journal of Abnormal and Social Psychology, 66,* 519–525.

Last, C. G, Hersen, M., Kazdin, A., Finkelstein, R., & Strauss, C. C. (1987). Comparison on DSM-III separation anxiety and overanxious disorders: Demographic characteristics and patterns of comorbidity. *Journal of the American Academy of Child Psychiatry, 26,* 527–531.

Last, C. G., & Strauss, C. C. (1990). School refusal in anxiety-disordered children and adolescents. *Journal of the American Academy of Child and Adolescent Psychiatry, 29,* 31–35.

Leonard, H. L., Lenane, M. C., & Swedo, S. E. (1993). Obsessive compulsive disorder. *Child and Adolescent Psychiatry Clinics of North America, 2,* 655–666.

McGee, R., Feehan, M., & Williams, S. (1995). Comorbidity of anxiety disorders in childhood and adolescence. In G. D. Burrows, W. Roth, & R. J. Noyes (Eds.), *Handbook of anxiety, Vol. 5.* Amsterdam: Elsevier.

Piacentini, J., Jaffer, M., Gitow, A., et al. (1992). Psychopharmacological treatment of child and adolescent obsessive compulsive disorder. *Psychiatric Clinics of North America, 15,* 87–107.

Reiter, S., Kutcher, S., & Gardner, D. (1992). Anxiety disorders in children and adolescents: Clinical and related issues in pharmacological treatment. *Canadian Journal of Psychiatry, 37,* 432–438.

Reynolds, C. R., & Richmond, B. O. (1985). *Revised children's manifest anxiety scale.* Los Angeles, CA: Western Psychological Service.

Ronen, T. (1996). Self-control exposure therapy for children's anxieties: A preliminary report. *Children and Family Behavior Therapy, 18,* 1–17.

Rutter, M., McDonald, H., LeCouteur, A., Harrington, R., Bolton, P., & Bailey, A. (1990). Genetic factors in child psychiatric disorders-II: Empirical findings. *Journal of Child Psychology and Psychiatry, 31,* 39–83.

Sandoval, J., & Echandia, A. (1994). Behavioral assessment system for children. *Journal of School Psychology, 32,* 419–425.

Scott, W., Scott, R., & McCabe, M. (1991). Family relationships and children's personality: A cross-source comparison. *British Journal of Social Psychology, 30,* 1–20.

Silverman, W. K. (1994). Structured diagnostic interviews. In T. H. Ollendick, N. J. King, & W. Yule (Eds.), *International handbook of phobic and anxiety disorders in children and adolescents.* New York: Plenum.

Silverman, W. K., Cerny, J. A., & Nelles, W. B. (1988). The familial influence in anxiety disorders: Studies on the offspring of patients with anxiety disorders. In B. B. Lahey & A. E. Kazdin (Eds.), *Advances in clinical child psychology, II.* New York: Plenum.

Silverman, W. K., & Nelles, W. B. (1988). The anxiety disorders interview for children. *Journal of the American Academy of Child Psychiatry, 27,* 772–778.

Snyman, J. H., & Rensburg, E. (1992). Family functioning of anxious primary school pupils. *South African Journal of Psychology, 22,* 240–246.

Spielberger, C. D. (1973). *Manual for the state-trait anxiety inventory for children.* Palo Alto, CA: Consulting Psychologists.

Strauss, C. (1991). Assessment of anxiety in children. In R. J. Prinz (Ed.), *Advances in Behavioral Assessment of Children and Families.* London: Jessica Kingsley.

Strauss, C., Last, C., Hersen, M., & Kazdin, A. (1988). Association between anxiety and depression in children and adolescents with anxiety disorders. *Journal of Abnormal Child Psychology, 15,* 57–68.

Treadwell, K. R., & Kendall, P. C. (1996). Self-talk in youth with anxiety disorders: States of mind, content specificity, and treatment outcomes. *Journal of Consulting and Clinical Psychology, 64,* 941–950.

Welner, Z., Reich, W., Herjanic, B., Jung, K. G., & Amado, H. (1987). Reliability, validity, and parent-child agreement studies of the diagnostic interview for children and adolescents (DICA). *Journal of the American Academy of Child and Adolescent Psychiatry, 26,* 649–653.

White, M., & Epston, D. (1990). *Narrative means to therapeutic ends.* New York: Norton.

9

A Family Perspective on Assessing and Treating Childhood Depression

Nadine J. Kaslow
Michelle B. Mintzer
Lindi Ann Meadows
Chandra M. Grabill

Twelve-year-old Henry had been seen in family therapy for two years due to his older sister Sarah's serious symptoms of anorexia nervosa, binge-eating/purging type, and significant rage reactions. Throughout the family therapy, it was evident that Henry had an underlying dysthymic disorder, as evidenced by chronic dysphoria, low self-esteem, and difficulty making decisions. In addition, he was socially isolated and did not want to spend time with peers. His grades were good, and he was very creative. He was quiet during family therapy sessions and saw no reason why he needed to participate. As his sister returned home from long-term treatment out of state but continued to evidence significant rage reactions and bulimic symptoms, Henry's parents became more discouraged, frustrated, and frightened. His mother became more depressed and tearful, and his father, who historically had a bad temper, became more despondent. Concurrent with this, Henry developed symptoms consistent with a major depressive disorder, single episode, superimposed on his dysthymic disorder. Specifically, he reported feeling sad and unable to enjoy himself. Even playing computer games and doing art projects were no longer fun for him. He appeared more

*slowed down and lethargic, verbalized feeling like he hated himself,
and felt guilty about not being more accepting of his sister and her
problems. He told his parents on a number of occasions that he felt
there was no point in living and that they would be better off if he
were dead, as they would have one less thing to worry about.*

Depression runs in families (Hammen, 1991). Compared to families of nondepressed psychiatric controls, families with a depressed child are five times
more likely to have a history of lifetime depressive disorder and twice as likely
to have recurrent episodes of depression (Kovacs, Devlin, Pollock, Richards, &
Mukerji, 1997). In addition, mood disorders in youth frequently develop and/or
are maintained within the context of maladaptive family patterns (e.g., Kaslow,
Deering, & Ash, 1996; Kaslow, Deering, & Racusin, 1994; Oster & Caro,
1990; Sholevar, 1994), and adverse childhood experiences have been associated with earlier onset and greater chronicity of depression (e.g., Hammen,
1991). Despite family history and family functioning data, little attention has
been paid to family treatment for depressed youth. This chapter reviews the
pertinent literature and offers guidelines for clinicians evaluating and treating
families with a depressed youth.

Assessment

Intake Assessment

To evaluate depression in a young person, the family therapist must gather information about the child's symptoms and functioning from the child, his or her
parents, teachers, and other informants (e.g., siblings, peers). In addition to
assessing the depressed child, an evaluation should be conducted with each family member. Each person's psychological symptoms, life events, and functioning across cognitive, affective, interpersonal, adaptive behavior, and family
domains should be ascertained. Assessment of all family members is recommended, as family members may model depressive behaviors, parental depression can influence parenting behaviors, and depressed youths often reside in
families characterized by problems with emotion regulation and communication
styles that reinforce or perpetuate the child's depression. This assessment should
include both clinical interviews and self- and other-report paper and pencil measures. The clinical interviews should include all family members together and
separate interviews with individual family members, at the clinician's discretion.

Once all the information has been gathered, the therapist and family must collaboratively integrate all the data to diagnose the child's depression and formulate the social context in which it is embedded. This is crucial with depressed youths, as there is typically a lack of agreement among informants regarding these children's symptom picture and other aspects of family functioning. Appropriate treatment recommendations can be made based on this collaborative formulation.

Typical Symptoms

The most common symptoms associated with childhood depression are listed in the *DSM-IV* (American Psychiatric Association [APA], 1994) under the categories of major depressive disorder (MDD) and dysthymic disorder (DD) and include the symptoms under the MDD category listed in the section related to specific culture, age, and gender features. Most depressed children come to family therapists' offices with some combination of the following symptoms: depressed or irritable mood; anhedonia (inability to experience pleasure); decreased weight or appetite or failure to make expected weight gains; sleep disturbance; psychomotor agitation or retardation; fatigue or loss of energy; feelings of worthlessness, low self-esteem, or inappropriate guilt; concentration difficulties or indecisiveness; thoughts of death and/or suicide; somatic complaints; feelings of helplessness; and social withdrawal. For the therapist to diagnose depression, the child's symptoms must cause impairment, must reflect a change from baseline, and may not be due to uncomplicated bereavement. In determining the specific *DSM-IV* depression diagnosis that should be utilized, the clinician needs to gather information about the duration and severity of the symptoms and whether the child's symptoms reflect a maladaptive reaction to one or more stressors.

Questions To Ask

Racusin and Kaslow (1991) outlined questions to be used in a family diagnostic interview to evaluate for depression in an elementary school–aged child. With regard to psychological symptoms, the family therapist should ask each family member, including the child, about the following:

- child's mood (e.g., is he sad or irritable?)
- ability to have fun (e.g., what does the child enjoy doing?)
- vegetative symptoms (e.g., have you noticed the child having any problems with his sleep, appetite, energy levels?)

- suicidality (e.g., has the child remarked that he feels like hurting himself or wishing he was dead?)

Questions regarding the child's cognitive functioning should address:

- changes in school performance (e.g., has there been a decline in the child's school performance?)
- the child's causal attributions for negative events (e.g., does the child blame herself for bad things?)
- the child's view of herself, the world, and the future (How does the child feel about herself? Does she seem to feel hopeless about things getting better?)

It is also important to ask how the family attributes negative things that happen to the child and how critical family members are of one another. Inquiries regarding the child's emotional functioning might address:

- feelings expressed by the child, specifically sadness, irritability, apathy, boredom, and anger
- the child's capacity to tolerate dysphoria without becoming emotionally overwhelmed
- how other family members assist the child in dealing with his or her emotional life (e.g., what do you do when the child seems really sad?)

With regard to interpersonal functioning, the family therapist might inquire about:

- the child's friends (e.g., number of friends, degree of closeness, typical activities)
- the child's degree of involvement with peers
- the child's skills in getting along with adults
- the degree to which other family members are engaged in social relationships outside the home

Finally, with regard to family functioning, specific attention should be paid to:

- how the family handles negative events (e.g., divorce, death)
- level of family closeness and support
- degree of parental control of the children
- how the family handles conflict
- communication patterns in the family

Assessment Instruments

To properly assess the depressed child, the family therapist should collect information through unstructured and semi-structured clinical interviews, questionnaires, and observation. A review of semi-structured clinical interviews and questionnaires can be found in Reynolds and Johnston's (1994) *Handbook of Depression in Children and Adolescents.* The most commonly used self-report measure is the Children's Depression Inventory, and the most often used semi-structured clinical interviews are the Diagnostic Interview Survey for Children and the Schedule for Affective Disorders and Schizophrenia in School-Aged Children. These semistructured interviews, along with questionnaires regarding psychological symptoms other than depression, need to be administered to inform clinicians about comorbid psychiatric conditions and symptoms. Family interaction patterns associated with depression in children can be evaluated via standard family observational techniques. Measures may be given to ascertain the cognitive, affective, interpersonal, and family functioning of all family members (Schwartz, Kaslow, Racusin, & Carton, 1998).

Comorbid Conditions

Most depressed children meet criteria for at least one comorbid condition. Typically, they also have symptoms of anxiety, attention deficit, disruptive behavior, eating, and substance-related disorders (e.g., APA, 1994).

IN FAMILY THERAPY sessions it appeared that Henry's symptom picture was worsening, and it became necessary to do a thorough assessment of his depression. The family therapist asked Henry to complete a Children's Depres-sion Inventory, and he obtained a score of 26, which is consistent with clinically significant levels of depressive symptoms. In addition, the therapist asked Henry's parents and his primary teacher to complete the Children's Behavior Checklist and the Teacher Rating Form, respectively. These assessments revealed that Henry exhibited clinically significant levels of problems on the following subscales: anxious/depressed, withdrawn, and social problems. In addition, there was some deterioration in his school performance and he was refusing to spend time outside of school with peers. Henry did not meet diagnostic criteria for any *DSM-IV* diagnoses other than major depressive disorder and dysthymic disorder. The parents reported that because they were so overwhelmed with Sarah's difficulties, they had less time and energy to devote to Henry and to address his emotional distress. They felt very guilty about this, which further served to worsen their own depressive feelings.

Family Dynamics

Common Dynamics

Depressed youths and their siblings describe their families as less cohesive, supportive, and adaptable and more controlling and conflictual than do their nondepressed peers (for a review see McCauley & Myers, 1992). Depressed children also report less secure attachment to their parents than do children with psychiatric difficulties other than depression or children with no history of psychological problems. Family therapists often portray parents of depressed youths as controlling, autocratic, and likely to use coercive behavior. Thus, these family environments are less rewarding and more aversive (for reviews see Kaslow et al., 1994, 1996; Kaslow & Racusin, 1994; McCauley & Myers, 1992; Schwartz, Gladstone, & Kaslow, 1997). The communication patterns of both depressed parents and parents of depressed children with their offspring are often negative, critical, and hostile (Chiariello & Orvaschel, 1995). Children who are depressed, as well as those with depressed parents, are less likely to reciprocate positive family behaviors and more likely to communicate in ways that elicit negative parental responses. These reactions perpetuate the child's depressive behavior and interfere with the development of healthy self-esteem and adaptive interactions (Chiariello & Orvaschel, 1995).

Structure

Family therapists are likely to encounter depressed children in divorced families, single-parent families, and/or families of low socioeconomic status. Often these children reside in families who have experienced many negative life events, notably loss and child maltreatment (Lizardi et al., 1995).

Boundaries

Very little has been written about boundaries in families with depressed children. This probably reflects both a lack of empirical attention to this structural characteristic and the fact that boundary impairments do not appear to be the central problem in families with a depressed youth.

Cohesion

When working with the family of a depressed child, family therapists are likely to observe that family relationships lack closeness and support and that the children often feel rejected (for reviews see Kaslow et al., 1994, 1996; Kaslow

& Racusin, 1994; McCauley & Myers, 1992; Schwartz et al., 1997). Some have argued that a low level of family cohesion is the factor that contributes most to the development of depression in a young family member. This is particularly true in families that also are marked by high levels of conflict (Sheeber, Hops, Alpert, Davis, & Andrews, 1997). In addition, parents of depressed children provide low rates of positive reinforcement and positive affect. The family therapist is also likely to see that the depressed child's lack of positive communication and emotional expression toward others in his or her family contributes to this atmosphere of limited cohesion and support.

Power

Families with depressed youths are marked by inappropriate levels of family control. Family therapists often observe parents in these families attempting to control their children's behavior, suppress their children's input into their own lives, and curtail their children's emotional self-expression. This parenting style may initially result in children's compliant behavior; however, because these children are unlikely to develop age-appropriate levels of independence, they will likely feel increasingly negative about themselves and hopeless about their future. This results in their feeling powerless and behaving in a passive manner, which in turn may perpetuate their parents' oppressive behaviors (for a review see Kaslow et al., 1996).

Subsystems

The most salient subsystems in families with a depressed child, the parent-child and marital subsystems typically are marked by conflict and difficulties with conflict resolution, particularly vis-à-vis child-rearing decisions (Burbach & Borduin, 1986; Sanders, Dadds, Johnston, & Cash, 1992). In families of depressed children characterized by conflict, the children are more likely to manifest impaired social and academic performance (Chen, Rubin, & Li, 1995).

Strengths and Competencies

Despite the fact that parental depression is a risk factor for childhood depression, youths with one depressed parent and a positive bond with their nondepressed parent appear to be buffered to a large extent from the negative effects of the depressed parent's condition (Tannenbaum & Forehand, 1994). Children who encounter stressful situations are less vulnerable to depression if their families are cohesive, and this is particularly true for girls (Rubin et al., 1992).

Emotional Climate

Research on the emotional climate of families of children with depressive disorders reveals that, compared to normal controls and children with schizophrenia spectrum disorders, children with depressive disorders are more likely to have parents who are critical and emotionally overinvolved (high expressed emotion) (Asarnow, Tompson, Hamilton, Goldstein, & Guthrie, 1994). In a related vein, high rates of maternal criticism are a risk factor for either major depressive disorder or dysthymic disorder in an offspring (Schwartz, Dorer, Beardslee, Lavori, & Keller, 1990). Not surprisingly, depressed children who reside in families characterized by high levels of expressed emotion have a poorer outcome than depressed youths from families with low levels of expressed emotion (Asarnow, Goldstein, Tompson, & Guthrie, 1993).

AN ASSESSMENT OF Henry's family's dynamics revealed the following. Although historically the family had been very cohesive, his sister's illness had reduced the level of family closeness and intensified his parents' need to be more controlling. As a result, Henry felt less securely attached, particularly to his mother, as she had become the primary caretaker for his older sister. The family had little time to have fun together, and family outings typically were marked by Sarah's temper tantrums when she did not get her own way. The kitchen cabinets were locked in an effort to reduce Sarah's binging, but this made Henry feel less comfortable in his own home. Due to his parents' increasing depression and anxiety, their communications with Henry were less supportive, and they had less energy to relax and have fun as a family. Henry felt helpless in the face of his sister's rage reactions, and he often would retreat to his bedroom when she became verbally and physically out of control, thereby increasing his sense of isolation, despair, hopelessness, and helplessness.

Developmental Issues

How Depression may Affect the Child's Development

A number of authors have found that there are maladaptive consequences of depression on children's development (Lewis, 1991). Depressed affect has been associated with decreases in cognitive performance and learning, less altruism, less resistance to temptation, and negative reactions from others. Children's ability to cope with negative situations may also be decreased by depression. For example, Garber and Dodge (1991) note that depressed children report being more likely to withdraw and less likely to engage in behavioral or problem-focused coping strategies than nondepressed children. Thus, depressed children's deficits in emotional functioning, school performance, and interpersonal interactions appear to impair their capacity for age-appropriate and adaptive functioning (Kaslow & Racusin, 1990).

How Children at Different Developmental Stages Manifest Depression

Depression in preschoolers is difficult to evaluate since children at this stage have difficulty verbalizing emotional states and reflecting on their inner worlds. However, researchers have identified several symptoms associated with depression in preschoolers, including anger and irritability, sad facial expression, lability, somatic complaints, feeding and sleep problems, lethargy, excessive crying, hyper- or hypoactivity, decreased socialization, tantrums, separation anxiety, and anhedonia.

Children between the ages of 6 and 8 years old tend to express their inner experiences through behavioral problems. Therefore, a pattern of prolonged unhappiness, decreased socialization, sleep problems, irritability, lethargy, poor school performance, accident-proneness, phobias, separation anxiety, and attention-seeking behaviors are associated with depression in children of this age group.

Nine- to 12-year-olds are better able to verbalize their feelings, and thus are more likely to voice feelings of low self-esteem and helplessness when depressed. Other symptoms, such as irritability, depressed mood, sad expression, aggression, lethargy, guilt, poor school performance, phobias, and separation anxiety, are also part of the presentation of depressed older school age children. During this stage, more severe symptoms, such as suicidal ideation, hallucinations, and self-destructive behaviors, may accompany depression.

Other Individual/Developmental Issues Related to Depression in Children

Many studies have noted that depressive disorders are common among children referred for mental health evaluations. For example, Kolvin and coworkers (1991) found that one in three outpatients at a child psychiatric department had significant depression and one in four had major depression. Therefore, it is crucial to include an assessment of depression in children who are referred to mental health practitioners.

The comorbidity of depression with other psychiatric diagnoses has been a consistent research finding (Harrington, 1994). This highlights the necessity for a thorough evaluation of mood symptoms, even when children present with other significant problems. It also should be noted that depressed children often present with somatic complaints. Somatic complaints may be equivalent to a depressive complaint in adults, as children often manifest their distress via behavioral and physical symptoms. Therefore, it is important to assess mood symptoms in children with unexplained physical complaints.

HENRY'S DEPRESSIVE symptoms, in combination with stress in the home, appeared to be interfering with his age-appropriate social development. While older childhood and preadolescence are times in which peer relationships are central, Henry's discomfort with his peers, including his unwillingness to socialize with his peers either in his home or outside of school, served to further exacerbate his depressive symptoms. His father made genuine efforts to engage him in Boy Scouts, but Henry remained on the periphery at scouting activities. His parents, cognizant of his need for peer interactions, made a number of efforts to engage him in other activities with his peers, but Henry refused all such attempts.

Medication

For adults, the effectiveness of antidepressant medication is well established, but the relatively few studies of the usefulness of antidepressant medications in children have yielded mixed results. A review of placebo-controlled studies of tricyclic antidepressants (e.g., imipramine, nortriptyline, amitriptyline) in children between ages 6 and 18 years found that the difference between treatment with medication and placebo was too small to be clinically significant (Hazell, O'Connell, Heathcote, Robertson, & Henry, 1995). Also, tricyclic antidepressants often are associated with significant side effects in children, especially cardiac changes, and an overdose is potentially lethal (Ryan, 1992). However, over the past two decades, these medications have been used in clinical practice with depressed children.

The reports that selective serotonin reuptake inhibitors (SSRIs) are efficacious in the treatment of adults with major depression have led to the use of these medications in children. SSRIs include fluoxetine (Prozac), sertraline (Zoloft), paroxetine (Paxil), and fluvoxamine (Luvox). These medications have a relatively benign side-effect profile, low lethality after an overdose, and are easily administered with once-per-day dosing. From 1989 to 1994, SSRI prescriptions for children and adolescents increased fourfold (Birmaher, Ryan,

Williamson, Brent, & Kaufman, 1996). Early open studies demonstrated the effectiveness of treating depressed adolescents with fluoxetine (Boulos, Kutcher, Gardner, & Young, 1992; Colle, Belair, DiFeo, Weiss, & LaRoche, 1994). However, a placebo-controlled double blind study of a small sample of adolescents did not find significant differences between treatment with fluoxetine and placebo (Simeon, Dinicola, & Ferguson, 1990). More recently, a more methodologically sound eight-week double blind study on a large sample of children and adolescents by Emslie and colleagues (1997) found fluoxetine superior to placebo in treating acute depression. These children had severe, persistent depressive symptoms. Despite the lack of a great number of methodologically sophisticated studies documenting the usefulness of medication in treating depressed children, many child psychiatrists advocate their use. More controlled studies with large samples are needed before definitive statements can be made about the efficacy of SSRIs for treating childhood depression.

When a child is taking medication prescribed by a child psychiatrist, it is important for the therapist and physician to maintain ongoing communication in addition to having active contact with the family regarding the child's medication regimen. This is most often accomplished through phone calls and correspondence. It is helpful to the psychiatrist to hear from another professional about the course of the child's depressive symptoms over time (e.g., if they are improving, staying the same, or getting worse). Since the therapist may be more aware of stressors or positive changes potentially affecting the child's depressive symptoms, it would be helpful for the physician to be told about any changes in the family system that may be affecting the symptoms. It is also desirable for the therapist to be informed by the psychiatrist of any changes in the medication, as well as medication dosage or possible side effects, since these factors may exert an impact on the child's symptoms and treatment course.

THE FAMILY THERAPIST discussed with the family the possibility of a medication evaluation by a child psychiatrist for Henry's depressive symptoms. However, Henry adamantly refused to take medications. In addition, his parents were reluctant to have him placed on medications, particularly since he was not evidencing any of the neurovegetative symptoms of depression (sleep, appetite, or concentration problems). They were willing to reconsider this decision if his depression persisted more than three months, or if his symptoms worsened significantly. However, this discussion ultimately led to the mother deciding to seek a psychiatric evaluation for her own depressive symptoms, resulting in the initiation of a Prozac trial. Henry's mother's symptoms began to improve significantly, and a few weeks later, as his own symptoms persisted, he announced that he would like to get some medicine too. He was placed on Prozac 10 mg qam and had a positive response.

Research

There are three burgeoning bodies of research pertinent to the treatment of depressed youths: (1) treatment programs that include a parent component, (2) programs that include a family component, and (3) programs for families with both a depressed youth and a depressed parent. The relevant studies for each are reviewed below.

Stark, Rouse, and Livingston (1991) compared self-control therapy, which is a cognitive-behavioral intervention, to a traditional counseling condition. For the cognitive-behavioral groups, monthly family meetings encouraged parents to assist their children in applying new skills learned in the treatment and to increase the frequency of positive family interactions. For the traditional counseling group, monthly family meetings addressed improving communication and increasing pleasant family events. Although children receiving self-control therapy improved more than their peers in the traditional counseling group, it was unclear if this was related at all to the differences in the two sets of parent meetings. This study did demonstrate, however, the feasibility of including a parent component in the treatment of depressed children. Lewinsohn, Clarke, Hops, and Andrews (1990) compared the relative efficacy of cognitive-behavioral group treatment for the adolescent only, cognitive-behavioral group treatment for the adolescent and separate sessions for the parents, and a wait-list control. Adolescents in both treatment groups improved more than their counterparts in the control group. There was a trend suggesting that the adolescent and parent condition was more effective than the adolescent-only condition, yet few between-group differences reached statistical significance. Thus, this study lends only partial support to the inclusion of a separate parent intervention for depressed youth. Most recently, Brent, Poling, McKain, and Baugher (1993) demonstrated the feasibility, acceptability, and, to some degree, the efficacy of a psychoeducational program for parents of adolescents with mood disorders.

The only empirical study to specifically examine a family intervention for depressed youths (adolescents) was conducted by Brent and coworkers (1997), who compared cognitive, family (systemic behavior family therapy), and supportive therapies. Participants in both active interventions improved more than those in the supportive therapy group. However, adolescents receiving the cognitive-behavioral intervention demonstrated the greatest treatment gains, and their parents found that treatment to be the most credible. Again, this study demonstrates questionable efficacy for a family component to the treatment of depressed youth. It should be noted that this study was conducted with adolescents, not elementary-school–aged children, and thus the relevance of these findings to younger children is questionable.

Beardslee and his colleagues have compared the responses of children and families to two preventive intervention strategies (clinician-facilitated, manual-based, psychoeducational preventive interventions versus a standardized lecture-group discussion) that were designed to diminish risk to children in families in which one or both parents suffered from a mood disorder (Beardslee, Wright, Rothberg, Salt, & Versage, 1996; Beardslee et al., 1997). Results revealed that although both preventive interventions produced changes in behaviors and attitudes, parents in the clinician-facilitated intervention reported more benefit. Similarly, children in the clinician-facilitated group reported greater understanding of parental affective disorder and demonstrated improved adaptive functioning after the intervention.

Treatment Plan

Interpersonal family therapy (IFT) is a model for assessing and intervening with families of depressed school-age children in 16 sessions (Kaslow & Racusin, 1994; Racusin & Kaslow, 1991). This framework incorporates family systems theory, cognitive-behavioral psychology, object relations theory, and developmental psychopathology. The family intervention is based on the principle that the reduction of children's depressive symptoms is done by focusing on current difficulties as they reflect dysfunctional family interactional processes.

Session Participants

Ideally, the initial assessment should include the identified patient, the parent(s) or principal caretakers, the depressed child's siblings, and other significant family members (e.g., grandparents living in the home, stepparents, step- or half-siblings). This format enables the clinician to obtain information about each family member and their interactions, especially as they contribute to the precipitation and maintenance of the child's depressive symptoms. Given the high rates of parental psychopathology in families of depressed children, the clinician will want to evaluate the parents' psychiatric status. Also, in families with one depressed parent, the strengths of the nondepressed parent need to be assessed, since this can influence the intervention process (Sholevar, 1994).

The decision of who should participate in each of the initial evaluative sessions depends on a number of factors. The family constellation (e.g., nuclear, single-parent, stepfamily), the custody status of the identified patient, the family living situation, and the age of the participants are all significant. If the family is intact, then all family members residing in the home participate in the first evaluation session. Subsystems of the family may be asked to participate in subsequent assessment sessions. In single-parent families, the family unit with whom the child primarily lives should attend the initial evaluation session. If possible, subsequent assessment sessions should include all the family subsystems in which the child is involved. From the information obtained during the evaluation phase, the clinician defines the main tasks of the intervention phase. These tasks determine who should participate in the subsequent intervention sessions and in what pattern.

Treatment Goals and Progress

The initial phase of IFT has several goals, notably those of joining with the family in a manner that permits subsequent assessment and therapeutic intervention, carrying out the assessment, sharing the results of the assessment with the family, and educating the family about depression as it is expressed in their particular family. Based on the data gleaned from the assessment, problems and goals are defined in behavioral and interpersonal terms (Shaffi & Shaffi, 1992). Subsequent interventions are designed to ameliorate psychological symptoms, enhance the quality of the family interactions, and improve functioning in cognitive, affective, interpersonal, and adaptive behavior domains.

When to Collaborate with Other Systems

Since children have significant ongoing relationships with others outside the nuclear family (e.g., in school, recreational groups, religious groups, and with extended family members), it is often important to involve these systems in the assessment and treatment of the depressed child and his or her family. Many clinicians have noted a low concordance between parents' and children's ratings of the child's depressive symptoms using standardized interview instruments (for a review, see Kazdin, 1994). This may be due to the fact that children usually give a better account of internalizing symptoms, while parents are more aware of overt behavior difficulties. Parental information may also be influenced by a parent's own psychopathology, which highlights the importance of obtaining information not only from the parents, but from other collateral sources.

Involving other systems in treatment can be helpful in optimizing the therapeutic potential of all the environments in which a child interacts. For example, if a depressed 4-year-old has tantrums and a labile mood in preschool, it would be helpful to communicate with the teacher to learn how the child's difficulties manifest in the school setting. This also would provide an opportunity to explain the nature of the child's problems to the teacher so the child is not labeled in a negative fashion. If the teacher is amenable, the therapist can offer support and suggestions on how to handle the child's behaviors and help increase the child's confidence and self-esteem in school.

When extended family members have ongoing contact with the child, they may be enlisted to offer support for the depressed child and his family. For example, a grandparent, aunt, or uncle may be asked to spend special one-on-one time with the child on a regular basis to help enhance his or her self-image and decrease his or her negative, attention-seeking behaviors. This also may be supportive to the nuclear family by providing an additional source of nurturance for the child.

Coordination of Treatment with Other Professionals

When a depressed child is having difficulties, a number of professionals may become involved with the family. In some schools, case conferences are held where the therapist, child psychiatrist (if the child is on medication), and the parents are invited to meet with the teacher, school psychologist, and other relevant school personnel. This affords an opportunity for all the professionals to share their understanding of the child's difficulties and coordinate their treatment efforts. Unfortunately, because depressed children often present as sad and withdrawn but are not disruptive in the classroom environment, school-based case conferences may not be initiated by school personnel. In such instances, it behooves the clinician to work with the family and the school in arranging such a meeting. When network meetings are not feasible, telephone calls, letters, case note reviews, and the collection of information from as many sources as possible can greatly enrich treatment.

If a child is receiving medication for his or her depressive symptoms or comorbid psychiatric disorders, it is important for the family and the therapist to maintain communication with the psychiatrist to help coordinate treatment.

If the child presents with suicidal thoughts, all appropriate members of the treatment team should be involved in assessing the potential risk of self-harm and making appropriate disposition decisions. Since many depressed children present with somatic complaints (e.g., headaches, stomachaches), it may be important to communicate with the child's pediatrician. Since some physical problems (e.g., inflammatory bowel disease, endocrine disorders) may cause significant depression, the child should have a physical examination to rule out any organic basis for the mood disorder. Laboratory studies to look for signs of anemia, infection, or metabolic abnormalities also should be part of the medical work-up.

Interventions

Sessions 1 and 2: Joining and Assessment

The primary tasks of the first two sessions are to (1) join with the family and (2) provide a comprehensive assessment of the family system. To join with families with a depressed child, the clinician must empathize with the vicissitudes of depression in the family and child, while maintaining clinical objectivity and communicating hope. This approach expresses respect for the family's distress and belief in their potential to effect positive change via modification of distorted cognitions. Joining also aids in the reparation of disrupted family attachments and leads to the development of more positive, secure, and developmentally appropriate relationships (Diamond & Siqueland, 1995). This helps ameliorate the current depression and family members' vulnerability to future depression and improves overall family functioning.

Since assessment is integral to IFT, sessions 1 and 2 entail a comprehensive assessment of the child's and family's current functioning across a broad range of domains. This assessment has been discussed previously and thus will not be the focus here.

Session 3: Feedback and Disposition

The goals of the third session are to (1) ascertain the need for adjunctive treatment resources, (2) determine if family treatment is the treatment of choice, (3) provide assessment feedback to the family and collaborate with them in devising a treatment plan, and (4) educate the family about depression. Since the fourth goal is unique to working with families with a depressed child, it is to this component of the session that we now turn our attention.

To educate the family about various topics related to the child's depression and to family interventions, the therapist should dialogue with the family while imparting information and answering questions. This educational approach empowers families by reducing their bewilderment regarding the child's difficulties, increasing their sense of hope for change, and laying the groundwork for subsequent interventions. The clinician and family should discuss the psychological symptoms associated with depression, functional domains affected by depression, common precipitants of depression, and the IFT approach to treatment. When a positive family history for mood disorders suggests that the child's depression partially expresses an underlying biological vulnerability, data regarding the genetics and biological vulnerability of mood disorders should be provided (Shulman, Tohen, & Kutcher, 1996). While such information may be painful for the family to hear, it may reduce the extent to which the child is blamed and/or feels guilty for depressive symptoms. The family therapist may also want to recommend self-help books and other reading materials that address childhood depression and other related problems (e.g., divorce, parental death, self-esteem). Many families appreciate reading books such as *The Optimistic Child: A Revolutionary Program that Safeguards Children against Depression and Builds Lifelong Resilience* (Seligman, Reivich, Jaycox, & Gillham, 1995).

Session 4: Psychological Symptomatology

The goals of session 4 are to (1) teach strategies to alleviate specific depressive symptoms, (2) identify precipitants of depressive reactions and teach the child and family more adaptive ways to cope with these stressors, and (3) reframe the child's psychological symptoms and decrease scapegoating of the depressed child. This session targets only the behavioral and vegetative symptoms of depression, since the affective and cognitive sequelae of the disorder are addressed in later sessions. For example, a suicidally depressed youth who does not require hospitalization may respond to a suicide contract combined with cognitive and problem-solving interventions targeting his or her suicidality. Similarly, interventions may be designed to target sleep, appetite problems, and/or other behavioral or vegetative symptoms.

As the session shifts to the relation between stress and depression, it is useful for the therapist to ask about family events (e.g., divorce, death, discord) that may have precipitated or be maintaining the child's depression. Attention should be paid to family members' interpretation of these events and the therapist should challenge distorted interpretations and help the family devise strategies for addressing these stresses. The clinician and family should ascertain potential future stressors both within and outside the family and work together to devise a plan to manage these stresses.

To address the final aim of this session, the therapist should help the family to understand the links among the child's depression, family problems, and family interactions regarding the child. In this discussion and throughout the intervention it behooves the therapist to block scapegoating or blaming of the depressed child or other family members for the child's difficulties. Rather than blaming the child for personal or family problems, the child's depression should be framed by the therapist as emblematic of multiple determinants, including family interactional processes, individual child factors, and genetic or biological predispositions. Reframing alleviates the child's self-blame and guilt, and thus may improve the child's self-esteem.

Sessions 5 and 6: Cognitive Functioning

The goals of sessions 5 and 6 are to (1) provide education about the negative cognitive triad, depressogenic attributional patterns, and faulty information processing, (2) teach ways to identify depressive cognitive patterns, and (3) challenge and change the depressive cognitive patterns within the family system that maintain or exacerbate the child's depression. The therapist educates the family members about cognitive patterns associated with the child's depressive feelings and behaviors. It is useful to explain the concept of the negative cognitive triad to help the family understand that depression is associated with a pervasive negative view, such that the depressed child feels badly about him- or herself (low self-esteem), feels the world is a negative place, and feels hopeless about the future. In addition, the therapist should communicate that depressed youths tend to make systematic errors in thinking that reinforce negative beliefs, regardless of evidence to the contrary.

Next, the clinician helps family members to identify the presence of automatic thoughts in their everyday lives by attending to each family member's descriptions and perceptions of life events and encouraging each member to be cognizant of those thought patterns associated with dysphoric affect. The primary goal of these sessions is to challenge and change those maladaptive cognitive processes that maintain or exacerbate the child's depression; particular attention should be paid to modifying depressive cognitions evidenced in dysfunctional parent-child interactions.

Sessions 7 and 8: Affective Functioning

The goals of sessions 7 and 8 are to (1) teach family members to label and verbalize both negative and positive affects and (2) educate the family regarding adaptive strategies for affect regulation. Children and their families first need to be instructed in basic labels for different emotions (e.g., anger, sadness, fear, happiness) and how to differentiate various feelings. Initially, this instruction should be done in a relatively neutral context, such as through the use of board games like the "Talking, Feeling, and Doing Game" or feeling posters. Once all family members have an understanding of the range of positive and negative emotions, they can use the acquired communication skills to discuss times when they have experienced various feelings. They are also encouraged to label and express their feelings toward one another. The final step in teaching family members to label and verbalize their feelings is helping them identify the links among events, thoughts, and emotions for positive and negative affective states.

These sessions should also help the child acquire developmentally appropriate cognitive, behavioral, and interpersonal strategies for affect regulation that are consistent with parental rules. For example, parents may encourage their child to discuss feelings when upset, rather than act out in behaviorally maladaptive ways or withdraw and emotionally "shut down." Parents may need to demonstrate appropriate conditions under which to express particular emotions, methods for expressing and regulating these emotions, and consequences accruing from such emotional expression (Garber & Dodge, 1991). The therapist must attend to the presence of parental depression and its effects on the child. Family intervention entails helping the depressed parent modulate affective distress more adaptively in order to provide a context supporting healthy emotional development in the child.

Sessions 9 and 10: Interpersonal Functioning

The goals of sessions 9 and 10 are to (1) improve interpersonal problem-solving skills and increase positive communication within the family, (2) assist the child in the development of social and relationship skills in order to improve his or her interpersonal functioning with peers, and (3) increase involvement in pleasurable activities with peers. Depressed children often exhibit deficits in pleasurable interpersonal functioning with siblings and peers, and the families of depressed children frequently have difficulties with interpersonal problem-solving and communication. The therapist can identify the family's communication strengths and deficits, reframe the family's problems in interactional terms, and help the family correct negative communication patterns consistently. Family members can be taught to utilize interpersonal problem-solving skills to resolve difficulties in and out of the family. Parents can help their children solve interpersonal problems by teaching strategies for responding to difficult social situations, encouraging active rather than passive approaches to increasing their social networks, and challenging negative cognitions children may have about how peers view them. Finally, the family is encouraged to engage in pleasurable family activities. It is important that parents participate in adult activities as a couple and with peers in order to model appropriate interaction skills for their children.

Session 11: Adaptive Behavior

The goals of session 11 are to (1) educate the family about age-appropriate adaptive behaviors and (2) facilitate acquisition and utilization of age-appropriate adaptive behaviors. Depressed children are often delayed in their acquisition of age-appropriate adaptive behavior skills in three areas: communication, daily living skills, and socialization. Since problems in socialization are addressed earlier in the treatment, this session focuses on age-appropriate communication and daily living skills. The family is educated in these areas so that expectations for the child's performance are neither too high nor too low. The therapist should explain the ways in which the child's depression and family patterns have delayed the child's acquisition of age-appropriate adaptive behaviors. For example, the child's deficits in communication skills can be addressed by pointing out ways family members speak for the depressed child, ignore the child's efforts to communicate, or refute or devalue the child's assertions. To address deficits in communication, the clinician can teach communication skills by first providing didactic information and then having the family practice the skills, first with neutral and then with affect-laden topics, both in and out of session. The child's impaired utilization of age-appropriate daily living skills should also be addressed. First, when children have not acquired these skills because of inadequate parenting, the parents are helped to teach their child these skills systematically. Second, when children fail to utilize acquired age-appropriate daily living skills, parents are supported in developing strategies to encourage and reinforce their child's use of these skills. Third, other family members are encouraged to help the depressed child engage in more self-care activities.

Sessions 12 and 13: Family Functioning

The goals of sessions 12 and 13 are to (1) identify dysfunctional family interaction patterns, and (2) promote changes in the structure of the family system. In this session, the therapist can identify maladaptive interactional patterns by "mapping" the family structure with a focus on subsystems, boundaries, and family members' roles. The therapist also can help the family discover the intrapsychic and interpersonal mechanisms that maintain depression within the family system. To address the identified maladaptive patterns, the therapist assists the family in making structural changes by strengthening the executive subsystem, restructuring the familial hierarchy, and facilitating changes in the family rules and interaction sequences maintaining undesirable behaviors. New interaction patterns can be practiced in session so that the therapist can give feedback, and the effects of these patterns can be discussed and understood. Additionally, the family is encouraged to implement these new patterns and strategies outside of therapy in order to generalize these skills and prepare to depart from therapy.

Sessions 14–16: Review, Synthesis, and Postassessment

The goals of sessions 14–16 are to (1) review information provided in prior sessions and troubleshoot about problem areas, (2) evaluate the family's progress, and (3) address termination issues. It is common for families to experience a reemergence of psychological symptoms during the concluding phases of therapy. The therapist should acknowledge the family's previously demonstrated capacity to problem-solve and help the family to recognize and take responsibility for the gains that occurred during the intervention. To ascertain the family's progress in IFT, a posttreatment assessment, which is similar to the initial evaluation, should be conducted, and feedback about progress, strengths, and weaknesses should be given to the family during the last sessions. Finally, adequate time should be devoted to the process of termination during the last few sessions. The therapist should acknowledge the impending conclusion of treatment, focus on the grief evoked by the termination, and emphasize the family's acquired competence to deal more adaptively with distressing life events, capitalizing on the family unit as a resource for coping. The intervention concludes with a "soft therapy" termination, as an open-door policy is underscored in IFT.

IT IS IMPORTANT TO note that, at the beginning of therapy, after an initial assessment and evaluation of family functioning, the therapist joined with Henry's family by sharing with them the results of the evaluation and enlisting their help in defining the main task of the intervention. Henry's parents initially reported that the main reason they had come to therapy was to solve Henry's worsening problems of sadness, self-hatred, and social isolation. After meeting with the therapist several times, however, including sessions during which the therapist shared with them current views of childhood depression and its links to stress and family interactions, Henry's parents began to see the main task of therapy as a broader-based, family responsibility focused on improving the ways in which they, Henry, and Sarah related to each other. A favorite aunt of Henry's was enlisted in this effort, and she set aside an evening each week to take Henry shopping, to dinner, or to a movie. Eventually, Henry's aunt was able to encourage him to bring a schoolmate or neighbor along on their outings. Although Henry's teacher initially did not see the importance of a case conference on Henry's behalf, stating, "He's just quiet and apathetic," a meeting was scheduled at the urging of both Henry's psychiatrist and therapist. During this conference, Henry's teacher learned more about Henry, the stresses at home, and that Henry's depressed mood and detached manner reflected a transient rather than permanent state. His teacher reported that she now viewed Henry in a different light and would seek to encourage and involve him more in the classroom. "I always knew he was bright," she said, "I just thought he didn't care and his parents didn't care." This was a revelation to Henry's parents, who began to wonder what else they could do to help Henry in school. Henry's father began setting aside a special time several days a week to be available to help Henry with his homework. In addition, depressive cognitive patterns, such as the parents' worsening guilt about ignoring Henry and Henry's worsening guilt about ignoring his sister, began to be challenged by the therapist and were identified as maladaptive. All family members were educated about the pervasive negative views of self, world, and future experienced by people who are depressed. The evening that Henry spent with his aunt allowed Henry's parents an evening to work on their interactions with Sarah. All family members were then encouraged to share with each other their interactional experiences and to practice new, more adaptive ways of relating to one another during family therapy sessions. As Henry's mother's functioning continued to improve while on antidepressant medication, Henry's father became more open about verbalizing his anger rather than "feeling guilty" or acting it out. The therapist enlisted Henry's parents to set family rules for expressing emotional reactions. Times were set aside in therapy during which Henry was allowed to openly express his anger, sadness, or annoyance. The therapist joined with Henry by encouraging him to clarify his communications with his parents, and encouraged

Henry's parents to do the same with Henry. Initially timid, Henry blurted out during one especially emotional session, "Oh! You mean this isn't all my fault?" Henry's parents were stunned that Henry had ever considered taking so much blame. Sarah was equally surprised. With this burden lifted from him, and with the continued help of antidepressant medication, Henry's negative ruminations lessened. He began to talk more on the phone with his peers, and he put up new posters on his bedroom walls. Negative interactions among Henry and other family members decreased. Sarah's behavior, too, showed an improved ability to clarify her feelings and a sense of hope for some measure of control over her eating disorder. Henry's parents, who had given up spending time as a couple, began to do so again. In short, even though all of the family's problems had not been solved, the family itself began to reorganize around its newly acquired competencies. Not only had Henry's depressive symptoms decreased, but also the family as a whole had become a more interpersonally productive and adaptive system, leaving room for both Henry and Sarah to develop their own problem-solving skills within a context of emotional safety and supportive family interactions.

Conclusion

IFT not only offers families assistance in reducing their children's depressive symptoms, but it also provides this help through a mechanism that challenges and changes maladaptive family patterns. To the extent that the therapist can engage the family in this process of challenge and change, a restructuring of the family ensues, increasing overall adaptive functioning of the family in crisis. Because the therapist seeks to involve the family at all levels of treatment, including education about depression, a groundwork is laid for the family to increase everyday adaptive functioning and to handle future crises. Finally, the depressed child is seen by the therapist (and, if therapy is successful, by the family as well) both as an individual and as a family member, empowering the child to experience a valuable developmental balance between independence and interdependence while in relationship with others.

Nadine J. Kaslow, Ph.D., is Professor and Chief Psychologist, Emory University School of Medicine Department of Psychiatry and Behavioral Sciences, Atlanta, Georgia.

Michelle B. Mintzer, M.D., is Psychiatrist, MHM Correctional Services Inc., Atlanta, Georgia.

Lindi Ann Meadows, M.A., is a graduate student at Georgia State University, Atlanta, Georgia.

Chandra M. Grabill, Ph.D., is a Psychologist at Sexton Woods Psychoeducational Center, Chamblee, Georgia.

References

American Psychiatric Association. (1994). *Diagnostic and Statistical Manual of Mental Disorders* (4th ed.).Washington, DC: Author.

Asarnow, J. R., Goldstein, M. J., Tompson, M., & Guthrie, D. (1993). One-year outcomes of depressive disorders in child psychiatric inpatients: Evaluation of the prognostic power of a brief measure of expressed emotion. *Journal of Child Psychology and Psychiatry, 34,* 129–137.

Asarnow, J. R., Tompson, M., Hamilton, E. B., Goldstein, M. J., & Guthrie, D. (1994). Family-expressed emotion, childhood-onset depression, and childhood-onset schizophrenia spectrum disorders: Is expressed emotion a nonspecific correlate of child psychopathology or a specific risk factor for depression? *Journal of Abnormal Child Psychology, 22,* 129–146.

Beardslee, W. R., Wright, E., Rothberg, P. C., Salt, P., & Versage, E. (1996). Response of families to two preventive intervention strategies: Long-term differences in behavior and attitude change. *Journal of the American Academy of Child and Adolescent Psychiatry, 35,* 774–782.

Beardslee, W. R., Wright, E., Salt, P., Drezner, K., Gladstone, T. R. G., Versage, E., & Rothberg, P.C. (1997). Evaluation of children's response to two preventive intervention strategies over time. *Journal of the American Academy of Child and Adolescent Psychiatry, 36,* 196–204.

Birmaher, B., Ryan, N. D., Williamson, D. E., Brent, D. A., & Kaufman, J. (1996). Childhood and adolescent depression: A review of the past 10 years, Part II. *Journal of the American Academy of Child & Adolescent Psychiatry, 35,* 1575–1583.

Boulos, C., Kutcher, S. Gardner, D., & Young, E. (1992). An open naturalistic trial of fluoxetine in adolescents and young adults with treatment-resistant major depression. *Journal of Child and Adolescent Psychopharmacology, 2,* 103–111.

Brent, D. A., Holder, D., Kolko, D., Birmaher, B., Baugher, M., Roth, C., Iyengar, S., & Johnson, B. A. (1997). A clinical psychotherapy trial for adolescent depression comparing cognitive, family, and supportive therapy. *Archives of General Psychiatry, 54,* 877–885.

Brent, D., Poling, K., McKain, B., & Baugher, M. (1993). A psychoeducational program for families of affectively ill children and adolescents. *Journal of the American Academy of Child and Adolescent Psychiatry, 32,* 770–774.

Burbach, D. J., & Borduin, C. M. (1986). Parent-child relations and the etiology of depression: A review of methods and findings. *Clinical Psychology Review, 6,* 133–153.

Chen, X., Rubin, K. H., & Li, B. (1995). Depressed mood in Chinese children: Relations with school performance and family environment. *Journal of Consulting and Clinical Psychology, 63,* 938–947.

Chiariello, M. A., & Orvaschel, H. (1995). Patterns of parent-child communication: Relationship to depression. *Clinical Psychology Review, 15,* 395–407.

Colle, L. M., Belair, J. F., DiFeo, M., Weiss, J., & LaRoche, C. (1994). Extended open-label fluoxetine treatment of adolescents with major depression. *Journal of Child and Adolescent Psychopharmacology, 4,* 225–232.

Diamond, G., & Siqueland, L. (1995). Family therapy for the treatment of depressed adolescents. *Psychotherapy, 32,* 77–90.

Emslie, G. J., Rush, A. J., Weinberg, W. A., Kowatch, R. A., Hughes, C. W., Carmody, T., & Rintelmann, J. (1997). A double-blind, randomized, placebo-controlled trial of fluoxetine in children and adolescents with depression. *Archives of General Psychiatry, 54,* 1031–1037.

Garber, J., & Dodge, K. A. (Eds.). (1991). *The development of emotion regulation and dysregulation.* New York: Cambridge University.

Hammen, C. (1991). *Depression runs in families: The social context of risk and resilience in children of depressed mothers.* New York: Springer-Verlag.

Harrington, R. (1994). Affective disorders. In M. Rutter, E. Taylor, & L. Hersov (Eds.), *Child and adolescent psychiatry* (pp. 330–350). Oxford, England: Blackwell Science.

Hazell, P., O'Connell, D., Heathcote, D., Robertson, J., & Henry, D. (1995). Efficacy of tricyclic drugs in treating child and adolescent depression: A meta-analysis. *British Medical Journal, 310,* 897–901.

Kaslow, N. J., Deering, C. G., & Ash, P. (1996). Relational diagnosis of child and adolescent depression. In F. W. Kaslow (Ed.), *Handbook of relational diagnosis and dysfunctional family patterns* (pp. 171-185). New York: John Wiley.

Kaslow, N. J., Deering, C. G., & Racusin, G. R. (1994). Depressed children and their families. *Clinical Psychology Review, 14,* 39–59.

Kaslow, N. J., & Racusin, G. R. (1990). Childhood depression: Current status and future directions. In A. S. Bellack, M. Hersen, & A. E. Kazdin (Eds.), *International handbook of behavior modification and therapy* (2nd ed., pp. 649–667). New York: Plenum.

Kaslow, N. J., & Racusin, G. R. (1994). Family therapy for depression in young people. In W. M. Reynolds & H. F. Johnston (Eds.), *Handbook of depression in children and adolescents* (pp. 345–363). New York: Plenum.

Kazdin, A. E. (1994). Informant variability in the assessment of childhood depression. In W. M. Reynolds & H. F. Johnston (Eds.), *Handbook of depression in children and adolescents* (pp. 249–274). New York: Plenum.

Kolvin, I., Barrett, M. L., Bhate, S. R., Berney, T.P., Famuyiwa, O., Fundudis, T., & Tyrer, S. (1991). The Newcastle child depression project: Diagnosis and classification of depression. *British Journal of Psychiatry, 159*(suppl. 11), 9–21.

Kovacs, M., Devlin, B., Pollock, M., Richards, C., & Mukerji, P. (1997). A controlled family history study of childhood-onset depressive disorder. *Archives of General Psychiatry, 54,* 613–623.

Lewinsohn, P. M., Clarke, G. N., Hops, H., & Andrews, J. (1990). Cognitive-behavioral treatment for depressed adolescents. *Behavior Therapy, 21,* 385–401.

Lewis, M. (1991). *Child and adolescent psychiatry: A comprehensive textbook.* Baltimore, MD: Williams & Wilkins.

Lizardi, H., Klein, D. N., Ouimette, P. C., Riso, L. P., Anderson, R. L., & Donaldson, S. K. (1995). Reports of the childhood home environment in early-onset dysthymia and episodic major depression. *Journal of Abnormal Psychology, 104,* 132–139.

McCauley, E., & Myers, K. (1992). Family interactions in mood-disordered youth. *Child and Adolescent Psychiatric Clinics of North America, 1,* 111–127.

Oster, G. D., & Caro, J. E. (1990). *Understanding and treating depressed adolescents and their families.* New York: John Wiley.

Racusin, G. R., & Kaslow, N. J. (1991). Assessment and treatment of childhood depression. In P. A. Keller & S. R. Heyman (Eds.), *Innovations in clinical practice: A sourcebook: Vol. 10* (pp. 223–243). Sarasota, FL: Professional Resource Exchange.

Reynolds, W. M., & Johnston, H. F. (Eds.). (1994). *Handbook of depression in children and adolescents.* New York: Plenum.

Rubin, C., Rubenstein, J. L., Stechler, G., Heeren, T., Halton, A., Housman, D., & Kasten, L. (1992). Depressive affect in "normal" adolescents: Relationship to life stress, family, and friends. *American Journal of Orthopsychiatry, 62,* 430–441.

Ryan, N. D. (1992). The pharmacologic treatment of child and adolescent depression. *Psychiatric Clinics of North America, 15,* 29–40.

Sanders, M., Dadds, M. R., Johnston, B. M., & Cash, R. (1992). Childhood depression and conduct disorder: I. Behavioral, affective, and cognitive aspects of family problem-solving interactions. *Journal of Abnormal Psychology, 101,* 495–504.

Schwartz, C. E., Dorer, D. J., Beardslee, W. R., Lavori, P. W., & Keller, M. B. (1990). Maternal expressed emotion and parental affective disorder: Risk for childhood depressive disorder, substance abuse, or conduct disorder. *Journal of Psychiatric Research, 24,* 231–250.

Schwartz, J. A. J., Gladstone, T. R. G., & Kaslow, N. J. (1997). Depressive disorders. In T. H. Ollendick & M. Hersen (Eds.), *Handbook of child psychopathology* (3rd ed., pp. 269–289). New York: Plenum.

Schwartz, J. A. J., Kaslow, N. J., Racusin, G. R., & Carton, E. R. (1998). Interpersonal family therapy for childhood depression. In V. B. Van Hasselt & M. Hersen (Eds.), *Handbook of psychological treatment protocols for children and adolescents* (pp. 109–152). Hillsdale, NJ: Lawrence Erlbaum.

Seligman, M. E. P., Reivich, K., & Jaycox, L., & Gillham, J. (1995). *The optimistic child: A revolutionary program that safeguards children against depression and builds lifelong resilience.* Boston: Houghton Mifflin.

Shaffi, M., & Shaffi, S. L. (Eds.). (1992). *Clinical guide to depression in children and adolescents.* Washington, DC: American Psychiatric Press.

Sheeber, L., Hops, H., Alpert, A., Davis, B., & Andrews, J. (1997). Family support and conflict: Prospective relations to adolescent depression. *Journal of Abnormal Child Psychology, 25,* 333–344.

Sholevar, G. P. (1994). *The transmission of depression in families and children: Assessment and intervention.* Northvale, NJ: Jason Aronson.

Shulman, K. I., Tohen, M., & Kutcher, S. P. (Eds.). (1996). *Mood disorders across the life span.* New York: John Wiley.

Simeon, J., Dinicola, V., & Ferguson, H. (1990). Adolescent depression: A placebo-controlled fluoxetine treatment study and follow-up. *Progress in Neuropsychopharmacology and Biological Psychiatry, 14,* 791–795.

Stark, K. D., Rouse, L. W., & Livingston, R. (1991). Treatment of depression during childhood and adolescence: Cognitive-behavioral procedures for the individual and family. In P. Kendall (Ed.), *Child and adolescent therapy* (pp.165–206). New York: Plenum.

Tannenbaum, L., & Forehand, R. (1994). Maternal depressive mood: The role of the father in preventing adolescent problem behaviors. *Behavioral Research and Therapy, 32,* 321–325.

10

Creative Activities for Children of Divorce

Mariellen Griffith

Joyce Thiessen-Barrett

"Why did my parents divorce? Don't they know how angry I am feeling, and that it's wrecking my life? Why didn't I do something to save their marriage? Was the divorce my fault? Why did God let this happen? Will they ever get back together? Why didn't you ask for my opinion, what I wanted?"

Divorce is a major disruptive experience that occurs within the family and can have a negative emotional impact on all members. The degree of impact divorce has on children varies with circumstances, such as the overall quality of life, stability of the parents and home environment, and effective communication between the child and the parents and with the school (Kaslow, 1984; Wallerstein & Blakeslee, 1989; Wallerstein & Kelly, 1980).

Major changes that occur among family members as a result of divorce can be classified within four categories: (1) primary psychological or emotional responses with accompanying behavioral manifestations; (2) geographic changes influencing and/or compounding adjustment processes; (3) systemic alterations; and (4) economic issues affecting phenomenological adjustment (Hutchinson & Spangler-Hirsch, 1988–89).

The purpose of this chapter is to hear children from divorced families reflect on their fears, anxieties, and sense of loss. Interventions will help these children develop effective coping strategies and assist them in appropriately channeling their emotions and behaviors.

Problems and Development Issues

Within children there is an innate tendency toward psychological development that corresponds to the growth of the body and the gradual development of functions. Just as the baby develops on the physical level, there is a process of evolution in emotional development (Winnicott, 1965). However, when the emotional development is blocked through the trauma of divorce, problems may develop. Children may function on a younger level than what is expected at their present chronological age as they cope with the strong emotions of loss, guilt, anger, and abandonment.

Children's responses include a wide range of emotions that often resemble grief. Many children will go through this process experiencing shock and insecurity, fearing abandonment, feeling lonely from a lack of attention from parents or emotional needs not taken care of, feeling guilty for having caused the separation, and experiencing both despair that can lead to depression and anger directed inward or outward. The impact of the separation will be influenced by the degree of attachment the child feels to a parent or situation that is lost. Attachment implies the need for security and safety, and when this is threatened, as in divorce, grief-like behavior occurs (Holmes, 1993).

Divorce is a frightening experience. Although the fear may be real or imagined, the underlying concern for children is one of vulnerability and abandonment. Many children appear to believe that if the marriage can dissolve, so too can the parent-child relationship. Children may express concern over who will care for them. Wallerstein and Kelly (1980) found that the announcement of the intent to divorce was often brief and seldom accompanied by any explanation as to how the child would be affected. Children were not encouraged to express their feelings about the situation. Besides fear, sadness was another feeling among children in families where parents divorced. Wallerstein and Kelly (1980) reported that many children in their study were openly tearful or moody. Frequently, the children showed acute depressive symptoms such as sleep disturbances and difficulty in sustaining attention in school. Young children in preschool and elementary school were most concerned with the departure of the father. Boys between 6 and 12 were most likely to express feeling rejected by the departed father. This sense of rejection may lead children to wonder if they are still lovable. Consequently, most children wish to maintain contact with the absent parent and hope for reconciliation between their parents.

As a result of this sense of loss while experiencing powerful emotions, inappropriate coping mechanisms may surface. Children may develop aggressive, withdrawn, or depressed behaviors while demonstrating low achievement in school. Researchers have noted that problems stemming from a divorce seemed to interfere with academic achievement, cognitive development, peer relationships, relations with adults in positions of authority, and feelings of low self-esteem and low self-worth (Amato, 1993; Kalter, 1977; Wallerstein & Kelly, 1980).

To understand the differences between the normal development of children and development in those who have gone through a divorce process, we need to look at the developmental stages. Each stage entails social, emotional, physical, and cognitive changes. Tasks and skills at each stage of normal development must be mastered by children to prepare them for roles and tasks in later life. Successful mastery of these tasks enables children to deal with challenges presented in later stages of development. The family life-cycle developmental tasks run parallel to the developmental stages of the child. The stages are: the new family, where marriage occurs and the task of the spouses is to begin to separate from the families of origin and develop their independence by living apart from their families; the family with children, in which the task of the spouses is to assume the roles of mother and father with the arrival of the first child, providing for the physical and emotional needs of the child; the family with children in elementary school, where the roles of the parents are to teach the children appropriate behaviors and to develop relationships with family members and other people outside the home (Carter & McGoldrick, 1998). If there is a disruption in the normal stages of the family life cycle through divorce, there is likely to be disruption in the developmental cycle of the child.

For toddlers and preschoolers, one of the main tasks is to begin the process of separation and differentiation from their parents. Gradually they move away from home, toward neighborhood children, later playing with schoolmates. Guilt feelings can occur when, during a divorce, they sense the need to separate from the mother. Children may experience guilt when, during a divorce, they sense that the mother needs their companionship when the father is absent. Children from divorced families are vulnerable to making mistakes of not pleasing the mother or father and suffering the consequences. Most preschoolers have a beginning sense of morality, what is right or wrong, and the consequences and punishment associated with broken rules. This sense of vulnerability about making mistakes and being wrong leads to guilt and confusion. Wallerstein and Kelly (1980) have suggested that divorce is very hard for preschoolers since they often believe themselves to be the cause of the divorce because they were angry at a parent or didn't behave appropriately. Often preschoolers become insecure, dependent, and demanding. They may fear the loss of their home and the custodial parent. In addition, they may experience conflicts in loyalty to parents.

During elementary school, according to Erikson (1963), children are primarily engaged in developing their competency in the outside world. Their task is to adjust to school, become industrious, and develop productive work habits and social skills with agemates and adults. Wallerstein and Kelly (1980) found the effects of divorce to be more profound for children in the 6- to 8-year-old group. These children seem to be old enough to realize what is happening but lack adequate skills to deal with the disruption of divorce. The disruption at home may endanger the child's efforts to move forward. School performance may be severely affected by daydreaming or acting out behaviors, problems with peers may occur as the child acts out internal conflicts, and somatic illnesses can develop from the anxiety of the divorce, moving to another city, or the home situation. Anger is commonly expressed, especially toward the parent they think caused the divorce.

Many couples separate or divorce during the children's first eight years. Interruption in developmental learning at this stage can have major long-term effects (Frieman, 1993), and critical skill gaps may occur. It is difficult to remediate basic skills after the age of nine (Good & Shinn, 1996).

Possible solutions to the problems of children from divorced families have been proposed by many scholars (Amato, 1993; Guidubaldi, Cleminshaw, McLaughlin, & Perry, 1983; Kearney, 1993; Kurdek, Fine, & Sinclair, 1995). In a study of children who have adjusted well to parental divorce, Guidubaldi and colleagues (1983) noted the following specific characteristics: (1) having earlier and regular bedtimes; (2) viewing less television; (3) participating in organized afterschool activities; (4) having more contact with the noncustodial parent; (5) being encouraged by parents and teachers to engage in hobbies and to strive for academic excellence; (6) having parents who are less likely to use strong discipline or rejecting child-rearing practices; and above all (7) attending school in safe, orderly, and predictable environments.

Children who experience minimal loss of resources and minor stress following divorce are unlikely to experience a decrease in well-being (Amato, 1993).

In a study by Kearney (1993), children who were rated as coping well tended to score higher than those coping poorly on the Wechsler Intelligence

Scale for Children-Revised (WISC-R), thus suggesting that children who tend to cope well with stress, such as that resulting from divorce, may be at an advantage in testing situations.

When reviewing some of the literature on the link between school adjustment and family climate for divorced children, Kurdek and others (1995) found that successful achievement in school was linked to moderate levels of supervision by the parent, particularly for preteens and young adolescents, who are likely to test the limits of family control amid the chaos. Moderate levels of supervision may not only provide students with sufficient amounts of structure and guidance but also allow for personal control, which is important in the maintenance of good grades.

The literature suggests that the task at hand is to identify what factors or strategies will enable children to develop appropriate coping skills and meaningful support throughout the most difficult stages of the divorce process. Shapiro (1997) suggests that it is important to teach children the skills of problem-solving and solution-finding. Current research suggests that we have underestimated children's problem-solving abilities and that they can be developed by teaching children how to brainstorm multiple solutions to a problem. Focusing on solutions rather than on problems will make it much easier for children to overcome obstacles.

Shapiro (1997) refers to the work of Stephanie Thornton, a psychology professor at the University of Sussex, who quotes a wide range of research studies that suggest children are much more adept at problem-solving than was once thought. Thornton explains that when emotions are not involved, children instinctively learn many different strategies to solve a single problem. With interpersonal problems, the connection between the logical brain and the emotional brain may be short-circuited. In neurological terms, the amygdala loses its ability to form interconnecting pathways with the cortex, and so the child relies exclusively on emotional logic. Emotional logic, which forms the basis of intuition, may be sufficient to solve some types of problems. But when strong emotions are involved, only the dispassionate help of the cortex can guide the brain toward realistic and effective solutions to problems by establishing connecting pathways between the emotional and logical parts of the brain. Therefore, children need to learn how to generate solutions, applying the steps of problem-solving skills through game formats until it is an automatic reaction to encountering a problem. Problem-solving and solution-finding need to be integrated into a child's school curriculum and therapy process in order to strengthen the coping strategies of the child. Problem-solving and solution-finding skills, as well as creative outlets for expressing emotions, may carry the child into the adult years when, according to Wallerstein and Blakeslee (1989), the "sleeper effect" of post-divorce trauma may surface even if there had not seemed to be any serious problems at the time of the divorce.

Underlying Assumptions of Family Therapy

Both family and individual therapy are used to assist children during and following a divorce. There are several assumptions of family therapy underlying this work.

1. The family is seen as a whole, a system, rather than as a group of separate individuals.
2. Change affects the entire family rather than just one member.
3. The family is made up of multiple levels, including the parental level, the sibling level, the individual level, and the grandparental level; moreover, these levels interact with other systems, such as school, church, extended family, and social and medical institutions. Looking at individual members as subsystems of the larger family system will preclude isolating an individual from the rest of the family.
4. All members of the family contribute to the problem.

A multilevel approach (Feldman, 1992; Griffith & Coleman, 1988; Pinsof, 1993) is used to treat children and their parents after a divorce. A major goal is stabilization and maintenance of the family system so that its structure, organization, and interactions can support the children. Individual and family therapy integration proceeds through three main phases (Feldman, 1992; Griffith, 1997; Griffith & Coleman, 1988): (1) establishing rapport, assessment, developing a plan; (2) implementation of the treatment plan; and (3) closure and termination.

Phase 1: Establishing Rapport, Assessment, Developing a Plan

The first purpose of phase 1 is to establish rapport with each family member. This involves hearing the verbal voices and noticing nonverbal expressions and gaining an understanding of the problem, the symptoms manifested by family members, the interactions and interdependencies of family members, and their interactions with other systems involved such as the school. The second purpose is to stabilize the family, and the third, to analyze the data, conceptualize the problem, and set goals.

Therapy begins with the initial request for help. Questions are asked over the phone as to the nature of the problem, the emotions expressed and not expressed, and behaviors exhibited. Then an appointment is made. We ask the custodial parent and children to attend the first session. The noncustodial parent is invited at a later time.

When the family arrives for the first session the therapist initiates rapport-building by being friendly, establishes a safe and protective environment by being open and honest, and discusses both rules of confidentiality and rules for helping each other to feel safe in the clinic room. Puppets are brought out for family members to use to introduce themselves to the therapist. The therapist models the behavior by using a puppet to introduce the therapy session and role of the therapist. Later, paper and crayons are given to each family member and they are asked to draw their present family. Following the drawing, family members are asked to share their thoughts and feelings about the picture. Children may choose to communicate verbally or not. Many want to talk to the therapist about their picture. It is important for the therapist to accept and appreciate all family members as they are, whether they share verbally or not.

The Assessment Process

Assessment, involving formal and informal methods, may be conducted during the first two to three therapy sessions. Formal methods include standardized sets of questions or questionnaires designed to ascertain family members' sense of loss, their relationships with each other, the structure and rules of the family, the various and collective relationships to their environment and other systems, and how their needs are met. Projective drawing and questionnaires may be used for assessment. Common projective tools like the Kinetic Family Drawing (K-F-D) (Burns & Kaufman, 1970) and Kinetic-House-Tree-Person Drawings (K-H-T-P) (Burns, 1987) reveal the clients' feelings, self-concepts, and relationships to one another.

The informal process involves observing the behaviors and responses of individuals as they interact with each other while in family therapy. To gauge family interactions and dynamics, the therapist may ask family members to engage in an activity, for instance planning a picnic or party. A commonly used assessment and projective tool is the Beavers Timberlawn Family Evaluation Scale (Lewis, Beavers, Gossett, & Phillips, 1976).

At later sessions a grandparent or grandparents may bring the child if the parents are unable to attend. Grandparents provide support for the family and can be a good resource for eliciting information about family dynamics. During later sessions the noncustodial parent is asked to come to a session with the children with the permission of the custodial parent. The purpose of meeting with the noncustodial parent is to assess his or her parenting skills with the children and to have both parents maintain consistent child-rearing practices.

Family Dynamics

The dynamics of a divorced family differ from those of an intact family. Family members experience emotional stress that disrupts the normal family stage of development. As summarized from empirical research and clinical studies and observations, two major cluster of difficulties generally plague children during marital separation/divorce and afterwards: (1) the losses that they suffer as a result of the breakup, and (2) the effects of continuing parental discord. Consistent with a family systems perspective, we suggest that children may become a source of stress for their parents because of their being disturbed by the parental separation. Examination of the emotional triangle that frequently develops when a child lines up with one parent against the other can lead to amelioration of stress. Similarly, exploration of what is happening, with the parents and the children present, can elucidate patterns of "emotional blackmail." In many instances, children will exploit the parents' sense of guilt and uncertainty in order to gain what they want or punish the parents because of the marital discord and breakup (Nichols, 1985).

Montalvo (1982) has suggested that there are four interpersonal arrangements among divorcing families that affect the child: (1) a system with one compass (one parent in the family); (2) the crippled executive (the weak and helpless parent); (3) the uneven race (separated parents are not equal in resources); and (4) the abdication contest (parents wanting to give up their responsibility to their children). Other dysfunctional patterns are seen in which children assume or are put into the role of the missing spouse. These children will attempt to console the mother or father to make the parent feel better. Or they will assume duties around the house or apartment that the missing spouse had performed, such as taking out the garbage or sweeping the snow off the steps and sidewalks. Another problem surfaces when adults have little time to spend with the children. Each parent may have his or her own individual concerns and problems that get in the way of providing the attention that children need in order to be heard and understood and to strengthen the children's coping strategies.

When the custodial parent gives over power to the children, the children may become controlling and manipulating. However, children with too little information about relationships, society, and the world in general make attempts to control in a narcissistic way to the detriment of the family. To be effective, roles in a family must be in a hierarchy, in which the custodial parent is in control and the children are in a lesser role.

The nature of the relationship between child and parents is partially determined by the child's contributions to the mutually reciprocal and reverberating child-parent unit. Parents may respond differently to different children or to the same child at differing levels of development, depending upon the parent's own characteristics or need. Similarly, the child must adapt to the parents' characteristics, rhythms of work, sleep, and activity. The strength and resiliency of most children enable them to make these adaptations, although some do not adapt successfully, particularly in the disruptive crisis of divorce. An imbalance in family functioning and structure occurs and the child suffers the result. The child may become the emotional need satisfier for the custodial parent, the third leg in a triangle that separates the mother from the father. Or the child may become the scapegoat for the failure of the parents to communicate well with each other.

Treatment Considerations

Wallerstein and Kelly (1977) described an intervention process of six weekly sessions for divorced families held between one and six months following the divorce. The custodial and noncustodial parents came with the children for family sessions, as well as to individual sessions.

When providing treatment to a divorced family, the family therapist needs to have an ecological and multilevel perspective that takes in all of the systems involved. It is difficult to treat children in a one-parent family without considering all of the interactions and interrelationships with other agencies, such as the children's school. Problems can develop when a triangular pattern develops involving, for example, the school, the mother, and the child. Open communication between all parties is necessary for a consistent support.

To set goals and a treatment plan for therapy, it is important for the family therapist to be aware that the major problem for divorced children is loss—not just the loss of a noncustodial parent or, in joint custody, the parent who has moved out of the house or apartment, but also losses that come with a change in home or living environment, change of neighborhood, school, friends, and possible loss of a comfortable standard of living. The treatment plan must include techniques and methods for children to become aware of loss and practice effective methods and techniques to utilize family and individual resources, their coping mechanisms, personal strengths, and relationships with others. It is important for parents to learn to manage their own stress and loss reaction, to maintain an appropriate parental role, and to support the children as they express their emotions about loss in their own individual way. The focus is on the continuing need for the adults to provide parenting for their children (Nichols, 1984; Sager et al., 1983).

General Treatment Goals

The first goal in the treatment plan for custodial parents is to establish and enforce the rules and structure of the home. A second major goal is for family members to listen to and understand one another. The third goal is for each family member to work through their individual issues resulting from the losses occurring from the divorce by utilizing their personal and family strengths and resources.

Phase 2: Implementation of the Treatment Plan

During the second phase of individual and family therapy sessions the therapeutic plan is implemented.

Creative and Play Activities

Creative and imaginative play and art activities (Ariel, 1992; Griffith, 1997; Warren, 1996) are used in family therapy and individual play therapy with children. Warren (1996) points out that the creative process actively engages the senses and the emotions. These activities are used to promote health, encourage healing, and improve the quality of an individual's life.

In therapy, poetry, imagery, story telling, narrative writing, movement and dance, relaxation techniques, sandplay, and play activities can be used for self-expression and relief of the emotional distress that children may be experiencing. Play equipment (Gil, 1994; Hendricks & Wills, 1975; Kaduson & Schaefer, 1997; Schaefer & Cangelosi, 1993) includes puppets, felt board and felt cut-outs, dress-up clothes, doll house with furniture and little people, medical kit, kitchen stove and refrigerator, telephone, board games, and water basin or pan of water. Creative and play activities provide a language to express feelings, to draw off tensions, and to express well-being. Children need nonverbal avenues of expression, since many of them have not developed adequate verbal skills to express their thoughts and emotions.

Children are naturally creative in their play. Winnicott (1971), concerned about the origin of the creative impulse, saw play as expanding into creative living and into the whole cultural life of the individual. The baby whose mother provides the right conditions for creative living will use actual objects to be creative. The child who is deprived of a nurturing mother or caretaker may be restless and unable to play. When a child enters therapy and is given an opportunity to play, with the right conditions and facilitative relationship with the therapist, he or she will rediscover that creative impulse.

Before introducing creative play and art activities to family members, the therapist offers a free and protective therapeutic place, a container for all emotional and behavioral expressions a child may release in the room without fear of being rejected or abandoned. Children are respected and accepted for who they are, not who they should be. "We need to structure our sessions so that everyone, individually and collectively, feels secure" (Warren, 1996, p. 8). Rules are few but specific. Within the structure of starting and ending on time, rules are stated by the therapist as maintaining confidentiality and playing freely with anything in the room as long as they do not harm themselves or the therapist.

When children have experienced trauma and loss in divorced families, many of them have anesthetized or dissociated awareness of all or part of their bodies. They mute their sense of touch, smell, vision, or hearing. If these senses are awakened, children's memories of their losses will return, which may be too painful to experience. Beverly James (1994, pp. 68–71) has suggested some play activities to teach the children that it is safe now to experience their environment:

1. Stimulating and sharing: Boxes of textured materials, such as sandpaper, satin, and squishy things; small film containers of cotton balls scented with various aromas, lotions, and powder; oranges and small containers of chocolate pudding—all are props for games, play, and contests that wake up and stimulate the senses.
2. Music, dance, and movement: Using music can teach children to wake up, shake out, and reclaim their bodies. Basically the children must learn that it is safe to feel, to live, and to know who they are.
3. Self-identity work: Soliciting opinions about the youngster's feelings, thoughts, body experience, food, play, clothing, and music likes and dis-

likes can fit in almost anytime. Physical care of the child can also provide opportunities to identify and respect the child's uniqueness—hair color and texture, teeth, and body shape are subjects for comment.

4. The basket of feelings: A basket is provided that contains slips of paper with feelings or pictures of children's faces with different expressions of feelings written on them. The therapist talks about how everyone is different and invites the child to tell about his or her experiences by drawing a feeling from the basket. If a child draws a feeling of sadness, the therapist can say to the child: "Tell me what it was like when you felt sad. What happened?"

5. "Me" book: The child, with the therapist's assistance, creates a book that tells all about that child with drawings, collages, writings, and photos.

6. Stories, drama, art projects, sandtray work, puppets: Stories and drama allow children to practice the feelings of young animals and astronauts and everything in between. Art projects provide a means for showing feelings in a concrete way. Sandtray work and puppets help them relate important events in their lives, giving specific directions about how the characters feel and express emotions.

The therapist can be directive or nondirective in working with children. An example of being directive would be the therapist asking a child to sculpt a certain theme or feeling in clay. A nondirective approach would be to show children the creative materials and tell them that they can use anything they wish to express how they feel. Following the activity the therapist would talk with the child about the project.

The role of the therapist is to provide a safe and protected space. When one is truly present for children, whatever they are feeling frequently transforms spontaneously into another state of being, often the very thing that child was needing all along—a feeling of comfort, support, being loved, or being at peace. The therapist must be aware of one's own countertransference issues. These issues may create a tendency to collude with the child's pain, anguish, or trauma. The therapist must be aware of trying to fix the problem rather than allowing it to be. Allowing the child to experience the therapeutic process, the therapist must be present to whatever the child is experiencing and trust in the child's process (James, 1994).

Art Activities

Art materials and tools that can be used in a therapeutic session are: charcoal, pastels, paint, pens, brushes, canvas, board, clay, glue, scissors, crayons, ink pencils, construction paper, various sizes of paper, and pictures for collages.

Children can draw and paint to share their experiences with the therapist (Allan, 1988; Riley & Malchiodi, 1994; Warren, 1996). There are two main reasons that art expressions are important to the therapist. First, the image that the child produces is seen as an externalization of the inner perception or dialogue the child is having around some specific event or thought. Second, only through this image can the therapist regain some ability to understand the lost concrete thinking of childhood. Imagery and symbols are retained in the memory bank in a distinct way, one that is more archaic than verbal memories. "Objects in a drawing may represent the wishes and fears of the child who made the drawing, just as the events, actions, and objects in a dream represent the wishes and fears of the dreamer" (Levick, 1998, p. x). The therapist can step into children's drawings and let them teach the meaning of this visual narrative.

When the drawing or painting is accepted, honored, and validated by the therapist, the child feels validated. The drawing or painting shows what the child is feeling or thinking in a way that is safe and in his or her own language. These drawings and paintings can be a bridge between the child and the therapist (Kellogg, 1969; Oster & Gould, 1987), helping to establish a relationship that is built on trust and safety. Drawings can become vehicles for expression of fears, wish fulfillment, and fantasies, as well as concrete expressions of therapeutic goals. Also, they can be avenues for dealing with frustrations and impulses in the process of developing communication skills to enhance a person's self-worth.

An example of a therapeutic art project involves the therapist's asking children to draw a picture of their family before the divorce doing something. Later, the therapist asks them to draw a picture of their immediate family in the present doing something. Then the children are asked to talk about what they have drawn. Combining writing with drawing, a child can make a divorce storybook. If the child is unable to write, the therapist can record what the child says in a booklet that they make together, with the child providing the illustrations. The therapist can help the child to fold two to four sheets of paper together, punch holes in the center of the fold, use yarn in the holes and make a tie. A sheet of construction paper can be use for the cover.

Other drawing tools such as Draw-A-Person-In-The-Rain, The Scribble, and Draw-A-Story Game (Hammer,1967; Oster & Gould,1987), can be used to elicit additional information about the child's feelings or to allow the child to express feelings on paper.

Puppets

Puppets can be used for interview assessment and in therapy (Gil, 1994; Irwin, 1985; Mesalam & Griffith, 1993). To gain information about feelings and ideas and to hear their voices, a range of puppets is provided. Puppets include fantasy and real puppets, animals that are warm and fuzzy as well as fearful animals such as a wolf, bear, dinosaur, and alligator. Puppets can be aggressive, friendly, or neutral, representing a range of affects.

When children enter the therapy room and see a box filled with puppets, they often choose an animal to represent how they are feeling at that moment. When children are angry they usually will chose an aggressive-looking animal, such as a wolf or alligator. If they appear to be feeling sad or withdrawn, many of them will choose a soft, warm, or fuzzy animal like a kitten or rabbit.

For example, a 4-year-old-boy from a divorced home who was living with his mother chose a witch from all of the puppets placed before him. For a number of sessions he repeatedly hit and punched the witch, locked her away in the toy box, and said, "Bad witch." It may be that the witch represented the new woman in his father's life, in his eyes a potential "wicked stepmother," as in the story of Snow White.

Sandplay

A nonverbal therapeutic expression of inner feelings and thoughts, sandplay encourages the child to select symbols that speak for inner potentials. The expression of these potentials in sandtray scenes and enactments facilitates psychological development (Kalff, 1980). Sandplay is a creative medium through which the contents of the imagination are made real and visible. In addition, it provides a unique opportunity for the therapist to observe the processes of growth and healing. Miller and Boe (1990) and Boik and Goodwin (2000) have suggested matching stories with a powerful emotional element to sandplay themes.

Sandplay is the process, sandtray the medium, and the sand picture the finished product. The process begins when the therapist invites the child to play with the sand and to choose from an assortment of miniature toys and objects. The categories include people, buildings, vehicles, vegetation, structures, animals, natural objects such as shells and rocks, and symbolic objects such as treasure chests and wishing wells (Allan & Berry, 1993; Bradway & McCoard, 1997; Vinturella & James, 1987).

Two sandtrays (28½ x 19½) are made available to the client, one with dry sand and one with moist. Water is available in a pitcher if a client wishes to add water to make a pond. When sandtrays are introduced to clients, they are asked to choose the moist or dry sandtray to create a scene or picture. Then they are asked to look at all of the miniatures and choose the ones they wish to make a scene in the sand with. Dora Kalff, the founder of the International Society for Sandplay Therapy, invites clients to look over the shelves where she stores the miniatures until they find something that speaks to them, put it in the tray, and then add to it as they wish (Bradway, 1981).

Adults respond differently than children to sandplay. Children usually respond naturally and spontaneously to using sandplay and miniatures. Adults may initially express reluctance and discomfort in this unfamiliar environment (Mitchell & Friedman, 1994).

Initial sandtray scenes are significant in that clients not only express how they feel about therapy and how they see their problem and a possible solution, but also demonstrate signs of resistance if present. Weinrib (1983) warns that sometimes a first try is "just pretty," but that the second tray may go "right down." In other words, some clients intentionally select figures and create a scene that represents specific events or personal characteristics they want the therapist to note. This may continue for a short time; usually with the second try, however, the descent into the deeper realm of the psyche begins (Mitchell & Friedman, 1994).

In a study that demonstrated the effectiveness of sandplay in eliciting fantasy play, Volcani, Stollak, Ferguson, and Benedict (1982) investigated two pertinent therapeutic questions: Does sandplay elicit fantasy behaviors that can be measured? Is fantasy play in the sandtray linked to parents' perceptions of their own child-rearing behaviors? Ten normal-functioning Caucasian first-born boys (ages 7–9) from urban upper-middle-class, two-parent families were individually videotaped making three sandtrays over a two-week period. In addition, the children's parents completed two inventories regarding their perceptions of their caregiving behaviors.

Comparisons of the boys' sandplay and the parents' test results showed that behavior could be measured on nine dimensions: benevolence, adequacy, assertion, construction, dominance, propensity for imaginative play, aggression, dependence, and submission. Aggression was found to be the most common trait among these boys; therefore, aggressive behavior was not necessarily indicative of any psychological problem. Other findings were: a positive relationship between benevolence and fathers who saw themselves as effective in their childcare; boys who had mothers who rejected them demonstrated less benevolent behavior in the sandtray; boys of mothers who reported that they fostered autonomy in their children were found to be more dominant and assertive in their sandtrays. The researchers found that the sandtray technique is highly conducive to eliciting fantasy play in children.

School Intervention

If the child of divorced parents is not doing well academically or behaviorally in school, the family therapist will need to get permission from the custodial parent to visit the school and meet with the classroom teacher and school counselor. Aponte (1974), Lusterman (1985), and Griffith and Coleman (1988) have suggested ecological approaches to family and school problems. One approach is for the family therapist to bring the school personnel and the family members together in a joint interview. This meeting usually includes the child, the parents, and select relevant school personnel. Holding the interview at the school emphasizes that the school holds the primary responsibility for developing a remediation plan for the child, although the family is also expected to make changes. The family/school interview is presented as an efficient and economical approach to problems involving family and school. It is helpful to the child experiencing divorce if the parent and family therapist visit the school counselor and classroom teacher together, thus presenting a unified team. Most children want their teachers to know what they are experiencing, to understand why they may not always be able to pay attention to the lesson at hand, and to have patience with them. However, children have a difficult time sharing their feelings and worries with others.

Besides showing concern about a possible gap in academic skills, the parent and family therapist need to articulate their belief in the importance of creative outlets for developmentally appropriate emotional expression. The children's teacher, school counselor, and parents need to agree on providing opportunities for students to express their feelings through dramatic play, expressive art materials such as paint and clay, music and movement, relevant literature, and conversations about their situation (Frieman, 1993), either in the school or with the family therapist using creative art and play therapy techniques.

Family Strengths and Resources

In the past family therapists viewed the single-parent family as psychopathological, an unstable family with numerous problems. Recent family therapy literature has instead emphasized family strengths and resources. Family members are viewed in terms of their roles, functions, and responsibilities, not as persons who are pathological. Children are seen not only as recipients and reactors, but also as strengths and supports. Larger systems, previously viewed as hostile or peripheral (e.g., schools, hospitals), are engaged in a mutually cooperative venture. There is respect for each family's unique and individual character. This respect for clients allows therapists to encourage families to be direct and authentic, respectful and compassionate, and honest and challenging. Such a therapist accepts the idea that family members have their own experiences and their own integrity (de Shazer, 1985; Nichols & Schwartz, 1995; O'Hanlon & Weiner-Davis, 1989; White & Epston, 1990).

Solution-oriented therapists oppose the ideas that problems serve ulterior motives and that people are ambivalent about their problems. They assume that clients really do want to change. Much of the work for solution-focused therapists lies in the negotiation of a goal that is achievable. Solution-focused therapists borrow from constructivists the idea that there is no absolute reality, so therapists shouldn't impose what they think is normal on clients. Meanings are arrived at in a therapeutic conversation that appears more like a process of negotiation than the development of understanding. Changing language is powerful, because as the client and therapist talk more and more about the solution they want to construct together, they come to believe in the truth or reality of what they are talking about (Berg & de Shazer, 1993).

Many divorced families already have the skills to solve their problems, but often they have lost sight of these abilities because the loss and change in family structure have caused so many problems that their strengths have been crowded out of the picture. Sometimes a simple shift in focus from what's not going well to what family members are already doing that works reminds them of their resources. Using the "exception question" ignores the picture of the problem and directs them to explore the times before the divorce and even since when the problems weren't there. By exploring these times and what was different about them, clients find clues to what they can do to recapture and expand those exceptions. In addition, clients may find that when they are able to change the problem, their outlook toward it changes. It seems less oppressive and more controllable.

Some of the major resources for children include parental support (emotional support, practical help, guidance, supervision, and role modeling), as well as parental socioeconomic resources. Children with high levels of resources not only have opportunities to develop social and cognitive forms of competence, but are better able to deal with stressful life situations than are other children.

Werner and her colleagues (Werner, 1989; Werner & Smith, 1992) and Bernard (1999) have found many stress-resistant children who survived chronic poverty, family conflict, abuse, and parental mental illness. Werner (1989) describes four characteristics typical of these children:

1. Resilient children are able to "recruit" a nurturing surrogate parent, who could be a teacher, baby-sitter, nanny, member of the clergy, parent of a friend, relative, coach, or housemother in an orphanage.
2. Resilient children have good social skills and a strong desire to help others. They are friendly and well-liked by their classmates and usually have one or several close friends.
3. Resilient children have hobbies and creative interests.
4. Resilient children seem to have faith that things will work out as well as can be reasonably expected and that the odds can be surmounted.

Resilient children demonstrate the tremendous capacity of human beings to survive difficult conditions. They are able to develop a healthy detachment from the disturbed environment or parents, such as in divorce; a supportive relationship with a family therapist, teacher, or school counselor; and activities that provide meaning, such as hobbies, sports, and friendship.

Family therapy and creative art and play activities are effective tools to use with children of divorce who may have lost their resiliency, since a supportive relationship within a safe environment is provided. Nichols (1985) has suggested that play therapy may help many preschool and school-age children express and act out reactions of loss, fear, and bewilderment.

Filial Therapy, Reading Books, Storytelling

As another way to build custodial strengths and resources, filial therapy (Van Fleet, 1994) joins two important strategies: playing with children and parent education through direct involvement in the change process. Parents become the primary change agents as they learn to conduct child-centered play sessions with their children. Special times are set aside at home for one parent and one child to use special art materials, toys, books, games, and play activities. These materials are stored in a box and used only during that special time. The custodial parent and child are encouraged to play together, do art activities, tell stories (Gil, 1994; Webb, 1991), or read storybooks (Pardeck, 1990) for 30 minutes to an hour per day or whenever a time can be arranged. This format permits optimal relationship development and attention to the child's needs. The therapist teaches communication skills of attending, reflecting, empathizing, and restating content to the custodial parent to enhance the parent's ability to listen to the voice and language of the child.

Phase 3: Closure and Termination

At some point, therapy ends, either because the agreed-upon number of sessions is reached or because family members decide that they do not wish to continue with therapy. To prepare family members for termination, during a session before the final one they are asked to think about what they liked or disliked about therapy. During the last session they are asked to share their thoughts. One method of evaluation is to ask family members to summarize what changes have occurred and whether or not the presenting goal or goals have been met. Family members can be given paper and crayons and asked to illustrate how they feel about the changes while they were in therapy. Another method is to review any personal changes family members have made either behaviorally or emotionally. Family members can express themselves verbally or through art materials. A third method is to discuss resources and a support system outside of therapy. The following questions are asked: Are grandparents or aunts or uncles available to provide support? Do the children belong to any clubs or organizations outside of school? Does the family attend church services or Sunday school? Are there friends to relate to?

A family art picture may be the final activity for the family. Family members are shown pictures that they drew during the first few weeks of therapy. The therapist asks family members to share how they felt when they first started coming to therapy. Then he or she asks them to draw, color, or paint a picture of their present family doing something that makes them feel happy and cared for.

Before the family leaves, we schedule a date for a "follow-through" session a month away. An additional session can provide information to the therapist concerning whether changes have been stabilized, support systems are intact, and the family is stable and functioning well.

Case Illustration

This case of a divorced, single mother and two children extended over twelve weekly sessions beginning in October and ending in March.

Anita, a recently divorced, single parent, was 44 years old and the mother of Sue, 8, and Jerry, 5. They had moved from another city to be close to the children's uncle, Anita's brother. She had initially called for an individual appointment concerning her depression, which followed the recent divorce and a move to a new city. She also expressed concern that her children were not adjusting well to the divorce, the new apartment, or the city. She did not have a job.

Presenting Problem and First Session

I (MG) met the family in the reception room, greeted them with handshakes and a friendly smile, and took them to my office. The mother was quiet and withdrawn. The daughter was bouncy and talkative. The son was clinging to his mother, not saying a word but looking down at his feet. I shared with the family members the procedures of family therapy, explaining context of the session, fees, length of sessions, taping, and forms to complete. While the mother was filling out the intake form (a short form asking for presenting problem, family history, medications, and referral information) and a permission to see the children, I asked the children to draw a family doing something (Burns, 1982), with the message that later they would be asked to talk about their drawing.

After taking care of the paperwork, I showed the family members a box of puppets and asked them to pick one to introduce themselves. I also chose a puppet to model the behavior and help family members feel comfortable and at ease. I introduced my puppet self and told them that I was happy to meet them. The son picked a wolf and began growling. He did not tell his name until his mother encouraged him. He said his name quietly while looking at the floor. His sister chose a Dalmatian dog wearing a firefighter hat, started barking, and then shared her name. The mother reached for the magician puppet, saying that she had to create miracles to keep the family together.

The final activity was a discussion about family rules. I began by asking questions of the children concerning bedtimes, homework, taking care of themselves, and completing chores around the house. I turned to the mother and to confirm the family rules, consequences for breaking rules, and rewards for following them. From my notes, I then formulated the list of family rules and rewards. Having agreed on the rules, the family members said they would report in the next session on whether the children complied and how the mother enforced the rules. Each child was handed a chart of behaviors with spaces for stickers to be placed by each responsibility carried out. Every day the mother and the children were to check the desired behaviors exhibited on the chart and place stickers after the stated behavior.

Aware of the studies related to children's adjustment to divorce (Amato, 1993; Guidubaldi et al., 1983; and Kearney, 1993), I emphasized the importance of the children's having earlier and regular bedtimes, viewing less television, and experiencing positive child-rearing practices.

Session Two

A week later the children greeted me enthusiastically, saying that they had followed through with the family rules. The mother, however, asserted that Jerry had had an angry outburst and started hitting his sister. The mother said that she had told him to stop but he ignored her. Finally she left the room in despair, not knowing what to do. I led a discussion of alternative ways to help Jerry with his anger. Anita decided that she would try to give him a five-minute time-out in his room. Jerry said that he would try to listen to his mother and go to his room. Sue said that she wouldn't fight back if he hit her.

Next the family was asked to do a family sculpture, a technique for assessing emotional closeness and distancing (Papp, Silverstein, & Carter, 1973). Each family member was asked to take turns showing how close and how distant family members were to each other. Jerry put Sue next to his mother and placed himself in front of his mother, putting her arms around him. When Sue took her turn, she placed herself closer to her mother and her brother farther away. He expressed his unhappiness by moving closer to his mother. The mother voiced some difficulty in carrying out the directions. Finally, with encouragement, she put her arms around the children and held them close to her. When the family members were asked to share their feelings and thoughts about the sculpting, the mother and daughter responded by saying it was "fun" or "okay." The son said nothing but focused on his mother for a response.

When asked what they did for fun, the daughter raised her hand and began talking about her new friends, new school, and her wish to have a pet. The son looked down and was quiet. The mother said that they were new to the city, having moved to be close to her family, and she needed to find a job, since the father was not always prompt with support and it wasn't enough to live on anyway. Near the end of the session I said that during the next visit the hour would be divided in half. All three of them would meet with me during the first half-hour; during the second half-hour the children would meet with me and do some creative art and play activities. The purpose of separating the children from the mother was to allow them to voice their feelings and thoughts about the divorce without fear of saying something that might hurt her feelings.

Since Anita expressed concern about her medication and needed to find a physician to continue her prescription, I gave her names of several psychiatrists and suggested she have an evaluation with the results sent to my office. In addition, the Minnesota Multiphasic Personality Inventory (MMPI) (Hathaway & McKinley, 1943) was given to the mother to assess her anxiety, depression, and potential for suicide. When asked directly about suicidal ideation, she admitted to having thoughts of suicide but said that she wouldn't carry them out because of the children. No formal diagnosis was given until the report from the psychiatrist was received.

At the end of the second session, we set together an outcome goal: Therapy would have a positive effect upon the children's ability to resolve their grief issues and adjust to the many changes in their lives. Specific goals were: Jerry and Sue would carry out the family rules listed on the chart; family members would listen to each other carefully to understand what each person was saying; and no one would interrupt other persons when they were talking. All of the family members were cooperative. Jerry was shy at first, but with encouragement from his mother and sister he followed through with the tasks.

Assessment Results and Family Dynamics

From the assessment process of the first two sessions, I noted that mother had relaxed her parental role by not maintaining the structure and rules of the family organization. The children reacted to this with anxieties and fears. Bedtime seemed to have become a difficult problem, since the children did not want to sleep in their own bedroom. They crawled into bed with the mother, and since she enjoyed their company she was allowing them to sleep with her. Jerry regressed developmentally by demonstrating separation anxiety, clinging to his mother, and having guilt feelings about his anger toward his father. Anita said that Jerry had asked many questions about the absence of his father, raged when his father didn't maintain contact, then expressed sadness to his mother that he missed his father. It appeared to Anita that Jerry had a difficult time accepting the feelings of anger and yet love for his father. In addition, he did not wish to go to kindergarten, preferring to stay home with his mother. It appeared that the mother was contributing to the problem by spending much of the day sleeping or worrying about her situation. I hypothesized that Jerry sensed that his mother was depressed and didn't want to be alone. It was difficult for him to leave her and go to school. When he was at home he clung to her and tried to make her happy.

Sue had been close to her father and was experiencing grief and sadness due to the absence of his emotional closeness and protection. She had nightmares and was performing at an academic level lower than she had achieved in the past. In addition, she felt responsible for her brother, realizing that her mother was weak and no longer able to enforce family rules. She would tell Jerry what to do, and he would do whatever she said, even if it wasn't appropriate. Weiss (1979) suggests that children of divorced parents learn to suppress the need for their parents' nurturance while becoming prematurely aware of adult concerns. This has a negative effect on young children. Winnicott (1965) and Wallerstein and Kelly (1980) have discussed the vulnerability of preschool children with divorced parents, in that they may become insecure, dependent, and demanding. They may fear the loss of their home and the custodial parent and experience conflicts in loyalty to parents.

The mother reported that her brother, who was living nearby, was hovering over her, trying to tell her what to do. She had a difficult time telling him to give her space so that she could learn to be independent because she needed his support and the resources he provided.

General Treatment Goals

The first goal was for Anita to successfully resume parenting by establishing and enforcing the rules and structure of the home. The second goal was for all family members to be listened to and understood, particularly in conversations between the mother and the children. The third goal was for each family member to work through his or her particular individual issues as a result of the divorce. For example, mother needed to manage her depression and resume the role of the parent in the family, Sue had to give up the parental role and deal with the reality of the divorce and her feelings of loss of father, home, friends and school, and Jerry needed to resolve his feelings of abandonment, learn to express his anger appropriately, and deal with his guilt and anger toward his father for not communicating.

In an individual session the mother developed personal goals to deal with her depression. She stated that one goal was to take her medication faithfully. A second was not to sleep during the day but to carry out the chores that she had outlined for herself. The third was to maintain her role as a parent in the family and enforce the rules of the house with her children. The fourth was to find support in a church, and the last was to begin looking for a job so that she could become more independent financially and not depend upon family members for financial support.

Jerry and Sue would be included in family therapy to discuss the divorce situation and ways to resolve their feelings of loss. This placed responsibility for resolution of their family issues on the shoulders of all family members. No one family member, that is, Anita, was left feeling that she alone bore the responsibility for taking care of the family and trying to make life better. The children felt that they were being listened to and could voice their feelings and thoughts in the sessions.

The importance of including children in family therapy was documented in a study by Stith, Rosen, McCollum, Coleman, and Herman (1996) of children between the ages of 5 and 13 who had participated in at least four family therapy sessions. They said that they are more comfortable with therapy when they knew what was going on. In addition, they seemed to appreciate the goals of therapy: to solve problems and increase the satisfaction of everyone with the way the family operates.

Session 3

The therapeutic plan was implemented. The mother and her two children met for four sessions, each of which was split in half. The first half was the family session; then the children were seen for either individual or sibling sessions. Anita, who had requested individual sessions to work on her depressive feelings and behaviors, was seen at another time during the week.

The format of the family session consisted of a review of the past week in terms of activities, communication with father, and compliance with the rules of the home. Following the check-in session, creative family activities were enacted to enhance family communication, build safety and trust, and increase the strength and resources in the family.

Puppets were used to help Jerry and Sue communicate their feelings and thoughts. It is important for children to be heard, understood, and accepted, and the use of puppets in therapy facilitates their ability to communicate. Anita, Sue, and Jerry were asked to each select a puppet and together, as a family, tell a story with a beginning, middle, and end. They told a story about moving from their former home to the new city, finding an apartment, and going to a new school.

As the therapist I observed and facilitated the conversations. If family members hesitated, I would reflect their behavior and follow through with a word of encouragement. For example, "Jerry, it seems that you may not wish to help your mother and Sue to tell a family story because I am watching. Just pretend that I am not here and that you are at home playing with each other. Then you will find that this game is fun."

In the sibling and individual sessions that occurred during the last half of the therapy hour, the children had a choice of puppets, drawing, painting, or playing in the sand. Sue chose to paint pictures using paint with glitter. Jerry chose sandplay.

Session 4

During the family session I helped Sue and Jerry confront the reality of divorce. The family members were asked to draw pictures of their family doing something together before the divorce. Sue drew the whole family at a carnival in the city where they used to live. The family was depicted riding on a roller coaster. In her story she shared her feelings of having fun being together. Jerry resisted the drawing exercise at first. With encouragement from his mother he drew his former house. His story was about the time when the family lived in the house and he and Sue had their own bedrooms and a yard to play in. Then they were asked to draw a picture of their present family life and talk about that. Sue drew a large apartment building with a Christmas tree showing in the window of their apartment. She said that she was looking forward to Christmas. Jerry drew his mother and sister sitting at the kitchen table eating dinner. After completing the drawing, Jerry was silent for a few minutes. When asked to tell his story, he went to his mother and whispered in her ear. He wanted her to tell the story for him. She began telling his story. Soon he interrupted her and finished his story with a smile on his face. From this drawing experience Jerry and Sue were able to accept the reality of the divorce and realize that they will not be moving back to their former home. Jerry was still experiencing grief and loss but realized that he can still enjoy being with his mother and sister in his new home.

Puppets were selected at the beginning of the sibling session. Sue chose a fluffy, soft kitten and said that she wanted a kitten for Christmas. She was going to ask her mother for a baby kitten. Later, as a Christmas present Sue received a kitten from her mother, which she kept in her room. Sue felt that her mother had listened to her and felt that she was responsible enough to take care of a kitten.

Session 5

The family's first experience with the sandtray was when the mother, Sue, and Jerry created a family picture. Sue selected a cat from the miniatures to put into the sandtray. At first Jerry hesitated and didn't know what to do. Sue started to tell him what to do. However, the mother told Sue that Jerry needed to choose for himself. I was pleased that mother was able to demonstrate positive parenting skills. On his own, Jerry sculpted a mountain and put rocks on top. He stood back and looked very pleased. The mother selected a clear quartz and placed it near the son's mountain. When the family was asked to tell a story everyone responded with positive feelings about the new family home and environment. The mother expressed her feelings by saying that she was glad that the whole family was in therapy. Sue wished for a cat, and Jerry liked to imagine that he was standing on the mountain and feeling strong. I sat quietly observing the family play in the sand. Family members were talking and listening to each other in a respectful way. Later, I commented on their behaviors and complimented them on cooperating to create a scene. They smiled and wanted me to take a picture of what they had created. A picture was taken and given to them.

Session 6

A turning point occurred in therapy when the children made a sandplay picture together depicting the apartment and neighborhood. Sue was feeling better because her mother was reasserting parental control over the family and so Sue did not have to feel so responsible for her brother and mother. The act of making an apartment in the sand, which Jerry put fences around, inspired Sue to comment that she felt safe in her new home and neighborhood. Jerry felt safe but missed his old house.

During the family session we discussed school work and play activities at home and in the neighborhood. The mother was concerned that there were no children in the neighborhood for the children to play with. Sue interrupted her mother and asked if she could invite some school friends to play with her. The mother said, "That is a good idea. I didn't think of that." Sue smiled and seemed pleased that her mother listened and accepted her idea.

One of the goals of therapy is for family members to develop effective communication skills with one another. It appeared that Sue and her mother were demonstrating these skills. I complimented Sue and her mother for the positive communication and suggested that they continue practicing these skills at home.

School Intervention

During the first month of family therapy I received permission from the mother to visit with Sue's and Jerry's teachers and school. The teachers and school counselor were pleased to talk to me. As a result of the meetings, both teachers said that they would offer support and understanding to the children and give the children a homework checklist for the mother to initial after they had completed their homework. The school counselor said that she was starting a new program for children of divorce and would ask the mother if she would give the children permission to attend.

Session 7

After six sessions and three months of therapy the mother brought Jerry, without Sue. She said that Sue was no longer having nightmares and did not want to come to therapy any longer. She was developing more friends at school, her grades were back in their normal range, and she wanted to take dancing lessons that met at the same time as the therapy sessions. I was pleased by the mother's comments that Sue had felt she worked through her issues and did not need to attend therapy but wanted to taking dancing lessons to be with her friends. I believe that children often know what they need from therapy and try to accomplish their goals. I accepted Sue's wish to terminate therapy and attend dancing lessons instead.

Jerry wanted to continue therapy. He enjoyed drawing pictures and playing in the sand. Anita said that Jerry seemed angry and hurt that his father had not called for a number of weeks. In therapy he was aggressive with toys and finally took the telephone and told his father how angry he was. In the sand he took light and dark soldiers and set them opposite to each other, enacting a battle or war. He added tanks and airplanes. Then he played war for most of the session. I followed Jerry's lead, reflecting on his behavior and feelings of anger. Experiencing the acceptance and permission to act out his feelings allowed Jerry to work through his anger toward his father.

Sessions 8 and 9

Jerry spent a couple weeks playing out his anger in the sand and painting pictures. He did not share his feelings with me or talk about his paintings. He appeared to be involved in the process of working on his anger and abandonment feelings. One week when Anita and Jerry arrived for therapy, she said that instead of waiting for their father to call, Sue and Jerry had called him and talked for a long time. Following that telephone call Jerry's sandplay did not appear as hostile and angry as it had previously. The dark and light soldiers were still fighting one another, but Jerry had added a rescue team composed of two soldiers carrying a stretcher toward the battle and then putting one soldier on the stretcher and carrying him to safety.

Session 10

The father, responding to my invitation, came to a therapy session with the other family members. On the phone I had told him that the children were feeling abandoned and he needed to reassure them that he was still available for them. He had not realized his importance to the children and agreed to come to one family session. There were several purposes for the session: (1) to help the father realize the importance of hearing his children's concerns; (2) to assist the parents in maintaining consistent rules at both homes; and (3) enable the parents not to belittle each other in front of the children but instead to maintain open, respectful communications. My role was to act as a facilitator and guide to accomplish these purposes. When the family came together, Sue and Jerry were so excited about seeing their father that they began talking to him about wishing to see him and talk to him more often. He said that he would make an attempt to follow through. Also, he invited them to spend a week with him over the holiday break at Christmas. With my encouragement the parents and children reviewed family structure and rules. The father agreed to be consistent in the household rules but asked Sue and Jerry to remind him of them. The session seemed to have resolved feelings of abandonment and insecurity for Sue and Jerry. They felt reassured that their father had not abandoned them, that he still loved them and wanted to spend time with them. Anita no longer felt that she was the sole parent raising the children. The father said that he would try to become consistent in sending her the monthly check for child support.

Inclusion of the father and extended family members can reduce the tension between the divorcing spouses and reassure the children that not all important figures in their world are leaving them. The major goal of inviting father into family therapy is to continue vital parenting functions while the marital relationship is dissolving (Beal, 1980).

Session 11

In Jerry's sandplay, symbols showing that conflicts were being resolved began to appear. Instead of battles and soldiers appearing in the sand, a circular mound was formed in the center, allowing the blue color of the bottom of the sandtray to show. There were families of animals in the picture. The scene was peaceful and nurturing. Jerry seemed to have worked through his anger toward his father and was adjusting to living in a one-parent family. Also, I sensed that Jerry had accepted my presence in the room and felt free and safe in the environment that we had created together.

Family Strengths and Resources

It was important for the mother to regain her strength and resources in the one-parent family and to be consistent and firm about family rules. In individual and family sessions I encouraged and supported Anita to maintain her role as a parent. After a few weeks of her being consistent, Sue and Jerry were able to follow the rules. Sometimes they had to be reminded, but on the whole they were responsible. I encouraged the development of social resources outside the family. Problem-solving techniques were used to facilitate the awareness of available resources. The problem was stated, "Find places or activities in the city to assist the family support system." I asked the children and the mother to remember what they did in their former city that helped them to feel supported. The mother said the church; the children said the school. Other places that were mentioned were the YWCA, Girl and Boy Scouts, and visiting relatives and friends in their homes. Then I asked how the family could find these resources. The children suggested that they could talk to their teachers and school counselors about the divorce and difficulty being in a new school. They were encouraged to ask about the program for children in divorced families.

Other resources were discussed. The mother said that she was thinking about taking the children to a church for Sunday school services. She was personally interested in joining a group at the church for divorced single parents. As a family they had investigated the neighborhood parks and canals. Jerry said that he liked to feed the ducks in the park. In addition, the mother was beginning to feel stronger and began looking at the section in the newspaper advertising employment.

To increase the family resources within the home, there were three activities that were suggested to the mother. The first activity was *reading books* (Pardeck, 1990) to the children. She was given a list of children's books on divorce available at the public library (see Table 10.1). She went to the library, picked out some books on divorce, and read them to the children at bedtime. After several days, reading became a family ritual every evening. After a couple of weeks the children began picking out other books at the library and asked the mother to read to them. A favorite book was on problem-solving.

The second activity was *storytelling* (Gil, 1994; Peo, 1993; Webb, 1991). Besides telling each other stories or mutual story telling, one particular activity combined story telling with art. The family was asked to make a book about the divorce together. Instructions were given to the mother and children on constructing a book. In the book they could draw illustrations and write a script of

TABLE 10.1
BOOKS FOR YOUNG CHILDREN

Brown, M. (1986). *Dinosaur's divorce.* New York: Little, Brown.

Caines, J. (1977). *Daddy.* New York: HarperCollins.

Clinton, L. (1974). *Everett Anderson's year.* New York: Holt, Rinehart & Winston.

Gardner, R. A. (1970). *The boys and girls book about divorce.* New York: Bantam.

Hazen, B. S. (1978). *Two homes to live in: A child's eye view of divorce.* New York: Human Sciences.

Helmering, D. W. (1981). *I have two families.* Nashville, TN: Abington.

Krementz, J. (1996). *How it feels when parents divorce.* New York: Knopf.

LeShan, E. (1978). *What's going to happen to me?* New York: Four Winds.

Mayle, P. (1988). *Divorce can happen to the nicest people.* New York: Harmony.

Miner, G., & Whiteman, T. (1990). *How Russell got his red bike with training wheels.* Wayne, PA: Fresh Start.

Navarra, T. (1989). *On my own: Helping kids help themselves.* New York: Barron's Educational Series.

Rogers, F. (1996). *Let's talk about it: Divorce.* New York: Family Communications.

Sharmat, M. (1980). *Sometimes mamma and papa fight.* New York: HarperCollins.

Sprague, G. (1992). *My parents got a divorce.* Elgin, IL: Chariot.

Stern, A., Stern, E., & Stern, E. S. (1997). *Divorce is not the end of the world, Zoe's and Evan's coping guide for kids.* Berkeley, California: Tricycle.

Stinson, K. (1984). *Mom and dad don't live together anymore.* Toronto: Annick.

Zolotow, C. (1971). *A father like that.* New York: HarperCollins.

---

their experiences. The family told me of the book's success and, after it was completed, brought it in to show me. The children reported that on car trips that they would make up stories to tell one another or take turns starting a story and letting the other person finish it.

The third activity was learning *filial therapy* (Van Fleet, 1994), as described earlier. This promoted an open, cohesive family climate, which fostered healthy and balanced child development in all spheres: social, emotional, intellectual, behavioral, physical, and spiritual.

The mother was excited about finding a way to spend "quality" time with her children one at a time. At first they both wanted to be with their mother at the same time using the activities in the box. After setting some limits and explaining the purpose of the activity, the children agreed to abide by the rules. When the mother would spend time with one child, the other child would become resourceful and find other things to do.

Closure and Termination

For the final two sessions of a six-month treatment process (12 sessions of individual and family therapy), Anita, Sue, and Jerry attended the therapy session. They talked about how the family goals were being met, such as both children completing chores and doing homework. The mother had started a new job, and financial worries had lessened. The father was communicating with the children on a weekly basis, and the children were adjusting well in school. The children had learned new coping skills, such as talking about how they feel with their mother, who was listening to them and accepting their feelings and thoughts, and successfully accepting a "time out" period if they lost control of their emotions or started hitting one another. The children had made new friends in school and in church.

The final activity was for all three to draw a picture together showing how they felt about their family. The picture was of mother and Sue and Jerry playing together in the park with the new kitten.

An appointment for a follow-up session was made a month later to support and assist family members to maintain the changes they had made. When they came back for that follow-up session, they shared what they were doing, including the fun activities the children were experiencing with their mother and also with their father. The children appeared to have adjusted to the divorce and subsequent losses.

Conclusion

Creative and imaginative therapeutic techniques within a therapeutic environment can relieve the emotional distress that children experience when a divorce occurs within the family. Through a variety of expressive art, sandplay, and creative activities, developing family strengths and resources within a safe and trusting environment, and a facilitating relationship with the family therapist, children can work through the stressful events and develop new and appropriate coping and problem-solving skills that may last a lifetime.

In the case study individual and family therapeutic strategies were integrated to assist family members to cope with internal and/or external reality. Each approach reinforced the therapeutic relationship, which provided trust and safety in a protected space. The integration of these two approaches helped in developing a mutually acceptable treatment plan and in devising interventions that were congruent with the therapeutic needs of the family.

Mariellen Griffith, Ed.D., is a marriage and family therapist in private practice, Bloomington, Illinois.

Joyce Thiessen-Barrett, M.Ed., is special education coordinator, Wichita Public Schools, Wichita, Kansas.

References

Allan, J. (1988). *Incapes of the child's world: Jungian counseling in schools and clinics.* Dallas, TX: Spring.

Allan J., & Berry, P. (1993). Sandplay. In C. E. Schaefer & D. M. Cangelosi (Eds.), *Play therapy techniques* (pp. 117–123). Northvale, NJ: Jason Aronson.

Amato, P. R. (1993). Children's adjustment to divorce: Theories, hypotheses, and empirical support. *Journal of Marriage and the Family, 55,* 23–38.

Aponte, R. N. (1994). The family-school interview: An ecostructural approach. In *Bread and spirit: Therapy with the new poor* (pp. 83–97). New York: Norton.

Ariel, S. (1992). *Strategic family play therapy.* New York: Wiley.

Beal, E. W. (1980). Separation, divorce, and single-parent families. In E. A. Carter & M. McGoldrick (Eds.), *The family life cycle: A framework for family therapy* (pp. 241–264). New York: Gardner.

Bernard, B. (1993). Fostering resiliency in kids. *Educational Leadership, 51,* 44–49.

Berg, I. K., & de Shazer, S. (1993). Making numbers talk: Language in therapy. In S. Friedman (Ed.), *The new language of change.* New York: Guilford.

Boik, B. L., & Goodwin, E. A. (2000). *Sandplay therapy: A step-by-step manual for psychotherapists of diverse orientations.* New York: Norton.

Bradway, K. (1981). A woman's individuation through sandplay. In K. Bradway (Ed.), *Sandplay studies: Origins, theory, and practice* (pp. 93–100). San Francisco: C.G. Jung Institute.

Bradway, K., & McCoard, B. (1997). *Sandplay: Silent workshop of the psyche.* New York: Routledge.

Brown, M. (1986). *Dinosaur's divorce.* New York: Little, Brown.

Burns, R. C. (1982). *Self-growth in families: Kinetic family drawings (K-F-D) research and application.* New York: Brunner/Mazel.

Burns, R. C. (1987). *Kinetic-house-tree-person drawings (K-H-T-P).* New York: Brunner/Mazel.

Burns, R. C., & Kaufman, S. H. (1970). *Kinetic family drawings (K-F-D): An Introduction to understanding children through kinetic drawings.* New York: Brunner/Mazel.

Caines, J. (1977). *Daddy.* New York: HarperCollins.

Carter, B., & McGoldrick, M. (Eds.). (1998). *The expanded family life cycle: Individual, family and social perspectives* (3rd ed.). Boston: Allyn & Bacon.

Clinton, L. (1974). *Everett Anderson's year.* New York: Holt, Rinehart & Winston.

de Shazer, S. (1985). *Keys to solutions in brief therapy.* New York: Norton.

Erikson, E. H. (1963). *Childhood and society* (2nd ed.). New York: Norton.

Feldman, L. B. (1992). *Integrating individual and family therapy.* New York: Brunner/Mazel.

Frieman, B. B. (1993). Separation and divorce: Children want their teachers to know—Meeting the emotional needs of preschool and primary school children. *Young Children, 48,* 58–63.

Gardner, R.A. (1970). *The boys and girls book about divorce.* New York: Bantam.

Gil, E. (1994). *Play in family therapy.* New York: Guilford.

Good, R., & Shinn, M. (1996). *On curriculum-based measurement and special needs children.* Workshop presentation at the University of Oregon, Department of School Psychology.

Griffith, M. (1997). Empowering techniques of play therapy: A method for working with sexually abused children. *Mental Health Counseling. 19,* 130–142

Griffith, M., & Coleman, R. (1988). *Family therapy: An ecological perspective.* Greeley, CO: Health Psychology.

Guidubaldi, J., Cleminshaw, H. K., Perry, J. D., & McLaughlin, C. S. (1983). The impact of parental divorce on children: Report on the nationwide NASP study. *School Psychology Review, 12,* 300–323

Hammer, E. F. (1967). *Clinical applications of projective drawings.* Springfield, IL: Charles C. Thomas.

Hathaway, S., & McKinley, J. C. (1943). *Minnesota multiphasic personality inventory (MMPI).* Minneapolis, MN: National Computer Systems, Inc.

Hazen, B. S. (1978). *Two homes to live in: A child's eye view of divorce.* New York: Human Sciences.

Helmering, D. W. (1981). *I have two families.* Nashville, TN: Abington.

Hendricks, G., & Wills, R. (1975). *The centering book: Awareness activities for children, parents, and teachers.* Englewood Cliffs, NJ: Prentice-Hall.

Holmes, J. (1993). *John Bowlby and attachment theory.* London: Routledge.

Hutchinson, R. L., & Spangler-Hirsch, S. L. (1988–89). Children of divorce and single parent lifestyles: Facilitating well-being. *Journal of Divorce, 12,* 5–24.

Irwin, E. (1985). Puppets in therapy: An assessment procedure. *American Journal of Psychotherapy, 39,* 389–399.

James, B. (1994). *Handbook for treatment of attachment-trauma problems in children.* New York: Free.

Kaduson, H., & Schaefer, C. (1997). *101 favorite play therapy techniques.* New York: Aronson.

Kalff, D. (1980). *Sandplay: A psychotherapeutic approach to the psyche.* Santa Monica, CA: Sigo.

Kalter, N. (1987). Long-term effects of divorce on children: A developmental vulnerability model. *American Journal of Orthopsychiatry, 57,* 587–600.

Kaslow, F. W. (1984). Divorce: An evolutionary process of change in the family system. *Journal of Divorce, 7,* 21–39.

Kearney, C. A. (1993). Depression and school refusal behavior: A review with comments on classification and treatment. *Journal of School Psychology, 31,* 267–279.

Kellogg, R. (1969). *Analyzing children's art.* CA: Mayfield.

Krementz, J. (1996). *How it feels when parents divorce.* New York: Knopf.

Kurdek, L. A., Fine, M. A., & Sinclair, R. J. (1995). School adjustment in sixth graders: Parenting transitions, family climate, and peer norm effects. *Child Development, 66,* 430–445.

LeShan, E. (1978). *What's going to happen to me?* New York: Four Winds.

Levick, M. (1998). *See what I'm saying: What children tell us through their art.* Dubuque, IA: Islewest.

Lewis, J. M., Beavers, W. R., Gossett, J. T., & Phillips, V. A. (1976). *No single thread: Psychological health in family systems.* New York: Brunner/Mazel.

Lusterman, D. (1985). An ecosystemic approach to family-school problems. *The American Journal of Family Therapy, 13,* 22–30.

Mayle, P. (1988). *Divorce can happen to the nicest people.* New York: Harmony.

Mesalam, B., & Griffith, M. (1993). Using puppets to facilitate the acceptance of a second mother by a four year old boy. *Association for Play Therapy, Inc. Newsletter, 12,* 2–4.

Miller, C., & Boe, J. (1990). Tears into diamonds: Transformation of child psychic trauma through sandplay and storytelling. *The Arts in Psychotherapy, 17,* 247–257.

Miner, G., & Whiteman, T. (1990). *How Russell got his red bike with training wheels.* Wayne, PA: Fresh Start.

Mitchell, R. R., & Friedman, H. S. (1994). *Sandplay past, present & future.* New York: Routledge.

Montalvo, B. (1982). Interpersonal arrangement in disrupted families. In F. Walsh (Ed.), *Normal family processes* (pp. 277–296). New York: Guilford.

Navarra, T. (1989). *On my own: Helping kids help themselves.* New York: Barron's Educational Series.

Nichols, M. P., & Schwartz, R. C. (1995). *Family therapy concepts and methods* (3rd ed.). Boston: Allyn & Bacon.

Nichols, W. C. (1984). Therapeutic needs of children in family system reorganization. *Journal of Divorce, 7,* 23–44.

Nichols, W. C. (1985). Family therapy with children of divorce. *Journal of Psychotherapy and the Family, 1,* 55–68.

O'Hanlon, W. H., & Weiner-Davis, M. (1989). *In search of solutions: A new direction in psychotherapy.* New York: Norton.

Oster, G. D., & Gould, P. (1987). *Using drawings in assessment and therapy.* New York: Brunner/Mazel.

Papp, P., Silverstein, O., & Carter, E. (1973). Family sculpting in preventive work of well families. *Family Process, 12,* 197–212.

Pardeck, J. T. (1990). Using bibliotherapy in clinical practice with children. *Psychological Reports, 67,* 1043–1049.

Peo, B. (1993). The healing magic of myth: Allegorical tales and the treatment of children of divorce. *Child and Adolescent Social Work Journal, 10,* 97–106.

Pinsof, W. M. (1993). Integrative problem-centered therapy: A synthesis of family and individual therapies. *Journal of Marital and Family Therapy, 9,* 19–35.

Riley, S., & Malchiodi, C. (1994). *Integrative approaches to family and art therapy.* Chicago: Magnolia Street.

Rogers, F. (1996). *Let's talk about it: Divorce.* New York: Family Communications.

Sager, C. J., Brown, H. S., Crohn, H., Engel, T., Rodstein, E., & Walker, L. (1983). *Treating the remarried family.* New York: Brunner/Mazel.

Schaefer, C. E., & Cangelosi, D. M. (Eds.). (1993). *Play therapy techniques.* Northvale, NJ: Jason Aronson.

Shapiro, L. E. (1997). *How to raise a child with a high E. Q.* New York: HarperCollins.

Sharmat, M. (1980). *Sometimes mamma and papa fight.* New York: HarperCollins.

Sprague, G. (1992). *My parents got a divorce.* Elgin, IL: Chariot.

Stern, J., Stern, E., & Stern, E. S. (1997). *Divorce is not the end of the world: Zoe's and Evan's coping guide for kids.* Berkeley, CA: Tricycle.

Stinson, K. (1984). *Mom and dad don't live together anymore.* Toronto: Annick.

Stith, S. M., Rosen, K. H., McCollum, E. E., Coleman, J. U., & Herman, S. A. (1996). The voices of children: Preadolescent children's experiences in family therapy. *Journal of Marital and Family Therapy, 22,* 69–86.

Van Fleet, R. (1994). *Filial therapy: Strengthening parent-child relationships through play.* Sarasota, FL: Professional Resource.

Vinturella, L., & James, R. (1987). Sandplay: A therapeutic medium with children. *Elementary School Guidance & Counseling, 21,* 229–238.

Volcani, Y., Stollak, G., Ferguson, L., & Benedict, H. (1982). *Sandtray play: Children's fantasy play and parental caregiving perceptions.* Paper presented at the Annual Meeting of the American Psychological Association, Washington, DC.

Wallerstein, J., & Blakeslee, S. (1989). *Second chances: Men, women and children a decade after divorce.* New York: Ticknor & Fields.

Wallerstein, J., & Kelly, J. B. (1977). Divorce counseling: A community service for families in the midst of divorce. *Journal of the American Academy of Child Psychiatry, 14,* 23–29.

Wallerstein, J., & Kelly, J. B. (1980). *Surviving the breakup: How children and parents cope with divorce.* New York: Basic.

Warren, B. (Ed.). (1996).*Using the creative arts in therapy.* New York: Routledge.

Webb, N. B. (Ed.). (1991). *Play therapy with children in crisis: A casebook for practitioners.* New York: Guilford.

Weinrib, E. L. (1983). *Images of the self: The sandplay therapy process.* Boston: Sigo.

Weiss, R. S. (1979). Growing up a little faster: The experience of growing up in a single parent household. *Journal of Social Issues, 35,* 97–111.

Werner, E. (1989). High risk children in young adulthood: A longitudinal study from birth to 32 years. *American Journal of Orthospsychiatry, 59,* 72–81.

Werner, E., & Smith, R. (1992). *Overcoming the odds: High risk children from birth to adulthood.* Ithaca, NY: Cornell University.

White, M., & Epston, D. (1990). *Narrative means to therapeutic ends.* New York: Norton.

Winnicott, D. W. (1965). *The family and individual development.* London: Tavistock.

Winnicott, D. W. (1971). *Playing and reality.* New York: Routledge.

Zolotow, C. (1971). *A father like that.* New York: HarperCollins.

11

Oppositional Behavior in Children

James P. Keim

The younger of Robert and Carol's two children, Sally, age 14, was becoming increasingly confrontational and disobedient. Although Sally's behavior difficulties had been limited to home over the last two years, she had recently begun to act out with one of her high school teachers. Carol sought therapy after an embarrassing confrontation at the mall. Carol had gone to the mall to retrieve Sally, and the two got into a loud and physical confrontation. It began when Carol walked up to Sally and told her that she was coming home. Sally defiantly said "no," and returned to her conversation with two friends. When Carol repeated her demand, Sally reminded her of how she didn't do the things that Sally asked her to do and then gave examples of how she had failed to follow through with promises. As Carol began to defend herself, her stance shifted from that of a reasonable, responsible parent to that of an obstinate, argumentative sister. Carol was seized by the feeling that she was losing the argument. In a passionate effort to reestablish her parental authority, Carol backed away from the argument and told Sally that she was coming home at that very instant. When Sally again said no, her mother grabbed her by the back of her sweater and began leading her out the door. Sally responded by pulling her mother's hair and swearing at her. The two began pulling each other's hair and screaming at each other until a nearby security officer intervened.

For the parent or teacher, oppositional behavior presents a challenge to personal authority. For the therapist, the challenge is not only to understand the

278

nature of the current conflict but also to catalyze a more benevolent vision of influence and change. Toward this end, I have developed a four-step intervention for highly disruptive oppositional behavior. Emphasizing the power of soothing, this approach begins with a redefinition of oppositional behavior and proceeds with specific therapeutic interventions.

The struggle of oppositional behavior is of particular interest because of the degree that it questions the very nature of authority, benevolence, and power. In addressing these issues from a systemic perspective, one must consider that a child's perception of authority is necessarily going to be different from that of the adults in the system. Taking this alternative view into consideration and making it a focal point of intervention is central to the intervention offered below.

Parental Authority

Baumrind's (1967) research on the relationship between parental authority styles and child mental health and functioning has had an important impact on developmental psychology and continues to be a basis for research (Kochanska, 1990; Lamborn, Mounts, Steinberg, & Dornbusch, 1991; Larzelere, Baumrind, & Polito, 1998; Weiss & Hechtman, 1986). The authoritarian-authoritative range described by Baumrind has been shown to be an effective variable in predicting issues such as personality, academic achievement, adolescent drug use, and parental potential for child abuse (Baumrind & Moselle, 1985; Cohen, Dunbar, Barch, & Braver, 1997; Steinberg, Fletcher, & Darling, 1994; Weiss & Hechtman, 1986). Baumrind's work has also led to research showing that parents and their children often have different conceptualizations of how power and authority are expressed in the family (Cohen et al., 1997; Smetana, 1995).

Many family therapy interventions focus on constructs parallel to Baumrind's authority-authoritarian range, including but not limited to Patterson's concept of coercive parenting (Patterson, 1982), structural (Minuchin, 1974; Minuchin, Montalvo, Guerney, Rosman, & Schumer, 1967) and strategic (Haley, 1976, 1980; Madanes, 1981, 1984) concepts of balanced hierarchy and authority, and the parenting skills addressed in multitarget ecological treatment (Chamberlain, 1994) and in functional family therapy (Alexander & Parsons, 1973). Each of these therapy models constructs authority as being earned through structure, benevolence, and consistency of reinforcement rather than through fear of retribution.

The interplay of interactional and authority dynamics in childhood behavioral problems received increased attention in the American Psychiatric Association's (APA) *Diagnostic and Statistical Manual of Mental Disorders, Fourth Edition* (*DSM-IV*) (1994). In the definition of oppositional defiant disorder, it is noted that "There may be a vicious cycle in which the parent and child bring out the worst in each other. Oppositional Defiant Disorder is more prevalent in families in which child care is disrupted by a succession of different caretakers or in families in which harsh, inconsistent, or neglectful child-rearing practices are common" (p. 92). Although this is an interesting start, a family therapist is likely to seek a more detailed interactional view of oppositional behavior.

The Individual Description of Oppositional Behavior

The *DSM-IV* definition of oppositional defiant disorder (ODD) begins with the following description:

> The essential feature of Oppositional Defiant Disorder is a recurrent pattern of negativistic, defiant, disobedient, and hostile behavior toward authority figures that persists for at least 6 months (Criterion A) and is characterized by the frequent occurrence of at least four of the following behaviors: losing temper (Criterion A1), arguing with adults (Criterion A2), actively defying or refusing to comply with the requests or rules of adults (Criterion A3), deliberately doing things that will annoy other people (Criterion A4), blaming others for his or her own mistakes or misbehavior (Criterion A5), being touchy or easily annoyed by others (Criterion A6), being angry and resentful (Criterion A7), or being spiteful or vindictive (Criterion A8). To qualify for Oppositional Defiant Disorder, the behaviors must occur more frequently than is typically observed in individuals of comparable age and developmental level and must lead to impairment in social, academic, or occupational functioning (see Criterion B). (APA, p. 91)

The complete description of ODD in *DSM-IV* differentiates it from developmentally normal oppositional behavior. This *DSM* description can be a useful start for the family therapist, since it is immediately recognizable to any parent, teacher, or therapist working with oppositional behavior. The label "oppositional" also succeeds in being appropriately descriptive and yet does not sound intimidatingly scientific until the term "disorder" is added to it.

One problem with the *DSM* definition of ODD is that the addition of behavior involving major violations of rights of others requires a change in diagnosis to conduct disorder (CD). Like many other clinicians and researchers (Loeber, Lahey, & Thomas, 1991), I (Keim, 1998) do not believe that it is helpful to view oppositional youth who act out in ways that involve major violations of rights of others as necessarily being qualitatively different from those who do not. In other words, oppositional behavior is best thought of as having degrees of acting out against others, the most serious of which involve major violations.

For the family therapist, the ODD label in the *DSM* has the additional limitation of not describing an interactional dynamic that could inform systemic intervention. The family therapist may start with the ODD description, but, in order to organize an intervention, a more detailed interactional description of oppositional behavior must be created.

Moving to the Interactional View

The interactional description of oppositional behavior includes two characteristics common in family therapy diagnosis. First, the problem description simultaneously suggests intervention. Second, the problem description is viewed as a pragmatic, simplified construction and not as a concrete reality. Following the commonly employed traditions described above, the variables addressed here have been chosen because focusing on them is likely to facilitate change. The central variables or constructs to be addressed are:

1. win/lose construction of disagreements or issues of influence
2. outcome and process orientation
3. hierarchy conflict

Win/Lose Construction of Disagreements or Issues of Influence

A win/lose conversation is one structured in a competitive way, such that parties taking part perceive that the outcome is going to make one party the loser and one party the winner. Called a zero-sum game in the language of game theory (Watzlawick, Bavelas, & Jackson, 1967), this construction became better known as a win/lose competition (Fisher & Ury, 1981; Pruitt, 1983). Gregory Bateson pointed out the potential dangers of applying win/lose dichotomies in situations where such outcomes were an illusion; in Bateson's view, the mismatch between win/lose construction and a context that does not allow for clear winners and losers can lead to dangerous escalations rather than collaborative agreements (Bateson, Haley, Jackson, & Weakland, 1956; Haley, 1981). Interestingly, this conflict between win/lose construction and a context that is not win/lose provides a means of describing how oppositional conflicts escalate between youth and adult authority figures.

Oppositional behavior is characterized by win/lose construction of both disagreements and negotiation of influence/control. For the sake of abbreviation, disagreements and negotiation of influence/control shall be referred to in this chapter as "difficult conversations." Successful therapy of oppositional behavior, regardless of the model used, seems to move the youth and adults involved from a tendency to engage in a win/lose construction of difficult conversations to more collaborative, win/win constructions that still respect the different levels of authority of all involved. When oppositional behavior escalates, there is an increase in the explosiveness and frequency of difficult conversations with a win/lose construction.

In order for a conversation to successfully integrate a win/lose construction, both the child and the adult authority figure must be attempting to "win" the conversation. In the observation of the author, win/lose construction of difficult conversations tends to start as a pattern between a youth and a single adult authority figure who consistently joins the child in win/lose conversations. If oppositional behavior progresses, the child attempts to bring the win/lose style into conversations with others who may be attempting win/win constructions. This tendency to bring a conversational structure that is occurring in one set of interactions (with a significant other) into other relationships is described in the strategic tradition as "metaphorical interaction." Metaphorical interaction is the attempted repetition of structures that characterize one significant set of relationships into other relationships (other schools of therapy describe this simply as generalization of communication patterns from one relationship to others).

Another characteristic of win/lose arguments is the tendency of both children and adults to involve third parties in the disputes. The adult-child arguments take on a win/lose structure, much like a debating team or courtroom argument; the two sides argue in a way that does not lead to collaboration but is instead intended to impress a third party (in the case of the debating team and courtroom the third party triangulated into the argument is the judge/jury). To the degree that the youth succeeds in triangulating with other adults against an adult authority figure, the win/lose arguments seem to become even more dichotomized and the oppositional behavior tends to escalate. If, during a difficult conversation, an adult consistently engages in a win/win style of communication while the youth consistently engages in a win/lose style, the argument tends not to escalate out of control (e.g., shouting, extreme anger, threats). The adult maintaining the win/win style will, however, still find the win/lose structure of the oppositional youth irritating and highly draining, and so any intervention that addresses the efforts to maintain win/win construction must also coach the adult in handling the resultant irritation. A win/win construction does not imply equality of power between those involved in the negotiation. It does imply that the goal for each party is to feel that the exchange has been fair without denying differences in power and social hierarchy.

An example of the win/lose and win/win construction can be found in dialogue recorded during the therapy of Anna, a 10-year-old girl with very oppositional behavior who is one of a number of siblings adopted simultaneously by the same parents. Anna initiates a conversation with her two parents by complaining about consequences given at home for bad behavior.

ANNA: Why do you give consequences for everything? Because . . . (*does not continue*)
FATHER: Come, tell us how you feel about consequences. (*Father pats seat next to him on the sofa, beckoning the daughter to sit and join her parents for conversation.*)
ANNA: Well, you won't change it.
FATHER: Well, just tell us how you feel.
ANNA: No!

Anna has stated that she does not see the use of discussing the issue unless her parents back down and give in to her demands. Blackmail such as this represents a moment of extreme win/lose construction of conversation.

Win/win or win/lose constructions of conversation do not necessarily involve overt negotiation. A win/win dialogue might merely involve an implicit exchange whereby each party agrees to respectfully listen to the words and feelings of the other party. It is just such an implicit contract that is constructed in the next lines of dialogue.

MOTHER: But we do care.
THERAPIST: And after that, let's talk about ballet and at what point after you move (it can restart) . . .
ANNA: I'm not interested in it anymore.

THERAPIST: . . . and everything is settled down in your lives and everything is
            back on track . . .
ANNA: I'll tell you how I feel about consequences 'cause it's the only
            time you'll listen to me.

With these words, Anna steps out of a win/lose construction and allows for
win/win by accepting the implicit arrangement whereby both she and her parents will exchange respectful listening to the other's complaints. Later still in
the dialogue, the topic returns to Veronica, Anna's 17-year-old sister by birth,
and Veronica's plan to leave home and attend school in California. Anna complains to her parents about it, and they respond.

FATHER: Tell us, tell us what you'd like to happen if, if you had, if you
            could choose what would happen. And Veronica wasn't making a
            choice for herself and we didn't have any choices. What would
            you choose? What would you choose with Veronica?
ANNA: I don't know.
FATHER: Would you like to her to stay forever and ever . . .
ANNA: No.
FATHER: . . . and be with us always?
THERAPIST: Sounds nice, but . . .
FATHER: It would be nice to have everybody all the time. Would you like
            her to stay a little bit longer before she goes away? Would you like
            to be able to talk to her more?
ANNA: (*She respectfully looks at her father, drops her head, and then
            begins to shed tears in a comfortable manner.*)

In this last section of dialogue, Anna momentarily participates without any sense
that meeting her needs must come at the expense of another party. At this point,
the dialogue is win/win as Anna affirms her father's role as parent and soother
and expects and receives empathy for the pain over her sister's leaving home.

Outcome and Process Orientation

The concepts of outcome and process orientation are pragmatic constructs:
practical, oversimplified ways of describing complex interaction. The terms
refer to whether the strongest reinforcement is the process or the outcome of
conversation, as the examples below illustrate.
    To show process orientation, we might use the hypothetical example of

Scott, who attended a two-hour Japanese tea ceremony. Scott's primary goal in attending the tea ceremony was not to get a cup of tea; his focus was on what was communicated in the process of the ceremony. His interest was in experiencing the calm, respect, and fellowship communicated in the ceremony. Because Scott's major reinforcement was the process and not the outcome (getting a cup of tea), the interaction would be described as *process oriented.*

To describe outcome orientation, let us use the hypothetical story of Sandra. Sandra wanted a quick cup of tea before work. She decided to use the drive-through window of a fast-food restaurant, gave her order to a plastic clown equipped with a microphone, paid a cashier, and received the tea. It took Sandra only two minutes to get the tea, and this short wait made her happy because she had to get to work. The major reinforcement from the tea-obtaining process came from the outcome, receiving a cup of tea. The process of obtaining the tea was not a major reinforcement unless, for example, Sandra received deep emotional satisfaction from speaking to a plastic clown. As the major reinforcement for the interaction was the outcome (just getting the tea), Sarah's interactions would be described as *outcome oriented.*

Now that we see the difference between outcome and process orientations, we can apply these concepts to interactions with ODD youths. During a confrontation between an oppositional youth and an authority figure, the child is usually focused on the process of the confrontation while the adult is focused on its outcome. Neither process nor outcome orientations are by themselves problematic. The issue with regard to oppositional behavior is the mismatch that occurs when one party in a confrontation if focused on outcome and the other on process. This difference in focus leads to painful escalations when confrontations arise. Writers such as Deborah Tannen (1991) and John Gray (1992) have described the painful escalations that happen in the context of same-generation, male-female differences in process and outcome communication. These gender-related escalations have their counterpart in intergenerational communication problems, and oppositional behavior is a prime example.

If we wish to examine the tendency of the child to focus on the process of communication during confrontation, then three aspects of process orientation are especially worthy of study. During confrontation, the process-oriented child is especially focused on determining the following three issues:

1. the timing of the confrontation
2. the content and direction of communication during the confrontation
3. the mood of the confrontation

Meanwhile, the adult in the confrontation tends to focus on determining:

4. the outcome of the confrontation.

As mentioned earlier in this chapter, the oppositional child is focused on "winning" difficult conversations. The concept of process orientation helps us to understand just what winning is for the oppositional child: The winner is not the one who determines the outcome as much as the one who determines the process. The winner is to a large extent the one who determines the timing, content and direction, and mood of a difficult conversation.

Hierarchy of Interaction

Oppositional kids are often described as "kids who are growing up too fast." Oppositional arguments are classically ones where the child is attempting to deal with adults as equals and the adults are trying to define the relationship as one between adult authority figures and a child who should be obedient.

The concepts of complementary and symmetrical relationships, drawn from systems theory as expressed by Bateson in *Naven* (1958), are applicable here. Writing in 1981, Haley described these terms:

> A symmetrical relationship is one where the two people exchange the same sort of behavior. For example, one gives something and the other gives something. A complementary relationship is one where they exchange different behavior. For example, one gives something and the other receives it. (Haley, 1981, p. 25)

In a symmetrical relationship, roles can be traded without requiring a relabeling of the defining relationship. For example, a husband and wife can trade the roles of homemaker and breadwinner without violating our modern concept of husband and wife. However, in a complementary relationship, the trading of roles can lead to a relabeling of the relationship. For example, if in a military unit an officer begins to take orders from an enlisted man, it is the enlisted man who is actually the leader and the officer who is actually the follower. In the second example, the trading of roles contradicted the previous relationship definition, and the example is thus one of a complementary relationship.

In oppositional relationships between adults and youth, the adults are attempting to define the relationship as being complementary (adult in charge, child obedient) and the child is attempting to define the relationship with adults as being symmetrical (adult and child having equal say). The concept of hierarchy spells out in detail the concepts behind a complementary relationship between adult and child.

In the context of this therapy with children and adolescents, the hierarchy of interaction describes the degree to which parents and children interact in age- and role-appropriate ways (Haley, 1976, 1980; Minuchin, 1974). The concept of hierarchy used in this chapter is typical of the Washington School (Haley and Madanes), which does not view hierarchy as necessarily creating problems; rather, the construct of hierarchy is viewed as being helpful in describing and solving problems.

Table 11.1 describes the responsibilities that play a strong part in determining who is functioning as an adult in a social system. To the degree that children assume the roles described in Table 11.1, they tend to perceive of themselves as adult-like and claim the authority of adults during confrontation (attempt a complementary definition of the relationship). To the degree that adults carry out the responsibilities below in a benevolent fashion, and to the degree that there is balance between the "hard" and "soft" sides of hierarchy, adults tend to increase their benevolent ability to guide and protect children. A child's ability to function in an age-appropriate manner is maximized when adults in the social system carry out these duties in a balanced fashion.

TABLE 11.1
HIERARCHY OF INTERACTION

The Hard Side of Hierarchy	The Soft Side of Hierarchy
who makes the rules	who soothes whom
who defines the punishments	who provides reassurance to whom
who carries out punishments	who protects whom
who tells whom what to do	who has responsibility for expressing love, affection, and empathy
who has final responsibility for making major decisions	who is the provider of good things and good times
who is responsible for making others feel safe and provided for	who usually determines the mood of situations
	who has the responsibility to listen to whom

Oppositional children are characterized by age-inappropriate assumption of hard and soft hierarchy responsibilities; they tend to take on these roles for themselves or allow the duties to be carried out by peers instead of by the proper adults (parents, teachers, etc.) in their social system. Successful therapy with oppositional children usually results in adults' reassuming these hierarchical responsibilities in a way that allows the child to function in a more age-appropriate way. In other words, the relationship retakes a complementary form.

To the degree that a youth tries to assume adult-like authority by trying to take the hard side of hierarchy in relationships with adults, the child is described as a being a "high-hierarchy" child. If a child is not high-hierarchy, the situation would not be described as oppositional and our intervention would not be applied. High-hierarchy youths are characterized by overt claims to adult-like authority, such as, "If I can't discuss what I want to discuss, I'm walking out of here right this second."

At the Washington School, the concept of low-hierarchy also exists. The low-hierarchy child functions with less authority than most other similarly-aged children and is much less able than the average child to confront or challenge adult views. Low-hierarchy children tend to be treated in family therapy in very different ways from high-hierarchy kids. With a low-hierarchy child, the therapy works to empower the youth to be age-appropriate by allowing the youth to have more adult-like authority. An example of this in a therapy session is a therapist's having to work hard to make a youth feel safe in making a request for change from a parent.

With a high-hierarchy child, the therapy works to empower the child to have more age-appropriate functioning by removing the perceived need to exert adult-like authority. Confrontations with high-hierarchy children are more overtly focused on the hard side of hierarchy (where the youth's requests for control and authority are overt). The confrontations with low-hierarchy children tend to be more overtly focused on the soft side of hierarchy (the expressed needs of the youth are more oriented towards receiving soothing and expression of love). Problems of high-hierarchy children tend to involve overt confrontation. Problems with low-hierarchy children tend to involve covert symptoms and behaviors that do not directly challenge the authority of adults in face to face confrontations (Madanes, 1981, 1984).

The concepts of high and low hierarchy exist solely to guide the therapist in choosing an intervention. These distinguishing labels are needed because different interventions are used depending on whether a child exerts too little or too much overt influence over adults.

The Interactional Assessment of Oppositional Behavior

Using the definitions described above, an assessment can be made of oppositional behavior. A youth would be considered oppositional only if these four criteria were met:

1. The youth habitually challenges in an overt and confrontational fashion the authority of adults (a summary of the *DSM* definition).
2. The youth tends to automatically construct difficult conversations as being win/lose propositions.
3. The youth tends to be process oriented during difficult conversations, while the adult is outcome oriented.
4. The youth tends to be high hierarchy and attempts to define the relationship with adult authority figures as being symmetrical, while the adults try to define the relationship as being complementary.

In the interactional tradition, these behaviors would not be constructed as a result of a "personality" problem but rather as a maladaption to relationships with authority figures.

The degree of oppositionality can be described using the following four-level system:

1. Mild and occasional oppositional behavior. Child still at times is open to the parent's soothing, and the parent is usually able to maintain an adult stance during arguments. Oppositional behavior usually takes place in only one context, such as school or home.
2. Oppositional behavior still does not commonly involve major violations of rights of others but is consistent, not just occasional. Parents sometimes have difficulty maintaining an adult stance during confrontations. The oppositional behavior takes place in the home and in other contexts (for example, in a particular class at school).
3. The behavior involves serious violations of rights of others and is consistent. Parents feel like they have lost power "over" the child. The behavior usually takes place with any authority figure who is responsible for setting limits and with whom there is a personal relationship.
4. The oppositional child is willing to escalate in a violent or dangerous fashion when faced with reasonable attempts by the immediate family to set limits. The intervention of institutions beyond the immediate family is required.

Comorbidity

A major issue in the conceptualization of ODD in the *DSM-IV* is its relationship to conduct disorder (CD). Most professional journal articles on ODD that have appeared since 1985 include a focus on its relationship to either attention-deficit disorders or CD. Some researchers (e.g., Schachar & Wachsmuth, 1990), view ODD as being a less severe version of CD and most research demonstrates some degree of correlation between the two diagnoses as they are defined in the *DSM* (Lahey et al. 1990; Loeber & Schmaling, 1985). Some studies choose not to differentiate between ODD and CD and lump these into a single category (e.g., Bird et al., 1988; Werry, Elkind, & Reeves, 1987).

ODD is most often referenced in journal articles as a comorbid factor in CD and attention-deficit/hyperactivity disorder (ADHD). ODD is more common in children with ADHD (Biederman et al., 1997; Bird et al., 1988), and the comorbidity of ODD and ADHD results in significantly more negative interactions with school and family (Kuhne, Schachar, & Tannock, 1997).

I suspect that, just as ODD is significantly more stressful in the presence of ADHD, it may also be significantly more stressful when it is comorbid with obsessive-compulsive disorder (OCD). Specifically, the nagging of parents that most children undertake and that is more strident in kids with ODD is especially hard on adults when combined with a obsessive-compulsive energy, focus, and frequency.

Family Associations

Oppositional behavior has been found to be associated with various family situations. After summarizing the data on family dynamics, the *DSM-IV* notes that ODD

> appears to be more common in families in which at least one parent has a history of a Mood Disorder, Oppositional Defiant Disorder, Conduct Disorder, Attention-Deficit/Hyperactivity Disorder, Antisocial Personality Disorder, or a Substance-Related Disorder. In addition, some studies suggest that mothers with a Depressive Disorder are more likely to have children with oppositional behavior, but it is unclear to what extent maternal depression results from or causes oppositional behavior in children. Oppositional Defiant Disorder is more common in families in which there is serious marital discord. (APA, p. 93)

Such associations between ODD and family interaction have been found in numerous studies. Stouthamer-Loeber & Loeber (1986) concluded that ODD symptoms relate to the amount of direct, coercive conflict within the family. Frick, Lahey, Loeber, and Stouthamer-Loeber (1992) found that poor parental adjustment, supervision, and persistence in discipline are associated with ODD.

Developmental Issues

Some degree of oppositional behavior is normal in preschool years, but there is no empirical basis for diagnosing children under the age of five with ODD (Loeber et al., 1991). As noted by Loeber, Lahey, and Thomas,

> Studies that have reported age of onset for disruptive behavior disorders have rarely referred to ODD as separate from CD. . . . In summary, the findings show that, although initially there is some overlap between the age of onset of ODD and CD symptoms for boys, the latter continue to emerge past the typical age of onset for the former. (1991, p. 383)

Excluding adolescent oppositional behavior, some argue that oppositional behavior represents a failure to grow past normal preschool oppositionality (Patterson, 1982).

Treatment Plan

There are four stages to the intervention. The first has two goals: (1) to help parents get past issues of blame and instead focus on solving the problem and (2) through reframing to create an empowering definition of the problem, usually by focusing the parents on differences in adults' and oppositional children's perceptions of power. Stage 1 is usually achieved in the first and second sessions, and there is usually an interval of one or two weeks between sessions.

Stage 2 focuses on disengaging adults from the exhausting and disempowering fights with the youth. One goal is to have the adults determine their own mood rather than allowing the child to do so. The second stage also begins interventions directed at increasing the amount of parent-inspired intimacy with the child in question. Attempts are made to strengthen the support network of the adults by, for example, focusing on the parents' marriage or connections with adult friends.

The third stage focuses on balancing positive and negative reinforcements and thus begins active efforts to change the child. This stage pays careful attention to communication strengths and weaknesses, to "tagging," to the construction of a linked system of cooperative and noncooperative consequences, and to the careful balancing of positive and negative interaction.

The fourth stage has two goals: (1) to help the parents move from merely maintaining their own preferred mood to actively attempting to change the child's mood from a negative to a positive state and (2) to enable them to discuss in an empathic and competent manner the most difficult and painful topic in the system. For soothing to have a profound impact on parental authority, it must be able to be delivered by the adult in highly challenging interaction.

Stage 1: From Blame to Empowering Descriptions

One of the characteristics of successful therapy is being able to move beyond the focus on who or what is to blame to the conversation "what do we do about this now?" (Miller, Duncan, & Hubble, 1997). The adults involved in oppositional confrontations commonly expect that the therapist or other adults in the system blame them for the child's behavior. Dealing with issues of perceived blame through open discussion and diplomatic involvement of parties labeled as agents of blame is essential before the therapy can progress.

Part of moving beyond blame is developing a more empowering view of oppositional behavior to replace the blame ideology. One empowering approach is to share the observation that oppositional youth are process oriented and that this interferes with the function of normal rules and consequences. Since normal rules and consequences tend not to work for oppositional kids, unusual steps must be taken.

Some of the steps in stage 1 include:

1. The parents are told that the child is not mean-spirited or bad but has oppositional tendencies and that the child perceives confrontation in a different way. The therapist says that the child is process oriented, explains the meaning, and finds examples in the case material provided by the family's description of the problem.
2. Reframing should avoid blaming the parents. The therapist explains that, because of the process orientation of the child, normal ways of disciplining the child often do not work. The therapist states that, if the parents have had problems, it was probably because they were doing the normal thing, which works with 85% of the population. This is important for reducing blame. The therapist further stresses the difference

between intervention and causation, explaining that asking the parents to undertake a task does not in any way suggest that they have done something wrong in the past.

3. The most important issue for the parents to understand is that the child loves them or they wouldn't be having these problems.

4. In the child's absence, the therapist encourages the parents and other adults involved to voice how angry they have been with the child and how they have felt that they were losing the power struggle. This is to ensure that the adults sense that the therapist knows just how difficult the situation is. The therapist joins with the adults over how normal it is to feel resentment and then expresses confidence that the parents can turn the situation around in a loving and gentle way. The therapist also emphasizes that it is understood that the parents love the child very deeply.

Stage 2: Beginning the Gentle Disempowerment of the Child

By the time that most families with an oppositional child come to therapy, the adults in the system are too burned out to behave immediately in the warm and empathic manner. Stage 2 works on increasing the energy and confidence of the adults by giving them permission to stop repeating usually successful parenting strategies that do not seem to work with their child and by focusing the adults on self-care during and outside of confrontations with their child. This initial avoidance of unsuccessful strategies is inspired by Watzlawick, Weakland, and Fisch (1974). Stage 2 includes the following steps:

5. The child has been inadvertently empowered and must be disempowered in a gentle and loving way. The child's interest in power is reframed as a loving attempt to become the parent of his parents.

6. The therapist describes the mechanics of the approach. Successfully dealing with oppositional behavior involves paying careful attention to the child's idea of what power is. The adults are urged to focus on how oppositional youth perceive power to be the ability to determine the mood of the parents and household, the timing of confrontations, and content and direction of conversation. Adults tend to perceive power as the ability to determine the outcome of the confrontation. Thus, adults view power as the outcome of the argument, and oppositional children view power as determining the way the argument went.

7. The therapist and parents review specific ways to avoid confrontations that empower the child, using examples of situations that will probably

occur in the next week. The parents are directed to act out in the session how they will respond. Special attention is given to ensuring that the parents respond in a firm, empathic, nonreactive, and optimistic fashion.

8. Strengthening the support network of adults is vital. The therapist must be very careful to stress practical change and self-care without becoming stuck in a discussion of who or what is to blame. For example, if the parents themselves suggest that marital tension has contributed to the child's problems, the therapist should respond with a neutral comment and let the parents view themselves as the source of this criticism.

   a. Adults are warned that trying to change a child with oppositional tendencies places great strain on the relationships. Adults are asked to take countermeasures such as repeating previously successful strategies for dealing with major emotional strains (restarting exercise classes, taking a short trip, etc.).

   b. The parents are told that one of the best ways to show children that they are on a separate, different hierarchical level is for the parents to go out for fun without their children. This contradicts the child's view that she or he is equal to the parents.

   c. Parents are asked to display overt affection for one another in front of the empowered child for the very same reason that they are asked to go out on dates—it emphasizes that there is a special relationship between the parents that is different from either parent's relationship with the child. If the parents are divorced or if their relationship is not romantic, appropriate collaborative gestures are helpful (for example, honestly complimenting and noting the competence of the other parent in the presence of the child).

   d. The parents are asked to use affectionate gestures (if they are currently involved with one another) or openly recall pleasant memories during difficult confrontations with the youth; this helps them to maintain control in emotional situations. For example, a couple may agree that if one kisses the other on the ear during a confrontation with the child, that is a nice way of noting that the other is losing control. Having the parents practice in the session makes use of such triggering signs much more likely.

9. The therapist emphasizes that parent-child intimacy is one of the foundations of parental authority and, if necessary, takes steps to improve the level of family intimacy.

Stage 3: Rules and Consequences

One of the most important moments in addressing oppositional behavior is the delivery by parents of positive and negative consequences. Negative consequences work only in a benevolent system where there is a healthy ratio of positive to negative interactions (Parsons, Siegel, & Cousins, 1997). One characteristic of successful approaches to oppositional behavior is that there is great emphasis on working within the endurance of parents. Such an approach emphasizes practicality and consistency of consequences over their "size," the idea that the punishment needs to fit the crime is very disempowering when youth misbehave as often as oppositional youth do. The following steps are associated with stage 3:

10. The therapist asks the parents to complete a list of existing rules and consequences. Don't be surprised if they tell you that there are no rules or consequences right now. If there are existing rules and consequences, ask the parent(s) if it might be possible to alter the rules. State that the normal approach alone won't work with oppositional children and request that the parents create with you an abnormal set of rules and consequences especially for oppositional behavior. Note that the reason that you are abandoning some existing rules is not that these rules are "wrong" but that the rules are for normal behavior, not oppositional behavior. If there are no rules and consequences, request that the therapy session be dedicated to drawing up a list.
11. Clearly write the rules and consequences on paper to be posted at home. Post the rules even if the child can't read because they are truly more for the parents than for the child.
12. The attitude of the parent(s) while giving a consequence must be firm, empathic, and nonreactive.
13. The therapist must pay attention to parental endurance when designing rules and consequences. Consequences should not be hard on the parents. Any punishment for the child that turns out to be harder on the parents only empowers the child.
14. One approach to consequences for oppositional situations is to avoid compliance-dependent punishments. For example, a punishment of having to rake leaves gives the child many ways to not comply. Taking away a toy or music tape when the child is not home is a punishment that requires no cooperation from the child.

15. Cooperation with a compliance-dependent consequence can be achieved with a two-tier consequence system in which a compliance-based consequence is "backed up" with a noncompliance-based consequence. Two-tier describes a system in which a second consequence is given until or unless the first consequence is completed. For example, until the leaves are raked, the television will remain locked in a closet, or, unless the leaves are raked by Friday, the television will be locked away for the weekend.

16. Use traditional positive reinforcements for good behavior, such as giving a star for a good day and a special prize for seven good days in a row. Self-help books on child-rearing are full of these sorts of positive reinforcement ideas. Encourage the parents to find or invent their own positive reinforcements.

17. There must be scheduled, regular parent-child fun that is never interfered with by consequences or other events. As noted in the hierarchy chart, being the provider of good things and good times is part of what gives adults authority, and it is important to avoid a degree of punishment that disempowers a parent by removing this provider role. Balanced systems require that consequences and positive interaction coexist.

18. The ability to decide when a confrontation will take place is central to the child's perception of who is in control. Don't let the child determine the timing of a confrontation if possible. Obviously, there are situations such as serious fights where the parent has no choice but to intervene at that time. However, if possible, it should be the parent who decides the timing of a confrontation. And, no matter how one intends the situation to progress, giving a punishment is always a confrontation. Let it be at the parent's timing, not the child's.

Giving punishments is one of the hardest things to do if one is trying to remain in control of one's mood. Parents should announce punishments at a time when they feel calm, centered, and in control. If the child picks the timing of the confrontation, it is almost guaranteed that it will be at a moment when the parent is tired, in a rush to get somewhere, or otherwise distracted. If the parent has a partner, I often recommend that punishments not be given out until both adults are at home and can discretely coach one another to be calm and empathic while giving the punishment. If the parent does not have a partner, an adult friend or neighbor will do.

Thus, contrary to traditional behaviorism, the exact punishment for breaking a serious rule should sometimes not be announced at the time of the bad behavior. It is better to tag significant bad behavior. Tagging is when a parent, teacher, or other authority figure tells the child that the parent is aware of the bad behavior and will deal with it later. It is appropriate only to tag bad behavior if it seems to the adults that the child is purposefully provoking the adult or if the adult is not in the best of conditions to control his or her own mood through a confrontation.

I have noticed that many oppositional youths have information-processing problems. Great care needs to be taken to ensure that the communication strengths and weaknesses of the child are respected during delivery and discussion of consequences. Coaching parents to use more facial expression, for example, might be particularly important with a youth whose auditory processing difficulties make it difficult for him to understand the emotional spin of verbal communication. This is especially important during moments of increased anxiety, when standard information-processing abilities are lowered.

Stage 4: Soothing the Oppositional Youth

The fourth stage moves the parents from merely focusing on maintaining a loving attitude themselves to actively changing the child's mood from negative to positive. The test of the parents' soothing ability is their competent and empathic handling of the most challenging discussions in the system.

The therapist coaches the parents in techniques that change the child's mood from a negative, escalating, inappropriately powerful one to a positive one appropriate for the child's age. The parent realizes that part of the power of parenting comes from the ability to soothe a child in an appropriate manner.A goal is to get the child to seek help in a positive way from the parent when the child realizes that his or her mood is off.

One strategy of mood changing is the age-old approach of parental reinterpretation, the interpretation by parents that the child's anger and aggressiveness are a sign that the youth is in pain or is experiencing anxiety and needs to talk about it. One example of parental reinterpretation used with young and mildly oppositional children is playful diversion, for example, turning the child's initiation of defiant behavior into a joke or game. The response to "I won't do that" might be that the parent tickles and kisses the child while mimicking the youngster in a playful way. The younger child will often go along with the game and pretend that she was actually just playing with the parent instead of trying to be defiant.

Another example of parental reinterpretation is metaphorical diversion, an age-old parenting approach that is most commonly used with older children. With metaphorical diversion, the parent chooses to openly interpret a child's defiant behavior as a sign that something important and serious needs to be discussed. For example, a parent might react to an adolescent's defiant comment by choosing to respond as if the comment were a sign that the child (a) was not feeling well, (b) had had a bad day at school, or (c) was depressed about something. Metaphorical diversion works only if the parent is being empathic and the symbolic interpretation, for example, that the child is not feeling well, is to some degree true. Ideally, this sort of diversion leads to a conversation about something that is truly bothering the child.

The therapist coaches the parents in metaphorical diversion and other techniques to find out from the child what is really bothering him or her. Often the poor communication that characterizes oppositional situations prevents necessary conversations from taking place. It is almost as if the oppositional child, through negative behavior, is giving the parents an excuse to avoid talking about certain sensitive topics. The therapist coaches the parents to keep the conversation on track, so that the child feels safe discussing even the "hottest" topics in the family.

The therapist coaches the parents to break stereotypes of family interaction that the child holds. This may involve getting parents to enjoy and practice stepping out of behavioral ruts. The therapist also continues coaching parents to take care of themselves so that they have sufficient energy and a balanced sense of their own lives. The parents must seem competent to the child in leading their own lives if the child is not to worry about them, and one of the most important ways for parents to demonstrate this is by having fun that does not involve the oppositional child.

The central intervention of stage 4 involves coaching adults to soothe a youth not only in common disagreements but also in relation to the most central pains in the young person's heart. This coaching usually includes helping adults to pursue a conversation about a painful issue in an empathic manor. Very oppositional youths will severely test adults before making themselves vulnerable through receipt of soothing; accepting soothing from an adult leads a youth to feel age-appropriate, and this is not always a safe feeling. In the case described earlier, Anna (the 10-year-old girl who is one of a number of siblings adopted simultaneously by one couple) did not feel safe in expressing her pain over her sister's leaving home until she had severely tested her parents. Anna insulted her parents in the most powerful way she knew and did so over a dozen times during this conversation. The parents, however, had been coached for almost two months (not in the presence of the child) and could recognize her acting out as a test that would allow Anna to feel safe offering up her pain to them for soothing. The parents thus responded with soothing.

The conversation below began with the parents' asking Anna how she felt about her older sister's leaving home. The parents and the therapist knew that this was the most pressing issue in Anna's heart at the moment through common sense (Veronica had been the one stable caretaking figure in her life) and through Anna's own words. Anna responded to the parents' request by having a tantrum in the office. The parents then switched to soothing, and then back to the issue of Veronica; they repeated this process of alternately soothing and seeking to discuss the issue so vital to Anna. The dialogue transcribed below begins with a return to soothing conversation, which takes the form of the adults' speaking in a complimentary way to each other about Anna; such indirect soothing is used when direct soothing would overwhelm the child.

MOTHER: Anna gave me a wonderful massage last night.
THERAPIST: Did she?
MOTHER: Yeah. She wanted me to come into her bed, and I went into her bed, and she just gave me a really nice massage. She's very good at that.
ANNA: Next time I'll be sure to kill you.
THERAPIST, MOTHER, FATHER: Mmmm.

The parents have been coached to respond in this situation to the murder threat by soothing the child. Previously, the mother had left the room when the issue of murder came up.

MOTHER: I know she's feeling mad.
FATHER: I, I think, we know that you don't mean those things you say.
ANNA: Phahhhhhhh!
FATHER: We know that you're upset.
THERAPIST: You know, Veronica will always be in the family, but you know, she's at the age where she's going to be making her own decisions and going on with her life and career.
MOTHER: Yeah, when Veronica first came to us, she'd been with her mom for 10 years. Ten long years. And so her mom is—basically that's her mom. You guys . . .
FATHER: In her mind, that's her mom for life . . .
MOTHER: . . . even after she came to us.
FATHER: . . . no matter what.

THERAPIST: Because at that age, especially, when you're 10, the person that you look at as your mom is the person you've considered your mom.

FATHER: Um-hm.

ANNA: Well, I still consider her my mom, my old mom, but you guys just came and adopted us and now you're treating us like we're nothing!

This myth that the children were kidnapped is interesting, but it would be a diversion to discuss it now as the child knows that it is not true. She is actually testing the parents. They must respond in an empathic and soothing manner.

FATHER: I hope not. You're very special.

ANNA: And you call people selfish!

THERAPIST: But, but you can understand . . .

ANNA: And you lie!!

THERAPIST: . . . how, when, um, how it's very upsetting for them when Veronica's . . .

FATHER: Yeah.

ANNA: No! Why don't you listen to me?!!

FATHER: Well, I think he was, don't you?

ANNA: No, no! I am sick of Mom calling me selfish, because that is not true.

MOTHER: You're . . .

ANNA: And I'm sick . . . No! I'm sick of you calling me selfish, I'm sick of you lying, 'cause I know when you're lying, 'cause your cheeks turn bright pink.

THERAPIST: Why don't you let her know that you know, just remind her that . . .

ANNA: And every time we go out somewhere . . .

THERAPIST: . . . the decision's up to Veronica, that you've asked her to come back, but Veronica's going to decide . . .

ANNA: . . . everytime we go out somewhere, if I haven't been behaving how you want me to you don't let me eat . . .

THERAPIST: . . . and she'll always be around and . . .

ANNA: . . . starve me or make me eat bad food, so disgusting.

THERAPIST: . . . and, um . . .

ANNA: I'm talking!

THERAPIST: . . . what, um, and it's okay for her to feel, you know, strange about it.

MOTHER: Yeah, I think it would be . . .

FATHER: Yeah, that's something that might be helpful for you to know, Anna. That sometimes kids do feel bad about something, like you feel bad about Veronica leaving, but we all have to accept it. Eventually Veronica gets old enough to make those choices for herself and we know you feel bad.

Some minutes later, the soothing continues as the adults talk to each other in a way that is complimentary to Anna.

FATHER: Even without toe shoes, she can stand on the tip of her toes.

THERAPIST: That's incredible.

MOTHER: Yeah.

THERAPIST: That's incredible.

FATHER: Very well coordinated. And lately she's learning gymnastics routines. She can do a back walkover very gracefully.

ANNA: Back walkover, front, front, back flip . . .

FATHER: . . . front flip . . .

THERAPIST: Um-hm.

ANNA: . . . splits. I can do anything I want to do.

FATHER: . . . cartwheel . . .

ANNA: Right now, I don't want to do anything.

FATHER: And we went to sort of a western dinner at the elementary school and they were teaching line dancing.

MOTHER: Yeah, yeah.

FATHER: And Anna went up and volunteered to be the partner for the guy who was teaching it.

THERAPIST: Um-hm.

FATHER: And he demonstrated the steps and she got it right away.

MOTHER: She's very gifted and very loving. She can be extremely loving sometimes and real caring.

THERAPIST: Tell her how much you like that.

ANNA: Say anything and I'll kill you!

The threat of murder is usually a conversation buster, but the therapy has coached the parents to vary their responses.

MOTHER: See, it makes me feel really good when she's really loving, 'cause it just shows me that she can . . .

ANNA: Hold on, I'm putting down every word of this!

MOTHER: . . . she can have a good life when she's like that.

FATHER: Yeah. And it shows that she has the capacity for very positive feelings.

MOTHER: Yeah.

FATHER: I think when somebody has that ability that, even though it gets clouded by bad feelings sometimes, they can always go back to the good feelings.

THERAPIST: Um-hm.

FATHER: We're very lucky.

MOTHER: She's very beautiful when she's like that. When she's very giving, her whole being is like really radiant, and it's really beautiful.

THERAPIST: Um-hm.

MOTHER: And everybody wants to be with her.

THERAPIST: Um-hm.

FATHER: Veronica has that trait, too. She can be just a very, very good friend.

THERAPIST: Um-hm. (*pause*) What do you miss most about Veronica? (*pause*) Anna, what do you miss most about Veronica?

MOTHER: Oh, let's see. I guess I miss those traits, those warm traits, you know, those traits where she's . . .

ANNA: I miss Veronica because you take her away. No. You want to hear why I'm saddest? Because you take everything that's important to me away. Veronica's important to me and you just take her away from me.

FATHER: And you feel a great loss.

After more than a dozen serious provocations were met with soothing, Anna felt safe enough to open up to her parents about her pain over Veronica's leaving. This greatly empowered the parents, because they proved they could handle the "hottest" topic in the system in a warm and empathic manner. Using the construct of the hierarchy chart, the parents have proved successful at soothing and thus have helped Anna to feel safe in being age-appropriate. In succeeding in soothing their child, the father and mother have greatly enhanced their own perception of their competence as parents. It is the ability to soothe in the most difficult of moments that, when paired with consistent and clear consequences, begins to change oppositional behavior to more age-appropriate behavior. One conversation does not create this change; it is the integration of the process into the interactional patterns of the family that addresses the behavior, and accomplishing this takes many soothing, but difficult, conversations.

Other Guidelines for the Four-Step Intervention

1. Oppositional behavior on the part of parents should be thought of as a sign that they feel blamed by the therapist. The amount of parental collaboration with the therapist is usually inversely proportional to the degree that parents feel that the therapist is blaming them. Therapists are often portrayed in the media as blaming parents, so it is best to be proactive, assume that being blamed is an issue before it manifests, and deal with it in direct and overt discussion early in the case.

2. When first describing this approach to parents, caution the parents to be patient and not expect too much from themselves when it comes to the speed with which they adapt these techniques. The most common reason for parents to drop out of therapy is a pace that is too fast. If, during the first week of this program, the parents employ on just one occasion the techniques described, they are to be congratulated. It is my experience that parents usually adapt the full approach rather quickly, but telling parents this puts too much pressure on them. Of course, with more serious behavior, the therapist must push for faster change. For an example of how to motivate parents very quickly to assume a new approach and change a serious oppositional sequence, see the atom bomb technique of Jerry Price (1996).

3. Note that this approach does not in any way depend upon the child's cooperation with the therapist. It is designed to work even if, in the case of a teenage client, the kid refuses to come in and the parents must come in alone. It is important to let the parents know that the child does not have the power to sink the therapy by not attending.

4. The therapist must model the appropriate mood for the family. Remember that the fashion in which a directive is given influences the mood with which the parents will carry it out. The mood of the parents when interacting with the child should be nonreactive (in the sense described by Murray Bowen [1972]), optimistic, warm, caring, and firm. This is also the mood to be modeled by the therapist. By "optimistic," we mean that the parents should act around the child as if they completely

expect the kid to follow their instructions; this attitude should be main-tained even when the child is threatening noncompliance.

5. Pay close attention to issues related to parental endurance in confronta-tions with children. Oppositional kids are masters at button-pushing. Emphasize that parents must choose their battles wisely and never let the child choose the battle; in order to do this, the parent must feel all right about making strategic retreats from the child. Ask parents how long they can reasonably expect to withstand a verbal onslaught before they retreat strategically. Discuss the specifics of how parents will complete the retreat before their endurance runs out. Then discuss what to do if they find that they have run out of patience.

6. This approach emphasizes helping the parents to avoid inappropriate and disempowering discussions with the child. However, the therapist should be sure that there is a proper time and place for legitimate complaints of the child to be aired.

7. Don't be surprised if the child declares that he or she hates you as a ther-apist. No matter how nice you are, once the child picks up on the fact that you are involved in his or her gentle disempowerment, you will be in the dog house. Think of poor treatment at the hands of the oppositional child as a chance to model control of mood for the parents. Emphasize to par-ents that this approach is designed to work without the cooperation of the oppositional child and that they should not be surprised or overly wor-ried when the child refuses to come to therapy.

Conclusion

The challenge for the psychotherapist is to focus on those few variables that are most likely to facilitate change (Haley, 1976). In the context of oppositional behavior, I have, through clinical observation, identified several important vari-ables. One begins by viewing oppositional youths as trying to assume the authority of adults through controlling behaviors that focus both on the hard side of hierarchy and on the construction of interaction as being zero-sum (win/lose) conflicts. Four important moments of escalation are when the adult authority figures (a) also focus on the hard side of hierarchy to the exclusion of soft-side responsibilities, (b) join in the construction of difficult discussion as being win/lose competitions, (c) replace normal consequences that no longer seem to work with verbal attempts to inflict emotional pain, and (d) triangulate with the youth against other adults. The four-stage intervention proceeds beyond avoiding the four types of escalation to actually turning them into opportunities for authority figures to express consistency, empathy, and, when appropriate, soothing.

The art involved in the therapy of oppositional behavior is the maintenance of a cooperative relationship with the adult authority figures and, if possible, the youth as well. Blame is continually addressed, and the involvement of third parties is scrutinized. Pacing according to the often-injured endurance of the adults is critical, and coaching self-care is required in order to give parents and others the energy and empathy to treat the youth warmly in difficult moments. Change tends to bring the realization that power within a family is determined not so much by the ability to control (which adults and oppositional youths are often equally skilled at) as by the ability of one party to soothe and fulfill the emotional needs of the other. It is only when power is additionally defined in terms of soothing and meeting emotional needs that adults are able to assume a benevolent authority and youths resume age-appropriate functioning that marks the resolution of oppositional behavior.

James P. Keim, M.S.W., L.C.S.W., is an internationally known presenter in private practice in Ft. Collins, Colorado.

References

Alexander, J. F., & Parsons, B. V. (1973). Short-term behavioral intervention with delinquent families: Impact on family process and recidivism. *Journal of Abnormal Psychology, 51,* 219–225.

American Psychiatric Association. (1994). *Diagnostic and statistical manual of mental disorders* (4th ed.). Washington, DC: Author.

Bateson, G. (1958). *Naven.* Stanford, CA: Stanford University Press.

Bateson, G., Haley, J., Jackson, D., & Weakland, J. (1956). Toward a theory of schizophrenia. *Behavioral Science, 1,* 251–264.

Baumrind, D. (1967, February). Child care practices anteceding three patterns of preschool behavior. *Genetic Psychology Monographs, 75*(1), 43–88.

Baumrind D., & Moselle, K. A. (1985, Spring-Summer). A development perspective on adolescent drug abuse. *Advances in Alcohol and Substance Abuse, 4*(3-4), 41–67.

Biederman, J., Faraone, S. V., Park, K. S., Rater, M., Russell, R. L., & Weber, W. (1997, December). Correspondence between DSM-II-R and DSM-IV attention-deficit/hyperactivity disorder. *Journal American Academy of Child and Adolescent Psychiatry, 36*(12), 1682–1687.

Bird, H. R., Canino, G., et al. (1988). Estimates of the prevalence of childhood maladjustment in a community survey in Puerto Rico. *Archives of General Psychiatry, 45,* 1120–1126.

Bowen, M. (1972). Being and becoming a family therapist. In A. Ferber, M. Mendelsohn, & A. Napier (Eds.), *The book of family therapy.* New York: Science House.

Chamberlain, P. (1994). *Family connections: A treatment foster care model for adolescents with delinquency.* Eugene, OR: Castalia.

Cohen J. D., Dunbar, K. O., Barch, D. M., & Braver, T. S. (1997, March). Issues concerning relative speed of processing hypotheses, schizophrenic performance deficits, and prefrontal function: Comment on Schooler et al. *Journal of Experimental Psychology: General, 126*(1), 37–41.

Fisher, R., & Ury, W. (1981). *Getting to yes.* Boston: Houghton-Mifflin.

Frick, P. J., Lahey, B. B., Loeber, R., & Stouthamer-Loeber, M. (1992). Familial risk factors to oppositional defiant disorder: Parental psychopathology and maternal parenting. *Journal of Consulting and Clinical Psychology, 60*(1), 49–55.

Gray, J. (1992). *Men are from mars, women are from venus.* New York: HarperCollins.

Haley, J. (1976). *Problem-solving therapy.* San Francisco: Jossey-Bass.

Haley, J. (1980). *Leaving home: The therapy of disturbed young people.* New York: McGraw-Hill.

Haley, J. (1981). *Reflections on therapy and other essays.* Rockville, MD: Triangle Press.

Keim, J. (1998). Strategic family therapy. In F. Dattilio (Ed.), *Case studies in couple and family therapy.* New York: Guilford.

Kochanska, G. (1990, December). Maternal beliefs as long-term predictors of mother-child interaction and report. *Child Development, 61*(6), 1934–1943.

Kuhne, M., Schachar, R., & Tannock, R. (1997, December). Impact of comorbid oppositional or conduct problems on attention-deficit hyperactivity disorder. *Journal American Academy of Child and Adolescent Psychiatry, 36*(12), 1715–1725.

Lahey, B. B., Loeber, R., Stouthamer-Loeber, M., Christ, M. A., Green, S., Russo, M. F., Frick, P. J., & Dulcan, M. (1990, July). Comparison of DSM-III and DSM-III-R diagnoses for prepubertal children: Changes in prevalence and validity. *Journal American Academy of Child and Adolescent Psychiatry, 29*(4), 620–626.

Lamborn, S. D., Mounts, N. S., Steinberg, L., & Dornbusch, S. M. (1991, October). Patterns of competence and adjustment among adolescents from authoritative, authoritarian, indulgent, and neglectful families. *Child Development, 62*(5), 1049–1065.

Larzelere, R. E., Baumrind, D., & Polite, K. (1998, March). Two emerging perspectives of parental spanking from two 1996 conferences. *Archives of Pediatric and Adolescent Medicine, 152*(3), 303–305.

Loeber, R., Lahey, B., & Thomas, C. (1991). Diagnostic conundrum of oppositional defiant disorder and conduct disorder. *Journal of Abnormal Psychology, 100*(3), 379–390.

Loeber, R., & Schmaling, K. B. (1985, June). Empirical evidence for overt and covert patterns of antisocial conduct problems: A meta-analysis. *Journal of Abnormal Child Psychology, 13*(2), 337–353.

Madanes, C. (1981). *Strategic family therapy.* San Francisco: Jossey-Bass.

Madanes, C. (1984). *Behind the one-way mirror: Advances in the practice of strategic therapy.* San Francisco: Jossey-Bass.

Miller, S., Duncan, B., & Hubble, M. (YEAR). *Escape from babel.* New York: Norton.

Minuchin, S. (1997). *Families and family therapy.* Cambridge, MA: Harvard University Press.

Minuchin, S., Montalvo, B., Guerney, B., Rosman, B., & Schumer, F. (1967). *Families of the slums.* New York: Basic.

Parsons, J. T., Siegel, A. W., & Cousins, J. H. (1997, August). Late adolescent risk-taking: Effects of perceived benefits and perceived risks on behavioral intentions and behavioral change. *Journal of Adolescence, 20*(4), 381–392.

Patterson, G. R. (1982). *Coercive family interactions.* Eugene, OR: Castalia.

Price, J. (1996). *Power and compassion.* New York: Guilford.

Pruitt, D. G. (1983, November-December). Strategic choice in negotiation. *American Behavioral Scientist, 27,* 167–194.

Schachar, R., & Wachsmuth, T. (1990). Oppositional disorder in children: A validation study comparing conduct disorder, oppositional disorder, and normal control children. *Journal of Child Psychology and Psychiatry, 31,* 1089–1102.

Smetana, J. G. (1995, April). Parenting styles and conceptions of parental authority during adolescence. *Child Development, 66*(2), 299–316.

Steinberg, L., Fletcher, A., & Darling, N. (1994, June). Parental monitoring and peer influences on adolescent substance use. *Pediatrics,* (6, Pt. 2), 1060–1064.

Stouthamer-Loeber, M., & Loeber, R. (1986, December). Boys who lie. *Journal of Abnormal Child Psychology, 14*(4), 551–564.

Tannen, D. (1991). *You just don't understand: Women and men in conversation.* New York: Ballantine.

Watzlawick, P., Bavelas, J., & Jackson, D. (1967). *The pragmatics of human communication.* New York: Norton.

Watzlawick, P., Weakland, J., & Fisch, R. (1974). *Change: Principles of problem formation and problem resolution.* New York: Norton.

Weiss, G., & Hechtman, L. (1986). *Hyperactive children grown up.* New York: Guilford.

Werry, J. S., Elkind, G. S., & Reeves, J. C. (1987, September). Attention deficit, conduct, oppositional, and anxiety disorders in children: III. Laboratory differences. *Journal of Abnormal Child Psychology, 15*(3), 409–428.

12

Attention-Deficit/Hyperactivity Disorder: Working with Children and Their Families

Michol Polson

Family therapy has devoted little attention to the treatment of families with children with attention-deficit/hyperactivity disorder (ADHD), despite the fact that ADHD is the most researched and written-about childhood problem (Barkley, 1987, 1991; Breen & Altepeter, 1990; DuPaul, Guevremont, & Barkley, 1991). Children with ADHD and their associated difficulties comprise the most prevalent clinical population in child and adolescent mental health settings (Barkley, 1997; Weissberg, Caplan, & Harwood, 1991).

ADHD embodies a chronic childhood disturbance characterized by an inability to maintain attention focus, high levels of impulsive behavior, and difficulty regulating motor activity (APA, 1987; Barkley, Fischer, Edelbrock, & Smallish, 1990; Barkley, Guevremont, Anastopolous, & Fletchner, 1992; Hechtman & Weiss, 1986). Approximately 3 to 5% of school age children appear to have this problem, with boys outnumbering girls in ratios from 6:1 to 9:1 (Fehlings, Roberts, Humphries, & Dawe, 1991; Barkley, 1990; Szatmari, Offord, & Boyle, 1989). Research also seems to support an additional characteristic of ADHD: deficits in the ability to regulate behavior appropriately to conform to rule-governed situations. It may appear at times as if the child has a built-in resistance to complying with family and classroom rules. A child's chronic inability to regulate his or her behavior due to ADHD strains teachers, parents, siblings, and extended family members. Eventually, the majority of parents with children with ADHD seek some form of intervention (usually medication) to better manage the child's misbehavior and diminished task performance. By mid-adolescence, 70 to 80% of children will have received psy-

308

chopharmacological intervention at the behest of their parents (Rosenberg, Holttum, & Gershon, 1994).

The purpose of this chapter is to provide family therapists or those interested in doing family therapy with a basic understanding of ADHD and ways to treat children with ADHD by involving family members in treatment. The diagnostic criteria for ADHD in the *DSM-IV*, procedures for assessing and diagnosing ADHD, common psychopharmacological interventions, developmental stages for ADHD, and typical dynamics of families with children with ADHD will be discussed. The chapter will end with the presentation of a treatment approach for families with preadolescents with ADHD. This approach reduces disruptive behavior, increases child compliance with rules in the home, and strengthens parenting cooperativeness and consistency.

DSM-IV Diagnostic Categories for ADHD

According to the *DSM-IV* (APA, 1994), the primary characteristics for ADHD are inattentiveness, impulsivity, and hyperactivity. These "markers" must be manifest *more frequently and severely* than in other age-appropriate peers. Thus a 6-year-old with ADHD must be *much more* inattentive, impulsive, or hyperactive than other 6-year-old children. In effect, the child who is properly diagnosed would definitely stand out as having *consistent, repetitive* patterns of criteria behavior compared to his or her peers who might *at times* be inattentive or impulsive or engage in restless motor behaviors.

Inattentiveness is described as problematic behaviors or impairment in a child's ability to retain sequential information in short-term memory retention (Barkley, 1994; Quinn, 1994). This impairment obstructs a child's ability to properly organize task performance. One often sees this in a child's inability to understand homework directions, complete homework assignments properly, or remember the sequence of instructions for home chores.

Impulsivity focuses on a child's inability to control reactivity to multiple, simultaneously occurring stimuli. This may confuse the family therapist since children are by definition impulsive. As stated previously, this impulsivity must be much more *severe* and *repetitive* than in other age-appropriate children. Most 6-year-old children like to climb things; many 6-year-old children with ADHD like to climb higher and take more dangerous risks. For example, such a child might climb a 12-feet-tall play slide and then jump off the top just to see what happens.

The last marker, *hyperactivity,* describes a child's inability to control rest-less verbal or motor activity. The classic behavior is a child's tendency to fid-get in a seated position, but it may also include excessive or loud talking. The *DSM-IV* places hyperactivity and impulsivity together, so the diagnosing clin-ician must look at the criteria for both.

Oppositional Defiant Disorder (ODD) and Conduct Disorder (CD)

Various authors have suggested that approximately 50% of children with ADHD (e.g., Barkley, 1990) will qualify for a comorbid diagnosis of opposi-tional defiant disorder (ODD) or conduct disorder (CD). ODD is a recurring pattern of negativity, hostility, and defiance toward fulfilling environmental demands (APA, 1994). CD is an advanced form of ODD where the individual has little regard for the rights or property of others and may engage in delin-quency. Since ADHD is not "curable," much of what one focuses on changing in family therapy are the noncompliant behaviors of ODD.

Therapists should assess for ODD or CD when assessing for ADHD. Bear in mind that ODD does not necessarily occur together with ADHD. Nevertheless, it should always be examined to rule out since it reflects a hard-ened resistance to environmental demands—precisely what the family therapist will begin to introduce with the family.

Frontal Lobe Disinhibition and Barkley's Developmental Model of Self-Control

The concepts *attention deficit* and *hyperactivity* used as the core of the diag-nosis for ADHD in the *DSM-IV* reflect research that began in the 1960s. Indeed, both concepts characterize ADHD symptomology but *not its causes.* Advances in research, particularly in brain mapping technologies (CAT, MRI, PET) are changing the notion of the underlying brain structures and mecha-nisms of patients with ADHD.

In the late 1980s researchers began to focus on the neurobiology of ADHD in an effort to determine the causal components or structures in the brain. These researchers began to study the prefrontal lobes of the cerebral cortex. The pre-frontal lobes perform *executive functions;* that is, the ability of the brain to uti-lize effective problem-solving strategies to resolve a present difficulty. Chief among these executive functions is the capacity to *inhibit improper choices.* Individuals who have a dysregulation of these executive functions will make impulsive choices, have less organizational ability, and respond more to dis-tracting environmental stimuli. For example, an individual who exhibits restless motor behavior or attentional distractibility is manifesting the inability of the prefrontal lobes to inhibit behavioral and cognitive hyperresponsivity to internal and environmental stimuli. Patricia Quinn, one of the leading authors on ADHD, states,

> It is now generally believed that ADHD is a result of the *disinhibition of the frontal lobes,* where the frontal lobes fail to inhibit emotional responses, inappropriate cognitive or psychological responses, and behavioral impulses. (1995, p. 22)

Russell Barkley (1997) proposes a comprehensive "hybrid model of executive functions," which links the latest information on neurobiology with a brain information-processing theory. This model is impressive because it is the first holistic model that explains how the brain processes work together to produce the characteristics of ADHD. Barkley borrows Bronowski's (1977) theory on the internalization of speech development and adapts it to a neurological model of the prefrontal lobes' executive functions. Behavioral impulses are inhibited, according to Barkley, through four executive functions that "permit self-control so as to anticipate change and the future, thereby maximizing the long-term outcomes or benefits for the future" (p. 154). One of Barkley's most startling assertions is that ADHD creates a distortion of the sense of psychological time for the individual. For example, children with ADHD live more in the present, governed by present-time impulses. Because ADHD creates a diminished sense of the past and future, children with ADHD find it more difficult to create adaptive behavior and control their impulses. To make proper choices, all individuals must link present stimuli with past consequences in order to properly regulate present stimuli to attain future goals. In other words, children with ADHD, especially when in a state of high emotional arousal (anger, sadness, defiance, etc.), may find it extremely difficult to connect to past consequences in memory and link them to future outcomes in order to make the appropriate choices in the present. Parents find it maddening when a child can, *after the fact,* recite perfectly the choices he or she should have done, but *at the moment* made the wrong choice(s). It is the rare parent who does not want, at that moment, to berate the child for his or her apparent stupidity. Yet Barkley's model explains in a clearly straightforward manner how the ADHD child's brain works to make such choices. It is highly recommended reading for the family therapist who wishes to understand ADHD on more than a superficial level.

In the next decade or two, the current usage of "ADHD" most probably will change to a different construct, perhaps BID (behavioral inhibition disorder; Barkley, 1994) or some variant, reflecting the etiological change in focus from symptoms to causes.

Procedures for Assessing and Diagnosing ADHD

Most prominent ADHD clinicians and researchers advocate a triad approach to diagnosis (Barkley, 1990; DuPaul & Stoner, 1994). This is a careful gathering and sifting of evaluative information to reach a tentative diagnostic conclusion. Unfortunately, many children are medicated by well-intended physicians simply upon the "diagnosis" of ADHD by the teacher or parent.

The triad method of diagnosing for ADHD consists of empirical assessment, behavioral observation, and a medical evaluation. Several empirical instruments are widely used for diagnosing ADHD. These include the Child Behavior Checklist: Parent, Teacher Report Forms, (Achenbach & Edelbrock, 1983) and Conners Parent and Teacher Rating Scale (Goyette, Conners, & Ulrich, 1978).

Behavioral observations, the second part of the triad diagnosis, should take place in as naturalistic a setting as possible (Barkley, 1994), such as in a task-oriented classroom setting (not play activities or recess) or with the child's family. A child's interactions with his or her parent(s) and sibling(s) can be observed in a structured, rather boring therapy room setting. The therapist may need to observe the child on more than one occasion in order to get an accurate sense of the child's behavior.

The final component of the triad diagnosis is a complete medical evaluation. Therapists working with children with ADHD should identify physicians in their community who really understand the disorder and who utilize caution in diagnosing and medicating these children.

Medicating ADHD Children

More literature exists on the psychopharmacological treatment of ADHD than any other treatment modality. Indeed, psychoactive medication of children with ADHD is the most common intervention, affecting some two million children annually (Rosenberg et al., 1994). In most cases, medication will comprise the only intervention these children ever receive (Ruel & Hickey, 1992). By the time children with ADHD are in their early teens, 70 to 80% will have experienced a medication trial (Weiss & Hechtman, 1993). Most children on medication show an improved ability to concentrate, do schoolwork, and inhibit their behavior. The accumulated body of empirical evidence shows that medication works better than any other intervention to improve ADHD symptomology; however, little research exists documenting the effectiveness of medication over years or even decades (Rosenberg et al., 1994).

Of these medications, the stimulant medications *Ritalin* (menthylphenidate), *Dexedrine* (dextroamphetamine), and *Cylert* (pemoline) are the first-line choices for treating ADHD (Rosenberg et al., 1994; Wilens & Biederman, 1992). Other medications, such as the tricyclic antidepressants *Norpramine* (desipramine), *Trofranil* (imipramine), *Prozac* (fluoxine), and *Wellbutrin* (bupropion), have a high use as replacement choices for stimulant medications that either do not work for the child or cause severe side effects. Family therapists working with children with ADHD *must* have a working knowledge of the commonly used psychoactive medications. Parents generally have many questions regarding medications and the consequences of medicating children.

To Medicate or Not to Medicate?

Many children with ADHD are already taking psychotropic medication when they come to the therapist. The family therapist who believes that medication is unnecessary or inappropriate may find him- or herself in a power struggle with the parents and/or school system. I generally encourage the use of medication as *one of several interventions*. If the child is on medication, I support it. If the child is not, I encourage parents to consider a medication trial for a month to see if it improves inattentiveness and task performance; however, I also stress very strongly that improvements in misbehavior due to medication effects may not last more than three months. Psychotropic medication will not erase recurrent episodes of misbehavior in the long run nor expunge the maladaptive patterns of thought and behavior that the child has learned to cope with ADHD (Rosenberg et al., 1994). In addition, medication does not change entrenched maladaptive family patterns around the child's behavior. It will not make parents more consistent in their structuring of the home environment nor will it make ineffective parenting more effective. In the short run, medication may give the parents and/or the teacher respite from the child's misbehavior, long enough to implement changes in the structure of the child's environment. Ten to 30% of children with ADHD will respond so positively to medication that little other intervention is necessary (Barkley, 1997; Weiss & Hechtman,

1993). Such children may have more mild symptoms, a higher than average IQ, a more structured, nurturing home environment, and an absence of comorbid learning disabilities, oppositional defiant disorder, or conduct disorder.

Developmental Issues

The literature on developmental stages and ADHD is voluminous. Those interested in more in-depth information are encouraged to read the literature reviews in Barkley (1990) and Weiss and Hechtman (1993).

Infants

Weiss & Hechtman (1993) indicate that very few studies exist to legitimately document ADHD in infants. Anecdotal information suggests that children later diagnosed with ADHD may present with the following as infants and toddlers: difficult-to-soothe crying; restless, disturbed sleep followed by screaming; feeding difficulties—crying or screaming during feeding; little-to-no smiling; and aversion to cuddling and physical touch (Weiss & Hechtman, 1993). When assessing for potential infant evidence of ADHD symptomology, some parents will report similar anecdotal information. While this constitutes interesting supportive testimony, it does not a diagnosis make.

Preschoolers

Barkley (1990) suggests that one can begin to identify some children who truly have ADHD, especially combined type, by their displays of what he calls "negative temperament." These temperament qualities have a neurological basis, and result in "early and relatively persistent personality characteristics of children" (p. 108). A child possessing such qualities may exhibit the following, compared to other similar aged children: overactivity, higher emotional and behavioral intensity, more inattentiveness, negative mood, quick irritability or anger, and aggression toward other children. It is not uncommon for preschoolers with ADHD symptoms to have been "kicked out" of several daycare facilities because of their aggressive behavior.

Preschoolers who have ADHD frequently have accidents because of fearless, impulsive, or inattentive behavior. Child Protective Services may become involved as the result of the child's injuries. Barkley (1990) reports that parents of preschoolers with ADHD must child-proof their home because of the destructive nature of the child's play. Noncompliance with rules and instruction is very common. Approximately 30 to 60% are actively defiant or oppositional (Cohen & Mindle, 1983). Some preschoolers' neurological systems may have some developmental delay or actual impairment. This may produce toilet-training difficulties and motor/speech delays. Significant delays in bowel/bladder control may also occur.

Preschoolers with ADHD cause their parents, especially mothers, a great amount of stress. Compared to mothers of children who do not have ADHD, these mothers give more commands, directions, criticism, supervision, and punishment. Parents of preschool children with ADHD also measure higher on parenting stress *than parents with older ADHD children* (Barkley, 1990).

Middle Childhood

When the child with ADHD enters middle childhood, parents must deal with not only at-home problems but also the increased pressure of problems from school. The major burden usually centers on poor academic performance and in-school disruptive and noncompliant behavior. Some researchers have speculated that up to 50% of children with ADHD need special education services because of academic difficulties (Lerner, Lowenthal, & Lerner, 1995; McKinney, Montague, & Hocutt, 1993).

Children with ADHD also begin to experience more pronounced social rejection during middle childhood. Because they have poorer self-monitoring skills than their peers, they typically commit more social gaffes. In structured and free-play activities, many of their peers find their temper, intensity, and intrusiveness overwhelming. Barkley (1990, 1997) indicates that children with ADHD are unable to modify the behaviors that provoke this rejection due to their lack of self-awareness and age-appropriate self-monitoring skills.

During middle childhood, most children with ADHD begin to show evidence of other coexisting disorders. By ages 7 to 10, 30 to 50% will have developed patterns of conduct disorder and antisocial behaviors (Barkley, 1990). Children who have ADHD as the only diagnosable disorder will be in the minority; these children tend to have problems primarily with academic achievement and will not have the wider repertoire of disruptive behaviors.

Adolescence

Many parents and mental health professionals believe that by early to mid adolescence, ADHD symptomology begins to disappear. Longitudinal studies suggest otherwise: Wender (1995) indicates that 60 to 70% of children with ADHD continue to exhibit ADHD as adults; Barkley (1990) claims 70 to 80%;

and Weiss and Hechtman (1993) state 50% have symptoms in adulthood (age 18 and older). Whatever the true figure, it is clear that most adolescents with ADHD will experience symptomology. Typically these symptoms take the form of low self-esteem, poor school performance, major depression/dysthymia, and disruptive peer relationships (Weiss & Hechtman, 1993), in addition to hyperactivity, impulsivity, and behavioral disinhibition. Many parents will seek family, marital, or individual child-centered therapy for assistance to resolve these problems.

Some families will see an increase in antisocial behavior by the adolescent. Barkley (1990) suggests that 25 to 35% will show antisocial tendencies, qualifying for a dual diagnosis of ADHD and conduct disorder. Children who have this dual diagnosis will as a rule have an inflated sense of the use of unhealthy power tactics to carry out their will. Family therapists who wish to develop a sense of cooperative behaviors among family members may find themselves frustrated by such children who do not want to cooperate or who do not see the value of it. By the time their adolescent with ADHD has reached age 14 or 15, some parents may have lost the battle for internal leadership in their home. A family therapist may have to assist the parent(s) to access community resources (e.g., police, truancy officer, juvenile case workers) to bring a recalcitrant child into compliance with basic parental requests.

In his review of the ADHD literature, Barkley (1990) suggests that the following factors best predict adolescent outcome:

- family socioeconomic status and general level of intelligence
- degree of peer relationship problems
- degree of aggressiveness and conduct problems in childhood
- degree of psychopathology in parents
- degree of conflict and hostility in parent-child interactions
- adolescent academic achievement

Family therapists may wish to use these factors as foci for initiating family and individual change.

Family Dynamics

During the past two decades, a great deal of data have accumulated on shared characteristics of families with ADHD children. To work effectively with families of children with ADHD it is important to focus on their strengths and successes. The therapist must understand the impact of ADHD on the child, parents, siblings, and family system.

> ADHD results . . . in a persuasive impact on the *day-to-day adaptive functioning of individuals* [italics added] having this disorder. As a consequence, ADHD is not a disorder of attention—it is a developmental disorder of inhibition, self-control, and time. (Barkley, 1997, p. x)

The patterns of behavioral interactions in families with children with ADHD are clearly different from those in families with children who do not have ADHD. There are higher rates of conflict, negative communication, and levels of expressed anger (Barkley, Guevremont, Anastopoulos, & Fletchner, 1991; DuPaul, Guevremont, & Barkley, 1991; Whalen & Henker, 1991). If the child has developed comorbid symptoms of ODD or CD, the family will experience greater levels of aggression and noncomplaint behavior from the child and perhaps between siblings (Barkley, 1987; Barkley, DuPaul, & McMurray, 1990). These comorbid externalizing behaviors are actions that violate social rules and expectations (Kazdin, 1987, 1991). Thus, a child with ADHD who also has ODD/CD has major impairment in his or her ability to change and participate in the family in a more cooperative way.

Children with ADHD require more time-intensive direction, control, suggestion, and encouragement from parents to get them to focus on assignments and comply with directives. Parents may find this especially vexing as the usual approaches to parenting advocated by parenting books and talk shows do not work as effectively (Pisterman, McGrath, Firestone, & Goodman, 1989). Both parents and siblings tend to have higher levels of psychological distress and psychological disorders (Barkley, 1990). A number of studies suggest that the adults in 38 to 50% of families of children with ADHD may qualify for at least one psychiatric diagnosis (Wender, 1995). Marital discord also occurs more frequently; married couples with children with ADHD tend to separate or divorce at a rate of approximately 75% (Barkley, 1990).

These statements may appear to blame children with ADHD for marital or family discord. Unfortunately, many therapists may concentrate too myopically on the personal flaws of the parents or on poor parenting skills. One must also acknowledge the intertwined reciprocal impact of the child on the parents and siblings, which contributes to feelings of anger, harshness, or rejection toward the child. Naturally, therapists will work to reduce or eliminate these feelings among family members. Yet one must take care in the beginning of therapy to not challenge or invalidate the experiences of the other family members when they describe the impact of the child's *behavior* on them.

Treatment

As mentioned previously, psychopharmacological treatment comprises the most widely used intervention for children with ADHD. In terms of psychotherapy, the most common forms of therapy are individual play therapy, self-control training, social skills training, and ADHD peer group therapy (Barkley, 1990). These therapies have either an individual or a group focus, typically with little parental or family involvement. Those who do value family involvement usually emphasize parent counseling, parent training in contingency management, and parent education (Barkley et al., 1992; Conoley & Conoley, 1991; Fauber & Long, 1991; Kazdin, 1991; Kazdin, Seigal, & Bass, 1992; Pisterman, Firestone, McGrath, & Goodman, 1992; Strayhorn & Weidman, 1989). These therapies do the opposite of individual and group modalities with children with ADHD—that is, they involve the parents but exclude the rest of the family.

Prior Research on Family Interventions

Despite the significant amount of outcome research on children with ADHD, in terms of stimulant medication and school-based interventions, very little literature exists that describes family-centered models for therapy with children with ADHD and their families. Anastopoulos and Barkley (1990) report that no more than ten studies have been published regarding parent training/parent counseling and their impact on child compliance. Only two studies have focused on behavioral parent training *concurrent with* parent counseling (Pisterman et al., 1989, 1992 ; Pollard, Ward, & Barkley, 1983). In other words, it is very uncommon to find information on *how to teach parents more effective parenting skills while at the same time providing them therapy to change their parenting efforts.*

This lack of published information on parent or family intervention is puzzling, given that most parents are challenged by ADHD children in ways unique to other children, especially in the manifestation of extreme behavior such as aggression or entrenched defiance. Families seeking clinical intervention often feel oppressed, defeated, and to some extent overwhelmed by the demands in managing an ADHD child's attitudinal and behavioral problems. In cases with two parent/caretaker families, the couple may experience a great deal of interpersonal conflict over management of the child. The chronic distress of parenting a noncompliant child with ADHD compels many parents to seek treatment, often centered on the child alone rather than family.

The ADHD Family-Centered Model

This section of the chapter provides a family therapy model for families with children with ADHD. The approach is targeted at reducing problems of disruptiveness and noncompliance and focuses on:

- getting parents (or involved adult extended family members) to work together on establishing firm rules, behavior constraints, and holding the child(ren) responsible for behavior
- getting children out of parental roles
- developing parental and child support networks
- preventing family members from accommodating to the child's misbehavior
- developing more positive, warm, and nurturing patterns of interaction within the family

A plethora of interventions and interventive approaches exists to guide the therapist in working with ADHD children. However, relatively few concentrate on introducing change to the entire family system.

Because ADHD is a chronic condition, this model assumes that the family has learned to accommodate to the rapidly shifting behavior and temperament characteristics of the child. This accommodation may have produced unhealthy family patterns of interaction (structure). These unhealthy transactional patterns may also have existed prior to the birth of the child. However, over time the addition of the child with ADHD seriously strains patterns of family organization that lack flexibility.

Assessment and Assumptions

The ideal model of healthy family functioning has functional, generational, and subsystem boundaries, a clear parent/child hierarchy, flexibility in the family interactional patterns, and parents who work together cooperatively rather than against each other (Aponte, 1992; Colapinto, 1988; Figley & Nelson, 1990; Minuchin, Rosman, & Baker, 1978; Szapocznik, Hervis, Rio, & Mitrani, 1991).

The ADHD family-centered model assumes that despite the challenges presented by the child with ADHD, the parents will still have to manage the child in order to successfully launch him or her into adulthood. Therefore, we presume that the inability of the parents to get the child to comply and assume greater self-control depends largely on the structural problems in the family organization (Minuchin, 1974; Minuchin & Fishman, 1981; Nichols & Schwartz, 1998).

The therapist should assess first for general structural flaws or deviations from the ideal model of family functioning in three primary areas: (1) interactions between parents in the executive subsystem; (2) interactions between the partners in the marital subsystem if two parents and/or caretaker are present; and (3) the nature of the boundary between the executive subsystem and the child with ADHD. This includes assessing the nature of the parental hierarchy to determine the extent to which the parent(s) exhibits "leadership behavior" (Szapocznik et al., 1991) over the child subsystem in general and the child with ADHD in particular. This includes the extent to which a parent is able to get the child with ADHD to comply and the nature of the child's interaction with the parent before and after compliance requests. It is important to pay particular attention to any interactional patterns that reveal the nature of the boundary between the parent(s) and child. Also of importance is the manner in which the parents, if two are present, mutually support each other. Who makes the decisions? How do they cooperate? And, most significantly, how do they either block or fail to support each other in managing the noncompliant child? Treatment is aimed at altering interactional patterns primarily between four areas: (1) parent 1–child, parent 2–child; (2) parent-parent; (3) child-siblings; and (4) school-child.

It is also assumed that changes with the child with ADHD will generalize to the other children in the family, if present. With the assessment, modification of structural problems, and the introduction of effective behavior-modification skills, the child with ADHD will become more compliant and the family stress will decrease.

The parenting techniques used for compliance are intended to change the ineffective, repetitious patterns of family organization that block the effective management of noncompliant behaviors. If the interactions around parenting the child with ADHD appropriately are inconsistent, and the executive adult leadership of the family is poorly maintained through either rigid or diffuse boundaries, then the child's natural inclination toward noncompliance and disruptiveness flourishes.

An important theme of this model is that ADHD constitutes a "chronic" condition. Simply parenting the child well will not cure ADHD symptomology. In most cases when the child's pattern of noncompliance increases, the parents need to examine their family organizational patterns around the child. In many cases, parents will also need to ask about changes in the child's peer relationships or a lapse in classroom structure.

Goals of the Model

The family-centered model focuses on the missing transactional patterns—that is, the patterns that would exist in the family system if it were healthy. This focus on missing patterns and their eventual establishment to ensure healthy functioning emphasizes a health-oriented quest for change rather than a deficit perspective. The therapist does not ask him- or herself, "What is *wrong* with this family?" or "How in the world did the family get into this mess?" Instead the therapist asks, "What is the *presenting problem* as defined by the family?" and "What new patterns of interaction in the family could help the family *better manage* the problem?" Families with a child with ADHD bring a wide range of individual and family problems to therapy, which represent obstacles to healthy family functioning.

Assessing the presenting problem and setting the goals of therapy rest on the belief that problems of noncompliant and disruptive behavior from the child are maintained by unhealthy patterns of family interaction around the ADHD. These unhealthy transactional patterns are the *result,* not the *cause,* of the presenting problems. The therapist emphasizes coping with ADHD, not curing it, and preventing moderate or severe ADHD symptomology through more structured parenting and healthier patterns of family organization. The therapist also teaches the parents when to expect and how to manage episodes of mild ADHD symptomology.

Since ODD and CD so frequently accompany ADHD, a goal of the ADHD family-centered model is to prevent the child from developing these disorders. This is accomplished by:

- getting parent(s) to work together on discipline, holding the child consistently responsible for misbehavior
- teaching respect for adult authority, and rules through rewards and punishments
- removing children from parental roles
- developing support networks for the adult(s)

- focusing on marital dynamics if problems interfere with effective parenting
- stopping family members from accommodating to the child's misbehavior
- providing assessment or treatment for individual problems (e.g., adult depression, impulse control, single parent issues, etc.) if necessary for increased family functioning

The Therapy Environment

Ideally, all family members living with or involved with the parenting of the child with ADHD comes to the initial session. If the child is in foster care, the foster parent most involved in the care of the child and the case manager/therapist should come to the first session.

Unlike more child-centered therapy or play therapy, therapists working with children with ADHD and their families avoid providing toys, art supplies, or other amusements in the therapy room. Because the children have a hyper-responsivity to *novel, external* stimuli, they may tend to display more *muted* ADHD-related behaviors during the initial sessions. Novel settings capture any child's attention but it may captivate the child with ADHD even more. For example, parents often express confusion over the struggle to get the child to calm down, read a book, or do homework—but hand the controls to Nintendo, Sega Genesis, or Play Station to the ADHD child and he or she will sit *quietly, absorbed for hours.*

Therapists must take care not to accommodate to the family's behavior in order to objectively observe the child's at-home behaviors and the parents' responses to them. These behaviors can be encouraged in the artificial environment of the therapy room by making the environment "boring" for the child. When children feel bored they tend to behave disruptively, triggering the parents' typical responses, and thus recreating as much of the at-home dance as one can hope for in the therapy room. The therapist thus gains a glance of the family's dynamics by witnessing the child's noncomplaint and disruptive behaviors and the family's management of them.

Case Illustration

Phase 1: Assessment Procedures During the Initial Two Sessions

The initial phone intake carried the usual red flags for a possible ADHD diagnosis: Seven-year-old Scott has social problems at school and difficulty with anger and aggressiveness. His parents, both aged 28, are college graduates and have two other children. Scott is their first child and is in the first grade. The child has not been assessed for ADHD by the school, physician, or a previous psychotherapist. Prior to beginning the assessment session, the parents fill out a form in which they are asked to list the problems or difficulties they would like to see changed. They state:

1. Very quick to get angry, throws tantrums, hits and kicks walls, throws things.
2. He needs to be the focus of attention for everyone. If someone else is getting more attention than him, he does whatever it takes to get their attention, good or bad.

THE THERAPIST HAS four goals in the initial assessment session, which typically takes 70 to 90 minutes. These goals are: joining with the ADHD family system, taking a psychoeducational approach, creating enactments to reveal family structure affected by ADHD dynamics, and observing and commenting on spontaneous interactions. The assessment of family organization occurs over one to two sessions. If families come in a state of crisis, the therapist may have to delay the structured assessment until the crisis alleviates.

Families who have children with ADHD generally have had dozens of encounters with "experts" (teachers, neighbors, mental health specialists, etc.), who have provided them with ideas on what to do regarding their child. They come to therapy because these ideas did not work or the family has not implemented them properly. Family members are highly sensitive to feeling blamed for their parenting efforts. The therapist should take great pains to use neutral language when asking questions or making observations. An appropriate use of humor may add to the family's capacity to trust. In other words, the therapist must present a different "expert" image than what the family, especially the parents, have learned to expect. The capacity of the family to trust the therapist relies heavily on the therapist's acceptance and nonblaming stance. Working hard to achieve this with the family during the first two to three sessions will create goodwill between therapist and parent(s), necessary to sustain the challenges to the family structure that the therapist will later introduce.

THE PARENTS SIT together on the loveseat sofa in my office. The three children, ages 7, 6, and 3, sit on the chairs next to the sofa initially, but soon begin to wander around the room. The parents appear angry and yet somewhat apprehensive. The next 15 minutes may be the most important in the entire therapy process. My primary task is to get the parents to trust me and obtain some sense of my competency in working with their child's issues.

I interact some with the children but focus the majority of my attention on the parents. After obtaining some preliminary information, I ask the parents to tell me what they hope to see change as a result of coming to therapy. I get an earful quickly. While listening to the content, I scan the children's behavior every 15 to 20 seconds and then look back at the parents. I may say, "I want you to know that what you have to say is very important and I am listening to you, but I also want to know what the kids do while you talk so I will be looking at them quite a bit." At this point, I do not speak much to the children but simply observe them.

THERAPISTS WORKING with children with ADHD and their families often go overboard trying to make the child or children feel comfortable during the initial session, but do very little to make the parents feel comfortable. In the ADHD family-centered model, the parents—not the children—are the most important players in the family sessions. This model emphasizes interacting and paying attention primarily to the parent(s), at least in the beginning sessions.

THE PARENTS EXPRESS a great deal of anger and frustration regarding Scott. Their glances toward him are shot through with irritation and defeat. He wanders around the room and appears not to hear them. I know better. To the child, this is an old story, one he has heard numerous times. He hears it at home and now he will hear it from the school for the next 11 years. The child has already internalized the classic ADHD messages about self from significant others: difficult, frustrating, unlikeable, unlovable, school failure, no friends, etc. I believe the parents love their son, yet their language does not reflect this. Their language echoes the powerlessness they experience as they attempt to manage the child's difficult behavior on a day-to-day basis. Now, they have the school system pressuring them to correct something they cannot even correct at home. Despite their best attempts, Scott has remained unresponsive and his unmanageability has increased.

THERAPISTS MUST remember that families with children with ADHD have higher rates of negative parent-child interactions, harsh or commanding parenting, and more parental/peer rejection than families of children who do not have ADHD. As indicated previously, these families are different. Still, it can tear at one's heartstrings to hear how parents and siblings talk about the child. Such talk needs to stop but not necessarily in the first few sessions. Therapists who become reactive or who want to protect the child run the risk of alienating the parents. The therapist must remember that raising most children with ADHD is a difficult task. It is not easy and it is often unpleasant to live with an ADHD child. The therapist should take note of the intensity of these comments, assess more, and then work quickly to help the parents better manage the child so these feelings can ease or heal.

The assessment combines basic structural family therapy assessment tools (enactments, looking for spontaneous interactions) with in-depth assessment of ADHD symptomology. Inexperienced therapists or therapists unfamiliar with ADHD may want to adhere rather strictly to the following guidelines over several cases until the basic session dynamics are learned. More experienced therapists or those who are familiar with ADHD may want to eschew the familiar and try out the unfamiliar.

Therapists need to remember that a successful assessment requires joining or relationship skills. These families want to experience the therapist as trustworthy, on their side, and able to help them live more peacefully.

AT THE END OF the first session, I give the parents an assessment package to fill out and bring to the next session. The package includes a Child Behavior Checklist (CBCL)-Parent Form, Conners-Parent Form, and a Barkley's Home Situation questionnaire. I ask them to have Scott's first-grade teacher fill out a Child Behavior Checklist-Teacher Form and a Conners-Teacher Form. Finally, I give the parents a copy of the *DSM-IV* criteria for ADHD and ODD and ask them to review the information and circle the items that describe their child.

When the parents bring back the completed questionnaires I see that Scott's scores on the CBCL Parent and Teacher Forms are above the 98th percentile on Attention Problems and Aggressive Problems. He also scores above the 98th percentile on the Conners Parent and Teacher Forms for Learning Problems, Impulsive-Hyperactive, and the Hyperactivity Index. On the *DSM-IV* criteria, the parents have circled 16 out of 18 criteria for ADHD and 7 out of 8 for ODD. I inform the parents that the instruments and *DSM-IV* suggest a diagnosis of ADHD, Combined Type, but that I want to see the family for at least one more session (three sessions total) before I feel more certain. I will also ask them to take Scott to their pediatrician for a medical evaluation.

Phase II: Using Psychoeducation as Intervention

Depending on the family issues and dynamics, either during the second session or at the beginning of the third, I take a psychoeducational approach. Psycho-education in this model consists of a series of themes and information provided to the family. Information on ADHD and repetitive themes are repeated throughout the assessment phase (two to three sessions), as opportunities present themselves. These opportunities occur especially when parents solicit information or the child manifests behavior particularly characteristic of children with ADHD.

Most parents have a number of questions regarding the etiology, character-istics, and developmental course of ADHD. Of particular importance in answering questions and providing information is the weaving of nonjudg-mental themes on ADHD, which serves to reduce the family's emotional inten-sity and often hostile attitude toward the child (Gingerich, Golden, Holley, & Nemser, 1992). I adhere to a core perspective on ADHD, which I communicate to families in a series of repetitive "frames" (Minuchin & Fishman, 1981). DuPaul, Guevremont, and Barkley (1991) express this core perspective, upon which many nonjudgmental themes are drawn:

> ADHD is a developmental disorder of self-control and social conduct that is chronic and without cure. An attitude of "coping" rather than "curing" is frequently communicated by the clinician, intimating that treatment may lead to the reduction of problems but not necessarily their complete elimination. (p. 120)

One theme emphasizes that dysfunctional family patterns do not generate the ADHD symptoms in a child. This theme is important because I do not believe that the family *needs* a symptomatic child with ADHD or even *wants* the child to behave as he or she does to directly or indirectly stabilize the family sys-tem (Haley, 1980; Nichols, 1987). I assume that the family feels oppressed, defeated, and, to some extent, overwhelmed by the demands of managing an ADHD child's attitudinal and behavioral problems. Sharing information about the characteristics, etiology, medication, and developmental course and adult outcome of children with ADHD is especially vital to assist parents and family members to develop a sense of mastery in coping with ADHD.

As a part of the model, it is critical that family members have information to take home and read. As a rule, I offer Parker's (1994) *The ADD Hyperactiv-*

ity Workbook for Parents, Teachers, and Kids and refer them to local or state parent support groups. I also provide a variety of articles about ADHD from popular magazines.

In addition, I rely on personal disclosure when appropriate, in a limited fashion. Many parents feel empowered when they are told that their experiences are common to many families with ADHD children. The therapist may empathize with the parents, indicating that he or she would be similarly distressed to have children who behaved in such a manner. The therapist may also relate personal reactions to children or family situations presented in other cases of families with children with ADHD. I have two children with ADHD and tend to draw upon personal experiences to both join with families and also inform as part of the psychoeducational approach.

Phase III: Providing Alternative Ways of Interacting Around the Child

Once the therapist has diagrammed the family structure (family mapping) following the first or second session, he or she is then in a position to begin actively introducing opportunities for change. For example, if the parents indicate that they argue with each other over how to manage their child with ADHD or other children in the family, the structural family map should indicate a rigid boundary between the parents in the executive subsystem. A structural goal could be to alter the restricted and conflictual interactions between the parents. Therapeutic interventions would then be directed toward getting the parents to experience success in mutually supporting and assisting each other in efforts to manage the child. Parents would learn new patterns of consulting and conflict management to function more as a parental team than as two divided parents in a chaotic home. They would also learn parenting skills that are more appropriate for raising children with ADHD.

The therapist, in effect, seeks opportunities to alter old patterns while at the same time teaching and reinforcing new parenting skills. As the parents focus on implementing these new skills, the mapped faulty structure should reveal itself, allowing the therapist multiple opportunities within each session to target and then direct the parents to interact in a different manner. Over the course of several sessions, the therapist will consistently redirect the parents to behave differently when the old structure appears. Backing up the redirection of behavior with repetitive, multiple cognitive constructions (Minuchin & Fishman, 1981) may gradually replace the faulty transactions that support the family's inability to manage the ADHD child's noncompliant behavior. Hopefully the family then develops more healthy patterns between parents and between parents and children.

Parenting Sheets

A virtual plethora of interventions and interventive approaches exists to guide the therapist. However, relatively few concentrate on changing the entire family system. Most focus on training the parent in child behavior management without the child's participation. Altering interactions between parents and children *concurrently* is rare.

I HAVE, AT THIS POINT observed Scott's family during three family sessions and have a basic understanding of the parents' organizational patterns of managing Scott. I have done little to structure the session time. I have observed the parents' approach to dealing with Scott when he wanders around my office, going through my desk drawers, etc. Their management of his misbehavior is too permissive, too little concerned about his going through my office items. The parents do not look at each other when talking or dealing with Scott. It seems clear that they are unused to working as a co-parenting team. They underreact and do not cue each other in on the child's misbehavior. It appears that they simply want Scott to behave better without putting in the hard parenting work to make it happen.

THE PARENTING techniques I use for compliance were especially constructed to assist the alteration of dysfunctional transactions blocking the effective management of compliant behaviors. Assuming that the parents are presenting with problems of managing noncomplaint child behavior, the therapist begins the second session with the following statement:

> This session I would like to conduct an experiment. I would like to introduce to you some new skills that may help you manage your child/ren's behavior more effectively. Let me show you some simple rules first and then I would like to practice the rules for the rest of the session. Since this is an experiment I'm not sure how things will turn out but let's give it a try. Is this acceptable to you (ask each parent)? I have 10 sheets describing these rules which I would like to go through one at a time with you and then we will practice them.

The therapist then goes through each sheet (table 12.1). If the child is 7 or older, the therapist can create more trust with the parents by asking their permission for the ADHD child to read the ADHD parenting sheets. Appropriate humor should accompany this when possible so that the presentation of this material does not feel grim or retaliative. The underlying tone should be that the parents will now take greater leadership of the family. The child or children should get the message that the parents want to establish a different hierarchy within the family with the collaboration of the therapist whom at this moment stands on the parents' side.

TABLE 12.1
PARENTING SHEETS USED IN THE ADHD FAMILY-CENTERED MODEL
TO CHANGE NONCOMPLIANT BEHAVIOR

---

1. If you live under my roof, you *MUST*:
   - Respect my authority over you!
   - Obey my rules!

2. As long as you live under my roof, you *MUST* obey *ALL* of my rules.

3. Rules are when I *SAY* to you:
   - No . . .
   - Don't . . .
   - Stop . . .
   - Do this . . .

4. You *BREAK* my rules when you:
   - Defy me!
   - Talk back to me!
   - Ignore me!
   - Dawdle!

5. When you decide that **you do not want to obey** my rules, then:
   You will get to sit in **time-out!!**

6. *TIME-OUT RULES:*
   - Never get off the chair!
   - Do not turn around!
   - **Begin with one minute per year of age.**

7. *RESTRAINT RULES:*
   - One minute per year of age.

TABLE 12.1 (continued)

- Back in time-out to finish the **original** time-out.
- Add two minutes to the previous restraint time until the child sits the entire **original** time-out.

8. ***GUIDLINES FOR PARENTS:***
   - Never allow your child to **argue** with you about time-out.
   - Never allow your child to **talk back to you.**
   - If this happens, be **silent,** and put your child in time-out.

9. ***AFTER THE TIME-OUT:***
   - Ask your child why he or she had to sit in time-out.
   - If he or she will not comply, then place the child back in time-out.
   - Otherwise, **hold** the child for a few moments and say that you **love** him or her.

10. ***FOR COUPLES WITH CHILDREN WITH ADHD:***
    - Never argue **in front** of the kids about enforcing the rules.
    - Work together as a team or the kids will **divide** you.
    - Be consistent in applying the parenting sheets—**inconsistency** makes child misbehavior **stronger.**

11. ***FOR ALL PARENTS WITH A CHILD OR CHILDREN WITH ADHD:***
    - Your child is **not** in your home to love you.
    - You must get your **love** from other adults.
    - If you have an **intense need** to have your child to give love to you, then you **will *not*** be consistent with the parenting sheets because the child **will not** give love to you.

The therapist then asks the parents for three misbehaviors they would like to see eliminated or reduced in the child. Parents often name problems outside their home environment, such as classroom behavior or peer interactions. However, while resolving these outside-the-home problems is important, it is best to begin within the home where the parents have the most control. Once the family and/or parents have experienced more success in managing their home environment, then the therapist can quickly shift to assisting them in resolving problems outside the home. This frame has worked in nearly all cases in my experience. A few parents, however, will insist on wanting to work on problems outside the home. It is better to honor the wishes of the parent than to engage in a power struggle. Therapy will therefore follow more of a general structural family therapy approach than the more prescribed ADHD family-centered model.

Once the parents have described the three problems, therapy should begin with the third misbehavior. Parents will generally name the most vexing problem first, followed by the second and third. Naturally, they will want to fix the most difficult problem now rather than later. However, they face a greater possibility of failure if they begin with the most challenging misbehavior. Parents will need to practice implementing the parenting sheets, which are not as easy as they appear; therefore, the parents are best served by starting with an easier problem to fix. The therapist asks the parents to practice the parenting sheets over the next week *only* with the third targeted misbehavior and *only* with the child with ADHD. If other children reside in the home, one may stifle protests by the ADHD child (and sometimes parents) that the other children's turn will come. The parents are to do what he or she would normally do with misbehavior by the other child(ren).

I am asking you to try this as an experiment. Remember that most experiments in the beginning have a fairly high chance of failure. What I am asking you to do might not work well or perhaps not at all.

This frame allows the parents some room to feel hopeful if they struggle with implementing the parenting sheets. It also provides the therapist with an exit should the parent not implement the sheets properly or consistently. Many parents will insist that they have tried time-out and that it fails to work; they may begin introducing the steps in the parenting sheets inconsistently, never quite believing they can work; or they may feel such desire to stop the misbehaviors that they target every misbehavior they see the first week. The therapist must lower their expectations for rapid and all-encompassing change within two to three weeks.

It is also critical that the therapist provides a framework for time-out as an intervention to reduce noncomplaint behavior. Time-outs work poorly with children with ADHD unless they *stay* in time-out. Physical restraint or a holding technique used in conjunction with time-out tends to produce an effective intervention. The justifications for these techniques are detailed next.

Time-out with physical restraint. Children with ADHD usually require strong behavioral interventions to motivate their behavior. Common consequences or reinforcements, normally powerful enough to shape non-ADHD behavior, often fail with ADHD children (Barkley, 1990; Haenlein & Caul, 1987; Quay, 1988). If used consistently, a combination of time-out and physical restraint is an extremely useful and powerful motivator to reduce noncomplaint behavior.

Time-out refers to removing a child from rewards, reinforcement, and attention. Upon misbehaving, the child is placed in a quiet and boring setting where little enjoyment is possible. For example, the child may be placed on a chair in a boring corner of a room where the parent can continue to observe the child.

For the technique to work, the child must *stay* in time-out. Children with ADHD have a well-deserved reputation for defeating time-out. There are a variety of ways to make time-out work. One is to continue pushing the child back into the chair. Another is to add minutes. I teach parents to use physical restraint (Barkley, 1990) as the *best* method for keeping the child in the time-out chair. Restraint is done by placing the child on the parent's lap and crossing the child's arms across his or her chest. The parent holds the child's crisscrossed arms by the wrists at the child's shoulder level. The parent must take care not to pull hard on the wrists, which may displace the shoulder joints. I model crossing the arms across the child's chest, holding the wrists like one would to grasp the handle bars of a bicycle, and positioning the elbows on top of each other. This prevents the wrists and arms from being pulled too much but still immobilizes the child. The parent should be advised to avoid using restraint if he or she feels extremely angry or out of control.

The parent holds the child in this manner for the length of the time-out period and then places the child back on the chair. For the larger or stronger child, a floor restraint can be used. This is done by placing the child prone on the floor, arms to the sides, and hands flat at the sides of the pelvis. The parent then lies lengthwise on the child placing a firm body weight over the child's pelvis; but avoids placing weight on the ribcage. The parent must use *enough* weight to render the child immobile but without crushing or injuring the child. Restraint is used *only* when the child refuses to sit in time-out. Restraint is modeled first by the therapist and then the parents are asked to restrain their child with the therapist observing. The parents are then shown how to use this method in the *therapy room first* when the child misbehaves. Parents will need to be strongly encouraged to use this method; the restraint feels more punishing to parents than children, especially in applying the time-out-restraint cycles consistently.

The sensation of restraint is very uncomfortable to the child. Children eventually prefer to sit in time-out than receive physical restraint. The child must sit in time-out for the entire time-out period. If the child violates the time-out rules (sheet 6), then he or she receives restraint. For example, if a 7-year-old ends up in time-out, he or she should have a 7-minute time-out. If the child breaks the time-out rules, then he or she receives a 7-minute restraint. The child then must go back to time-out and repeat the 7-minute period. If he or she breaks the time-out again, then the child receives a 9-minute time-out. When completed the child goes back to time-out for 7 minutes. If time-out is broken, an 11-minute time-out is applied, and so forth. Eventually, even the most stubborn child will learn that a time-out feels better than restraint and will comply with the time out. I have worked with children who have deeply entrenched patterns of defiance toward the parent and who need several cycles of time-out and restraint before they choose to comply. The record goes to a very powerful 9-year-old boy who went 17 time-out–restraint cycles before agreeing to sit in time-out. In my clinical experience, by sessions 5 to 7 very few parents need to use restraint on a daily basis. Children learn very quickly to avoid restraint and comply with time-out.

The third and successive sessions. The third therapy session focuses on getting the parents to work cooperatively around the parenting sheets. In this way the therapist directs the parents to interact in new structural patterns as they implement the parenting rules. Each succeeding session focuses on the success/inability of the parents to use the parenting sheets. The therapist continues to direct the family in altering ineffectual interactional patterns, emphasizing the importance of parenting consistency to alter transactional patterns and manage the child's behavior. It may take several sessions of practice around the child's misbehavior to break entrenched patterns of family behavior. It may also prove important to begin time-outs with the other children by the third or fourth session.

Many therapists find the use of structural intensity to break impasses in controlling the child difficult or distasteful. However, given the nature of most families with children with ADHD, it cannot be avoided. For example, the therapist needs to concentrate especially on issues of power and control between parents and/or the child and parents, as some two-parent families have developed strong patterns of noncooperativeness between the parents.

Children with ADHD often have a special talent for dividing parents who fight with each other, thus avoiding the consequences of their misbehavior. The therapist must get these parents to stop fighting and work together—a very difficult task, especially if one parent has an enmeshed relationship with the child. Some children appear to break time-out in order to obtain the physical contact with the parent in the restraint. In this case, the therapist may coach the parents to give the child more physical contact of an appropriate nature. For example, all children enjoy being held for a while or engaging in horseplay with the parent. If a parent does not like physical contact with the child, he or she will need structural intensity to move past the initial stage of inertia.

SCOTT IS QUITE used to my office by now; the novelty of the setting and family therapy process has worn off. He begins to go through my desk drawers. The parents seem oblivious to this. I ask gently, "Should he be doing that?" The father tells him to stop several times. The mother is silent. Scott ignores them. They do not use the information from the ADHD parenting sheets I had them tape on the wall at home. They look back at me with a powerless gaze.

I ask the mother to state a rule to Scott using one of the "No," "Don't," "Stop," "Do this" statements about going through my desk. I do this because I have learned that teaching her son accountability is more difficult for her than nurturing him. Disciplining Scott feels harsh or mean to her. Protecting his feelings feels more natural and in line with her beliefs in mothering. However, at this moment Scott needs correction for his misbehavior. I ask the mother to place the child in the time-out chair. She does and he immediately leaps off with a defiant glare. The mother looks powerless. I ask her to place him in a sitting restraint. She does and for the next 7 minutes of the restraint, I sit next to her and offer encouragement for doing something that feels so against the grain. She then places the child in time-out again. The child has not learned; after one minute he gets off the chair. Restraint is once again necessary to teach Scott to stay in the chair. I ask the mother to perform the restraint again, and have the father offer encouragement and coaching through the intense unpleasantness of the restraint.

We do this for one more round until Scott decides to comply with sitting in time-out for 7 minutes. The parents feel exhausted but determined to carry this out at home. I repeatedly point out the importance of supporting each other and cueing each other to act quickly in dealing with Scott's misbehavior.

THE THERAPIST SHOULD also emphasize the importance of intermittent, random variable reinforcement schedules in strengthening child noncompliance. Too many parents tire of the constant vigilance over the ADHD child. Parents come home from work feeling tired, faced with the daunting tasks of fixing dinner, checking homework, and then having several episodes of time-out and restraint to deal with. After a few sessions, parents may see improvement and then slack off. Therapists should expect this and bring it to the attention of the parents as quickly as possible.

Phase IV: Maintaining Changes

Once the parents are able to manage the child's behavior, then the therapist may begin to space the sessions out every two weeks to see if the new structure has replaced the inadequate structure. The therapist may want to encourage a booster session every three to six months for a period of time. Parents should also be encouraged to join and participate in their local CHADD chapter (Children and Adults with Attention-Deficit/Hyperactivity Disorder). One can find the local chapter by contacting CHADD on the Internet.

Many parents of children with ADHD may want to initiate marital or individual therapy after the child's misbehavior begins to subside. Marital therapy may become especially relevant if the parents become aware of their inability to work together in parenting which highlights their marital weaknesses.

As INDICATED IN the chapter, many parents of children with ADHD struggle with significant personal issues such as mood and anxiety disorders, anger, impulse control, adult survivor issues, etc. Although most family therapy encompasses eight to twelve sessions, additional sessions may prove necessary for some families should the parents choose to work on additional marital and/or individual issues, particularly those that interfere with their ability to parent effectively and consistently.

Michol Polson, Ph.D., is Marriage and Family Therapist, Family Resource Center, Idaho Falls, Idaho.

References

Achenbach, T., & Edelbrock, C. (1983). *Manual for the child behavior checklist and revised child behavior profile.* Burlington, VT: University of Vermont.

American Psychiatric Association. (1994). *Diagnostic and Statistical manual of mental disorders* (4th ed.). Washington, DC: Author.

Anastopoulos, A., & Barkley, R. (1992). Attention-deficit/hyperactivity disorder. In C. E. Walker, & M. C. Roberts (Eds.), *Handbook of clinical child psychology* (2nd ed.). New York: John Wiley.

Aponte, H. (1992). Training the person of the therapist in structural family therapy. *Journal of Marital and Family Therapy, 18,* 269–281.

Barkley, R. A. (1987). The assessment of attention-deficit/hyperactivity disorder. *Behavioral Assessment, 9,* 207–233.

Barkley, R. A. (1990). *Attention-deficit/hyperactivity disorder: A handbook for diagnosis and treatment.* New York: Guilford.

Barkley, R. A. (1991). Diagnosis and assessment of attention-deficit/hyperactivity disorder. *Comprehensive Mental Health Care, 1,* 27–43.

Barkley, R. A. (1994). The assessment of attention in children. In G. R. Lyon (Ed.), *Frames of Reference for the assessment of learning disabilities: New views on measurement issues.* Baltimore, MD: Paul H. Brookes.

Barkley, R. A. (1997). *ADHD and the nature of self-control.* New York: Guilford.

Barkley, R., DuPaul, G., McMurray, M. (1990). Comprehensive evaluation of attention deficit disorder with and without hyperactivity as defined by research criteria. *Journal of Consulting and Clinical Psychology, 58,* 775–789.

Barkley, R., Fisher, M., Edelbrock, C., & Smallish, L. (1990). The adolescent outcome of hyperactive children diagnosed by research criteria: An 8-year prospective follow-up. *Journal of the American Academy of Child and Adolescent Psychiatry, 29,* 546–557.

Barkley, R., Guevremont, D., Anastopoulos, A., & Fletchner, K. (1992). A comparison of three family therapy programs for treating family conflicts in adolescents with attention-deficit hyperactivity disorder. *Journal of Consulting and Clinical Psychology, 60,* 450–462.

Barkley, R., Anastopoulos, A., Guevremont, D., & Fletchner, K. (1991). Adolescents with ADHD: Patterns of behavioral adjustment, academic functioning, and treatment utilization. *Journal of the American Academy of Child and Adolescent Psychiatry, 30,* 752–761.

Breen, M., & Altepeter, T. (1990). Situational variability in boys and girls identified as ADHD. *Journal of Clinical Psychology, 46,* 486–490.

Bronowski, J. (1977). *A sense of the future: Essays on natural philosophy.* Cambridge, MA: Massachusetts Institute of Technology Press.

Cohen, N., & Mindle, K. (1983). The "hyperactive syndrome" in kindergarten children: Comparison of children with pervasive and situational symptoms. *Journal of Child Psychology and Psychiatry and Allied Disciplines, 24,* 443–455.

Colapinto, J. (1988). Teaching the structural way. In H. A. Liddle & C. Douglas (Eds.), *Handbook of family therapy training and supervision* (pp. 17–37). New York: Guilford.

Conners, C. K. (1989). *Conner's Parent and Teacher Questionnaire.* North Tonawanda, NY: Multi-health Systems.

Conoley, J., & Conoley, C. (1991). Collaboration for child adjustment: Issues for school and clinic-based child psychologists. *Journal of Consulting and Clinical Psychology, 59,* 821–829.

DuPaul, G., Guevremont, D., & Barkley, R. (1991). Attention-deficit/hyperactivity disorder in adolescence: Critical assessment parameters. *Clinical Psychology Review, 11,* 231–245.

DuPaul, G., & Stoner, G. (1994). *ADHD in the schools: Assessment and intervention strategies.* New York: Guilford.

Fauber, R., & Long, N. (1991). Children in context: The role of the family in child psychotherapy. *Journal of Consulting and Clinical Psychology, 59,* 813–820.

Fehlings, D., Roberts, W., Humphries, T., & Dawe, G. (1991). Attention-deficit/hyperactivity disorder: Does cognitive behavioral therapy improve home behavior? *Journal of Developmental and Behavioral Pediatrics, 12,* 223–228.

Figley, C., & Nelson, T. (1990). Basic family therapy skills, II: Structural family therapy. *Journal of Marital and Family Therapy, 16,* 225–239.

Gingerich, E., Golden, S., Holley, D., & Nemser, J. (1992). The therapist as psychoeducator. *Hospital and Community Psychiatry, 43,* 928–930.

Haenlein, M., & Caul, W. (1987). Attention-deficit disorder with hyperactivity: A specific hypothesis of reward dysfunction. *Journal of the American Academy of Child and Adolescent Psychiatry, 26,* 356–362.

Haley, J. (1980). How to be a marriage therapist without knowing practically anything. *Journal of Marital and Family Therapy, 6,* 385–391.

Hechtman, L., & Weiss, G. (1986). Controlled prospective fifteen-year follow-up of hyperactives as adults: Non-medical drug and alcohol use and anti-social behavior. *Canadian Journal of Psychiatry, 31,* 557–567.

Kazdin, A. (1987). *Conduct disorders in childhood and adolescence.* Newbury Park, CA: Sage.

Kazdin, A., (1991). Effectiveness of psychotherapy with children and adolescents. *Journal of Consulting and Clinical Psychology, 59,* 785–789.

Kazdin, A., Seigal, J. C., & Bass, D. (1992). Cognitive problem solving skills training and parent management training in the treatment of antisocial behavior in children. *Journal of Consulting and Clinical Psychology, 60,* 733–747.

Lerner, J., Lowenthal, B., & Lerner, S. (1995). *Attention deficit disorders: Assessment and teaching.* Pacific Grove, CA: Brooks/Cole.

McKinney, J., Montaque, M., & Hocutt, A. (1993). Educational assessment of students with attention deficit disorder. *Exceptional Child, 60,* 125–131.

Minuchin, S. (1974). *Families and family therapy.* Cambridge, MA: Harvard University Press.

Minuchin, S., & Fishman, C. (1981). *Family therapy techniques.* Cambridge, MA: Harvard University Press.

Minuchin, S., Rosman, B., & Baker, L. (1978). *Psychosomatic families: Anorexia nervosa in context.* Cambridge, MA: Harvard University Press.

Nichols, M. (1987). The individual in the system. *Family Therapy Networker, 11,* 33–38, 85.

Nichols, M., & Schwartz, R. (1998). *Family therapy: Concepts and methods* (4th ed.). Boston, MA: Allyn & Bacon.

Parker, H. C. (1994). *The ADD hyperactivity workbook for parents, teachers, and kids* (2d ed.). Manasses Park, VA: Impact.

Pisterman, S., Firestone, P., McGrath, P., & Goodman, J. (1992). The role of parent training in treatment of preschoolers with ADHD. *American Journal of Orthopsychiatry, 62,* 397–408.

Pisterman, S., McGrath, P., Firestone, P., & Goodman, J. (1989). Outcome of parent-mediated treatment of preschoolers with attention deficit disorder with hyperactivity. *Journal of Consulting and Clinical Psychology, 57,* 628–635.

Pollard, S., Ward, E., & Barkley, R. (1983). The effects of parent training and Ritalin on the parent-child interactions of hyperactive boys. *Child and Family Behavior Therapy, 5,* 51–69.

Rosenberg, D. R., Holttum, J., & Gershon, S. (1994). *Textbook of pharmacotherapy for child and adolescent psychiatric disorders.* New York: Brunner/Mazel.

Quay, H. (1988). The behavioral reward and inhibition system in childhood behavior disorders. In L. M. Bloomingdale (Ed.), *Attention deficit disorder, Vol. 3: New research in attention, treatment, and psychopharmacology* (pp. 176–186). Oxford, England: Pergamon.

Quinn, P. O. (Ed.). (1994). *ADD and the college student: A guide for high school and college students with attention deficit disorder.* Washington, DC: Magination Press/American Psychological Association.

Quinn, P. O. (1995). Neurobiology of attention deficit disorder. In K. Nadeau (Ed.), *A comprehensive guide to attention deficit disorder in adults: Research, diagnosis, and treatment* (pp. 18–31). New York: Brunner/Mazel.

Ruel, J., & Hickey, P. (1992). Are too many children being treated with methylphenidate? *Canadian Journal of Psychiatry, 37,* 570–572.

Strayhorn, J., & Weidman, C. (1989). Reduction of attention deficit and internalizing symptoms in preschoolers through parent-child interaction training. *Journal of the American Academy of Child and Adolescent Psychiatry, 28,* 888–896.

Szapocznik, J., Hervis, O., Rio, A., & Mitrani, V. (1991). Assessing change in family functioning as a result of treatment: The structural family systems rating scale. *Journal of Marital and Family Therapy, 17,* 295–310.

Szatmari, P., Offord, D., & Boyle, M. (1989). Ontario Child Health Study: Prevalence of attention deficit disorder with hyperactivity. *Journal of Child Psychology and Psychiatry and Allied Disciplines, 30,* 219–230.

Weiss, G., & Hechtman, L. (1993). *Hyperactive children grown up: ADHD in children, adolescents, and adults* (2nd ed.). New York: Guilford.

Weissberg, R., Caplan, M., & Harwood, R. (1991). Promoting competent young people in competence-enhancing environments: A systems-based perspective in primary prevention. *Journal of Consulting and Clinical Psychology, 59,* 830–841.

Wender, P. (1995). *Attention-deficit/hyperactivity disorder in adults.* New York: Oxford University Press.

Whalen, C., & Henker, B. (1991). Social impact of stimulant treatment for hyperactive children. *Journal of Learning Disabilities, 24,* 231–241.

Wilens, T., & Biederman, J. (1992). The stimulants. *Psychiatric Clinics of North America, 15,* 191–122.

III
ADDITIONAL PERSPECTIVES

13
Engaging Families in Therapeutic Play
Eliana Gil
Barbara Sobol

A mother, father, and 10-year-old child were referred by a reunification worker at the Department of Social Services, with a specific consultation question: Is this family ready to have the sexually abusive father return home? The therapist had tried several sessions of verbal therapy and still felt uneasy and uncertain, unable to pinpoint her concern. She conferred with me, and I suggested she try a family puppet interview. After asking the family to select puppets and construct a story with a beginning, middle, and end, the family told the following brief story: A mother and daughter, living together, were concerned about how to keep safe from a bee that kept flying around, trying to sting them. They told the bee to scat, they built nets around the house, and they used pesticides, but the bee persisted until finally he bit the girl. The girl was rushed to the doctor's office and the doctor told her that it would be quite important to make sure she could be safe from other bee stings. The girl then faced the bee, insisting that he must stay away and talk to his bee friends whenever he had the urge to sting anyone. Mother likewise said she felt that it was too hard to keep the bee out since he was small and slippery. At the end of the story, and while the family members were putting away their puppets, the bee once again snuck over and stung the girl. When the therapist pointed this out, the father, now putting away the bee puppet said, "That wasn't a

sting, it was a kiss." Mother and child proclaimed that it seemed like
a sting, not a kiss. The therapist concluded that it was not safe for
this family to reunify at this time, especially since the father could
not tell the difference between a sting and a kiss, and the mother
and daughter could not feel safe with a bee they could not control.
Additional offender-specific therapy was recommended for the
father as well as ongoing treatment for the mother and daughter.

A Rationale for the Use of Play with Families

Family therapists have a rich history of creativity and original thought. Loathe to rest on their laurels, their recent innovations include constructivist, narrative, and solution-focused therapies. Several books have promoted applicability of these techniques with children (Araoz & Carrese, 1996; Freeman, Epston, & Lobovits, 1997; Smith & Nylund, 1997).

It seems mystifying that, in this context of imaginative and spirited theory and technique, there has been relatively limited attention to utilizing specific techniques designed to elicit fuller participation from young children in family sessions. Miller (1994) aptly points to territoriality and exclusivity in both family and play therapy models as one of the reasons for this lack of integration. On the other hand, she emphasizes a growing consensus that play in family therapy has a positive impact and notes, "Metaphor allows children to express themselves within play, a developmentally less intimidating prospect than verbally facing their parents" (p. 15). Green (1994) suggests that a lack of training in utilization of play in family therapy prevents clinicians from employing this medium. He notes that training in child therapy has been woefully absent from major training curricula, and he calls for the incorporation of these techniques to develop confidence and motivation in family therapists who work with children.

Several authors have encouraged family therapists and other clinicians to keep children in the forefront, not only during assessment sessions but also throughout the treatment process (Andreozzi, 1996; Combrinck-Graham, 1989; Kilpatrick & Holland, 1995; Wachtel, 1994; Zilbach, 1986). A few writings have focused on the use of play in family therapy (Ariel, 1992; Gil, 1994; Griff, 1983; Schaefer & Carey, 1994) or on integrating play as a way to enhance family-child interactions (B. Guerney, 1964; L. Guerney, 1997).

Observing Therapeutic Family Play

Most family therapists are skilled in the observation of family interactions. Family therapy training emphasizes the observation of clinical videotapes, live family sessions, and reflecting teams. Therapists learn to observe families in minute detail, documenting factors such as hierarchical structure and organization, boundaries, communication styles, emotional connectedness, and many subtle variables such as family cohesion, rigidity, and access to internal or external resources. The family's broader cultural context is considered highly relevant to family functioning, and clinicians are encouraged to view the family with attention to class and gender variables (see, for example, Bograd, 1991; Gibbs & Huang, 1998; Ho, 1987; McGoldrick, Anderson, & Walsh, 1991; Wen-Shing & Hsu, 1991).

Family Dynamics

Obviously, a focused observation of family interactions aids in the assessment and treatment process. Another valuable layer of useful information can be gleaned through the observation of family play dynamics. Specifically, the integration of play tasks into family sessions allows therapists windows of insight into the following categories:

- *Ability and willingness to organize around a task.* When family members are asked to participate in a low-risk, low-demand activity, clinicians observe the family's ability to cooperate with each other; leadership styles; use of democratic or autocratic systems; the utilization and delegation of power; alliances and collusions; who is included and excluded; ability to negotiate and reach consensus; and relationship to success, failure, or stalemates.
- *Level of contact.* When family members cooperate in a play activity, clinicians can document the use, abuse, or exclusion of physical contact; type and level of affective contact; whether genuine or false contact is made and tolerated; and whether contact appears comfortable or uncomfortable, rewarding or unrewarding.
- *Level of enjoyment.* When a play activity is introduced into the context of therapy, family members may experience joy, spontaneity, increased energy, and a sense of delight and surprise. Clinicians can note whether the family enjoyment appears low, moderate, or high, and if specific family members encourage or discourage enjoyment and relaxation.

• *Level of insight.* As family members engage in play activities, the process of creating or constructing, as well as the final product, can elicit individual or collective insights. The discussions that pertain to the process or content can be used to uncover camouflaged issues that might surprise, frighten, or perplex the family.

• *Collective unconscious.* As families are asked to select or create object symbols and develop thematic materials both individually and collectively, the collective unconscious is sparked. According to Jung (1964), we are all symbolically connected with our historical and primitive development, so that certain images, or archetypes, communicate meaning on an unconscious level.

Family play therapy provides ample data about the interplay between individual and systemic issues and how family members contribute and react to one another, constructing an organizational style that can help or hinder when obstacles arise.

Process and Content

The observation of family play occurs primarily on two levels: process and content.

Process

To illustrate process it might be interesting to note the level of enthusiasm, disinhibition, creativity, intensity, and pleasure with which an individual approaches and engages in the task. Some people who appear tense and emotionally shut down seem to come to life when they manipulate puppets, briskly smear paints on canvas, or use their hands to create three-dimensional objects. It is interesting to watch highly verbal individuals struggle with nonverbal expression, and it is likewise fascinating to witness the emergence of verbal expression in direct response to creative symbol images. At the same time, the individual's enthusiasm and creative energy may diminish as he or she responds to the forces of the system involved in a collective task.

Process information also includes stylistic differences: Some family members work alone; some seek constant approval, possibly emulating or finding stimulation in others' work. Some family members become secretive about their projects, showing them off only after others have shown theirs, even requiring pushing and prodding to reveal their products. Others work hard to obtain attention. The level and type of nonverbal and verbal communication will obviously have an impact on outcome. For example, some parents or partners constantly push, prod, question, ridicule, or support each other. Sometimes family members are harsh and unforgiving, pointing and laughing at each other's work. Other times, they are remarkably kind and encouraging, making positive comments, showing interest, or requesting information. Table 13.1 provides an example of the observational categories that can be seen and measured during family play sessions. As you can see, some of these categories are quantitative (e.g., number of positive statements made) and some are qualitative (type of affect).

Content

When discussing content, the second dimension of observation, most family therapists refer to the topic or issue discussed. For family play therapists, content involves not only what is being said, but also what is suggested through symbol, metaphor, and metaphor language. Content also refers to the actual product, art image, or story that is created. Depending on the level of training you have had, content may have more or less significance during or after the family session.

When the content is available, it is important to document how family members label the work, how they react to it, and whether or not symbol language emerges. One or more of the family members may repeat specific phrases, demonstrate an interest in a particular aspect of the play, or assign meaning for another family member. Our experience has been that families can keep symbolic meaning alive, help it thrive, or stifle future development. Likewise, a therapist can reintroduce the content of previous family play sessions by using specific language developed by the family, bringing out specific toys or symbols, reviewing art work or videotapes, or asking family members to remember or reenact play aspects.

One 5-year-old child was in therapy because she was struggling to cope with a drug-addicted mother who visited the child sporadically. This child was fiercely loyal to her mother and denied feeling disappointed or angry when her mother did not keep scheduled visits. She could speak about her mother only in glowing terms. She had a number of minor symptoms but the most worrisome was her tendency to develop somatic complaints. She was often sick with stomachaches, headaches, and general physical discomfort.

I (EG) used a storytelling technique with her and told her a story about a little squirrel whose mother left her alone for long periods of time. (As I was telling the story I paused to give the child the opportunity to help me develop

---

TABLE 13.1
Sample of Observational Categories* for Observing Family Play Therapy Sessions

---

PARENTAL AFFECT

____ None observed ____ Tense and guarded ____ Open laughter and delight

____ Tears (sadness) ____ Raised voices (excitement) ____ Raised voices (anger)

____ Affect differential to family members

PARENT INTRUSION

____ Continually asked questions, directed, made commands about others' art

____ Did not intrude into anyone's art process

____ Encouraged or helped in nondirective ways

PARENTAL PRAISE

____ None present ____ Praised own art work ____ Praised others' art work

PARENTAL COMPLIANCE

____ No compliance ____ Complied some of the time

____ Complied most of the time ____ Complied always

PARENTAL COMMUNICATION

____ No verbal statements ____ Some verbal statements

____ Many verbal statements

____ Number of supportive statements

____ Number of critical or harsh statements

USE OF PUNISHMENT OR THREATS

____ None used ____ Some used ____ Many used

____ Number of statements including threats or punishments

These factors are observed between parent and child(ren), between adults, between siblings, and in the differential uses initiated by parents or children.

*Observational categories are selected by clinicians based on their theoretical frameworks.

---

the story. She gave the squirrel both her own name and her age.) This child, who usually could not identify her own feelings, quickly responded to the part of the story in which I said, "The squirrel's mommy went away for long periods of time, and the squirrel didn't know when she would see her mommy again. She worried about her mommy, and she felt sad and lonely, but sometimes she was just plain mad at her mom for leaving her alone in the woods." With tears welling in her eyes, she said, "I feel all those ways too. I wish my mom wouldn't go far."

As we kept talking about the squirrel's plight, the child was able to acknowledge her own feelings by empathizing with the character in the story. In future sessions, when this little girl wanted to talk about her feelings about mom, she would go and grab the squirrel puppet. The squirrel became the symbol that communicated the child's readiness to face her difficult emotions.

Similarly, in the example given at the beginning of the chapter the therapist who worked with the family reported that after constructing the story, the mother and daughter often made reference to the "stinging bee" or problems they were having with "the bee." The stinging bee metaphor was code language for the sexual offending behavior and seemed to increase the family's willingness to bring up and discuss these important issues without feeling threatened or ashamed. Both clinician and family can get to the point quickly and easily by using metaphor language or symbols replete with personal meaning.

I try to videotape family play sessions so that families have the opportunity to view the tapes together. Young children seem to like viewing the tapes repeatedly. Parents often notice specific aspects of the story, the family interactions, or the potential meanings that they might have missed early on. This subsequent viewing allows for a deepening of the work in which family members make personal associations or insights about the stories they have told, or other products they have created.

Promoting Therapeutic Goals Through Therapeutic Play

Once the process and content material has been evaluated by clinician and family, there may be ways to promote therapy goals by using family play therapy techniques. For example, many families come into treatment because they feel emotionally disconnected or because the parents feel that their children are out of control. It behooves us to observe how family members interact with each other in order to better understand how the problems emerge and how they are being sustained within the family system.

Family play techniques allow us not only to view interactional patterns but also to give family members opportunities to view each other differently, to have an enjoyable and rewarding interaction with each other, and to work on their problems in a different way, as in this family: Instead of talking about Scotty, who was seen as out of control, the family talked about a baby raccoon who was mischievous and could not make any friends. We then worked on helping the raccoon within the context of family play therapy sessions. In one meeting, the family built a safe environment for a miniature raccoon, making sure all his needs were met so he wouldn't have to go scavenge next door. In another session we had the raccoon pick out a friend, and then everyone contributed ideas for how to approach someone you wanted to befriend. The family members had fun while they helped Scotty resolve his problem. Scotty was more receptive because he wasn't identified as a problem child, but rather, a child with a behavioral problem.

Another family I worked with was very concerned about sibling aggression. The children, Anna, 7, and John, 9, were extremely competitive with each other and could not tolerate one getting more attention than the other. Because John was physically aggressive with his sister, he often got negative attention from his parents. The more negative attention he got, the more he longed for approval from them. The end result was that he resented his sister and saw her as responsible for his plight.

I started by asking the family to make a family sand tray (Boik & Goodwin, 2000) in the hopes that they could negotiate the limited space of the sandbox in such a way that the children got equal attention. The children fought over wanting the same miniature, and John eventually grabbed an object out of his sister's hand. At that point the parents became angry with John and John became sullen. As he withdrew the family created a world in the sand—a world with no place for John. As an afterthought, the father took some things out so that John could put down whatever he wanted, but by then it was too late.

We watched the videotape of this session the following week. I asked the parents to watch closely, since I thought it might contain some important information about how the "familiar pattern" they had described to me repeated itself in the family play session. We paused the tape at the point when the kids were arguing over one miniature, and I asked the parents to discuss what was happening. They both reported that they had not been aware of this when it was going on. "I didn't notice there was a problem until John yanked that out of her hand."

Instructed to watch the tape again, the parents noticed that there were two identical miniatures that could have been chosen but the children were fighting over one. The father then asked the children, "Didn't you see the other one?" "Yes," they both said. "Then why didn't you just use both of them?" John responded, "I picked it first and then she had to have it because I wanted it."

Mother asked Anna if that was accurate and she said it was but added, "John gets mean with me. If he had just asked me nice I would have given it to him."

After we discussed how this dynamic contributed to the overall problem of John eliciting negative attention, I asked the family to build another world in the sand, this time paying special attention to everyone having enough space and everyone negotiating to get needs met. They completed a highly cohesive sand world in which everyone felt validated.

When they returned the following week I had made an enlarged transparency of the picture I took of the sand tray, and I used an overhead projector to shine it on the wall. The family members were quite impressed with their work and they took turns telling about the worlds they had built and the reasons they had chosen the objects in the tray.

This kind of positive family experience motivates people to work harder to achieve the desired results. This family told family puppet stories, made a family aquarium, designed a soccer game based on John's interest in the game, and effectively replaced dysfunctional interactional patterns with more rewarding ones. The parents understood that they were catching John being bad instead of trying to catch him being good. They made efforts to give him spontaneous positive attention and he responded in kind. Anna did not take the change smoothly, preferring it when John was in the background. I did some individual work with her to help her tolerate sharing the limelight. (She made up a story about a Broadway star with an understudy who was mad because she never got sick. I introduced the notion that even Broadway stars need some rest so they can go shopping or ice skating or do something fun. Eventually she relented and shared the stage with the understudy every now and then.)

Integrating Family Play Sessions

The most frequently asked questions are: "When do you use family play sessions?" "How often do you use them?" "Do you use them with every family you see?" Fortunately, there are no rigid rules. You can select family play therapy sessions whenever you deem them useful or appropriate.

Family play therapy sessions can be initiated by clinician or client at any time. They will yield helpful diagnostic data early in therapy. It is possible to do first-visit play therapy sessions when clinicians feel comfortable doing so or to wait until four or five verbal therapy sessions have taken place.

Family play therapy sessions can be used for a variety of reasons: when there are young children in the family who are bored or disinterested in traditional verbal therapy; when the family has reached a therapeutic impasse; when families are not verbally-oriented; when family members are overly analytical or cerebral; when you hope to change flat family dynamics; when you feel the family is unable to disclose underlying concerns due to shame or discomfort; to build or solidify the therapeutic alliance; to promote specific therapeutic goals; to encourage new family relational patterns and to introduce the concept of laughter and play as a conduit to change; and to increase a family's sense of well-being. Too often clinicians are working with highly stressful family situations fraught with tension and distress. Family play sessions are simply another way to try to alleviate overwhelming stress and create optimism and hope.

When families come for their intake sessions, clinicians usually inform them as to their theoretical orientation and give them an idea of the course of therapy. Family play therapists say, "I am a family play therapist, which means that from time to time I will ask you and your children to come in for play therapy sessions using puppets, art, sand, games, or other play activities. I may ask to see your children alone, in sibling sessions, with one or the other parent, or with everyone in the family present."

We almost always make a written contract that states the presenting problem as defined by the parent and lists three goals with a time frame for improvement. We are guided by the work of Kiresuk and Sherman (1968) regarding goal attainment scaling, a structure we find particularly helpful. After listing the goals (or scales), the indicators (what behavioral change we will see to prove the goal is being met), the time frame (by when we expect to see change), we add one more column, "What play therapy technique can best help us to promote this goal?" This goal-oriented approach increases the likelihood of helping family members meet their goals, which by definition will give therapist and client a sense of accomplishment.

Therapeutic Play Techniques

A number of family play therapy techniques are listed in the following pages. However, clinicians are encouraged to design their own techniques fueled by their personal interests or those of the family. As you read these, allow yourself to make associations to other activities that you can then invent and promote.

Family Puppet Sessions

This technique was developed by Irwin and Malloy (1994) as a structured interview technique with families. Over the years, I (EG) have expanded this technique to include a more active therapeutic component, as described elsewhere (Gil, 1994). I find that this type of family play therapy has immeasurable value since it allows the family to communicate symbolically, decrease defenses, experience individual and collective pleasure, and develop an enhanced mechanism for interacting.

Description. Family members are asked to look at the assembled puppets and find those that are interesting to them. Once they make their selections, family members are asked to make up a story with a beginning, middle, and end and to use their puppets to formulate and then act out their story.

After listening to the story, Irwin and Malloy do a formal closure with specific questions, such as "Which character is most/least like each of you?" "Does this story remind you of anything that's going on in your real life?" "What is the moral of this story?" or "If you had to give this story a title, what would it be?" I prefer to delay the formal closure, instead seizing an opportunity to expand and work within the metaphor. In other words, I encourage clinicians to engage in a therapeutic dialogue with the puppet characters, staying within the story rather than closing it down prematurely. This expanding strategy will be demonstrated in the case discussions that follow.

Instructions. The instructions to the family are very straightforward: "Pick out some puppets that seem interesting to you for whatever reason. Once you've made your choices let me know."* The clinician then states, "I would like you to make up a story that has a beginning, middle, and end. There are only two rules: First, you must make up the story rather than tell a story you've heard or seen at the movies, like Prince of Egypt or Lion King. Second, once you tell the story you must act it out with the puppets rather than narrate it. Most people need about 20 to 25 minutes to make up their story. If you finish earlier simply let me know. I will be your audience as you tell me your story."

Tools required. You need a sufficient selection of puppets, probably 20 to 30. The puppets should have the potential for symbolic use. For example, you should select puppets associated with danger or threat (e.g., shark, tarantula), as well as those associated with polar feelings such as compliance or vulnera-

---

*I have learned to avoid limiting the number of puppets that people choose. How individuals select puppets is informative. A child who has to have more than anyone else communicates his or her needs: perhaps the child feels neglected in the family; perhaps the child needs to feel special or different. Enmeshed family members may need to pick the same puppet, or sometimes one individual's choice (a fish) may set the tone for everyone else (turtle, seahorse, whale, starfish), indicating that person's influence over the family.

bility (lambs, deer, baby chickens). Be sure to include some that have universal meaning, such as a wizard, a fairy godmother, or an alien. In addition, those in positions of authority are included (policemen, teachers, doctors). Try to have animal and human puppets, and make sure the human puppets are culturally diverse. Lastly, it is helpful to include puppets that symbolize transformation (e.g., a caterpillar that turns into a butterfly). The most popular among my puppets are the turtle, the fox, and the owl (suggesting issues of safety or shyness, slyness and quickness, and wisdom).

I recommend videotaping the stories not only because family members enjoy watching their stories at home but also because the stories are often told so quickly that it can take several viewings to fully observe interactions between family members and story development (process and content). In addition, it is interesting to videotape the family's rehearsal of the story and then compare it to the telling of the story. Sometimes the two are identical, and other times the variations that occur are quite meaningful and ignite important discussion. It is likely that in the telling of the story momentum develops that might elicit unconscious material that then contributes to straying from the original script.

Follow-up. When the family returns to therapy the following week, we view the tape together without interruption. Family members are then asked for their thoughts and feelings about the story they told or the dialogue after the story. (On occasion, family members have been given a homework assignment and are asked to report on that.) Clinicians come prepared to make comments or observations, usually expressing curiosity about one thing or another. It is important to keep clinical interpretations to a minimum while still encouraging family members to be introspective.

Sometimes family members ask to view their tapes over and over again. Other times they want to tell a new story, and still other times they quickly make associations between the story and a particular family problem. It is not unusual for the metaphor of the story to become integrated into the family's language. For example, a family who told a story about a shark who was being held prisoner in a cage understood the symbolism in that metaphor. Father had left the family to have an extramarital affair and when he returned the children did not trust him and were angry with him. When they told their story, father, who self-selected the shark puppet, was captured and put in a cage. The children, who acted as "sea hunters," would feed him a fish from time to time but would not let him out until he promised he would not go around threatening to eat every fish in sight. Mother was an octopus who would not come near the cage but preferred to go about her business, collecting food for a rainy day when there would be little to eat on the bottom of the sea.

In verbal therapy sessions the children would refer to "the shark in the cage," when they wanted to talk about their father and how angry they were at him. Father would also make reference to feeling like "an outsider, someone who was looking in, not knowing what to do to get himself free." Mother described her situation when father was gone by saying, "there was never enough time to get everything done between work, picking the kids up, arranging for sitters, making dinner. I often longed for extra arms, like the octopus. But now that I know that I can get along without him, I'm not afraid anymore."

This family was able to reunify after mother and children held father accountable and father apologized to them. His final statement was, "I know that there are other fish in the ocean, but I want to make a home with my wife and kids and I won't be chasing after those fish anymore."

Family Art Evaluation (FAE)

Kwiatkowska (1978) wrote extensively about family art evaluations, which she created as a diagnostic tool in her work with schizophrenic families. The short form of her evaluation consists of having family members draw a series of four pictures; one of the pictures is a joint family activity. She developed a detailed rating sheet for documenting the vast information gleaned from the evaluation. This particular evaluation tool was designed to be used by trained art therapists. We are hopeful that more and more family therapists will become trained to integrate modifications of these techniques into their work, particularly as a way to observe family dynamics in action. Such adaptations work well in clinical practice, although those conducting research with this technique are advised to follow Kwiatkowska's original designs. Here we describe our modification of the FAE.

Tools required. Standing easels, 11" x 24" white paper, boxes of Nupastels, black magic markers, wet towels, and enough space for setting up easels in a semi-circle.*

Description. The family art evaluation requires each family member to produce four individual drawings, and the entire family to do one art task. The

---

*Many clinicians do not have the office space that allows for setting up standing easels in semi-circles. They have also expressed concern about the cost of purchasing numerous easels. Office supply stores and art stores have a variety of standing easels at reasonable prices. Recently, we have seen small easels that stand on top of tables. In addition, pieces of paper can be clipped to large pieces of foam board available in art stores, or they can be placed on walls with blank paper underneath.

joint family art task can be either a scribble drawing or a mural. For a family scribble drawing, everyone in the family is asked to make a scribble on a blank piece of paper. The scribbles should be made with broad sweeping arm motions with a light pastel. Family members then look at all the scribbles, turning them over, until they jointly select one scribble that looks like it has possibilities to be made into a family picture. Family members are asked to look at the scribbles and see if they see images that could be better defined by coloring them in, making new lines, or adding or emphasizing colors. Because this is a family task, members are encouraged to discuss and make a joint selection and then to participate together in the creation of a picture.

The family mural is made on a very large piece of paper taped onto a wall. The family is asked to think about a picture they would like to make together and then to proceed to make it. These tasks are designed to challenge family members to participate in a shared creative activity.

Instructions. These sessions will take longer than the standard 50 minutes. Family members are asked to come early enough in the evening so that they do not tire, and parents are asked to give their children a snack so they aren't distracted by hunger. Usually, the session takes about 90 minutes. It's important to remember that setting up and dismantling equipment may take extra time. In addition, art will need to be organized and, in some cases, photographed.

The instructions to the family are as follows: "You will be asked to make four individual pictures and one joint picture. You will not be evaluated for your artistic ability. This is simply another way that families communicate with each other. Please do not be too elaborate in your pictures, since we have a limited amount of time for each one. After each picture you'll get a chance to look at each other's work and make brief comments or ask questions. For the first picture, make a picture of anything you want, anything that comes to mind (a free drawing)."

The second task is to "make a picture of your family including yourself. You may make a picture of the family as it really looks, or you can use lines, shapes, colors, and images to show how you feel about the people in the family, including yourself."

The third task is to make a scribble. Therapists should have family members make broad sweeping motions in the air with a light pastel, and then put the same motion on a piece of paper. Once individual scribbles are completed, the family is asked to choose one scribble to develop into a picture by adding lines, colors, shapes, or images. The family must select the scribble and discuss the picture together.

The fourth and final task is a repetition of the first free drawing: "Make a picture of anything you want, anything that comes to mind."

Follow-up. Evaluation works best when the art is discussed and reviewed several times. It is extremely useful to follow the family art evaluation session with a processing session, where any thoughts, feelings, or insights since the evaluation can be discussed. After the therapeutic dialogue, the art work is taped onto the wall so the family can view the pictures anew. More discussion regarding the pictures ensues; finally, a portion of the videotape can be shown for additional comments.

During the evaluation, or in a session following the evaluation, the clinician can give the family feedback on both process and content.

A mother and her two children (Concha, 14, and Tomas, 10) participated in a family art evaluation. Father was unable to attend the first few sessions, and apparently his absence caused the adolescent girl to feel anger and disappointment. The critical production of this family's art evaluation was a family picture that they entitled "The Piranha from Hell." In this picture, a giant fish had a man in his mouth and the man was bleeding as the fish was saying "Aaaahhh" (as in yummy). When the family sat down to look at their joint creation, mother got teary-eyed when she learned that Concha saw the man in the fish's mouth as her father. "That's not nice," mother said, "Why do you have your poor father being eaten by the fish?" Her daughter immediately felt protective of her teary mother and said, "It's just 'cause he didn't come tonight and I'm mad at him." Concha's final art work (task 4) was an apology to her mother for making her cry. "I'm sorry," the picture stated, "I love you all."

When the family returned for a follow-up session, they were quite stunned by the intensity of the piranha drawing. They made some comments about mother's artistic ability, how much they enjoyed doing art, how it was too bad Dad hadn't been able to participate. Finally, my cotherapist and I (EG) said, "We are quite struck with the image of The Piranha from Hell, and it has made us concerned about what might be going on in the family that you would create this very powerful image." This comment led to a more open discussion of what was going on at home. Tomas reported feeling worried. When we asked what his worst worry was, he wrote on a piece of paper and passed us a note that said, "That my dad will hit my mother or my sister." We asked Tomas to show the note to his mother, who then was able to report a history of domestic violence and a recent episode in which Concha had been physically abused.

This family had a lot on its mind. Individual family members were frightened about violence they wanted to deny or avoid. Mother had hoped that the violence would resolve itself on its own but had recently begun to realize that it might not. In the family there was an unspoken agreement not to reveal these family secrets; yet once they engaged in art work the images spoke volumes. Through the art the family was able to communicate without betrayal. When witnessing the powerful image they created, however, they were no longer able to protect the father and deny the problem. It took the therapist's comments to help the family make the transition from silence to disclosure.

It is interesting to note that the therapists had not suspected domestic violence, or any kind of violence, until they saw the piranha picture, which had a very disturbing impact. Part of the value of a family art evaluation is that the art speaks to the clinician and the clinician has countertransference responses not only to the family but to the images that the family produces. The therapists knew the family had some kind of problem and that they had to make comments designed to elicit more information.

This is a dramatic example of the power of art. The initial therapeutic comments should first and foremost support the family's observations. Later the therapist should make comments without suggesting meaning. It is very important for family members to allocate meaning to their own symbols rather than being told what symbols represent. Therapists can certainly pose questions and "wonder out loud" without providing answers or interpretations. During the follow-up session, the therapist is engaging family members in "left brain activity," so that they are stimulated to self-evaluate both individual and collective connections and meanings. Sometimes, families engage in their own evaluation with little directive from the clinicians. I have found it useful to alert families to the possibility that they may have insights about the art evaluation when they least expect it, and that they should make an effort to jot down their associations, insights, questions, or comments.

The overall goal of the family art evaluation is to provide an opportunity for family members to communicate and express themselves in a different way. Families can also have positive experiences that will promote a sense of well-being and competence. Because many adults have had unfortunate experiences with art in their pasts (for example, getting poor marks or being made to feel inadequate), they may have initial resistance to the project. Conversely, some family members take to the task quite freely, relieved at not having to communicate verbally. Kwiatkowska's pioneering work with the family art evaluation has been carried on by a handful of art therapists who recognize its value and usefulness and teach the FAE in their classes (authors Gil and Sobol included).

Other art therapists have promoted the use of art work in families (see, for example, Burns, 1990; Gillespie, 1994; Landgarten, 1987) and suggested a multitude of creative and enjoyable tasks that can be undertaken by families.

Family Sand Worlds

Sand therapy appears to be swelling in popularity (Mitchell & Friedman, 1994). More and more adult and child therapists are using this technique as their chosen modality or as an adjunct to other forms of therapy. Two primary sand therapy techniques, sandplay (Kalff, 1980; Ryce-Menuhin, 1992) and sand tray (Lowenfeld, 1939) are used primarily with individuals (adults and children). Even the Erica Method (Sjolund, 1993), an evaluation method using sand, sand tray, and miniatures, is restricted to use by individuals. While attempts to use sand therapy with couples or families have been infrequently documented, the family sand therapy technique holds great promise and is utilized by many professionals with training in sand therapy and family therapy (Carey, 1991, 1999; Boik & Goodwin, 2000).

Many professionals find family sand trays, like family art evaluation, overwhelming, intimidating, or cumbersome to conduct. In my (EG) experience as a trainer, these resistances have been both expectable and easily overcome. The best results are achieved when clinicians have an opportunity to do the task rather than observe one. Those interested in working with sand are referred to a new work that provides the basics in an accessible and comprehensive way without focusing exclusively on one theory (Homeyer & Sweeney, 1999).

Description. The family sand tray technique consists of asking family members to create a scenario in the sand, using whatever miniatures they like.

Tools required. A sand tray on a stand so that adults and children can work with it easily; fine sand; water; a set of miniatures representing plants, minerals, animals, people, buildings, bridges, and so forth.

Instructions. "As you can see, this is a sand tray filled with very fine sand. (Touching the sand) Most people find that the sand feels very good on their hands. (Pushing away sand to reveal the blue bottom) Some people have commented that this looks like water. I'd like you to use as few or as many miniatures as you like to create a scene in the sand. There is no right way or wrong way of doing this; each family has its own way, which is just fine. Remember to decide together as a family what you will build in the sand, and develop your idea together as a family."

Those familiar with sandplay therapy will feel comfortable with the phrase "using the miniatures, build whatever you like in the sand." Those who have used the sand tray technique may ask the family to use the miniatures to build a world in the sand tray.

Follow-up. We have found it useful to give the builder a little time before engaging in an intellectual discussion that may disrupt the building process. Many clients describe feeling self-absorbed, almost as if in a trance, as they do sandplay; others have commented on the spiritual journey, which has been emphasized by sand therapy pioneers. Because of this, we believe that the therapeutic dialogue, which probably solidifies the conscious and unconscious links, can wait until future sessions. It should not be rushed. Addressing these issues over time allows for a natural processing of material, increased opportunity for insight and closure, and a deepening of alternative meanings.

It is always useful to give families an opportunity to create something in the sand tray that emerges totally from their unconscious. In this way, this particular technique is nondirective in nature. However, it is also possible to elicit unconscious responses in family members when the clinician is more directive with the instructions, as in the following case. Recently, I (EG) met with a mother and five children whose physically abusive father had recently been convicted and now awaited sentencing. The children were shy and uncomfortable when talking, so I decided to give them a concrete task that could help them express how they were feeling. I set out two sand trays, one with dry sand and one with wet sand, and said, "I would like you to build two worlds. In World 1, build a world that shows your thoughts and feelings about home when your dad lived with you. In World 2, build a world that shows your thoughts and feelings about home now that your dad does not live with you." I then asked the family to select the sand tray they would use to construct World 1. They unanimously picked the wet sand to create the world that included Dad. While they worked together to build this world, their affect was constricted and tense. Mother chose two elderly people sitting on a bench with their backs to each other. She also placed an oblong shape in the sand, which the children then reinforced with fences that had no entry or exit. The children contributed a variety of objects, mostly soldiers with guns who were "killing people" and tombstones for the people who had already been killed. Godzilla was introduced as a threatening and powerful figure about to "wipe everyone out," and there was fire in two of the corners. In addition, a rubber knife was placed on one of the fences, indicating danger and violence. The family seemed rushed in constructing this world, and one of the children voiced relief at moving to the next sand tray. "Okay," he said, "now for the good stuff."

As they moved to World 2, the affect changed significantly as the youngest child stated, "This is the calm world and no bad things happen here." That world had a big house for the family, churches, trees, children playing, flowers, beads, and many, many maternal figures taking care of children, all in an open environment without fences. The difference in the family's collective affect during the building of the worlds was striking, so much so that when the children started singing "Joy to the World," it seemed quite appropriate.

There were some insights given at the end of the session, but verbal communication was not required since the children had discharged and processed many of their thoughts and feelings about Dad's presence and absence. It was clear that they now felt safe, secure, and hopeful. Future sessions addressed their father's incarceration, their parents' divorce, and their adjustment to a new family configuration without an involved father figure.

Family Collage

Description. Family members select and cut out pictures from magazines and newspapers, arranging them onto a large piece of paper or construction paper. Collages can be spontaneous or in response to specific suggestions (see below).

Tools required. Scissors, glue, diverse magazines, construction paper, magic markers.

Instructions. Family members are asked to select pictures, cut them out, and then arrange them together on a large piece of construction paper. This particular exercise is totally projective in nature and may provoke anxiety due to the lack of instruction (as to which pictures to cut out or themes to develop). It also requires family cooperation as pictures are arranged on a single piece of construction paper. Clinicians may observe process issues such as who leads, follows, contributes, and withdraws, as well as efforts to be visible, invisible, or make space. The size of the pictures may suggest issues such as intrusion, enmeshment, or need for power. The content of the images may communicate intra- or interpersonal dynamics, preoccupations, obsessions, or concerns.

A more directive way of collage-making requires family members to cut out pictures and arrange them on a single easel-size paper, but provides a clear suggestion, such as:

- Make a collage of a happy time in your family.
- Make a collage of a crisis time in your family.
- Make a collage of an ideal family environment.
- Make a collage of achievement or success.

- Make a collage of anxious, uncomfortable feelings.
- Make a collage of calm, relaxing feelings.
- Make a collage of how to problem solve.
- Make a collage of positive self-esteem.
- Make a collage of effective communication.

Directives can be selected based on the family's presenting problem or specific therapy goals.

Follow-up. Once the collage is completed, family members are asked what it was like to make the product. A brief discussion about the actual experience of constructing a joint project (process observations) may ensue. Next, family members may be asked to look at the finished product and ask questions, make comments, or share their reaction. During these conversations, it is important to note how family members interact with each other and the level and type of support and communication they demonstrate. For example, some family members limit their support to specific people, ignoring others. Some family members restrict all comments to negative or harsh statements. Some give ample praise. The actual construction and process yield invaluable data regarding the family's relational interactions.

Family Play Genograms

The family play genogram was created in collaborative fashion. I (EG) was invited to teach play therapy and family play therapy at the Family Institute of New Jersey (FINJ) by the Institute's Director, Monica McGoldrick, a well-known family therapist, author, and one of the clinicians who has most promoted and developed the use of the genogram (McGoldrick & Gerson, 1985; McGoldrick, Gerson, & Shellenberger, 1999). As I watched faculty and students present cases with attention to large family systems chronicled in genograms, the idea of family play genograms surfaced. Simply put, the idea integrated play and play symbols with genograms as a way to enrich what was understood about each family member. Individually, family members are asked to choose a symbol that best represents their thoughts and feelings about each other. An alcoholic parent, for example, might be assigned a beer bottle by one family member, a baseball bat by another, and an alarm clock by a third. This might depict the fact that this family member spent most of his time listening to ball games on the radio and drinking himself to sleep, often neglecting important family activities or work commitments. This technique has great potential to help clinicians during history-taking and assessment. In addition, symbols can be requested that depict the nature of the relationships between specific family members.*

Description. The family play genogram utilizes the standardized graphic representation of family members, eliciting an expanded mode of communication. In essence, the family cooperates in the construction of a large genogram (of their nuclear and extended family) on easel-size paper (18" x 24"). The clinician can draw the basic symbols for mother, father, children, and then obtain information about family members' names and ages. Once the genogram is drawn and information is documented, family members are asked to choose one object (miniature) that most represents their thoughts and feelings about each person in the genogram, including themselves, and place it within each person's symbol.

Tools required. Large easel-size paper (18" x 24"); thick black magic markers; miniature objects such as those used for sand therapy. Although it is not necessary to have hundreds of miniatures for this task, it is best to include a representative sample of standard categories included in sand therapy (humans, zoo animals, farm animals, plants and minerals, transportation, and objects representing death, birth, religion, royalty, and magic or fantasy). A suggested list of objects is presented in Table 13.2. It is important to provide small pieces of clay that can be molded into objects that are not available and to give permission to write words that suggest absent symbols. In addition, family members can bring to the next session objects that they feel best illustrate their emotions or thoughts about themselves or a specific family member.

Instructions. As mentioned above, once the genogram is complete, family members are asked to look at available miniatures and select an object that conveys their thoughts and feelings about each family member and themselves.

Follow-up. Once all the objects have been placed, family members are asked to sit back and take a look at the genogram, ask clarifying questions, or make generic comments about the process. A discussion ensues about each family member, and the collective symbols, perceptions, memories of, or associations to that person are explored. Once individuals are discussed and each person has an opportunity to say a few words about his or her choice of object, family members may be asked to choose a symbol that best describes the nature of the relationship between dyads. For example, one adult woman chose

---

*One of FINJ's graduates, Deborah Buurma, has begun the Family Play Therapy Project in Metuchen, NJ. Ms. Buurma has collected photographs of many family play genograms and has done workshop presentations highlighting this idea and its application.

TABLE 13.2
BASIC LIST OF MINIATURES FOR SAND THERAPY

PEOPLE
  Family sets
    different ethnicity, ages, sizes
  Children
    nude and dressed
    infants through adolescence
  Older grandparent figures
  Brides and grooms
    ethnically diverse
    separate and together
  Professions
    police, judge, physician, nurse,
    firemen, sports figures
  Army
    tanks and equipment
    wounded with stretchers
  Historical
    cave people or aborigines
    knights and royal figures
    cowboys, Indians, settlers
    modern figures
ANIMALS
  dinosaurs, zoo animals, farm animals,
  domestic animals, insects and butterflies
NATURE
  trees, bushes, rocks, water (wells,
  lakes), volcano, cave, sea shells

VEHICLES
  cars, trucks, airplanes, boats,
  motorcycles, ambulance, school bus,
  police car
BOUNDARIES
  fences, popsicle sticks, cardboard and
  foam board
STRUCTURES
  buildings, churches, schools, bridges,
  wells
MINERALS
  copper, sandshells, eye of the tiger,
  crystals, colored beads, dinosaur tears
FANTASY
  wizard, castle, fairy godmother,
  dragons, angels, fairies, space aliens
RELIGIOUS
  minister, priest, rabbi, nun, bible,
  crosses, devil, Buddha, wise meditating
  men
OTHER
  weird or scary characters, twigs, rocks,
  pine cones, art materials, cross-cultural
  items
  Clay for sculpting desired objects

a high-rise building to symbolize her relationship to her mother, because she saw her as cold and inaccessible. This same woman chose a lighthouse to represent her relationship to her father, because she felt that he continued to be a source of guidance, direction, and comfort for her. When I asked her to pick a symbol to represent her parents' relationship to each other, she chose two soldiers carrying a stretcher with a wounded hero. She said she thought of her father as a wounded hero whose only chance to be nurtured was to be taken to the hospital to be cared for by a nurse. "In other words," she added, "he's been shut out by my mother all these years and I think he's given up trying to get any warmth from her." She cried as she looked at the symbols she had laid on the paper and felt their emotional impact.

These family sessions should not be rushed. It may take a full session to complete the genogram if all family members are present. Usually there is sufficient time to complete the genogram and select objects to be placed on each family member. A second session might focus on discussion of chosen objects, and a third session might discuss relational issues. This particular way of utilizing a genogram is quite helpful in eliciting cognitive as well as emotional descriptions of relationships between family members.

Family genograms are photographed, and family members are offered one picture while another remains with the therapist, with the family's consent.

Family Environments

Description. This technique was created by Sobol and Schneider (1998) for use with children. Clients are asked to select a small animal and then build an environment for the chosen figure.[*]

Tools required. Plastic animal figures of same size, usually available at five-and-dime stores in plastic bags. A combination of wild, zoo, and farm animals are included. In addition, a variety of materials are provided for the environment, including wood pieces, foam board, string, spools, rocks, sand, fabric, beads, glue, tape, staples, and hammer and nails. The creation of the environment is done under clinical supervision.

Instructions. Clients are asked to select the animal that they wish to work with. Once selections are made, the other animals are put away. Family members are then asked to create an environment for their creature using the materials provided.

Although the initial directive allows for projective work, once the first environment is completed and processed it may be useful to provide specific directives (based on the original work or treatment goals), such as:

• Make a safe environment.
• Make a dangerous environment.

---

[*]We continue to expand this technique. One of us (BS) recently suggested that children select a baby, a threatening object, and a protector. The other (EG) has suggested that children choose any animal plus Sobol's suggested protector and dangerous figures. This serves to externalize vulnerability, external danger, and internal resources. Children have responded quite well.

• Make a "fantasy" or ideal environment.
• Make an environment that you would like to live in.

Once individual family members have constructed their own environments, they are asked to tell others about it. To help them elaborate, clinicians might use prompting statements or questions such as:

• Tell me about this environment.
• What kind of an environment is this?
• What's the creature's favorite part of the environment?
• How does the creature spend his or her time?
• What things does the creature wish for that s/he doesn't have?
• Who would the creature talk to if s/he had a problem?
• I wonder how the creature likes living here.

After this therapeutic dialogue, this technique is expanded into a family technique, in which family members are given a large sheet of construction paper and asked to arrange their environments so there is cohabitation between the creatures. At this point clinicians again observe process and content issues, such as closeness or distance of environments, how environments are connected or protected (e.g., fences or walkways), and whether common space is filled in with shared items such as food, water, sunlight, or signs.

Some families negotiate this project very well, building cooperative walls and communal drinking wells. Other families isolate their environments in corners of the paper, resisting cohabitation or shared interactions. How families negotiate this task speaks volumes about family boundaries, perceptions of family relationships, and systemic issues, such as family cohesion, open or closed system, and level and type of rewarding/unrewarding interactions.

Follow-up. As with other projects, there is great value in eliciting a therapeutic dialogue about both process and content issues. Once family members share their perceptions, clinicians can "wonder out loud" or offer their observations for discussion. Environments can also be revisited later in therapy or during termination sessions. Some family members insist on taking their projects home; others prefer that their therapists hold onto the projects.

As therapy progress is made, clinicians might ask clients to do the exercise again, this time showing new ways of building or connecting their environments. Sometimes family members ask to repeat the project or suggest a variation.

Family Aquarium

Description. Family members are asked to draw, cut out, and decorate fishes, and then arrange them on a large piece of blue construction paper, called an aquarium.*

Tools required. White paper, pencils, markers, scissors, glitter, glue, colored strings, feathers, beads, crystals, blue construction paper.

Instructions. Family members are first given 8½" x 11" white sheets of paper and asked to draw a picture of any fish they like. Younger children may be given stenciled drawings of a variety of fish so they can select the fish they wish to be. Both adults and children then decorate their fish using magic markers or any other decoration they wish. Children will need help, and clinicians should observe parent-child interactions around helping rather than taking the helper role during the task.

It usually takes one full session to draw and decorate the fish. Family members are asked to leave their fish in the office for use in the next session. If children insist on taking their fish, parents are asked to bring them next time. On occasion, they are forgotten and the children may need to make new fish. Some children can be persuaded to leave their fish if they get to take a Polaroid picture or a photocopy of the fish with them.

The next phase of this task is to have the family arrange their fish on the large blue piece of construction paper to create a living environment in the aquarium. Family members spontaneously discuss water temperature, food, and other environmental objects like sand, other sea life, and places for fish to hide or sleep. It is interesting to note the family's tendency to make the environment safe, dangerous, nurturing, comfortable, and so forth. Once the aquariums are completed, the clinician initiates a therapeutic dialogue encouraging the family to view the whole product, ask questions, make comments, and so forth.

Follow-up. In the following weeks, the family is asked to revisit their work. This can be done by looking at 5" x 7" pictures of the family's work or by showing a transparency on an overhead projector. Enlarging pictures of the

---

*Many clients have suggested a variation to this exercise, finding an aquarium too limiting. Instead, they have put their fish in oceans, lakes, and ponds. In some cases I (EG) give clients the option of creating any environment for their fish; other times I prefer the aquarium because it forces the issue of more stable or permanent boundaries, which may be symbolically significant.

family's work tends to give it extra import and validates and values the work itself. Clinicians can ask if family members have had other thoughts or feelings, either about making the aquarium or about the product itself.

One family was amazed by the fact that their aquarium was divided into an upper and lower half. The father was in the top half, moving up toward the surface, while the mother and two small daughters were swimming in circular fashion on the bottom of the sea. The 4-year-old blurted out, "Where's Daddy going?" and then, "Daddy, where are you going?" The father said sadly, "You know I have to go to work." "Besides," he added, "there's no room left for me down there." This family system was in turmoil because the father was absent so frequently and the mother had turned to the children to get her affection needs met. When father did come home early, he felt as if his wife had no time for him. He also felt that his children preferred to be with their mother, in part because the mother made an effort to keep the children away from their father so that he could rest. All these issues were raised as a result of making the aquarium.

The smallest child in this family asked to make another aquarium four months later, and it seemed as though the problem situation had improved considerably. The second aquarium had all four fishes on the bottom half of the aquarium, watching television and playing with marbles. Father was prominently featured resting on his easy chair with the little fish swimming in and out of the legs of the chair.

Family Vase

Description. Family members draw individual flowers of their choice, then color and decorate them. Later they make a floral arrangement in a real or constructed vase.

Tools required. Paper, magic markers, crafts for decoration (glitter, sparkles, colored strings, fabrics, and so forth), and construction paper for making a vase, or a real flower vase.

Instructions. Family members are told to think about the type, color, and shape of flower that they would like to draw. Then they draw and decorate their flowers separately. Once all the flowers are complete, they are asked to place them in a vase, carefully making a floral arrangement to their liking.

Follow-up. This project is discussed by first inquiring what it was like to draw and decorate the flowers. Family members can make spontaneous comments about the pictures, and they may ask each other questions about their selection of flower or decorations. Once this conversation is concluded, the process of making a joint floral arrangement is discussed.

Family Garden

Description. Family members make garden plots in which flowers or vegetables are "grown." These garden plots are then arranged on a large piece of construction paper.

Tools required. White paper with equal-size rectangles drawn in pencil; colored magic markers; a large piece of green construction paper.

Instructions. Family members are given equal-size rectangles labeled "garden plots." They are told to decide what kind of flowers, fruits, or vegetables they wish to grow in their plots, and to fill in the rectangles with drawings of these objects. Once completed, these rectangles are arranged on a large piece of green construction paper, and family members are asked to make decisions about how to make their gardens grow effectively.

Follow-up. Discussions are held about individual choices. In addition, the arrangement of the plots on the limited space is also reviewed. It is interesting to note whether the family designs the necessary resources to create optimal conditions for the gardens to thrive. Some families quickly identify the need to share irrigation, fertilizer, fencing, crosswalks, shade, and sun. Some families come back weeks later with ideas to add insecticides, scarecrows, or to somehow assist in the protection and production of their crops.

Family Carnival Rides

Description. Family members draw or construct individual carnival rides and then arrange them on a piece of construction paper, with careful attention to creating the kind of carnival they like. Most families decide to make the carnivals fun, safe, and financially successful.

Instructions. Family members are asked to think of a carnival ride that they can draw or construct in some way. Once individual rides or carnival activities are ready, they are asked to arrange the material on a piece of construction paper, deciding ahead of time what kind of carnival they wish to construct. In addition to the qualities of the carnival (such as safe and successful), family members are asked to think about other facets of the carnival's operation (cost of rides, length of rides, height and age requirements, and so on).

Follow-up. Conversations are replete with symbolism as family members decide the types of ride they wish to contribute. In addition, constructing a carnival poses important questions for the family about issues such as boundaries, structures, action, and safety.

One family came to treatment because the 8-year-old son had been physically abused by his alcoholic mother. When making the carnival rides, mother chose to construct a roller coaster and she made it really steep with very dangerous turns. During the construction process she commented, "They say a few kids fell out of this ride once so that will tell you something about how high and fast it goes." Her husband responded, "That's so typical—scare the kids to death." Father chose to be the "funny mirrors," because he was always fascinated at how different people could look in those mirrors. He volunteered that when he saw himself in the mirrors it was "the only time I ever thought I looked good." He added, "I'll be the funny mirrors so that people will feel good when they come see me." In making this choice father spoke of his low self-esteem and desire to please others.

Finally, the abused 8-year-old said he didn't want to be a ride because they were all too scary. When his parents told him he had to be something, he chose to be the person who admitted passengers to ride the "crazy cars." "I get to decide who goes in and I won't let little kids in because they get crashed into by the bigger kids." He also stated, "If kids are mean, I'll tell them they gotta get out." This was a veiled reference to his own sense of vulnerability and his desire to "kick Mom out" when she was drinking or abusive. It also suggested this child's desire to be in control, a compensatory trait often found in children who feel powerless and vulnerable.

Clinicians may pose questions to family members to draw out the symbolism. The following questions can be conducive to discussion:

- Tell me about this ride.
- Who likes to use this ride?
- Are there any rules about who can get into this ride?
- Are there any dangers to this ride?
- What precautions are taken to make sure people are safe when they use this ride?
- How much does it cost to get on this ride?
- What's your favorite ride in this carnival?
- What kinds of families go to carnivals?

The Planetary System

Description. Every family member makes a picture of a planet. They arrange their planets on a large piece of construction paper.

Tools required. Drawing paper, magic markers, scissors, construction paper.

Instructions. To select, draw, and decorate a planet, which they will place on a large piece of blue construction paper representing the heavens.

Follow-up. The choice of planets, as well as the experience of cooperating to construct a model planetary system, is discussed.

Fruit Salad

Description. Family members are asked to select, purchase, and bring their favorite fruit, as well as some "dressing" for the fruit salad, to the therapy session. Fruits are then washed, cut, and arranged to make a fruit salad, and family members prepare the dressing. Family members may eat the salad in the session or take it home for later consumption.

Instructions. Together, parents and children go to the store to select and purchase the items for this task. They are asked to prepare their fruits for the salad and decide together on the type and quantity of dressing desired.

Follow-up. Family members are asked to talk a little about their selections as well as the process of preparing the salad. In addition, family members discuss the ease or difficulty with which they agreed on a dressing for their salad.

Case Illustration

Bo, a 6-year-old Asian-American boy, was referred to me (BS) by his first grade teacher. Vera, a well-educated Asian-American single mother in her early thirties, brought Bo into therapy. During our intake session, she described that Bo was having numerous problems both at school and at home. He routinely disrupted his first grade classroom with tantrums and had become increasingly verbally aggressive toward the other children. At times he seemed grandiose— he would strut or pace in class, lecturing the children on his intellectual superiority. At home, Vera said, Bo was argumentative, threw tantrums, and acted "like a little tyrant" with her and with her parents, with whom they lived. Both she and her parents felt emotionally drained, having tried punishments, "lectures," and even bribes. Recently, they had begun to blame one another for their misery at home.

The social history revealed a complex family situation, one in which Bo's behavior may have been a way to elicit outside intervention for the family and particularly to get help for his depressed mother. Vera was the oldest of three children born to a Chinese couple who had immigrated to the United States when she was about eight. An introverted, gifted child, Vera became a high achiever in school, but she described herself as an unhappy and rebellious girl, eager—from the time she was a teenager—to break free from her family's expectations and the rather formal cultural milieu at home. At 20 she had dropped out of college and, on the rebound from an earlier, failed relationship, married an American of whom her parents vehemently disapproved. Bo was born less than a year later, six weeks premature. There was concern that he had suffered some neurological damage, although nothing was apparent at the time. Within about another year, the marriage fell apart. Vera says that her husband had lied to her about both his personal and family history; moreover, he had squandered their joint savings. Humiliated and impoverished, Vera left her husband and returned to her parents' home. Over the next few years, she finished college and entered medical school, while her parents supported her and Bo. Her husband had left the country and was not involved with his son.

Vera said that she suffered her humiliation silently in order to avoid conflict with her parents. For the same reason, she urged Bo to be quiet and well behaved. She had little time or energy for her son. At night, after studying late, Vera would come home exhausted. With effort, she would read a bedtime story to Bo, who was always waiting up well past his bedtime. Their interaction was tense and perfunctory; often the "story" was a tale told "to build character." By her description, the joy Vera once had experienced at the sight of her newborn had turned to an oppressive sense of burden.

Much of Bo's increasingly disruptive behavior stayed out of public view until he started kindergarten, where he was seen as extremely bright but troubled. The detentions, then suspensions that began in first grade caused Vera embarrassment, anger, and stress at her hospital internship. At home, she felt a lack of sympathy and understanding. But aside from an occasional blow-up, she continued to keep her feelings to herself and to exert pressure on Bo to behave. A pattern developed: Typically, Vera would attempt to influence Bo through reasoning or "moral instruction." When that failed, she would cajole or plead, and soon after, grow angry and resort to shaming him or threatening to leave. Any successes she had were short-lived. By the time they were referred to therapy, Bo was wreaking defiant mischief at home, disobeying even the most reasonable rules concerning hygiene and dinner manners.

Bo presented in therapy as a bright, scrubbed, chatty little boy with adult mannerisms and sophisticated speech. He was eager to show me his knowledge of Asian history, computers, and weapons. Vera was extremely tense. She had difficulty identifying positive qualities in her son. Often she wanted to begin sessions by reading from a notebook in which she had logged his daily misbehaviors. From the outset some of their patterns of interaction were clear. Both mother and son used words in attempts to be powerful, but their words were ineffective. Bo's dazzling displays of information did not gain him any praise from his mother. Vera's categories of faults and elaborate lectures did not bring about behavior change. Each seemed to be shouting into the wind, and most early family sessions led to one or another of Vera's triad of reactions: derision, pity, or self-blame. Especially notable in these sessions was Vera's inability to "tune in" to Bo's use of symbolic language and behavior. Sometimes when Vera was talking about his faults, Bo would move about the room, picking up a toy sword and lunging at the air or raising an imaginary AK47 and making "gun noises." Vera would invariably cut off this behavior, unable to respond to Bo's play as his symbolic attempts at self-defense against her stream of harsh invective.

Several weeks into therapy, I decided to do a family art evaluation (FAE) as an assessment, to refine my understanding of the emotional dynamics of their interaction. I also wanted to provide an activity in which Vera and Bo could interact in a new, *nonverbal,* and possibly more positive way. It was important to me to establish a context for the therapy in which the tyranny of words would be lessened. Additionally, I felt that the art experience might show strengths in the relationship that had been masked by the predictable and rigid pattern of interaction. I wondered what symbols and metaphors might emerge as important—other than the ever-present guns and swords. I wondered if I could discover ways to help Vera provide structure, boundaries, and emotional resources for Bo. Although the grandparents had participated in many of the family sessions, they did not wish to attend a session in which art would be the primary treatment technique.

Family Art Evaluation

The family did the modified version of the FAE described earlier (see Kwiatkowska, 1978). Each did a free drawing, a family portrait, and a warm-up scribble drawing. Together, they did a mural, which was followed by individual final free drawings.

In the first drawing, both Bo and his mother were understandably anxious and had a hard time *not* engaging verbally. Bo drew a portrait of his mother but talked incessantly. His provocative language embarrassed Vera, who reacted predictably. However, even while reacting, she was able to draw a simple outline of a Volkswagen Beetle, and she was surprised and pleased at her own skill. She remarked, "Owning a car would give me some freedom. I could come and go as I please. I could even take Bo places."

In the second drawing (family portrait), Bo continued to try to get his mother's attention by provocative remarks. When Vera threatened to leave—again, the predictable response—Bo quieted down to draw. He made a family of wobbly stick figures in which one figure seemed to be holding a smaller figure in its jaws, while two other figures made vertical bookends to this pair. Later he identified these as himself and his mother at the center, flanked by grandmother and grandfather. Here the art product caught Bo's symbolism and preserved it on paper, so that it was hard to ignore or dismiss. Vera's drawing was also startling in its symbolism. She drew Bo and herself as two children fused into a single unit, with torsos that were joined at the hip and only three visible legs. The eyes are empty, "Orphan Annie" eyes. The whole image was done in a pale green line. When we looked at the drawings together, Bo shouted, "Hey! Where's my other leg?" The drawing suggested that Vera may experience Bo as inseparable from herself. I wondered (to myself) if she identified with Bo as the unhappy child she felt herself to have been. Or was he for her a "mark of Cain," that is, living proof of her own failures and shame? Remembering Vera's description of her initial joy at his birth, I wondered how much she had once dreamed that her little boy would be instead the living proof of her own worth.

The warm-up scribble was unremarkable. For process reasons, I decided to forego the development of a "joint scribble" in favor of a "family mural." I was concerned that the scribble, which requires working at very close quarters, might force them back into their pattern of conflict. I taped a large piece of mural paper to the wall and gave the instructions to "make a picture together *as a family* on any theme you wish." Given a directive and ample space, Vera and Bo appeared to relax. Their interaction took on a pleasant, if primitive, quality of harmonious cooperation and even playfulness. Vera allowed her son to be in charge of choosing a theme, much the way any mother might allow her infant to take the lead in floor play. She made several appropriate suggestions for a theme and allowed Bo to make the final choice. Bo chose "the universe" as the theme. He began at once to give his mother directions as to the size, color, and position of the planets—giving himself a chance to show off his knowledge of these things—while she did the actual drawing. She was able to ignore an occasional verbal provocation, and in the end they were both pleased and proud of their work. From my vantage point, I observed a graceful interaction where argument had the quality of playful banter. The physical movements between them were softer and more fluid than I had ever seen.

In the brief discussion period after the drawing was done, this playful fluidity entered their verbal interaction. As Vera complained that they had drawn the solar system and not the universe, Bo went back to the drawing. With a piece of black pastel chalk, he drew a circle completely around the large composite image of the sun and planets. "See," he said, "everything inside the circle is the solar system; what is outside the circle is the universe." They both laughed at this clever solution to the problem, and I noted silently that he also had beautifully illustrated the importance of boundaries.

For the last drawing, Vera used many colors to draw a beach scene that included herself and Bo as separate but adjacent figures in identical bathing suits and sunglasses. She also draw a male lifeguard—clearly, said Vera, an imagined new love interest for her. She remarked that a beach would be a place she might take Bo if they had a car. On his paper Bo continued the space theme in a contented manner. The harmonious feeling between them seemed to carry over as they left the session to go home.

By providing much rich process and content information, the FAE helped me to refine and redirect the goals of the family sessions. Because the attachment and identification issues seemed so strong (and mostly negative), I planned to support whatever positive connections I had seen between Vera and Bo, while coaching Vera in efforts to differentiate. For example, I encouraged her to seek peer activities and friends for Bo and to develop her own friendships. Remembering the images from the FAE, I knew it was important to tread carefully. I wanted to ensure that as Bo began to feel some freedom from the jaws he had created to represent his mother, Vera would not feel ripped away from her image of herself and Bo as inseparably fused. To avoid the continued distortion of words, I continued to explore emotions nonverbally. Play and art activities would provide Vera with the opportunity to be playful while maintaining her dignity as a mother and would offer Bo continued opportunity to express himself symbolically in a way his mother could both tolerate and eventually understand.

Over the next few months, I made several efforts to effect change in the family interactional patterns in keeping with this overall treatment direction. Additionally, a more thorough exploration of possible neurological difficulties was undertaken. After a neurological examination and a psychiatric examination provided somewhat contradictory diagnoses for Bo, Vera consented reluctantly to a trial of Ritalin for possible ADHD. However, as this seemed to increase Bo's aggressive behavior and tantrums, it was discontinued. Vera and her parents found themselves in rare agreement in their reluctance to explore further the use of medication and in their willingness to pursue a change in Bo's school placement. The proposed more restrictive school setting required that Bo be labeled an "emotionally disturbed" child. As hard as it had seemed for Vera to praise her son's good qualities, it appeared equally hard for her to accept that her son was, in her words, "defective."

The new school program and a caring teacher with clear expectations proved very helpful and for several months Bo's behavior at school improved dramatically. Encouraged, Vera also agreed to place Bo in a half-day school program the following summer. But throughout the winter and spring months, Bo continued to spend long hours after school either riding his bike or in the company of his grandparents, waiting for his mother to come home from the hospital. Vera herself continued to seem depressed and withdrawn. In individual therapy sessions, Bo was able to express some of his anger and sadness in clay sculpture and sand tray stories. He particularly seemed to relish making sand worlds in which he had complete control over his characters. Observing him at play, I noted that before he could express compassion for his characters, he needed to first establish a complete sense of control over their "lives." In family sessions, I continued my efforts to balance coaching Vera in setting limits and encouraging positive interactions with Bo. With the latter goal in mind, I invited Vera and Bo to do some sand trays together.

First Family Sand Tray

Having been told the week before that we would be working in the sand tray, Vera and Bo came ready to "make a world, together" in the dry sand tray. However, Vera was uneasy. She wanted to discuss "negative behaviors." For several minutes, she sat silently with her behavior notebook open and her hands in her lap, while Bo began to fill the tray with a variety of monsters, dragons, dinosaurs, rocks, and plastic soldiers. Slowly, her attention was drawn to the tray. She complained to Bo that he had not left enough room for her to create her part of the world. Just as he had done in the family mural, Bo responded not with his usual argumentativeness but with a gesture of goodwill, setting up a fence line that gave his mother about a quarter of the tray space. He watched intently as his mother chose a cottage, two nuns, a church, some trees, several children, a tiny wizard, and several domestic animals to arrange in her corner. He asked appropriately child-like questions: "Why did you put a wizard in your world? Who are those children? Why are there nuns?" She answered that the wizards and nuns were spiritual figures who could help her to create a peaceful, happy scene. Spontaneously, Bo moved his fence line to make more room for his mother's world. Without asking, he placed a figure of a puppy near the children, and before his mother could comment (or protest), he said that the puppy represented himself. The aura of mutual deference, playfulness, and gracefulness (the fluidity I had seen fleetingly in the mural exercise) had happened again.

Following this peak of graceful interaction, the story changed. Bo seemed to have an intuitive understanding of his own vulnerability and of the fragile nature of his alliance with his mother. Perhaps to buttress their relationship, he built a high mound of sand near the fence, placed some of his monsters on it, and began to give names to particular monster figures. The first monster he called "my father" and the second he named as "your boss." Vera laughed and soon joined in the game: "This is your old principal" and "this is the social service worker." Together, they identified a number of common "enemies." The play had now taken on a new quality; Bo seemed to be colluding with his mother, perhaps for the purpose of keeping her engaged. I felt there was some manipulation going on that Vera did not recognize. She also seemed not to recognize the inappropriate alliance they were creating of "you and me against the world." I felt troubled as they left the session hand in hand. How quickly an inappropriate alliance had turned into a less-than-wholesome bond! While Bo had actually succeeded in engaging his mother, it seemed to be at the cost of having to collude with her anger.

Between Sessions

As in verbal therapy, the therapist who uses play or art is faced with choices, among them: to allow the theme to develop further; to redirect the play (if the family does not seem ready to process the material); or to interpret the play or art. In the case of Vera and Bo, I was concerned about the collusion that I saw as their joint attempt to fill intertwined emotional needs. Despite their obvious intellectual strengths, I felt that Vera and Bo would reject any effort I might make to address their relationship directly or through verbal interpretation of their process. In the enjoyable play environment of the sand tray, however, they might be able to address such issues continuously at the level of the metaphor. Later, the metaphor might become an internalized model for "real world" behavior.

Second Family Sand Tray

For the next family sand tray, the only directive I gave was in the form of a speculative remark: "I wonder what kind of a world you will make today." Both Vera and Bo seemed eager to develop a theme similar to the first tray, a world in which Bo demarcated his own area to be filled with aggressive figures of all sorts, while his mother again created a peaceful village. They seemed to know that they were far from having exhausted this scenario as an avenue toward deep and largely unexpressed thoughts and feelings. When the basic village had been laid out, Bo again placed the figure of the puppy in his mother's village scene. He then placed a small gorilla next to the puppy and identified it as his father. Vera said she really did not want the gorilla in the scene, but she let it stay, as if recognizing that she should not cut off her son's attempts to open an exploration of this sensitive topic. But then she added a horse and said that this represented her wished-for new husband (and new father for Bo). While neither said more on this subject, both were able to sustain the play for several minutes longer. Bo chose a clay arch and placed it at the border of the village. He placed some soldiers near the gate; from their placement it was hard to tell if the soldiers were poised to attack or to defend the village. When I asked about this, Bo turned the soldiers so that they were clearly defending the village from the horde of beasts advancing from his side of the tray.

Third Family Sand Tray and Family Art Session

Two weeks later, Bo entered the family session extremely anxious and agitated. Perhaps the previous session's unexplored theme of the "new father" needed more verbal processing before we could return safely to expressive work. At least, that was my hypothesis. Whatever the cause, Bo's agitation and Vera's response to it (angry criticism) suggested that I needed to use this session to decrease, if possible, the level of emotional volatility. Bo had already wheeled out the sand tray and was rather wildly stirring up the sand. I decided to redirect the session and suggested that we use the time to "both play and talk." We could use clay to make some objects that we might need for future sand tray stories. Because the "clay" was paper pulp clay, a non-messy and fairly dry material, there was little danger that Bo would get out of control. He could continue to use physical energy, but perhaps in a manner more narrowly focused than sand tray work. Vera, Bo, and I gathered around a table and began to manipulate small pieces of the pulp "clay" that I had broken off from the large block. To help direct the session, I said that I thought I would like to make a clay bridge for use in the sand tray. Bo followed my modeling almost immediately and said that he was going to make a boat. Vera hesitated and said nothing at first, but soon she began shaping her piece of clay. We talked about sand trays, establishing some distance from the sand tray work itself. The activity was calming. Within about 20 minutes, we each had made a miniature for the tray. We spent the final minutes of the session discussing our pieces and cleaning up together. Bo had made a long barque and had embedded a large flat gold bead in the prow. The piece showed a level of investment and focus unusual for him. His boat, he said, was meant to carry people and animals to faraway places. Vera had made a small, rather constricted piece, a bench that she could "just sit on" if she were tired. I finished my small bridge. We agreed to make another tray in a few weeks.

Between Sessions

The clay session had been a response to my observation that the family had hit upon a fragile topic (new husband, new father) and that delving into this theme too quickly might increase anxiety without offering therapeutic help. Between sessions I reflected on where the play therapy and art therapy might now lead.

I had been struck by how intently this little boy followed his mother's cues, adjusting his words and movements to fit hers. He seemed to know instinctively that in order to achieve a feeling of well-being he must track and meet his mother's emotional needs. But because Vera's responses to him were—for him—unpredictable, Bo had developed a number of strategies to keep himself emotionally safe. These ranged from hostile behavior that pushed her away to rather coy behavior that invited closeness. He could play both "monster" and "puppy." Each of these reflected a genuine emotional state, yet each had a manipulative potential that often came into play. Sadly for Bo, neither monster nor puppy aspects of his personality could control his mother's responses, at least not for more than a moment or two.

Bo seemed stuck in a pattern of urgent and largely unconscious behavior ploys to manipulate his mother. Any direct expression of his need, hurt, and anger—especially at home—risked the loss of his mother's good will. Symbolic expression often invited a similar risk. In the family sessions, Vera's individual needs began to drive the play stories. Bo gradually had begun to abandon genuine symbolic expression in favor of acting the compliant child. I felt that it was critical to reestablish the family play and art as an emotionally safe activity. In the clay session, the parallel shared activity appeared to be just such a safe zone, free from secret collusion, blame, or other manipulation. I had also observed that in the sand tray sessions, both Vera and Bo had seemed genuinely grateful and happy during certain moments, but that these moments were short-lived. To support the goal of emotional safety, I decided to continue to adhere to a simple technique: I would continue to invite Vera and Bo into a clearly demarcated "play world," different from the "real world," in which I set the rules and in which both mother and child could feel free to "just play."

Fourth Sand Tray

In the earlier sand trays, the complementary themes of danger/aggression and peace/safety had emerged. Mainly Bo had been the source of the dangerous images and Vera, of the peaceful ones. In this session, I asked them to work together to create a world that would "feel like a safe place" to both of them.

Bo began by selecting monsters and aggressive animal figures and placing them randomly throughout the tray. Vera waited until he took a break. Then she made a ring of large, smooth stones around the figures that were closest to the center of the tray, effectively corralling them into a defined area. Bo seemed eager to play and helped to build the stone wall another layer higher and to move some of the outlying figures into the center. When all the dangerous animals were within the circle, Vera chose additional jungle animals and placed them in a ring around the perimeter of the stone wall. These she identified as figures that were guarding the dangerous figures. Again, Bo helped. There was little verbal exchange as they worked. When they stood back to look at the tray, Bo said, "These are the bad guys who want to kill everybody in the world and they have to be locked up." I was happy to see that Bo himself had introduced the concept of *containment* into the therapeutic play and I noted aloud that they had worked together to keep the bad guys from getting out of control. Aloud, I wondered what could happen to help these bad guys to feel less angry.

In this session, in keeping with my concern that, given the opportunity, Bo and Vera would fall back into their collusive ways or hostile ways of relating, I devoted much time to the housekeeping aspects of the art session: photographing the sand tray image, putting away the figures, sweeping up. This activity gave Vera and Bo ample time to shift away from the play world back into the real world.

Several more sand tray sessions took place before a change in agency policy and insurance considerations required that the family transfer to a new clinic. As I ended my phase of the work with the family, I tried to consolidate the work that had been done in both the play and verbal sessions. In the last sessions, I maintained the emphasis on shared activity, pacing the work (not rushing headlong into deep and fragile emotional material), and on sustaining positive interaction as more important than uncovering or exploring content. I continued to support the idea of individual therapy for Vera and more supervised peer activity for Bo.

Concluding Remarks about this Case

Art and play were part of a network of therapeutic modalities used in this very complex, long-term case. I felt that the sustained work in play and art therapy had established an arena in which to practice good object relations and had reinforced the more positive experiences of differentiation between this deeply and ambivalently attached mother and son. Maintaining a balance between the expression/exploration of unmet emotional needs and the need to address matters of behavior and boundaries was possible through diligent attention to the events in each session. The play was most effective when Vera allowed herself to "just" draw and play. At those times she was able to safely access moments of uncomplicated pleasure with her son. And within the safety of "only play," Bo could suspend his manipulations and enjoy the emotional availability of his mother. I felt that these were indeed precious moments.

Many months later, Vera consented to enter individual therapy and to see Bo's issues as enough separate from hers to allow renewed exploration of medication and more intensive school services to address his individual needs. Because the art and play sessions tended to be untainted by the tyranny of words in this family, they were excellent vehicles for addressing the need for emotional bonding. Healthy bonding was the critical foundation on which I had hoped to develop more appropriate separation and differentiation, so necessary for successful work with families.

Summary

There are few limits to the variety of family activities that might encourage family members to interact with each other in new and enjoyable ways. These tasks demand certain things from family members: First and foremost, family members must access and utilize their creative imagination, selecting symbol objects and allowing for metaphoric communication. Secondly, individuals are often invited to engage with each other in a shared activity resulting in a tangible product, which the family can then observe, touch, feel, manipulate, photograph, and possibly take home. Third, family members are challenged to view each other in a new and different light.

Clinicians create opportunities to observe and experience the family on a deeper level than that provided by verbal communication. When people limit their communication to words, they usually struggle to find ways to make themselves heard or understood. Often, disagreements arise when individuals "can't find the right words" or can't quite get across their critical ideas.

When symbolic language is used, some matters become more clear. An explosive father who chooses to grow small white roses in his garden may be showing a part of himself not readily visible to his family. Likewise, an oppositional, defiant child who chooses a turtle that is afraid to make friends may be communicating his fear and anxiety in social settings.

Family members deserve an opportunity to have novel interactions with each other that might surprise or delight them. Much too often, families in crisis have negative or neutral interactions with each other, and they become accustomed to high levels of stress and pain, ignoring the possibilities of play, laughter, and heightened emotional contact.

Play is a serious matter, and can be used with families who present with very serious concerns. Family play therapy is optimistic and harnesses the family's inherent abilities to access and utilize internal strengths. At those very moments when clinicians feel most overwhelmed and flat, unable to determine how to proceed, family play therapy creates openings, elicits energy, and, at the very least, gives everyone a new interactive experience.

Family play therapy creates openings. It invites clinician and therapist alike to interact in less guarded, more expressive ways. Inevitably, what is shared has a deep impact on clinicians and clients alike and can contribute to meaningful insights, motivation to seek or try new interactions, and eventual behavioral change.

Eliana Gil, Ph.D., is Director of Abused Children's Treatment Services, Inova Kellar Center, Fairfax, Virginia.

Barbara Sobol, M.A., A.T.R., L.P.C., is Clinical Service Coordinator, Health and Human Services Community Partnership for Children, Youth and Families, Montgomery County, Maryland.

References

Araoz, D. L., & Carrese, M. A. (Eds.). (1996). *Solution-oriented brief therapy for adjustment disorders: A guide for providers under managed care.* New York: Brunner/Mazel.

Ariel, S. (1992). *Strategic family play therapy.* New York: Wiley.

Andreozzi, L. L. (1996). *Child-centered family therapy.* New York: Wiley.

Bograd, M. (Ed.). (1991). *Feminist approaches for men in family therapy.* New York: Harrington Park.

Boik, B. L., & Goodwin, E. A. (2000). *Sandplay therapy: A step-by-step manual for psychotherapists of diverse orientations.* New York: Norton.

Burns, R. C. (1990). *A guide to family-centered circle drawings.* New York: Brunner/Mazel.

Carey, L. (1991). Family sandplay therapy. *Arts in Psychotherapy, 18,* 231–239.

Carey, L. J. (1999). *Sandplay therapy with children and families.* Northvale, NJ: Aronson.

Combrinck-Graham, L. (Ed.). (1989). *Children in family contexts: Perspectives on treatment.* New York: Guilford.

Freeman, J., Epston, D., & Lobovits, D. (1997). *Playful approaches to serious problems: Narrative therapy with children and their families.* New York: Norton.

Gibbs, J. T., & Huang, L. N. (Eds.). (1998). *Children of color: Psychological interventions with culturally diverse youth.* San Francisco, CA: Jossey-Bass.

Gil, E. (1994). *Play in family therapy.* New York: Guilford.

Gillespie, J. (1994). *The projective use of mother-and-child drawings: A manual for clinicians.* New York: Brunner/Mazel.

Green, R. J. (1994). Foreword. In E. Gil, *Play in family therapy.* New York: Guilford.

Griff, M. D. (1983). Family play therapy. In C. E. Schaefer & K. J. O'Connor (Eds.), *Handbook of play therapy* (pp. 65–76). New York: Wiley.

Guerney, B. (1964). Filial therapy: Description and rationale. *Journal of Consulting Psychology, 28,* 303–310.

Guerney, L. (1997). Filial therapy. In K. J. O'Connor & L. M. Braverman (Eds.), *Play therapy theory and practice: A comparative presentation* (pp. 131–159). New York: Wiley.

Ho, M. K. (1987). *Family therapy with ethnic minorities.* Newbury Park, CA: Sage.

Homeyer, L. E., & Sweeney, D. S. (1999). *Sandtray: A practical manual.* Canyon Lake, TX: Lindan.

Irwin, E. C. & Malloy, E. S. (1994). Family puppet interview. In C. Schaefer & L. Carey (Eds.), *Family play therapy* (pp. 21–34). Northvale, NJ: Aronson.

Jung, C. G. (1964). *Man and his symbols.* New York: Dell.

Kalff, D. (1980). *Sandplay, a psychotherapeutic approach to the psyche.* Santa Monica, CA: Sigo.

Kilpatrick, A. C., & Holland, T. P. (1995). *Working with families: An integrative model by level of functioning.* Boston: Allyn & Bacon.

Kiresuk, T., & Sherman, R. E. (1968). Goal attainment scaling: A general method for evaluating comprehensive mental health programs. *Community Mental Health Journal, 4,* 443–453.

Kwiatkowska, H. Y. (1978). *Family therapy and evaluation through art.* Springfield, IL: Charles C. Thomas.

Landgarten, H. B., (1987). *Family art psychotherapy: A clinical guide and casebook.* New York: Brunner/Mazel.

Lowenfeld, M. (1939). The World pictures of children: A method of recording and studying them. *British Journal of Medical Psychology, 18,* 65–101.

McGoldrick, M., Anderson, C. M., & Walsh, F. (Eds.). (1991). *Women in families: A framework for family therapy.* New York: Norton.

McGoldrick, M., & Gerson, R. (1985). *Genograms in family assessment.* New York: Norton.

McGoldrick, M., Gerson, R., & Shellenberger, S. (1999). *Genograms: Assessment and intervention* (2nd ed.). New York: Norton.

Miller, W. (1994). Family play therapy: History, theory, and convergence. In C. Schaefer & L. Carey (Eds.), *Family play therapy* (pp. 3–20). Northvale, NJ: Aronson.

Mitchell, R. R., & Friedman, H. S. (1994). *Sandplay: Past, present and future.* London: Routledge.

Ryce-Menuhin, J. (1992). *Jungian sandplay: The wonderful therapy.* London: Routledge.

Schaefer, C. E. & Carey, L. (Eds.). (1994). *Family play therapy.* Northvale, NJ: Aronson.

Sjolund, M. (1993). *The ERICA method: A technique for play therapy and diagnosis: A training guide.* Greeley, CO: Carron.

Smith, C. & Nylund, D. (1997). *Narrative therapies with children and adolescents.* New York: Guilford.

Sobol, B., & Schneider, K. (1998). Art as an adjunctive therapy in the treatment of children who dissociate. In J. L. Silberg (Ed.), *The dissociative child: Diagnosis, treatment, and management* (2nd ed., pp. 191–218). Lutherville, MD: Sidran.

Wachtel, E. F. (1994). *Treating troubled children and their families.* New York: Guilford.

Wen-Shing, T., & Hsu, J. (1991). *Culture and family: Problems and therapy.* New York: Haworth.

Zilbach, J. J. (1986). *Young children in family therapy.* New York: Brunner/Mazel.

14

Involving Fathers in Children's Therapy

Richard L. Meth

Like most second-year graduate students in the marriage and family therapy training program, Sherri wanted the opportunity to watch me work with a family and was pleased we could arrange to see the Miller family together. As we entered the waiting room, Laura Miller and her 12-year-old daughter, Jessica, greeted us for their first family session. Sherri looked surprised and said, "I thought that when I spoke with you over the phone I indicated that your husband was expected to attend today's first meeting." As Sherri's supervisor, I had made special arrangements to be at this first intake session, so it was understandable that Sherri was a bit embarrassed by Dave Miller's absence.

Appearing frustrated and defensive, Laura explained, "You know, my husband's been so busy with work, he's absolutely beat when he comes home. I know he should be here for Jessica, but you have to understand that he's not been easy to approach about this counseling. Actually, Dave doesn't think we should be here because he believes it's the school's responsibility to provide a counselor, since they're the ones who think there's a problem. To tell you the truth, neither one of us has a problem with Jessica at home. It's just that I'm more willing to be here. If I would have pushed this with Dave we would have had a major argument right when he walked in the door."

I would like to express my appreciation to Dr. Ronald P. Rohner, Professor Emeritus at the University of Connecticut, for the ideas and encouragement he provided during the preparation of this chapter.

Since it seemed awkward to let this conversation continue in the waiting room in front of other clients, I suggested that we move to the therapy room. In the therapy room Sherri reminded Laura that our regular clinic protocol was to see both parents for the intake appointment. Knowing that the chances of ever seeing Dave would be greatly diminished if we saw Laura and Jessica without him, Sherri boldly suggested that we reschedule for another time when Dave could be present. She also handed Laura a brief statement describing how we work with families, a routine part of our center's informed consent package.

Although Laura's facial expression told me this did not sit well with her, I agreed completely with Sherri. Laura agreed to call Sherri the next day to reschedule another session at a time when Dave could attend. After three days without a phone call, Sherri called me and nervously asked whether she had made a mistake and "lost the family." I supported the position she had taken with Laura and suggested that she wait a bit longer before she called them. Nearly a week later Laura called and indicated that Dave had reluctantly agreed to come in for the intake appointment.

When Sherri and I finally saw the family, Dave was much more cooperative and engaged than we had expected. In fact, during the first session we discovered that Dave had been quite involved in raising his daughter during her early years. However, like so many parents, Dave found negotiating Jessica's transition into adolescence difficult. Parenting styles that worked for Dave during Jessica's childhood now produced constant struggles with his daughter. In the past two years Laura often felt compelled to intervene between Jessica and her father when their interactions became too heated. As a parent Dave had become increasingly withdrawn, accepting the position that most of the parenting should now fall on Laura's shoulders. When he read our center's "philosophy on the family" hand-out, which Laura had left for him, Dave was surprised that we expected him to be actively involved in the therapy. He had figured that this was something his wife would take care of.

Should we be surprised by Dave's reaction or is this common among fathers? Does this only occur with fathers of adolescents and not young children? While the dynamics in this family are certainly more complex and extensive than what is suggested by this overview of the initial visit, the Millers are a good example of what many of us see in our daily practices. Mothers often bring their children to therapy because this is considered part of their parenting domain. With families like the Millers, involving fathers in their children's therapy may pose a formidable challenge. Yet, when a therapist focuses exclusively on the child's problematic behavior, a great deal of information about the family may be lost. In other words, a clinician who sees a child alone, or sees the child with only one parent (usually the mother), loses the rich, systemic perspective made available by seeing the whole family.

Beginning with a historical perspective, this chapter presents a blueprint that will enable clinicians to understand the barriers that interfere with fathers' involvement in therapy. Interventions and case examples will be used to illustrate ways that clinicians can promote greater involvement of fathers in therapy.

A Historical Perspective

Men's participation in child-rearing activities and expectations for greater paternal involvement in the family have increased considerably in the past twenty years. In part due to the social and demographic shifts that have occurred in families since the 1970s, men are now expected to participate directly in child care and other household activities that both men and women have long considered "women's work." Research conducted over the last two decades has consistently demonstrated the degree to which fathers play a number of significant roles in addition to that of breadwinner, including care provider, moral guide, role model, companion, and teacher (Biller, 1971, 1974; Lamb, 1981; Lamb, Pleck, Charnov, & Levine, 1987; Lamb, Pleck, & Levine, 1985; Radin, 1981; Russell, 1986). This research underscores the need for practitioners to pay close attention to the ways we may unknowingly exclude fathers from therapy, particularly when that therapy involves their children (Pleck, Lamb, & Levine, 1986). As we will see later in this chapter, some of the more contemporary therapeutic models, especially those that operate from a systemic framework, have been especially vigilant in challenging clinicians who have ignored or devalued fathers' involvement in children's therapy.

As we trace the concept of fatherhood from the seventeenth to the twentieth century, we find that the defining element of fatherhood that has endured to the present day is that of the father as the economic provider. Yet in the past twenty years, a large body of research has emerged that convincingly illustrates how much more extensively and positively fathers exert influence over their children. Even though much of the research has demonstrated the benefits of increased paternal involvement, fathers' behavior has been slow to change (Palkovitz, 1984). Furthermore, many fathers are still unlikely to participate in family therapy without a struggle. Why fathers' behavior has been slow to change and why practitioners still struggle to have fathers participate in therapy are two questions this chapter will address.

As indicated above, research on paternal behavior and fathering over the past fifteen to twenty years has clearly documented the important positive influence that fathers can have on their children's development (Cowan & Bronstein, 1988; Lamb, 1981,1997; Phares, 1997; Pleck, 1997). Even with such well-documented findings, mythical and anachronistic notions about the traditional role of the father in the family still exert a strong influence on current paternal behavior. In order to understand and appreciate the lasting power of such notions, we must examine them from both historical and sociocultural perspectives.

For last 200 years, a mother's love has been generally considered paramount in child development (Kagan, 1978; Stearns, 1991). During the seventeenth and eighteenth centuries, fathers were viewed as stern patriarchs. However, British and American diaries from that era frequently reported fathers' delight in a child's birth (Stearns, 1991). Father-son relations were considered to be especially strong, as men worked hard to teach their sons how to farm and care for their land. Some have even argued that fathers of colonial New England showed a keen interest in the social and emotional development of their young children (Rotundo, 1993). During that time men generally worked the land and thus did not have to stray far from home to provide economically for the family. Many researchers/historians believe that this created natural opportunities for men to be actively involved in daily child-rearing activities.

The industrial revolution changed this, however, as men left the homestead to find employment opportunities in factories or other industrial settings. The image of father changed to that of a distant breadwinner. As men in America continued to seek employment away from their homes, increasingly in developing urban centers, the responsibilities of child-rearing fell almost entirely on the mother. Men came to equate their success as husbands and fathers with their ability to provide economically for their families (Stearns, 1991). Although the amount of time fathers spent with their children was minimal, most fathers believed that they were doing a good job as long as they worked hard and provided adequately for the family. They did not feel that their absence deprived their children in any way.

The popular press had little regard for increased paternal involvement or concern that fathers could play a role in raising healthy children. Ellner (1973) reviewed every magazine article related to child-rearing in the first six months of 1950, 1960, and 1970, and found only 3 (2%) of the 177 articles dealt with fathers. Similar findings were reflected in the professional literature. Peterson, Becker, Hellmer, Shoemaker, and Quay (1959) reviewed the literature on parent-child relations from 1929 to1956 and found that approximately 170 publications dealt with mother-child relations, with only 12 (7%) of these addressing any aspect of the father-child relationship. Phares and Compas (1992) reviewed every article in 8 clinical and adolescent journals from 1984 to1991. The authors wanted to explore possible gender bias in the reporting of parental influences in child and adolescent psychopathology. They found that 48% of the articles reviewed included only mothers, whereas 1% included only fathers. Finally, Nash (1965) argued that the available information about fathers came from mothers because researchers made the implicit assumption that fathers themselves were inaccessible due to out-of-home economic responsibilities.

Prior to the 1960s and 1970s, behavioral scientists assumed that fathers were unimportant to the healthy development of their children (Nash, 1965). Fathers were thought to be peripheral to the job of raising children because children spent most of their time with mothers. The popular press and television seemed to reinforce the notion of the father as not only peripheral but also ineffectual, mindless, and incompetent (Mackey, 1996). Conversely, mothers were viewed as central to the family, especially with regard to raising children. When problems with children arose, mothers were typically blamed or expected to intervene and change the child's behavior. By accepting this premise of the mother's centrality, mental health professionals, in general, participated in the tendency to make mothers solely responsible for child-rearing. In fact, most of the well-known, highly respected child guidance clinics, in the business of helping troubled children by providing the highest quality of care, seldom included fathers in therapy.

Fatherhood as a Cultural Construction

Why have fathers been virtually excluded for nearly a century from the study of parent-child relations and the treatment of children? Much of behavioral science can be a value-laden enterprise, though this is mostly unintended and often goes unrecognized (Kaplan, 1964). Research questions that are regarded as appropriate or sensible at a particular point in time usually fall within a matrix of cultural beliefs widely accepted by the dominant population and, certainly, of beliefs held by the scientific community. The issue of fatherhood is a case in point. According to Rohner (1997), fatherhood "is a cultural construction and once formulated, has implications for the subsequent behavior of those who share the beliefs and assumptions defining that construction" (p. 6).

It is important to underscore the meanings commonly associated with fatherhood and fathering behaviors and recognize the constraints placed on one's behaviors when these meanings are accepted as being true. Moreover, to understand fully the cultural construction of fatherhood, one must understand how society has constructed its counterpart, motherhood. Furthermore, we must recognize that both of these constructions are greatly influenced by cultural conceptions of masculinity and femininity. For instance, child care has generally been associated with feminine behavior. For more than a century, raising children, clearly defined as the woman's role, has been viewed by many men and women as unmasculine. A common theoretical assumption held as recently as the 1970s and 1980s asserted that fathers' major contribution to child development was indirect, through their economic, social, and emotional support of mothers (Biller, 1993; Hetherington, Cox, & Cox, 1979; Maccoby & Martin, 1983). This premise highlights the pervasive and powerful influence of the cultural construction of fatherhood as it has existed in Western culture.

The cultural construction of fatherhood widely held prior to the 1970s and still very present today has two components. The first asserts that fathers are essentially incompetent and may even be biologically unsuited for the job of child-rearing. The maternal counterpoint here is that women are genetically programmed to nurture and care for children. The second asserts that fathers' influence in child development is unimportant or, at the very least, peripheral or indirect. The maternal counterpoint here is that mothers' nurturing and competent maternal care provides everything that children need for normal, healthy development.

The internalization of these cultural beliefs has had sometimes unintended and unrecognized but nonetheless real consequences. First, fathers were kept out of the mainstream of behavioral science research until late into the twentieth century. Second, the mental health profession often ignored fathers and systematically excluded them from therapy that involved their children. Because it was assumed axiomatically that only mothers were important in child development, researchers tended to study mostly mothers' behavior. And clinicians, many of whom occupied the role of mother or father in their own families, were too embedded within the prevailing cultural norms to see how their construction of fatherhood perpetuated the tradition of excluding fathers from therapy.

Recognition of the Role of Fathers in Child Development

Over the past twenty years, many behavioral scientists have begun to acknowledge that fathers should not be overlooked in child development and family studies research. Today, in fact, there is widespread acceptance of the notion that fathers are often affectively and formatively prominent in the development of children (Lamb, 1997). Recent research has highlighted fathers' influence on children's attitudes and behaviors toward educational and vocational choice (Bozett & Hanson, 1991). In addition, this body of research has demonstrated how paternal involvement contributes to the child's socially appropriate gender role identity, academic performance, and moral development (Bronstein & Cowan, 1988; Jordan, Radin, & Epstein, 1975; Mackey, 1996; Phares, 1997; Pleck, 1997).

As indicated earlier, fathers play multifaceted roles in the development of their children. Whether through direct or indirect contact, fathers affect their children by being more than simply the family breadwinner. Research has shown that fathers actively teach their children about the world and relationships and influence their children's perceptions of growing up male or female (Bronstein, 1988). Furthermore, fathers' self-perceived competence in interacting with children has been associated with their involvement (Baruch & Barnett, 1986; McHale & Huston, 1984). In other words, through various parenting activities, men learn that they positively influence the lives of their children, that they are a valuable part of the parenting process. They also discover that their increased involvement creates a greater intimacy with their children (Haas, 1988). Besides the noted benefit of greater feelings of competence that increased paternal involvement has on children, spouses feel more supported when fathers are involved in child-rearing activities, and this increased participation also tends to enhance the quality of the mother-child relationship (Lamb, 1997). Father involvement has been shown to increase when the wife's educational level increases, if the father has had a positive relationship with this father, and if the father has a liberal attitude toward gender (Pleck, 1997). But liberal attitudes toward gender may first necessitate a reexamination of the cultural construction of gender, or specifically, a challenge to traditional ideas about masculinity and femininity.

Many believe that the advent of the feminist movement, with its call for gender equality in the workplace and partner equality in the home, led to this reexamination and the subsequent increase in paternal involvement (Rohner, 1997). At that time, mothers were entering the out-of-home workforce in unprecedented numbers. In 1960, for example, fewer than 40% of mothers worked outside of the home (Biller, 1993). But by 1972 almost 50% were working outside of the home and by 1990 over 90% were (Biller, 1993). As greater numbers of mothers began working, the feminist movement called for fathers to become more involved in child care and household tasks (Biller, 1993; Bronstein, 1988; Griswold, 1993). Men responded to these changes their wives were making and demanding of them by reexamining their role as fathers and by redefining traditional gender roles (Jain, Belsky, & Crnic, 1996). This in turn led researchers to study the impact of the changing father role and explore the effects of increased paternal involvement. For the first time, child development and family studies specialists were keenly motivated to study fathers directly (Bronstein & Cowan, 1988; Parke, 1985).

But many men were not prepared to make this transition toward redefining long-standing, traditional beliefs and values about child-rearing and household responsibilities. This became a tumultuous time for men and women, and these new mandates for change caused enormous upheaval in their relationships. As men were challenged to change their attitudes and behaviors as husbands and as fathers, few had anything but traditional male role models to guide them. Many saw these models as anachronistic and unworkable given the changes taking place in the family. Unable to draw from what was learned and familiar, many men withdrew from their families. One study that examined how these changing times were affecting men concluded that fathers "may be spending great amounts of time in their work role in order to avoid the responsibilities of the father role because they lack the knowledge/skills to be comfortable in that role" (Price-Bonham & Skeen, 1979).

It is not the intent of this chapter to provide an in-depth analysis of the competing social, political, economic, and cultural forces associated with the feminist movement that eventually politicized fatherhood in America (Griswold, 1993). I simply want to recognize that due to the direct and indirect effects of the feminist movement, individuals holding onto old cultural constructions of fatherhood were challenged to change and adapt. The "new father" role required men to reorder priorities and engage in behaviors that were unfamiliar to them. Levant (1988) described this as the "ultimate act of pioneering" because men had to learn how to be different from their fathers. But there were other challenges facing the family besides men's struggle to learn new behaviors. It was also a time when women were attempting to relinquish control over a domain that for nearly a century was considered solely theirs. These sociocultural influences led to the construction of the psychological barriers that prevent many men from increasing their involvement in the fathering role.

Barriers to Increased Paternal Involvement

Understanding Initial Resistance

Without question, one of the things that clinicians find most frustrating as they work with troubled children and their families is the reluctance of fathers to participate in their children's therapy. To some extent, a father's willingness to attend therapy may reflect the degree to which he is involved in the fathering role aside from being the family breadwinner. Even in this postfeminist era, many men still regard mothers as the experts in dealing with the daily care of their children. How many clinicians attempting to schedule an appointment with a family reach the father who says, "Hold on, you'd better talk to my wife"? Though not necessarily based on much data, the impression is that this is a man who is minimally involved in his family and holds onto the traditional notion that the socioemotional development of his children falls within the mother's domain. The clinician now has several questions to ponder: Will this man be involved in his child's therapy? Does he know anything about his kids? To what extent is he involved in daily child-rearing activities?

Often, the struggle to involve the father begins even before the family calls to schedule the first therapy appointment. Clinicians typically discover that the father has been conspicuously absent from school meetings arranged by teachers, social workers, guidance counselors, or other school administrators. Sometimes schools encourage both parents to be involved, but frequently fathers are excused from attending daytime meetings because "it's hard for them to get away from work." Naturally, when fathers' participation in school meetings is easily excused, it sets an unfortunate precedent that does not bode well for a father's eventual involvement in their child's therapy. In most instances, mothers make the initial call to the clinic or to the clinician's private office, although some suggest there is increasing evidence that fathers are taking a more active role in this process (Pleck et al., 1986).

At this early point, it becomes crucial for the practitioner to understand what contributes to a father's reluctance to participate in the therapy. In most instances, there is no one single factor but rather a complex maze of issues that must be unraveled in order to involve the reluctant father and develop a positive and trusting therapeutic relationship. Notice here that I deliberately avoid using the term "resistant," a term that not only has been overused but can at times be pejorative and insensitive to men with deeply ingrained barriers that keep them from participating in therapy. For many men these barriers have evolved naturally, beginning in early childhood and continuing into adulthood, along with their sense of manhood.

Consequences of the Male Script

Some of the barriers to involvement in therapy evolve from a man's boyhood experience of observing his own father. Many men have grown up with fathers who were physically unavailable, working long hours away from home to provide for their family. The legacy left by fathers who did not participate in any of the daily child-rearing activities would be that their sons could not access an image of a father who directly engages in child-rearing activities. In other words, this is not part of what men do. As I've indicated elsewhere (Meth, 1990), boys learn that on the road to becoming a man there is a script that they are to follow closely if they are to develop a strong, masculine self-concept. This script, a basic blueprint for what it means to be a man, provides boys with strict mandates for what they can and cannot do as men. Many of these mandates separate attitudes and behaviors into the two distinct categories of masculine and feminine. Such a dichotomy does not allow for much flexibility; rather, it becomes clear to boys that they are to think, feel and act in ways distinctly different from girls. For example, as young boys are socialized, they learn they should not express certain emotions that could leave them looking weak or vulnerable. Adhering to such a mandate increases boys' tendency to detach from their emotions. So when men become fathers, they lack what Levant (1995) calls "the skill of emotional awareness," a skill that is basic to attending to the needs of their children. Thus, many men view raising children as an emotional enterprise best left to women. Although men are mostly oblivious to the impact of gender role socialization, it nevertheless contributes to their sense of incompetence and creates barriers to change.

It has been argued that a major factor responsible for men's avoiding therapy is that the process of therapy is antithetical to their sense of masculinity (Meth, 1990). In other words, men view therapy as an activity in which they are expected to talk about themselves in ways that are uncomfortable and, more importantly, unfamiliar. They are uncomfortable because this is something they not only don't do with any regularity but also have avoided their entire life. Men believe therapy will require them to express their feelings and emotions, a process they have always viewed as feminine. Being asked to reflect on their behavior as husbands or fathers may cause men to feel incompetent in either area, and naturally they will try to avoid facing this sense of failure.

Having a life script firmly grounded in traditional and dichotomous gender roles and holding firm to the belief that child care is a mostly feminine activity create serious dilemmas for men. As I described above, the unwritten script that guides men through adolescence into manhood limits their choices. Our society, as well as many others, has dichotomized gender roles so that behaviors are either masculine or feminine. Fatherhood does not change the core beliefs when men are systematically exposed to messages that reinforce this dichotomy. However, clinicians can challenge these core beliefs and assist men in learning how these beliefs have contributed to their peripheral role in the family.

Absence of Father Role Models

Another major barrier that interferes with greater paternal involvement is the absence of father role models from childhood. Many men observed and internalized the paternal behavior of a father who functioned almost entirely as an economic provider. For the most part, these men are simply following cultural proscriptions and modeling their own fathers. These men believe not only that it is acceptable to work hard to achieve financial stability and provide a good home, but also that this is the definition of a successful father. The prevailing attitude is that "it worked for him, so why shouldn't it work for my family?" While these men are willing to attribute their fathers' failure to spend time with them to the cultural expectations of the times, few are willing to acknowledge the impact of their fathers' absence. To do so could mean that they would need to address the multiple layers of emotion created by their father's absence. As indicated earlier, early in life men learn to detach themselves from profoundly painful emotions; in this instance, emotions such as disappointment, anger, sadness, and loss frequently sit just beneath the surface. Because these emotions are deeply buried, it becomes very difficult for clinicians to access them in therapy. Conversely, there may be times when a clinician decides it is not wise to pursue such buried emotions. The case study presented later elaborates on this.

Therapist Biases

Another barrier that may interfere with involving fathers in their children's therapy comes unknowingly from therapists themselves. Clinicians bring to their work their own assumptions, biases, and beliefs, which unquestionably influence they way they proceed with families. That is, therapists may have blind spots around issues that concern their own fathers. For example, a therapist who grew up in a family where the parents assumed traditional parental roles may not attempt to foster greater paternal participation in families, particularly when that is indicated. As we think about involving fathers in their children's therapy, we need to pay attention to what this arouses in us. Do we make assumptions based solely on our experience with our own fathers? Do we anticipate certain kinds of fathering behaviors from various ethnic or socioeconomic groups? When we make these kinds of assumptions we create unnecessary obstacles that may affect the therapeutic process.

For example, I recently supervised a young woman who was treating a first-generation Italian-American family. The family consisted of the parents, Joe, age 52, his wife, Marie, age 50, and their three children, Joe Jr., 19, Anna, 16 (the identified patient), and Tommy, 14. When I discovered that dad did not attend the first session (and was not scheduled to come in for the next one), I asked the therapist how she made the decision to exclude the dad. Her response was both honest and telling: "I'm very familiar with these kinds of families and, believe me, fathers don't want to be involved in things like therapy. It would be like pulling teeth to get him involved." When we discussed her family-of-origin experience, her own father, and how that might not necessarily be the model for all Italian-American families, she recognized how her biases might be impeding her work with this family.

Mothers as Gatekeepers

Another common barrier to greater paternal involvement is the way mothers function as gatekeepers for their children. As indicated earlier, women as well as men have been raised to believe that the daily care of children is the mother's job. This means that not only do men view themselves as incompetent in child care, but some women share this belief as well. If a woman doubts a father's ability to act responsibly with his children, she may not show much enthusiasm for increasing his involvement. Although Brooks (1995) and Gilbert (1993) find that women in dual-career families want their spouses to increase their participation in parenting activities, women may also interfere or discourage their spouse's child-care activities.

Beth and Wayne Alexander are a good example of such a family. Since both work full-time, the expectation they both expressed was that they share the parenting responsibilities of their three children, Brian, 17, Erin, 15, and Kim, 9. Beth and Wayne had been arguing frequently, mostly around issues that concerned Erin. Beth felt that Wayne was using a double standard with the kids, by allowing Brian greater freedom than Erin. Like most adolescents, Erin tested the limits imposed by her parents but mostly with her dad, regularly trying to undermine his authority. Since Beth worked weekends, Wayne was often the parent who had to deal with Erin's busy social life. Recently Wayne had been spending more time than usual at work and making himself less available at home; consequently, Beth was feeling more burdened. After being confronted by Beth in the session, Wayne responded in a way that revealed underlying assumptions and helped move the therapy forward. He turned to Beth and in a sarcastic tone said, "Why do you care so much that I'm not there? You always have something negative to say about what I do when I am there, particularly when it comes to Erin. So am I really needed?"

Involving Fathers in Therapy: Interventions

Inviting Fathers To the First Session

Of all the interventions at the therapist's disposal, perhaps the most important one occurs even before therapy begins, that is, when the decision is made about whom to invite to the first session. When therapists request that both parents attend (if both parents live together), they send the message that both are critical to the process of helping their child. Therapists should clearly convey their belief that the father's participation is no less important than the mother's. Although clinicians often anticipate the traditional response—that fathers have to work and cannot attend—they should be prepared to explain that therapy cannot begin until both parents can attend. If the clinician caves in and accepts the premise that the father is too busy to attend, a significant tactical error is made, creating a potentially irreversible situation in which the father's involvement is lost.

In the initial contact, the therapist should convey with great confidence how things will change only if both parents participate in the beginning. I even told one parent during the first phone contact that I would be doing the family a grave disservice if I didn't wait and meet with both mother and father *at the same time*. Clinicians who hold firm to this position must be prepared to find alternative appointment times more convenient for the family. A therapist who is dedicated and committed to working with fathers must be willing to be flexible. Our clinic offers Saturday morning appointments in addition to evening times during the week. This sends a clear message to families: It is vitally important for *both* parents to participate in the child's therapy, and we will find a time when this will work.

Sometimes families have had negative experiences with prior treatment, prompting the husband to swear that he will never go back again. Here it can be helpful to fish for more information during the initial phone contact, since you want to learn why the previous therapy was a failure in their eyes and avoid repeating that experience. It may be that one or both parents felt blamed by the therapist, or maybe one or both parents felt threatened by the therapist's suggestion that they examine their own relationship. Men are often oriented to work toward a specific goal within a prescribed period of time, and the father may have felt that the therapy lasted "too long" without producing results. At that point, the best strategy is to try to "buy" at least one session. In other words, the therapist should acknowledge that some therapy does go longer than needed, but explain that not all therapists practice the same way. I have found that men like to hear that I will recommend stopping the therapy if it becomes unproductive for the family. Try to get a commitment from the father to attend at least one session, which leaves the door open for bargaining for additional sessions. It is best to avoid a struggle in the first phone contact.

Structuring the First Session

Once the clinician feels confident that the father will attend the first session, the next task is to decide how to structure this session. To emphasize the centrality of both parents, the clinician should direct questions to *both parents.* Even when the mother appears to be the primary spokesperson or presents herself as the most knowledgeable resource regarding the child, directing questions to the father implies that his contribution is valued. In other words, therapists do not want to unknowingly perpetuate the myth that fathers are incompetent. This means that the therapist must actively block the father's attempts to defer to his wife when asked directly about his child. The therapist should step in when this occurs and challenge the father who believes he has nothing to offer. Sometimes it is simply a matter of saying to the father, "I know your wife spends lots of time with your child, but I'm struck by how much you greatly underestimate what *you know* about your child. Right now I think what you have to say could be enormously helpful to me in working with your family." Fathers need to know that their perspective is a necessary part of their child's therapy. Solutions to problems can only occur with their input.

The way in which we ask questions, that is, whether we ask questions designed to elicit feelings versus thoughts or ideas, is critical when working with fathers. It is important that the clinician carefully track the father's way of talking about his child and related concerns and use parallel language when asking a question. In other words, if a father talks about his child from a cognitive perspective, using phases like "I think that my son . . ." or "I believe that my daughter . . . ," the therapist should structure questions using his words. For example, the therapist may look at the father and ask, "So what do you believe may be underlying some of your daughter's concerns?" In general, we must recognize the degree to which many men are uncomfortable and unfamiliar with language that calls for identification of affect. If one of our goals is to join with fathers so they feel welcomed and valued in the therapeutic process, it is wise to ask cognitive questions until we learn that other kinds of questions can be asked. For example, rather than ask a father how he feels about his son's behavior in school, the therapist might ask, "So what do you think about what your son did in school the other day?" Talking in a language that men are familiar with will encourage further participation.

Using familiar metaphors also helps to increase the comfort level with men who from the start are uneasy about being in therapy. For example, I recently saw Roy, a skilled mechanic in an automobile repair shop. When Roy indicated in the waiting room that he would only be coming for this first session, I knew I had to find a way to engage him. Roy worked with cars, not exactly my specialty area but something I know a little about. Appearing genuinely curious, I asked Roy about the kinds of engines he worked on. He was eager to answer, of course, since talking about work was preferable to talking about life at home. But when his wife Betty began to talk about the problems that brought the family to therapy, Roy appeared to drift away and detach from the conversation. "So," I said to Betty, "what you're telling me is that the family doesn't seem to be firing on all cylinders. Have you asked Roy what he thinks the solution might be, because I think he might have some ideas about what needs fixing." Using a metaphor from Roy's work world seemed to reengage him in the therapy.

Direct Communication from the Therapist

Fathers need to hear directly from the therapist how important they are throughout the therapeutic process. Although I indicated earlier that this message needs to be conveyed during the first phone contact, transmitting it only through the mother can create several problems. First, the therapist does not know how the mother plans to convey this message. While we would like to assume that this will be discussed by the parents in a positive way, a father's lack of involvement in the family may have become a source of resentment and marital tension, resulting in the mother saying abruptly, "The therapist said you have to attend the session, since you're also a parent in the family." Second, if the therapist doesn't have direct contact with the father, he or she misses the opportunity to ask him what questions he has regarding the therapy. Additionally, by soliciting the father's input about the child, the therapist demonstrates that the father, as well as the mother, is an expert regarding the child. This helps to dispel the myth that the fathers are incompetent when it comes to their children.

Some fathers who come into therapy reluctant to express themselves immediately become targets of criticism by other family members. It is not uncommon to hear a father berated for being quiet or not offering an opinion. So not to stifle future participation, the therapist should support the father to participate on his own terms, reframing his silence as having merit. For example, instead of agreeing with the mother that he needs to contribute more, the therapist could note that it is good to have someone in the family who watches carefully and is introspective. When therapists remove the expectation of immediate participation, we accept unconditionally the father's style and increase the chance that he will continue to participate in therapy.

A Psychoeducational Approach

Clinicians can effectively engage men in a therapeutic process by utilizing a psychoeducational approach (Meth, 1995). This is an approach that teaches, explains, and clarifies information relevant to men and their significant others. Through such an approach, the clinician fosters a dialogue that helps men develop a deeper understanding of the impact that gender role socialization has had on their lives. The clinician can help men discover (often for the first time) the pervasive effects of gender role socialization on their lives, and in particular what gender role socialization has taught them about what they can or cannot do. Unlike some therapeutic models that require specific types of interventions at the beginning, middle, and end of therapy, a psychoeducational approach enables the clinician to provide information at any time. That is, at any point during the therapy it is beneficial to talk with men about the things they learned about being a man that serve as obstacles to greater paternal participation. It is important to note here that clinicians can use a psychoeducational format with men individually or in the presence of their partners. As I indicated earlier, women enter relationships with notions about men based on their own socialization experience. Most importantly, a psychoeducational format enables women to learn that men do not deliberately choose these obstacles that interfere with fathering; rather, they result from the powerful impact of gender role socialization.

Case Illustration: Working with One Father in Therapy

The following case presents excellent examples of some the barriers to therapy previously discussed. Tim, a 38-year-old computer programmer and father to 8-year-old Jeremy, had been fairly uninvolved in his son's life since his birth. His wife, Judy, a 37-year-old attorney, was openly critical of Tim's behavior toward his son and expressed her frustration to whomever would listen. She said she had grown impatient with her husband's short temper and lack of interest in their son. The school guidance counselor referred the family to therapy after a few incidents where Jeremy punched classmates. When Joan, the family therapist assigned to the intake, first got the referral, Judy requested that she and Tim come in without Jeremy for the first session. Joan reluctantly agreed, thinking that at least the mom and dad would provide some vital background information. Tim and Judy appeared to be arguing about something when Joan greeted them in the waiting room. In the initial session, Tim was defensive and visibly upset by Judy's accusation that his erratic behavior toward his son was responsible for Jeremy's problem. Apparently each blamed the other for Jeremy's problem. Because Tim had recently started a new job after a long period of unemployment, he was working long hours to make a favorable impression and move up in his department. He was angry that Judy failed to recognize and appreciate the sacrifices he was making for the family. He also indicated that he was doing the best he could, certainly "a lot better than my own father."

When presented with this kind of information, the temptation for most clinicians is to explore Tim's experience in his family of origin and link this to his relationship with his son. However, this kind of intervention must be handled delicately and patiently. First, the clinician must not forget that, since the family entered therapy because of Jeremy's problematic behavior, that is the first order of business. They will not readily shift away from the individual identified as "the patient" to another family member's issues. Regardless of how committed the clinician is to a systemic focus, it is highly unlikely that the family will initially share that view. Also, we must not underestimate the impact of asking Tim to talk more about his relationship with his father, with or without his partner present, this early in the therapy. Perhaps a good metaphor to illustrate my point is when you ask your dentist to examine a sensitive tooth. If the dentist probes carefully and quickly diagnoses the problem, there is minimal discomfort and you feel ready to proceed with the prescribed treatment. If your dentist probes too quickly and deeply and doesn't notice the pain you're having, you'll become increasingly uncomfortable and consider leaving the office before the tooth is treated.

Although Tim spoke openly about his desire to be a better father than his father was, he did not offer much insight into his feelings about his dad. He did, however, provide some additional clues indicating that his father spent little time with him. "At least sometimes I read a story to Jeremy. My father never came close to doing that. I guess he was too busy working two jobs," Tim stated. This is a moment in therapy that can challenge the clinical judgment of the therapist. Does the therapist use this disclosure as a bridge to explore the apparent unresolved issue of paternal deprivation? Is Tim ready to address these issues now? Or is it too early for Tim to open the floodgates of feelings that he may be unprepared to explore? Rather than ask Tim to delve into the complex issues and deep emotions connected to his father, Joan decided to take an approach that she considered less threatening. "So, how is it for you to sit with Jeremy and read to him? Is it something you enjoy doing, or do you find that it's not a fulfilling activity for you?"

Tim's response was something Joan would not have predicted this early in the therapy. "I don't know how to say this so it doesn't come out wrong," Tim said hesitantly, "but when I'm on Jeremy's bed reading to him, I feel myself getting annoyed. . . . I just want to leave. Actually, I'm embarrassed to admit this, but I get really angry at Jeremy when he tries to manipulate me into reading more than one book—I mean, he's lucky I'm even reading him one." As Tim and Joan began talking about Tim's becoming a more involved father, it was clear that spending more "quality time" with Jeremy triggered painful feelings and disturbing memories. Disappointment, anger, and chronic feelings of emptiness that lingered from Tim's childhood experience of paternal deprivation had constantly overwhelmed him since Jeremy's birth. (Tim did not directly express these feelings; rather, it was Joan's sense that these feelings were pervasive in this session.) When he sat with his son, images of what Tim wanted but never had with his father appeared without warning. At his point Joan's thoughts were not about Jeremy's issues but, rather, about Tim's deep psychic wounds. Although the parents anticipated bringing Jeremy in for a second session, Joan was uncertain about how to proceed and told the family she would call them in a few days.

Later, in supervision, Joan was both excited and anxious about the first session but also perplexed about how to proceed. She knew it was important to see the entire family for the next session, yet she did not want to lose the momentum and rapport she had established with Tim. I asked Joan to think about Tim's response to the first session. While it appeared to go well, I suggested that talking about these issues might cause Tim considerable anxiety. Furthermore, it is likely that Tim would experience a profound sense of ambivalence about revisiting these issues in another session. In other words, while a part of Tim may have felt an enormous sense of relief at being able to talk about his childhood memories, another part of him may have felt frightened and overwhelmed by the underlying feelings these issues aroused in him. There are several issues to think about, I suggested to Joan. First, Tim did not come in asking to look at his childhood experiences with his father, so what rationale would she provide for changing the direction of the therapy? Second, is Joan certain that Jeremy's acting out is solely related to the father-son relationship and not to other factors in the family that the therapy may need to examine? Because it was important to see Jeremy interact with his parents, Joan decided to see the whole family for the second session.

In that session Jeremy entered the therapy room and immediately began to play with some toys he found near the play area. Even before the parents sat down Joan sensed that Tim was irritated about something. Apparently there had been an incident in the waiting room that resulted in Tim yelling at Jeremy. But Tim's irritation was not with Jeremy; he was angry at his wife. "Every time I correct Jeremy," Tim explained, "Judy gets next to him and comforts him, as if I've just done some horrible thing. It makes me look like a jerk and I'm getting sick of it." Judy defended her actions by pointing out to Joan that in the past week Tim had been unusually inpatient with Jeremy. "You really need to change the way you relate to our son," said Judy in a tone that suggested Judy was issuing Tim an ultimatum. Two things struck Joan at that moment. First, she was concerned about the enormous amount of anger Judy had toward Tim. Second, she was curious about Tim's increased impatience in the past week and how it related to the material that came out in the first session. Joan decided to pursue Judy's anger and found that it were issues from Judy's family of origin that exacerbated the conflict between Tim and her.

During Judy's childhood her family struggled financially and moved frequently to find less expensive housing. Apparently Judy's father went from job to job and never found any stable employment. This often required Judy's mother to work several part-time jobs to support the family. As she and Joan discussed this history and its effect on current relationships, Judy realized that Tim's recent period of unemployment triggered many painful memories for her and brought up much of the suppressed anger she still carried. As Tim listened, he realized that his wife's constant criticism had made him feel more and more inadequate as a husband and a provider. Joan sensed that it may have been difficult for Tim to figure out whether Judy was angry at him for failing as a father or as a provider. Although Tim learned very little from his father about how to be a father, he thought he was doing the best he could with Jeremy. Not only did Tim feel this was never acknowledged by Judy, but he also felt unfairly criticized by her. It was at this point that Joan knew what direction to take with this family. Neither Judy nor Tim disagreed with Joan's rationale for proceeding in the next session without Jeremy. They both recognized how past issues from their family of origin interfered with daily parenting activities.

In the supervision that followed the second session, Joan and I discussed why she chose to pursue Judy's anger and not Tim's issues brought up during the first session. Joan admitted that Tim looked depressed in the session; at first she was not clear why she decided to take a different direction. With some further prodding, she realized that she did not want to "pathologize" Tim. When I asked her to clarify what she meant, Joan recalled the way her own family dwelled on her father's depression during her adolescence. "Unfortunately for our family my father saw a therapist only once and decided it was not for him; it was too bad, because he could have used the help," said Joan. At that moment she realized that she did not pursue Tim's depression because she was afraid she might scare him away from the therapy—just like her dad.

Ignoring Tim's depression in the second session was not a major clinical blunder. In fact, Tim's concerns about his depression surfaced in the third session when he acknowledged he had felt irritable for years but was reluctant to look at it as a problem. At his point in the therapy, Tim was less defensive than he would have been in the first session. Since he was not feeling "blamed" for Jeremy's problems, he was more willing to examine his moodiness and how it affected his fathering. Tim even suggested that he might come in for an individual session to "get rid of the baggage from my family" that he knew was interfering with his relationship with Jeremy. Knowing that Judy's presence at this session could greatly increase her empathy and understanding of Tim's struggle with fatherhood, Joan asked Tim if he would mind if Judy attended.

Tim and Judy's fourth meeting primarily focused on issues from Tim's family of origin.

In the fifth session Joan worked with Judy and Tim on their coparenting relationship. By now each showed considerable empathy and listened more effectively to each other's concerns. While Tim continued to experience occasional periods of irritability, Judy said she did not expect miracles but hoped that Tim's relationship with Jeremy would continue to grow. Tim admitted that he wanted to do more with Jeremy but did not feel comfortable in play. One of the ways clinicians can help men become more comfortable interacting with their children is to schedule sessions with the father and child without the mother present. As planned, Tim brought Jeremy to the sixth session without his wife and, after some encouragement from Joan, played games on the floor with Jeremy for nearly the entire session. Joan's main goal for this session was for Tim to leave the clinic feeling an increased sense of competence as a father. As Jeremy and Tim were leaving, Jeremy asked Joan if he and his dad could come back again next week and play. Joan sensed Tim's joy and relief when he heard this.

After one more session with Tim and Jeremy, Judy came back with Tim for a final session. As Tim and Judy reviewed the work they had done, Joan reminded them of what they were able to accomplish in such a short time. Tim even asked where he could continue to get therapy for himself if his irritability remained a problem. Joan found out several weeks later that Tim had joined a men's support group.

Conclusion

While all of us would agree that fathers are important to their children, fathers can be difficult to engage in the therapeutic process when their children are referred for therapy. Nevertheless, the literature has been clear that children benefit from greater rather than less paternal involvement. Beginning with a historical perspective, this chapter has shown why men have been so difficult to engage in therapy and examined many of the barriers that prevent greater involvement. A number of interventions have been described and a detailed case study has been presented to provide the reader with some basic skills in working with fathers. Finally, as clinicians it is imperative that we look at our own biases and blind spots so we don't add to the barriers that already exist in working with men.

Richard L. Meth, M.S.W., Ph.D., is Clinical Director, Child and Family Services of Pioneer Valley, Springfield, Massachusetts.

References

Baruch, G. K., & Barnett, R. C. (1986). Consequences of fathers' participation in family work: Parents role strain and well being. *Journal of Personality and Social Psychology, 51,* 983–992.

Biller, H. (1971). *Father, child and sex role.* Lexington, MA: D.C. Heath.

Biller, H. (1974). *Paternal deprivation: Family, school, sexuality, and society.* Lexington, MA: D.C. Heath.

Biller, H. (1993). *Fathers and families: Paternal factors in child development.* Westport, CT: Auburn House.

Bozett, F., & Hanson, S. (Eds.). (1991). *Fatherhood and families in cultural context.* New York: Springer.

Bronstein, P. (1988). Father-child interaction: Implications for gender role socialization. In P. Bronstein & C. Cowan (Eds.), *Fatherhood today: Men's changing role in the family* (pp. 107–126). New York: Wiley.

Bronstein, P., & Cowan, C. (Eds.). (1988). *Fatherhood today: Men's changing role in the family.* New York: Wiley.

Brooks, G. A., & Gilbert, L. A. (1995). Men in families: Old constraints, new possibilities. In R. F. Levant & W. S. Pollack (Eds.), *A new psychology of men* (pp. 252–279). New York: Basic.

Cowan, C. P., & Bronstein, P. (1988). Fathers' roles in the family: Implications for research, intervention, and change. In P. Bronstein & C. P. Cowan (Eds.), *Fatherhood today: Men's changing role in the family* (pp. 341–347). New York: Wiley.

Ellner, J. (1973). *Recent changes in American child-rearing practices 1950 through 1970.* Unpublished manuscript. Center for the Study of Parental Acceptance and Rejection, University of Connecticut, Storrs, CT.

Gilbert, L. A. (1993). *Two careers/one family: The promise of gender equality.* Newbury Park, CA: Sage.

Griswold, R. L. (1993). *Fatherhood in America: A history.* New York: Basic.

Haas, L. (1988). *Understanding fathers' participation in child care: A social constructionist perspective.* Paper presented to the National Council on Family Relations, Philadelphia.

Hetherington, M., Cox, M., & Cox, R. (1979). Divorced fathers. *Family Coordinator, 25,* 417–428.

Jain, A., Belsky, J., & Crnic, K. (1996). Beyond fathering: Types of dads. *Journal of Family Psychology, 10,* 431–442.

Jordan, B., Radin, N., & Epstein, A. (1975). Paternal behavior and intellectual functioning in preschool boys and girls. *Developmental Psychology, 11,* 407–408.

Kagan, J. (1978, August). The parental love trap. *Psychology Today, 54,* 57, 58, 61, 91.

Kaplan, A. (1964). *The conduct of inquiry: Methodology for behavioral science.* Scranton, PA: Chandler.

Lamb, M. E. (1981). *The role of the father in child development* (2nd ed.). New York: Wiley.

Lamb, M. E. (1997). Fathers and child development: An introductory overview and guide. In M. E. Lamb (Ed.), *The role of the father in child development* (pp. 1–18). New York: Wiley.

Lamb, M. E., Pleck, J. H., Charnov, E.L., & Levine, J. A. (1987). A biosocial perspective on paternal behavior and involvement. In J. B. Lancaster, J. Altman, A. Rossi, & L. R. Shepard (Eds.), *Parenting across the life span: Biosocial perspectives* (pp. 11–42). New York: Academic.

Lamb, M. E., Pleck, J. H., & Levine, J. A. (1985). The role of the father in child development: The effects of increased paternal involvement. In B. Lahey & A. Kazdin (Eds.), *Advances in clinical child psychology* (Vol. 8, pp. 229–266). New York: Plenum.

Levant, R. F. (1995). Towards the reconstruction of masculinity. In R. F. Levant & W. S. Pollack (Eds.), *A new psychology of men* (pp. 229–251). New York: Basic.

Levant, R. F., & Kelly, J. (1989). *Between father and child.* New York: Viking.

Maccoby, E. E., & Martin, J. A. (1983). Socialization in the context of the family: Parent-child interaction. In E. M. Hetherington (Ed.), *Socialization, personality, and social development* (Vol. IV, 4th ed., pp. 1–101). New York: Wiley.

Mackey, W. C. (1996). *The American father: Biocultural and developmental aspects.* New York: Plenum.

McHale, S. M., & Huston, T. L. (1984). Men and women as parents: Sex role orientations, employment, and parental roles with infants. *Child Development, 55,* 1349–1361.

Meth, R. L. (1990). The road to masculinity. In R. Meth & R. Pasick (Eds.), *Men in therapy: The challenge of change* (pp. 1–38). New York: Guilford.

Meth, R. L. (1995). *Refusing to shed their mask: Working with men in therapy.* Paper presented at the annual meeting of the American Association of Marriage and Family Therapy, Baltimore, Maryland.

Nash, J. (1965). The father in contemporary culture and current psychological literature. *Child Development, 36,* 261–291.

Palkovitz, R. (1984). Parental attitudes and fathers' interactions with their five-month-old infants. *Developmental Psychology, 20,* 1054–1060.

Parke, R. D. (1985). Foreword. In S. M. H. Hanson & F. W. Bozett (Eds.), *Dimensions of fatherhood* (pp. 9–12). Beverly Hills: Sage.

Peterson, D., Becker, W., Hellmer, L., Shoemaker, D., & Quay, H. (1959). Parental attitudes and child adjustment. *Child Development, 30,* 119–130.

Phares, V. (1997). Psychological adjustment, maladjustment, and father-child relationships. In M. E. Lamb (Ed.), *The role of the father in child development* (3rd ed., pp. 261–283). New York: Wiley.

Phares, V., & Compas, B. (1992). Role of fathers in child and adolescent psychopathology: Make room for daddy. *Psychological Bulletin, 111*(3), 387–412.

Pleck, J. (1997). Paternal involvement: Level, sources, and consequences. In M. E. Lamb (Ed.), *The role of the father in child development* (3rd ed., pp. 66–103). New York: Wiley.

Pleck, J., Lamb, M., & Levine, J. (1986). Epilogue: Facilitating future change in men's family roles. In R. A. Lewis & M. Sussman (Eds.), *Men's changing roles in the family* (pp. 11–16). New York: Haworth.

Price-Bonham, S., & Skeen, P. (1979). A comparison of Black and White fathers with implications for parents' education. *Family Coordinator, 28*(1), 53–59.

Radin, N. (1981). The role of the father in cognitive, academic, and intellectual development. In M. E. Lamb (Ed.), *The role of the father in child development* (pp. 379–428). New York: Wiley.

Rohner, R. (1997). *The importance of father love: History and contemporary evidence.* Unpublished manuscript, Center for the Study of Parental Acceptance and Rejection, University of Connecticut, Storrs, CT.

Rotundo, E. A. (1993). *American manhood: Transformations in masculinity from the revolution to the modern era.* New York: Basic.

Russell, G. (1986). Primary caretakers and the role sharing fathers. In M. E. Lamb (Ed.), *The father's role: Applied perspectives* (pp. 29–60). New York: Wiley.

Stearns, P. N. (1991). Fatherhood in historical perspective: The role of social change. In F. W. Bozett & S. M. H. Hanson (Eds.), *Fatherhood and family in cultural context* (pp. 28–52). New York: Springer.

15

Resilience in Children

Bonnie Klimes-Dougan
Kimberly T. Kendziora

By most definitions, Victoria would be characterized as resilient. Victoria is an attractive 34-year-old, Caucasian female who has been married for nine years. She has worked for the government as a lawyer in the same job for six years. Her husband is also a professional. She often gets together with friends and enjoys leisure activities, including horseback riding and reading. Except for an occasional call from a brother asking for money, another brother distraught by his severed parental rights, or her mother asking for legal advice, the chaos and abuse she experienced growing up is a distant memory.

Victoria was the oldest child of four and the only daughter born to parents living in a rural setting. She was a cheerful infant and the favored child. While well-intending, her teen mother was emotionally unavailable and was often negligent in caring for Victoria (e.g., rarely changing her diapers, leading to chronic diaper rash). Although bright, her father was uneducated, illiterate, and made very little money in a succession of jobs as an unskilled laborer. The family relied on public assistance to make ends meet, and discussions around their financial woes often led to physical altercations between Victoria's parents. As the children grew, they were all physically abused by their father. Whether due to being the favored child or being clever at avoiding conflictual situations, Victoria was less often the target of her father's physical abuse than her siblings. She was not spared, however, for her father sexually abused her and one of her siblings over a period of several years.

From a young age, Victoria was given the charge of supervising her younger brothers. When her 2-year-old brother was found several miles from the house, she was severely punished for shirking her duties. When Victoria was 6 her parents separated for a year. Her mother left with a boyfriend, and Victoria went to live with a beloved aunt who had periodically cared for her as an infant. Although she entered first grade without any preparation, she thrived under the loving care of her aunt. By the end of first grade she was at the top of her class and well liked by her teacher and peers. Victoria returned to her family when her parents got back together the following year. During her early elementary school years, Victoria developed an interest in reading and could frequently be found in the library engrossed in a romance novel.

The conflict between her parents persisted and after numerous temporary separations her parents divorced when she was in junior high school. In an effort to obtain custody of Victoria, her father sent her to a boarding academy. She experienced a major depressive episode while at boarding school and, with the encouragement of her boyfriend, sought treatment for the first time. She continued to date this boyfriend after graduation. Her boyfriend was from a family that highly valued education and, when he mentioned that he could not see himself marrying someone that hadn't completed college, Victoria promptly enrolled. She struggled with her classes and the finances to get through. Upon completing college she went on to law school and soon after married her long-time boyfriend.

We have said that Victoria is resilient. What do we mean by resilience? In physical science, resilience is the capacity of a strained body to recover its size and shape after some deformation caused by compressive stress. Rubber balls are resilient, and light bulbs are not. In psychology, resilience may be thought of as that process of functioning as well or better than unstressed individuals in the face of adversity. This topic of study arose when researchers realized that there were some people who "worked well, played well, loved well, and expected well" despite major life stresses (Werner & Smith, 1992, p. 262). Resilience in people is the process of bouncing back like a rubber ball in circumstances where other, more vulnerable individuals would shatter like a light bulb. Resilience, then, requires two conditions: (1) the person must be, now or in the past, exposed to adversity, and (2) the person must be doing well.

Resilience in the Context of Risk

The first part of our definition of resilience requires that children be exposed to *adversity, stress,* or *risk.* A risk factor is any individual or environmental characteristic that increases the likelihood of some negative outcome. Examples of risk factors are poverty, marital conflict, or child abuse. Having a mentally ill parent is also a potent risk factor. In fact, the literature on resilience in children grew from early studies of "invulnerable" children—those who had schizophrenic parents, yet were free of psychological disturbance (Garmezy, 1971).

One may ask, are protective factors specific to the nature of the risk conditions the individual is exposed to? Garmezy (1985) has speculated that protective factors may be nonspecific. They may operate in a general way across a variety of contexts, stressors, and risk factors. For example, social competence has been found to be a protective factor in samples identified based on maternal depression, poverty, or multiple risk factors (e.g., Garmezy, 1987; Radke-Yarrow & Sherman, 1990; Werner, 1993). There are several reasons why the protective factors may be similar for children from various family contexts. One explanation is that there are multiple risks associated with many of these family environments. Rutter (1979) found that risk variables (e.g., parental psychopathology) did not lead to an increased rate of psychiatric disorder in children if they occurred in isolation. The presence of two or more concurrent variables increased the risk for problems. In their work with offspring of mentally ill mothers, Sameroff (Sameroff, Seifer, Baldwin, & Baldwin, 1993) has stressed that the cumulative effect of these chronic adversities places children at risk. Families selected for evidence of maternal depression were found to be more likely to evidence multiple risks (e.g., marital conflict, divorce, and financial stress). It is likely that even when diverse selection criteria (e.g., maternal depression, children living in poverty) are identified to study the topic of resilience, the composition of the samples is quite similar in that they are largely made up of families that have experienced numerous, concurrent risk factors over a prolonged period of time.

A second explanation can be found in Gotlib and Avison's (1993) conceptualization of risk. They identified classes of family environments that are likely to place children at risk for psychopathology that include (1) social disadvantage (e.g., poverty), (2) disrupted family structures (e.g., divorce, unmarried mothers, death of a parent), and (3) parental psychopathology (parental depression, schizophrenia, alcoholism). Then they proceeded to suggest that all these family environments increased the risk of psychopathology and that the manifestation of psychopathology in these diverse family environments was quite similar. For example, even though children of depressed parents are at risk for depression, they are also at risk for other emotional and behavioral problems, not unlike children of divorced parents or socioeconomically disadvantaged children. In an attempt to explain the commonality of outcomes, they suggested those two high-level constructs of marital/family conflict and parental emotional unavailability may mediate child risk in most of these family environments that place children at risk. We propose that it is likely that children who possess characteristics that enable them to cope with marital/family conflict and parental emotional unavailability are one important group of children who are identified as resilient.

Resilience as Outcome

Regarding the second part of the definition, resilience is not something that can logically be said to exist in a child who has never been significantly stressed. Nor is it a static, preexisting quality, such as having a high IQ, a supportive family environment, or an encouraging teacher. Although these things are certainly important, they are more properly identified as *protective factors* or *buffers*. These factors reduce the probability that maladaptation will occur when confronted with stress. However, like many protective factors, resilience can be taught or encouraged.

One may wonder why a chapter on resilience exists in a volume on treating presumably poorly functioning children. There are several reasons for this. First, in incorporating families into children's therapy, one might discover a sibling who has been exposed to many of the same risks and hazards as the target child, but who nonetheless is functioning well. In fact, some research has identified a family pattern in which the presence of behavior problems and a negative/conflictual parent-child relationship for one sibling actually *protects* the other sibling from having problems (Reiss et al., 1995). The process of examining how a sibling could be functioning well while a target child is not may uncover some resources or skills that could be taught or reinforced in the affected youth.

A second reason to study resilience is that important lessons may be learned from studying the coping skills of those who have passed, seemingly unimpeded, through difficult childhoods. What factors are associated with resilient outcomes? How can these factors be fostered in children whose psychological health is at risk?

Third, it is conceivable that children may be resilient with respect to some outcomes but not others. Just as risks must always be defined in relation to specific outcomes (Rutter, 1987), resilience may not be universal across domains. Cowan, Cowan, and Schulz (1996) pointed out that the same quality (for example, shyness) may place a child at risk for one outcome (depression), but may in fact serve as a protective factor with respect to a second outcome (conduct problems or delinquency). Likewise, a youth living in conditions of dire risk who functions well in school and maintains her responsibilities at home (overt competence) may still suffer from some feelings of anxiety or depression (covert distress; Luthar, 1993).

The purpose of this chapter is to discuss some core concepts of resilience, focusing on aspects that may be particularly applicable to therapists who are working with children and children's families. We start by providing an overview of research on this topic. Individual, family, and community factors associated with resilience are reviewed. Relevant principles of developmental psychopathology and transactional theories are highlighted with regard to resilience. In the final section of this paper, we conclude with some remarks about how to foster resilience.

Correlates of Resilience

Research on Resilience

The discipline of developmental psychopathology provides principles that guide the examination of resilience (Cicchetti, 1984; Sroufe & Rutter, 1984). "Developmental psychopathology may be defined as the study of the origins and course of individual patterns of behavioral maladaptation" (Sroufe & Rutter, 1984, p. 18). This approach is used to identify which factors place children at risk and which factors are associated with successful adaptation. Furthermore, a developmental psychopathology perspective emphasizes the importance of successful adaptation for a given developmental period. Given that developmental tasks vary with age, it follows that protective factors may also differ with age.

The focus on resilience as an outcome is also relevant to this approach. The goal is to identify characteristics that predict adaptation at some later point. Because the highest risk period for psychopathology is adolescence and early adulthood, what might look like resilience in childhood may be risk not yet manifest. The impact of cumulative stress must also be acknowledged when identifying resilient children. As Farber and Egeland (1987) found with their study of abused preschoolers, the number of competent children declined over time. Furthermore, behavior that is normative for one developmental period may be considered pathological when it persists. For example, negativism, fears, and obsessional qualities are normative in toddlers and preschoolers, but when these characteristics persist into childhood they may be symptoms of emotional and behavioral problems. Consequently, in the study of resilience there are inherent weaknesses of one-time assessments.

Longitudinal studies are necessary to determine whether children who are identified as resilient continue to do well in terms both of adaptive behavior and of emotional health (Farber & Egeland, 1987). Without these types of assessments, intervention and prevention programming may overlook those in need of attention. There are three main studies that have followed large groups of subjects (more than 200) from childhood into adulthood. The Kauai study (e.g., Werner, 1993; Werner & Smith, 1992) was epidemiological in nature, studying almost 700 children born on a Hawaiian island in 1955 and following them up at ages 1, 2, 10, 18, and 32. Of the Kauai children, 30% were at high risk due to various socioeconomic, biological, or family factors. Of the high-risk children, one-third were resilient. Rutter (e.g., Rutter, 1976; Rutter, 1979; Rutter, Maugham, Mortimore, & Ouston, 1979) studied a sample from the Isle of Wight (England) and urban London who experienced multiple risks. In Project Competence, Garmezy and Masten (e.g., Garmezy, 1985; Garmezy, Masten, & Tellegen, 1984) studied a sample from urban environments in the mainland United States. In summarizing the literature on resilience, these researchers (e.g., Garmezy, 1985) have reached considerable consensus in grouping protective factors into three broad categories that serve as the predictive correlates of resilient outcomes: (1) individual characteristics of the child, including dispositional attributes, (2) a supportive family milieu, and (3) availability of external support in the community for the child and their parent(s). The correlates of resilience reviewed in the subsequent sections are believed to transact with one another. That is, characteristics of the individual affect the responses of the family and larger community. Likewise, the resources available in the family and community are believed to affect the child by promoting resilience.

Individual Characteristics Associated with Resilience

We begin by stating that the discussion of individual characteristics associated with resilience is largely gleaned from Werner's (1993, 1995) developmental review of the resilience literature. Soon after birth, some infants exhibit characteristics associated with resilience. These infants appear to successfully elicit positive attention from their caregivers and are typically described as "easy" babies. They tend to be active, alert, responsive, and sociable.

In the preschool period, those who combined autonomous behavior with the ability to ask for help when needed had favorable outcomes. Resilient preschoolers were socially oriented and developmentally advanced. That is, they were skilled in communication, locomotion, and self-help skills. They also were found to be self-confident, independent, and capable of producing change in frustrating situations.

A sense of competence and self-efficacy is the hallmark of successful adaptation under conditions of stress for those in middle childhood. Resilient children are typically characterized as possessing good problem-solving and communication skills. While some longitudinal studies have noted the relationship between intelligence and resilience (e.g., Werner & Smith, 1982), there is little evidence that high intelligence alone promotes effective coping. As Luthar notes (Luthar & Zigler, 1991), high intelligence may be associated with an increased sensitivity to stressors and heighten the child's susceptibility to risk. Strong interests in hobbies and other leisure pursuits like sports, reading, or stamp collecting may also buffer children from the stressors they encounter. These interests may allow the child to remain somewhat detached from the stressors of the environment (Worland, Weeks, & Janes, 1987) or serve as an emotional refuge. Resilient children do not necessarily abide by the sex-stereotype norms that are typically so evident during this developmental period. For example, resilient boys tend to be emotionally expressive and resilient girls tend to be autonomous and independent. Moreover, an attributional style and patterns of coping that may allow them to deal effectively with challenging situations characterize resilience in middle childhood. Resilient children typically have a positive self-concept, flexible coping strategies, and an internal locus of control.

Many of the protective factors associated with resilience in middle childhood are also found in resilient adolescents (Werner, 1990). Resilient adolescents tend to have an internal locus of control and positive self-concept. They are responsible, achievement oriented, and socially mature. Both resilient males and females are likely to possess "feminine attributes," such as being gentle, nurturant, and socially perceptive.

In summary, several themes emerge in this developmental approach to classifying individual characteristics associated with resilience. First, the child's temperament appears to be a core factor associated with resilience. In early infancy "easy" babies are resilient. In preschool and middle childhood, socially competent children are resilient. Second, children who are developmentally advanced or show evidence of excelling in an area of special interest are more likely to be resilient. While some of these factors are likely to be nurtured within the child's environment (e.g., interest in stamp collecting), it has also been recognized that some of the core correlates associated with resilience (e.g., temperament, intelligence) may reflect genetically influenced characteristics (Luthar & Zigler, 1991; Rende & Plomin, 1993). We turn now to examine how these individual characteristics influence what support systems are available to the individual within the family and the larger community.

Family Factors Associated with Resilience

Family factors have been associated with resilient outcomes across the course of development. We have already noted that babies, who do well later despite challenges, tend to be active, alert, responsive, and sociable—that is to say, "easy." It is important to note that such individual factors, which are powerfully influenced by genetics (temperament or physical appearance), in turn influence family factors that further contribute to the individual child's resilience. Unfair as it may seem, some children who are born with certain individual assets attract further relational assets.

A good example may be found in the study by Langlois, Ritter, Casey, and Sawin (1995). These researchers observed mothers feeding and playing with their firstborn infants while they were still in the hospital after giving birth and again when the infants were three months old. Mothers of more attractive infants were more affectionate and playful compared with mothers of less attractive infants. In contrast, new mothers with less attractive infants were more likely to engage in routine caregiving rather than affectionate behavior. This preference for attractiveness may also be innate, as infants themselves show similar preferences (e.g., Samuels, Butterworth, Roberts, & Graupner, 1994).

With the caveat in place that family factors are not independent of individual factors, let us also note that family factors are enormously important to children's resilience to stress. Family factors are so central that many resilience researchers have selected their samples based upon them. In this vein, offspring of parents with schizophrenia (e.g., Garmezy, 1974, 1987), alcoholism (e.g., Werner, 1986), and depression (e.g., Hammen, 1997; Radke-Yarrow & Brown, 1993) have been studied. Additionally, the resilience of children of divorce (e.g., Emery & Forehand, 1994; Hetherington, 1991), children of parents prone to child abuse (e.g., Erickson, Egeland, & Pianta, 1989; Farber & Egeland, 1987), and teenage parents (e.g., Apfel & Seitz, 1997; Osofsky, Hann, & Peebles, 1993) have been studied as high risk groups.

From these and other studies, we have learned that a close bond between child and caregiver is among the most important family factors associated with resilience. In infancy, the resilient child seems more likely to have acquired the attention of a competent and emotionally stable caregiver who cares deeply about the child's well-being. It is important to note that this caregiver need not be a biological parent. Werner (1993) found that grandparents, older siblings, and other substitute caregivers supplied much of this important nurturing for young children.

The role of the father may also be important. In the Rochester Child Resilience Project (Cowen, Work, & Wyman, 1997), a study of poor, young, inner-city children exposed to serious and chronic life stressors, researchers found that stress-resistant children tended to have families with child care support for the mother during infancy, both in general and specifically from a father figure. Further research is needed in clarifying the role of the father, for not all studies have noted the role of the father as being critical for resilience (e.g., Werner, 1993).

Another provocative finding from the Rochester study was that the absence of a prolonged separation from the primary caregiver was associated with resilient outcomes. This could be interpreted in a number of ways. One is that the primary caregivers have made the care of their infants a priority in their lives, and they have avoided any voluntary periods of separation. Another is that the caregivers of resilient children were themselves more stable and less prone to problems such as addiction or mental illness that could result in a prolonged separation from their babies.

Beyond infancy, the developmental periods of early and middle childhood have their own sets of challenges and tasks. Children become more connected to the world outside their homes (school, friends, etc.), and their competence there can foster the emergence of resilience. Nevertheless, family factors remain important as children grow older. A sound parent-child relationship is associated with resilience during these developmental periods (warm, caring interactions, use of competent discipline, and involvement in common activities; Cowen, Work, & Wyman, 1997; Gribble et al., 1993). Even when mothers are mentally ill, if they are able to display responsiveness, availability, and warmth, their children are much more likely to become resilient (Musick, Cohler, & Dincin, 1982). In these cases, it was also helpful when the mentally ill mothers encouraged their children to avail themselves of alternative care-giving environments. The centrality of a parent-child relationship that is both warm and structuring may well be an extension of the caring bond that is so protective during the first year of life.

Other family characteristics have been associated with resilience in children. Resilient children have been found to be family favorites (Radke-Yarrow & Brown, 1993). Birth order is another characteristic that may be associated with resilience. In the Kauai Longitudinal Study, most of the resilient boys were firstborn and had no siblings following them for at least 20 months (Werner, 1985). In cases of father absence due to death, divorce, or desertion, being first or second born (particularly in families with four or fewer children spaced at least two years apart) was associated with greater responsibility and social maturity for both boys and girls. One mechanism potentially responsible for this birth order effect may be what Rachman (1979) has called *required helpfulness*. Some aspects of the chore of caring for younger siblings may be functional in fostering strength and competence in resilient children.

Socialization practices within the family have been found to interact with gender in the prediction of resilience. Werner (1985) found that for boys, households with more structure, clearer rules, good supervision, a strong father or father figure, and encouragement of emotional expressiveness were protective from negative outcomes. For girls, households combining an emphasis on independence, an absence of overprotection, and emotional support from the primary caregiver were more likely to be associated with resilience (Werner & Smith, 1982). For girls raised in poverty, steady employment of the mother outside the home has been shown to be protective (Werner, 1993). This may be due to the fact that low-income working mothers are themselves resilient. Stegelin and Frankel (1993) highlight the existence of single, working mothers who do cope in the face of limited energy, resources, and structural support systems. These women demonstrate unusual problem-solving skills and personal strength, serving as a model of resilience for their children.

External Resources Associated with Resilience

Positive outcomes tend to be associated with a high use of community support systems. It should be noted that the literature reviewed is primarily relevant to middle childhood. And yet, infants and preschoolers may also benefit greatly by external support systems. A relevant example is found in the research of Field and her colleagues with infants of depressed mothers (Field et al., 1988; Pelaez-Nogueras, Field, Cigales, Gonzalez, & Clasky, 1994). Compared to infants of well mothers, these infants had lower interaction scores (e.g., less attentiveness, lower activity levels, more fussiness) with both their mothers and unfamiliar nondepressed adults. However, infants of depressed mothers showed more positive expressions with other familiar adults (e.g., familiar nursery school teacher). The authors interpreted these findings to mean that other caretakers may serve to compensate for or buffer the effects of a depressed mother.

Although professional help may occasionally be the venue of choice, resilient children and their families are more likely to have an informal network of relationships within the community (summarized by Luthar & Zigler, 1991; Werner & Smith, 1982). Resilient school-aged children tend to be well liked by their peers. Here again it may be their personal characteristics that others are drawn to. That is, the social interactions of resilient children have been characterized by humor, empathy, or social expressiveness.

Mentoring relationships have been found to be associated with resilience. Teachers are an important source of support for resilient children (Rutter et al., 1979; Wallerstein & Blakeslee, 1989; Werner, 1995). They support children by listening to them, challenging them, or rooting for them. Teachers also serve as positive role models. Other community resources may also serve as protective factors. Extended kin, neighbors, clergy, coaches, and others in the community may provide supportive functions to children at risk. For example, religious beliefs and practices have been associated with resilience (Park & Cohen, 1988). In addition to the mentoring relationships potentially available in this setting, church affiliation has been found to provide stability and meaning in the lives of resilient children.

Numerous studies have found that high-risk children who successfully utilize social support systems within the community are resilient (e.g., Garmezy, 1985; Werner, 1993). However, Rhodes (1994) identifies a number of ambiguities in this research. What is the direction of the relationship between community sources of support and resilience? Some have placed the emphasis on the predisposition of the youth, in that they are good at recruiting mentors or garnering social support. Others have speculated that social support serves to buffer children from the high levels of stress. There are also differing views regarding how the support mechanism might function. Some researchers seem to suggest that mentors may serve to compensate for an absence of a strong parental bond. Others imply that mentors serve as a supplemental support by reducing the child's dependence on immediate family members for support. Little is known about either type of bond. In what ways do natural helping relationships differ from assigned mentoring relationships? How might the intensity of the relationship be linked to child resilience? Freedman (1988) pointed out that some bonds are characterized by extraordinary commitment, while others may be described as helpful neighborliness. Clarification of these issues is necessary for planning successful interventions to promote resilience. These issues will be addressed in the final section of the chapter.

Incorporating Resilience into Children's Therapy: Lessons to be Learned

In addition to understanding the conditions under which psychopathology may be averted, the study of resilience may be relevant for guiding treatment. "For clinicians, intervention in the lives of high-risk children and youth means an attempt to tilt the balance from vulnerability to resiliency, either by *decreasing* an individual's exposure to biological risk factors or stressful life events, or by *increasing* the number of protective factors (problem-solving skills, sources of support) that she or he can draw upon" (Werner, 1989, p. 172). We turn now to a discussion on how to foster resilience. The approach taken here is to parallel the research on resilience by outlining possible points of intervention on the individual, family, and community resources. With regard to each of these points of intervention, particular emphasis is placed on how to incorporate the family into the child's therapy.

The first lesson to be learned from the literature on resilience is that there are likely to be numerous individual characteristics that are associated with resilience. In working with children and their families, it is important for the therapist to be informed about the range of protective factors. For example, an individual may learn new ways to respond to the stress he or she encounters. However, other attributes like intelligence, physical attractiveness, and birth order may be less amenable to change. Implying that interventions aimed at facilitating adaptive coping "level the playing field" would be misleading. The informed therapist will be able to acknowledge the role these attributes may potentially play in facilitating or interfering with successful adaptation of the individual. Indeed, part of the assessment process involves acknowledging factors in the client that are potentially amenable to change and those less so.

With this cautionary note in mind, we turn now to one area of research that holds a great deal of promise with regard to intervention. There is growing evidence that the amount of stress that is endured by the individual is not necessarily closely linked with risk; rather, the methods one uses to cope with the stress encountered are more likely to influence adaptation (e.g., Folkman & Lazarus, 1986). But what is meant by the term *coping?* Defining the construct has proven to be a paramount challenge (e.g., Compas, Worsham, & Ey, 1992; Folkman, 1991). Perhaps one of the more accepted definitions is provided by Folkman and Lazarus (1980): "the cognitive and behavioral efforts made to master, tolerate, or reduce external and internal demands and conflicts among them" (p. 223). The two domains of coping that have received the greatest attention in the literature are problem-focused coping and emotion-focused coping. In short, problem-focused coping entails acting on the problem that is the source of stress. Emotion-focused coping pertains to the acting on (or regulating) the emotion related to a stressful event.

Typically individuals possess an arsenal of strategies that might be used when stress is encountered. Problem-solving strategies are the most commonly used approach. The findings in the literature on resilience (e.g., Werner & Smith, 1982) are similar to other studies of risk populations (e.g., Billings & Moos, 1984), in that problem-focused coping is typically associated with psychological health. Although emotion-focused coping may be associated to some degree with maturity (Compas, Worsham, & Ey, 1992), reliance on emotion-focused coping has been linked with various forms of psychopathology, including depression (e.g., Billings & Moos, 1984).

Despite these overall patterns between coping and risk found in the literature, there is considerable evidence to suggest that a more detailed analysis of emotion-focused and problem-focused coping will be helpful when planning interventions. Some have stressed the importance of a repertoire of coping responses that can be applied flexibly according to characteristics of the stressor (Compas, Malcarne, & Fondacaro, 1988). Others have noted that some aspects of emotion-focused coping are adaptive and others are less so. Nolen-Hoeksema (1991) and her colleagues have focused their study on two types of emotion-focused coping, rumination and distraction. They found that depressed adults tended to focus attention on negative emotions. Furthermore, subjects with depressive symptoms who were asked to ruminate became more depressed compared to those who were asked to use distraction (Nolen-

420   Children in Therapy

Hoeksema & Morrow, 1993). With few exceptions (e.g., Klimes-Dougan et al., 1997), ruminative coping responses have not been examined in children or adolescents, although it is likely that Nolen-Hoeksema's approach to facilitating more adaptive coping strategies may be useful with this population.

The issue of how appraisals relate to adaptive coping has received considerable attention as well. Much of the literature has focussed on perceptions of control. Folkman (1984) hypothesized that problem-focused efforts are more adaptive when applied to events that are under the individual's control and emotion-focused coping is more adaptive when the situation is recognized as uncontrollable. Although the research supports the relationship between problem-focused coping and perceptions of control, emotion-focused coping appears to be more closely linked to emotional arousal (reviewed by Compas, 1995). Examples of how the appraisal process might be crucial for dealing with a number of family disruptions are provided. Beardslee and Podorefsky (1988) noted the importance of accurately appraising a stressor in offspring of depressed parents. They found that resilient youth were able to appraise the stress associated with their parent's depression realistically and act in a manner that was congruent with this appraisal. They found that it was helpful for the youth to realize that their parent's behavior was largely beyond their control and have applied these findings when conducting preventative interventions with offspring of depressed parents (Beardslee, 1990). Similarly, some interventions targeting children whose parents have divorced attempt to affect appraisals by clarifying confusing or upsetting information (Pedro-Carroll, 1997). Presumably this process of clarification allows the child to apply coping strategies more adaptively.

How might intervention enhance coping efforts of children and adolescents? Compas (1995) suggests a sequential and hierarchical model for adolescents, consisting of three levels. The first level involves the promotion of effective coping with normative stresses. Psychoeducational programs that are taught in the school may represent primary prevention efforts. The second and third levels require more targeted interventions for youth who are experiencing acute stress (e.g., divorce) and severe chronic stress (e.g., poverty or parental mental illness). Specialized efforts in the form of individual and group therapy would be necessary to promote coping strategies that match the situational demands.

The second lesson to be learned is that coping takes place within the context of the family system. Families may serve as resources for effective coping as well as impediments to effective coping (Compas & Epping, 1993;

McClellan & Trupin, 1989). Families may serve as sources of information and social support. Also, some coping strategies are adopted as a result of the instruction, reinforcement, and modeling provided by parents and other family members (Compas, Worsham, & Ey, 1992). There is some evidence to suggest that the coping patterns are similar for family members (e.g., Klimes-Dougan & Bolger, 1998). Finally, families provide rules and enact regulatory processes that influence the coping processes used by the individual.

Interventions targeting families may be one of the most important ways in which resilience is fostered. Pellegrini (1990) has set forth a convincing argument as to why such an approach may be important:

> Whereas no risk or protective factor has emerged, or is likely to emerge, as the single variable whose presence or absence accounts for vulnerability or resilience across the lifespan, a case can be made that family discord or harmony constitutes a "first among equals." Harmonious family relationships seem to lay the foundation of feelings of security and control in young children which, in turn, appear to account for their ability to modulate affect, establish positive social relationships, and successfully negotiate the variety of developmental tasks and challenges that children confront. (p. 206)

The recommended type of intervention involving the family may differ according to the presenting problems. Marital therapy may be recommended for some families, parent training for others, and for still others structural or systemic family therapy approaches. Therapeutic efforts should be aimed at decreasing family discord, facilitating a supportive and warm family environment, and promoting the implementation of competent discipline. Thus, assessment and interventions that focus on the family will undoubtedly prove to be one of the most effective means of fostering resilience.

A third lesson to be learned is that community resources are important in promoting resilience. Multiple stresses in the child's environment often necessitate the support of those outside the family (Wolin & Wolin, 1993). The previous discussion about external support systems is relevant in this regard. Parents may need to be encouraged to allow their children to have these supplemental support systems. A depressed mother may not look to others, who may be capable of temporarily relieving her burden of parenting. Intervention goals promoting social support may be largely a matter of case management. Often the therapist must be the impetus for acquiring this support through agencies like Big Brother, Girl Scouts, and others. Furthermore, it is likely that efforts to educate the public about the role of mentors and others outside the family in promoting resilience would be worthwhile. Brooks (1994) and others have targeted teachers and school counselors to inform them of the potential importance of their relationship with at-risk children.

Providing social support for the parents may also be important and may have both direct and indirect effects. There is considerable evidence to suggest that parents with adequate social networks are more likely to provide supportive environments to their children (e.g., Brown & Harris, 1978). Olds and colleagues (1998) concluded from the results of their studies and a review of other studies that comprehensive prenatal and early childhood home visitation programs administered by trained nurses can affect early risks and reduce conduct disorder and antisocial behavior among children and youth born into at-risk families. They hypothesized that the support provided to these mothers was an important factor in accounting for these findings. Indeed, mothers who lived alone made the greatest improvements. Perhaps these mothers were able to benefit most from the support and information provided.

In conclusion, the lessons learned from the study of resilient children indicate that interventions aimed at individual, family, and community levels all may lead to better outcomes for children. Clinicians are accustomed to attending to risks and challenges in children's environments, but attention to protective factors that may foster resilience could also be profitable. Perhaps through supporting and building upon these strengths, the mental health community can help children not only survive but flourish.

Bonnie Klimes-Dougan, Ph.D., is Assistant Professor of Psychology, The Catholic University of America, Washington, D.C.

Kimberly T. Kendziora, Ph.D., is a research analyst at the American Institutes for Research, Washington, D.C.

References

Apfel, N., & Seitz, V. (1997). The firstborn sons of African American teenage mothers: Perspectives on risk and resilience. In S. S. Luthar, J. A. Burack, D. Cicchetti, & J. R. Weisz (Eds.), *Developmental psychopathology: Perspectives on adjustment, risk, and disorder* (pp. 486–506). New York: Cambridge University.

Beardslee, W. R. (1990). Development of a clinician-based preventive intervention for families with affective disorders. *Journal of Preventive Psychiatry and Allied Disciplines, 4,* 39–61.

Beardslee, W. R., & Podorefsky, M. A. (1988). Resilient adolescents whose parents have serious affective and other psychiatric disorders: Importance of self-understanding and relationships. *American Journal of Psychiatry, 145,* 63–69.

Billings, A. G., & Moos, R. H. (1984). Coping, stress, and social resources among adults with unipolar depression. *Journal of Personality and Social Psychology, 46,* 877–891.

Brooks, R. B. (1994). Children at risk: Fostering resilience and hope. *American Journal of Orthopsychiatry, 64,* 545–553.

Brown, G. W., & Harris, T. (1978). *Social origins of depression: A study of psychiatric disorder in women.* New York: Free.

Cicchetti, D. (1984). The emergence of developmental psychopathology. *Child Development, 55,* 1–7.

Compas, B. E. (1995). Promoting successful coping during adolescence. In M. Rutter (Ed.), *Psychosocial disturbances in young people: Challenges for prevention* (pp. 247–273). New York: Cambridge University.

Compas, B. E., & Epping, J. E. (1993). Stress and coping in children and families: Implications for children coping with disaster. In C. F. Saylor (Ed.), *Children and disasters* (pp. 11–28). New York: Plenum.

Compas, B. E., Malcarne, V. L., & Fondacaro, K. M. (1988). Coping with stressful events in older children and young adolescents. *Journal of Consulting and Clinical Psychology, 56,* 405–411.

Compas, B. E., Worsham, N. L., & Ey, S. (1992). Conceptual and developmental issues in children's coping with stress. In A. M. La Greca, L. J. Siegel, J. L. Wallander, & C. E. Walker (Eds.), *Stress and coping with child health* (pp. 7–24). New York: Guilford.

Cowan, P. A., Cowan, C. P., & Schulz, M. S. (1996). Thinking about risk and resilience in families. In E. M. Hetherington & E. A. Blechman (Eds.), *Stress, coping, and resiliency in children and families* (pp. 1–38). Mawah, NJ: Lawrence Erlbaum.

Cowen, E. L., Work, W. C., & Wyman, P. A. (1997). The Rochester Child Resilience Project (RCRP): Facts found, lessons learned, and future directions divined. In S. S. Luthar, J. A. Burack, D. Cicchetti, & J. R. Weisz (Eds.), *Developmental psychopathology: Perspectives on adjustment, risk, and disorder* (pp. 527–547). New York: Cambridge University.

Emery, R. E., & Forehand, R. (1994). Parental divorce and children's well-being: A focus on resilience. In R. J. Haggerty, L. R. Sherrod, N. Garmezy, & M. Rutter (Eds.), *Stress, risk, and resilience in children and adolescents: Processes, mechanisms, and interventions* (pp. 64–99). New York: Cambridge University.

Erickson, M. F., Egeland, B., & Pianta, R. (1989). The effects of maltreatment on the development of young children. In D. Cicchetti & V. Carlson (Eds.), *Child maltreatment: Theory and research on the causes and consequences of child abuse and neglect* (pp. 647–684). New York: Cambridge University.

Farber, E. A., & Egeland, B. (1987). Invulnerability among abused and neglected children. In E. J. Anthony & B. J. Cohler (Eds.), *The invulnerable child* (pp. 253–288). New York: Guilford.

Field, T., Healy, B., Goldstein, S., Perry, S., Bendaell, D., Schanberg, S., Zimmerman, E. A., & Kuhn, C. (1988). Infants of depressed mothers show "depressed" behavior even with non-depressed adults. *Child Development, 59,* 1569–1579.

Folkman, S. (1984). Personal control an stress and coping processes: A theoretical analysis. *Journal of Personality and Social Psychology, 46,* 839–852.

Folkman, S. (1991). Coping across the life span: Theoretical issues. In E. M. Cummings, A. L. Greene, & K. H. Karraker (Eds.), *Life-span developmental psychology: Perspectives on stress and coping,* (pp. 3–19). Hillsdale, NJ: Lawrence Erlbaum.

Folkman, S., & Lazarus, R. S. (1980). An analysis of coping in a middle-aged community sample. *Journal of Health and Social Behavior, 21,* 219–239.

Folkman, S., & Lazarus, R. S. (1986). Stress processes and depressive symptomatology. *Journal of Abnormal Psychology, 95,* 107–113.

Freedman, M. (1988). *Partners in growth: Elder mentors and at-risk youth.* Philadelphia, PA: Public/Private Ventures.

Garmezy, N. (1971). Vulnerability research and the issue of primary prevention. *American Journal of Orthopsychiatry, 41,* 101–116.

Garmezy, N. (1974). The study of competence in children at risk for severe psychopathology. In E. J. Anthony & C. Koupernik (Eds.), *The child in his family: Vol. 3. Children at psychiatric risk* (pp. 77–98). New York: Wiley.

Garmezy, N. (1985). Stress-resistant children: The search for protective factors. In J. E. Stevenson (Ed.), *Resent research in developmental psychopathology* (pp. 213–233). Oxford: Pergamon.

Garmezy, N. (1987). Stress, competence, and development: Continuities in the study of schizophrenic adults, children vulnerable to psychopathology, and the search for stress resistant children. *American Journal of Orthopsychiatry, 57,* 159–174.

Garmezy, N., Masten, A. S., & Tellegen, A. (1984). The study of stress and competence in children: A building block for developmental psychopathology. *Child Development, 55,* 97–111.

Gotlib, I. H., & Avison, W. R. (1993). Children at risk for psychopathology. In C. G. Costello (Ed.), *Basic issues in psychology* (pp. 271–319). New York: Guilford.

Gribble, P. A., Cowen, E. L., Wyman, P. A., Work, W. C., Wannon, M., & Raoof, A. (1993). Parent and child views of the parent-child relationship and resilient outcomes among urban children. *Journal of Child Psychology and Psychiatry and Allied Disciplines, 34,* 507–519.

Hammen, C. (1997). Children of depressed parents: The stress context. In S. Wolchik & I. Sandler (Eds.), *Handbook of children's coping: linking theory and intervention* (pp. 131–157). New York: Plenum.

Hetherington, E. M. (1991). The role of individual differences and family relationships in children's coping with divorce and remarriage. In P. A. Cowan & E. M. Hetherington (Eds.), *Family transitions: Advances in family research series* (pp. 165–194). Hillsdale, NJ: Lawrence Erlbaum.

Klimes-Dougan, B., & Bolger, A. K. (1998). Coping with maternal depressed affect and depression: Adolescent children of depressed and well mothers. *Journal of Youth and Adolescence, 27,* 1–15.

Klimes-Dougan, B., Simon-Thomas, J., Osman, K. S., McBride, A. M., Buchalter, A. J., & Welsh, J. D. (1997, April). *The experience, expression, and regulation of sadness and anger: Implications for the development of psychopathology.* Poster presented at the biennial meeting of the Society for Research in Child Development, Washington, DC.

Langlois, J. H., Ritter, J. M., Casey, R. J., & Sawin, D. B. (1995). Infant attractiveness predicts maternal behaviors and attitudes. *Developmental Psychology, 31,* 464–472.

Luthar, S. S. (1993). Annotation: Methodological and conceptual issues in research on childhood resilience. *Journal of Child Psychology and Psychiatry and Allied Disciplines, 34,* 441–453.

Luthar, S. S., & Zigler, E. (1991). Vulnerability and competence: A review of the research on resilience in childhood. *American Journal of Orthopsychiatry, 61,* 6–22.

McClellan, J., & Trupin, E. (1989). Prevention of psychiatric disorders in children. *Hospital and Community Psychiatry, 40,* 630–636.

Musick, J. S., Cohler, B. J., & Dincin, J. (1982). *Risk and recovery in the children of mentally ill mothers.* Chicago: Department of Mental Health and Developmental Disabilities.

Nolen-Hoeksema, S. (1991). Responses to depression and their effects on the duration of depressive symptoms. *Journal of Abnormal Psychology, 100,* 569–582.

Nolen-Hoeksema, S., & Morrow, J. (1993). Effects of rumination and distraction on naturally occurring depressed mood. *Cognition and Emotion, 7,* 561–570.

Olds, D., Hendreson, C., Kitzman, H., Eckenrode, J., Cole, R., & Tatelbaum, R. (1998). The promise of home visitation: Results of two randomized trials. *Journal of Community Psychology, 26,* 5–21.

Osofsky, J.D., Hann, D. M., & Peebles, C. (1993). Adolescent parenthood: Risks and opportunities for mothers and infants. In C. H. Zeanah (Ed.), *Handbook of infant mental health* (pp. 106–119). New York: Guilford.

Park, C., & Cohen, L. H. (1988). Religious beliefs and practices and the coping process. In B. N. Carpenter (Ed.), *Personal coping: Theory, research, and application* (pp. 185–198). Westport, CO: Praeger.

Parker, G. R., Cowen, E. L., Work, W. C., & Wyman, P. A. (1990). Test correlates of stress affected and stress resilient outcomes among urban children. *Journal of Primary Prevention, 11,* 19–35.

Pedro-Carroll, J. (1997). The Children of Divorce Intervention Program: Fostering resilient outcomes for school-aged children. In G. W. Albee & T. P. Gullotta (Eds.), *Primary prevention works. Issues in children's and families' lives, Vol. 6.* (pp. 213–238). Thousand Oaks, CA: Sage.

Pelaez-Nogueras, M., Field, T., Cigales, M., Gonzalez, A., & Clasky, S. (1994). Infants of depressed mothers show less "depressed" behavior with a familiar caregiver. *Infant of Mental Health Journal, 15,* 358–367.

Pellegrini, D. S. (1990). Psychosocial risk and protective factors in childhood. *Developmental and Behavioral Pediatrics, 11,* 201–209.

Rachman, S. (1979). The concept of required helpfulness. *Behavior Research & Therapy, 17,* 1–6.

Radke-Yarrow, M., & Brown, E. (1993). Resilience and vulnerability in children of multiple-risk families. *Development & Psychopathology, 5,* 581–592.

Radke-Yarrow, M., & Sherman, T. L. (1990). Hard growing children who survive. In J. E. Rolf, A. S., Masten, D. Cicchetti, K. Nuechterlein, & S. Weintraub (Eds.), *Risk and protective factors in the development of psychopathology* (pp. 97–119). New York: Cambridge University.

Reiss, D., Hetherington, E. M., Plomin, R., Howe, G. W., Simmens, S. J., Henderson, S. H., O'Connor, T. J., Bussell, D. A., Anderson, E. R., & Law, T. (1995). Genetic questions for environmental studies: Differential parenting and psychopathology in adolescence. *Archives of General Psychiatry, 52,* 925–936.

Rende, R., & Plomin, R. (1993). Families at risk for psychopathology: Who becomes affected and why? *Development and Psychopathology, 5,* 529–540.

Rhodes, J. E. (1994). Older and wiser: Mentoring relationships in childhood and adolescence. *Journal of Primary Prevention, 14,* 187–196.

Rutter, M. (1976). Isle of Wight studies, 1964-1974. *Psychological Medicine, 6,* 313–332.

Rutter, M. (1979). Protective factors in children's response to stress and disadvantage. In M. W. Kint & J. E. Rolf (Eds.), Primary prevention in psychopathology, Vol. 3: Social competence in children (pp. 49–74). Hanover, NH: University Press of New England.

Rutter, M. (1987). Psychosocial resilience and protective mechanisms. *American Journal of Orthopsychiatry, 57,* 316–331.

Rutter, M. (1989). Isle of Wight revisited: Twenty-five years of child psychiatric epidemiology. *Journal of the American Academy of Child & Adolescent Psychiatry, 28,* 633–653.

Rutter, M., Maughan, B., Mortimore, P., Ouston, J., with Smith, A. (1979). *Fifteen thousand hours: Secondary schools and their effects on children.* Cambridge, MA: Harvard University.

Sameroff, A. J., Seifer, R., Baldwin, A., & Baldwin, C. (1993). Stability of intelligence from preschool to adolescence: The influence of social and family risk factors. *Child Development, 64,* 86–97.

Samuels, C. A., Butterworth, G., Roberts, T., & Graupner, L. (1994). Facial aesthetics: Babies prefer attractiveness to symmetry. *Perception, 23,* 823–831.

Sroufe, L. A., & Rutter, M. (1984). The domain of developmental psychopathology. *Child Development, 55,* 17–29.

Stegelin, D. A., & Frankel, J. (1993). Families of lower-income employed mothers. In J. Frankel (Ed.), *The employed mother and the family context. Focus on women series* (Vol. 14, pp. 115–131). New York: Springer.

Wallerstein, J. S., & Blakeslee, S. (1989). *Second chances: Men, women, and children a decade after divorce.* New York: Basic.

Werner, E. E. (1985). Stress and protective factors in children's lives. In A. R. Nicol (Ed.), *Longitudinal studies in child psychology and psychiatry.* New York: Wiley.

Werner, E. E. (1986). Resilient offspring of alcoholics: A longitudinal study from birth to age 18. *Journal of Studies on Alcohol, 47,* 34–40.

Werner, E. E. (1989). Vulnerability and resiliency: A longitudinal perspective. In M. Brambring, F. Loesel, & Skowronek (Eds.), *Children at risk: Assessment, longitudinal research, and intervention. Prevention and intervention in childhood and adolescence* (Vol. 7, pp. 158–172). Berlin: Walter De Gruyter.

Werner, E. E. (1990). Protective factors and individual resilience. In S. J. Meisels & J. P. Shonkoff (Eds.), *Handbook of early childhood intervention* (pp. 97–116). New York: Cambridge University.

Werner, E. E. (1993). Risk, resilience, and recovery: Perspectives from the Kauai Longitudinal study. *Development and Psychopathology, 5,* 503–515.

Werner, E. E. (1995). Resilience in development. *Current Directions in Psychological Science, 4,* 81–85.

Werner, E. E., & Smith, R. S. (1982). *Vulnerable but invincible: A study of resilient children.* New York: McGraw-Hill.

Werner, E. E., & Smith, R. S. (1992). *Overcoming the odds: High-risk children from birth to adulthood.* Ithaca: Cornell University.

Wolin, S., & Wolin, S. (1993). *The resilient self: How survivors of troubled familes rise above adversity.* New York: Villard Books.

Worland, J., Weeks, D. G., & Janes, C. L. (1987). Predicting mental health in children at risk. In E. J. Anthony & B. J. Cohler, (Eds.), *The invulnerable child.* New York: Guilford.

16

Children's Social and Emotional Development: Applications for Family Therapy

Robert E. Nida

Sarah Pierce

Our lives are bound together with the lives of others; still, we remain selves—flesh and blood persons, with private hopes and ambitions, motives and expectations, quirks and foibles, and potential for creative growth.

Michael Nichols, *The Self in the System*

. . . After all, a person's a person, no matter how small.

Dr. Seuss, *Horton Hears a Who!*

Dr. Seuss's well-known children's book begins with Horton the elephant "enjoying the jungle's great joys" by relaxing in a pool of water located in the "Jungle of Nool." Suddenly Horton hears a small noise and stops splashing to look toward the sound. He discovers that the noise is coming from a small speck of dust blowing past in the air. He reasons that there must be someone on top of that small speck of dust, "some creature of very small size, too small to be seen by an elephant's eyes." He then discovers that there is a "person" on the particle of dust who has "no way to steer" and decides that he had better rescue this individual, "because, after all, a person's a person, no matter how small." In the spirit of Horton's discovery, we remind the reader of a very fundamental fact, that despite their small size, children are persons too, and to a considerable extent dependent upon the people and places that surround them.

428

Of equal importance is the fundamental concept that in the course of growing up children undergo important developmental changes and face a number of challenging tasks. Developmental theory and research indicate that there are predictable sequences of growth and change that occur across childhood. While most children experience typical sequences of development, at some point in time they may experience physical, emotional, and behavioral problems that are usually transient in nature. These problems often result from the stresses of development and interactions with societal expectations (Schroeder & Gordon, 1991). Family therapists are faced with the challenge of helping families whose children experience emotional and behavioral problems, as well as helping parents manage life stressors and support children's normal growth and development. Knowledge of the age-related changes in development and the mechanisms that underlie behavior and development may add considerably to the therapist's repertoire of therapeutic and intervention techniques.

The purpose of this chapter is to provide a brief overview of social and emotional development in children, as well as to consider various developmental issues that may relate to the therapeutic process. The socioemotional behavior and development of children is increasingly being recognized as having considerable clinical relevance (Campbell, 1990; Hartup, 1989; Lewis, 1989; Schroeder & Gordon, 1991), since the child's emotional signals and cues may serve as an indicator of his or her state of being. Recently, the emotional well-being and moral character of children have received prominent attention in the popular literature. For example, Goleman (1995) developed the concept of "emotional intelligence" (i.e., the ability to control one's emotional reactions and "read" the signals of others), while Coles (1997) has written extensively about children's "moral intelligence." The work of Goleman and Coles follows that of developmentalists who introduced the concept of "social competence"—the ability to engage peers and adults in a friendly and cooperative manner and to be resourceful and achievement-oriented (Anderson & Messick, 1974; Baumrind, 1967; Connelly & Bruner, 1974; White, 1985). Thus, the quality of social relationships serves as an indicator of the child's social well-being. The formation of friendships, for example, is considered to be a "developmental advantage" in socioemotional development (Hartup, 1989). Conversely, peer rejection in childhood is considered to be a risk factor and has been consistently found to relate to later adjustment problems (Coie & Dodge, 1983; Parker & Asher, 1987).

Throughout this chapter we will consider a number of topics relevant to family therapists' work with children. We begin with a brief mention of developmental and family theory, pointing out several developmental trends. Our discussion of socioemotional development begins with the examination of the self system, which is divided into four parts: (1) the self-concept, (2) self-esteem, (3) the moral self, and (4) the social self. The section on emotional development includes coverage of the expression of emotions and emotion regulation. We conclude our discussion by briefly summarizing a childhood assessment and intervention system developed by Schroeder and Gordon (1991). We focus primarily on socioemotional development with some reservation, because we recognize that the child is a whole person—physical, cognitive, emotional, and social—and that these domains are highly related or connected. We are necessarily highly selective in our coverage of social and emotional development, presenting what we consider to be clinically relevant behavior and abilities. In addition, it is beyond the scope of this chapter to present a complete and integrated view of development. At best, limited integration occurs as we consider how certain developmental systems, both biological and psychological, are related to social/emotional functioning.

Family and Developmental Perspectives of the Child

Family Systems Theory

Family systems theory tends to focus on interpersonal relationships between family members as the fundamental unit of analysis. Although family systems theory assigns to the child some measure of autonomy and individual functioning, he or she is ultimately beholdened to and maintained by homeostatic features of the family system. Deviations or perturbations on the part of the child are seen as the result of interactional patterns between family members. The mechanisms of change and the regulation of behavior are primarily external to the child. The problems children experience are viewed as being a function of the interpersonal context or being "systemic." As Minuchin (1985) explains, "if the individual is part of an organized family system, he or she is never truly independent and can only be understood in context" (p. 290).

Developmental Theory

The field of human development also recognizes the family as the primary context for the child, with the most pervasive influence over him or her. Yet, developmentalists are more inclined to describe the child as a developing individual who functions in a dynamic, continuous, and reciprocal process of interaction with his or her environment, including relationships and contexts beyond the family (Magnusson, 1988). Furthermore, human development is seen as the outcome of an enduring interplay between biology and experience. Ecological or transactional theories propose, for example, that developmental change (both positive and negative) is the result of the "transactional dialogue among each child with his or her unique biological/genetic makeup, the physical and social environment, and the cultural milieu into which he or she is born" (Schroeder & Gordon, 1991, p. 4).

Developmental Systems Theory

More recently, other scholars have advanced developmental systems theory as a theoretical perspective to account for the complexity of human development. Developmental systems, as proposed by Gottlieb (1996), recognizes that human development occurs as a function of ongoing, mutual interactions among many systems. Systems are hierarchical in nature and include such levels as DNA, RNA, protein synthesis, cells, organs, neurophysiological systems, and psychological systems, as well as systems that are external to the individual (e.g., the family and the broader social networks in which the family is embedded). Developmental systems theory recognizes systemic origins of behavior and development, but takes into consideration systems that are "internal" and "external" to the individual. For example, emotion regulation involves the interplay of cognitive strategies (a psychological system) and neuroregulatory processes (a biological system). Furthermore, internal systems generally interact within the context of some system external to the child, such as the family, school, or peer group. Developmental systems theory recognizes the ongoing and reciprocal influences that various systems have on the developing person. Thus, there are both "bottom up" and "top down" influences. See Efran, Greene, and Gordon (1998) and Reiss (1995) for further discussion of the integration of family studies/therapy and human development.

Trends in the Field of Child Development

Paralleling changes in developmental theory, the field of child development has witnessed several important trends in research and application. The first trend is an increasing emphasis on individual differences in development rather than relying solely on normative descriptions of behavior and development. Individual differences refer to the extent children vary along certain dimensions such as temperament, learning styles, personality, intelligence, information-processing abilities, experience, etc. The normative approach was based on epigenetic or maturational theory (e.g., G. Stanley Hall, Arnold Gesell, Erik Erikson), which regarded child development as a genetically determined, automatically unfolding series of events. In normative approaches, measurements of behaviors are taken on large numbers of children and age-related averages are computed to represent typical development (Berk, 1996). The concept of developmental milestones, or the average age at which children acquire various skills and abilities, grew out of this tradition. Although developmental milestones serve as an indispensable tool by which to delineate typical from atypical development, strict adherence to milestones may result in a failure to account for differences in the rates and patterns of change. Most developmentalists do not think of children as simply being "average" or "above average"—like the children of Lake Wobegon (Keilor, 1985)! Rather, children are "alike but different."

The second major trend is the increasing attention to biological factors that influence development across time and that may contribute to differences in the rates and patterns of change. It is now well established that genes are part of a multilevel system that influences a broad range of developmental outcomes such as cognitive functioning, personality differences, and psychopathology (Reiss, 1995). Other biological factors may include underlying neurophysiological systems (e.g., neural pathways, hypothalamic-pituitary-adrenocortical system) that are consistently related to certain behaviors (e.g., self-regulation), and neurochemical systems such as hormones and neurotransmitters (i.e., chemical messengers) that have been found to influence physical maturation (e.g., puberty) and attentional capacity (e.g., ADHD), respectively. Most importantly, developmentalists are especially interested in the ways that these biological systems interact within social contexts (e.g., Magnusson, 1988).

The third trend concerns an orientation toward information-processing, such as social problem-solving skills. Social problem-solving skills are a vital part of the child's growing repertoire of cognitive abilities, which in turn may affect the quality of his or her social interactions with others. Children vary in their ability to interpret social cues in the environment and then use their skills to mediate social interactions with peers and family members (e.g., Dodge, Pettit, McClaskey, & Brown, 1986; Pettit, Dodge, & Brown, 1988).

Children's Socioemotional Development

The Self System

In this section we focus our attention on different components of the self system, a psychological system that includes the self-concept, self-esteem, the moral self, and the social self, which includes relationships with other children. Nichols (1987), calling upon family therapists to recognize the role of the individual in the family system, argues that at the heart of the individual are the inner workings of the self, or the "self in the system." He proposes that family therapists may have to shift their attention to individual dynamics, especially when traditional interventions do not work or when individual members are unwilling and unable to change. We embrace this challenge by calling upon family therapists to consider developmental changes of self that occur throughout childhood. See Breunlin, Schwartz, and Kune-Karrer (1992) and Harter (1999) for further discussion of intrapsychic constructs and clinical applications.

The self has been described as the core of the personality and perhaps the most important construct of socioemotional development. Knowledge of self offers the child a sense of permanence and continuity that endures despite momentary changes in the environment and fluctuations in mood (Damon, 1983). According to Brooks-Gunn and Lewis (1982), the acquisition of the self by the end of the second year not only facilitates the acquisition of social knowledge, but also underlies social competence, peer relations, gender identity, and empathy. Erikson's psychosocial theory proposes that defining oneself is really an organizing theme of life and is also the cornerstone of social and emotional development. During the child's quest for identity, the child must gain a sense of security, control, and competence as he or she interacts with the environment.

Harter's (1999) recent analysis describes the central organizational and functional contributions of the self system across childhood. In examining the development of the self, Harter argues that the construction of the self is the result of both cognitive and social processes. From a cognitive-developmental framework, the construction of the self inevitably occurs due to the mind's powerful ability to organize and interpret experience. Citing cognitive-developmental theory, Harter notes, "Our species has been designed to actively create theories about one's world, to make meaning of one's experiences, including the construction of a theory of self" (p. 8). Due to the abilities and limitations of each developmental period, however, age-related changes in the structural content of self-representations are evident. In the section below we will highlight some of these developmental changes.

While children are active agents in their own development, the construction of the self is also the result of socialization processes. Socialization experiences with caregivers, teachers, and peers produce individual differences in the content of self-representations and whether self-evaluations are positive or negative. How children are treated will determine whether the child comes to view the self as "competent versus incapable, as lovable versus undeserving of others' affection, as worthy of esteem versus lacking value" (Harter, 1999, p. 9).

Self-evaluations that comprise much of the self system are also accompanied by "self-conscious" emotions such as pride and shame. Self-conscious emotions, which are thought to be largely the result of socialization experiences, may have either developmental benefits or liabilities. Children who receive praise and encouragement for their efforts will develop a sense of pride in their accomplishments. Conversely, children who are habitually criticized for their performance will develop a sense of shame that can be emotionally debilitating. Thus, the self system can be viewed as a repository of our many experiences. Each of these themes will be addressed in subsequent sections.

The self system, as described by Harter, is consistent with the concept of "internal working models" initially advanced by Bowlby (1980). Internal working models are defined as emotionally ladened mental representations of the self and others which are derived from interactional experiences. These models function outside of conscious awareness to direct attention and organize memory in such a way as to guide interpersonal behavior and the interpretation of social eperience. Speaking of the internal working model's role as "organizers of experience and filterers of information," Belsky & Pensky (1988) stress the "active role of the individual in interpreting the experienced world and the inclination to assimilate information into pre-existing models" (p. 198). Internal working models are believed to have their origins during infancy, undergo developmental changes across childhood, and are carried forward into adulthood. By the adult years these models become rather resistent to change, yet they are susceptible to modification. "Interpersonal development," according to Belsky and Pensky, "is likely to be conservative, as a result, as the individual disregards inconsistent information or reinterprets it, rather than modify his/her model" (p. 198). The concept of internal working models, therefore, offer a compelling explanation as to why individuals can be so resistent to change during therapy.

Self-Knowledge

The emergence of self-knowledge, or self-awareness, occurs during the second year of life. Two ways to investigate the development of self-awareness are through the emergence of self-recognition and the systematic progression of self-definitions. Self-recognition refers to the ability of infants to correctly identify images of themselves. Lewis and Brooks (1978) conducted a clever study to examine the emergence of self-recognition. They examined infants between 9 and 24 months of age to determine when infants can understand the significance of their own reflection in a mirror. Mothers surreptitiously placed a spot of rouge on their infant's nose and, after a time, had the infants look at themselves in the mirror. None of the 9- to 12-month-old babies responded to the mark of rouge on their faces; rather, they tried to touch the "baby in the mirror." Approximately 25% of the babies in the 15- to 18-month age range and 75% of the 21- to 24-month-olds attempted to touch or wipe the mark off their face, as if to say, "That's me." Self-recognition represents one of the crowning achievements of infancy. Infants who have not achieved self-recognition by the end of the second year may be at risk for developmental delay.

Once self-recognition has emerged during late infancy, changes in self-definition continue in a predictable progression during early and late childhood. Self-definition begins with the development of the "verbal self," which emerges with the acquisition of language. The young toddler describes herself in terms of personal pronouns ("I" or "me" versus "you"), personal attributes ("big," "little," "curly hair"), and possessions ("mine" versus "yours"). Later self-descriptions may include such statements as "I play" or "I can do this." Such verbalizations serve as indications that the establishment of self is well under way. Adults can facilitate infants' self-awareness and social development by: (1) holding young babies in front of a mirror and playing games such as touching and naming body parts or making faces (e.g., "Look, see _____ in the mirror?"), (2) taking the baby's picture at various ages and looking at the pictures together with the baby, pointing out such characteristics as hair and eyes, (3) playing interactive games such as "peek-a-boo" and "pat-a-cake" as soon as the baby can reciprocate such interactions and increasing the complexity of games as the infant gets older (e.g., "tea parties"), (4) playing games using various body parts (e.g., "This little piggy"), (5) providing culturally and developmentally appropriate toys, books, and materials, (6) providing infants with opportunities to interact with other infants, children, and adults, and (7) encouraging independence and self-sufficiency (Snow, 1998). Infant social skills are best assessed in natural contexts such as play (Odom & Munson, 1996). *The Transdisciplinary Play-Based Assessment* (TPBA) is a widely used measure (Linder, 1993). Other standardized instruments to assess social skills of infants include the *Vineland Adaptive Behavior Scales* (Sparrow, Balla, & Cicchetti, 1984) and the *Battelle Developmental Inventory* (Newborg, Stock, Wnek, Guiduabaldi, & Sviniski, 1988).

The Categorical Self

During the early childhood years, the "categorical" self emerges, as children become increasingly able to define themselves along a number of dimensions

and categories, including age, size, gender, beliefs, values, and activity preferences. Young children will often define themselves according to age ("I'm
three years old"), gender ("I'm a girl"), physical dimensions ("I have brown
hair and blue eyes"), or physical skills ("I can run fast," "I can hop on one
foot!"). The young child also defines the self in terms of preferences ("I like
ice cream," I love my cat Rudy") and possessions ("I have a flashlight and
keys"). Self-representations during this period remain highly differentiated or
isolated from one another. Due to their cognitive limitations, young children
may be unable to provide integrated and coherent descriptions of self. Among
preschoolers there is typically an absence of the more higher-order psychological dimensions of self that characterize self-definitions of older children and
adolescents (Damon & Hart, 1982).

As the young child's self-concept expands, so does the need for the expression of self. Young children express themselves in a variety of "voices"
(Edwards, Gandini, & Forman, 1996). The Reggio Emilia approach to early
education draws attention to the many natural symbolic languages that children
use to express themselves. For example, children communicate and represent
their understandings, feelings, and creative selves through written and spoken
words, drawings, paintings, drama, movement, dance, music, imaginary play,
sculptures in clay, and other creative materials (Hendrick, 1997). Young children also take great pride in mastering various tasks, such as running fast, hop-
ping, climbing, coloring, cutting with scissors, identifying letters and numbers,
and completing a puzzle. A preschooler who approaches an adult and proudly
announces, "I can hop on one foot," and then begins to hop not only is expressing his self but is also involved in an act of self-definition. What often appear
to be simple acts to adults may well be significant accomplishments to the
child.

The Psychosocial Self

The definition of self changes during the elementary school years as self-rep-
resentation shifts from concrete categories to more psychological dimensions.
The "psychosocial self" includes such psychological traits as trust, honesty,
truthfulness, friendliness, and sincerity, and competencies such as "I am good
at multiplying" or "I am a very good cellist." Between 5 and 7 years of age,
children's self-descriptions continue to share features that are characteristic of
preschool years; that is, their accounts may remain fairly positive, and children
may continue to overestimate their abilities. However, notable advances in self-
representation occur at this time. References to various social skills, cognitive

abilities, and athletic talents become more commonplace. Children also begin to acquire the ability to coordinate various features of self that were once compartmentalized. For example, they may be able to combine a number of their competencies (e.g., running, throwing, schoolwork; having friends in the neighborhood, at school and at church) (Harter, 1999).

Advances in cognitive ability during middle to late childhood allow for the formation of higher-order generalizations or concepts of self. Older school children and adolescents begin defining themselves in terms of their traits, motivations, and interpersonal affiliations, such as "I think I'm generous" and "when I see homeless people, I try to be kind" (Damon & Hart, 1982). The use of self-descriptive trait labels are often used. Frequently used trait labels include "popular," "nice," "helpful," "smart," "mean," and "dumb" (Harter, 1999). During the elementary school–age years, children begin making social comparisons; that is, they judge their appearance, abilities, and behavior in relation to those of others. How the child is perceived by others in various social networks, such as the classroom, neighborhood, playground, or community center, becomes incorporated into the child's sense of self. George Herbert Mead (1934) referred to the psychosocial self as the "looking-glass self," noting that our identity may be a reflection of how other people react to us, that is, one's self-definition is the image seen in the social mirror (Shaffer, 1988). The ability to incorporate the opinions of others brings new vulnerabilities that may have clinical implictions. During this period children become increasingly vulnerable to negative evaluations of self. Therapists may need to determine whether the unfavorable self-evaluations are realistic and to make interventions if deemed necessary (Harter, 1999).

School-age children also become increasingly concerned with acquiring skills that will enable them to achieve more "real world" accomplishments. The acquisition of these skills is defined predominantly in the context of formal school. Entry into school brings with it exposure to the technology of school society: books, maps, films, computers, microscopes, multiplication tables, and arts and crafts (Berk, 1996). Learning and instruction can also occur in other social settings, including clubs, parks, camps, organizations, neighborhoods, and recreational facilities. The challenge for the child is to develop a sense of competence as worker and learner. Parents can facilitate the child's sense of self by encouraging participation in a variety of school-related and extracurricular activities. Involvement in organized activities provides opportunities to establish constructive social relationships and achieve some measure of success with a sport, hobby, sport, or artistic pursuit.

Self-Esteem

The second component of the self system is self-esteem. Our understanding of self-esteem has evolved from the description "the feeling side of self" to a person's perceived competence and conceptions of control over oneself and one's life (Harter, 1990, 1999). Self-esteem involves two components: cognitive judgment of one's abilities or appearance, and the affective reaction to that judgment. Children with high self-esteem have more positive evaluations of self, whereas children with low self-esteem have more negative evaluations of self. Self-esteem is a very important component of self-development, because children's evaluations of their personal competencies affect emotional experiences, future behavior, and long-term psychological adjustment (Harter, 1999).

Young children's self-esteem is not as well defined as that of older children (Harter, 1983). Before age 6 or 7, young children are not able to reflect accurately on a wide range of activities. When asked how well they can perform a particular task or activity, most preschoolers will rate their own ability very high. For example, young children may indicate that they are very proficient at remembering, running fast, or throwing a ball, when in fact they may perform quite poorly at these tasks. It is important to understand that these distortions of self are normative in that they reflect cognitive limitations and not a deliberate attempt to deceive the listener (Harter, 1999). Young children's evaluations of self are supported by parental attributes of acceptance, patience, and encouragement. Parents would do well to avoid being overly disapproving and critical of their children, especially when their youngsters attempt new tasks or take initiative. Children also gain a measure of self-worth from initiating and mastering various challenges in their environment, such as riding a tricycle, climbing, running, jumping, cutting with scissors, and learning basic concepts. Young children manifest their self-esteem in their behavior, or what Harter (1999) refers to as "behaviorally presented self-esteem" (p. 19).

The development of self-esteem becomes much more defined as the child reaches 6 or 7 years of age. At this age children become even more aware of their abilities and are capable of addressing their performance across a wide range of tasks and contexts. Harter (1983, 1990), who has examined school-aged children's perceptions of self or their "perceived competence," finds that self-worth is hierarchically organized. That is, children form three separate self-esteems—academic, physical, and social. Academic self-worth includes performance in different school subjects, social self-worth includes peer and parental relationships, and physical self-worth includes physical ability and physical appearance. Harter (1990) proposes that school-age children combine their separate self evaluations into a general sense of self-worth. By third grade children become fairly accurate in their ability to perceive their competencies in different areas either favorably or unfavorably. Thus, children's self-esteem becomes fairly well established by middle childhood. It may, however, depend upon the situation or context in which the child finds herself (e.g., school, playground, computer clubs) or different areas of competence. For example, children who are less competent in sports or other physical activities may derive a great deal of self-worth from academic performance or from developing good social relationships. Parents can help foster their child's self-esteem by building on the child's strengths (helping the child find her niche), encouraging involvement in appropriate clubs and recreational activities, and closely monitoring the child's academic achievement and social adjustment in the classroom. Harter (1982) has developed the *Perceived Competence Scale for Children,* a 28-item scale that evaluates school-aged children's competencies in the areas mentioned above. Also available is *The Pictorial Scale of Perceived Competence and Social Acceptance for Young Children,* a 24-item scale for children between the ages of 4 and 7 (Harter & Pike, 1984).

Social cognitive processes, such as self-perception, contribute to children's conceptions of self. Bandura (1986, 1989) proposes that self-efficacy—the child's perception of his or her competence in dealing with the environment—mediates behavior. According to Bandura, various behaviors in the academic, social, and recreational arenas are affected by self-efficacy. Children may have the necessary skills for mastering a task, but if they do not perceive themselves as capable of actually using their skills, they may fail or not even attempt the tasks (see Miller, 1993, for an excellent review of Bandura's theory). For example, children may assign their failures and successes on a task to either ability or effort (Chapman & Skinner, 1989). Children who are high in academic self-esteem develop mastery-oriented attributions. They believe that their successes are due to ability, a characteristic they can count on in the future when faced with new challenging tasks. Conversely, these same children may attribute failure to insufficient effort or to the fact that the task was just too difficult and beyond their range of ability. These attributions provide the child with a sense of control over the environment and enable the learner to maintain a positive and enthusiastic approach to learning.

Unfortunately, not all children hold such positive mastery-oriented attributions. Some children, those who have experienced repeated failures, may develop a sense of learned helplessness. Children with learned helplessness attribute failure to a lack of ability, a fixed characteristic of the self that cannot be changed. When faced with a challenging task, they experience anxiety or a sense of loss of control. Children who have acquired a sense of learned helplessness have a tendency to give up on a variety of tasks. Several instruments are available to measure children's orientation in the classroom and other social settings. Harter (1981) has developed a self-report scale of intrinsic versus extrinsic orientation in the classroom. Two other instruments that measure internal-external locus of control are the *Nowicki-Strickland Locus of Control Scale for Children* (Nowicki & Strickland, 1973) and the *Multidimensional Measure of Children's Perceptions of Control* (Connell, 1980).

The Moral Self

A number of developmental researchers propose the development of the conscience—the sense of right and wrong—as a central construct of social-emotional development. In describing conscience formation, Kochanska (1993) states, "the gradual developmental shift from external to internal regulation that results in a child's ability to conform to societal standards of conduct and to restrain antisocial or destructive impulses, even in the absence of surveillance, is the essence and hallmark of successful socialization" (p. 325). Kochanska proposes that conscience includes two basic components: affective and behavioral. The affective component concerns the emotional discomfort (e.g., anxiety, guilt, and remorse) a child displays in the face of actual or potential wrongdoing. The behavioral component involves the capacity for behavioral control (e.g., resisting a forbidden impulse or executing a desirable act) in settings where standards of conduct apply.

Parental socialization patterns marked by "positive affect states" combined with "inductive reasoning" are associated with optimal conscience formation (Hoffman, 1988; Kochanska, 1993). In the presence of emotionally supportive caregiving, the very young child is more likely to make reference to or "read" the available social cues of his or her caregiver and learn to respond accordingly. Parents communicate prohibitions by expressing disapproval or warning during the process of affective communication. Because the infant or young child has developed a trusting relationship with the caregiver, such "emotional signals function as inhibitors of forbidden acts—first, when the parent is physically present and can be referenced, and later (around 30 to 36 months) even when the parent is absent" (Kochanska, 1993, p. 326). Eventually the code becomes internalized and children carry these prohibitions with them in the absence of the caregiver. The work by Kochanska suggests a sensitive period (roughly 14 to 36 months), when the internalization of moral rules and principles that leads to the self-regulation of moral conduct takes root.

While developmental research indicates that consistent, sensitive, and contingent parental interactions serve as a major factor in the socialization of conscience, Kochanska notes that individual differences in temperament also affect the process. For example, children who are moderately anxious and more easily aroused are much more likely to internalize parental prohibitions. Temperamental qualities also relate to the child's behavioral control or response inhibition. Children who have poor inhibitory control may not be as attentive to parental prohibitions. Parents of impulsive children may need to employ more assertive parenting strategies, such as consistent follow-through, providing concrete and explicit expectations and rules, and maintaining appropriate boundaries and limits. On the other hand, reasoning and induction may be more effective with children who are temperamentally less impulsive. The research literature also indicates that highly impulsive children whose parents create unpredictable and chaotic environments may develop serious deficiencies in conscience formation. Conversely, children with high inhibitory tendencies who are reared in highly structured environments may develop "an overcontrolled pattern, marked by strict and rigid adherence to standards of conduct at the cost of their spontaneity" (Kochanska, 1993, p. 340).

Conscience formation follows a developmental course, emerging in the latter part of infancy with the gradual internalization of parental prohibitions and culminating with the establishment of an internal code of conduct by late childhood (i.e., 12 years of age). The early and gradual internalization process can be gauged by both nonverbal and verbal expressions of the young child. A toddler may exhibit discomfort when seeing the destruction of property such as a toy or a piece of furniture by commenting, "Uh-oh!" Some toddlers may display guilt reactions by lowering their heads and gradually lifting their eyes in the direction of an authority figure. By around 3 years of age one may see children's guilt reactions following misbehavior. Young children may exhibit displeasure upon witnessing an act of aggression or comment on other children's actions, "Jimmy's not nice to me." Likewise, if they misbehave, they may comment on their own actions, "I naughty, I broke the vase." By the end of early childhood children learn to abide by a set of moral rules, such as "Be kind to others" and "Don't take toys from others." It is also not uncommon to hear young children say, "Tell the truth," "You're not supposed to take things without asking," or "You went first last time." At other times one may witness the internalization of a parent's voice, as when the child says, "Didn't you hear Mommy, we'd better not eat these cookies!" In summary, young children are much more dependent upon external controls, such as supervision, direct instruction, modeling of appropriate behaviors, and the use of rewards and punishment, than their older counterparts.

The Development of Self-Control and Prosocial Behavior

The positive side of conscience formation leads to self-control and the expression of prosocial behaviors. Self-control, in the moral sense, involves inhibiting behaviors that conflict with a moral course of action. Compliance and delay of gratification are considered to be two important indicators of self-control. Compliance, the voluntary obedience to adult commands and requests, emerges between 12 and 18 months of age and is generally established by 3 or 4 years of age. During the early childhood years, most children are fairly compliant and gain a measure of satisfaction by helping their parent(s) with household tasks. Delay of gratification involves the ability of a child to hold impulses in check before acting. Children between 12 and 18 months of age have great difficulty delaying gratification. Delay strategies typically begin to take effect between 3 and 4 years of age (Maccoby, 1980).

Cognitive advances, such as the ability to take another's perspective, enable the child to recognize other people's thoughts and actions and foster empathy, the child's ability to respond sympathetically to other children. Perspective-taking and empathy play a significant role in fostering prosocial behaviors. Prosocial behaviors refer to actions that are intended to benefit another person or group of people without the anticipation of being rewarded. Such actions often entail some cost, self-sacrifice, or risk on the part to the individual (Mussen & Eisenberg-Berg, 1977). Examples of prosocial behaviors include helping, sharing, sympathy, kindness, turn-taking, generosity, altruism, and concern for others. Prosocial children are more apt to help others in time of need, share their toys, provide affection (e.g., hugs and pats), express verbal sympathy, and play well with others. Young children who display prosocial behaviors are more likely to establish patterns of social competence. Socially competent children tend to display the following characteristics: (1) social responsibility—behavior which is friendly, facilitative, and cooperative, (2) independence—behavior that is purposeful and self-determining, (3) achievement orientation—behavior in which children seeks intellectual challenges and problem solves persistently, and (4) vitality—lively and vigorous appearance (Baumrind, 1967). Parenting styles marked by nurturance and control (which we will discuss later) tend to promote social competence.

The Development of Negative Behaviors

The other side of conscience development is seen in children who display patterns of behaviors that are inconsistent with the social rules that most societies follow. A major goal of parenting is to socialize children to conform to socially acceptable standards of conduct. As children become more independent, their desires often come into conflict with those of their parents and other caregivers. As a result, children may display "negative" behaviors, including temper tantrums, whining or crying, demanding attention, noncompliance, and aggression. For most children these negative behaviors are usually transient and considered "normal" based on the developmental age of the child (e.g., temper tantrums of the toddler, the whining of a preschooler, adolescent rebellion). Some children exhibit negative behaviors with greater intensity and/or frequency that may persist well into childhood (Schroeder & Gordon, 1991). Unfortunately, other children may develop "antisocial" patterns that are more serious in nature and persist into later childhood and adolescence. Antisocial behaviors are defined as actions taken to deliberately harm or injure another person such as fighting, stealing, cheating, lying, delinquency, cruelty to animals, and the destruction of property. Negative behaviors, as opposed to antisocial ones, can be a challenge for clinicians trying to determine what is "normal" and transient versus "clinically significant."

The two types of negative/antisocial behavior that have received considerable attention in the literature are noncompliance and aggression. Noncompliance is generally defined as not following directions, disregarding requests, or doing the opposite of what is asked, but it may also include such behaviors as tantrums, whining, talking back, and holding one's breath. (Schroeder & Gordon, 1991). Since most children are noncompliant from time to time, it can be difficult to differentiate between "normal" and "problem" noncompliance. Research indicates that normal compliance to parental commands ranges from roughly 50% to 75%, whereas problem children exhibit compliance to parental commands approximately 40% of the time or less (Forehand, Gardner, & Roberts, 1978). An effective way to distinguish normal and problem noncompliance is to consider such dimensions as frequency, severity, duration, persistence, and context (discussed later in the chapter). For example, when a negative behavior persists over a relatively long period of time (3 to 6 months), is frequent (occurs on a daily basis), and becomes increasingly severe, a long-term problem may be developing. Noncompliance is a central feature of opositional defiance disorder (ODD), a clinical disorder of childhood (American Psychiatric Association, 1994).

Across the early childhood years there seems to be a gradual shift from undirected anger to true aggression (anger focused on a specific person) (Maccoby, 1980). Temper tantrums and the early expression of anger, as witnessed in infants and toddlers, are considered to be initial forms of aggression. "Aggression" may be defined as physically aggressive acts against another person (hitting, kicking, biting, and fighting), verbal aggression (threats, tattling, teasing, name calling) and symbolic aggression (threatening gestures, chasing, making faces) (Schroeder & Gordon, 1991). Between 2 and 4 years of age two forms of aggression emerge—instrumental and hostile. The most common form of aggression is known as "instrumental," that is, aggression with the intent of obtaining something. For example, if a child wants a particular toy or is defending his space, he may hit, push, or shout at another child. Most developmental researchers consider instrumental aggression normative for young children. With increased age, instrumental aggression typically declines, as children learn various techniques such as compromise and sharing. "Hostile" aggression takes on a deliberate tone, where the child purposefully hits, insults, or tattles in order to injure another person. Hostile aggression increases between 4 and 7 years of age, but generally does not occur as much as children's friendly interactions with others (Shantz, 1987). Boys are more likely to become engaged in hostile aggression than girls, but there are no sex differences in rates of instrumental aggression. As we will discuss later, early peer relationships serve as the context in which children first learn to master their aggressive impulses and behavior. The unique egalitarian relationships found within the peer group, as opposed to hierarchical relationships within families, allow children opportunities to initiate aggressive acts and successfully or unsuccessfully resolve conflict (Hartup, 1983a).

More serious antisocial behaviors may appear in middle childhood and adolescence. Antisocial behavior patterns are obviously not considered normative and may signal the presence of a childhood "conduct disorder." As defined by the American Psychiatric Association (1994), a conduct disorder involves the repetitive and persistent pattern of behavior in which the basic rights of others or major age-appropriate societal norms or rules are violated.

There are a number of available treatment approaches for negative and aggressive behaviors. Social skills training, cognitive skills training, early education programs, and parent training programs have been found effective (Dumas, 1989; Kazdin, 1987; Schroeder & Gordon, 1991). For aggressive children, social problem-solving training has been found to be effective. In this form of training, children are taught how to resolve social conflicts through discussing and role-playing successful strategies. For young children, therapists may use puppets to act out common conflicts and then discuss effective and ineffective ways of resolving the conflicts (Feis & Simons, 1985). Finally, standardized questionnaires specific to child behavior problems include the *Child Behavior Checklist* (CBCL; Achenbach & Edelbrock, 1983) and the *Eyberg Child Behavior Inventory* (ECBI; Eyberg & Ross, 1978). *The Child Behavior Checklist* provides summary scores representing "internalizing" and "externalizing" problems. The scale can also measure social competence. The *Conners Parent Rating Scale* (Goyette, Conners, & Ulrich, 1978) is designed to measure the presence of problems with hyperactivity and/or attention.

Child-Rearing Practices Associated with Self-Esteem and Social Competence

Developmental research indicates that complex interactions between parents (e.g., personality characteristics and developmental history), children (e.g., unique child characteristics), and broader social networks (e.g., peer relationships and friendships) contribute to the development of both positive and negative outcomes for children (Belsky, 1984; Belsky & Pensky, 1988; Schroeder & Gordon, 1991). Research on developmental process has moved away from unidirectional models (e.g., parent-to-child interactions) and has focused instead on the reciprocal influences between the children and family members. For example, Thomas, Chess, and Birch (1968) introduced the concept of "goodness of fit" or the interrelationship between the caregiver/environment and the individual characteristics of the child that either support or interfere with optimal development.

A special form of communication, known as "interactional synchrony" (also referred to as "attunement") between parent and infant is most effective in promoting emotional well-being (Stern, 1985). Generally speaking, interactional synchrony describes whether caregivers and their infants appear to be coordinated behaviorally and are also physiologically harmonious during early interactions (Field, 1985). Interactional synchrony may be best described as a "sensitively tuned emotional dance, in which the mother (caregiver) responds to infant signals in a well timed and appropriate fashion. Both partners match emotional states, especially positive ones" (Berk, 1996, p. 270). Examples of interactional synchrony are as follows: if the baby smiles at dad, dad smiles back, or if the baby cries, dad responds by offering comfort or meeting the baby's need, or if the toddler gives dad a toy, dad receives the toy (and of course quickly gives the toy back!). Through supportive interactional experiences, infants come to believe that those around them will offer comfort and security. Thus, their "internal working model" of the world shapes their interpretation, expectation, and understanding of how others will respond (Bowlby, 1980).

As children grow older, certain parenting behaviors are correlated with optimal child functioning. The work of Baumrind (1967) demonstrates that during the early childhood years parents who express high levels of nurturance and control tend to foster social competence. Parental modeling of appropriate behaviors (Bandura, 1977; Grusec, 1988), as well as the use of induction or reasoning and consistent discipline (Hoffman, 1988) is related positively to internal control, self-esteem, prosocial behaviors, and intellectual achievement during the elementary school years (Coopersmith, 1967; Hoffman, 1988; Kochanska, 1993; McCall, Appelbaum, & Hagarty, 1973). Induction, a type of parenting practice that involves the use of reasoning and questioning to draw the child's attention to the effects of his or her misbehaviors on others, has been found to be especially effective. After witnessing an altercation with another child, the adult might reason with the child in the following ways, "That hurt Johnny when you pushed him off the swing," or "How do you think Johnny felt when you pushed him off of the swing?" According to Belsky (1984), "across childhood, parenting that is sensitively attuned to children's capabilities and to the developmental tasks they face promotes a variety of highly valued developmental outcomes including emotional security, behavioral independence, social competence, and intellectual achievement" (p. 85). The reader is referred to Belsky (1984) and Belsky and Pensky (1988) for an excellent and in-depth discussion of multiple determinants of developmental and family process. One useful assessment instrument that provides a measure of the degree of stress in the parent-child relationship is the *Parenting Stress Index* (PSI; Abidin, 1990). The scale is composed of two broad categories: stress that results from characteristics of the parents, and stress that results from characteristics of the child.

The Social Self: Child-Child Interactions

The establishment of peer relationships and friendships is an essential component of child development. Hartup (1983a) relates that "experience with peers is not a superficial luxury to be enjoyed by some children and not by others, but is a necessity in childhood socialization. And among the most sensitive indicators of difficulties in development are failure by the child to engage in the activities of the peer culture and failure to occupy a relatively comfortable place in it" (p. 220). The developmental consequences of deficient peer inter-action (withdrawal, isolation, rejection) tend to be related to patterns of mal-adjustment, such as anxiety, inappropriate aggressiveness, and lower childhood competence (Hartup, 1970). By contrast, positive involvement with peers appears to have developmental benefits and is related to childhood compe-tence, adjustment, and emotional security. Relationships with other children, particularly those who share a positive orientation to life, are considered to be an indispensable source of social support and may serve to buffer the child from other adversities in the environment.

Benefits of Peer Involvement

Interactions with peers offer children opportunities and experiences that may not be available in the family, where sibling relationships are defined hierar-chically. Children are capable of deriving a number of developmental benefits from interacting with peers, such as fostering the capacity to relate to others, the development of social control, and the acquisition of social values (Hartup, 1983b). Additionally, peer interaction allows children to master their aggres-sive impulses within the context of the peer culture rather than within the con-text of the family or school, provides a context for the socialization of sexuality, offers opportunities to test moral rules, and enables children to resolve anxiety and emotional disturbances (Hartup, 1983b).

The Development of Friendships

Satisfying friendships (special relationships marked by attachment and com-mon interests) also provide children with a sense of belonging and emotional support (Hartup, 1983b; Rubin & Coplan, 1992). Children's friendships undergo developmental changes in the ways they are established and main-tained. Children between the ages of 3 and 5 typically view friends as "momen-tary physical playmates," that is, whomever one is playing with at a particular time (Rubin, 1983). As Rubin (1983) notes, "children at this stage (3 to 5 years of age) reflect only on the physical attributes and activities of playmates, rather than on psychological attributes such as personal needs, interests, or traits" (p. 250). By the early primary years, children often establish close friendships to one or two playmates in particular. They will begin inviting "favorite" friends over to play or express a desire to play at another friend's house. By the end of the elementary school years children begin to understand friendships as involv-ing "intimate and mutual sharing" and as sources of intimacy and support

(Rubin, 1983). Unfortunately, not all children are able to establish close relationships with others. As we will discuss later, peer rejection may place children at risk for later maladjustment (Kupersmidt, Coie, & Dodge, 1990). Adults can foster the formation of young children's friendships by providing children with opportunities to play with others. For many young children, attending preschool and day care programs that promote social interaction serves to facilitate social development

The Development of Peer Relations

As the child's social world broadens, developmental changes in peer relationships occur. Starting around age 3, children actively seek the companionship of other children (Ellis, Rogoff, & Cromer, 1981). Children become increasingly interactive and skilled at initiating and maintaining social exchanges (Rubin & Coplan, 1992). During early childhood, peer relationships occur primarily within the context of play, progressing from fairly independent or parallel play activities to associative and cooperative play episodes (Rubin, Watson, & Jambor, 1978). A variety of play experiences with other children provides youngsters with opportunities to learn important social skills, such as cooperation, turn-taking, sharing, and empathy. More advanced forms of play, such as cooperative play (when children orient towards a common goal) and sociodramatic play (when two or more children adopt a make-believe theme and act it out) have been found to promote cognitive, academic, and socio-emotional development in young children (Smilansky, 1968; Smilansky & Shefatya, 1990).

Entry into school marks the beginning of a significant increase in peer contact. Across middle childhood children display a strong desire for peer companionship. As school-age children congregate together—in school, neighborhood, or shopping malls—they create a definite social structure of leaders and followers to ensure that the goals of the peer group will be met. A "peer group" is formed as the result of these informal social networks. According to Hartup (1983b), peer groups are characterized by peer participants who feel a strong desire to belong to the social unit, generate shared norms or rules of conduct beyond those maintained by society, and develop a hierarchical social structure of roles and relationships that govern their interaction with one another. The practices of these informal groups lead to a peer culture that typically consists of a special vocabulary, dress code, and place to congregate during leisure hours. These customs bind children together, creating a sense of group identity.

A significant number of children, however, lack access to peers or may not be able to easily join a peer group or make friends. Using sociometric techniques, researchers often classify children into one of the following categories: (1) popular children (those accepted by most peers and rejected by few), (2) amiables or accepteds (those who receive fewer positive nominations than the "popular" children but still obtain a majority of positive nominations, (3) isolates or neglectees (children who receive few positive nominations or negative nominations and who seem to "fall between the cracks"), and (4) rejectees (those who are rejected by many peers and accepted by only a few).

Longitudinal studies examining the developmental pathways of children of varying peer status have produced interesting findings. The children classified as either classroom superstars or amiables are more likely to retain their high peer status throughout their school experience. Conversely, isolates and rejectees—who are low in peer acceptance—appear to be at greater risk for subsequent developmental problems. It may not be as bad to be ignored by one's peers as to be rejected. Isolates tend at least to have a chance to change their social status and improve their peer status through a change of classroom or by making friends with a popular child (Coie & Dodge, 1983). Rejectees, unfortunately, are likely to experience serious adjustment problems later in life, and are considered to be at risk for developmental problems such as aggression, school drop-out, and juvenile delinquency (Cowen, Pederson, Babigan, Izzo, & Trost, 1973).

Individual Differences in Peer Involvement

A number of behavioral, cognitive, and biological factors may operate to influence the course of peer relationships. One of the most commonly cited correlates of peer acceptance is social competence. Socially competent children are skilled at initiating and maintaining positive relationships and are also skilled at repairing relationships when conflicts arise. Socially competent children, particularly the popular ones, are less likely to draw unwarranted attention to themselves and are not overbearing. Popular children also tend to be prosocial in orientation; for example, they are viewed as cooperative, friendly, sociable, and sensitive by peers, teachers, and observers (Dodge, 1983; Rubin, Hymel, LeMare, & Rowden, 1989). On the other hand, the most commonly cited correlate of peer rejection is aggression (Coie & Kupersmidt, 1983).

Researchers have also examined the relationship between social information-processing skills and peer acceptance. For example, Rubin and Krasnor (1983) propose that when children are faced with a social dilemma their thinking follows a sequential order. First, they select a social goal or a cognitive representation of the desired outcome. Second, they examine the task environment by interpreting all the relevant social cues. Third, they select strategies, which involves generating possible plans of action for achieving the perceived social goal. Fourth, children evaluate the outcome of the strategy by assessing the situation to determine the relative success of the course of action in achieving the social goal. If the initial strategy is unsuccessful, the child may repeat it, select a new strategy, or abandon the situation altogether. Aggressive and rejected children demonstrate notable deficits in performance at various stages of this model (Rubin & Coplan, 1992).

Children with higher perceived social competence (awareness of their personal social skills) tend to be more popular with peers. Self-efficacy judgments play an important role in the quality of peer relationships. Self-efficacy concerns the degree to which children believe they can successfully perform behaviors that are necessary for achieving desired outcomes (Bandura, 1977). Positive correlations have been found between children's social self-efficacy judgments and sociometric nominations scores (Ladd & Price, 1987; Rubin & Coplan, 1992).

Emotional Development

The Expression of Emotion

In the book, *Life Among Giants,* Young (1966) describes the spontaneous and transient nature of young children's emotions in a rather amusing and informative manner. Young writes, "Children consider how they feel the single most important factor in their respective universe, and they have the tendency to feel strongly about almost everything that affects their universe. In fact, children don't go in much for the so-called mild emotions. They take their feelings straight without sugar or cream!" (p. 13). By 3 years of age children are experiencing variety of emotions, such as the basic emotions of joy, sadness, anger, fear, excitement, and interest, in addition to the more complex emotions, including empathy, pride, guilt, shame, and embarrassment. While emotions become increasingly complex and elaborate across childhood, there are also individual differences in emotional expression. Children may vary in the intensity, frequency, duration, predominence, and lability of their emotional expression (also known as "emotion dynamics"). Perhaps most importantly, emotions play an important functional and organizational role in development and behavior. For example, joy, anger, sadness, frustration, and the social emotions of guilt and pride are all necessary for healthy functioning. Emotions may also serve as coping mechanisms, such as when a child experiences fear when threatened, sadness when a pet is lost or dies, and anger when goals are blocked. The inability to access certain emotions, such as the expression of joy and happiness or the absence of guilt and remorse in response to wrongdoing, may signal that there is a problem (Cole, Michel, & Teti, 1994).

Along with the use of standardized assessment instruments, knowledge of emotional development may help the therapist to determine the child's internal state. This becomes especially relevant for children who are nonverbal or who have a difficult time articulating their personal experiences. Identification of a child's emotional style also enables parents and therapists to provide a "goodness-of-fit" between a child and the environment. Research also indicates that personal emotional styles may become fairly established in the early years, and that these styles often show remarkable stability across time (Denham, 1998). Parents and teachers have long been able to identify children's emotional styles, such as "She's got such a sunny disposition" or "He is down right grumpy!" Knowledge of emotional style enables adults to tailor socialization experiences that either encourage the appropriate expression of emotion or to implement interventions designed to alter styles that may interfere with interpersonal functioning.

The Development of Emotions

As with most socioemotional constructs, emotions follow a developmental course. Infants are equipped with a number of primary emotions (Izard, 1993), such as distress, interest, excitement, disgust, sadness, pleasure, surprise, anger, wariness, and rage. Primary emotions are manifested by characteristic facial expressions in the first six months of life. Basic emotions are further classified as either positive or negative emotions, which become more differentiated with increases in age (Lewis, 1989).

Interest and joy, two positive emotions, have received considerable attention in the developmental literature. Interest is displayed at the beginning of life, and occurs in response to the human face and voice, as well as a variety of other stimuli (e.g., various patterns, objects, toys, lights). Increasing interest in the external environment becomes especially evident by 4 to 6 months of age. When infants are disinterested in their surroundings at this age, we might suspect a lack of stimulation in the home or a developmental delay. Smiling, the facial display of the affect joy, appears in the first two months but is thought to be related to reflex action. The true "social smile, " often accompanied by plea-surable cooing, appears after the second or third month (Sroufe & Waters, 1976). The social smile becomes increasingly differentiated over the next 6 to 8 months, and during the latter half of the first year infants typically smile in response to familiar people and events. Laughter occurs first between 3 to 4 months, generally in response to playful interactions with the baby, such as kissing the tummy or verbalizations such as "I'm going to get you!"

Secondary or more complex emotions such as empathy, pride, shame, embarrassment, and guilt emerge between 18 months and 4 years of age. Secondary emotions are often referred to as "self-conscious emotions," because they require a self system and involve injury to or enhancement of our sense of self (Campos, Caplovitz, Lamb, Goldsmith, & Stenberg, 1983). According to Lewis (1989), self-conscious emotions appear in two phases. The first class of self-conscious emotions appear between 18 and 24 months of age, and include embarrassment, empathy, and envy. The second class of self-con-scious emotions—guilt, shame, and pride, emerge some time between the sec-ond and third year of life.

Empathy, which has received considerable attention in the research litera-ture, involves the child's ability to recognize and respond sympathetically to the feelings of others. Often referred to as a "social" emotion (Denham, 1998), empathy is thought to underlie the development of prosocial behaviors (Mussen & Eisenberg-Berg, 1977). Young children are able to feel empathy and respond to others in a variety of ways (Denham, 1998). Children as young as 18 months of age have been observed to respond sympathetically to others in distress as evidenced by their facial expressions (e.g., knit brows), verbal-izations (e.g., "Mary sad, Mary sad,") and actions (e.g., hugging, patting). Effective techniques found to foster empathy are verbal labeling of emotions and empathy training. For very young children, an adult may wish to provide a verbal label that signifies the emotion that the child is experiencing (e.g., "You are sad that your hampster died," "You are feeling angry."). Concrete statements such as these help children understand what they are feeling. Empathy training involves going beyond labeling the emotion by informing children of the consequence of their actions. For example, an adult may respond to an aggressive act by stating, "How do you think Jimmy felt after you hit him?" If the child is unable to respond to the question, the adult may then add, "When you hit other children it hurts!" Child rearing has a particular impact on the socialization of empathy. Parents who are warm and nurturing, who exhibit empathetic concern for their children, and talk about the importance of kindness have preschoolers who are more likely respond to the needs of others (Zahn-Waxler & Radke-Yarrow, 1990).

The emotions of guilt, shame, and pride, also known as "moral"emotions, correspond with the development of conscience and involve the socialization of standards and rules. Some investigators continue to combine guilt and shame into one "feel-bad-about-performance" emotion, and pride into the "feel-good-about-performance" emotion (Denham, 1998). However, guilt and shame have their unique emotional and functional properties. Shame and guilt are elicited when a standard of behavior is not attained. The emotion of guilt involves a particular behavior, or the feeling that "I did a bad thing." According to Denham, "Children and adults experiencing guilt often report a nagging concentration on the specific transgression—thinking of it over and over, wishing they had behaved differently or could undo the bad deed" (1998, p. 40). Likewise, the emotion of shame can occur as the result of a specific behavior or transgression. But the consequences of shame extend well beyond guilt where the feeling is seen as a reflection of one's worth as an individual. Shame involves the feeling that "I am bad" or that "I am an unworthy person." As Denham states, "People in the midst of a shame experience often report a sense of shrinking, of 'being small.' They feel worthless, powerless, and exposed" (1998, p. 40). A preponderance of shame can interfere with interpersonal relationships, erode one's self-concept, and lead to various forms of psychopathology (Tangney, Burggraf, & Wagner, 1995).

Whereas shame tends to be emotionally debilitating and leads individuals to develop avoidant patterns of behavior, a reasonable level of guilt is more likely to "keep people constructively engaged in interpersonal situations" (Denham, 1998, p. 41). In response to feelings of guilt, children are more likely to take corrective actions with others such as apologizing, confessing, or making amends. A number of researchers view "shame-free" guilt as having an important developmental function, motivating children to adopt positive interpersonal behaviors. Thus, as conscience formation takes hold and "Jiminy Cricket" begins to speak, children are more apt to exhibit empathy, take personal responsibility for their actions, manage their anger in constructive ways, and adhere to the rules of society (Tangney & Fischer, 1995).

Pride, on the other hand, corresponds with the child's achievements and personal accomplishments, and is displayed when the child is able to evaluate him- or herself against the standard and finds that his or her behavior exceeded the standard. Pride reflects delight in one's achievement. In turn, the child may say, "I have done something well." Adult instruction plays a pivotal role in when to feel proud or ashamed. For example, when parents recognize the accomplishments of their children (e.g., "Wow, look how far you kicked the ball!"), they help to foster pride. Conversely, when parents say, "You never do anything right!" they are fostering feelings of shame. An appropriate balance of adult instruction leads to a healthy compliment of these two emotions. Providing children with a opportunities to take initiative and to be industrious enables the child to experience a measure of success, which in turn helps to foster the child's pride in his or her accomplishments. Children are likely to experience successful task performance when they are provided with developmentally appropriate curriculum and instructional practices. Appropriately challenging tasks that are within the child's level of mastery lead to feelings of success rather than failure.

Shame and pride are measured by examining children's behaviors and body posture (Lewis, Alessandri, & Sullivan, 1992; Stipeck, Recchia, McClintic, 1992). Investigators have measured these two emotions after presenting children with either easy or difficult tasks, and evaluating whether the children experienced success or failure with them. Shame is indicated when a child's shoulders are hunched; hands are down and close to the body; arms or hands are placed in front of the face or across the body. Shame is also indicated when a child shows avoidant postures, with head and chin down, body to one side or squirming, turning away, lowered eyes with gaze downward, pouting, frowning, lower lip tucked between the teeth, withdrawal from the task situation, or negative self-evaluative remarks such as "I can't do it." Pride is evident when a child adopts an open, erect posture, with shoulders back, head up, and/or arms open and up. Additional behaviors include smiling, pointing at the outcome, applauding, verbalizing positive self-statements ("Look at what I did!), calling attention to the product, or looking up for additional approval.

Childhood Fears and Anxiety

In the normal course of development, many children experience fear or anxiety. Fear is defined as a normal physiological reaction to a real or perceived threat, which disappears with the withdrawal of the danger. The stimuli that provoke fear change developmentally in a way that corresponds with the child's increasing cognitive and physical abilities (Schroeder & Gordon, 1991). For example, children's vivid imaginations and difficulties in separating appearance from reality account for some early childhood fears. As their representational capacity develops, some children may imagine such things as ghosts, monsters, and the bogey man. Young children may dream about such events and have a difficult time separating their dreams from reality. Fortunately, common fears are transient in nature and typically last no more than a few months. Common fears for 2- and 3-year-olds include, but are not limited to, imaginary creatures, burglars, auditory stimuli (e.g., trains and thunder), animals, the dark, being alone, and disconcerting visual stimuli (masks). For children between the ages of 4 and 5, fears may include the dark, wild animals, parents' leaving at night, loud stimuli (fire engines), injury, falling, and dogs. School-age children may fear such things as natural disasters (fire, flood), failure and criticism, minor injuries, danger (burglars, getting lost), death, and medical and dental procedures. Parents who deal with these fears through understanding and patience help their children resolve them by acknowledging the child's feelings, encouraging the child to talk about them, and offering reassurance until the fear declines. Intensity and persistence of the fear give an indication of whether it will develop into an ongoing problem (Morris & Kratochwill, 1983). If a child's fear is very intense, persists for a long time, interferes with daily activities, and cannot be reduced through various management procedures, the fear may have reached the level of a phobia. If phobias are present, the child may need to receive specific treatment or therapy.

Anxiety is defined as an internally cued aversive emotional state with no specific focus or obvious external trigger (Schroeder & Gordon, 1991). Two forms of anxiety that emerge during infancy are often of particular interest and concern to parents: separation anxiety and stranger anxiety. Separation anxiety, showing distress following the departure of a familiar caregiver, appears around 6 months of age, increases in intensity until about 15 months of age, and declines in a gradual fashion (Kagan, Kearsley, & Zelazo, 1978). Stranger anxiety, showing distress response in the presence of unfamiliar adults, appears after 6 months of age. Both of these emotional responses are considered normal, provided levels of intensity are appropriate. In fact, these emotions, along with interest and pleasure directed toward familiar persons, signal the presence of attachment to a caregiver. Excessive anxiety involving separation from the attachment figure or home may signal the presence of separation anxiety disorder (American Psychiatric Association, 1994).

Emotion Regulation

Most developmental researchers have concerned themselves primarily with the functional and organizational aspects of emotions that serve to establish, maintain, or disrupt relationships between children and other people (Campos, Campos, & Barrett, 1989; Denham, 1998; Greenspan & Greenspan, 1985). The regulatory and functional aspects of emotion are especially important during infancy and childhood, since emotion organizes the development of early social relationships (Sroufe, Schork, Motti, Lawroski, & LaFreniere, 1984) and underlies self-regulatory behaviors and other inhibitory controls such as conscience (Cicchetti, Ganiban, & Barnett, 1991; Kochanska, 1993). In addition, as Cole, Michel, and Teti (1994) point out, a number of emotion-related symptoms comprise the *DSM-IV* diagnostic criteria (American Psychiatric Association, 1994) for oppositional defiant disorder, conduct disorder, attention-deficit/hyperactivity disorder, and anxiety disorder.

Emotion regulation is generally defined as the processes or strategies that are used to manage emotional arousal so that successful interpersonal functioning is possible (Calkins, 1994). Those studying emotion regulation recognize that both underlying neurophysiological systems and socialization experiences play a significant role in emotion regulation. Neurophysiological systems include regions of the brain associated with arousal and fear (e.g., amygdala, limbic system, hippocampus) or specific neuroregulatory systems such as the hypothalamic-pituitary-adrenocortical (HPA) system that underlies reactions to stress and uncertainty. Early socialization experiences contribute directly and indirectly to the child's ability to regulate emotion. Researchers tend to agree that the child's ability for self-control is the result of the interplay between these underlying neuroregulatory systems and parent-child interactions. There are also individual differences in emotion regulation that may be attributed to within-child characteristics (learned strategies, temperament, and cognitive abilities) and early socialization experiences (both implicit and explicit socialization practices) (Calkins, 1994).

Factors within the Child

Learned Strategies

As children's social information-processing skills develop, they learn when it is appropriate to regulate displays of affect and develop the ability to apply various strategies to suit the circumstances. As Calkins (1994) notes, children learn to interpret available cues in the environment before "generating a suitable emotion-regulating response." It should be noted that many of these "learned" strategies emerge spontaneously, as is true for other cognitive strategies. By 3 to 4 years of age, the young child may learn to blunt unwanted stimuli by restricting sensory input by, for example, covering eyes or ears to block out a scary sight or sound. Other coping strategies include self-comforting ("Mommy said she'll be right back"), changing one's goals (deciding that one doesn't want to play after being excluded from a game), seeking a parent for help, distraction techniques (focusing attention elsewhere), or taking control of the situation (Stansbury & Gunnar, 1994; Thompson, 1994). With increases in age, these strategies tend to become more efficient and sophisticated.

Physiological Basis for Emotion Regulation

The ability of an infant or young child to regulate emotion is dependent, in part, upon the progressive maturation of a number of neuroregulatory systems to a point where they are functional and organized. Cortical inhibitory controls over arousal emerge gradually during infancy and may not become fully functional until early childhood (Kagan, 1994). However, individual differences in neural circuitry and other neuroregulatory systems have been linked to children's ability to regulate their emotions (and behavior) (Fox, 1994; Greenspan, 1992; Greenspan & Greenspan, 1985). Differences in neural circuits or "wiring" may predispose children to certain emotional states and arousal levels. Simply put, it may be easier for some children to control displays of emotion based on the efficiency of various neuroregulatory systems.

The role of temperament as an individual difference factor in emotion regulation has received a great deal of attention from developmental researchers (Calkins, 1994; Gunnar, 1994; Gunnar, Tout, de Haan, Pierce, & Stansbury, 1997; Kagan, 1994). Temperament is generally referred to as the behavioral style of a child's interaction with the environment. According to Kagan, temperament is defined as the "psychological qualities that display considerable variation among infants and young children and, in addition, have a relatively, but not indefinitely, stable physiological basis that derives from the individual's biological constitution" (1994, p. 16). The dimensions of temperament that tend to receive the most attention from researchers and clinicians, and are also most noted by parents, include activity levels, reactivity, irritability, mood, attentiveness, adaptability, ease of being soothed, impulsivity, sociability, approach to or avoidance of novelty, ease as well as intensity of arousal in reaction to stimulation, and regulation of arousal states (Buss & Plomin, 1984; Cary & McDevitt, 1978; Rothbart, 1981; Thomas & Chess, 1977). Buss and Plomin (1984) propose four temperament variables: (1) activity levels (total energy output); (2) emotionality (intensity of reaction or level of arousal); (3) sociability (affiliativeness or a desire to be with others); and (4) impulsivity (response latency).

Kagan, Reznick, and Snidman (1987, 1988) have studied two types of children that vary with respect to temperament qualities. The children are known as "inhibited" and "uninhibited," and they present very different behavioral profiles in response to similar environments or identical stimuli. Inhibited children tend to become quiet, vigilant, restrained, and avoidant while they assess the situation and their personal resources before acting. Uninhibited children react with spontaneity to the same situation. The situations that elicit the two patterns of responses tend to be encounters with unfamiliar events, objects, people, and contexts. Inhibited and/or highly reactive infants and children may react with distress to novelty, be it toys, classrooms, shopping malls, grocery stores, or a visit to a relative's house. Stimuli such as crowdedness, congestion, and noise may also elicit very different reactions from children based on their temperament.

Kagan and his colleagues also stress that socialization experiences, primarily in the home, play a significant role in the development and maintenance of these two styles. If parents or caregiving adults accept the avoidant behaviors of the inhibited child, the inhibition may become more entrenched. On the other hand, if caregivers gently encourage the child to approach unfamiliar objects, people, and places or prepare the child for novelty, it is more likely that the inhibited style will not become strong. In summary, Kagan (1994) notes "the development of a stable inhibited behavioral style requires a combination of a low threshold of reactivity in the limbic sites—the temperamental component—and a social environment that either encourages or fails to discourage timidity" (p. 21).

Recently, a great deal of attention has been directed to children diagnosed with "sensory integration disorder" (SI). Children with SI have a difficult time processing information received through the senses (Ayers, 1979; Kranowitz, 1998), leading to individual differences in sensory reactivity and sensory processing. Their central nervous systems have difficulty analyzing, organizing, or connecting (integrating) sensory messages, which interferes with daily living skills. Some children with SI problems tend to be overly sensitive and seek less stimulation (e.g, avoid touch, refuse to wear certain clothes, resist certain foods, withdraw from others, and experience more emotional outbursts). Other children with SI may be undersensitive and seek more stimulation (e.g., playing in the mud, grabbing other children and adults, seeking loud sounds, preferring spicy foods, and failing to recognize cues from others). Sensory integration problems may also impair the child's adaptive, motor, or academic development and learning. For a more complete discussion of sensory and neurodevelopmental problems see Kranowitz (1998), Greenspan (1992), and Greenspan and Meisels (1984).

The hypothalamic-pituitary-adrenocortical (HPA) system is also an important component of emotional reactivity. Cortisol, which is the primary hormonal product of the HPA system in humans, plays a significant role in emotion regulation and stress resistance. Cortisol circulates at basal levels to serve an important homeostatic function in humans and becomes elevated in response to stress (Gunnar, Marvinney, Isensee, & Fisch, 1989; Stansbury & Gunnar, 1994). Research has shown that children's cortisol levels rise in response to stressors such as venipuncture and vaccinations (Gunnar, Malone,Vance, & Fisch, 1985) and challenging social situations in the classroom (e.g., cleaning and putting up toys before they are finished playing, waiting to play with a desirable toy, separation from mother when left with a busy caregiver, or playing with an unfamiliar peer) (Granger, Stansbury, & Henker, 1994; Stansbury & Gunnar, 1994). It also appears as if HPA functioning varies according to the temperament of the child. Significantly higher cortisol elevations have been found in shy (inhibited) children, as compared to outgoing (uninhibited) children (Calkins, Fox, & Marshall, 1996; Zimmermann, 1998).

Factors within the Caregiving Environment

Socialization experiences, primarily within the context of the family, have the most pervasive influence on the development of emotion regulation. Parental sensitivity (a parent's contingent, consistent, warm responses to the child's needs) has been identified as an important mediator in both emotional and behavioral regulation (Jacobvitz & Sroufe, 1987; Sethre-Hofstad, 1998; Silverman & Ragusa, 1990). Sensitive caregivers are better able to interpret and empathize with their children's feelings and respond appropriately to their children's distress, thereby helping to facilitate the regulation of emotion. Socialization experiences are either "implicit," occurring in the interactive experiences between the child and parent, or "explicit," involving training, that is, modeling, reinforcement, or discipline (Calkins, 1994).

Implicit Experience

A substantial body of work has focused on the relationship between an infant's attachment to his or her primary caregiver and emotion regulation. An attachment relationship (mentioned earlier) is generally defined as an emotionally enduring tie to a significant other person (Maccoby, 1980). On the positive side, attachment relationships can be described as strong emotional ties we feel for special people in our lives that lead us to feel pleasure and joy when we interact with them and to be comforted by their nearness during times of distress (Berk, 1996). Ainsworth (1967), following the work of Bowlby, found qualitative differences in attachment relationships. Infants were found to form "secure" or "anxious" attachment relationships. A secure attachment relationship promotes healthy emotional growth and development and provides the child with a sense of emotional security and predictability about the world. Anxious patterns of attachment are marked by insecurity (ambivalence) or withdrawal (avoidance).

Sroufe and his colleagues (Sroufe, 1983; Sroufe & Fleeson, 1986; Sroufe & Waters, 1977) have studied the long-term consequences of attachment relationships. They found that securely attached infants, as compared to anxiously attached infants, exhibit a different behavioral profile across the early childhood years. Infants who receive consistent, responsive care in the first year of life, and are securely attached, are more likely to develop positive social relationships and remain emotionally healthy in childhood. Conversely, infants who experience erratic care, marked by intrusive or hostile interactions, and are avoidant-anxiously attached, are more likely to become isolated and socially withdrawn. Children who receive unresponsive care, and are ambivalently-anxiously attached, are more likely to be disruptive and difficult. Disturbances in social relatedness may indicate the presence of childhood disorder known as reactive attachment disorder of infancy or early childhood (American Psychiatric Association, 1994).

Sensitive parenting not only serves to promote healthy attachment relations, but has also been found to provide a protective biological function, "inoculating" an infant against ongoing stress and adversities (Shore, 1997). Gunnar and her colleagues (Gunnar, Larson, Hertsgaard, Harris, & Brodersen, 1992; Gunnar, Mangelsdorf, Larson, & Herstgaard, 1989; Gunnar, Marvinney, Isensee, & Fisch, 1989) have measured children's reactions to stress by measuring their salivary cortisol levels. These researchers have found that stress and traumatic events can elevate an individual's cortisol level. Highly sustained levels of cortisol may, in turn, have a negative effect on the immune and central nervous systems. Over time, elevated cortisol levels have the potential to make the brain vulnerable to processes that destroy neurons or reduce the number of synaptic connections in certain regions of the brain. Thus, ongoing stressful or traumatic experiences are believed to elevate cortisol levels and, in turn, undermine neurological development, placing children at risk for cognitive, motor, and social delays. Gunnar's work also suggests that infants who receive warm, responsive, and nurturing care are less likely than other children to react to stress by producing cortisol. When they do react to stress, their HPA system is able to regulate cortisol production more efficiently. Similar responses have been found with elementary school children with secure attachment relationships (Egeland, Carlson, & Sroufe, 1993).

Explicit Socialization Experiences

Children benefit from interactions with parents who actively attempt to socialize them by incorporating explicit methods to regulate emotions and behaviors. Parents, who display positive affect and who exhibit such behaviors as caring, nurturing, empathy, and helping others serve as powerful models for their children. In her work on parenting styles, Baumrind (1967) found a relationship between parenting styles and children's self-regulation. Parents who incorporate higher levels of nurturance and control (i.e., discipline) tend to have children who display higher levels of social competence and independence. Various discipline techniques, especially induction, have been shown to relate not only to conscience development, but also to self-control. Furthermore, some parents actively attempt to instruct their children in ways to manage their frustration, anger, and fears. As the result of a myriad of both informal and formal socialization processes, most children will begin to shift from external sources of control to internal ones by the middle childhood years.

Positive Child Guidance Techniques and Early Educational Practices

Practices used by many early childhood educators are effective in helping young children regulate their emotions. These practices include, but are not limited to: (1) redirection ("Why don't you either play in the block area or at the art table?"), (2) helping children use their words to express themselves ("Ask Melanie if you can have a turn"), (3) verbally labeling the child's emotions ("I know you're upset"), (4) make-believe and sociodramatic play that give children opportunities to express emotions, (5) puppets that represent certain feelings or behavioral styles such as turtles, alligators, koala bear, (6) art work such as painting or drawing that provides children with opportunities to express themselves nonverbally, (7) "writing" a story about how the child feels, (8) soothing music written for children, and (9) attachment or transitional objects such as stuffed animals, blankets, and pillows. Finally, responsive statements can be used to assist children in understanding their innermost feelings. For example, if a child says to the adult, "My puppy got killed and I cried," the adult might respond by saying, "You were sad about your puppy dying. You just felt like crying." Statements such as these validate the child's feelings and show understanding. The good news for many parents is that the young child's increasing awareness and use of any number of strategies means that intense outbursts become less frequent over the preschool years!

Verbal Self-Regulatory Strategies

More recently, researchers have focused on the role of language as a mediating factor in self-regulation (Berk & Winsler, 1995). Vygotskian theory provides a valuable framework for understanding the central role that language plays in the development. During the early childhood years, children begin to bring their actions under the control of thought, and the acquisition of language serves as the central tool for such an accomplishment. By the age of 3 or 4 children begin to acquire verbal dialogues, particularly from conversations they experience with adults and more capable peers. Initially, their "self-directed" speech occurs aloud, as when a child is playing or working on a problem. For example, while working on a puzzle, a child may say, "I wonder where this piece goes? I'll bet it goes down here." Young children use self-directed speech as a means to guide their interactions across a number of settings (e.g., play, problem solving, and transitions) (Berk, 1996; Berk & Landau, 1993). Around 6 or 7 years of age, their self-directed speech becomes increasingly silent. Finally, around age 8 the self-directed speech goes "underground" and becomes what Vygotsky referred to as "inner speech," the silent conversations that one has with oneself. Inner speech serves an important cognitive and self-regulatory function.

Researchers have examined the crucial role that relationships between adults and children play in children's self-regulatory problems. For example, parents of children with attention-deficit/hyperactivity disorder (ADHD) are more likely to adopt interaction patterns that inhibit the child's use of private speech and inner speech and, in turn, undermine the child's self-regulatory abilities. Parents of children with ADHD are consistently more controlling and negative, issue more verbal commands, more often physically direct the child during an activity, and are less responsive (Danforth, Barkley, & Stokes, 1991).

Winsler and his colleagues (Winsler, 1995; Winsler, Diaz, McCarthy, Bird, & Feldman, 1995; Winsler, Diaz, & Montero, 1997) have found that parents of children with ADHD engaged in less effective scaffolding when involved in a joint problem-solving task. Scaffolding is a interactional pattern whereby an adult (or more capable peer) offers a support system that is sensitively tuned to the child needs. During scaffolding, the adult gradually turns the responsibility of the task over to the child as necessary. Other elements of scaffolding consist of well-timed verbal statements ("Which puzzle piece might fit here?" or "Do you see pieces that have the same shape?"), emotional support and reassurance

("Now you're getting it!" "Great, you did it!"), and goal directed partnership (the participants in the social interaction negotiate, or compromise, while working toward a shared view of the situation—one that falls within the child's range of ability). Vygotskian researchers claim, and have supportive evidence, that the quality of the parent-child and teacher-child interactions serve to either support the child's self-regulatory capacities or undermine this process. Berk and Winsler (1995) make the point well: "Since self-regulation emerges from other-regulations and social environments differ to the extent to which they provide effective scaffolding, children's self-regulatory capacity is influenced by the quality of other-regulatory support in adult-child communication, to which both partners contribute" (p. 91).

Evaluating Emotion Regulation

Developmental researchers have employed various dimensions to evaluate emotion regulation (Cole, Michel, & Teti, 1994; Thompson, 1994). Cole and colleagues (1994) make the distinction between emotion regulation and emotion dysregulation in an effort to differentiate between adaptive (or typical) and maladaptive (atypical) emotional patterns in children. Emotion dysregulation concerns patterns of emotional expression that serve to jeopardize or impair functioning and that may, in turn, become symptoms of psychopathology. Thompson (1994) suggests the concept of "emotion dynamics" as a means to distinguish emotion regulation and dysregulation. The dimensions of emotion dynamics include frequency, intensity, duration, and recovery from emotional responses. Frequency measures the number of episodes that occur in a given day or week: are the episodes occurring several times a day throughout the week? Intensity involves the magnitude of the emotional expression or outburst, including such behaviors as crying, howling, screaming, kicking, hitting, bitting, and rigid posturing. Duration concerns the length of time the emotional expression lasts. Recovery involves the child's ability to regain composure. When emotional outbursts are frequent, intense, and last 10 to 15 minutes, we might conclude that the child has problems managing his or her emotions.

Assessment of Children's Behavior

Epidemiological studies indicate that approximately 10 to 15% of all children in the United States have significant problems that warrant mental health services (Kazdin, 1987; Goldberg, Roghmann, McInery, & Burke, 1984). Additionally, research studies estimate that by the end of high school approximately 20% of children will have "special needs," requiring the provision of extra-educational services and attention (Farran & Shonkoff, 1994). Two percent of the population of special needs children experience disabilities such as deafness, blindness, autism, orthopedic impairment, or significant cognitive delays. These children occupy what is known as the "normative" category of special needs. The remaining 18% of the child population constitutes what is referred to as "non-normative" categories, including such labels as "learning disabled," "speech or language impaired," "mildly mentally retarded," and "hyperactive" (Tomlinson, 1982).

Given these prevalence rates, family therapists will encounter children with a variety of developmental problems across the physical/motor, cognitive, language, social, and emotional domains. Knowledge of the child's developmental status will enable the clinician to evaluate the behavior of the child in comparison with that of children of the same age or developmental level. Behavior that is considered a problem at one developmental level may be normal at another. A 2-year-old who has temper tantrums, for example, has a problem that may be considered "normal" or common for that age, whereas a 10-year-old who continues to tantrum has a more significant problem. As Schroeder and Gordon (1991) note, one of the primary roles of the clinician "is to decide whether the behavior of concern is more or less than one would expect of any child at that age and in that environment" (p. 54).

We have found the Comprehensive Assessment-to-Intervention System (CAIS) (Schroeder & Gordon, 1991) to be a valuable resource for clinicians working with children. We conclude this chapter by presenting a very abbreviated version of the CAIS. In our opinion, the CAIS is an indispensable tool for evaluating the many issues and factors that must be taken into account when identifying and treating children with emotional and behavioral problems.

The CAIS is comprised of six sections: (1) Clarifying the Referral Question, (2) Determining the Social Context, (3) Assessing General Areas, (4) Assessing Specific Areas, (5) Determining the Effects of the Problem, and (6) Determining Areas for Intervention. To provide the reader with a feel for this system, we briefly summarize the sections on assessing general and specific areas. The assessment of general areas includes: (1) developmental status of the child, (2) parent and family characteristics, (3) environmental characteristics, (4) consequences of the behavior, and (5) medical/health status of the child. Assessment of a particular behavior (e.g., high activity level, emotional outbursts) falls under the category of "specific areas." The specific assessment includes six aspects of behavior (which the reader will find similar to Thompson's emotion dynamics presented above): (1) persistence of behavior—how long has it been going on? (e.g., "Jack has been whining and crying a lot since the birth of his baby brother 6 months ago"), (2) changes in behavior—is the behavior becoming worse? (e.g., "Jack has gotten much more clingy and anxious whenever I take him to day care"), (3) severity of behavior—is the behavior very intense or dangerous, or "low-level" but annoying? (e.g., "Jack refuses to go to bed at night and has nightmares three to four times a week. He often leaves his room and ends up sleeping on the sofa in our living room"), (4) frequency of behavior—has the behavior occurred only once or twice, or many times? (e.g., "Jack has been caught stealing crayons and other school supplies in the classroom since the beginning of the school year"), (5) situation specificity—does the behavior occur only at home or in a variety of settings? (e.g., "Jack sticks his tongue out at me at home, and now he is doing the same thing to his teacher!"), and (6) type of problem—is the behavior a discrete problem or a set of diffuse problems? (e.g., The child begins to exhibit a variety of problematic behaviors both at home and at school. In all likelihood these problems would impair his functioning and development unless immediate intervention took place.)

Conclusion

We began this chapter with Horton relaxing in the Jungle of Nool. In time he hears a small voice and, pausing to listen, he discovers a "creature of very small size." Horton decides to rescue this creature and is eventually successful in helping this "person" find his way home. The decision to become a family therapist carries with it an enormous responsibility. Family therapy also offers the therapist many rewarding opportunities to help children (and families) to live productive and satisfying lives. In our clinical and research experience, we have enjoyed working with children. They have taught us many things about living well. As we close this chapter, we leave you with the example set by Horton: Listen to the voice of the child!

Robert E. Nida, Ph.D., is Associate Professor, Department of Child Development and Family Relations, East Carolina University, Greenville, North Carolina.

Sarah Pierce, Ph.D., is Associate Professor, School of Human Ecology, Louisiana State University, Baton Rouge, Louisiana.

References

Abidin, R. R. (1990). *Parenting Stress Index Manual* (3rd ed.). Charlottesville, VA: Pediatric Psychology Press.

Achenbach, T. M., & Edelbrock, C. (1983). *Manual for the Child Behavior Checklist and Revised Child Behavior Profile.* Burlington, VT: University Associates in Psychiatry.

Ainsworth, M.D.S. (1967). *Infancy in Uganda: Infant care and the growth of attachment.* Baltimore, MD: The Johns Hopkins Press.

American Psychiatric Association. (1994). *Diagnostic and statistical manual of mental disorders* (4th ed.). Washington, DC: Author.

Anderson, S., & Messick, S. (1974). Social competence in young children. *Developmental Psychology, 10,* 282–293.

Ayers, J. (1979). *Sensory integration and the child.* Los Angeles: Western Psychological Services.

Bandura, A. (1977). *Social learning theory.* Englewood Cliffs, NJ: Prentice Hall.

Bandura, A. (1986). *Social foundations of thought and action.* Englewood Cliffs, NJ: Prentice Hall.

Bandura, A. (1989). Social cognitive theory. In R. Vasta (Ed.), *Annals of child development, Vol. 6* (pp. 1–60). Greenwich, CT: JAI Press.

Baumrind, D. (1967). Child care practices anteceding three patterns of preschool behavior. *Genetic Psychology Monographs, 75,* 43-88.

Belsky, J. (1984). Determinants of parenting. *Child Development, 55,* 83–96.

Belsky, J., & Pensky, E. (1988). Toward an emergent family system. In R. E. Hinde, & J. Stevenson-Hinde (Eds.), *Relationships within families: Mutual influences* (pp. 193–217). Oxford: Clarendon.

Berk, L. (1996). *Infants, children, and adolescents* (2nd ed.). Boston: Allyn & Bacon.

Berk, L. E., & Landau, S. (1993). Private speech of learning disabled and normally achieving children in classroom academic and laboratory contexts. *Child Development, 64,* 556–571.

Berk, L., & Winsler, A. (1995). *Scaffolding children's learning: Vygotsky and early childhood education.* Washington, DC: NAEYC.

Bowlby, J. (1980). *Attachment and loss: Loss, sadness, and depression, Vol 3.* New York: Basic.

Bretherton, I. (1985). Attachment theory: Retrospect and prospect. In I. Bretherton & E. Waters (Eds.), Growing points of attachment theory and research. *Monographs of the Society for Research in Child Development, 50* (1–2, Serial No. 209).

Bretherton, I., & Waters, E. (Eds.). (1985). Growing points of attachment theory and research. *Monographs of the Society of Research in Child Development, 50* (1–2, Serial No. 209).

Brofenbrenner, U. (1988). Interacting systems in human development: Research paradigms, present and future. In N. Bolger, A. Caspi, G. Downey, & M. Moorehaise (Eds.), *Persons in context: Developmental processes.* New York: Cambridge University Press.

Brofenbrenner, U. (1989). Ecological systems theory. In R. Vasta (Ed.), *Six theories of child development: Revised formulations and current issues (Vol 6.).* Greenwich, CT: JAI Press.

Brooks-Gunn, J., & Lewis, M. (1982). The development of self-knowledge. In C. Kropp & J. Krawkow (Eds.), *The child: Development in social context* (pp. 333–387). Reading, MA: Addison-Wesley.

Breunlin, D., Schwarz, R., & Mac Kune-Karrer, B. (1992). *Metaframeworks: Transcending the models of family therapy*. San Francisco: Jossey-Bass.

Buss, A. H., & Plomin, R. (1984). *Temperament: Early developing personality traits*. Hillsdale, NJ: Erlbaum.

Calkins, S. D. (1994). Origins and outcomes of individual differences in emotion regulation. In N. A. Fox (Ed.), The development of emotion regulation: Biological and behavioral considerations. *Monographs of the Society for Research in Child Development, 59* (2–3, Serial No. 240).

Calkins, S. D., Fox, N. A., & Marshall, T. R. (1996). Behavioral and physiological antecedents of inhibited and uninhibited behavior. *Child Development, 67,* 523–540.

Campbell, S. B. (1990). *Behavior problems in preschool children*. New York: Guilford.

Campos, J., Campos, R., & Barrett, K. (1989). Emergent themes in the study of emotional development and emotional regulation. *Developmental Psychology, 25,* 394–402.

Campos, J. J., Caplovitz, K. B., Lamb, M. E., Goldsmith, H. H., & Stenberg, C. (1983). Socioemotional development. In M. M. Haith & J. J. Campos (Eds.), *Handbook of child psychology. Vol. 2: Infancy and developmental psychobiology* (4th ed., pp. 783–915). New York: Wiley.

Carey, W. B., & McDevitt, S. C. (1978). Revision of the Infant Temperament Questionnaire. *Pediatrics, 61,* 745–739.

Chapman, M., & Skinner, E. A. (1989). Children's agency beliefs, cognitive performance, and conceptions of effort and ability: Individual and developmental differences. *Child Development, 60,* 1229–1238.

Cicchetti, D., Ganiban, J., & Barnett, D. (1991). Contributions from the study of high-risk populations to understanding the development of emotion regulation. In J. Gerber & K. A. Dodge (Eds.), *The development of emotion regulation and dysregulation*. New York: Cambridge University Press.

Coie, J. D., & Kupersmidt, J. (1983). A behavioral analysis of emerging social status in boys' groups. *Child Development, 54,* 1400–1416.

Coie, J. D., & Dodge, K. A. (1983). Continuities and changes in children's social status: A five-year longitudinal study. *Merrill-Palmer Quarterly, 19,* 261–282.

Coie, J. D., & Dodge, K. A. & Coppotelli, H. (1982). Dimensions and types of social status: A cross-age perspective. *Developmental Psychology, 18,* 557–570.

Cole, P. M., Michel, M. K., & Teti, L. O. (1994). The development of emotion regulation and dysregulation: A clinical perspective. In N. A. Fox & J. J. Campos (Eds.), The development of emotion regulation: Biological and behavioral considerations. *Monographs of the Society for Research in Child Development, 59* (2–3, Serial no. 240).

Coles, R. (1997). *The moral intelligence of children*. New York: Random House.

Connell, J. P. (1980). *A multidimensional measure of children's perceptions of control*. Unpublished masters thesis, University of Denver.

Connelly, J. J., & Bruner, J. S. (Eds.). (1974). *The growth of competence*. London: Academic Press.

Coopersmith, S. (1967) *The antecedents of self-esteem.* San Francisco: W.H. Freeman.

Cowen, E. L., Pederson, A., Babigan, H., Izzo, L. D., & Trost, M. A. (1973). Long-term follow-up of early detected vulnerable children. *Journal of Consulting and Clinical Psychology, 41,* 438–446.

Damon, W. (1983). *Social and personality development.* New York: Norton.

Damon, W., & Hart, D. (1982). The development of self-understanding from infancy through adolescence. *Child Development, 53,* 841–864.

Danforth, J. S., Barkley, R. A., & Stokes, T. F. (1991). Observations of parent-child interactions with hyperactive children: Research and clinical applications. *Clinical Psychology Review, 11,* 703–727.

Denham, S. A. (1998). *Emotional development of young children.* New York: Guilford.

Dodge, K. A. (1983). Behavioral antecedents of peer status. *Child Development, 54,* 1386–1399.

Dodge, K. A., Pettit, G. S., McClaskey, C. L., & Brown, M. M. (1986). Social competence in children. *Monographs of the Society for Research in Child Development, 51* (1, Serial No. 213).

Dumas, J. E. (1989). Treating antisocial behavior in children: Child and family approaches. *Clinical Psychology Review, 9,* 197–222.

Edwards, D., Gandini, L., Forman, G. (Eds.). (1996). *The hundred languages of children: The Reggio Emilia approach to early childhood education.* Greenwich, CT: Ablex.

Efran, J. S., Greene, M. A., & Gordon, D. E. (1998, March/April). Lessons of the new genetics: Finding the right fit for our clients. *Family Therapy Networker, 22*(2), 26–41.

Egeland, B., Carlson, E., & Sroufe, L. A. (1993). Resilience as process. *Development and psychopathology, 5,* 517–528.

Ellis, S., Rogoff, B., & Cromer, C. C. (1981). Age segregation in children's social interactions. *Developmental Psychology, 17,* 399–407.

Erikson, E. (1950). *Childhood and society.* New York: Norton.

Eyberg, S. M., & Ross, A. W. (1978). Assessment of child behavior problems: The validation of a new inventory. *Journal of Clinical Child Psychology, 7,* 113–116.

Farran, D. C., & Shonkoff, J. P. (1994). Developmental Disabilities and the concept of school readiness. *Early Education and Development, 5,* 141–151.

Feis, C. L., & Simons, C. (1985). Training preschool children in interpersonal cognitive problem solving skills: A replication. *Prevention in Human Services, 3,* 59–70.

Field, T. (1985). Attachment as psychobiological attunement: Being on the same wavelength. In M. Reite & T. Field (Eds.), *Psychobiology of attachment and separation.* New York: Academic.

Forehand, R. L., Gardner, H., & Roberts, M. (1978). Maternal response to child compliance and noncompliance: Some normative data. *Journal of Clinical Child Psychology, 7,* 121–124.

Fox, N. A. (1994). The development of emotion regulation: Biological and behavioral considerations. *Monographs of the Society for Research in Child Development, 59* (2–3, Serial No. 240).

Goldberg, I. D., Roghmann, K. J., McInery, T. K., & Burke, J. D. (1984). Mental health problems among children seen in pediatric practice: Prevalence and management. *Pediatrics, 73,* 278–293.

Goleman, D. (1995). *Emotional intelligence.* New York: Bantam.

Gottlieb, G. (1996). Developmental psychobiological theory. In R. B. Cairns & G. H. Elder (eds.), *Developmental science: Cambridge studies in social and emotional development* (pp. 63–77). New York: Cambridge University Press.

Goyette, C. H., Conners, C. K., & Ulrich, R. F. (1978). Normative data on the revised Conners Parent and Teacher Rating Scales. *Journal of Abnormal Child Psychology, 6,* 221–236.

Granger, D., Stansbury, K., & Henker, B. (1994). Preschoolers behavioral and neuroendocrine response to social challenge. *Merrill-Palmer Quarterly, 40*(2), 190–211.

Greenspan, S. (1992). *Infancy and early childhood: The practice of clinical assessment and intervention with emotional and developmental challenges.* Madison, CT: International Universities Press.

Greenspan, S., & Greenspan, N. (1985). *First feelings: Milestones in the emotional development of your baby and child.* New York: Viking.

Greenspan, S., & Meisels, S. (1986). Toward a new vision for the developmental assessment of infants and young children. In S. Meisels & E. Fenichel (Eds.), *New visions for the developmental assessment of infants and young children* (pp. 11–26). Washington, DC: Zero to Three.

Greenspan, S., & Wieder, S. (1998). *The child with special needs: Encouraging intellectual and emotional growth.* Reading MA: Perseus.

Grusec, J. E. (1988). *Social development: History, theory, and research.* New York: Springer-Verlag.

Gunnar, M. (1994). Psychoendocrine studies of temperament and stress in early childhood: Expanding current models. In J. Bates & T. Wachs (Eds.), *Temperament: Individual differences at the interface of biology and behavior* (pp. 175–198). Washington, DC: American Psychological Association.

Gunnar, M. R., Larson, M., Hertsgaard, L., Harris, M., & Brodersen, L. (1992). The stressfulness of separation among nine-month-old infants: Effects of social context variables and infant temperament. *Child Development, 63,* 290–303.

Gunnar, M. R., Mangelsdorf, D., Larson, M., & Hertsgaard, L. (1989). Attachment, temperament, and adrenocorital activity in infancy: A study of psychoendocrine regulation. *Developmental Psychology, 25,* 355–363.

Gunnar, M., Malone, S., Vance, G., & Fisch, R. O. (1985). Coping with aversive stimulation in the neonatal periods: Quiet sleep and plasma cortisol levels during recovery form circumcision in newborns. *Child Development, 56,* 824–834.

Gunnar, M., Marvinney, D., Isensee, J., & Fisch, R. O. (1989). Coping with uncertainty: New models of the relations between hormonal behavioral and cognitive processes. In D. Palermo (Ed.), *Coping with uncertainty: Biological, behavioral, and developmental perspectives.* Hillsdale, NJ: Erlbaum.

Gunnar, M.R., Tout, K., de Haan, M., Pierce, S., & Stansbury, K. (1997). Temperament, social competence, and adrenocortical activity in preschoolers. *Developmental Psychobiology, 31,* 65–85.

Harter, S. (1981). A new self-report scale of intrinsic versus extrinsic orientation in the classroom: motivational and informational components. *Developmental Psychology, 17,* 300–312.

Harter, S. (1982). The perceived competence scale for children. *Child Development, 53,* 87–97.

Harter, S. (1983). Developmental perspectives on the self-system. In E. M. Hetherington (Ed.), *Handbook of child psychology, Vol. 4: Socialization, personality, and social development* (4th ed., pp. 275–385). New York: Wiley.

Harter, S. (1986). Processes underlying the construction, maintenance and enhancement of self-concept in children. In S. Suhls & A. Greenwald (Eds.), *Psychological perspectives of the self* (Vol. 3, pp. 136–182). Hillsdale, NJ: Erlbaum.

Harter, S. (1990). Issues in the assessment of the self-concept of children and adolescents. In A. LaGreca (Ed.), *Through the eyes of a child* (pp. 292–325). Boston: Allyn & Bacon.

Harter, S. (1999). *The construction of the self: A developmental perspective.* New York: Guilford.

Harter, S., & Pike, R. (1984). The pictorial scale of perceived competence and social acceptance for young children. *Child Development, 55,* 1969–1982.

Hartup, W. W. (1970). Peer interaction and social organization. In P.H. Mussen (Ed.), *Carmichael's manual of child psychology. Vol 2* (pp. 361–456). New York: John Wiley.

Hartup, W. W. (1983a). Peer interactions and the behavioral development of the individual child. In W. Damon (Ed.), *Social and personality development: Essays on the growth of the child.* New York: Norton.

Hartup, W. W. (1983b). Peer relations. In E. M. Hetherington (Ed.), *Handbook of child psychology, Vol. 4: Socialization, personality, and social development* (4th ed., pp. 103–106). New York: Wiley.

Hartup, W. W. (1989). Social relationships and theory developmental significance. *American Psychologist, 44,* 120–126.

Hendrick, J. (1997). *First steps toward teaching the Reggio way.* Upper Saddle River, NJ: Merrill.

Hoffman, M. L. (1988). Moral development. In M. H. Bornstein & M. E. Lamb (Eds.), *Developmental psychology: An advanced textbook* (2nd ed., pp. 497–548). Hillsdale, NJ: Erlbaum.

Isabella, R., & Belsky, J. (1991). Interactional synchrony and the origins of infant-mother attachment: A replication study. *Child Development, 62,* 373–384.

Izard, C. (1993). Organizational and motivational functions of discrete emotions. In M. Lewis & L. Haviland (Eds.), *Handbook of emotions* (pp. 631–641). New York: Guilford.

Jacobvitz, D., & Sroufe, L. A. (1987). The early caregiver-child relationship and attention-deficit disorder with hyperactivity in kindergarten: A prospective study. *Child Development, 58,* 1496–1504.

Kagan, J. (1994). On the nature of emotion. In N. A. Fox (Ed.), The development of emotion regulation: Biological and behavioral considerations. *Monographs of the Society for Research in Child Development* (59, Serial Nos. 2–3).

Kagan, J., Kearsley, R. B., & Zelazo, P. R. (1978). *Infancy: Its place in human development.* Cambridge, MA: Harvard University Press.

Kagan, J., Reznick, J. S., & Snidman, N. (1987). The physiology and psychology of behavioral inhibition in children. *Child Development, 58,* 1459–1473.

Kagan, J., Reznick, J. S., & Snidman, N. (1988). Biological bases of childhood shyness. *Science, 240,* 167–171.

Kazdin, A. E. (1987). Treatment of antisocial behavior in children: Current status and future directions. *Psychological Bulletin, 102,* 187–203.

Keilor, G. (1985). *Lake Wobegon days.* New York: Penguin.

Kochanska, G. (1993). Toward a synthesis of parental socialization and child temperament in early development of conscience. *Child Development, 64,* 325–347.

Kranowitz, C. S. (1998). *The out-of-sync child: Recognizing and coping with sensory integration dysfunction.* New York: Perigie/Putnam.

Kupersmidt, J. B., Coie, J. D., & Dodge, K. A. (1990). The role of poor peer relationships in the development of disorder. In S. R. Asher & J. D. Coie (Eds.), *Peer rejection in childhood* (pp. 274–305). Cambridge: Cambridge University Press.

Ladd, G. W., & Price, J. M. (1987). Predicting children's social and school adjustments following the transition from preschool to kindergarten. *Child Development, 58,* 1168–1189.

Lewis, M. (1989). Emotional development in the preschool child. *Pediatric Annals, 18,* 316–327.

Lewis, M., Alessandri, S. M., & Sullivan, M. (1992). Differences in shame and pride as a function of children's gender and task difficulty. *Child Development, 63,* 630–638.

Lewis, M., & Brooks, J. (1978). Self-knowledge in emotional development. In M. Lewis & L. Rosenblum (Eds.), *The development of affect* (pp. 205–226). New York: Plenum.

Linder, T. (1993). *Transdisciplinary play-based assessment* (rev. ed.). Baltimore: Brookes.

Maccoby, E. (1980). *Social development: Psychological growth and the parent-child relationship.* New York: Harcourt Brace Jovanovich.

Magnusson, D. (1988). *Individual development from an interactional perspective: A longitudinal study.* Hillsdale, NJ: Erlbaum.

Malaquzzi, L. (1993). History, ideas, and basic philosophy. In C. Edwards, L. Gandini, & G. Forman (Eds.), *The hundred languages of children. The Reggio Emilia approach to early childhood education.* Norwood, NJ: Abby.

McCall, R. B., Appelbaum, M. I., & Hagarty, P. S. (1973). Developmental changes in mental performance. *Monographs of the Society for Research in Child Development, 38* (3, Serial No. 150).

Mead, G. H. (1934). *Mind, self, and society.* Chicago: University of Chicago Press.

Miller, P. H. (1993). *Theories of developmental psychology* (3rd ed.). New York: Freeman.

Minuchin, P. (1985). Families and individual development: Provocations form the field of family therapy. *Child Development, 56,* 289–302.

Morris, R., & Kratochwill, T. (1983). *Treating children's fears and phobias: A behavioral approach.* Elmsford, NY: Pergamon.

Mussen, P., & Eisenberg-Berg, N. (1977). *Roots of caring, sharing, and helping: The development of prosocial behavior in children.* San Francisco: Freeman.

Newborg, J., Stock, J., Wnek, L., Guiduabaldi, J., & Sviniski, J. (1988). *Battelle developmental inventory screening test.* Chicago: Riverside.

Nichols, M. D. (1987). *The self in the system: Expanding the limits of family therapy.* New York: Brunner/Mazel.

Nowicki, S., Jr., & Strickland, B. R. (1973). A locus of control scale for children. *Journal of Consulting and Clinical Psychology, 40,* 148–154.

Odom, S., & Munson, L. (1996). Assessing social performance. In M. McLean, D. Bailey, & M. Wolery (Eds.), *Assessing infants and preschoolers with special needs* (2nd ed., pp. 398–343). Columbus, OH: Merrill.

Parker, J. G., & Asher, S. R. (1987). Peer relations and later adjustment: Are low-accepted children "at risk"? *Psychological Bulletin, 102,* 357–389.

Pettit, G. S., Dodge, K. A., & Brown, M. M. (1988). Early experience social problem-solving patterns, and children's social competence. *Child Development, 59,* 107–120.

Reiss, D. (1995). Genetic influence of family systems: Implications for development. *Journal of Marriage and the Family, 57,* 289–302.

Rothbart, M. K. (1981). Measurement of temperament in infancy. *Child Development, 52,* 569–578.

Rothbart, M. K. (1989). Temperament in childhood: A framework. In G. A. Kohstam, J. E. Bales, & M. K. Rothbart (Eds.), *Temperament in childhood.* Chichester: Wiley.

Rubin, Z. (1983). What is a friend? In W. Damon (Ed.), *Social and personality development: Essays on the growth of the child.* New York: Norton.

Rubin, K. H., & Coplan, R. J. (1992). Peer relationships in childhood. In M. H. Bornstein & M. E. Lamb (Eds.), *Developmental psychology: An advanced textbook* (3rd. ed). Hillsdale, NJ: Erlbaum.

Rubin, K. H., Hymel, S., LeMare, L. J., & Rowden, L. (1989). Children experiencing social difficulties: Sociometric neglect reconsidered. *Canadian Journal of Behavioral Science, 21,* 94–111.

Rubin, K. H., & Krasnor, L. R. (1983). Age and gender differences in the development of a representative social problem solving skill. *Journal of Applied Developmental Psychology, 4,* 463–475.

Rubin, K. H., Watson, K. S., & Jambor, T. W. (1978). Free-play behaviors in preschool and kindergarten children. *Child Development, 49,* 539–536.

Schroeder, C. S., & Gordon, B. N. (1991). *Assessment and treatment of childhood problems: A clinician's guide.* New York: Guilford.

Sethre-Hofstad, L. (1998, March). *Maternal sensitivity, cortisol, and emotion regulation: Relations between mothers and preschool-aged children in response to stress.* Paper presented at the Fifteenth Biannual conference on Human Development, Mobile, AL.

Shaffer, D. R. (1988). *Social and personality development* (2nd ed.). Belmont, CA: Wadsworth.

Shantz, C. U. (1987). Conflicts between children. *Child Development, 58,* 283–305.

Shore, R. (1997). *Rethinking the brain: New insights into early development.* New York: Families and Work Institute.

Silverman, I. W., & Ragusa, D. M. (1990). Child and maternal correlates of impulse control in 24-month-old children. *Genetic, Social, and General Psychology Monographs, 116*(4), 435–473.

Smilansky. S. (1968). *The effects of sociodramatic play on disadvantaged children: Preschool children.* New York: Wiley.

Smilansky, S., & Shefatya, L. (1990). *Facilitating play: A medium for promoting cognitive, socio-emotional and academic development in young children.* Gaithersburg, MD: Psychosocial & Educational Publishers.

Snow, C. W. (1998). *Infant development* (2d. ed.). Upper Saddle River, NJ: Prentice Hall.

Sparrow, S., Balla, D., & Cicchetti, D. (1984). *Interview edition, expanded form manual, Vineland adaptive behavior scales.* Circle Pines, MN: American Guidance Service.

Sroufe, L. A. (1983). Infant-caregiver attachment and patterns of maladaption in preschool: The roots of maladaption and competence. In M. Perlmutter (Ed.), *Development and policy concerning children with special needs* (Minnesota Symposia on Child Psychology, Vol. 16), Hillsdale, NJ: Erlbaum.

Sroufe, L. A., & Fleeson, J. (1986). Attachment and the construction of relationships. In W. Hartup & Z. Rubin (Eds.), *Relationships and development* (pp. 51–72). Hillsdale, NJ: Erlbaum.

Sroufe, L. A., Schork, E., Motti, F., Lawroski, N., & LaFreniere, P. (1984). The role of affect in social competence. In C. E. Izard, J. Kagan, & R. B. Zajonc (Eds.), *Emotions, cognition, and behavior.* Cambridge: Cambridge University Press.

Sroufe, L. A., & Waters, E. (1976). The ontoagenesis of smiling and laughing: A perspective on the organization of development in infancy. *Psychological Review, 83,* 173–189.

Sroufe, L. A., & Waters, E. (1977). Attachment as an organizational construct. *Child Development, 48,* 1184–1199.

Stansbury, K. & Gunnar, M. R. (1994). Adrenocortical Activity and emotion regulation. In N. A. Fox (Ed.), The development of emotion regulation: Biological and behavioral considerations. *Monographs of the Society for Research in Child Development, 59* (2–3, Serial No. 240).

Stern, D. N. (1985). *The interpersonal world of the infant.* New York: Basic.

Stipeck, D., Recchia, S., & McClintic, S. (1992). Self-evaluation in young children. *Monographs of-st the Society for Research in Child Development, 57* (1, Serial No. 226), 1–84.

Tangney, J. P., Burggraf, S. A., & Wagner, P. E. (1995). Shame-proneness, guilt-proneness, and psychological symptoms. In J. P. Tangney & K. W. Fischer (Eds.), *Self-conscious emotions: The psychology of shame, guilt, embarrassment, and pride* (pp. 347–367). New York: Guilford.

Tangney, J. P., & Fischer, K. W. (1995). *Self-conscious emotions: The psychology of shame, guilt, embarrassment, and pride.* New York: Guilford.

Thomas, A., & Chess, S. (1977). *Temperament and development.* New York: Brunner/Mazel.

Thomas, A., Chess, S., & Birch, H. B. (1969). *Temperament and behavior disorders in children.* New York: New York University Press.

Thompson, R. (1994). Emotion regulation: A theme in search of definitions. In N. Fox (Ed.), The development of emotion regulation: Biological and behavioral considerations. *Monographs of the Society for Research in Child Development 59* (2–3, Serial No. 240).

Tomlinson, S. (1982). *A sociology of special education.* London: Routledge & Kegan Paul.

White, B. (1985). *The first three years of life* (rev. ed.). Englewood Cliffs, NJ: Prentice. Hall.

Winsler, A. J. (1995). The social origins and self-regulatory quality of private speech in hyperactive and normal children. *Dissertation Abstracts International, 55*(7), 1885A. (University Microfilms No. 9430018).

Winsler, A. J., Diaz, R. M., McCarthy, E. M., Bird, R. L., & Feldman, A. (1995). *Early verbal self regulation in children at-risk for Attention-Deficit Hyperactivity Disorder.* Poster presented at the Biennial Meeting of the Society for Research in Child Development.

Winsler, A. J., Diaz, R. M., & Montero, I. (1997). The role of private speech in the transition from collaborative to independent task performance in young children. *Early Childhood Research Quarterly, 12,* 59–79.

Young, L. (1966). *Life among the giants.* NY: McGraw-Hill.

Zahn-Waxler, C., Kochanska, G., Krupnich, J., & McKnew, D. (1990). Patterns of guilt in children of depressed and well mothers. *Developmental Psychology, 26,* 51–59.

Zahn-Waxler, C., & Radke-Yarrow, M. (1990). The origins of empathetic concern. *Motivation and Emotion, 14,* 107–130.

Zimmermann, L. K. (1998, March). *Emotion regulation and cortisol elevation in shy three-year-old children.* Paper presented at the Fifteenth Biannual Meeting of the Conference of Human Development, Mobile, AL.

17

Involving Parents in Children's Therapy

C. Everett Bailey

Catherine E. Ford Sori

"I scheduled another client for you," the receptionist informed me. "A parent called and said she wanted to bring her child in because she is having problems with her," she continued.

"Did the parent say anything about coming to the session?" I wondered.

"No. She said she just wanted an appointment for her child."

Cynically, I thought, another parent dropping off a child to be "fixed." But, how do I persuade parents to participate in therapy without blaming them? Should I just see the child for a couple of sessions and then focus treatment on the parents? If I focus treatment on the parents, do I stop treating the child? If I involved both parents and children in sessions, how would I do it?

Most therapists are confronted with these issues and questions when a child is presented for therapy. Currently, most therapists approach children's problems either by treating the child alone, usually through play therapy, or by treating the parents alone. As marriage and family therapists, we believe that such a dichotomous approach to treatment is unnecessary and that it is important to have both parents and children involved in treatment. Family therapy and individual child therapy can complement each other to develop the most effective treatment for both children and parents. Nevertheless, studies indicate that marriage and family therapists often do not treat parents and children together. In fact, children are often excluded from family therapy, while family therapists focus on treating parents, even when a child is the identified patient (Johnson & Thomas, 1999; Korner & Brown, 1990). At times it may be important to see the child alone as part of treatment. Yet, our ultimate goal is to help improve the parent-child relationship. In doing so, we can build a long-term foundation that will help the family resolve any future problems they encounter. However, to accomplish this, parents must be involved in children's therapy.

In this chapter, we discuss the process of involving parents in their children's therapy. First, we offer a rationale for why it is important to involve parents in children's treatment. Second, we discuss reasons why parents have not been traditionally involved in their children's therapy. Next, we introduce a multimodal approach for treating children that emphasizes parental involvement. Then, we briefly summarize two common approaches to treating children's problems: play therapy (e.g., Landreth, 1991) and parent management training (e.g., Briesmeister & Schaefer, 1998). We also describe treatments that involve both parents and children in therapy and illustrate them with brief case studies. Finally, we present an extended case study that demonstrates a multimodal approach to therapy and the importance of involving parents in children's treatment.

Parental Involvement in Children's Therapy

We believe there are several reasons why parents ought to be involved in their children's therapy. The most salient is that research in both the child development and family fields gives strong evidence that children's problems are determined by many factors. This belief is in stark contrast to the long-established systemic notion that a child's problems are symptomatic of marital problems or family dysfunction (Montalvo & Haley, 1973; Olson, 1970). Although children can experience externalizing and internalizing disorders as a result of marital conflict (Cummings & Davies, 1994; Fincham, 1998), research also shows that genetics (Plomin & Rutter, 1998), temperament difficulties (Sanson & Rothbart, 1995), parental psychopathology (Field, 1995), sibling relationships (Brody & Stoneman, 1996), physical illness and disabilities (Rolland, 1994), economic and social factors (Hoff-Ginsberg & Tardif, 1995), and peer relationships (Ladd & Le Sieur, 1995) are all factors that influence children's behavior. In order to assess and treat all of these factors, parents must be involved. Parents provide critical information that is necessary to conduct a thorough assessment, including information about the child's development and family background. Parents are the experts when it comes to their child. In addition to providing important background information, parents can identify both the child's and the family's strengths that will enable the child to overcome his or her problems. This information and support from the parents is paramount in helping the child change and maintain therapeutic gains.

Therapists can also observe parental functioning and parent-child dynamics in session when they involve parents. This "live" observation is necessary to understand the impact that the parent-child interaction has on the child's functioning. Often the parent-child relationship becomes dominated by the problem, focusing exclusively on the child's negative behavior, while disregarding the child's good behavior and inherent strengths. In response, children resent and resist their parents, often escalating their negative behavior. Thus, to ultimately help the child change, therapists need to help parents change unhealthy parent-child interactions that maintain the problem.

A third reason for parental involvement is that parents who are having problems with a child need support and encouragement. Not only do parents affect children; they are also greatly affected by their child's problems. At the point that they bring the child into therapy parents may feel discouraged and "worn down." Moreover, parents frequently blame themselves and feel blamed by others (e.g., teachers, doctors, other family members) for their child's problems. Most parents take their child's problems personally and often carry a burden of shame and guilt for contributing to or causing their child's problems. In addition, they often feel inadequate and confused about how to help their child. All of these feelings undermine their confidence in their parenting. As a result, they often come to therapy feeling frustrated and hopeless. Of course, any parent experiencing such feelings is going to struggle in their parenting, even under the best conditions. Therapists can provide a supportive environment where parents can start to understand both their own role and their child's role in the problem. Therapists can also identify strengths and resources that parents can draw on when dealing with their child's problem.

A fourth reason to involve parents is that the child may be adversely affected by the parent's problems. Marital discord or a parent's own mental illness (e.g., depression, substance abuse) may be contributing to the child's difficulties. If the parents are not involved in treatment, then the therapist will never know if the parents' marital relationship or individual functioning is undermining the child's progress in therapy.

Finally, the goal of therapy should be to help parents to help their children. Treatment should focus on improving the parent-child relationship, thereby creating a context for the child to change. If parents are excluded from treatment, then the emphasis remains on the individual child's behavior and the only relationship that is improved is the therapist-child relationship. Treatments insensitive to the contextual factors affecting children's behavior run the risk of only providing symptom relief and not long-term treatment gains. For example, Estrada and Pinsof (1995) report that children from families with multiple risk factors (e.g., marital discord, parental psychopathology, social-cognitive deficits, socioeconomic disadvantage) show fewer therapeutic gains and are less likely to maintain those gains over time.

Why Parents Are Not Involved in Therapy

Historically, parents have not been involved in children's therapy because traditional child psychotherapy has been approached from a psychoanalytic perspective. In the psychoanalytic approach the therapist uses play to gain access to the child's inner life. Thus, the main focus of therapy is on the child's intrapsychic process and exploring the unconscious. This is best done through analysis of the transference in the therapist-child relationship. Since the child's problems stemmed from the unconscious and the inclusion of more than one person in therapy would contaminate the transference, parents were not included in the therapy. In a similar fashion, play therapists are trained to work individually with a child. Play therapists engage the child in play to help him or her express and resolve a traumatic experience. Generally, the parents are not involved in treatment and the therapist usually does not inform the parent about what goes on in the child's therapy (Landreth, 1991).

As a result of this history, parents may not expect to be involved in treatment. They are probably not familiar with the systemic approach that stresses the inclusion of multiple family members, especially the parents. Family therapists, therefore, may need to educate parents about the systems approach to therapy. One analogy that most parents can relate to is comparing the family system to a mobile. When one of the parts of the mobile moves it affects the other parts. Similarly, when one family member is having problems it impacts other members of the family and vice versa. All family members should be involved in order to assess accurately how each family member is affected by the problem.

Another reason parents might not initiate involvement in therapy is they are afraid of being blamed for their child's problems. Parents tend to be defensive about their parenting because they fear that they may have caused their child's problem. They fear that the therapist may point to them as the source of the child problems (e.g., they didn't toilet-train the child properly). Because of these concerns, therapists need to establish a strong therapeutic alliance with the parents. This can be done by being nonjudgmental, supportive, and sympathetic to the parents' challenges. Therapists should be empathic and discover a personal experience or feeling that will help them relate to the parents' struggles, even if they, themselves, are not a parent. In addition, therapists can acknowledge the parents' desire to be good parents and the concern they show by seeking help for their child. Clinicians can also build trust by finding something that they respect or admire about the parents; something that they think the parents are doing well. It is easy for both parents and clinicians to focus on deficits—in the child, parents, and family. We believe it is vital to the therapeutic alliance and to the outcome of therapy to help parents shift their focus from deficits to family strengths and past resiliencies (Walsh, 1998). Pointing out parental strengths and resiliencies will help reconstruct the parents' self-confidence and build a relationship of trust with the therapist. Therapists should avoid pathologizing parents or blaming them for the child's problems. Building a strong therapeutic alliance by gaining the parents' trust, is critical groundwork that must be laid before attempting to intervene. Unless a therapist disarms the parents' fear and defensiveness by establishing a relationship of safety and trust, parents will remain resistant to change and want the therapy to stay focused on their child.

Another way to persuade parents to participate in therapy is to let them know that they are an important resource for their child. Therapists can stress to parents that their child needs their support to make and maintain behavioral changes. Parents, then, can act as cotherapists or consultants to the therapist and be invited to play a positive role in helping their child to change.

Multimodal Approach to Working with Children

In our work with children and their families, we have found that it is important to assess and treat both individual and relationship issues. We believe that to effectively treat children a therapist needs to be able to assess and treat six different areas:

1. the individual child who is the identified patient
2. the individual functioning of each parent
3. the child's relationship with each parent
4. the marital relationship
5. sibling relationships
6. the overall family relationships, including multigenerational relationships

First, individual child therapy may be called for to help children heal from traumatic experiences, resolve internalized conflicts, and gain mastery over their environment. In many cases if the child's individual issues are not addressed they may continue to foster problems in the parent-child relationship. The same can be said for individual therapy with the parents. Many of the parents' past issues tend to surface in the parent-child relationship. These issues are largely a result of their experience in their family of origin. Unless some of these issues are addressed in the parents' individual therapy it will be difficult to help the parents make any effective changes in the parent-child relationship.

In addition to addressing individual issues, it is also necessary to assess and treat different family relationships. Of vital importance is the parent-child relationship. If the parent-child relationship is dysfunctional (i.e., the parents are abusive or neglectful), the child will continue to manifest problem behavior, even if individual therapy with the child is "successful." The interaction between a parent and child can create problems that did not otherwise exist. Individually or in other relationships, the parent/child may be asymptomatic; however, the parent-child interaction can serve as a catalyst for problems. As a result, it is important that the therapist assess and treat each parent's interaction with the child. The therapist also needs to consider the marital relationship or, in some cases, the impact of marital dissolution on the children. Research documents the negative impact that marital discord has on children's adjustment. If a therapist observes a significant amount of interparental conflict, it is important to include marital therapy as part of the treatment plan. Finally, because of the dynamics that other children create in a family system it is important to assess the interaction of the entire family. Cross-generational alliances, differential treatment of siblings by parents, unresolved family-of-origin issues that are affecting current parental or family functioning, or other family problems affecting a child's behavior may not manifest themselves unless all family members are seen and assessed in therapy. This often calls for individual, dyadic, couple, and whole-family assessment. All of these types of therapy may not be necessary in every case. However, because a child's development is multi-determined, a therapist must assess and be prepared to treat each of the above areas, if necessary, in order to ensure the most effective treatment for children and their families.

The Use of Play Therapy in Treating Children's Problems

For many individually trained child therapists, the primary therapeutic approach to treating children's problems is play therapy. A play therapist "provides selected play materials and facilitates the development of a safe relationship for the child to fully express and explore self (feelings, thoughts, experiences, and behaviors) through the child's natural medium of communication, play" (Landreth, 1991, p. 14). Landreth goes on to say, "Children are able to use toys to say what they cannot say, do things they would feel uncomfortable doing, and express feelings they might be reprimanded for verbalizing. Play is the child's symbolic language of self-expression and can reveal (1) what the child has experienced; (2) reactions to what was experienced; (3) feelings about what was experienced; (4) what the child wishes, wants, or needs; and (5) the child's perception of self" (p. 15). Although play therapy is an effective way to help the child deal with his or her individual issues, parents are often not involved in treatment. Generally, parental involvement is limited to providing background information about the child's problem, even though such information is not considered essential. Play therapists believe that if parents are included in treatment, the same therapist should not see both the child and the parents. If parent involvement is needed, parents should be referred to another therapist in order to prevent interference with the therapist-child relationship. If a play therapist does meet with the parents, it is recommended that they meet at a time when they do not have the child with them, or the therapist split the session and spend half the time with the parents and half the time with the child. Even though some play therapists may involve parents in the child's therapy, play therapists contend that children can change their behavior without their parents' involvement or the parents changing their own behavior (Landreth, 1991). Although this may be true in cases where the child is dealing with a singular traumatic event, many childhood problems are more complex and will not be resolved in the long term unless parents and other family members are involved in treatment.

The Use of Parent Management Training in Treating Children's Problems

In contrast to child play therapy, which focuses almost exclusively on the child, parent management training (PMT) focuses treatment on parents. In the psychological literature, PMT has gained wide acceptance and empirical support in treating a broad range of childhood disorders (Briesmester & Schaefer, 1998). Grounded in behaviorism and social learning theory, PMT teaches parents specific parenting skills that will help them alter interactions with their child and decrease the child's problem behavior. Treatment does not typically involve the child. Instead, parents are taught social learning principles and procedures such as positive reinforcement (e.g., praise, tokens, or points), mild punishment (e.g., use of time out or loss of privileges), negotiation, and contingency contracting. Once parents become proficient in these procedures than the focus shifts to applying them to the child's specific problem behavior (Estrada & Pinsof, 1995).

Play therapy and PMT certainly provide some benefits by addressing the individual functioning of children and parents. However, these methods do not acknowledge, nor address, the impact that family relationships have on a child's behavior. Yet, the research literature shows that parenting and child development is largely affected by several factors beyond the individual (Bornstein, 1995; Belsky, 1984). This implies that in addition to assessing and treating individual issues, effective treatment must address parent-child, marital, and family dynamics.

Treatment Approaches Involving Both Parents and Children

Parent-Child Interaction Therapy

Parent-child interaction therapy (PCIT) (Eyberg 1988; Eyberg & Boggs, 1998) is an extension of PMT. PCIT is divided into two components, which integrate behavioral family therapy with the general principles of traditional play therapy. Each component is taught to the parents alone in a didactic session. The first component is child-directed interaction (CDI) and is the part that distinguishes PCIT from PMT. In these sessions, parents learn and practice skills that will enhance parent-child interaction. The skills they learn are based on the basic rule to follow the child's lead during the play session. Parents are also given three Don't rules: don't give commands, don't ask questions, and don't criticize. In addition, parents are instructed to describe what the child is doing during play, imitate what the child is doing, reflect what the child says during play, and praise the child. These guidelines help parents minimize negative interaction and establish a positive parent-child relationship that will serve as the foundation for effective behavior change. After the parents learn these rules, then children are included in the sessions. In these conjoint sessions, a parent plays with the child while the therapist and the other parent observes them through a one-way mirror. During the session, the therapist coaches the parents and provides positive feedback on their demonstrated skills.

When parents become proficient in parent-child play, treatment moves on to the second phase, parent-directed interaction (PDI). During this phase, rather than just responding to child-initiated play, parents are directed to lead the activity. Parents are instructed to give clear, direct commands that require child compliance. If the child complies then the parent gives labeled praise that tells the child specifically what the parent likes about his or her behavior. If the child does not comply then the parent initiates a time-out procedure. Once the child complies consistently in sessions, then parents begin to give commands related to the child's presenting problems. The total therapy program takes an average of 9 to 12 sessions.

The strength of PCIT is its inclusion of both parents and children in treatment. Although it can be effective in changing the parent-child interaction, we believe that it is too didactic and narrow in its focus on behavior, excluding emotions and other family dynamics.

PMT and PCIT can be effective by teaching the parents behavior-management skills that change the parent-child interaction and help reduce the child's behavior problems. This is an important step, especially when parents are initially angry and frustrated with their children. However, simply eliminating symptoms is often not enough. Child behavior problems are often a symptom of an underlying problem (e.g., ADD, peer problems, fears or anxieties, depression in the child and/or a parent, marital conflict that is being detoured through a child). Often, eliminating a symptom without addressing larger systemic issues results in a different set of symptoms cropping up in the same child or another family member (V. Thomas, personal communication, 1999).

Filial Therapy

Filial therapy (Johnson, 1995; Landreth, 1991; VanFleet, 1994) is another approach developed to address children's behavior problems by improving the parent-child relationship through play. In weekly training sessions, often conducted in groups, parents are taught to conduct child-centered play sessions with their children. During this training, parents are taught four basic skills: structuring skills, empathic listening, child-centered imaginary-play skills, and limit-setting skills (VanFleet, 1994). Parents learn how to conduct play therapy sessions with their children by observing play sessions, receiving skills training, and doing role-plays. After completing the training, parents receive supervision, either live or videotaped, while they conduct play sessions with their children. The following is a description of a case that utilized filial therapy within a multimodal approach that also included individual therapy for the parents and marital therapy.

THE COX FAMILY WAS African-American, and consisted of Charlene, the mother, Clarence, the father, and their 6-year-old daughter, Clarissa ("Rissa"). Clarence and Rissa were extremely close, while Charlene was emotionally disengaged from her daughter, and quite resentful of Dad's attention to Rissa. The child often defied her mother, knowing that Clarence usually took her side against Charlene. This resulted in Charlene often feeling frustrated and angry with both. Charlene openly stated that she wanted to send "that devil child" to live with relatives in another state. However, Mom was very attached to her two pit bulls and three cats. Rissa often teased the dogs, and on more than one occasion had come close to being bitten. Clarence, who usually worked the afternoon shift, worried about Rissa when he was not home. He was the nurturing parent, the one who tucked Rissa in bed and played with her.

As I (CS) came to know the family better, it became apparent that there was a clear division of loyalty in this family. In an individual session, Clarence confided that if he had to choose between Charlene and Rissa, he would choose his daughter. On the other hand, when I addressed the need for Charlene to take steps to ensure her daughter's safety from the dogs, she made it clear that her pets were more important to her than her daughter. Charlene seemed to have little interest in being a parent. Both parents had a simple, child-like quality. In fact, it seemed that Clarence, Charlene, and Rissa were all siblings.

Their previous therapist had done excellent work in engaging this family, and in improving communication about these difficult issues. She had found that what worked best was to hold conjoint sessions to improve the marital relationship, along with individual sessions with Mom to meet her individual needs, and family sessions to try to strengthen the mother-daughter relationship.

In individual sessions with Charlene, I learned that she had not wanted children, and that the pregnancy was unplanned. She only went through with the birth because Clarence threatened to leave her if she aborted. She had never wanted Rissa and had never felt close to her. Instead, she felt Rissa had robbed her of Clarence's attention and loyalty.

As I explored Charlene's childhood, it became apparent why it had been difficult for her to bond with Rissa. Charlene had been a "change baby" and was raised in a poor, rural area in Alabama. Throughout her childhood, Charlene's mother locked her in the attic every day, while her parents ran a small grocery store below. She was forced to stay up there all day in the summers, and afternoons and evenings in the winters, with no food, water, or bathroom. There she played alone with a few simple toys. Charlene had no recollection of ever being hugged, read to, played with, kissed, or tucked in bed by either of her parents. It had been five years since she had last seen them, and she spoke to them only about once a year. They took no interest in Rissa. It seemed that children were not valued in her family.

Clarence was raised by his mother after his father deserted the family when he was 5. His mother was warm and had a positive outlook on life, despite hard times and few resources. This seemed to be a trait she passed on to her son.

As Charlene and I explored her family of origin in individual sessions, she was gradually able to see patterns and to understand why her mother had such a difficult time showing affection. A turning point in therapy occurred when Charlene was able to get in touch with her profound sense of loss, loneliness, and isolation in her childhood. As she described what it was like to never to have been shown love by her mother, I asked her how she thought this might have affected her. Charlene wondered aloud if Rissa felt the same way toward her as she did toward her mother. With tears in her eyes, she vowed to be a better mother than her mother had been.

I seized this opportunity to suggest integrating filial therapy with continued individual and family sessions. (Note: I decided not to include Dad in the filial therapy training, because the goals were to enhance the mother-child relationship, and to empower her as a parent to manage Rissa's behavior. Clarence was already overfunctioning as a parent.) In marital sessions Clarence agreed to support and encourage Charlene, to try to parent more as a team, and to spend more time with his wife.

In the first individual filial training session, when I asked Charlene what toys Rissa played with, she replied she did not know. She flatly stated she had never seen Rissa play, since she always sent her to her room. Rissa was overjoyed when she learned that Mom was going to play with her. However, it proved to be very difficult for Charlene to play with her child. As I observed from a corner of the room, I was touched by Rissa's repeated attempts to engage her mother in play. Charlene, however, kept sending her daughter back to another table to play alone so she could finish her own drawing. Charlene truly had never learned how to play with anyone. She was trying, but was utterly unaware of her child's emotional needs.

As the filial training progressed, changes began to emerge in Charlene's parenting. First, she recognized how to apply the limit-setting skills she learned in filial therapy to other times, such as when she tried to get Rissa to shut off the television and go to bed. For example, she would say, "Rissa, you have five minutes left to watch television before getting ready for bed." Rissa's compliance in filial therapy sessions also began to generalize to her behavior at home.

During the same time, Charlene continued in individual therapy. Individual sessions provided her with the support, empathy, and esteem she had missed in childhood. Over time Charlene seemed to literally "grow up" as I encouraged and complimented her on her efforts to be a loving parent. As she worked in individual sessions to label and experience her own emotions, Charlene was increasingly able to play with her child and empathically mirror Rissa's emotions in child-centered play sessions. Rissa had been starving for this attention from her mother, and simply glowed as Mom played with her. Within a few weeks, she was cuddling up in Mom's lap in family sessions, asking Mom to read to her! Charlene, initially uncomfortable with this, responded to my encouragement to cuddle and read to her daughter.

I also continued conducting marital sessions with Charlene and Clarence. Charlene felt slighted by her husband, who often sided with their daughter. Couple therapy helped to adjust the cross-generational alliance that existed between Clarence and Rissa and left Charlene feeling emotionally isolated (which was reminiscent of her childhood experience of being locked in the attic). Clarence began to shift his allegiance away from Rissa and became much more attentive to Charlene. They occasionally even had a "date." As their marital relationship improved, they also began to function more as a parenting team. Clarence reduced his overfunctioning parental role and supported Charlene in becoming an "expert" on parenting her daughter.

As Charlene's image of herself as a parent began to change, so did her relationship with Rissa. Her image of Rissa shifted from a "devil-child" to a more normal, but sometimes difficult child. As Charlene's needs were met through her marriage, she seemed to grasp the fact that parenting was not just about making her daughter mind, but also about showing her love and affection. Now instead of calling her names, she wanted to find ways to improve her parenting skills and to build her daughter's self-esteem. She became so enthused that she often brought a book on parenting to session in order to discuss specific parts that struck her. One major shift occurred when Charlene decided to get involved in her daughter's education. She worked to save money to purchase special materials at the teacher's store in order to work with her daughter at home. She even felt empowered enough to contact the school to advocate for special testing for Rissa. At the same time, Charlene's relationship with her widowed mother was also changing. She had several important conversations with her mother and was excitedly planning a trip to visit.

This multimodal approach that emphasized filial therapy training along with individual and family therapy sessions benefited the entire family. Both the family structure and levels of intimacy were enhanced. Individual sessions helped Charlene deal with her own difficulties with intimacy, which stemmed from her own childhood. With filial training Charlene's self-esteem as a parent soared and her bond with Rissa improved considerably. Couple therapy strengthened the marital bond, as Clarence shifted his primary loyalty from his daughter to his wife. As Charlene felt her needs were being met by Clarence, she was able to be more invested in meeting her daughter's needs. Although the family still had areas they could improve in, the parents had definitely moved along a continuum from poor parenting to "good enough" parenting. Such changes could not have occurred without integrating all of the different approaches.

FILIAL THERAPY CAN BE a valuable treatment component when working with children. It improves the parent-child relationship by empowering the parent to help the child deal with his or her own psychological problems, rather than the therapist helping the child. However, as a sole treatment, its use is limited. Although filial therapy teaches parents how to conduct effective play therapy sessions, the large majority of parent-child interactions occur outside of a play session. Certainly empathic listening and limit setting skills can be generalized beyond play sessions, but parents still need help changing ineffectual moment-to-moment interactions with their children, which can exacerbate or create children's problem behavior. In addition, not all parents are interested in making the necessary investments of time and energy to learn filial therapy and practice it at home.

Family Play Therapy

Family play therapy (Gil, 1994) engages both parents and children in a joint play activity. Such activities include family puppet interviews, family art therapy, mutual storytelling, or playing a board game (see chapter 13 in this book for more activities). Family play therapy engages both parents and children in therapy while providing the clinician an opportunity to observe family dynamics. The purpose of family play therapy is to move therapy from the intellectual and cerebral world familiar to adults to the world of metaphor, imagination, and creativity familiar to children. In the process, family play therapy facilitates change. Through the metaphor of play activities, children are able to express the feelings and experiences that they otherwise would not feel comfortable doing or have the ability to express verbally. Parents also gain insight into their child's inner world and feelings, revealing how certain events have affected them. Family play therapy can have a catalytic affect by infusing energy into therapy that has become flat or stifled because family members have remained disconnected, uncommunicative, superficial, or intellectual in their interaction. It is also a medium that breaks down defenses, while providing a positive, enjoyable interaction, giving distressed families temporary relief from their problems. In addition, it allows family members to break the negative cycle of interaction and to see each other differently.

In contrast to filial therapy, the family play therapist is an active participant in the play session. Rather than teaching parents play therapy skills, the therapist concentrates on helping the parents understand how children experience their world and how family interactions and experiences may be contributing to the child's problems. The therapist "enters" the family's metaphor by exploring, challenging, questioning, and encouraging ongoing interactions between family members. Once the family has participated in the play activity, the therapist invites each family member to describe their play experience. During this processing the therapist highlights parallels between the family's play and the family's presenting problems.

Because of its ability to involve both parents and children in therapy, while allowing the therapist to observe family dynamics in vivo, we feel that family play therapy is a useful treatment component when working with children. It can be very effective as a part of a larger treatment plan that could include individual sessions with a parent, marital therapy, or play therapy sessions with a child. The following is an example of how family play therapy was used to decrease parental pathologizing of a child, and to promote healthy family relationships. I (CS) will highlight a few of the family play techniques that were utilized in the different phases of family therapy.

CELIA ROSEN INITIATED therapy for her 8-year-old daughter, Pamela. Celia was a single parent with two children. Herself an only child, Celia came from a Jewish family, and she had inherited a large fortune from her grandparents. Currently she had chosen not to work in her field, which was finance.

At the beginning of the first session, I (CS) first saw Mom alone. Celia recounted that she was "at the end of her rope" with Pamela, and seeing me was a last resort before she sent the child to live with her father, Dick. (Pamela had been in individual play therapy for six months prior to seeing me.) Celia explained that she and Dick divorced when Pamela was 4, shortly after the birth of their second child, Peter. Dick, an out-of-work attorney, was in and out of their lives. Celia and Dick had tried reconciling on several occasions, but it always ended the same way: Dick taking off without saying goodbye, after he had talked Celia into giving him large sums of money for "investments," and Celia crying and depressed. Frequently, Pamela erupted in violent temper tantrums, during which she screamed at Mom. Pamela was the angriest child I had ever met. These tantrums often occurred when her father was in town or when Mom was going on a date.

Pamela was very sullen at our first meeting. I asked if she wanted to have Mom come in, or if she wanted to come in alone. She decided to come in alone. Still not talking, she begrudgingly allowed me to read the Dinosaur Divorce book to her. Pamela was fascinated with the pages about feelings little dinosaurs have when parents divorce. She identified with the pictures of sadness, fear, and anger. When I asked if she wanted to show the book to Mom, she responded with enthusiasm. As Pamela read the book to her Mother, her mother's face softened. They talked together about how confusing it can be to feel so many emotions at once. Mom reassured Pamela that there was nothing she had said or done that had caused her parents to divorce. It was a powerful session with more happening in one family session than had occurred previously in six months of individual child play therapy. Later Mom told me that she was amazed that Pamela was actively engaged in the therapy process. Celia also said she was excited about being involved in the therapy as well.

Frequently I used bibliotherapy and art in family sessions to help Pamela and her brother, Peter (age 3 1/2 at our first meeting) express their feelings and to promote more open family communication. In one family session, Mom read another book about divorce to her children. When I asked Pamela to draw what divorce felt like, she drew a heart with a ragged split down the middle. One side was blue, the other red. I asked her to tell us about her drawing and she said, "It's called 'Mad-Sad.' This is my heart. The red side is for Dad—it's mad. The blue side is for Mom—it's sad." I was stunned by how clearly Pamela had depicted the division and pain she felt. Mom and Peter drew their own pictures, and we all talked about hurting hearts and how to help them stop hurting and start to heal.

In another family therapy session, I asked each family member to draw a picture of the family doing something fun together before the divorce. Pamela drew a picture of the family on a camping trip sitting around a huge fire toasting marshmallows. Pamela sat on one side of the fire with Dad, while Peter and her Mother sat on the opposite side of the fire. The fire was a huge barrier between the two sides, and seemed about to engulf everyone. This drawing provided an opportunity for the family to talk about how many ways they all missed Dad, and their family camping trips. (My goal was to have the three of them eventually all on the same side of the fire!)

As I observed the family interactions during the family sessions, I could see how Celia's interaction with each of the children contributed to Pamela's problems. Pamela was clearly the "bad child," and indeed often seemed to do her best to provoke Mom. On the other hand, Peter could do no wrong in Mom's eyes. Pamela clearly resented all the attention shown her brother. However, Pamela was such an angry and resistant child that Celia found it very difficult to be affectionate with Pamela. Having family sessions also helped to identify the interactional sequence that maintained the problem. When Pamela and Peter had a disagreement, Peter would wail as if injured, and Mom would intervene. Mom would get angry, yell at Pamela, and send her to her room, while she held and comforted Peter. Identifying this pattern laid the groundwork for the following play therapy intervention.

During one family therapy session I asked the family to make a family video. The purpose was to have the family role-play a recent argument they had, then to switch roles and re-enact the same scene. The purpose of the activity is to break up rigid patterns of interaction and increase each family member's ability to understand how others feel. The idea is that once the emotions around an interaction change, the family cannot fight the old way anymore, because the rules and roles have been altered (Sori, 1998).

The family re-enacted a recent argument where Pamela and Peter had been playing with dolls on the floor. Peter wanted Pamela's doll, and tried to grab it from her. Pamela resisted, they struggled, and Pamela angrily pushed Peter away. Peter burst into loud, heartwrenchng sobs. Mom ran in from the kitchen, snatched up Peter, and screamed at Pamela to go to her room. Pamela stomped her feet, stood her ground, and shouted back. They then replayed the whole scene, but this time Mom and Pamela reversed their roles. They had a tremendous amount of fun doing this activity, announcing the scenes, and dancing and bowing at the end of the "show." The family watched themselves on TV afterwards, and the results of this intervention were amazing. For the first time Mom understood how she favored Peter, and she experienced firsthand what it felt like to be Pamela and always take the blame while her brother "got away with it." This was a major turning point for Mom. After this she made a conscious decision to start being both more affectionate to Pamela (and to work harder at "catching her being good") and to set limits with Peter (e.g., ignoring whining and crying, giving both children time-outs when they fought). Pamela also realized "how hard it is to be the mom."

Another family play therapy activity that I used in family sessions was the "Talking Feeling Doing Game." The children loved this game, which promotes open communication about both light and more serious topics. The fun the family was experiencing in sessions began to generalize to home. Mom was so enthused that she bought several games to play at home with the children. She planned a special camping trip to the mountains, just for the three of them. Celia also started putting Peter to bed before Pamela, which greatly pleased Pamela. This allowed for special "Pamela time," where Mom and Pamela would play a game, cuddle on the couch to watch television, or simply lie in Mom's bed and have "girl-talks."

Over time there were marked improvements in Pamela's behavior. As she learned to say how she felt (often through the modality of play) and Mom responded appropriately, she did not need to *act out* her sad and mad feelings. Her expression softened, and she smiled more often. The intensity of the fights with her brother gradually diminished, and she and Mom became more affectionate with each other. The tantrums were reduced in both number and severity, but occasionally resurfaced when Mom dated. However, in therapy Pamela was able to tell Mom that her tantrums were attempts to protect Mom from being hurt again. Mom reassured Pamela that she could take care of both herself and her children.

At termination the family drew a final picture for me: "My Family Then . . . My Family Now." In the "then" picture, each drew themselves how they were when they first came to see me. They were all yelling and fighting, with angry reds, blacks, and dark blues. The "Family Now" picture showed them on a recent vacation to the ocean. They were all laughing on the sunny beach and swimming together in beautiful water. This vividly punctuated the changes that had occurred over the course of therapy. As we shared our tears and hugs good-bye, Pamela shyly gave me her recent school picture so I would not forget her—as if I ever could!

The day after writing the above case study I received a card from Celia. It contained a picture of the three of them, with Pamela (now 12) standing slightly above and behind her mother and brother, smiling brightly, with an arm draped around each of their shoulders. In the card Mom wrote: "Look at Pamela's smile, I think we found it! Thanks again for everything. Love, Celia."

The success of this case was due to the family play therapy techniques that engaged both the children and mother. Through bibliotherapy, drawings, enact-ments, role-plays, and games, the rigid roles and patterns of communication in the family were broken up. This family discovered new ways to experience each other and to have fun again. In addition, Pamela was finally able to grieve the divorce, Mom was helped to change the way she interacted with Pamela and Peter, enabling the family to restructure in a healthy way. Family play ther-apy was the primary modality that facilitated all this.

Case Illustration: Engaging and Empowering
Parents through Play

The following is an extended case study that illustrates how parents who are reluctant to participate in their son's therapy were gradually won over and became active participants. As these parents became engaged in family play therapy, individual and conjoint sessions, and filial therapy, they became agents of change for their son and family. As a result of therapy, the parents became a resource to their child and advocates in dealing with larger social systems, such as the courts and physicians.

Geraldo, age 12, was referred for therapy by the juvenile court system. His Mexican-American family lived on a small farm in a rural area. Geraldo, the eldest of two children, had been charged with sexually molesting a 6-year-old girl in a neighbor's barn on 2 occasions. The father, Marcus, called for the first appointment. Although I (CS) requested that the whole family attend the first session, Marcus and Geraldo arrived alone. Geraldo had a severe harelip (I later learned the children at school called him "Split Lip"). Geraldo appeared to be anxious, and was extremely talkative and pleasant, although his speech was incoherent. He seemed genuinely happy to meet me.

I met first with Marcus alone. When I inquired as to why Mom and the rest of the family were not present, he said his wife just was not up to coming. He told me that since the problem clearly involved only Geraldo, they did not feel it was necessary for anyone else to come. I accepted this news for now. I went on to gather some background information, hear his story about what had happened, and ask what he hoped to accomplish in coming to therapy.

Marcus told me that Geraldo was in a self-contained special education classroom in the fifth grade in a rural elementary school. He had failed first grade, and could not read at all. Geraldo had no friends and the children at school shunned him and made fun of him because of his appearance and speech. However, he had become friends with several adult neighboring farmworkers.

It was with a great deal of shame that Marcus shared the details of why they were referred to therapy. Marcus related that the sister of one of Geraldo's classmates had told her mother that, on two occasions, Geraldo had forced her into the barn and molested her. Dad was clearly in anguish over his son's behavior. His hope in coming to therapy was to understand how this could have happened, and to have some reassurance that it would never happen again. Dad was clearly eager to "get this therapy business over with," and he asked me how many times I would need to meet with his son. At this point I explained that the best way I knew to understand the problem and help Geraldo was to meet with the whole family. Dad was skeptical, but agreed to bring his wife and daughter to the next session.

I did not know quite what to expect as I met alone with Geraldo for the first time. My guess was that he would either deny the whole thing, or not want to talk about it. To my surprise he was eager to tell me. When I asked him why he thought he was in my office, his reply was so rapid and jumbled that it was difficult to follow. While he was clearly anxious, it was also obvious that his IQ was below the normal range, and he had other developmental problems. Traditional "talk therapy" would be difficult with this child.

Instead, I asked if he would like to play with some puppets. Geraldo selected three puppets: a small, sad looking puppy, a larger lion puppet, and a gorilla. Without prompting, he quickly began to "tell me" what had happened in the barn. Amazingly, as he told this story, his speech slowed down and it was easier to understand him. Geraldo showed me how the puppy puppet had ridden his bike over to see the gorilla puppet, whom he had thought was a nice gorilla. Soon, however, the gorilla got "mean," refused to play, and went into his house. The lion puppet, who had been standing off to the side, then said to the puppy (clearly Geraldo), "I'll play with you—let's go in the barn. I've got a surprise." Geraldo then enacted how the lion suggested they take off their pants and show each other their "privates." It was clearly the lion who molested the puppy. Geraldo said, "The puppy was so scared—he didn't know what to do!" (An alarm went off in my head, because if the story had happened the way Geraldo described it, he seemed more of a victim than a perpetrator.)

Geraldo seemed happy to re-enact the entire story for his father and me. His Dad was amazed at the story, and at Geraldo's eagerness to "tell" it. Geraldo also used puppets and dolls to show us how he and his Dad had gone to the police station where he was "arrested" because he was a bad, bad boy! His father confessed that this had been a humiliating event, and that he and his son had been forced to sit and wait for three hours. Dad had threatened Geraldo that if he ever did anything like this again, the police would take him away to live in an awful place with other bad boys, and he would never see his family again! Geraldo was terrified of this. He had frequent nightmares about this "home for bad boys" and about a monster trying to swallow him up. His father had taken him to see the priest, with whom he prayed to be good again. Obviously, Dad was using the "boys home" as a threat to ensure Geraldo's good behavior, but his child was terrorized by what might happen to him.

Dad was fascinated with how Geraldo "talked" through his play, and was very willing to participate in therapy after that first session. However, it took several more sessions before Dad trusted me enough to bring in Mom and Geraldo's sister, Theresa (age 8). In the sessions with Dad, Geraldo used the dolls and puppets often to re-enact the events in the barn. His story never changed, but his speech continued to gradually improve.

Dad and I discussed what might have made Geraldo especially vulnerable to the events in the barn. It sounded like Geraldo was so happy to have a friend who wanted to play with him, but that he did not know how to set appropriate boundaries. Dad and Geraldo had several conversations about boundaries and right and wrong. Geraldo admitted that what the little girl did confused him. He knew it was wrong, but it felt very good. With my coaching, Dad and Geraldo used puppets to role-play how to say no and leave a situation that could get him into trouble. Dad also used male and female dolls to explain sex to his son. Consistent with his value system, Dad explained that sex is a wonderful thing that God created to be enjoyed between a man and his wife.

These frank discussions were entirely new to father and son, and gave Marcus a sense of actively doing something to prevent anything like this from happening again. In individual sessions Marcus admitted he had never felt close to his son, and that he really did not know him well. As he described their family life, it seemed that both parents had been pretty distant from Geraldo, and that Geraldo had largely been left to fend for himself. I asked Marcus what he thought life was like for Geraldo who was friendless, scorned by his peers, yet doggedly cheerful and resourceful enough to initiate friendships with adults. Dad's eyes moistened, as he seemed to consider this for the first time. When Geraldo returned to the room, Marcus told him *he* was not a "bad boy," but *what had happened* in the barn was bad. With tears in his eyes he hugged his son and, in a husky voice, told him he loved him. He then asked if Geraldo would like to toss a ball in the yard that evening after chores.

In another session Geraldo and Dad discussed his continuing nightmares of being in the "house for bad boys" with a monster trying to swallow him. He often woke everyone with his screams of terror. At my prompting, Dad told Geraldo that he would not have to go to the "house" if he made sure that what happened in the barn never happened again. Geraldo jumped up and promised profusely that he would never ever let that happen again! When Dad asked how he could be sure, he and Dad again used the puppets to role-play how Geraldo could set boundaries, say no, and get on his bike and go home.

To help him conquer his fears, I asked Geraldo to draw a picture of the "house for bad boys and the monster." He drew a terrifying scene of darkness, with an ugly blue monster, teeth barred, threatening a tiny figure crying in a corner of the paper. Dad and I each held a corner of this picture, and Geraldo, using a toy sword, attacked the drawing. As he tore the picture to shreds he shouted that he could beat the monster and rescue the little boy! After this session the nightmares quickly diminished, and stopped altogether within a few weeks.

Up to this point, I had not yet been successful in getting the rest of the family to come to therapy. Therefore, I was pleased when Geraldo's Mom, Elena, and sister, Theresa, came to the next session. Theresa seemed normal in both appearance and intelligence, and was passing in school. She had heard her brother talk about playing in therapy, and wanted her chance to play and have fun!

First I met with Mom and Dad alone. Elena told me that, after hearing what was happening in therapy sessions, she felt comfortable enough to attend. I then saw Elena alone, and invited her to tell her story. She began to cry as she described the shame she felt Geraldo had brought to their family. She now jumped every time the telephone rang, cried a lot, and seldom talked to anyone or left the house anymore. She had told no one, and she and Marcus just could not talk about it. Later in a conjoint session, I encouraged Marcus and Elena to share their pain and disappointment with each other. They took turns describing how they had been such careful parents, never letting "bad" kids come over, attending Mass regularly, and working hard to provide for their children. They were bewildered by how this could have happened. As they shared their guilt and feelings of failure and shame, they both cried. At my encouragement, they held and comforted each other. Afterward Elena said she felt very relieved to have a safe place to talk about all this.

As we continued to meet in conjoint and family sessions, I was able to slowly gather more information about Geraldo and his family. Mom shared that she had never learned to read and had been in special education classes herself. She and Marcus had met in church. In an individual session Marcus, who had considered entering the priesthood, confessed he married Elena because he both admired her spirit and he felt sorry for her. He had never dated much and, like his son, had had few friends growing up on an isolated farm. He and Elena shared the dream of instilling their strong Catholic values in their children and building a family of which they could be proud. In conjoint sessions they were able to share their feelings of failure and then to explore their strengths and examples of past resiliency as a couple and family.

As they shifted their focus from pathology to strengths, Marcus and Elena were able to identify ways in which they were good, loving parents. For example, they attended church together as a family. Marcus worked long hours to provide a better life for his children than he had had growing up. Elena always cooked hot meals and made sure the children were in bed by 9 o'clock.

Emphasizing their strengths as parents empowered them to help Geraldo heal from this experience and become active advocates for him, especially within the school system. At some point, they had received paperwork about Geraldo from the school. They admitted that neither of them understood the papers or what the school psychologist had told them. Dad said, "Just so I don't find out my son will be cleaning stables all his life!" However, an IQ test taken the previous school year revealed that Geraldo's overall IQ was 79. He was somewhat impulsive in school, and his talking sometimes got him in trouble. I encouraged them to ask for a consultation with school officials, and that I would be happy to attend with them. At this conference the parents learned about Geraldo's limitations and special needs, as well as his strengths. After this meeting both parents felt relieved and encouraged, and Dad was motivated to help Geraldo more with homework.

At our next session, I asked the family to participate in family play therapy. I asked them to make up a story together that had a beginning, a middle, and an end, but was not a story they already knew, like Snow White (Irwin & Malloy, 1975). I left the room while they worked on their story, and then came back in for the "performance." All the puppets, dolls, and stuffed animals were sitting in a circle around the perimeter of the room. Using the sad puppy puppet again, Geraldo went around to each animal, inviting each one to come to his birthday party. Geraldo did all the talking. As each parent and his sister took turns holding up the animals, Geraldo spoke for each. "I can't come, I have to do homework" said the white kitten. "My Mommy won't let me," said the lamb. "I don't want to come to your house!" said the angry gorilla. One by one, all the animals refused his invitation. Finally the bumblebee flew over to Geraldo and said, "See, I have beautiful magic wings . . . and a stinger! I could sting them all, like this!" The bee proceeded to sting all the animals, who yelled and fell over. "Oh, let me fly with you," said Geraldo's puppy. And off they flew to "beeland" to be with all the friendly bees who wanted to play with the puppy.

In this story Geraldo helped Marcus and Elena understand how lonely and friendless he felt. We discussed the fact that his desire for friends could make him so anxious to please that he could be vulnerable. They were even able to see the dangers in him seeking out older male adults as special friends. They had been concerned about Geraldo's long absences from home, but had not set any limits. Using the puppets we explored separately with both Geraldo and Theresa whether any other violations had occurred. The parents then worked together to limit Geraldo's excursions, and they used the puppets to role-play the new rules. Geraldo practiced using the puppy puppet to ask, "What time is it? I have to be home by 4 o'clock."

We spent several sessions exploring the parent's beliefs about allowing their children to have friends over, and how they might help Geraldo improve his social skills. Eventually the parents relented and invited one child from "a nice family" over on the following Saturday. Geraldo was ecstatic!

To help this day go well for Geraldo, we used a family session to teach him how to make friends and to talk to other kids. Dad explained how to ask a question and then wait for an answer before asking another question. To teach this skill we used a small rubber ball and role-played. Geraldo would ask a question like "What's your favorite television show?" as he tossed the ball to Dad. "The Simpsons. What's yours?" Dad replied, as he tossed the ball to Mom. "I like Oprah. What about you, Theresa?" And on it went. This helped Geraldo learn to wait for an answer. The family got a lot of enjoyment from this "game." Dad and Geraldo often played this game, even while working in the barn or driving in the pickup. And Mom and Geraldo started playing checkers together, first in my office, and then at home. It was apparent that the family was learning to enjoy being together in a new way.

I complimented Marcus and Elena for their active participation in Geraldo's treatment, and for their willingness to try family play therapy, which they found they enjoyed. At this point in therapy, I felt that Elena's relationship with the children could be enhanced through filial therapy. In the next session I explained the basics of filial therapy, and they were eager to learn. During the training Elena's self-esteem seemed to soar as she increased her ability to set limits and identify her children's feelings. Elena even found some inexpensive puppets, which were Geraldo's favorite toys in therapy, to use for filial therapy at home.

About this time Mom received a call from Geraldo's probation officer. Another child in the school had come forward to reveal that the little girl who had accused Geraldo of sexually abusing her had actually abused him. This corroborated Geraldo's story that he had been a passive participant in the incidents in the barn. The other family was now mandated for therapy, and Geraldo's parents were both relieved and elated at the confirmation that their son had been telling the truth that he had not initiated the sexual encounter.

As we approached terminating therapy, I no longer felt that Geraldo was on his own, but was now a member of the family. Geraldo had a clear and well-rehearsed strategy of how to get himself out of any threatening situation. He clearly knew right from wrong, and knew the behavior in the barn was wrong. His horrible nightmares had ended and he was sleeping all night. He was able to talk to his parents about his feelings and he was slowly improving his social skills. Remarkably, his speech was much improved. Marcus and Elena said they were feeling much better about themselves and how they had handled the situation. They felt they were working through this together, and felt closer than ever before as a couple. Elena was no longer feeling depressed.

I wrote my summary letter to the court with reasonable assurance that therapy was successful and that Geraldo was not likely to be involved in any sexual misconduct in the future. As the court date neared, the family again used puppets to role-play what this experience might be like. Dad shared that he felt much more confident and empowered when they went to court the second time, and he was able to love and support his son through that difficult experience. The charges against Geraldo were dismissed.

When I called the family about six months later to follow up, Dad told me that they were all doing well. The parents had even taken Geraldo back to the doctor to reevaluate his harelip. The doctor had referred them to a specialist who was going to perform surgery as soon as school was out! This was true evidence of the second-order change that had occurred in this family—the shift in the parents' ability to want to know their son and to empathize with his pain had empowered them to muster their resources to help him.

THE INVOLVEMENT OF the parents was vital to the successful outcome of this complicated case. The parents needed to understand the complexities of what had happened and gain a sense of actively preventing future problems. Geraldo was vulnerable because he was so lonely, even in his own family. The therapeutic outcome would not have been the same if Geraldo had been seen alone, as the parents originally requested. It is likely that the parents would have remained angry with their son, yet have been too ashamed to talk to each other or anyone else. Certainly Geraldo had a lot shame and fear that could have been resolved through individual play therapy. However, just as important as helping Geraldo heal, was the healing that took place in the parents' marriage and between the parents and Geraldo. These changes needed to occur within the family, not with the therapist.

It is important to recognize that therapy with this family involved a multimodal approach that was designed to meet the needs of the family at different stages of treatment. Individual child therapy was used initially to help Geraldo "tell" his story. Puppets were used in family play therapy as a means for Dad to teach his son about boundaries, right and wrong, and sex. Individual and marital sessions offered this hurting couple an opportunity to share their grief and pain and to explore new ways to parent their children. Filial play therapy training broadened the parent's skills at limit-setting, empathizing, and playing with their children. This was especially helpful for mother and son. Each of these approaches contributed to the overall success of this case, while no singular approach would have been nearly as effective.

Conclusion

Involving both parents and children together in therapy is a challenging task. Children must be engaged in a medium that they are comfortable and familiar with, such as play. Parents are more comfortable with talk therapy and do not see the therapeutic value of play. As a result we can sympathize with the dilemma of focusing treatment on either the child or the parents. Yet, the family, and particularly the parents, is the greatest source of support and strength for children. Therefore, it is essential to create new treatment approaches that will help therapists to involve parents in therapy. In this chapter, we have suggested a multimodal approach that combines individual and conjoint therapy and involves parents. We believe that using such an approach, which includes parents in children's therapy, will enable therapists to be more effective in providing long-term solutions to children's problems.

C. Everett Bailey, Ph.D., is Assistant Professor in the Marriage and Family Therapy Program, North Dakota State University, Fargo, North Dakota.

Catherine E. Ford Sori, Ph.D.(c), is Child and Family Associate, Cancer Support Center, Homewood, Illinois.

References

Belsky, J. (1984). The determinants of parenting: A process model. *Child Development, 55,* 83–96.

Bornstein, M. H. (Ed.). (1995). *Handbook of parenting.* Mahwah, NJ: Lawrence Erlbaum.

Briesmeister, J. M., & Schaefer, C. E. (Eds.). (1998). *Handbook of parent training: Parents as co-therapists for children's behavior problems* (2nd ed.). New York: John Wiley.

Brody, G. H., & Stoneman, Z. (1996). A risk-amelioration model of sibling relationships: Conceptual underpinnings and preliminary findings. In G. H. Brody (Ed.), *Sibling relationships: Their causes and consequences* (pp. 231–247). Norwood, NJ: Ablex.

Cummings, E. M., & Davies, P. (1994). *Children and marital conflict: The impact of family dispute and resolution.* New York: Guilford.

Estrada, A. U., & Pinsof, W. M. (1995). The effectiveness of family therapies for selected behavioral disorders of childhood. *Journal of Marital and Family Therapy, 21,* 403–440.

Eyberg, S. (1988). Parent-child interaction therapy: Integration of traditional and behavioral concerns. *Child and Family Behavior Therapy, 10,* 33–46.

Eyberg, S. M., & Boggs, S. R. (1998). Parent-child interaction therapy: A psychosocial intervention for the treatment of young conduct disordered children. In J. M. Briesmester & C. E. Schaefer (Eds.), *Handbook of parent training: Parents as co-therapists for children's behavior problems* (2nd ed.). New York: John Wiley.

Field, T. (1995). Psychologically depressed parents. In M. H. Bornstein (Ed.), *Handbook of parenting: Vol. 4. Applied and practical parenting* (pp. 85–99). Mahwah, NJ: Lawrence Erlbaum.

Fincham, F. D. (1998). Child development and marital relations. *Child Development, 69,* 543–574.

Gil, E. (1994). *Play in family therapy.* New York: Guilford.

Hoff-Ginsberg, E., & Tardif, T. (1995). Socioeconomic status and parenting. In M. H. Bornstein (Ed.), *Handbook of parenting: Vol. 2. Biology and ecology of parenting* (pp. 161–188). Mahwah, NJ: Lawrence Erlbaum.

Irwin, E. C., & Malloy, E. S. (1975). Family puppet interview. *Family Process, 14,* 179–191.

Johnson, L. (1995). Filial therapy: A bridge between individual child therapy and family therapy. *Journal of Psychotherapy, 6,* 55–70.

Johnson, L., & Thomas, V. (1999). Influences on the inclusion of children in family therapy. *Journal of Marital and Family Therapy, 25,* 117–123.

Korner, S., & Brown, G. (1990). Exclusion of children from family psychotherapy: Family therapists' beliefs and practices. *Journal of Family Psychology, 3,* 420–430.

Ladd, G. W., & Le Sieur, K. D. (1995). Parents and children's peer relationships. In M. H. Bornstein (Ed.), Handbook of parenting: Vol. 4. *Applied and practical parenting* (pp. 377–436). Mahwah, NJ: Lawrence Erlbaum.

Landreth, G. L. (1991). *Play therapy: The art of the relationship.* Bristol, PA: Accelerated Development.

Montalvo, B., & Haley, J. (1973). In defense of child therapy. *Family Process, 12,* 227–244.

Olson, D. H. (1970). Marital and family therapy: Integrative review and critique. *Journal of Marriage and the Family, 32,* 501–538.

Plomin, R., & Rutter, M. (1998). Child development, molecular genetics, and what to do with genes once they are found. *Child Development, 69,* 1223–1242.

Rolland, J. S. (1994). *Families, illness, & disability: An integrative treatment model.* New York: Basic.

Sanson, A., & Rothbart, M. K. (1995). Child temperament and parenting. In M. H. Bornstein (Ed.), *Handbook of parenting: Vol. 4. Applied and practical parenting* (pp. 299–321). Mahwah, NJ: Lawrence Erlbaum.

Sori, C. E. F. (1998). Involving children in family therapy: Making family movies. In L. L. Hecker & S. A. Deacon (Eds.), *The therapist's notebook: Homework, handouts, and activities for use in psychotherapy.* New York: Haworth.

VanFleet, R. (1994). *Filial therapy: Strengthening parent-child relationships through play.* Sarasota, FL: Professional Resource.

Walsh, F. (1998). *Strengthening family resilience.* New York: Guilford.

Indexes

Name Index

Abidin, R. R., 446
Achenbach, T. M., 195, 312, 445
Ackerman, N., xvii, 193
Adam, K. S., 114
Ainsworth, M. D. S., 460
Alessandri, S. M., 454
Alexander, J. F., 279
Allan, J., 254, 255
Allen, A. J., 193
Alpert, A., 221
Altepeter, T., 308
Amado, H., 195
Amato, P. R., 244, 245, 262
Anastopoulos, A., 308, 317, 318
Andersen, T., 66
Anderson, C. M., 343
Anderson, E. R., 410
Anderson, H. D., 18, 21, 47, 48, 49, 53, 59, 62, 67, 69, 70, 119
Anderson, R. L., 220
Anderson, S., 429
Andreozzi, L. L., 342
Andres, J., 221
Andrews, J., 226
Apfel, N., 415
Aponte, H., 319
Aponte, R. N., 257
Appelbaum, M. I., 446
Araoz, D. L., 342
Ariel, S., 251, 342
Asarnow, J. R., 222
Ash, P., 216, 220, 221
Asher, S. R., 429
Atkinson, L., 114
Avison, W. R., 409

Axiline, V. M., 183, 313
Ayers, J., 458

Babigna, H., 449
Bailey, A., 199
Baker L., 319
Balach, L., 193
Baldwin, A., 409
Baldwin, C., 409
Balla, D., 435
Bandura, A., 199, 439, 446, 450
Barch, D. M., 279
Barkley, R. A., 308, 309, 311, 312, 314–15, 316, 317, 318, 325, 326, 332, 462
Barnett, D., 456
Barnett, R. C., 389
Barrett, K., 455
Barrett, M. J., 138, 143, 185
Barrett, M. L., 223
Barrett, P. M., 193, 195
Bartholomew, K., 114
Baruch, G. K., 389
Bass, D., 318
Bateson, G., 281, 282, 286
Baugher, M., 226
Baumrind, D., 279, 429, 443, 446, 461
Bavelas, J., 281
Beal, E. W., 269
Beardslee, W. R., 222, 227, 420
Beavers, W. R., 248
Becker, W., 387
Beidel, D., 203
Belair, J. F., 225
Belsky, J., 390, 434, 445, 446, 482
Bendaell, D., 417

503

Subject Index